Bloom's Period Studies

BLOOM'S PERIOD STUDIES

Edwardian and Georgian Fiction

Edited and with an introduction by
Harold Bloom
Sterling Professor of the Humanities
Yale University

CHELSEA HOUSE
P U B L I S H E R S
A Haights Cross Communications Company ®
Philadelphia

©2005 by Chelsea House Publishers, a subsidiary of
Haights Cross Communications.

A Haights Cross Communications ◢ Company®

www.chelseahouse.com

Introduction © 2005 by Harold Bloom.

Printed and bound in the United States of America.

10 9 8 7 6 5 4 3 2 1

Library of Congress Cataloging-in-Publication Data

Edwardian and Georgian fiction / [edited by] Harold Bloom.
    p. cm. — (Bloom's period studies)
  Includes bibliographical references and index.
  ISBN 0-7910-8319-5 (alk. paper)
  1. English fiction—20th century—History and criticism. 2. Great Britain—History—
Edward VII, 1901-1910. 3. Great Britain—History—George VI, 1936-1952. 4. Great
Britain—History—George V, 1910-1936. I. Bloom, Harold. II. Series.
  PR883.E34 2004
  823'.91209—dc22
                                2004028204

Contributing editor: Pamela Loos

Cover design by Keith Trego

Layout by EJB Publishing Services

All links and web addresses were checked and verified to be correct at the time of
publication. Because of the dynamic nature of the web, some addresses and links may
have changed since publication and may no longer be valid.

Contents

Editor's Note

My extensive Introduction traces the influences of Schopenhauer and allied speculative thinkers on a succession of novelists and story-writers from Thomas Hardy and Oscar Wilde through Joseph Conrad and Rudyard Kipling on to E.M. Forster.

Henry James, best of all American novelists, makes clear his preference for Joseph Conrad over H.G. Wells and Arnold Bennett.

A strong Marxist critic, Raymond Williams, also surveys the split between "materialists" like Wells and Bennett, and the rather more transcendent James, Woolf, and Forster, after which David Thorburn celebrates Joseph Conrad as a High Romantic.

The late literary and cultural critic Allan White considers the dialectic of revelation and concealment in the literature of Meredith, Conrad, and James.

In an overview, John Batchelor takes us from Kipling on to the advent of Conrad, while John McClure brilliantly explores the presence of colonialism in both Kipling and Conrad.

L.R. Leavis charts sexual nuances in George Gissing, Hardy, and D.H. Lawrence, after which Peter Keating surveys a varied tapestry from Hardy and Robert Louis Stevenson to Conan Doyle.

Hardy's last novel, *Jude the Obscure*, is contrasted by Annette Federico to Gissing's *The Whirlpool*, while the late Edward W. Said, father of anti-colonialist criticism, lingers ambiguously upon Kipling's *Kim*, at once an aesthetic delight and a wicked pleasure.

Malcolm Bradbury brings together Ford Madox Ford, Conrad, and Forster as pre-World War I seers greatly altered by its outbreak, after which David Trotter judges even Gissing and Bennett as evaders of Naturalism.

Bram Stoker's deliciously grisly *Dracula*, as interpreted by Nicholas Daly, makes a charming juxtaposition with Oscar Wilde's *Picture of Dorian Gray* and Walter Pater's sly critique of Wilde, as set forth by John Paul Riquelme, after which Jil Larson brings together Hardy and the later Victorian feminist writers, Sarah Grand and Olive Schreiner.

In this volume's final essay, Ruth Robbins interprets Lawrence's *The Rainbow*, and connects it to Forster's *A Passage to India*.

Introduction

I

For Arthur Schopenhauer, the Will to Live was the true thing-in-itself, not an interpretation but a rapacious, active, universal, and ultimately indifferent drive or desire. Schopenhauer's great work, *The World as Will and Representation*, had the same relation to and influence upon many of the principal nineteenth- and early twentieth-century novelists that Freud's writings have in regard to many of this century's later, crucial masters of prose fiction. Zola, Maupassant, Turgenev, and Tolstoy join Thomas Hardy as Schopenhauer's nineteenth-century heirs, in a tradition that goes on through Proust, Conrad, and Thomas Mann to culminate in aspects of Borges, and Beckett, the most eminent living writer of narrative. Since Schopenhauer (despite Freud's denials) was one of Freud's prime precursors, one could argue that aspects of Freud's influence upon writers simply carry on from Schopenhauer's previous effect. Manifestly, the relation of Schopenhauer to Hardy is different in both kind and degree from the larger sense in which Schopenhauer was Freud's forerunner or Wittgenstein's. A poet-novelist like Hardy turns to a rhetorical speculator like Schopenhauer only because he finds something in his own temperament and sensibility confirmed and strengthened, and not at all as Lucretius turned to Epicurus, or as Whitman was inspired by Emerson.

The true precursor for Hardy was Shelley, whose visionary skepticism permeates the novels as well as the poems and *The Dynasts*. There is some technical debt to George Eliot in the early novels, but Hardy in his depths was little more moved by her than by Wilkie Collins, from whom he also learned elements of craft. Shelley's tragic sense of eros is pervasive throughout Hardy, and ultimately determines Hardy's understanding of his strongest heroines: Bathsheba Everdene, Eustacia Vye, Marty South, Tess Durbeyfield, Sue Bridehead. Between desire and fulfillment in Shelley falls the shadow of the selfhood, a shadow that makes love and what might be called the means of love quite irreconcilable. What M.D. Zabel named as "the aesthetic of incongruity" in Hardy and ascribed to temperamental causes is in a profound way the result of attempting to transmute the procedures of *The Revolt of Islam* and *Epipsychidion* into the supposedly naturalistic novel.

J. Hillis Miller, when he worked more in the mode of a critic of consciousness like Georges Poulet than in the deconstruction of Paul de Man and Jacques Derrida, saw the fate of love in Hardy as being darkened always by a shadow cast by the lover's consciousness itself. Hugh Kenner, with a distaste for Hardy akin to (and perhaps derived from) T.S. Eliot's in *After Strange Gods*, suggested that Miller had created a kind of Proustian Hardy, who turns out to be a case rather than an artist. Hardy was certainly not an artist comparable to Henry James (who dismissed him as a mere imitator of George Eliot) or James Joyce, but the High Modernist shibboleths for testing the novel have now waned considerably, except for a few surviving high priests of Modernism like Kenner. A better guide to Hardy's permanent strength as a novelist was his heir D.H. Lawrence, whose *The Rainbow* and *Women in Love* marvelously brought Hardy's legacy to an apotheosis. Lawrence, praising Hardy with a rebel son's ambivalence, associated him with Tolstoy as a tragic writer:

> And this is the quality Hardy shares with the great writers, Shakespeare or Sophocles or Tolstoi, this setting behind the small action of his protagonists the terrific action of unfathomed nature; setting a smaller system of morality, the one grasped and formulated by the human consciousness within the vast, uncomprehended and incomprehensible morality of nature or of life itself, surpassing human consciousness. The difference is, that whereas in Shakespeare or Sophocles the greater, uncomprehended morality, or fate, is actively transgressed and gives active punishment, in Hardy and Tolstoi the lesser, human morality, the mechanical system is actively transgressed, and holds, and punishes the protagonist, whilst the greater morality is only passively, negatively transgressed, it is represented merely as being present in background, in scenery, not taking any active part, having no direct connexion with the protagonist. (Œdipus, Hamlet,

Macbeth set themselves up against, or find themselves set up against, the unfathomed moral forces of nature, and out of this unfathomed force comes their death. Whereas Anna Karenina, Eustacia, Tess, Sue, and Jude find themselves up against the established system of human government and morality, they cannot detach themselves, and are brought down. Their real tragedy is that they are unfaithful to the greater unwritten morality, which would have bidden Anna Karenina be patient and wait until she, by virtue of greater right, could take what she needed from society; would have bidden Vronsky detach himself from the system, become an individual, creating a new colony of morality with Anna; would have bidden Eustacia fight Clym for his own soul, and Tess take and claim her Angel, since she had the greater light; would have bidden Jude and Sue endure for very honour's sake, since one must bide by the best that one has known, and not succumb to the lesser good.

(*Study of Thomas Hardy*)

This seems to me powerful and just, because it catches what is most surprising and enduring in Hardy's novels—the sublime stature and aesthetic dignity of his crucial protagonists—while exposing also his great limitation, his denial of freedom to his best personages. Lawrence's prescription for what would have saved Eustacia and Clym, Tess and Angel, Sue and Jude, is perhaps not as persuasive. He speaks of them as though they were Gudrun and Gerald, and thus have failed to be Ursula and Birkin. It is Hardy's genius that they are what they had to be: as imperfect as their creator and his vision, as impure as his language and his plotting, and finally painful and memorable to us:

Note that, in this bitterness, delight,
Since the imperfect is so hot in us,
Lies in flawed words and stubborn sounds.

II

Alone among Hardy's novels, *Jude the Obscure* has three strong figures, all triumphs of representation: Sue, Jude, Arabella. Unfortunately, it also has little Father Time, Hardy's most memorable disaster in representation. Even more unfortunately, it is a book in which Hardy's drive to go on telling stories gives way to his precursor Shelley's despair that there is one story and one story only, the triumph of life over human integrity. As the most Shelleyan of Hardy's novels (except perhaps for *The Well-Beloved*, which precedes it in initial composition, though not in revision and publication), *Jude the Obscure* has a complex and perhaps crippling relation to *Epipsychidion*. Sue Bridehead is more Shelleyan than even Shelley's Emilia in that poem, and would have been better off married to Shelley than to Jude Fawley, which is not to say that poor Shelley could have survived the union any better than the unhappy Jude.

D.H. Lawrence, inevitably, was Sue's most articulate critic:

> Her female spirit did not wed with the male spirit: she could not prophesy. Her spirit submitted to the male spirit, owned the priority of the male spirit, wished to become the male spirit.

Sue needs no defense, least of all in 1986 when she has become prevalent, a subtle rebel against any dialectic of power founded wholly upon mere gender. Yet, within the novel, Sue is less a rebel than she is Jude's Shelleyan epipsyche, his twin sister (actually his cousin) and counterpart. She can live neither with Jude, nor without him, and their love is both narcissistic and incestuous, Hardy's metaphor for the Will to Live at its most destructive, because in Jude and Sue it destroys the most transcendent beings Hardy had ever imagined.

It will not suffice to call *Jude the Obscure* a tragedy, since what is most tragic in Jude and Sue is their Shelleyan transcendence. When Shelley attempted tragedy in *The Cenci*, he succeeded only by diverting the form into a lament for the descent of Beatrice Cenci to her father's level. But Jude and Sue cannot be said to descend, any more than Eustacia, Henchard, and Tess descend. The Will to Live in Hardy's cosmos is too terrible and too incessant for us to speak of it as debasing its subjects or victims. In a world dominated by drive, a spirit like Jude's is condemned to die whispering the Jobean lament: "Let the day perish wherein I was born." *Jude the Obscure* is Hardy's Book of Job, and like Job is too dark for tragedy, while unlike Job it is just the reverse of theodicy, being Hardy's ultimate declaration that the ways of the Immanent Will towards man are unjustifiable.

Few interchanges in literature are at once so pathetic and so charming as the intricate, Shelleyan dances of scruple and desire intertwined that involve Sue and Jude:

> He laughed. "Never mind," he said. "So that I am near you, I am comparatively happy. It is more than this earthly wretch called

Me deserves—you spirit, you disembodied creature, you dear, sweet, tantalizing phantom—hardly flesh at all; so that when I put my arms round you, I almost expect them to pass through you as through air! Forgive me for being gross, as you call it! Remember that our calling ourselves cousins when really strangers was a snare. The enmity of our parents gave a piquancy to you in my eyes that was intenser ever than the novelty of ordinary new acquaintance."

"Say those pretty lines, then, from Shelley's 'Epipsychidion' as if they meant me," she solicited, slanting up closer to him as they stood. "Don't you know them?"

"I know hardly any poetry," he replied, mournfully.

"Don't you?" These are some of them:

"'There was a Being whom my spirit oft
Met on its visioned wanderings far aloft.

. . . .

A seraph of Heaven, too gentle to be human,
Veiling beneath that radiant form of woman ... '"

"Oh, it is too flattering, so I won't go on! But say it's me!—say it's me!"

"It is you, dear; exactly like you!"

"Now I forgive you! And you shall kiss me just once there—not very long." She put the tip of her finger gingerly to her cheek, and he did as commanded. "You do care for me very much, don't you, in spite of my not—you know?"

"Yes, sweet!" he said, with a sigh, and bade her good-night.

It is Sue, right enough, and it is disaster. The true epigraph to *Jude the Obscure* comes at the climax of *Epipsychidion:*

In one another's substance finding food,
Like flames too pure and light and unimbued
To nourish their bright lives with baser prey,
Which point to Heaven and cannot pass away:
One hope within two wills, one will beneath
Two overshadowing minds, one life, one death,
One Heaven, one Hell, one immortality,
And one annihilation.

That "one will beneath" the "two overshadowing minds" of Sue and

Jude is the Immanent Will of Thomas Hardy, and it indeed does become "one annihilation."

III

Oscar Wilde was essentially a man of action displaced into a man of letters. In some curious sense, there is a sickness-unto-action in Wilde's life and work, a masked despair that led him to the borders of that realm of fantasy the Victorians called "nonsense" literature, the cosmos of Edward Lear. Wilde stands between a doctrine of momentary aesthetic ecstasies, phantasmagoric hard gemlike flames, and a vision of lyric simplification through aesthetic intensity, what Yeats called the Condition of Fire. Nonsense is the truest rejection of mere nature, and the strongest program for compelling nature to cease imitating itself and to imitate art instead.

In his collection of stories, I turn with pleasure to Wilde at nearly his most delightful, the nine fairy tales published originally as two volumes, *House of Pomegranates* and *The Happy Prince and Other Tales*. "The Young King" is a visionary narrative in the mode of Walter Pater's *Imaginary Portraits*, and suffers from being both too ornate and a touch too sentimental. But its hero, questing always for beauty crossed by the shadow of mortality, is one of Wilde's luminous Christ figures, and almost redeems the story from its baroque elaborations. Far better is the cruel and provocative "The Birthday of the Infanta," where the dancing dwarf's first sight of his own reflection is necessarily self-destructive, and represents Wilde's great theme of the narcissistic element in the death drive, beyond the pleasure principle. The story's closing outcry, the Infanta's "For the future let those who come to play with me have no hearts," can be considered one of Wilde's veracious if ironic mottoes.

"The Fisherman and His Soul," a much more ambitious story, is one of the authentic weird tales in the language, worthy of E.T.A. Hoffmann and better than anything by Poe. Its great figure is not the young Fisherman but his equivocal and dangerous Soul, or shadowy double, and its most ironic and telling moment, extraordinary in context, is the reunion between self and soul in the act of dying:

> And his Soul besought him to depart, but he would not, so great was his love. And the sea came nearer, and sought to cover him with its waves, and when he knew that the end was at hand he kissed with mad lips the cold lips of the Mermaid, and the heart that was within him, brake. And as through the fulness of his love his heart did break, the Soul found an entrance and entered in,

and was one with him even as before. And the sea covered the young Fisherman with its waves.

The last story to appear in *A House of Pomegranates*, "The Star-Child," may invest too much of its intensity in pathos, yet the hidden meaning redeems the hyperbolic sentiment, as this is clearly one of Wilde's allegories of his own malaise and quest for the mother. Freud's reading of the psychosexuality of Leonardo da Vinci is wholly relevant to "The Star-Child," where the child is Oscar and the mother is a displaced version of Lady Jane Wilde, who wrote poems and revolutionary articles for the Irish cause under the name Speranza and who was famous as the author-translator of *Sidonia the Sorceress*, a dubious work yet greatly admired by William Morris.

Freud, in his study of Leonardo, remarks that all great men must retain something of the infantile throughout their whole life, and certainly this was true of Wilde. But the sublime Oscar knew this of himself; what after all, whether of himself or others, did he not know? This may account for the marvelous bitterness that ends the tale of "The Star-Child." Though reconciled to this mother, and his father, the star-child Oscar cannot live and rule happily ever after:

> Yet ruled he not long, so great had been his suffering, and so bitter the fire of his testing, for after the space of three years he died. And he who came after him ruled evilly.

IV

Four of the five fairy stories in *The Happy Prince and Other Tales* are Wilde's masterpieces in this genre, being short, swift, and eloquently ironic. Only "The Devoted Friend" yields to its own bitterness, while "The Happy Prince" and "The Remarkable Rocket" are perfectly balanced between irony and pathos, and "The Nightingale and the Rose" and "The Selfish Giant" are more mixed successes, the first inclining too much to disillusion, while the second falls finally into Wilde's Christological obsessions.

The title story, "The Happy Prince," is consistently superb, but my own favorite passage in it comes with the introduction of the hero, the insouciant little Swallow, who comes upon a beautiful Reed and is "so attracted by her slender waist" that, for a time, he falls in love with her:

> "Shall I love you?" said the Swallow, who liked to come to the point at once, and the Reed made him a low bow. So he flew

round and round her, touching the water with his wings, and making silver ripples. This was his courtship, and it lasted all through the summer.

"It is a ridiculous attachment," twittered the other Swallows, "she has no money, and far too many relations"; and indeed the river was quite full of Reeds. Then, when the autumn came, they all flew away.

After they had gone he felt lonely, and began to tire of his ladylove. "She has no conversation," he said, "and I am afraid that she is a coquette, for she is always flirting with the wind." And certainly, whenever the wind blew, the Reed made the most graceful curtsies. "I admit that she is domestic," he continued, "but I love travelling, and my wife, consequently, should love travelling also."

"Will you come away with me?" he said finally to her; but the Reed shook her head, she was so attached to her home.

"You have been trifling with me," he cried. "I am off to the Pyramids. Good-bye!" and he flew away.

Delicious in its urbane control, the passage belongs to the higher sphere of nonsense literature, with Edward Lear and Lewis Carroll and *The Importance of Being Earnest*. What Wilde wrote of his greatest play is true also of the story of the Swallow and the Reed: "It is exquisitely trivial, a delicate bubble of fancy, and it has as its philosophy ... that we should treat all the trivial things of life seriously, and all the serious things of life with sincere and studied triviality."

In "The Nightingale and the Rose," as I have already intimated, Wilde unfortunately concludes by treating all the trivial matters trivially and all the serious issues too seriously, so that the tale falls short of the sublimities of true Nonsense. "The Selfish Giant" is better, if slighter, and has about it the Paterian sadomasochism that always attends Wilde when he celebrates "the wounds of Love." Bitterness, never much below the surface of Wilde's work, breaks through too strenuously in "The Devoted Friend," which, however, is saved by its beginning and end, where we inhabit the cosmos of the old Water-rat, the Duck, and the Green Linnet. In that world, prophetic of *The Wind in the Willows*, the divine Oscar cannot go wrong.

I am delighted to conclude my consideration of these stories with Wilde at his strongest, in "The Remarkable Rocket," perhaps the best of all his fairy tales. With earnest originality, Wilde places us in the psychic realm of royal fireworks, where we listen to the conversation of Roman Candles,

Catherine Wheels, Squibs, Bengal Lights, and the Remarkable Rocket himself, a veritable paragon of vainglory and self-importance. The Remarkable Rocket cannot be bothered to keep himself dry, since he is too concerned with giving pleasure only to himself: "The only thing that sustains one through life is the consciousness of the immense inferiority of everybody else, and this is a feeling that I have always cultivated."

Incapable of going off at the right time, the Remarkable Rocket fails to shoot up into the sky at the royal fireworks display. In a descending slide worthy of Thomas Pynchon, the Remarkable Rocket goes out to no effect whatsoever:

> Then he began to feel a curious tingling sensation all over him.
>
> "Now I am going to explode," he cried. "I shall set the whole world on fire, and make such a noise, that nobody will talk about anything else for a whole year." And he certainly did explode. Bang! Bang! Bang! went the gunpowder. There was no doubt about it.
>
> But nobody heard him, not even the two little boys, for they were sound asleep.
>
> Then all that was left of him was the stick, and this fell down on the back of a Goose who was taking a walk by the side of the ditch.
>
> "Good heavens!" cried the Goose. "It is going to rain sticks"; and she rushed into the water.
>
> "I knew I should create a great sensation," gasped the Rocket, and he went out.

The great line of Nonsense writers, from Lear and Carroll through Perelman and Pynchon, would not disown this grand epiphany, this fit conclusion to the narcissistic ego's orgy of self-love. Freud, who has his own recondite place among the seers of Nonsense, taught us that the ego must fall in love with an object other than itself in order to avoid becoming very ill indeed. "The Remarkable Rocket" is Wilde's parodistic presentation of this dark Freudian truth, and certainly is part of Wilde's permanent literary legacy, worthy of the genius who also gave us *The Importance of Being Earnest* and "The Decay of Lying."

V

The prose-poem is a notoriously difficult genre to transpose into English, and Wilde, at his best, superbly understood that to succeed in English it must become more parable than poem. His first prose-poem, "The Artist," fails because it lacks parabolic force, since its insight is too obvious. The reader performs no labor of understanding in moving from the image of "The Sorrow that Endureth for Ever" to the new image of "The Pleasure that Abideth for a Moment," or more simply, from the ideology of realism to the humane hedonism of Walter Pater.

But the next prose-poem, "The Doer of Good," is an extraordinary parable, celebrated by Yeats, though he regretted that Wilde may have spoiled it in the passage from oral recital to the ornate diction of the text. Jesus comes to four people he had healed or saved—the leper, the blind man, Mary Magdalen, and Lazarus—and they reply to the Christ in unanswerable paradoxes. The healed leper, now a reveler and a drunkard, asks: "How else should I live?" The cured blind man, now an idolator of the forgiven Magdalen, asks: "At what else should I look?" The Magdalen, who will not walk the way set forth by the normative Torah, is beyond asking anything and laughs that her own way "is a pleasant way." Finally, the resurrected Lazarus asks the overwhelming rhetorical question "What else should I do but weep?"

Yeats may have been too concerned about the ornateness of diction to have seen how subtly Wilde has arranged this poem in prose. Each time, Jesus touches again the person he has healed, saved, or resurrected by a previous laying on of hands, but each time the touch is different. He touches the former leper on the shoulder, the restored blind man on the hand, the Magdalen on her painted raiment, and the resurrected Lazarus, most erotically, on "the long locks of his hair." Each touch is precise, because each is a clear displacement of desire, as though Wilde's Jesus were restrained by his normative Judaic allegiances from yielding to his own true nature. The leper's shoulder is a displacement of his Dionysiac mouth or lips, now freed of sores, while the hand of the man formerly blind substitutes for his eyes. Painted raiment and the long hair of Lazarus manifestly become fetishes, in each case for sexual parts. Drink, sexual excess, despair of life itself; these are the reality that the Christ himself cannot abolish, the reality everywhere underlying Wilde's fantasy and wit.

Oscar Wilde's best prose poem, "The Disciple," written in 1893, represents the consummate expression of Wilde's psychological and spiritual sense of the abyss. It is difficult to see how a poem in prose could be better. The diction and prose rhythm, far from being ornate, are of a limpid clarity, graciously mitigating the savage irony of "The Disciple's" awareness of both natural and human limits.

When Narcissus died the pool of his pleasure changed from a cup of sweet waters into a cup of salt tears, and the Oreads came weeping through the woodland that they might sing to the pool and give it comfort.

And when they saw that the pool had changed from a cup of sweet waters into a cup of salt tears, they loosened the green tresses of their hair and cried to the pool and said, "We do not wonder that you should mourn in this manner for Narcissus, so beautiful was he."

"But was Narcissus beautiful?" said the pool."

Who should know better than you? answered the Oreads. "Us did he ever pass by, but you he sought for, and would lie on your banks and look down at you, and in the mirror of your waters he would mirror his own beauty."

And the pool answered, "But I loved Narcissus because, as he lay on my banks and looked down at me, in the mirror of his eyes I saw ever my own beauty mirrored."

Kierkegaard might have called this "The Case of the Contemporary Disciple Doubled." Narcissus never saw the pool, nor the pool Narcissus, but at least the pool mourns him. Wilde's despair transcended even his humane wit, and could not be healed by the critical spirit or by the marvelous rightness of his perceptions and sensations. Wilde, like Pater both a contemporary of Freud and a Freudian before Freud, as it were, anticipates the fundamental Freudian formula. All love initially is self-love, and can return to the ego when the object is withdrawn. The ego is always a bodily ego, and is necessarily a narcissistic ego, and so partly unconscious or repressed. These realizations, which in Pater and Freud led to Stoicism, in the more emotional and flamboyant Wilde could lead only to authentic despair.

Something of the same despair oddly vitalizes "The Master," where the despair mounts up to become a horror, where the homoerotic and masochistic would-be Christ weeps not for Jesus but for himself: "All things that this man has done I have done also. And yet they have not crucified me." Wilde, having rushed towards his own crucifixion by British society, in his long letter to Lord Alfred Douglas from Reading Gaol, January–March 1897 (*De Profundis*, as we now call it), insisted that Jesus, like Wilde himself, had created his own catastrophe out of profound imaginative need:

And it is the imaginative quality of Christ's own nature that makes him this palpitating centre of romance. The strange figures of poetic drama and ballad are made by the imagination of others, but out of his own imagination entirely did Jesus of Nazareth create himself. The cry of Isaiah had really no more to do with his coming than the song of the nightingale has to do with the rising of the moon—no more, though perhaps no less. He was the denial as well as the affirmation of prophecy. For every expectation that he fulfilled, there was another that he destroyed.

This Jesus is High Romantic rather than nihilistic, as though Wilde does not quite dare wholly to assimilate the Christ to himself. The fifth prose-poem, "The House of Judgment," embraces nihilism, when the Man assures God that he cannot be sentenced to Hell by the Deity "because in Hell have I always lived," or to Heaven, because it is unimaginable by men. When we reach the final prose-poem, "The Teacher of Wisdom," Wilde's complex bitterness gives us a parable of the sorrows of influence, of the loss that tuition causes in the teacher, rather than in the taught. "The Teacher of Wisdom" confirms Lord Henry Wotton's remark to Wilde's Dorian Gray that all influence is immoral, necessarily including Lord Henry's instruction of Dorian:

> Because to influence a person is to give him one's own soul. He does not think his natural thoughts, or burn with his natural passions. His virtues are not real to him. His sins, if there are such things as sins, are borrowed. He becomes an echo of someone else's music, an actor of a part that has not been written for him.

Closer even to "The Teacher of Wisdom" is Wilde's own bitterness in "The Portrait of Mr. W.H." "Influence is simply a transference of personality, a mode of giving away what is most precious to one's self, and its exercise produces a sense, and, it may be, a reality of loss. Every disciple takes away something from his master."

This is the loss experienced by the Teacher of Wisdom, who finally gives away completely his knowledge of God, only to be rewarded by the perfect love of God. If this seems sentimental to us, that may be because Wilde was enough of a Gnostic not to be able to convince himself that knowledge of God and love of God were antithetical to one another. We can believe that Wilde's deathbed conversion to the Church was simply a reaffirmation of his lifelong belief that Christ was an artist, not in Wilde a frivolous belief but an heretical one, indeed an aesthetic version of Gnosticism. Hence Wilde's preference for the Fourth Gospel, which he shrewdly regarded as Gnostic:

> While in reading the Gospels—particularly that of St. John himself, or whatever early Gnostic took his name and mantle—I see this continual assertion of the imagination as the basis of all spiritual and material life, I see also that to Christ imagination was simply a form of Love, and that to him Love was Lord in the fullest meaning of the phrase.

This is Wilde speaking out of the depths in *De Profundis*. G. Wilson Knight, startlingly linking Wilde and Christ, hints that the ideology of Wilde's homosexuality was its dominant element, involving the raising of love to the high realm of aesthetic contemplation. Without disputing Knight (or Wilde), one can observe that such an elevation is more like Pater than Plato, more like the lying against time that is the privileged moment than the lying against mortality that is the realm of the timeless Ideas. As Pater's most dangerous disciple, Wilde literalizes Pater's valorization of perception over nature, of impression over description.

VI

In Conrad's "Youth" (1898), Marlow gives us a brilliant description of the sinking of the *Judea*:

> Between the darkness of earth and heaven she was burning fiercely upon a disc of purple sea shot by the blood-red play of gleams; upon a disc of water glittering and sinister. A high, clear flame, an immense and lonely flame, ascended from the ocean, and from its summit the black smoke poured continuously at the sky. She burned furiously; mournful and imposing like a funeral pile kindled in the night, surrounded by the sea, watched over by the stars. A magnificent death had come like a grace, like a gift, like a reward to that old ship at the end of her laborious day. The surrender of her weary ghost to the keeper of the stars and sea was stirring like the sight of a glorious triumph. The masts fell just before daybreak, and for a moment there was a burst and turmoil of sparks that seemed to fill with flying fire the night patient and watchful, the vast night lying silent upon the sea. At

daylight she was only a charred shell, floating still under a cloud
of smoke and bearing a glowing mass of coal within.

Then the oars were got out, and the boats forming in a line
moved round her remains as if in procession—the longboat
leading. As we pulled across her stern a slim dart of fire shot out
viciously at us, and suddenly she went down, head first, in a great
hiss of steam. The unconsumed stern was the last to sink; but the
paint had gone, had cracked, had peeled off, and there were no
letters, there was no word, no stubborn device that was like her
soul, to flash at the rising sun her creed and her name.

The apocalyptic vividness is enhanced by the visual namelessness of the
"unconsumed stern," as though the creed of Christ's people maintained both
its traditional refusal to violate the Second Commandment, and its
traditional affirmation of its not-to-be-named God. With the *Judea*, Conrad
sinks the romance of youth's illusions, but like all losses in Conrad this
submersion in the destructive element is curiously dialectical, since only
experiential loss allows for the compensation of an imaginative gain in the
representation of artistic truth. Originally the ephebe of Flaubert and of
Flaubert's "son," Maupassant, Conrad was reborn as the narrative disciple of
Henry James, the James of *The Spoils of Poynton* and *What Maisie Knew*, rather
than the James of the final phase.

Ian Watt convincingly traces the genesis of Marlow to the way that
"James developed the indirect narrative approach through the sensitive
central intelligence of one of the characters." Marlow, whom James derided
as "that preposterous magic mariner," actually represents Conrad's swerve
away from the excessive strength of James's influence upon him. By always
"mixing himself up with the narrative," in James's words, Marlow guarantees
an enigmatic reserve that increases the distance between the impressionistic
techniques of Conrad and James. Though there is little valid comparison that
can be made between Conrad's greatest achievements and the hesitant,
barely fictional status of Pater's *Marius the Epicurean*, Conrad's impressionism
is as extreme and solipsistic as Pater's. There is a definite parallel between the
fates of Sebastian Van Storck (in Pater's *Imaginary Portraits*) and Decoud in
Nostromo.

In his 1897 Preface to *The Nigger of the "Narcissus*,*"* Conrad famously
insisted that his creative task was "before all to make you see." He presumably
was aware that he thus joined himself to a line of prose seers whose latest
representatives were Carlyle, Ruskin, and Pater. There is a movement in that
group from Carlyle's exuberant "Natural Supernaturalism" through Ruskin's

paganization of Evangelical fervor to Pater's evasive and skeptical Epicurean materialism, with its eloquent suggestion that all we can see is the flux of sensations. Conrad exceeds Pater in the reduction of impressionism to a state of consciousness where the seeing narrator is hopelessly mixed up with the seen narrative. James may seem an impressionist when compared to Flaubert, but alongside of Conrad he is clearly shown to be a kind of Platonist, imposing forms and resolutions upon the flux of human relations by an exquisite formal geometry altogether his own.

To observe that Conrad is metaphysically less of an idealist is hardly to argue that he is necessarily a stronger novelist than his master, James. It may suggest though that Conrad's originality is more disturbing than that of James, and may help explain why Conrad, rather than James, became the dominant influence upon the generation of American novelists that included Hemingway, Fitzgerald, and Faulkner. The cosmos of *The Sun Also Rises, The Great Gatsby*, and *As I Lay Dying* derives from *Heart of Darkness* and *Nostromo* rather than from *The Ambassadors* and *The Golden Bowl*. Darl Bundren is the extreme inheritor of Conrad's quest to carry impressionism into its heart of darkness in the human awareness that we are only a flux of sensations gazing outwards upon a flux of impressions.

VII

Heart of Darkness may always be a critical battleground between readers who regard it as an aesthetic triumph and those like myself who doubt its ability to rescue us from its own hopeless obscurantism. That Marlow seems, at moments, not to know what he is talking about is almost certainly one of the narrative's deliberate strengths, but if Conrad also seems finally not to know, then he necessarily loses some of his authority as a storyteller. Perhaps he loses it to death—our death, or our anxiety that he will not sustain the illusion of his fiction's duration long enough for us to sublimate the frustrations it brings us.

These frustrations need not be deprecated. Conrad's diction, normally flawless, is notoriously vague throughout *Heart of Darkness*. E.M. Forster's wicked comment on Conrad's entire work is justified perhaps only when applied to *Heart of Darkness*:

Misty in the middle as well as at the edges, ... the secret casket of his genius contains a vapour rather than a jewel.... No creed, in fact.

Forster's misty vapor seems to inhabit such Conradian recurrent modifiers as "monstrous," "unspeakable," "atrocious," and many more, but these are minor defects compared to the involuntary self-parody that Conrad inflicts upon himself. There are moments that sound more like James Thurber lovingly satirizing Conrad than like Conrad:

> We had carried Kurtz into the pilot house: there was more air there. Lying on the couch, he stared through the open shutter. There was an eddy in the mass of human bodies, and the woman with helmeted head and tawny cheeks rushed out to the very brink of the stream. She put out her hands, shouted something, and all that wild mob took up the shout in a roaring chorus of articulated, rapid, breathless utterance.
> "Do you understand this?" I asked.
> He kept on looking out past me with fiery, longing eyes, with a mingled expression of wistfulness and hate. He made no answer, but I saw a smile, a smile of indefinable meaning, appear on his colorless lips that a moment after twitched convulsively. "Do I not?" he said slowly, gasping, as if the words had been torn out of him by a supernatural power.

This cannot be defended as an instance of what Frank Kermode calls a language "needed when Marlow is not equal to the experience described." Has the experience been described here? Smiles of "indefinable meaning" are smiled once too often in a literary text if they are smiled even once. *Heart of Darkness* has taken on some of the power of myth, even if the book is limited by its involuntary obscurantism. It has haunted American literature from T.S. Eliot's poetry through our major novelists of the era 1920 to 1940, on to a line of movies that go from the *Citizen Kane* of Orson Welles (a substitute for an abandoned Welles project to film *Heart of Darkness*) on to Coppola's *Apocalypse Now*. In this instance, Conrad's formlessness seems to have worked as an aid, so diffusing his conception as to have made it available to an almost universal audience.

VIII

Lord Jim (1900) is the first of Conrad's five great novels, followed by what seems to me the finest, *Nostromo* (1904), and then by the marvelous sequence of *The Secret Agent* (1906), *Under Western Eyes* (1911), and finally *Victory* (1915). Of these, it seems clear that *Lord Jim* has the closest to universal appeal; I have rarely met a reader who was not fascinated by it. Martin Price, the subtlest of Conrad's moral critics, prefers *Lord Jim* to *Nostromo* because he finds that both the author's skepticism and the author's Romanticism are given their full scope in *Lord Jim* rather than in *Nostromo*. Doubtless this is true, but Jim himself lacks the High Romantic appeal of the magnificent Nostromo, and I prefer also the corrosive skepticism of Decoud to the skeptical wisdom of Marlow and Stein. Not that I would deprecate *Lord Jim*; had Conrad written nothing else, this single novel would have guaranteed his literary survival.

Aaron Fogel, writing on *Nostromo*, sees it as marking Conrad's transition from an Oedipal emphasis (as in *Lord Jim*) to a representation of the self's struggle against more outward influences. Certainly Jim's struggle does suit Fogel's formulation of the earlier mode in Conrad: "the denial, by internalization, of the Oedipal order of forced dialogue in the outside world—the translation of inquisition into an inner feeling of compulsion to quarrel with a forebear or with oneself." Though there is much of Conrad in Marlow, and a little of him in Stein, his true surrogate is surely Jim, whose dialectics of defeat are in some sense a late version of Polish Romanticism, of the perpetual defeat of Polish heroism. This is only to intimate that Jim's Byronism is rather more Polish than British. Jim rarely demands anything, and he never demands victory. One way of understanding the novel is to see how incomprehensible it would be if Conrad had chosen to make his hero an American.

Marlow, our narrator, becomes something like a father to Jim, in an implicit movement that has been shrewdly traced by Ian Watt. There is an impressive irony in the clear contrast between the eloquent father, Marlow, and the painfully inarticulate son, Jim. The relation between the two poignantly enhances our sense of just how vulnerable Jim is and cannot cease to be. Marlow is a survivor, capable of withstanding nearly the full range of human experience, while Jim is doom-eager, as much a victim of the Romantic imagination as he is a belated instance of its intense appeal to us.

Albert J. Guérard associated *Lord Jim* with *Absalom, Absalom!* (a not un-Conradian work) as novels that become different with each attentive reading. Jim's "simplicity" takes the place of the charismatic quality we expect of the Romantic protagonist, and Guerard sees Jim as marked by a conflict between personality and will. But Jim's personality remains a mystery to us, almost despite Marlow, and Jim's will is rarely operative, so far as I can see. What we can know about Jim is the enormous strength and prevalence of his fantasy-making powers, which we need not confuse with a Romantic imagination, since *that* hardly excludes self-knowledge. Indeed, the deepest puzzle of Jim is why should he fascinate anyone at all, let alone Marlow, Stein, Conrad, and ourselves? Why is he endless to meditation?

Everyone who has read *Lord Jim* (and many who have not) remember its most famous statement, which is Stein's:

> A man that is born falls into a dream like a man who falls into the sea. If he tries to climb out into the air as inexperienced people endeavour to do, he drowns—*nicht wahr?* ... No! I tell you! The way is to the destructive element submit yourself, and with the exertions of your hands and feet in the water make the deep, deep sea keep you up.

That describes Stein's Romanticism, but hardly Jim's, since Jim cannot swim in the dreamworld. When he seems to make the destructive element keep him up, as in Patusan, there would always have to be a Gentleman Brown waiting for him. An imagination like Jim's, which has little sense of otherness, falls into identification as the truly destructive element, and the error of identifying with the outrageous Brown is what kills Jim. Tony Tanner deftly compares Brown to Iago, if only because Brown's hatred for Jim approximates Iago's hatred for Othello, but Brown has a kind of rough justice in denying Jim's moral superiority. That returns us to the enigma of Jim: why does he make such a difference for Marlow—and for us?

We know the difference between Jim and Brown, even if Jim cannot, even as we know that Jim never will mature into Stein. Is Jim merely the spirit of illusion, or does there linger in him something of the legitimate spirit of Romance? Marlow cannot answer the question, and we cannot either, no matter how often we read *Lord Jim*. Is that a strength or a weakness in this novel? That Conrad falls into obscurantism, particularly in *Heart of Darkness*, is beyond denial. Is *Lord Jim* simply an instance of such obscurantism on a larger scale?

Impressionist fiction necessarily forsakes the Idealist metaphysics of the earlier Romantic novel, a metaphysics that culminated in George Eliot. Marlow beholding Jim is a concourse of sensations recording a flood of impressions; how can a sensation distinguish whether an impression is authentic or not? Yet Marlow is haunted by the image of heroism, and finds an authentic realization of the image in Stein. The famous close of Marlow's narrative invokes Jim as an overwhelming force of real existence, and also as a disembodied spirit among the shades:

> "And that's the end. He passes away under a cloud, inscrutable at heart, forgotten, unforgiven, and excessively

romantic. Not in the wildest days of his boyish visions could he have seen the alluring shape of such an extraordinary success! For it may very well be that in the short moment of his last proud and unflinching glance, he had beheld the face of that opportunity which, like an Eastern bride, had come veiled to his side.

"But we can see him, an obscure conqueror of fame, tearing himself out of the arms of a jealous love at the sign, at the call of his exalted egoism. He goes away from a living woman to celebrate his pitiless wedding with a shadowy ideal of conduct. Is he satisfied—quite, now, I wonder? We ought to know. He is one of us—and have I not stood up once, like an evoked ghost, to answer for his eternal constancy? Was I so very wrong after all? Now he is no more, there are days when the reality of his existence comes to me with an immense, with an overwhelming force; and yet upon my honour there are moments, too, when he passes from my eyes like a disembodied spirit astray amongst the passions of his earth, ready to surrender himself faithfully to the claim of his own world of shades.

"Who knows? He is gone, inscrutable at heart, and the poor girl is leading a sort of soundless, inert life in Stein's house. Stein has aged greatly of late. He feels it himself, and says often that he is 'preparing to leave all this; preparing to leave...' while he waves his hand sadly at his butterflies."

Stein's sadness is that he had hoped to find a successor in Jim and now wanes into the sense that he is at the end of a tradition. Enigmatic as always, Marlow cannot resolve his own attitude towards Jim. I do not suppose that we can either and I wonder if that is necessarily an aesthetic strength in Conrad's novel. Perhaps it is enough that we are left pondering our own inability to reconcile the authentic and the heroic.

IX

Endlessly enigmatic as a personality and as a formidable moral character, Conrad pervades his own books, a presence not to be put by, an elusive storyteller who yet seems to write a continuous spiritual autobiography. By the general consent of advanced critics and of common readers, Conrad's masterwork is *Nostromo;* where his perspectives are largest, and where his essential originality in the representation of human blindnesses and consequent human affections is at its strongest. Like all overwhelming originalities, Conrad's ensues in an authentic difficulty, which can be assimilated only very slowly, if at all. Repeated rereadings gradually convince me that *Nostromo* is anything but a Conradian litany to the virtue he liked to call "fidelity." The book is tragedy, of a post-Nietzschean sort, despite Conrad's strong contempt for Nietzsche. Decoud, void of all illusions, is self-destroyed because he cannot sustain solitude. Nostromo, perhaps the only persuasive instance of the natural sublime in a twentieth-century hero of fiction, dies "betrayed he hardly knows by what or by whom," as Conrad says. But this is Conrad at his most knowing, and the novel shows us precisely how Nostromo is betrayed, by himself, and by what in himself.

It is a mystery of an overwhelming fiction why it can sustain virtually endless rereadings. *Nostromo*, to me, rewards frequent rereadings in something of the way that *Othello* does; there is always surprise waiting for me. Brilliant as every aspect of the novel is, Nostromo himself is the imaginative center of the book, and yet Nostromo is unique among Conrad's personae, and not a Conradian man whom we could have expected. His creator's description of this central figure as "the Magnificent Capataz, the Man of the People," breathes a writer's love for his most surprising act of the imagination. So does a crucial paragraph from the same source, the Author's Note that Conrad added as a preface thirteen years after the initial publication:

> In his firm grip on the earth he inherits, in his improvidence and generosity, in his lavishness with his gifts, in his manly vanity, in the obscure sense of his greatness and in his faithful devotion with something despairing as well as desperate in its impulses, he is a Man of the People, their very own unenvious force, disdaining to lead but ruling from within. Years afterwards, grown older as the famous Captain Fidanza, with a stake in the country, going about his many affairs followed by respectful glances in the modernized streets of Sulaco, calling on the widow of the cargador, attending the Lodge, listening in unmoved silence to anarchist speeches at the meeting, the enigmatical patron of the new revolutionary agitation, the trusted, the wealthy comrade Fidanza with the knowledge of his moral ruin locked up in his breast, he remains essentially a man of the People. In his mingled love and scorn of life and in the bewildered conviction of having been betrayed, of dying betrayed he hardly knows by what or by whom, he is still of the People, their undoubted Great Man—with a private history of his own.

Despite this "moral ruin," and not because of it, Conrad and his readers share the conviction of Nostromo's greatness, share in his sublime self-recognition. How many persuasive images of greatness, of a natural sublimity, exist in modern fiction? Conrad's may be the last enhanced vision of Natural Man, of the Man of the People, in which anyone has found it possible to believe. Yet Conrad himself characteristically qualifies his own belief in Nostromo, and critics too easily seduced by ironies have weakly misread the merely apparent irony of Conrad's repeated references to Nostromo as "the magnificent Capataz de Cargadores." Magnificent, beyond the reach of all irony, Nostromo manifestly is. It is the magnificence of the natural leader who disdains leadership, yet who loves reputation. Though he is of the People, Nostromo serves no ideal, unlike old Viola the Garibaldino. With the natural genius for command, the charismatic endowment that could make him another Garibaldi, Nostromo nevertheless scorns any such role, in the name of any cause whatsoever. He is a pure Homeric throwback, not wholly unlike Tolstoy's Hadji Murad, except that he acknowledges neither enemies nor friends except for his displaced father, Viola. And he enchants us even as he enchants the populace of Sulaco, though most of all he enchants the skeptical and enigmatic Conrad, who barely defends himself against the enchantment with some merely rhetorical ironies.

Ethos is the daimon, character is fate, in Conrad as in Heraclitus, and Nostromo's tragic fate is the inevitable fulfillment of his desperate grandeur, which Conrad cannot dismiss as mere vanity, despite all his own skepticism. Only Nostromo saves the novel, and Conrad, from nihilism, the nihilism of Decoud's waste in suicide. Nostromo is betrayed partly by Decoud's act of self-destruction, with its use of four ingots of silver to send his body down, but largely by his own refusal to maintain the careless preference for glory over gain which is more than a gesture or a style, which indeed is the authentic mode of being that marks the hero. Nostromo is only himself when he can say, with perfect truth, "My name is known from one end of Sulaco to the other. What more can you do for me?"

X

Toward the end of chapter 10 of part 3, "The Lighthouse," Conrad renders his own supposed verdict upon both Decoud and Nostromo, in a single page, in two parallel sentences a paragraph apart:

A victim of the disillusioned weariness which is the retribution meted out to intellectual audacity, the brilliant Don Martin

Decoud, weighted by the bars of San Tomé silver, disappeared without a trace, swallowed up in the immense indifference of things.

The magnificent Capataz de Cargadores, victim of the disenchanted vanity which is the reward of audacious action, sat in the weary pose of a hunted outcast through a night of sleeplessness as tormenting as any known to Decoud, his companion in the most desperate affair of his life. And he wondered how Decoud had died.

Decoud's last thought, after shooting himself, was "I wonder how that Capataz died." Conrad seems to leave little to choose between being "a victim of the disillusioned weariness which is the retribution meted out to intellectual audacity" or a "victim of the disenchanted vanity which is the reward of audacious action." The brilliant intellectual and the magnificent man of action are victimized alike for their audacity, and it is a fine irony that "retribution" and "reward" become assimilated to one another. Yet the book is Nostromo's and not Decoud's, and a "disenchanted vanity" is a higher fate than a "disillusioned weariness," if only because an initial enchantment is a nobler state than an initial illusion. True that Nostromo's enchantment was only of and with himself, but that is proper for an Achilles or a Hadji Murad. Decoud dies because he cannot bear solitude, and so cannot bear himself. Nostromo finds death-in-life and then death because he has lost the truth of his vanity, its enchanted insouciance, the *sprezzatura* which he, a plebeian, nevertheless had made his authentic self.

Nostromo's triumph, though he cannot know it, is that an image of this authenticity survives him, an image so powerful as to persuade both Conrad and the perceptive reader that even the self-betrayed hero retains an aesthetic dignity that renders his death tragic rather than sordid. Poor Decoud, for all his brilliance, dies a nihilistic death, disappearing "without a trace, swallowed up in the immense indifference of things." Nostromo, after his death, receives an aesthetic tribute beyond all irony, in the superb closing paragraph of the novel:

Dr. Monygham, pulling round in the police-galley, heard the name pass over his head. It was another of Nostromo's triumphs, the greatest, the most enviable, the most sinister of all. In that true cry of undying passion that seemed to ring aloud from Punta Mala to Azuera and away to the bright line of the horizon, overhung by a big white cloud shining like a mass of solid silver, the genius of the magnificent Capataz de Cargadores dominated the dark gulf containing his conquests of treasure and love.

XI

Twenty years after writing his essay of 1943 on Kipling (reprinted in *The Liberal Imagination*, 1951), Lionel Trilling remarked that if he could write the critique again, he would do it "less censoriously and with more affectionate admiration." Trilling, always the representative critic of his era, reflected a movement in the evaluation of Kipling that still continues. I suspect that this movement will coexist with its dialectical countermovement of recoil against Kipling, as long as our literary tradition lasts. Kipling is an authentically *popular* writer, in every sense of the word. Stories like "The Man Who Would Be King," children's tales from the *Jungle Books* and the *Just-So Stories;* the novel *Kim*, which is clearly Kipling's masterwork; certain late stories and dozens of ballads—these survive both as high literature and as perpetual entertainment. It is as though Kipling had set out to refute the sublime function of literature, which is to make us forsake easier pleasures for more difficult pleasures.

In his speech on "Literature," given in 1906, Kipling sketched a dark tale of the storyteller's destiny:

> There is an ancient legend which tells us that when a man first achieved a most notable deed he wished to explain to his Tribe what he had done. As soon as he began to speak, however, he was smitten with dumbness, he lacked words, and sat down. Then there arose— according to the story—a masterless man, one who had taken no part in the action of his fellow, who had no special virtues, but who was afflicted—that is the phrase—with the magic of the necessary word. He saw; he told; he described the merits of the notable deed in such a fashion, we are assured, that the words "became alive and walked up and down in the hearts of all his hearers." Thereupon, the Tribe seeing that the words were certainly alive, and fearing lest the man with the words would hand down untrue tales about them to their children, took and killed him. But, later, they saw that the magic was in the words, not in the man.

Seven years later, in the ghastly Primal History scene of *Totem and Taboo*'s fourth chapter, Freud depicted a curiously parallel scene, where a

violent primal father is murdered and devoured by his sons, who thus bring
to an end the patriarchal horde. Kipling's Primal Storytelling Scene features
"a masterless man" whose only virtue is "the necessary word." But he too is
slain by the Tribe, or primal horde, lest he transmit fictions about the Tribe
to its children. Only later, in Freud, do the sons of the primal father
experience remorse, and so "the dead father became stronger than the living
one had been." Only later, in Kipling, does the Tribe see "that the magic was
in the words, not in the man."

Freud's true subject in his Primal History Scene was the transference,
the carrying-over from earlier to later attachments of an overdetermined
affect. The true subject of Kipling's Primal Storytelling Scene is not so much
the Tale of the Tribe, or the magic that was in the words, but the storyteller's
freedom, the masterless man's vocation that no longer leads to death, but that
can lead to a death-in-life. What Kipling denies is his great fear, which is that
the magic indeed is just as much in the masterless man as it is in the words.

Kipling, with his burly imperialism and his indulgences in anti-
intellectualism, would seem at first out of place in the company of Walter
Pater, Oscar Wilde, and William Butler Yeats. Nevertheless, Kipling writes
in the rhetorical stance of an aesthete and is very much a Paterian in the
metaphysical sense. The conclusion of Pater's *Renaissance* is precisely the
credo of Kipling's protagonists:

> Not to discriminate every moment some passionate attitude in
> those about us, and in the brilliancy of their gifts some tragic
> dividing of forces on their ways, is, on this short day of frost and
> sun, to sleep before evening. With this sense of the splendour of
> our experience and of its awful brevity, gathering all we are into
> one desperate effort to see and touch, we shall hardly have time
> to make theories about the things we see and touch. What we
> have to do is to be for ever curiously testing new opinions and
> courting new impressions.

Frank Kermode observed that Kipling was a writer "who steadfastly
preferred action and machinery to the prevalent Art for Art's Sake," but that
is to misread weakly what Pater meant by ending the conclusion to *The
Renaissance* with what soon became a notorious formula:

> We have an interval, and then our place knows us no more. Some
> spend this interval in listlessness, some in high passions, the
> wisest, at least among "the children of this world," in art and

song. For our one chance lies in expanding that interval, in getting as many pulsations as possible into the given time. Great passions may give us this quickened sense of life, ecstasy and sorrow of love, the various forms of enthusiastic activity, disinterested or otherwise, which come naturally to many of us. Only be sure it is passion—that it does yield you this fruit of a quickened, multiplied consciousness. Of this wisdom, the poetic passion, the desire of beauty, the love of art for art's sake, has most; for art comes to you professing frankly to give nothing but the highest quality to your moments as they pass, and simply for those moments' sake.

Like Pater, like Nietzsche, Kipling sensed that we possess and cherish fictions because the reductive truth would destroy us. "The love of art for art's sake" simply means that we choose to believe in a fiction, while knowing that it is not true, to adopt Wallace Stevens's version of the Paterian credo. And fiction, according to Kipling, was written by daemonic forces within us, by "some tragic dividing of forces on their ways." Those forces are no more meaningful than the tales and ballads they produce. What Kipling shares finally with Pater is a deep conviction that we are caught always in a vortex of sensations, a solipsistic concourse of impressions piling upon one another, with great vividness but little consequence.

XII

Kipling's authentic precursor and literary hero was Mark Twain, whose *Huckleberry Finn* and *Tom Sawyer* are reflected inescapably in *Kim*, certainly Kipling's finest achievement. "An Interview with Mark Twain" records Kipling's vision of the two hours of genial audience granted him, starting with Twain's "Well, you think you owe me something, and you've come to tell me so. That's what I call squaring a debt handsomely."

Kim, permanent work as it is, does not square the debt, partly because Kim is, as David Bromwich notes, both Huck Finn and Tom Sawyer, which is to confuse essentially opposed personalities. Since *Kim* is founded upon *Huckleberry Finn*, and not on *Don Quixote*, the mixing of Huck and Tom in Kim's nature brings about a softening of focus that malforms the novel. We cannot find Sancho Panza in Kim, though there is a touch of the Don, as well as of Nigger Jim, in the lama. Insofar as he is free but lonely, Kim is Huck; insofar as he serves the worldly powers, he is Tom. It is striking that in his "Interview with Mark Twain" Kipling expresses interest only in Tom Sawyer, asking Twain "whether we were ever going to hear of Tom Sawyer as a man." I suspect that some anxiety of influence was involved, since *Kim* is the son of the *Adventures of Huckleberry Finn* and not of the lesser novel.

Kim is one of the great instances in the language of a popular adventure story that is also exalted literature. *Huckleberry Finn* is too astonishing a book, too nearly the epic of the American consciousness, together with *Leaves of Grass* and *Moby-Dick*, to be regarded as what it only pretends to be: a good yarn. *Kim* stations itself partly in that mode which ranges from Rider Haggard, at its nadir, to Robert Louis Stevenson, at its zenith: the boy's romance crossing over into the ancient form of romance proper.

There are many splendors in *Kim*, but the greatest is surely the relation between Kim and his master, the lovable, half-mad Tibetan lama, who proves to be Kim's true father, and to whom Kim becomes the best of sons. It is a triumph of the exact representation of profound human affection, rather than a sentimentality of any kind, that can move us to tears as the book ends:

> "Hear me! I bring news! The Search is finished. Comes now the Reward.... Thus. When we were among the Hills, I lived on thy strength till the young branch bowed and nigh broke. When we came out of the Hills, I was troubled for thee and for other matters which I held in my heart. The boat of my soul lacked direction; I could not see into the Cause of Things. So I gave thee over to the virtuous woman altogether. I took no food. I drank no water. Still I saw not the Way. They pressed food upon me and cried at my shut door. So I removed myself to a hollow under a tree. I took no food. I took no water. I sat in meditation two days and two nights, abstracting my mind; inbreathing and outbreathing in the required manner.... Upon the second night—so great was my reward—the wise Soul loosed itself from the silly Body and went free. This I have never before attained, though I have stood on the threshold of it. Consider, for it is a marvel!"
>
> "A marvel indeed. Two days and two nights without food! Where was the Sahiba?" said Kim under his breath.
>
> "Yea, my Soul went free, and, wheeling like an eagle, saw indeed that there was no Teshoo Lama nor any other soul. As a drop draws to water, so my soul drew near to the Great Soul which is beyond all things. At that point, exalted in contemplation, I saw all Hind, from Ceylon in the sea to the Hills, and my own Painted Rocks at Suchzen; I saw every camp and village, to the least, where

we have ever rested. I saw them at one time and in one place; for they were within the Soul. By this I knew the Soul had passed beyond the illusion of Time and Space and of Things. By this I knew that I was free. I saw thee lying in thy cot, and I saw thee falling down hill under the idolater—at one time, in one place, in my Soul, which, as I say, had touched the Great Soul. Also I saw the stupid body of Teshoo Lama lying down, and the hakim from Dacca kneeled beside, shouting in its ear. Then my Soul was all alone, and I saw nothing, for I was all things, having reached the Great Soul. And I meditated a thousand years, passionless, well aware of the Causes of all Things. Then a voice cried: 'What shall come to the boy if thou art dead?' and I was shaken back and forth in myself with pity for thee; and I said: 'I will return to my chela, lest he miss the Way.' Upon this my Soul, which is the soul of Teshoo Lama, withdrew itself from the Great Soul with strivings and yearnings and retchings and agonies not to be told. As the egg from the fish, as the fish from the water, as the water from the cloud, as the cloud from the thick air, so put forth, so leaped out, so drew away, so fumed up the soul of Teshoo Lama from the Great Soul. Then a voice cried: 'The River! Take heed to the River!' and I looked down upon all the world, which was as I had seen it before—one in time, one in place—and I saw plainly the River of the Arrow at my feet. At that hour my Soul was hampered by some evil or other whereof I was not wholly cleansed, and it lay upon my arms and coiled round my waist; but I put it aside, and I cast forth as an eagle in my flight for the very place of the River. I pushed aside world upon world for thy sake. I saw the River below me—the River of the Arrow—and, descending, the waters of it closed over me; and behold I was again in the body of Teshoo Lama, but free from sin, and the *hakim* from Dacca bore up my head in the waters of the River. It is here! It is behind the mango-tope here—even here!"

"Allah Kerim! Oh, well that the Babu was by! Wast thou very wet?"

"Why should I regard? I remember the *hakim* was concerned for the body of Teshoo Lama. He haled it out of the holy water in his hands, and there came afterwards thy horse-seller from the North with a cot and men, and they put the body on the cot and bore it up to the Sahiba's house."

"What said the Sahiba?"

"I was meditating in that body, and did not hear. So thus the Search is ended. For the merit that I have acquired, the River of the Arrow is here. It broke forth at our feet, as I have said. I have found it. Son of my Soul, I have wrenched my Soul back from the Threshold of Freedom to free thee from all sin—as I am free, and sinless. Just is the Wheel! Certain is our deliverance. Come!"

He crossed his hands on his lap and smiled, as a man may who has won Salvation for himself and his beloved.

This long passage builds, through radiant apprehensions, to an extraordinarily controlled and calm epiphany of parental love. The vision of the lama, though it presents itself as the wise soul's freedom from the silly body, is clearly not dualistic, but is caused by the lama's honest declaration: "I was troubled for thee." Caught up in the freedom from illusion, and free therefore supposedly of any concern for other souls, like one's own, they are not, the lama is close to the final freedom: "for I was all things." The voice that cries him back to life is the voice of his fatherly love for Kim, and the reward for his return to existence, negating mystical transport, is his true vision of the River, goal of his quest. It breaks forth at his feet, and is better than freedom, because it is not merely solitary, but is Salvation for his beloved adopted son, as well as for himself.

Certainly this is Kipling's most humane and hopeful moment, normative and positive. *Kim* is, like its more masterly precursor work, *Huckleberry Finn*, a book that returns us to the central values, avoiding those shadows of the abyss that hover uneasily elsewhere in Kipling. Yet even here the darker and truer Kipling lingers, in the sudden vision of nothingness that Kim experiences, only a few pages before his final reunion with the lama:

At first his legs bent like bad pipe-stems, and the flood and rush of the sunlit air dazzled him. He squatted by the white wall, the mind rummaging among the incidents of the long *dooli* journey, the lama's weaknesses, and, now that the stimulus of talk was removed, his own self-pity, of which, like the sick, he had great store. The unnerved brain edged away from all the outside, as a raw horse, once rowelled, sidles from the spur. It was enough, amply enough, that the spoil of the *kilta* was away—off his hands—out of his possession. He tried to think of the lama,—to wonder why he had tumbled into a brook,—but the bigness of the world, seen between the forecourt gates, swept linked thought aside. Then he looked upon the trees and the broad fields, with the thatched huts hidden among crops—looked with strange eyes unable to take up the size and proportion and use of things— stared for a still half-hour. All that while he felt, though he could not put it into words, that his soul was out of gear with its surroundings—a cog-wheel unconnected with any machinery, just like the idle cog-wheel of a cheap Beheea sugar-crusher laid by in a corner. The breezes fanned over him, the parrots shrieked at him, the noises of the populated house behind—squabbles, orders, and reproofs—hit on dead ears.

"I am Kim. I am Kim. And what is Kim?" His soul repeated it again and again.

Despite the Indian imagery and the characteristic obsession of Kipling with machinery, the mark of Walter Pater's aesthetic impressionism, with its sensations beckoning us to the abyss, is clearly set upon this passage. Identity flees with the flux of impressions, and the dazzlement of "the flood and rush of the sunlit air" returns us to the cosmos of the conclusion to *The Renaissance*. Kipling's art, in *Kim*, is after all art for art's sake, in the dark predicate that there is nothing else. The extravagant fiction of the great love between an Irish boy gone native in India, half a Huck Finn enthralled with freedom and half a Tom Sawyer playing games with authority, and a quixotic, aged Tibetan lama is Kipling's finest invention, and moves us endlessly. But how extravagant a fiction it is, and had to be! Kipling refused to profess the faith of those who live and die for and by art, yet in the end he had no other faith.

XIII

E.M. Forster's canonical critic was Lionel Trilling, who might have written Forster's novels had Forster not written them and had Trilling been English. Trilling ended his book on Forster (1924) with the tribute that forever exalts the author of *Howards End* and *A Passage to India* as one of those storytellers whose efforts "work without man's consciousness of them, and even against his conscious will." In Trilling's sympathetic interpretation (or identification), Forster was the true antithesis to the world of telegrams and anger:

A world at war is necessarily a world of will; in a world at war Forster reminds us of a world where the will is not everything, of a world of true order, of the necessary connection of passion and prose, and of the strange paradoxes of being human. He is one of those who raise the shield of Achilles, which is the moral intelligence of art, against the panic and emptiness which make their onset when the will is tired from its own excess.

Trilling subtly echoed Forster's own response to World War I, a response which Forster recalled as an immersion in Blake, William Morris, the early T.S. Eliot, J.K. Huysmans, Yeats: "They took me into a country where the will was not everything." Yet one can wonder whether Forster and Trilling, prophets of the liberal imagination, did not yield to a vision where there was not quite enough conscious will. *A Passage to India*, Forster's most famous work, can sustain many rereadings, so intricate is its orchestration. It is one of only a few novels of this century that is *written-through*, in the musical sense of thorough composition. But reading it yet again, after twenty years away from it, I find it to be a narrative all of whose principal figures—Aziz, Fielding, Adela Quested, Mrs. Moore, Godbole—lack conscious will. Doubtless, this is Forster's deliberate art, but the consequence is curious; the characters do not sustain rereading so well as the novel does, because none is larger than the book. Poldy holds my imagination quite apart from Joyce's *Ulysses*, as Isabel Archer does in James's *Portrait of a Lady*, or indeed as Mrs. Wilcox does in Forster's *Howards End*, at least while she is represented as being alive. The aesthetic puzzle of *A Passage to India* is why Aziz and Fielding could not have been stronger and more vivid beings than they are.

What matters most in *A Passage to India* is India, and not any Indians nor any English. But this assertion requires amendment, since Forster's India is not so much a social or cultural reality as it is an enigmatic vision of the Hindu religion, or rather of the Hindu religion as it is reimagined by the English liberal mind at its most sensitive and scrupulous. The largest surprise of a careful rereading of *A Passage to India* after so many years is that, in some aspects, it now seems a strikingly *religious* book. Forster shows us what we never ought to have forgotten, which is that any distinction between religious and secular literature is finally a mere political or societal polemic, but is neither a spiritual nor an aesthetic judgment. There is no sacred literature and no post-sacred literature, great or good. *A Passage to India* falls perhaps just short of greatness, in a strict aesthetic judgment, but spiritually it is an extraordinary achievement.

T.S. Eliot consciously strove to be a devotional poet, and certainly did become a Christian polemicist as a cultural and literary critic. Forster, an amiable freethinker and secular humanist, in his *Commonplace Book* admirably compared himself to Eliot:

With Eliot? I feel now to be as far ahead of him as I was once behind. Always a distance—and a respectful one. How I dislike his homage to pain! What a mind except the human could have excogitated it? Of course there's pain on and off through each individual's life, and pain at the end of most lives. You can't shirk it and so on. But why should it be endorsed by the schoolmaster and sanctified by the priest until

the fire and the rose are one

when so much of it is caused by disease or by bullies? It is here that Eliot becomes unsatisfactory as a seer.

One could add: it is here that Forster becomes most satisfactory as a seer, for that is the peculiar excellence of *A Passage to India*. We are reminded that Forster is another of John Ruskin's heirs, together with Proust, whom Forster rightly admired above all other modern novelists. Forster too wishes *to make us see*, in the hope that by seeing we will learn to connect, with ourselves and with others, and like Ruskin, Forster knows that seeing in this strong sense is religious, but in a mode beyond dogmatism.

XIV

A Passage to India, published in 1924, reflects Forster's service as private secretary to the Maharajah of Dewas State Senior in 1921–22, which in turn issued from his Indian visit of 1912–13 with G. Lowes Dickinson. It was not until 1953 that Forster published *The Hill of Devi*, utilizing letters he had written home from India both forty and thirty years before. *The Hill of Devi* celebrates Forster's Maharajah as a kind of saint, indeed as a religious genius, though Forster is anything but persuasive when he attempts to sustain his judgment of his friend and employer. What does come through is Forster's appreciation of certain elements in Hinduism, an appreciation that achieves its apotheosis in *A Passage to India*, and particularly in "Temple," the novel's foreshortened final part. Forster's ultimate tribute to his Maharajah, a muddler in practical matters and so one who died in disgrace, is a singular testimony for a freethinker. *The Hill of Devi* concludes with what must be called a mystical apprehension:

> His religion was the deepest thing in him. It ought to be studied—neither by the psychologist nor by the mythologist but by the individual who has experienced similar promptings. He

penetrated into rare regions and he was always hoping that others would follow him there.

What are those promptings? Where are those regions? Are these the questions fleshed out by *A Passage to India?* After observing the mystical Maharajah dance before the altar of the God Krishna, Forster quotes from a letter by the Maharajah describing the festival, and then attempts what replies seem possible:

> Such was his account. But what did he feel when he danced like King David before the altar? What were his religious opinions?
>
> The first question is easier to answer than the second. He felt as King David and other mystics have felt when they are in the mystic state. He presented well-known characteristics. He was convinced that he was in touch with the reality he called Krishna. And he was unconscious of the world around him. "You can come in during my observances tomorrow and see me if you like, but I shall not know that you are there," he once told Malcolm. And he didn't know. He was in an abnormal but recognisable state; psychologists have studied it.
>
> More interesting, and more elusive, are his religious opinions. The unseen was always close to him, even when he was joking or intriguing. Red paint on a stone could evoke it. Like most people, he implied beliefs and formulated rules for behaviour, and since he had a lively mind, he was often inconsistent. It was difficult to be sure what he did believe (outside the great mystic moments) or what he thought right or wrong. Indians are even more puzzling than Westerners here. Mr. Shastri, a spiritual and subtle Brahmin, once uttered a puzzler: "If the Gods do a thing, it is a reason for men not to do it." No doubt he was in a particular religious mood. In another mood he would have urged us to imitate the Gods. And the Maharajah was all moods. They played over his face, they agitated his delicate feet and hands. To get any pronouncement from so mercurial a creature on the subject, say, of asceticism, was impossible. As a boy, he had thought of retiring from the world, and it was an ideal which he cherished throughout his life, and which, at the end, he would have done well to practise. Yet he would condemn asceticism, declare that salvation could not be reached through it, that it might be Vedantic but it was not Vedic,

and matter and spirit must both be given their due. Nothing too much! In such a mood he seemed Greek.

He believed in the heart, and here we reach firmer ground. "I stand for the heart. To the dogs with the head," cries Herman Melville, and he would have agreed. Affection, or the possibility of it, quivered through everything, from Gokul Ashtami down to daily human relationships. When I returned to England and he heard that I was worried because the post-war world of the '20's would not add up into sense, he sent me a message. "Tell him," it ran, "tell him from me to follow his heart, and his mind will see everything clear." The message as phrased is too facile: doors open into silliness at once. But to remember and respect and prefer the heart, to have the instinct which follows it wherever possible— what surer help than that could one have through life? What better hope of clarification? Melville goes on: "The reason that the mass of men fear God and at bottom dislike Him, is because they rather distrust His heart." With that too he would have agreed.

With all respect for Forster, neither he nor his prince is coherent here, and I suspect that Forster is weakly misreading Melville, who is both more ironic and more Gnostic than Forster chooses to realize. Melville too distrusts the heart of Jehovah and consigns the head to the dogs precisely because he associates the head with Jehovah, and identifies Jehovah with the Demiurge, the god of this world. More vital would be the question: what does Professor Godbole in *A Passage to India* believe? Is he more coherent than the Maharajah, and does Forster himself achieve a more unified vision there than he does in *The Hill of Devi?*

Criticism from Lionel Trilling on has evaded these questions, but such evasion is inevitable because Forster may be vulnerable to the indictment that he himself made against Joseph Conrad, to the effect that

he is misty in the middle as well as at the edges, that the secret casket of his genius contains a vapour rather than a jewel; and that we need not try to write him down philosophically, because there is, in this particular direction, nothing to write. No creed, in fact. Only opinions, and the right to throw them overboard when facts make them look absurd. Opinions held under the semblance of eternity, girt with the sea, crowned with the stars, and therefore easily mistaken for a creed.

Heart of Darkness sustains Forster's gentle wit, but *Nostromo* does not. Is there a vapor rather than a jewel in Forster's consciousness of Hinduism, at least as represented in *A Passage to India?* "Hinduism" may be the wrong word in that question; "religion" would be better, and "spirituality" better yet. For I do not read Forster as being either hungry for belief or skeptical of it. Rather, he seems to me an Alexandrian, of the third century before the Common Era, an age celebrated in his *Alexandria: A History and a Guide* (1922), a book that goes back to his happy years in Alexandria (1915–19). In some curious sense, Forster's India is Alexandrian, and his vision of Hinduism is Plotinean. *A Passage to India* is a narrative of Neoplatonic spirituality, and the true heroine of that narrative, Mrs. Moore, is the Alexandrian figure of Wisdom, the Sophia, as set forth in the Hellenistic Jewish Wisdom of Solomon. Of Wisdom or Sophia, Forster says: "She is a messenger who bridges the gulf and makes us friends of God," which is a useful description of the narrative function of Mrs. Moore. And after quoting Plotinus (in a passage that includes one of his book's epigraphs): "To any vision must be brought an eye adapted to what is to be seen," Forster comments:

> This sublime passage suggests three comments, with which our glance at Plotinus must close. In the first place its tone is religious, and in this it is typical of all Alexandrian philosophy. In the second place it lays stress on behaviour and training; the Supreme Vision cannot be acquired by magic tricks—only those will see it who are fit to see. And in the third place the vision of oneself and the vision of God are really the same, because each individual *is* God, if only he knew it. And here is the great difference between Plotinus and Christianity. The Christian promise is that a man shall see God, the Neo-Platonic—like the Indian—that he shall be God. Perhaps, on the quays of Alexandria, Plotinus talked with Hindu merchants who came to the town. At all events his system can be paralleled in the religious writings of India. He comes nearer than any other Greek philosopher to the thought of the East.

Forster's Alexandria is in the first place personal; he associated the city always with his sexual maturation as a homosexual. But, as the book *Alexandria* shrewdly shows, Forster finds his precursor culture in ancient Alexandria; indeed he helps to teach us that we are all Alexandrians, insofar as we now live in a literary culture. Forster's insight is massively supported by the historian F. E. Peters in the great study *The Harvest of Hellenism*, when he catalogs our debts to the Eastern Hellenism of Alexandria:

> Its monuments are gnosticism, the university, the catechetical school, pastoral poetry, monasticism, the romance, grammar, lexicography, city planning, theology, canon law, heresy, and scholasticism.

Forster would have added, thinking of the Ptolemaic Alexandria of 331–30 B.C.E., that the most relevant legacy was an eclectic and tolerant liberal humanism, scientific and scholarly, exalting the values of affection over those of belief. That is already the vision of *A Passage to India*, and it opens to the novel's central spiritual question: How are the divine and the human linked? In *Alexandria*, Forster presents us with a clue by his account of the Arian heresy:

> Christ is the Son of God. Then is he not younger than God? Arius held that he was and that there was a period before time began when the First Person of the Trinity existed and the Second did not. A typical Alexandrian theologian, occupied with the favourite problem of linking human and divine, Arius thought to solve the problem by making the link predominately human. He did not deny the Godhead of Christ, but he did make him inferior to the Father—of *like* substance, not of the *same* substance, which was the view held by Athanasius, and stamped as orthodox by the Council of Nicaea. Moreover the Arian Christ, like the Gnostic Demiurge, made the world;—creation, an inferior activity, being entrusted to him by the Father, who had Himself created nothing but Christ.
>
> It is easy to see why Arianism became popular. By making Christ younger and lower than God it brought him nearer to us—indeed it tended to level him into a mere good man and to forestall Unitarianism. It appealed to the untheologically minded, to emperors and even more to empresses. But St. Athanasius, who viewed the innovation with an expert eye, saw that while it popularised Christ it isolated God, and he fought it with vigour and venom. His success has been described. It was condemned as heretical in 325, and by the end of the century had been expelled from orthodox Christendom. Of the theatre of this ancient strife no trace remains at Alexandria; the church of St. Mark where

Arius was presbyter has vanished: so have the churches where Athanasius thundered—St. Theonas and the Caesareum. Nor do we know in which street Arius died of epilepsy. But the strife still continues in the hearts of men, who always tend to magnify the human in the divine, and it is probable that many an individual Christian today is an Arian without knowing it.

To magnify the human in the divine is certainly Forster's quest and appears to be his interpretation of Hinduism in *A Passage to India*.

Down in the sacred corridors, joy had seethed to jollity. It was their duty to play various games to amuse the newly born God, and to simulate his sports with the wanton dairymaids of Brindaban. Butter played a prominent part in these. When the cradle had been removed, the principal nobles of the state gathered together for an innocent frolic. They removed their turbans, and one put a lump of butter on his forehead, and waited for it to slide down his nose into his mouth. Before it could arrive, another stole up behind him, snatched the melting morsel, and swallowed it himself. All laughed exultantly at discovering that the divine sense of humour coincided with their own. "God is love!" There is fun in heaven. God can play practical jokes upon Himself, draw chairs away from beneath His own posteriors, set His own turbans on fire, and steal His own petticoats when He bathes. By sacrificing good taste, this worship achieved what Christianity has shirked: the inclusion of merriment. All spirit as well as all matter must participate in salvation, and if practical jokes are banned, the circle is incomplete. Having swallowed the butter, they played another game which chanced to be graceful: the fondling of Shri Krishna under the similitude of a child. A pretty red and gold ball is thrown, and he who catches it chooses a child from the crowd, raises it in his arms, and carries it round to be caressed. All stroke the darling creature for the Creator's sake, and murmur happy words. The child is restored to his parents, the ball thrown on, and another child becomes for a moment the World's desire. And the Lord bounds hither and thither through the aisles, chance, and the sport of chance, irradiating little mortals with His immortality.... When they had played this long enough—and being exempt from boredom, they played it again and again, they played it again and again—they took many sticks and hit them together, whack smack, as though they fought the Pandava wars, and threshed and churned with them, and later on they hung from the roof of the temple, in a net, a great black earthenware jar, which was painted here and there with red, and wreathed with dried figs. Now came a rousing sport. Springing up, they struck at the jar with their sticks. It cracked, broke, and a mass of greasy rice and milk poured on to their faces. They ate and smeared one another's mouths and dived between each other's legs for what had been pashed upon the carpet. This way and that spread the divine mess, until the line of schoolboys, who had somewhat fended off the crowd, broke for their share. The corridors, the courtyard, were filled with benign confusion. Also the flies awoke and claimed their share of God's bounty. There was no quarrelling, owing to the nature of the gift, for blessed is the man who confers it on another, he imitates God. And those "imitations," those "substitutions," continued to flicker through the assembly for many hours, awaking in each man, according to his capacity, an emotion that he would not have had otherwise. No definite image survived; at the Birth it was questionable whether a silver doll or a mud village, or a silk napkin, or an intangible spirit, or a pious resolution, had been born. Perhaps all these things! Perhaps none! Perhaps all birth is an allegory! Still, it was the main event of the religious year. It caused strange thoughts. Covered with grease and dust, Professor Godbole had once more developed the life of his spirit. He had, with increasing vividness, again seen Mrs. Moore, and round her faintly clinging forms of trouble. He was a Brahman, she Christian, but it made no difference, it made no difference whether she was a trick of his memory or a telepathic appeal. It was his duty, as it was his desire, to place himself in the position of the God and to love her, and to place himself in her position and to say to the God, "Come, come, come, come." This was all he could do. How inadequate! But each according to his own capacities, and he knew that his own were small. "One old Englishwoman and one little, little wasp," he thought, as he stepped out of the temple into the grey of a pouring wet morning. "It does not seem much, still it is more than I am myself."

Professor Godbole's epiphany, his linkage of Mrs. Moore's receptivity toward the wasp with his own receptivity toward Mrs. Moore, has been much

admired by critics, deservedly so. In this moment-of-moments, Godbole
receives Mrs. Moore into Forster's own faithless faith: a religion of love
between equals, as opposed to Christianity, a religion of love between the
incommensurate Jehovah and his creatures. But though beautifully executed,
Forster's vision of Godbole and Mrs. Moore is spiritually a little too easy.
Forster knew that, and the finest moment in *A Passage to India* encompasses
this knowing. It comes in a sublime juxtaposition, in the crossing between
the conclusion of "Part II: Caves" and the beginning of "Part III: Temple,"
where Godbole is seen standing in the presence of God. The brief and
beautiful chapter 32 that concludes "Caves" returns Fielding to a Western
and Ruskinian vision of form in Venice:

> Egypt was charming—a green strip of carpet and walking up and
> down it four sorts of animals and one sort of man. Fielding's
> business took him there for a few days. He re-embarked at
> Alexandria—bright blue sky, constant wind, clean low coast-line,
> as against the intricacies of Bombay. Crete welcomed him next
> with the long snowy ridge of its mountains, and then came
> Venice. As he landed on the piazzetta a cup of beauty was lifted
> to his lips, and he drank with a sense of disloyalty. The buildings
> of Venice, like the mountains of Crete and the fields of Egypt,
> stood in the right place, whereas in poor India everything was
> placed wrong. He had forgotten the beauty of form among idol
> temples and lumpy hills; indeed, without form, how can there be
> beauty? Form stammered here and there in a mosque, became
> rigid through nervousness even, but oh these Italian churches!
> San Giorgio standing on the island which could scarcely have
> risen from the waves without it, the Salute holding the entrance
> of a canal which, but for it, would not be the Grand Canal! In the
> old undergraduate days he had wrapped himself up in the many-
> coloured blanket of St. Mark's, but something more precious than
> mosaics and marbles was offered to him now: the harmony
> between the works of man and the earth that upholds them, the
> civilization that has escaped muddle, the spirit in a reasonable
> form, with flesh and blood subsisting. Writing picture post-cards
> to his Indian friends, he felt that all of them would miss the joys
> he experienced now, the joys of form, and that this constituted a
> serious barrier. They would see the sumptuousness of Venice, not
> its shape, and though Venice was not Europe, it was part of the
> Mediterranean harmony. The Mediterranean is the human norm.

When men leave that exquisite lake, whether through the Bosphorus or the Pillars of Hercules, they approach the monstrous and extraordinary; and the southern exit leads to the strangest experience of all. Turning his back on it yet again, he took the train northward, and tender romantic fancies that he thought were dead for ever, flowered when he saw the buttercups and daisies of June.

After the muddle of India, where "everything was placed wrong," Fielding learns again "the beauty of form." Alexandria, like Venice, is part of the Mediterranean harmony, the human norm, but India is the cosmos of "the monstrous and extraordinary." Fielding confronting the Venetian churches has absolutely nothing in common with Professor Godbole confronting the God Krishna at the opposite end of the same strip of carpet upon which Godbole stands. Forster is too wise not to know that the passage to India is only a passage. A passage is a journey, or an occurrence between two persons. Fielding and Aziz do not quite make the passage together, do not exchange vows that bind. Perhaps that recognition of limits is the ultimate beauty of form in *A Passage to India*.

HENRY JAMES

The New Novel

I

Still not to let go of our imputation of interest to some part at least of what
is happening in the world of production in this kind, we may say that non-
selective and non-comparative practice appears bent on showing us all it can
do and how far or to what appointed shores, what waiting havens and
inviting inlets, the current that is mainly made a current by looseness, by
want of observable direction, shall succeed in carrying it. We respond to any
sign of an intelligent view or even of a lively instinct—which is why we give
the appearance so noted the benefit of every presumption as to its life and
health. It may be that the dim sense is livelier than the presentable reason,
but even that is no graceless fact for us, especially when the keenness of
young curiosity and energy is betrayed in its pace, and betrayed, for that
matter, in no small abundance and variety. The new or at least the young
novel is up and doing, clearly, with the best faith and the highest spirits in the
world; if we but extend a little our measure of youth indeed, as we are happily
more and more disposed to, we may speak of it as already chin-deep in
trophies. The men who are not so young as the youngest were but the other
day very little older than these: Mr. Joseph Conrad, Mr. Maurice Hewlett
and Mr. Galsworthy, Mr. H.G. Wells and Mr. Arnold Bennett, have not quite
perhaps the early bloom of Mr. Hugh Walpole, Mr. Gilbert Cannan, Mr.

From *Notes on Novelists*. © 1914 by Charles Scribner's Sons.

Compton Mackenzie and Mr. D.H. Lawrence, but the spring unrelaxed is still, to our perception, in their step, and we see two or three of them sufficiently related to the still newer generation in a quasi-parental way to make our whole enumeration as illustrational as we need it. Mr. Wells and Mr. Arnold Bennett have their strongest mark, the aspect by which we may most classify them, in common—even if their three named contemporaries are doubtless most interesting in one of the connections we are not now seeking to make. The author of "Tono-Bungay" and of "The New Machiavelli," and the author of "The Old Wives' Tale" and of "Clayhanger," have practically launched the boat in which we admire the fresh play of oar of the author of "The Duchess of Wrexe," and the documented aspect exhibited successively by "Round the Corner," by "Carnival" and "Sinister Street," and even by "Sons and Lovers" (however much we may find Mr. Lawrence, we confess, hang in the dusty rear). We shall explain in a moment what we mean by this designation of the element that these best of the younger men strike us as more particularly sharing, our point being provisionally that Mr. Wells and Mr. Arnold Bennett (speaking now only of them) began some time back to show us, and to show sundry emulous and generous young spirits then in the act of more or less waking up, what the state in question might amount to. We confound the author of "Tono-Bungay" and the author of "Clayhanger" in this imputation for the simple reason that with the sharpest differences of character and range they yet come together under our so convenient measure of value by *saturation*. This is the greatest value, to our sense, in either of them, their other values, even when at the highest, not being quite in proportion to it; and as to be saturated is to be documented, to be able even on occasion to prove quite enviably and potently so, they are alike in the authority that creates emulation. It little signifies that Mr. Wells's documented or saturated state in respect to a particular matter in hand is but one of the faces of his *generally* informed condition, of his extraordinary mass of gathered and assimilated knowledge, a miscellaneous collection more remarkable surely than any teller of "mere" tales, with the possible exception of Balzac, has been able to draw upon, whereas Mr. Arnold Bennett's corresponding provision affects us as, though singularly copious, special, exclusive and artfully economic. This distinction avails nothing against that happy fact of the handiest possession by Mr. Wells of immeasurably more concrete material, amenable for straight and vivid reference, convertible into apt illustration, than we should know where to look for other examples of. The author of "The New Machiavelli" knows, somehow, to our mystified and dazzled apprehension, because he writes and because that act constitutes for him the need, on occasion a most desperate, of absorbing knowledge at the pores; the chronicler of the Five Towns writing so much more discernibly, on the other hand, because he knows, and conscious of no need more desperate than that particular circle of civilisation may satisfy.

Our argument is that each is ideally immersed in his own body of reference, and that immersion in any such degree and to the effect of any such variety, intensity and plausibility is really among us a new feature of the novelist's range of resource. We have seen him, we have even seen *her*, otherwise auspiciously endowed, seen him observant, impassioned, inspired, and in virtue of these things often very charming, very interesting, very triumphant, visibly qualified for the highest distinction before the fact and visibly crowned by the same after it—we have seen him with a great imagination and a great sense of life, we have seen him even with a great sense of expression and a considerable sense of art: so that we have only to reascend the stream of our comparatively recent literature to meet him serene and immortal, brow-bound with the bay and erect on his particular pedestal. We have only to do that, but have only also, while we do it, to recognise that meantime other things still than these various apotheoses have taken place, and that, to the increase of our recreation, and even if our limited space condemns us to put the matter a trifle clumsily, a change has come over our general receptive sensibility not less than over our productive tradition. In these connections, we admit, overstatement is easy and overemphasis tempting; we confess furthermore to a frank desire to enrich the case, the historic, with all the meaning we can stuff into it. So viewed accordingly it gives us the "new," to repeat our expression, as an appetite for a closer notation, a sharper specification of the signs of life, of consciousness, of the human scene and the human subject in general, than the three or four generations before us had been at all moved to insist on. They had insisted indeed, these generations, we see as we look back to them, on almost nothing whatever; what was to come to them had come, in enormous affluence and freshness at its best, and to our continued appreciation as well as to the honour of their sweet susceptibility, because again and again the great miracle of genius took place, while they gaped, in their social and sentimental sky. For ourselves that miracle has not been markedly renewed, but it has none the less happened that by hook and by crook the case for appreciation remains interesting. The great thing that saves it, under the drawback we have named, is, no doubt, that we have simply—always for appreciation— learned a little to insist, and that we thus get back on one hand something of what we have lost on the other. We are unable of course, with whatever habit of presumption engendered, to insist upon genius; so that who shall describe the measure of success we still achieve as not virtually the search for freshness, and above all for closeness, in quite a different direction? To this nearer view of commoner things Mr. Wells, say, and Mr. Arnold Bennett, and in their degree, under the infection communicated, Mr. D.H. Lawrence and Mr. Gilbert Cannan and Mr. Compton Mackenzie and Mr. Hugh Walpole, strike us as having all gathered themselves up with a movement never yet undertaken on our literary scene, and, beyond anything else, with an instinctive divination of what had most waved their predecessors off it. What had this lion in the path been, we make them out as after a fashion asking themselves, what had it been from far back and straight down through all the Victorian time, but the fond superstition that the key of the situation, of each and every situation that could turn up for the novelist, was the sentimental key, which might fit into no door or window opening on closeness or on freshness at all? Was it not for all the world as if even the brightest practitioners of the past, those we now distinguish as saved for glory in spite of themselves, had been as sentimental as they could, or, to give the trick another name, as romantic and thereby as shamelessly "dodgy"?—just in order *not* to be close and fresh, not to be authentic, as that takes trouble, takes talent, and you can be sentimental, you can be romantic, you can be dodgy, alas, not a bit less on the footing of genius than on the footing of mediocrity or even of imbecility? Was it not as if the sentimental had been more and more noted as but another name for the romantic, if not indeed the romantic as but another name for the sentimental, and as if these things, whether separate or united, had been in the same degree recognised as unamenable, or at any rate unfavourable, to any consistent fineness of notation, once the tide of the copious as a condition of the thorough had fairly set in?

So, to express it briefly, the possibility of hugging the shore of the real as it had not, among us, been hugged, and of pushing inland, as far as a keel might float, wherever the least opening seemed to smile, dawned upon a few votaries and gathered further confidence with exercise. Who could say, of course, that Jane Austen had not been close, just as who could ask if Anthony Trollope had not been copious?—just as who could *not* say that it all depended on what was meant by these terms? The demonstration of what was meant, it presently appeared, could come but little by little, quite as if each tentative adventurer had rather anxiously to learn for himself what *might* be meant—this failing at least the leap into the arena of some great demonstrative, some sudden athletic and epoch-making authority. Who could pretend that Dickens was anything but romantic, and even more romantic in his humour, if possible, than in pathos or in queer perfunctory practice of the "plot"? Who could pretend that Jane Austen didn't leave much more untold than told about the aspects and manners even of the confined circle in which her muse revolved? Why shouldn't it be argued against her that where her testimony complacently ends the pressure of appetite within us presumes exactly to begin? Who could pretend that the reality of Trollope didn't owe much of its abundance to the diluted, the quite extravagantly watered strain, no less than to the heavy hand, in which it continued to be ladled out? Who of the younger persuasion would not have been ready to cite, as one of the liveliest opportunities for the critic eager to see representation searching, such a claim for the close as Thackeray's sighing and protesting "look-in" at the acquaintance between Arthur Pendennis and Fanny Bolton, the daughter of the Temple laundress, amid the purlieus of that settlement? The sentimental habit and the spirit of romance, it was unmistakably chargeable, stood out to sea as far as possible the moment the shore appeared to offer the least difficulty to hugging, and the Victorian age bristled with perfect occasions for our catching them in the act of this showy retreat. All revolutions have been prepared in spite of their often striking us as sudden, and so it was doubtless that when scarce longer ago than the other day Mr. Arnold Bennett had the fortune to lay his hand on a general scene and a cluster of agents deficient to a peculiar degree in properties that might interfere with a desirable density of illustration— deficient, that is, in such connections as might carry the imagination off to some sport on its own account—we recognised at once a set of conditions auspicious to the newer kind of appeal. Let us confess that we were at the same time doubtless to master no better way of describing these conditions than by the remark that they were, for some reason beautifully inherent in them, susceptible at once of being entirely known and of seeming delectably thick. Reduction to exploitable knowledge is apt to mean for many a case of the human complexity reduction to comparative thinness; and nothing was thereby at the first blush to interest us more than the fact that the air and the very smell of packed actuality in the subject-matter of such things as the author's two longest works was clearly but another name for his personal competence in that matter, the fulness and firmness of his embrace of it. This was a fresh and beguiling impression—that the state of inordinate possession on the chronicler's part, the mere state as such and as an energy directly displayed, *was* the interest, neither more nor less, *was* the sense and the meaning and the picture and the drama, all so sufficiently constituting them that it scarce mattered what they were in themselves. Of what they were in themselves their being in Mr. Bennett, as Mr. Bennett to such a tune harboured them, represented their one conceivable account—not to mention, as reinforcing this, our own great comfort and relief when certain high questions and wonderments about them, or about our mystified relation to them, began one after another to come up.

Because such questions did come, we must at once declare, and we are still in presence of them, for all the world as if that case of the perfect harmony, the harmony between subject and author, were just marked with a flaw and didn't meet the whole assault of restless criticism. What we make out Mr. Bennett as doing is simply recording his possession or, to put it more completely, his saturation; and to see him as virtually shut up to that process is a note of all the more moment that we see our selected cluster of his interesting juniors, and whether by his direct action on their collective impulse or not, embroiled, as we venture to call it, in the same predicament. The act of squeezing out to the utmost the plump and more or less juicy orange of a particular acquainted state and letting this affirmation of energy, however directed or undirected, constitute for them the "treatment" of a theme—*that* is what we remark them as mainly engaged in, after remarking the example so strikingly, so originally set, even if an undue subjection to it be here and there repudiated. Nothing is further from our thought than to undervalue saturation and possession, the fact of the particular experience, the state and degree of acquaintance incurred, however such a consciousness may have been determined; for these things represent on the part of the novelist, as on the part of any painter of things seen, felt or imagined, just one half of his authority—the other half being represented of course by the application he is inspired to make of them. Therefore that fine secured half is so much gained at the start, and the fact of its brightly being there may really by itself project upon the course so much colour and form as to make us on occasion, under the genial force, almost not miss the answer to the question of application. When the author of "Clayhanger" has put down upon the table, in dense unconfused array, every fact required, every fact in any way invocable, to make the life of the Five Towns press upon us, and to make our sense of it, so full-fed, content us, we may very well go on for the time in the captive condition, the beguiled and bemused condition, the acknowledgment of which is in general our highest tribute to the temporary master of our sensibility. Nothing at such moments—or rather at the end of them, when the end begins to threaten— may be of a more curious strain than the dawning unrest that suggests to us fairly our first critical comment: "Yes, yes—but is this *all?* These are the circumstances of the interest—we see, we see; but where is the interest itself,

where and what is its centre, and how are we to measure it in relation to *that?*"
Of course we may in the act of exhaling that plaint (which we have just
expressed at its mildest) well remember how many people there are to tell us
that to "measure" an interest is none of our affair; that we have but to take it
on the cheapest and easiest terms and be thankful; and that if by our very
confession we have been led the imaginative dance the music has done for us
all it pretends to. Which words, however, have only to happen to be for us the
most unintelligent conceivable not in the least to arrest our wonderment as to
where our bedrenched consciousness may still not awkwardly leave us for the
pleasure of appreciation. That appreciation is also a mistake and a priggishness,
being reflective and thereby corrosive, is another of the fond dicta which we
are here concerned but to brush aside—the more closely to embrace the
welcome induction that appreciation, attentive and reflective, inquisitive and
conclusive, is in this connection absolutely the golden *key* to our pleasure. The
more it plays up, the more we recognise and are able to number the sources of
our enjoyment, the greater the provision made for security in that attitude,
which corresponds, by the same stroke, with the reduced danger of waste in
the undertaking to amuse us. It all comes back to our amusement, and to the
noblest surely, on the whole, we know; and it is in the very nature of clinging
appreciation not to sacrifice consentingly a single shade of the art that makes
for that blessing. From this solicitude spring our questions, and not least the
one to which we give ourselves for the moment here—this moment of our
being regaled as never yet with the fruits of the movement (if the name be not
of too pompous an application where the flush and the heat of accident too
seem so candidly to look forth), in favour of the "expression of life" in terms as
loose as may pretend to an effect of expression at all. The relegation of terms
to the limbo of delusions outlived so far as ever really cultivated becomes of
necessity, it will be plain, the great mark of the faith that for the novelist to
show he "knows all about" a certain congeries of aspects, the more numerous
within their mixed circle the better, is thereby to set in motion, with due
intensity, the pretension to interest. The state of knowing all about whatever it
may be has thus only to become consistently and abundantly active to pass for
his supreme function; and to its so becoming active few difficulties appear to
be descried—so great may on occasion be the mere excitement of activity. To
the fact that the exhilaration is, as we have hinted, often infectious, to this and
to the charming young good faith and general acclamation under which each
case appears to proceed—each case we of course mean really repaying
attention—the critical reader owes his opportunity so considerably and so
gratefully to generalise.

II

We should have only to remount the current with a certain energy to come straight up against Tolstoy as the great illustrative master-hand on all this ground of the disconnection of method from matter—which encounter, however, would take us much too far, so that we must for the present but hang off from it with the remark that of all great painters of the social picture it was given that epic genius most to serve admirably as a rash adventurer and a "caution," and execrably, pestilentially, as a model. In this strange union of relations he stands alone: from no other great projector of the human image and the human idea is so much truth to be extracted under an equal leakage of its value. All the proportions in him are so much the largest that the drop of attention to our nearer cases might by its violence leave little of that principle alive; which fact need not disguise from us, none the less, that as Mr. H.G. Wells and Mr. Arnold Bennett, to return to them briefly again, derive, by multiplied if diluted transmissions, from the great Russian (from whose all but equal companion Turgenieff we recognise no derivatives at all), so, observing the distances, we may profitably detect an unexhausted influence in our minor, our still considerably less rounded vessels. Highly attaching as indeed the game might be, of inquiring as to the centre of the interest or the sense of the whole in "The Passionate Friends," or in "The Old Wives' Tale," after having sought those luxuries in vain not only through the general length and breadth of "War and Peace," but within the quite respectable confines of any one of the units of effect there clustered: this as preparing us to address a like friendly challenge to Mr. Cannan's "Round the Corner," say, or to Mr. Lawrence's "Sons and Lovers"—should we wish to be *very* friendly to Mr. Lawrence—or to Mr. Hugh Walpole's "Duchess of Wrexe," or even to Mr. Compton Mackenzie's "Sinister Street" and "Carnival," discernibly, we hasten to add, though certain betrayals of a controlling idea and a pointed intention do comparatively gleam out of the two fictions last named. "The Old Wives' Tale" is the history of two sisters, daughters of a prosperous draper in a Staffordshire town, who, separating early in life, through the flight of one of them to Paris with an ill-chosen husband and the confirmed and prolonged local pitch of the career of the other, are reunited late in life by the return of the fugitive after much Parisian experience and by her pacified acceptance of the conditions of her birthplace. The divided current flows together again, and the chronicle closes with the simple drying up determined by the death of the sisters. That is all; the canvas is covered, ever so closely and vividly covered, by the exhibition of innumerable small facts and aspects, at which we assist with the most comfortable sense of their substantial truth. The sisters, and more particularly the less adventurous, are at home in their author's mind, they sit and move at their ease in the square chamber of his attention, to a degree beyond which the production of that ideal harmony between creature and creator could scarcely go, and all by an art of demonstration so familiar and so "quiet" that the truth and the poetry, to use Goethe's distinction, melt utterly together and we see no difference between the subject of the show and the showman's feeling, let alone the showman's manner, about it. This felt identity of the elements—because we at least consciously feel—becomes in the novel we refer to, and not less in "Clayhanger," which our words equally describe, a source for us of abject confidence, confidence truly *so* abject in the solidity of every appearance that it may be said to represent our whole relation to the work and completely to exhaust our reaction upon it. "Clayhanger," of the two fictions even the more densely loaded with all the evidence in what we should call the case presented did we but learn meanwhile for what case, or for a case of what, to take it, inscribes the annals, the private more particularly, of a provincial printer in a considerable way of business, beginning with his early boyhood and going on to the complications of his maturity—these not exhausted with our present possession of the record, inasmuch as by the author's announcement there is more of the catalogue to come. This most monumental of Mr. Arnold Bennett's recitals, taking it with its supplement of "Hilda Lessways," already before us, is so describable through its being a monument exactly not to an idea, a pursued and captured meaning, or in short *to* anything whatever, but just simply *of* the quarried and gathered material it happens to contain, the stones and bricks and rubble and cement and promiscuous constituents of every sort that have been heaped in it and thanks to which it quite massively piles itself up. Our perusal and our enjoyment are our watching of the growth of the pile and of the capacity, industry, energy with which the operation is directed. A huge and in its way a varied aggregation, without traceable lines, divinable direction, effect of composition, the mere number of its pieces, the great dump of its material, together with the fact that here and there in the miscellany, as with the value of bits of marble or porphyry, fine elements shine out, it keeps us standing and waiting to the end—and largely just because it keeps us wondering. We surely wonder more what it may all propose to mean than any equal appearance of preparation to relieve us of that strain, any so founded and grounded a postponement of the disclosure of a sense in store, has for a long time called upon us to do in a like connection. A great thing it is assuredly that *while* we wait and wonder we are amused—were it not for that, truly, our situation would be thankless enough; we may ask ourselves, as has already been noted, why on such ambiguous terms we should consent to be, and why the practice doesn't at a given moment break down; and our answer brings us back to that many-fingered grasp of the orange that the author squeezes. This particular orange is of the largest and most rotund, and his trust in the consequent flow is of its nature communicative. Such is the case always, and most naturally, with that air in a person who has something, who at the very least has much to tell us: we *like* so to be affected by it, we meet it half way and lend ourselves, sinking in up to the chin. Up to the chin only indeed, beyond doubt; we even then feel our head emerge, for judgment and articulate question, and it is from that position that we remind ourselves how the real reward of our patience is still to come—the reward attending not at all the immediate sense of immersion, but reserved for the aftersense, which is a very different matter, whether in the form of a glow or of a chill.

If Mr. Bennett's tight rotundity then is of the handsomest size and his manipulation of it so firm, what are we to say of Mr. Wells's, who, a novelist very much as Lord Bacon was a philosopher, affects us as taking all knowledge for his province and as inspiring in us to the very highest degree the confidence enjoyed by himself—enjoyed, we feel, with a breadth with which it has been given no one of his fellow-craftsmen to enjoy anything. If confidence alone could lead utterly captive we should all be huddled in a bunch at Mr. Wells's heels—which is indeed where we *are* abjectly gathered so far as that force does operate. It is literally Mr. Wells's own mind, and the experience of his own mind, incessant and extraordinarily various, extraordinarily reflective, even with all sorts of conditions made, of whatever he may expose it to, that forms the reservoir tapped by him, that constitutes his provision of grounds of interest. It is, by our thinking, in his power to name to us, as a preliminary, more of these grounds than all his contemporaries put together, and even to exceed any competitor, without exception, in the way of suggesting that, thick as he may seem to lay them, they remain yet only contributive, are not in themselves full expression but are designed strictly to subserve it, that this extraordinary writer's spell resides. When full expression, the expression of some particular truth, seemed to lapse in this or that of his earlier novels (we speak not here of his shorter things, for the most part delightfully wanton and exempt,) it was but by a hand's breadth, so that if we didn't inveterately quite know what he intended we yet always felt sufficiently that *he* knew. The particular intentions of such matters as "Kipps," as "Tono-Bungay," as "Ann Veronica," so swarmed about us, in their blinding, bluffing vivacity, that the mere sum

of them might have been taken for a sense over and above which it was
graceless to inquire. The more this author learns and learns, or at any rate
knows and knows, however, the greater is this impression of his holding it
good enough for us, such as we are, that he shall but turn out his mind and
its contents upon us by any free familiar gesture and as from a high window
forever open—an entertainment as copious surely as any occasion should
demand, at least till we have more intelligibly expressed our title to a better.
Such things as "The New Machiavelli," "Marriage," "The Passionate
Friends," are so very much more attestations of the presence of material than
attestations of an interest in the use of it that we ask ourselves again and again
why so fondly neglected a state of leakage comes not to be fatal to *any*
provision of quantity, or even to stores more specially selected for the ordeal
than Mr. Wells's always strike us as being. Is not the pang of witnessed waste
in fact great just in proportion as we are touched by our author's fine off-
handedness as to the value of the stores, about which he can for the time
make us believe what he will? so that, to take an example susceptible of brief
statement, we wince at a certain quite peculiarly gratuitous sacrifice to the
casual in "Marriage" very much as at seeing some fine and indispensable little
part of a mechanism slip through profane fingers and lose itself. Who does
not remember what ensues after a little upon the aviational descent of the
hero of the fiction just named into the garden occupied, in company with her
parents, by the young lady with whom he is to fall in love?—and this even
though the whole opening scene so constituted, with all the comedy hares its
function appears to be to start, remains with its back squarely turned,
esthetically speaking, to the quarter in which the picture develops. The point
for our mortification is that by one of the first steps in this development, the
first impression on him having been made, the hero accidentally meets the
heroine, of a summer eventide, in a leafy lane which supplies them with the
happiest occasion to pursue their acquaintance—or in other words supplies
the author with the liveliest consciousness (as we at least feel it should have
been) that just so the relation between the pair, its seed already sown and the
fact of that bringing about all that is still to come, pushes aside whatever veil
and steps forth into life. To show it step forth and affirm itself as a relation,
what is this but the interesting function of the whole passage, on the
performance of which what follows is to hang?—and yet who can say that
when the ostensible sequence *is* presented, and our young lady, encountered
again by her stirred swain, under cover of night, in a favouring wood, is at
once encompassed by his arms and pressed to his lips and heart (for
celebration thus of their third meeting) we do not assist at a well-nigh
heartbreaking miscarriage of "effect"? We see effect, invoked in vain, simply

stand off unconcerned; effect not having been at all consulted in advance she is not to be secured on such terms. And her presence would so have redounded—perfectly punctual creature as she is on a made appointment and a clear understanding—to the advantage of all concerned. The bearing of the young man's act is all in our having begun to conceive it as possible, begun even to desire it, in the light of what has preceded; therefore if the participants have *not* been shown us as on the way to it, nor the question of it made beautifully to tremble for us in the air, its happiest connections fail and we but stare at it mystified. The instance is undoubtedly trifling, but in the infinite complex of such things resides for a work of art the shy virtue, shy at least till wooed forth, of the whole susceptibility. The case of Mr. Wells might take us much further—such remarks as there would be to make, say, on such a question as the due understanding, on the part of "The Passionate Friends" (not as associated persons but as a composed picture), of what that composition is specifically *about* and where, for treatment of this interest, it undertakes to find its centre: all of which, we are willing however to grant, falls away before the large assurance and incorrigible levity with which this adventurer carries his lapses—far more of an adventurer as he is than any other of the company. The composition, as we have called it, heaven saving the mark, is simply at any and every moment "about" Mr. Wells's general adventure; which is quite enough while it preserves, as we trust it will long continue to do, its present robust pitch.

We have already noted that "Round the Corner," Mr. Gilbert Cannan's liveliest appeal to our attention, belongs to the order of *constations* pure and simple; to the degree that *as* a document of that nature and of that rigour the book could perhaps not more completely affirm itself. When we have said that it puts on record the "tone," the manners, the general domestic proceedings and *train de vie* of an amiable clergyman's family established in one of the more sordid quarters of a big black northern city of the Liverpool or Manchester complexion we have advanced as far in the way of descriptive statement as the interesting work seems to warrant. For it *is* interesting, in spite of its leaving itself on our hands with a consistent indifference to any question of the charmed application springing from it all that places it in the forefront of its type. Again as under the effect of Mr. Bennett's major productions our sole inference is that things, the things disclosed, *go on and on, in any given case, in spite of everything*—with Mr. Cannan's one discernible care perhaps being for how extraordinarily much, in the particular example here before him, they were able to go on in spite of. The conception, the presentation of this enormous inauspicious amount as bearing upon the collective career of the Folyats is, we think, as near as the author comes at any point to betraying an awareness of a subject. Yet again, though so little encouraged or "backed," a subject after a fashion makes itself, even as it has made itself in "The Old Wives' Tale" and in "Clayhanger," in "Sons and Lovers," where, as we have hinted, any assistance rendered us for a view of one *most* comfortably enjoys its absence, and in Mr. Hugh Walpole's newest novel, where we wander scarcely less with our hand in no guiding grasp, but where the author's good disposition, as we feel it, to provide us with what we lack if he only knew how, constitutes in itself such a pleading liberality. We seem to see him in this spirit lay again and again a flowered carpet for our steps. If we do not include Mr. Compton Mackenzie to the same extent in our generalisation it is really because we note a difference in him, a difference in favour of his care for the application. Preoccupations seem at work in "Sinister Street," and withal in "Carnival," the brush of which we in other quarters scarce even suspect and at some of which it will presently be of profit to glance. "I answer for it, you know," we seem at any rate to hear Mr. Gilbert Cannan say with an admirably genuine young pessimism, "I answer for it that they were really *like* that, odd or unpleasant or uncontributive, and therefore tiresome, as it may strike you;" and the charm of Mr. Cannan, so far as up or down the rank we so disengage a charm, is that we take him at his word. His guarantee, his straight communication, of his general truth is a value, and values are rare—the flood of fiction is apparently capable of running hundreds of miles without a single glint of one—and thus in default of satisfaction we get stopgaps and are thankful often under a genial touch to get even so much. The value indeed is crude, it would be quadrupled were it only wrought and shaped; yet it has still the rude dignity that it counts to us for experience or at least for what we call under our present pitch of sensibility force of impression. The experience, we feel, is ever something to conclude upon, while the impression is content to wait; to wait, say, in the spirit in which we must accept this younger bustle if we accept it at all, the spirit of its serving as a rather presumptuous lesson to us in patience. While we wait, again, we are amused—not in the least, also to repeat, up to the notch of our conception of amusement, which draws upon still other forms and sources; but none the less for the wonder, the intensity, the actuality, the probity of the vision. This is much as in "Clayhanger" and in "Hilda Lessways," where, independently of the effect, so considerably rendered, of the long lapse of time, always in this type of recital a source of amusement in itself, and certainly of the noblest, we get such an admirably substantial thing as the collective image of the Orgreaves, the local family in whose ample lap the amenities and the humanities so easily sit, for Mr.

Bennett's evocation and his protagonist's recognition, and the manner of the presentation of whom, with the function and relation of the picture at large, strikes such a note of felicity, achieves such a simulation of sense, as the author should never again be excused for treating, that is for neglecting, as beyond his range. Here figures signally the interesting case of a compositional function absolutely performed by mere multiplication, the flow of the facts: the Orgreaves, in "Clayhanger," are there, by what we make out, but for "life," for general life only, and yet, with their office under any general or inferential meaning entirely unmarked, come doubtless as near squaring esthetically with the famous formula of the "slice of life" as any example that could be adduced; happening moreover as they probably do to owe this distinction to their coincidence at once with reality and charm—a fact esthetically curious and delightful. For we attribute the bold stroke they represent much more to Mr. Arnold Bennett's esthetic instinct than to anything like a calculation of his bearings, and more to his thoroughly acquainted state, as we may again put it, than to all other causes together: which strikingly enough shows how much complexity of interest may be simulated by mere presentation of material, mere squeezing of the orange, when the material happens to be "handsome" or the orange to be sweet.

III

The orange of our persistent simile is in Mr. Hugh Walpole's hands very remarkably sweet—a quality we recognise in it even while reduced to observing that the squeeze pure and simple, the fond, the lingering, the reiterated squeeze, constitutes as yet his main perception of method. He enjoys in a high degree the consciousness of saturation, and is on such serene and happy terms with it as almost make of critical interference, in so bright an air, an assault on personal felicity. Full of material is thus the author of "The Duchess of Wrexe," and of a material which we should describe as the consciousness of youth were we not rather disposed to call it a peculiar strain of the extreme unconsciousness. Mr. Walpole offers us indeed a rare and interesting case—we see about the field none other like it; the case of a positive identity between the spirit, not to say the time of life or stage of experience, of the aspiring artist and the field itself of his vision. "The Duchess of Wrexe" reeks with youth and the love of youth and the confidence of youth—youth taking on with a charming exuberance the fondest costume or disguise, that of an adventurous and voracious felt interest, interest in life, in London, in society, in character, in Portland Place, in the Oxford Circus, in the afternoon tea-table, in the torrid weather, in fifty other immediate things as to which its passion and its curiosity are of the sincerest. The wonderful thing is that these latter forces operate, in their way, without yet being disengaged and hand-free—disengaged, that is, from their state of *being* young, with its billowy mufflings and other soft obstructions, the state of being present, being involved and aware, close "up against" the whole mass of possibilities, being in short intoxicated with the mixed liquors of suggestion. In the fumes of this acute situation Mr. Walpole's subject-matter is bathed; the situation being all the while so much more his own and that of a juvenility reacting, in the presence of everything, "for all it is worth," than the devised and imagined one, however he may circle about some such cluster, that every cupful of his excited flow tastes three times as much of his temperamental freshness as it tastes of this, that or the other character or substance, above all of this, that or the other group of antecedents and references, supposed to be reflected in it. All of which does not mean, we hasten to add, that the author of "The Duchess of Wrexe" has not the gift of life; but only that he strikes us as having received it, straight from nature, with such a concussion as to have kept the boon at the stage of violence—so that, fairly pinned down by it, he is still embarrassed for passing it on. On the day he shall have worked free of this primitive predicament, the crude fact of the convulsion itself, there need be no doubt of his exhibiting matter into which method may learn how to bite. The tract meanwhile affects us as more or less virgin snow, and we look with interest and suspense for the imprint of a process.

If those remarks represent all the while, further, that the performances we have glanced at, with others besides, lead our attention on, we hear ourselves the more naturally asked what it is then that we expect or want, confessing as we do that we have been in a manner interested, even though, from case to case, in a varying degree, and that Thackeray, Turgenieff, Balzac, Dickens, Anatole France, no matter who, can not do more than interest. Let us therefore concede to the last point that small mercies are better than none, that there are latent within the critic numberless liabilities to being "squared" (the extent to which he may on occasion betray his price!) and so great a preference for being pleased over not being, that you may again and again see him assist with avidity at the attempt of the slice of life to butter itself thick. Its explanation that it *is* a slice of life and pretends to be nothing else figures for us, say, while we watch, the jam super-added to the butter. For since the jam, on this system, descends upon our desert, in its form of manna, from quite another heaven than the heaven of method, the mere demonstration of its agreeable presence is alone sufficient to hint at our more than one chance of being supernaturally fed. The happy-go-lucky fashion of it is indeed not then, we grant, an objection so long as we do take in refreshment: the meal may be of the last informality and yet produce in the event no small sense of repletion. The slice of life devoured, the butter and the jam duly appreciated, we are ready, no doubt, on another day, to trust ourselves afresh to the desert. We break camp, that is, and face toward a further stretch of it, all in the faith that we shall be once more provided for. We take the risk, we enjoy more or less the assistance—more or less, we put it, for the vision of a possible arrest of the miracle or failure of our supply never wholly leaves us. The phenomenon is too uncanny, the happy-go-lucky, as we know it in general, never *has* been trustable to the end; the absence of the last true touch in the preparation of its viands becomes with each renewal of the adventure a more sensible fact. By the last true touch we mean of course the touch of the hand of selection; the principle of selection having been involved at the worst or the least, one would suppose, in any approach whatever to the loaf of life with the *arrièrepensée* of a slice. There being no question of a slice upon which the further question of where and how to cut it does not wait, the office of method, the idea of choice and comparison, have occupied the ground from the first. This makes clear, to a moment's reflection, that there can be no such thing as an amorphous slice, and that any waving aside of inquiry as to the sense and value of a chunk of matter has to reckon with the simple truth of its having been *born* of naught else but measured excision. Reasons have been the fairies waiting on its cradle, the possible presence of a bad fairy in the form of a bad reason to the contrary notwithstanding. It has thus had connections at the very first stage of its detachment that are at no later stage logically to be repudiated; let it lie as lumpish as it will—for adoption, we mean, of the ideal of the lump—it has been tainted from too far back with the hard liability to form, and thus carries in its very breast the hapless contradiction of its sturdy claim to have none. This claim has the inevitable challenge at once to meet. How can a slice of life be anything but illustrational of the loaf, and how can illustration not immediately bristle with every sign of the extracted and related state? The relation is at once to what the thing comes from and to what it waits upon —which last is our act of recognition. We accordingly appreciate it in proportion as it so accounts for itself; the quantity and the intensity of its reference are the measure of our knowledge of it. This is exactly why illustration breaks down when reference, otherwise application, runs short, and why before any assemblage of figures or aspects, otherwise of samples and specimens, the question of what these are, extensively, samples and specimens *of* declines not to beset us—why, otherwise again, we look ever for the supreme reference that shall avert the bankruptcy of sense.

Let us profess all readiness to repeat that we may still have had, on the merest "life" system, or that of the starkest crudity of the slice, all the entertainment that can come from watching a wayfarer engage with assurance in an alley that we know to have no issue—and from watching for the very sake of the face that he may show us on reappearing at its mouth. The recitals of Mr. Arnold Bennett, Mr. Gilbert Cannan, Mr. D.H. Lawrence, fairly smell of the real, just as the "Fortitude" and "The Duchess" of Mr. Hugh Walpole smell of the romantic; we have sufficiently noted then that, once on the scent, we are capable of pushing ahead. How far it is at the same time from being all a matter of smell the terms in which we just above glanced at the weakness of the spell of the happy-go-lucky may here serve to indicate. There faces us all the while the fact that the act of consideration as an incident of the esthetic pleasure, consideration confidently knowing us to *have* sooner or later to arrive at it, may be again and again postponed, but can never hope not some time to fall due. Consideration is susceptible of many forms, some one or other of which no conscious esthetic effort fails to cry out for; and the simplest description of the cry of the novel when sincere—for have we not heard such compositions bluff us, as it were, with false cries?— is as an appeal to us when we have read it once to read it yet again. *That* is the act of consideration; no other process of considering approaches this for directness, so that anything short of it is virtually not to consider at all. The word has sometimes another sense, that of the appeal to us *not*, for the world, to go back—this being of course consideration of a sort; the sort clearly that the truly flushed production should be the last to invoke. The effect of consideration, we need scarce remark, is to light for us in a work of art the hundred questions of how and why and whither, and the effect of these questions, once lighted, is enormously to thicken and complicate, even if toward final clarifications, what we have called the amused state produced in us by the work. The more our amusement multiplies its terms the more fond and the more rewarded consideration becomes; the fewer it leaves them, on the other hand, the less to be resisted for us is the impression of "bare ruined choirs where late the sweet birds sang." Birds that have appeared to sing, or whose silence we have not heeded, on a first perusal, prove on a second to have no note to contribute, and whether or no a second is enough to admonish us of those we miss, we mostly expect much from it in the way of emphasis of those we find. Then it is that notes of intention become more present or more absent; then it is that we take the measure of what we have already called our effective provision. The bravest providers and designers show at this point something still in store which only the second rummage was appointed to draw forth. To the variety of these ways of not letting our fondness fast is there not practically no limit?—and of the arts, the devices, the graces, the subtle secrets applicable to such an end what presumptuous critic shall pretend to draw the list? Let him for the moment content himself with saying that many of the most effective are mysteries, precisely, of method, or that even when they are not most essentially and directly so it takes method, blest method, to extract their soul and to determine their action.

It is odd and delightful perhaps that at the very moment of our urging this truth we should happen to be regaled with a really supreme specimen of the part playable in a novel by the source of interest, the principle of provision attended to, for which we claim importance. Mr. Joseph Conrad's "Chance" is none the less a signal instance of provision the most earnest and the most copious for its leaving ever so much to be said about the particular provision effected. It is none the less an extraordinary exhibition of method by the fact that the method is, we venture to say, without a precedent in any like work. It places Mr. Conrad absolutely alone as a votary of the way to do a thing that shall make it undergo most doing. The way to do it that shall make it undergo least is the line on which we are mostly now used to see prizes carried off; so that the author of "Chance" gathers up on this showing all sorts of comparative distinction. He gathers up at least two sorts—that of bravery in absolutely reversing the process most accredited, and that, quite separate, we make out, of performing the manœuvre under salvos of recognition. It is not in these days often given to a refinement of design to be recognised, but Mr. Conrad has made his achieve that miracle—save in so far indeed as the miracle has been one thing and the success another. The miracle is of the rarest, confounding all calculation and suggesting more reflections than we can begin to make place for here; but the sources of surprise surrounding it might be, were this possible, even greater and yet leave the fact itself in all independence, the fact that the whole undertaking was committed by its very first step either to be "art" exclusively or to be nothing. This is the prodigious rarity, since surely we have known for many a day no other such case of the whole clutch of eggs, and these withal of the freshest, in that one basket; to which it may be added that if we say for many a day this is not through our readiness positively to associate the sight with any very definite moment of the past. What concerns us is that the general effect of "Chance" is arrived at by a pursuance of means to the end in view contrasted with which every other current form of the chase can only affect us as cheap and futile; the carriage of the burden or amount of service required on these lines exceeding surely all other such displayed degrees of energy put together. Nothing could well interest us more than to see the exemplary value of attention, attention given by the author and asked of the reader, attested in a case in which it has had almost unspeakable difficulties to struggle with—since so we are moved to qualify the particular difficulty Mr. Conrad has "elected" to face: the claim for method in itself, method in this very sense of attention applied, would be somehow less lighted if the difficulties struck us as less consciously, or call it even less wantonly, invoked. What they consist of we should have to diverge here a little to say, and should even then probably but lose ourselves in the dim question of why so special, eccentric and desperate a course, so deliberate a plunge into threatened frustration, should alone have seemed open. It has been the course, so far as three words may here serve, of his so multiplying his creators or, as we are now fond of saying, producers, as to make them almost more numerous and quite emphatically more material than the creatures and the production itself in whom and which we by the general law of fiction expect such agents to lose themselves. We take for granted by the general law of fiction a primary author, take him so much for granted that we forget him in proportion as he works upon us, and that he works upon us most in fact by making us forget him.

Mr. Conrad's first care on the other hand is expressly to posit or set up a reciter, a definite responsible intervening first person singular, possessed of infinite sources of reference, who immediately proceeds to set up another, to the end that this other may conform again to the practice, and that even at that point the bridge over to the creature, or in other words to the situation or the subject, the thing "produced," shall, if the fancy takes it, once more and yet once more glory in a gap. It is easy to see how heroic the undertaking of an effective fusion becomes on these terms, fusion between what we are to know and that prodigy of our knowing which is ever half the very beauty of the atmosphere of authenticity; from the moment the reporters are thus multiplied from pitch to pitch the tone of each, especially as "rendered" by his precursor in the series, becomes for the prime poet of all an immense question—these circumferential tones having not only to be such individually separate notes, but to keep so clear of the others, the central, the numerous and various voices of the agents proper, those expressive of the action itself and in whom the objectivity resides. We usually escape the worst of this difficulty of a tone *about* the tone of our characters, our projected performers, by keeping it single, keeping it "down" and thereby comparatively impersonal or, as we may say, inscrutable; which is what a creative force, in its blest fatuity, likes to be. But the omniscience, remaining indeed nameless, though constantly active, which sets Marlow's omniscience in motion from the very first page, insisting on a reciprocity with it throughout, this original omniscience invites consideration of itself only in a degree less than that in which Marlow's own invites it; and Marlow's own is a prolonged hovering flight of the subjective over the outstretched ground of the case exposed. We make out this ground but through the shadow cast by the flight, clarify it though the real author visibly reminds himself again and again that he must—all the more that, as if by some tremendous forecast of future applied science, the upper aeroplane causes another, as we have said, to depend from it and that one still another; these dropping shadow after shadow, to the no small menace of intrinsic colour and form and whatever, upon the passive expanse. What shall we most call Mr. Conrad's method accordingly but his attempt to clarify *quand même*—ridden as he has been, we perceive at the end of fifty pages of "Chance," by such a danger of steeping his matter in perfect eventual obscuration as we recall no other artist's consenting to with an equal grace. This grace, which presently comes over us as the sign of the whole business, is Mr. Conrad's gallantry itself, and the shortest account of the rest of the connection for our present purpose is that his gallantry is thus his success. It literally strikes us that his volume sets in motion more than anything else a drama in which his own system and his combined eccentricities of recital represent the protagonist in face of powers leagued against it, and of which the dénouement gives us the system fighting in triumph, though with its back desperately to the wall, and laying the powers piled up at its feet. This frankly has been *our* spectacle, our suspense and our thrill; with the one flaw on the roundness of it all the fact that the predicament was not imposed rather than invoked, was not the effect of a challenge from without, but that of a mystic impulse from within.

Of an exquisite refinement at all events are the critical questions opened up in the attempt, the question in particular of by what it exactly is that the experiment is crowned. Pronouncing it crowned and the case saved by sheer gallantry, as we did above, is perhaps to fall just short of the conclusion we might reach were we to push further. "Chance" *is* an example of objectivity, most precious of aims, not only menaced but definitely compromised; whereby we are in presence of something really of the strangest, a general and diffused lapse of authenticity which an inordinate number of common readers—since it always takes this and these to account encouragingly for "editions"—have not only condoned but have emphatically commended. They can have done this but through the bribe of some authenticity other in kind, no doubt, and seeming to them equally great if not greater, which gives back by the left hand what the right has, with however dissimulated a grace, taken away. What Mr. Conrad's left hand gives back then is simply Mr. Conrad himself. We asked above what would become, by such a form of practice, of indispensable "fusion" or, to call it by another name, of the fine process by which our impatient material, at a given moment, shakes off the humiliation of the handled, the fumbled state, puts its head in the air and, to its own beautiful illusory consciousness at least, simply runs its race. Such an amount of handling and fumbling and repointing has it, on the system of the multiplied "putter into marble," to shake off! And yet behold, the sense of discomfort, as the show here works out, *has* been conjured away. The fusion has taken place, or at any rate *a* fusion; only it has been transferred in wondrous fashion to an unexpected, and on the whole more limited plane of operation; it has succeeded in getting effected, so to speak, not on the ground but in the air, not between our writer's idea and his machinery, but between the different parts of his genius itself. His genius is what is left over from the other, the compromised and compromising quantities—the Marlows and their determinant inventors and interlocutors, the Powells, the Franklins, the Fynes, the tell-tale little dogs, the successive members of a cue from one to the other of which the sense and the interest of the subject have to be passed on together, in the manner of the buckets of water for the improvised extinction of a fire, before reaching our apprehension: all with whatever result, to this apprehension, of a quantity to be allowed for as spilt by the way. The residuum has accordingly the form not of such and such a number of images discharged and ordered, but that rather of a wandering, circling, yearning imaginative *faculty*, encountered in its habit as it lives and diffusing itself as a presence or a tide, a noble sociability of vision. So we have as the force that fills the cup just the high-water mark of a beautiful and generous mind at play in conditions comparatively thankless—thoroughly, unweariedly, yet at the same time ever so elegantly at play, and doing more for itself than it succeeds in getting done for it. Than which nothing could be of a greater reward to critical curiosity were it not still for the wonder of wonders, a new page in the record altogether—the fact that these things are apparently what the common reader has seen and understood. Great then would seem to be after all the common reader!

RAYMOND WILLIAMS

A Parting of the Ways

In 1895 Hardy stopped writing novels. He was to live on and as a major poet until 1928, but there were to be no more novels. *Jude the Obscure* had been hysterically attacked as immoral—

> the experience completely curing me of further interest in novel-writing.

These attacks on *Jude*, as earlier on *Tess*, remind us of something we now easily forget: that of all nineteenth-century novelists Hardy was the most bitterly received, in his important work, by the English establishment. He is in this sense a true predecessor—though it is a lineage none of them wanted—of Joyce and Lawrence.

Hardy's stopping novel-writing was, of course, more complicated than that. But the date, 1895, can serve to indicate as well as single dates ever can a new situation in the English novel. I don't mean only that it feels like the end of that great nineteenth-century realist tradition. In a way we must not cut that off: the continuity from Hardy to Lawrence is central. But between *Jude the Obscure* and *Sons and Lovers* there is in effect a generation: a missing generation. Yet what happened between the 1890s and 1914 is of great critical importance for the novel. It is a period of crisis and of a parting of the ways. The different roads then taken and the disputes that accompanied each

From *The English Novel: From Dickens to Lawrence.* © 1970 by Raymond Williams.

creative choice connect in important ways to our own world. Some of the problems then raised we still haven't resolved. Indeed the central problem—the relation between what separated out as 'individual' or 'psychological' fiction on the one hand and 'social' or 'sociological' fiction on the other—is still, though perhaps in new ways, at the heart of our creative difficulties and concerns.

At the same time, as a lesser matter than that creative difficulty but of course affecting it (as a critical context, a critical vocabulary, inevitably does) we have to face the fact that academically, professionally the choice of roads has been overridden by a marked and settled preference. The fiction that emerged from one of these roads, from the 1890s to the 1920s, is still, oddly—it is even odder when Lawrence has somehow to be reconciled with it—recommended as 'modern'. It tells us a lot about contemporary Britain that 'modern' is that period of our grandfathers and great-grandfathers. But the record got stuck just there and it's been very difficult, for reasons we may see, to jerk it going again. That critical celebration of the 'modern' is, as you know, self-perpetuating and thriving.

Of course when I said there was a gap between Hardy and Lawrence you must have immediately been filling it in. The names are all there: James and Conrad; the early novels of Forster, indeed all but *A Passage to India;* and then of course that composite figure H.G.A.J. Wells-Bennett-Galsworthy, Esquire. It's all these I want to discuss (though I shall concentrate more specifically on Conrad later). Not because in taking them together I can hope to say enough that is specific and relevant to each particular writer; but because it is even more important, I think—important as a way of taking some decisive bearings—to see what the choices were, what the effects and consequences were; and to make this examination active, not just as so often a critical play-off of one group over another. The point of my argument, I can say now, is that the division of roads, the choices and the effects of the choices, are much too serious and complicated for that familiar demonstration and putting down. Virginia Woolf's essay *Mr Bennett and Mrs Brown* can be printed on vellum and given away as a presentation copy to anybody whose mind is already made up about those fateful issues (though perhaps not, it would cost a fortune given ordinary critical inertia). In any case I want to try to show that the issues are still very active and undecided; the issues I mean as they connect to our own active world.

1895. I've argued before that in the late 1870s, the early 1880s, the Victorian period ended. Of course the Queen lived on and it's not her fault but ours, our particular muddle, if we choose to describe our history by these single anointed lives. Socially, culturally, economically, politically, a new phase of our history began. It is quite identifiable, from the late 1870s to the war in 1914. And what is there as scattered accumulating evidence, over two decades, reaches a critical point in the 1890s. The last year of Hardy, the year of *Jude the Obscure*, is also the first year of Wells, the year of *The Time Machine*. Henry James covers the whole period of this visibly altering world. The important and characteristic critical quarrel between them, between Wells and James, reached its decisive point at the very end of the period, between 1911 and 1914. It is that world, that emerging deciding dividing world, that I want first to stress.

And here it is necessary to argue that in many other ways—other ways than in fiction—something important and decisive was happening in that period to what can be called the English tradition. Coming myself from a border area I'm always uneasy about these national names. I have to look both ways, over both shoulders at once. English literature; the English novel: these are literature, novels, in English; and there is already before this period, and increasingly important after it, the significant and creative work of American writers in English to be added but as a tradition—a vital tradition—in itself. All through the literature, men from other parts of the culture than the specifically English have contributed: Scots, Irish, Welsh. But on the whole, in the nineteenth-century novel, there is a very specific Englishness. Marian Evans had border connections, but her county is Warwickshire. The Brontës were Bruntys in County Down only a generation before the novelists, but the generation is all that now matters. Disraeli, yes; that's a case on its own but I'd settle for Beaconsfield, as he did; that's how the consciousness went. Meredith—I have to pronounce him in that English way because for him that is how it was, though in Wales the sound is quite different; Meredith the Englishman. And Dickens, Thackeray, Trollope, Elizabeth Gaskell, Thomas Hardy: English, English specifically. It isn't the origins that matter. It's the common consciousness, the common culture; a very specific set of common concerns, common preoccupations. Disturbed certainly; profoundly disturbed; that's what I've mainly been arguing. But with a creative confidence, a creative centre, that is there and impressive, continuously impressive: the English, specifically English, novel.

It's not been like that since and of course there are many reasons. Out of the profound disturbance from the 1830s to the 1870s something new was fashioned; something more openly confident, more settled, less rough at the edges; something English in a new sense, where many of the real difficulties begin. It appears in many ways but I'd settle for saying the formed self-confident insulated middle class. That class you could see coming, hear coming, all the way through the century, but now arrived and housed, settled in. The *English* middle class, English in a new sense—insulated and strong in their insulation just because, perhaps, that island within an island ruled an Empire, ruled half a world.

It's the point, as it happens, where English for me becomes problematic. I don't belong, don't wish to belong, to what English then means. But of course I respect it, I've had to, for some of the real things it is. In science particularly it is a superb culture; and in the technical and learned and administrative professions if not superb at least strong. But its weakness, its very deep weakness, is in ideas and imagination: not from some national quality, disquality—I don't accept that for a moment; it's untrue and unreal. It was in imagination and ideas, from Blake to Hardy and from Coleridge to Morris, that the specific greatness of something identifiably English—and English of the period after the Industrial Revolution, carrying on what was already a major imaginative and intellectual culture—was founded. But weak, problematic, at that particular time and in that particular place: the last decades of the nineteenth century, the first decade of our own.

It was, we must remember, a dominant culture, meant to be dominant, filtering other cultures, other classes, through its own curious mesh, and there again, clogging the mesh a bit, a new self-conscious experimental minority; getting out of line, speaking out of turn, bohemians and artists. Before that settlement, with all its supporting and interlocking and modernised institutions, much of the really creative work had come from other groups: from women, who had been very specifically excluded from the forming masculine world (the importance of women novelists in the nineteenth century is well known and remarkable); from mobile individuals, with what were called lower or lower-middle class associations—Carlyle, Dickens, Hardy. But in the new period this is much more marked; is indeed almost exclusive. And a new element enters that through the twentieth century—at least till the second war—stood out quite remarkably. Yeats, Shaw, Joyce, Synge, O'Casey; Henry James, T.S. Eliot, Pound; Conrad. Other nationalities, other conscious nationalities, and from these immigrants, these outsiders, the major imaginative work. Of course this is in part a response to Empire, just as the figures for genius in fifth-century Athens have to be qualified by where those figures came from to that decisive centre. But it's more than that. It's the cultural question that from this time on gets more and more asked: where, by the way, are the English? Well, Lawrence was to come, as Carlyle and Dickens and Hardy had come. But in this settling period, apart from Mr Forster, there is only that enigmatic figure Wells-Bennett-Galsworthy. And it's worth reflecting—indeed it's necessary to reflect—how much of the reaction against him, against them, has to do with a version, a subsequent version, of how narrow how unimaginative how upholstered and materialist the English—the English!—had become.

This fact of mobility and of alternative viewpoints comes profoundly, in this period, to affect the novel. There's a crisis I've been tracing through all the novelists so far, in their different ways: a crisis of language and form, a tension within language and form, which now comes to a new phase. In effect, I'd say, what had been a tension became now a split. Internal disturbances of the sort we saw in George Eliot and in Hardy became too strong, too restless, to be contained any longer within any single writer (though Lawrence tried, and we shall see what a struggle it was, what in the end it cost him).

Internal disturbances of language and form. But these, I've been saying all along, are problems of relationship, of essential relationship: to and with other people, other groups, other classes; but as these work through in any real experience disturbances of consciousness, the consciousness of the writer. Educated and customary, public and private—these are settling terms, quietening terms, for what were really, in all the most interesting, the most exposed minds, not definitions or categories but moving continuous and unconscious histories. And it wasn't that the new minds were any less serious. What they had to hold to, had to try to see whole, was in itself more complicated, more deeply dividing and disturbing.

It was not, for example, a less divided society in the 1890s than in the Two Nations of the 1840s. It was more advanced and more prosperous but it was also more rationally, more objectively and consciously and functionally divided.

> The great house, the church, the village, and the labourers and the servants in their stations and degrees, seemed to me, I say, to be a closed and complete social system. About us were other villages and great estates, and from house to house, interlacing, correlated, the Gentry, the fine Olympians, came and went.... I thought this was the order of the whole world.... It seemed to be in the divine order.

That's Wells, in *Tono Bungay*, on that Bladesover world in which his mother was a servant. Of course, if it were only that, it would be nothing new. It's the world Jane Austen described, the world George Eliot extended and then under pressure went back to for the ideas, for the talk. But Wells goes on:

> That all this fine appearance was already sapped, that there were forces at work that might presently carry all this elaborate social

> system in which my mother instructed me so carefully that I
> might understand my place, to Limbo, had scarcely dawned upon
> me....

And that's the real point: the consciousness, the gathering consciousness of
the end of a period; but of an end within something 'closed and complete',
something externally solid and absolute.

> It is like an early day in a fine October. The hand of change rests
> on it all, unfelt, unseen; resting for awhile, as it were half
> reluctantly, before it grips and ends the thing for ever. One frost
> and the whole face of things will be bare....

Or again, to explain and define, a new note: a new consciousness, self-
consciousness of the 'modern':

> England was all Bladesover two hundred years ago; ... it has had
> reform Acts indeed, and such-like changes of formula, but no
> essential revolution since then; ... all that is modern and different
> has come in as a thing intruded or as a gloss upon this
> predominant formula, either impertinently or apologetically.

It is the important Wells tone: something now easily, too easily dismissed;
overt and challenging, set up like a milepost along a brand new road that
hasn't yet been built. Yet what he says is obviously true, even of his own way
of saying it:

> all that is modern and different has come in as a thing intruded
> or as a gloss....

For the predominant formula at the time he was writing was not only a
traditional community—the country-house world of Bladesover. It was also
the inherited, the shaping form of the novel.

Now it is here, really, that the split takes place. To accept that world,
that form, was in a very deep way to accept its consciousness. Of course with
every kind of qualification and refinement; an intense pressure, a self-
conscious and intricate pressure within that imaginary, imaginative circle. To
question the circle itself, to examine the relations which composed it—
profound relations of property, income, work, education—was not only
radical in overt ways—asking radical questions, giving radical opinions. It

was a break in texture where consciousness itself was determined; an assault, or so it seemed, not only on the form of the novel but on an idea, *the* idea, of literature itself.

And this is Wells's importance, and the real significance of his quarrel with James. You've only to read the introduction to their exchanges—a modern introduction, by critical minds set firmly on one side of this argument, a set that goes almost too deep to be noticed—you've only to notice the tones, the terms, their familiarity in contemporary discussion, to see how central this difference is. To break out from Bladesover once you were really aware of it was to break every convention at once. It had been different for Hardy, away from that Home Counties, that determining world. Hardy lived still where England was active in all its main senses: a working relating society. That's why of course, very quickly, he was called—'placed' as—a regional novelist; or to take the word that was really to turn the trick, provincial. All that was not Home Counties—meaning that social formation that stretched from St James's to places like Bladesover but also to Calcutta and Boston—all the places and feelings of another England were provincial; let it have, in a folk way, its regional, its provincial works. But where consciousness was formed—in the schools, the colleges, the clubs, the country-houses—nobody supposed himself in the presence of a sector, a sect; he was now at the centre, the centre of the world; and a centre that could take over with its trained confidence all that England had been, all that literature had been.

Of course, at very different levels: all the way from *The Spoils of Poynton* to Galsworthy's *The Country House*. That's what's wrong, by the way, about that composite figure Wells-Bennett-Galsworthy. Bennett in all the work that matters, the very fine early work, is a located, that is to say an English novelist. The link, it might have been, from George Eliot and Hardy to Lawrence, who was very aware of him. But in this new phase, and of course in himself, without the staying-power, without the persistent creative autonomy: drawn in, sucked in, pushing in to that consuming reconciling centre. And Galsworthy was inside it from the beginning. Galsworthy writing that intensive internal study formally after Turgeniev, but Turgeniev was an exile, a real exile, and that made all the difference. Galsworthy, certainly, is self-critical, what is called satirical, but within limits of course: within that centre's limits. The farthest he really gets is the division, the superficial division, that was possible inside it: between business people and artistic people; conventional people and promiscuous people; sheep and black sheep. It's the same kind of novel only the tensions are all on the surface; not working, not disturbing but set—often effectively and memorably—in prepared situations, contrasting characters. And past these arranged confrontations, with their steady implication of change and reform, is a deciding continuity: a sense that this and only this is the human scale.

And then Wells is very different. He failed in the end; he emigrated to World Government as clearly as Lawrence to Mexico. But until 1914, until that real break that went beyond him, not only a restless energy—fashion is prepared to concede that to outsiders—but a creative energy, and a creative energy in fiction. His simplest successes are of course what are called the romances (that's placing again, very like 'provincial'). He avoids tearing that seamless cloth, that traditional texture of the novel, by taking his consciousness of change—his sense of history and of the urgency of transformation—outside that social fiction, that intensive realism, where in existing circumstances such questions could never be put; or rather, could be put as questions but could never become actions. The Morlocks and the Eloi at the end of the Time Machine; the alteration of consciousness in the passing of the Comet; the disturbance of conventions by the invisible man: these were real ways through, in an otherwise reconciling world. Kipps and Mr Polly, men on the run from the system: there we see the alternative: an irrepressible humour and energy, but not the humour and energy of Dickens, transforming a world; only the endlessly self-conscious, self-consciously perky, the almost apologetic assertion—over the shoulder, behind the hand—of a right to live.

I can feel with this strongly, as I felt strongly with Lewisham many years ago making schedules for exams: the first character in fiction I ever clearly identified with. But it's a game, you know (to revert to the idiom): only a game, old man. Like Orwell's Mr Bowling thirty years later in *Coming Up for Air*, it's a dog off leash; a gay dog, a sad dog. More like us, much more like us, that any Forsyte or Warburton, but still only in odd corners or doing a public act—a public act among friends. And nostalgic always, cosily nostalgic: an adolescent nostalgia, a whole world away from the bitter and tearing—yet then profoundly connecting—adult memories of George Eliot or Hardy or Lawrence. Of course we all wish there were a little pub by the river, where we could live and let live. We wish it when we're tired, or when general change is too hard or too disturbing. It's the appealing side, the nice side, of the petit bourgeois; with the emphasis on the small man, the little human peninsula, trying to forget what the high bourgeois mainland is like (and in that turning away there's some genuine warmth).

What it grows up into, unfortunately, is that consciousness Wells really does share with Bennett, and that's been very pervasive: a bouncing cheeky finally rampant commercialism: not Mr Polly but Northcliffe, and beyond him the *Daily Mirror* and ITV; the break-out—what's called a break-out—from Bladesover to Tono Bungay. It's because of this, I suppose, that the ghosts of Henry James and of Matthew Arnold are still so regularly summoned: an enclosed and intricate lamplit seriousness against all that cheerful bounce that so quickly becomes a mechanical thump, practically breaking your shoulder. It's a measure of our difficulty that we think it's there—only there—we've got to choose.

Yet what an odd thing it is that we have to say this about Wells, who could see worlds transformed, entire systems changed, a modern Utopia. That's the key of course: that last word, Utopia. Wells is unique in his time because he saw very clearly the scale of the change that was coming, the change that had to be fought for. He couldn't bring it together in any single form: the world as it is and the scale of the change. But he exploits the distance, the imaginative distance, with a skill that's the basis of both his comedy and his prophetics. It's a now familiar experience: the difference between the pace of history and the pace of a life: the difference, I mean, in deeply established, deeply customary and yet resourceful societies. We oughtn't to take too seriously his final abandonment of literature—I mean when he says he doesn't want it, can't use it, would rather write something else. We oughtn't to take this too seriously as a way of dismissing him, as a way of dismissing his problem, as it's possible to do if you think in conventional ways that you know what literature is, what that seamless texture is, what that circle—that conventional circle—encloses. Ever since Wells and still with real difficulty and urgency we have seen a confusion of forms, an overlapping of interests, a formal separation of imagination, social criticism and documentary which in practice keeps breaking down as the real interests rejoin. And the interaction of the interests (the older name of course is just general human experience) is where literature, inevitably, is.

What we have then to try to say, as precisely and as justly as we can, is what happened to literature, to that seamless literature, through all this disturbance. And we can only do this seriously if we acknowledge the disturbance; acknowledge, I mean, its necessity, its reality. If we say the disturbance is some system, call it sociology or materialism or technologico-Benthamism, we gain some rhetorical victories but at a terrible cost; at the expense, really, of any continuing literature, though with a residual emphasis—a very pure emphasis—on the achieved literature, the decided literature of the past. For the questions that fired Wells—very similar questions, for all the difference of tone, to the questions that fired Lawrence, and that are still very close to us—were necessary questions, running back to the disturbances of Dickens and George Eliot and Hardy.

What a stable society, a known civilisation, most evidently offers is a human emphasis, a place for human emphasis. Given that stability we can look long and deep; look at human possibility, at individual strengths and weaknesses, always intricately meshed with each other; look, examine, with a seriousness that depends, really, on certain other possibilities having been ruled out: say war, poverty, revolutionary conflict. The change of the novel in the mid-nineteenth century had been a change made necessary by just these disturbances: a sudden and desperate realisation of what was really at stake in all our active relationships.

This realisation came again at the turn of the century: as urgently, as unavoidably as in that generation of the 1840s, but now, we must see, with very different results. The new social and historical consciousness was more general, necessarily general, because the scale had widened. It wasn't only a crisis within a single society, a nation: that specific Englishness which was a strength, a focus, in the generation from Dickens to Hardy. Much wider issues, implicit before, now became explicit: war and imperialism, which then had been distant or marginal; poverty and revolution, which had new international bearings. It was a very much longer way—impossibly longer it seemed and can still seem—from those human crises, crises that do decide life, to what can be known directly and particularly as human crisis: that experience, that relationship—visible, tangible experience and relationship; the texture of what James so rightly called, emphasised as 'felt life'.

Not that war, imperialism, poverty, revolution were other than life; were simply abstractions called politics. 'Something other than human life': that phrase of Blake's is not to be transplanted, not when we really think of Blake, to processes which in the generations now living were to make their way into every experience and every relationship directly and indirectly, as George Eliot had foreseen. What I call the split, between the 1890s and the first war, was in a way inevitable; only a far-reaching change could have prevented it. But it is from that time on and especially in the novel that people tried to talk of 'social' and 'personal' as separable processes, separate realms. 'Social'—we've all seen it—became the pejorative 'sociological', and a 'sociological' interest was in 'something other than human life', in classes, statistics, abstract ideas, systems. 'Personal'—we may have noticed this less— became the whole of 'human'; the recommending, ratifying 'human'—love, friendship, marriage, death. And you can now very quickly start a fight anywhere between the claims of the definitions: which of the two is really substantial, decisive, important, significant. Schools clash or more often ignore and despise each other. 'Sociological' is a sneer you may think the last word until you hear 'literary' from the other side of the fence. Systems of all kinds (and this is really odd) rise to support each principality. The deciding reality is here, or here. False consciousness and superstructure, rationalisation and projection are the names for what the others are doing, for all they are doing. And at this new frontier, the writer can seem to be required to present himself with a clear identity paper: is he poet or sociologist? interested in literature or in politics? committed to reality or to the merely incidental and personal? What had been always precariously a republic of letters became this series of jealous and squabbling states and areas; in the end down to fields. And in the process, unnoticed, the seamless cloth of literature had been simply, impudently carried off.

I don't mean carried off by James: not in his work anyway, though the critical prefaces are different. It's very easy to raise, even to feel a prejudice against James: as Wells let it out in *Boon*—

> every light and line focused on the high altar. And on the altar, very reverently placed, intensely there, is a dead kitten, an eggshell, a piece of string.

That won't do at all, won't survive a few minutes' re-reading of James himself. Very serious human actions are at the centre of all his best work, and this means most of it. Very serious and material actions, as it happens. It is a much more materialist fiction than Wells, who is idealist, fantasist, to the core. James tells us how he would rewrite in his mind almost everybody he read; he even did this—it's a thought—to Wells' *First Men in the Moon*. But what he could really rewrite, what belongs in his dimension and would be much improved by it, is Galsworthy: that's where the conventional groupings really break down. He hasn't Galsworthy's interest in remedy, that is to say in change. He has excluded from the novel as any major element not morality, moralising (though people praise that exclusion, are glad to be free of didacticism, welcome the wrought work of life—art—that is there and wholly known). Any knowing, any showing, any *presentation*—to take the exact word for James—is moral inevitably. The selection and the placing are the judgments, of a sort that could be made especially by someone in his position; someone not in ordinary ways himself at stake and involved. But what he has really excluded is history: that other dimension of value which from Scott through Dickens and George Eliot and Hardy to Lawrence (but not to Joyce) has transformed prose fiction.

Some of the deepest and also some of the coarsest human problems are at the centre of James's work: people using each other, betraying, failing, destroying: not a small world in that sense, and certainly not relics or eggshells. Since an image has been offered I will suggest my own. Not an altar, there's nothing reverent. Past the qualifying assuaging oblique tone it's the reverse of reverent; even cruel when you get to the heart. But I remember that first scene in George Eliot's *Daniel Deronda*—that novel which in one of its parts has been rightly seen as a lead to James: that scene in

> one of those splendid resorts which the enlightenment of ages has prepared ... a suitable condenser for human breath belonging, in great part, to the highest fashion ... the atmosphere ... well-brewed to a visible haze.

What is happening is gambling, 'dull gas-poisoned absorption', though there is a detached observer and a little boy looking away towards the door. But that image of a table at which people come to play, making moves of the utmost seriousness and intricacy in which their lives are staked though the tone is still of a diversion, and with an imaginary circle cutting them off, really cutting them off, not only from where the money is made but from where the lives are made in direct relationship, in creation, in the real and connected care of life: that table, full of absorbed players speaking a language of their own, and the clear-eyed observer, seeing the game, the haze, so exactly, and the boy looking away to the door: that for me—I mean as an image—is the actual James world.

And this is why, I think, his art is so fine of its kind. The concentration, the working, are very remarkable. I have often thought reading James—*The Portrait of a Lady* is still the best example—that human speech in its intricacy, its particularity, its quality as a sequence, has never been better rendered. That it is the speech of a class makes, at first, little difference; all languages are in some sense particular. But then what also strikes me is that it is just this working, this rendering, that is the defining centre. I don't mean the defining of others, I mean the rendering, the preoccupied rendering, of a single reality 'well-brewed to a visible haze'. In James, that is to say, and the effect of this is very important, the emphasis has so shifted within an apparently continuous form—it is an emphasis that began to change, as I've argued, in George Eliot—that we call two kinds of fiction, two kinds of novel, by the same generic name—'psychological realism', when what has really happened is a transfer of process from the signified to the signifier; from the material to the work on material; from the life to the art.

The art, let's say quickly, is also life—that distinction won't ever really do except as a first approximation. The act of seeing, the act of making, the act of rendering and presenting is life itself of an intense kind. But of a kind, undoubtedly; a kind 'psychological realism' doesn't describe, define closely enough or perhaps define at all. What really matters in James is that act of signifying in which the novel becomes its own subject, as opposed to late Wells, in which the subject, the isolated subject, becomes the novel. Consciousness in James, to put it another way, is the almost exclusive object and subject of consciousness. This is the source of the perceptive brilliance and the ease of James's stories about writing and writers: *The Lesson of the Master, The Figure in the Carpet* or the relaxed connecting *Death of a Lion* or *The Next Time*. But in the larger works it's a thing in itself, and of course it reveals a great deal. Not a solipsist fiction. On the contrary. That's where the separation, the wrenching-apart of 'individual' and 'society' comes in to confuse us. Since consciousness is social its exploration, its rendering as a process, is connecting, inevitably. The figures that form there, figures of consciousness—of this or that done or said—are as moving, as connecting, as recognised as any figures in the world. More recognised we might even say; more tangible, tactile, by a curious paradox: more undeniably *there*—to come back to that word—than the figures less brewed in that visible haze; figures— but then not figures, men and women—who might get up and walk away, who are not accessible, not accessible and workable in that way, to the ever-conscious, not involved but absorbed novelist.

It's this, in the end, I mean by the split. Not just 'social' realism or 'psychological' realism, though that's a way of putting it: a pulling of life, in the scale and complexity of any now known community, one way or the other—their overt common acts in their social identities; or their unexpressed desires, attachments, movements in their personal identities. In the next generation it settled down like that: one kind of reality or the other seemed to have to be chosen. But in this decisive period it is still a problem of relationship, of the writer's relationship: what Wells hits (among many misses) when he says James relates before everything to 'The Novel'.

It comes out in another way as we see James's critical preferences, James's selection and rejection of ancestors: the tradition he tried to establish, though it sometimes embarrasses its subsequent propagandists. Flaubert: 'for many of our tribe at large *the* novelist' (and notice 'tribe'; the writing community is now the most known, the most knowable; that is the radical change). Flaubert's complications

> were of the spirit, of the literary vision, and though he was thoroughly profane he was yet essentially anchoretic.

That has a characteristic (if comically edged) brilliance; it is very exactly, very

referentially said. 'The spirit ... the literary vision.' But Dickens: *Bleak House,
Little Dorrit, Our Mutual Friend*—'forced ... laboured ... dug out as with a
spade and pickaxe' (the metaphors of work, in that tone, are precisely
revealing). Or again:

> A story based upon those elementary passions in which alone we
> seek the true and final manifestation of character must be told in
> a spirit of intellectual superiority to those passions.

'Intellect' and 'passions': that's one way of putting it, and the point about the
'spirit of intellectual superiority' is certainly relevant. We've been haunted by
that spirit, often in obviously borrowed or ill-fitting clothes, through so
many of the corridors of literary education.

But it's not really a matter of faculties of the mind; it's a relationship,
'intellect' and 'passions', between a novelist and 'his' characters; the
relationship I was defining in George Eliot and Hardy; between the novelist
and other people, at that depth where a society—a knowable society—is at
issue and is decided.

The most critical reference is to Tolstoy:

> the great illustrative master-hand on all this ground of
> disconnection of method from matter.

And Wells and Bennett are seen as Tolstoy's 'diluted' successors. It sounds
like a critical point; what is now usually taken as a critical point, something
about 'method' and 'matter'. But it is the terms that are revealing, since the
relationship James senses in Tolstoy—the relationship that disturbs and
indeed ought to disturb him—is not a matter of 'art' in his sense at all. It is
a matter of relationship between the writer and other men (and so between
the writer and his work, himself). There's a subsidiary answer, if you feel you
have to find one. Tolstoy works, creates, puts an intense life there, with a
range and a power of sustained attention against which James, obviously, is
minor. But that's not the main point. Tolstoy couldn't accept that version of
consciousness, of relationship, which was becoming—exclusively, even
arrogantly—'literature': that working, working over, working through, by
the last of the great men, the last hero, the novelist, the signifier. For always
beyond that lighted circle, that imaginative circle, was a stubborn active
connecting life: not 'matter' at all, and always challenging the
preoccupation—the *preoccupation*—with 'method'. So that 'social' and
'personal', 'public' and 'private', 'historical' and 'psychological' make no

sense in Tolstoy: make no sense of him in his sustained, his truly preoccupying and connecting life and art. The continuum of experience: that's one way of putting it. But it's never passive, never given. It's an active relationship, an exploration into consciousness which at its most intricate and intimate is a consciousness of others, and of others with us in history, in production, in the care and maintenance of life. Not matter then to be absorbed by a method; but an experience almost breaking, needing to break, any available signifying form; and yet in and through itself, in the pressure and structure of active experience, creating forms, creating life: *the* novelist, in and outside the tribe.

And when that pressure and struggle became too intense—too intense, I mean, in a society suspended, temporarily dominant, unable to change— there was a falling away into alternative concerns. Or concerns seen as alternative: the issues of history and society—what Wells went on to write about, to set up as props in his novels; or the close issues of personal life— what a late bourgeois literature, though not yet in full flight, selected, deliberately selected, as the only knowable reality, the only known and yet inevitably excluding community. There's no choice in the end between those two roads; no separable merit—I mean merit in emphasis—in either. It's like the choice, the related choice—the same choice in other terms—between art as a vehicle, the position Wells came to argue, and art as autonomous in its own clear circle, the position of James. That, it seems to me, is no choice at all: the terms, the questions, are just records of a failure. But as we put it that way, let's take care, respecting care, to emphasise the seriousness, the effort, the important and lasting energy of the attempt to keep hold, to keep going. In Forster, for example, we can see these radical impulses straining almost dislocating his early novels; the sense of strain, of inevitable but reluctant divergence as late as *A Passage to India*, and then the significant silence in this most honest, most self-appraising of our living writers. But the larger energies of Wells and of James—those figures who force us, forced each other, to an eventual contrast—these energies remind us of how much was at stake; of what a crisis it was, in that time, that period, that now wrongly seems static.

It is history now. The choices don't come in that open way again and what succeeds the division, the parting of the ways, is a renewal of energy, a renewal of the novel, as important as anything that preceded it. It's just that criticism, literary history hasn't really caught up; has taken the terms of that split and continued to apply them as a sort of prescription—actually a biased prescription, a symptom—when the real sickness is the separation into classes, into categories, into mutually hostile preoccupations and methods: the individual *or* society; public *or* private; social *or* literary studies.

What matters to us is the crisis itself: where what was and is most creative in the novel—the open response to an extending and active society, the similarly open response to intense and unique and connecting feeling—encountered major difficulties: difficulties of relationship and so difficulties of form: difficulties that connect and disturb through all the rest of our century.

DAVID THORBURN

Conrad and Modern English Fiction

T.S. Eliot borrowed famously from *Heart of Darkness* in his epigraph to "The Hollow Men": *Mistah Kurtz—he dead.* And however serviceable this borrowing may have been, it can also be said to crystallize the partial and limiting view of Conrad's work that this book has wished to qualify. To insist, as I have tried to do, on the way in which Conrad's major fiction describes and deeply values our fragile but genuine human connections is not to deny Conrad his melancholy. But it is to imply that the largely unqualified despair in Eliot's early poetry constitutes a special rather than a representative instance of the modernist imagination. Indeed, as I read and reread Conrad, fortifying my sense of his deep sympathies with that antiapocalyptic strain in Romanticism that Lionel Trilling describes in "Wordsworth and the Rabbis"[1] and that is dramatized so powerfully in poems like Wordsworth's "Tintern Abbey" and Keats's "To Autumn," I came increasingly to see that my notions about Conrad could be applied in some degree to James and to the major English novelists who immediately follow them.

There is a large irony in the fact that our revised understanding of the intimate links between the Romantics and the early modern poets has not been extended to the novelists of the same period. We have come to see that despite their aggressive insistence on their own distance from the nineteenth century, the modern poets were the heirs and continuers of the very tradition they claimed to subvert. But the related notion that the central figures in the

From *Conrad's Romanticism.* © 1974 by Yale University.

great modern novels may not be counterparts of J. Alfred Prufrock has yet to be widely acknowledged.

Though other influences are also involved, it is a remarkable tribute to Eliot's immense authority that the prevailing understanding of modern fiction should continue to center on the themes of barrenness and despair. In the famous review of *Ulysses*—paradoxically, an effort to defend Joyce's book from Richard Aldington's attack on its alleged perversity and formlessness— Eliot praises what he calls Joyce's "mythical method": a method, he says, that gives shape and significance "to the immense panorama of futility and anarchy that is contemporary history."[2] This is not, of course, a neutral critical description but a signal instance of a writer-critic reading his own practices and perceptions into the work of another. Embedded in Eliot's sentence, as in the essay as a whole, is the assumption that Joyce shared his sense of the world's "futility" and that Joyce's technical innovations embody just such a hopeless and crisis-ridden view. This association of technical innovativeness with a vision of despair dominated the Joyce scholarship until fairly recently, and continues, I think, to be largely characteristic of the general attitude toward writers like Conrad, Woolf, and Ford Madox Ford.

Gloom and apocalypse are, in any case, recurring themes for some of the most important critics of modern fiction. Erich Auerbach, for example, at the conclusion of what remains perhaps the single most impressive analysis of the essential techniques of modern fiction, speaks of the "air of vague and hopeless sadness" in Virginia Woolf's novels, of Joyce's "blatant and painful cynicism," of a "certain atmosphere of universal doom" and "hopelessness" that pervades modernist fiction generally.[3] And Irving Howe, a consistent and important champion of modernism, has repeatedly stressed its extremist and nihilistic impulses. "The 'modern,' " Howe summarizes in a recent book, "as it refers to both history and literature, signifies extreme situations and radical solutions. It summons images of war and revolution, experiment and disaster, apocalypse and skepticism; images of rebellion, disenchantment and nothingness."[4] Although this fearful catalogue may correspond in some degree to the work of Continental modernists, it seems to me to apply in the English tradition only to certain extremist and unrepresentative figures like the early Eliot.

Though I have no wish to deny modern fiction's recurring insistence on the radically problematic and even estranging aspects of experience, I cannot feel that Howe's, or Auerbach's, emphasis takes account of the powerfully antiapocalyptic temper of the great modern English novels, their shared respect for what Conrad calls "the irremediable life of the earth as it is." Ellmann's sense of this quality in Joyce has a brilliant conciseness:

"Joyce's discovery, so humanistic that he would have been embarrassed to disclose it out of context, was that the ordinary is the extraordinary."[5] This Joycean impulse to recover and to celebrate the ordinary has roots deep in Romanticism, of course, and is widely shared not only by Conrad but by other modern English writers as well. It is central, for instance, in Ford, whose great and still undervalued tetralogy is in part a meditation on the antiapocalyptic character of our individual lives. Against a backdrop of the most decisive public and political events, *Parade's End* shows us characters whose natures change only minimally; and whose desire to alter or to transform themselves is satisfied only ambiguously and incompletely. (This is why Tietjens himself is largely absent from the pages of the concluding volume of the tetralogy, having been drawn away from his simple country retreat and his new life as an antique dealer back to Groby, the ancestral home from which he had imagined himself to be finally free.) Ford's largest theme, in fact, might be said to be the disjunction between the enormous political eruptions that the society he describes is experiencing and the far more minimal and ordinary alterations that occur in the lives of his characters. This theme is elaborated most fully in the career of his protagonist, who in the course of his education—*Parade's End*, like many of the great English novels of the period, is a *bildungsroman* but about an adult—must come to terms with the simplest and most elemental facts about himself, must acknowledge that he is unhappy, that being a Tietjens of Groby does not exempt him from pain or simple human need or even— during the war—ambition for advancement. This small and basic insight Ford sees as a remarkable act of will and moral heroism. Just so, I think, in Joyce, Bloom's increasing capacity simply to confront directly the fact of Molly's infidelity and his own partial responsibility for it is a crucial drama of the book. Bloom changes little in *Ulysses*, advances only to a rich equanimity concerning the partialness of life, and the novel insists in every possible way on the ordinariness and simplicity of his consolations.

This emphasis on the ordinary, the simple human thing, is crucial, too, in Virginia Woolf, who finds in the most elementary human gatherings and undertakings—parties, dinners, moments of intimacy in conversation, public pageants that draw people briefly out of their separateness—a fragile but real counterforce to the fact that time passes and nothing endures but the neutral indifferent sea.

Even Lawrence, who loves apocalypse, has a way of acknowledging, if only in his best books, the world's resistance to the imagination of crisis and transformation. Lawrence, it would seem to me, is in fact at his most Romantic in those books—*Women in Love* far above all—in which the spirit's yearning for transcendence is mocked and frustrated, so that Lawrence is then able, like the Romantic poets of the century before him, to tell the truth not only about the yearning but also about what really happens to it in the world. Birkin weeping before Gerald's corpse—he had earlier said one oughtn't to waste tears on the dead—and Birkin in the last pages of the novel, returned to the England, to the very roof, he had thought to put behind him in his journey into fullness—this Birkin lives in a partial, indecisive world of simple human intimacies that is not entirely at odds with the world of Joyce or Woolf or Ford Madox Ford.

One way of clarifying these matters is to suggest that J. Alfred Prufrock, or Gregor Samsa, is a far less characteristic modernist figure than James's Strether, who disembarks in Europe to find himself in a new world of overwhelming complexity and nuance. If traditional moral assumptions and old stabilities are called into question for Strether, and if he feels the loss of such assurances acutely, he is conscious at the same time of the challenge and the variousness of the world he has entered. His position is endangered and precarious, but he has much to see and little inclination to despair. Strether can serve, I think, as an emblem not only for many of the protagonists of modern English fiction but also for the makers of it: for their shared sense of the difficulties, even the terrors, but also the excitements of the world they wished to render in art.

The formulations about the nature of modern fiction offered us by Virginia Woolf and Ford Madox Ford seem to me far more accurate and helpful than Eliot's review of Joyce. In Woolf's two major essays on modern fiction and in the extended reflections on fictional technique scattered through Ford's memoirs and other books, there is a remarkable accord. Both writers suggest that life as they see and understand it had not been adequately rendered in earlier novels, largely because older fictional methods are called into question by the modern awareness of the complexities of the inner life and by a recognition of the ways in which one's subjective vision selects and colors experience. Both, in their own ways, and Conrad, James, Lawrence, and Joyce in theirs, tried to devise techniques that would do justice to the new complexity they saw before them. They are all, except for Lawrence, suspicious of apocalypse. "Let us not take it for granted," Woolf writes, echoing many passages in Ford, "that life exists more fully in what is commonly thought big than in what is commonly thought small." And they reject conventional versions of plot and of literary structure. Here is Woolf speaking, then Ford:

> Examine for a moment an ordinary mind on an ordinary day. The
> mind receives a myriad impressions—trivial, fantastic,

evanescent, or engraved with the sharpness of steel. From all sides they come, an incessant shower of innumerable atoms; and as they fall, ... the accent falls differently from of old; the moment of importance came not here but there; so that if a writer were a free man and not a slave, if he could write what he chose, ... there would be no plot, no comedy, no tragedy, no love interest or catastrophe in the accepted style.... Life is not a series of gig lamps symmetrically arranged; but a luminous halo, a semi-transparent envelope surrounding us from the beginning of consciousness to the end. Is it not the task of the novelist to convey this varying, this unknown and uncircumscribed spirit, whatever aberration or complexity it may display, with as little mixture of the alien and external as possible?[6]

We agreed that the general effect of a novel must be the general effect that life makes on mankind. A novel must therefore not be a narration, a report. Life does not say to you: In 1914 my next door neighbour, Mr. Slack, erected a greenhouse and painted it with Cox's green aluminium paint.... If you think about the matter you will remember, in various unordered pictures, how one day Mr. Slack appeared in his garden and contemplated the wall of his house. You will then try to remember the year of that occurrence and you will fix it as August 1914 because having had the foresight to bear the municipal stock of the city of Liège you were able to afford a first-class season ticket for the first time in your life. You will remember Mr. Slack ... again [in] ... his garden, this time with a pale, weaselly-faced fellow, who touched his cap from time to time. Mr. Slack will point to his house-wall several times at different points, the weaselly fellow touching his cap at each pointing. Some days after, coming back from business you will have observed against Mr. Slack's wall.... At this point you will remember that you were then the manager of the fresh-fish branch of Messrs. Catlin and Clovis in Fenchurch Street.... What a change since then! Millicent had not yet put her hair up.... You will remember how Millicent's hair looked, rather pale and burnished in plaits. You will remember how it now looks, henna'd ... You remember some of the things said by means of which Millicent has made you cringe—and her expression! ... Cox's Aluminium Paint! ... You remember the half empty tin that Mr. Slack showed you ...

And, if that is how the building of your neighbour's greenhouse comes back to you, just imagine how it will be with your love-affairs that are so much more complicated....[7]

Both passages seem to me remarkably clear explanations for the unconventional methods of modern fiction. Both adhere firmly to a mimetic conception of literature, appealing directly to the real world, to the way things are or seem to us to be. And in neither passage is there the suggestion that the complexity of this reality is a cue for despair. The modern novelists realize, of course, that nihilism may be a logical consequence of the perception that the world's significance is subjective and private, and they give us characters—like Decoud, or Mr. Ramsay, or Stephen Dedalus—who are tortured and sometimes destroyed by this recognition. But being novelists and not metaphysicians they live with muddle and inconsistency more readily than some of their characters, and their "working assumptions," as Ian Watt has written of Conrad, "echo the greatest of English empiricists, who in *Twelfth Night* gave Sir Andrew Aguecheek the immortal words: 'I have no exquisite reason for 't, but I have reason good enough.'"[8]

The harshness but also the beauty of modern fiction, its tough honesty but also its odd exuberance, have an illuminating parallel in the writings of Freud. The Freud I have in mind is the stoic humanist who emerges from some of Lionel Trilling's essays and, most impressively, from Philip Rieff's great book.[9] Like the modern novelists who were, roughly, his contemporaries, this Freud is aware of the definitive inwardness of men, of their estrangement from themselves and from their fellows, of the tyranny of the trivial and the quotidian. But, again like the novelists, Freud's sense of our grave human limits leads not to despair but to a recognition of man's resilience and his capacity for that tough-minded candor which can lead to a minimal self-mastery and even, sometimes, to a kind of secular reverence for things as they are:

How [did Bloom enter the bed]?
With circumspection, as invariably when entering an abode (his own or not his own): with solicitude, the snake-spiral springs of the mattress being old, the brass quoits and pendent viper radii loose and tremulous under stress and strain: prudently, as entering a lair or ambush of lust or adder: lightly, the less to disturb: reverently, the bed of conception and of birth, of consummation of marriage and of breach of marriage, of sleep and of death.

Both Freud and these writers speak in their different ways especially of the essential human labor of perception, of seeing the world and the self clearly. They are antagonistic to lies and deception. Warily, mainly by implication and sometimes with terrible obliqueness the writers affirm the tough-minded clarity of Mrs. Ramsay:

> It will end, it will end, she said. It will come, it will come, when suddenly she added, We are in the hands of the Lord.
>
> But instantly she was annoyed with herself for saying that. Who had said it? Not she; she had been trapped into saying something she did not mean. She looked up over her knitting ... purifying out of existence that lie, any lie.

Freud's book about this particular lie, *The Future of an Illusion* (1927), focuses, like the novelists, on the theme of seeing and growing:

> True, man will then [having renounced religion] find himself in a difficult situation. He will have to confess his utter helplessness and his insignificant part in the working of the universe; he will have to confess that he is no longer the centre of creation, no longer the object of the tender care of a benevolent providence. He will be in the same position as the child who has left the home where he was so warm and comfortable. But, after all, is it not the destiny of childishness to be overcome? Man cannot remain a child for ever; he must venture at last into the hostile world.[10]

That these generalizations are fitted to Conrad I think is beyond question. Yet I would not insist on them too exclusively. For there is something quaint, old-fashioned about him, and one feels toward his work in some degree as his friends seem to have felt about his person: that he was uneasy not only in that place of exile whose language he appropriated and greatly honored, but also in the time in which he lived. There is a rich, simple nostalgia in him, and a decorousness and reticence not at all modern. He is different from Joyce and Woolf and his friend Ford, even less at home with them, finally, than the older James. The Singleton of modern literature, he stands nearer to Wordsworth than to Joyce.

Something of his special quality may be suggested by Walter Allen's distinction between two classes of novelists, the sophisticated and the naive:

> The sophisticated novelist is one who is aware, in the foreground of his consciousness, of his special relation as novelist to his subject-matter or to his readers often, indeed, to both. The naive novelist, on the other hand, is much more plainly the lineal descendant of the primitive story-teller. He takes his audience's interest for granted; he knows they want to hear a story. "Take my word for it, this is the way it happened," is his attitude.[11]

What is striking about Conrad, of course, is the extent to which he fits both of Allen's groupings. (So, too, he would seem to unite both the "drama" and the "romance" of Stevenson's famous definition: "Drama is the poetry of conduct, romance the poetry of circumstance.")[12] It is scarcely possible to imagine a more self-conscious writer than Conrad, to imagine anyone more aware of his special relation to his material and to his audience. Yet he is, like any writer of adventure fiction, clearly descended from the "primitive story-teller." Indeed, in *Lord Jim* and elsewhere both Conrad and Marlow presume upon and subtly exploit their audience's patience: "In regard to the listeners' endurance," Conrad writes in an author's note, "the postulate must be accepted that the story *was* interesting. It is the necessary preliminary assumption" (*Lord Jim*, p. vii).

Ford Madox Ford understood the mixed character of Conrad's fiction, and focused on it in a comparison between his collaborator and two of his famous contemporaries, James and Stephen Crane. James's people, Ford tells us, attend tea parties that are "debating circles of a splendid aloofness, of an immense human sympathy," while Crane is interested in

> physical life, in wars, in slums, in Western saloons, in a world where the "gun" was the final argument. The life that Conrad gives you is somewhere halfway between the two; it is dominated—but less dominated—by the revolver than that of Stephen Crane, and dominated, but less dominated, by the moral scruple than that of James.[13]

This judgment—like most of Ford's literary opinions—is particularly acute, for it is clear that in novel after novel Conrad tries to mingle the sophisticated and the primitive, tries to tell great old-fashioned stories complexly and fully. His subject matter is consistently that of the popular adventure story, his plots are nearly always potentially melodramatic, his rhetoric is always listing toward ornateness and excess. Yet his important work, far from succumbing to the simplification and banality inherent in these things, retrieves from them a rare and austere seriousness. And Conrad accomplishes this work of discovery and rescue, I hope the foregoing has shown, not by denying extravagance but by using it. Although, as I have argued, a principal concern of Conrad's narrative strategies is to deflect our attention away from such extravagance, his successful work never finally denies—is never finally afraid to make use of—the acts and gestures and circumstances that are characteristic of Stevenson and Kipling and Rider Haggard.

"I remember," writes Lionel Trilling, "with what a smile of saying something daring and inacceptable John Erskine told an undergraduate class that some day we would understand that plot and melodrama were good things for a novel to have and that *Bleak House* was a very good novel indeed."[14] One wants, I think, to say something of the same for Conrad, but with the emphasis upon his bloody combats and natural disasters, his pirate battles (as in the conclusion of *Lord Jim*) and his threatening seas (as in *Typhoon* and *The Shadow-Line*).

To say this is to reinforce Ford's estimate of Conrad, an estimate that implicitly clarifies Conrad's complex, mediating role in the development of modern fiction. Ford recalls that James described *Romance* as "an immense English Plum Cake which he kept at his bedside for a fortnight and of which he ate nightly a slice."[15] If James did not say that, he ought to have, for the remark's typically Jamesian mixture of courtesy and condescension suggests exactly how alien and "unserious" such a book must have appeared to the writer Conrad addressed in his letters as "très cher maître."[16]

Though Conrad is frequently (and justly) compared to James, from one angle there is no important modern novelist who less resembles him. For Conrad's complex narrative strategies examine not nuances of gesture, nor even, essentially, moral subtleties—even Marlow, after all, admits that Jim's case is "simple"—but crucial problems of conduct. These problems are profoundly moral and psychological, of course, but if they threaten psychic disintegration, the urgency with which they do so is a consequence primarily of the fact that these dilemmas of conduct also promise literal annihilation. The illusion, the mistake, even (most frighteningly) the mischance of calm or storm over which man has no control—these things can not only maim or undermine a man's sense of himself and his commitments in life, they can, quite simply, kill him. The threat of death or disintegration in Conrad's fiction is nearly always double: it is both spiritual or moral or psychological *and* at the same time palpably physical, something you feel on your pulses, something that happens *out there*, and happens to others outside yourself to whom you are bound by the ties of community:

When the time came the blackness would overwhelm silently the bit of starlight falling upon the ship, and the end of all things would come without a sigh, stir, or murmur of any kind, and all our hearts would cease to beat like run-down clocks.

It was impossible to shake off that sense of finality. The quietness that came over me was like a foretaste of annihilation.[17]

I take this passage to be representative of the double appeal of Conrad's finest work, which is modern and Romantic simultaneously. The spiritual, the interior testing mirrors the pressing physical ordeal that precedes and triggers it. And in what he himself would call this "purposely mingled resonance"—in this balance between the claims of external disaster and of psychic collapse, between the deed and the words that describe and evaluate the deed—we must see, I think, Conrad's lonely distinction.

NOTES

1. Trilling, *The Opposing Self,* pp. 118–50.

2. Originally published in the *Dial,* 75 (1923), 480–83, the review is accessible in Richard Ellmann and Charles Feidelson, Jr., eds., *The Modern Tradition* (New York, 1965), pp. 679–81.

3. Auerbach, *Mimesis,* trans. Willard R. Trask (Princeton, 1953), p. 551.

4. Irving Howe, *A World More Attractive* (New York, 1963), p. ix.

5. Richard Ellmann, *James Joyce* (1959; rpt. New York, 1965), p. 3.

6. Virginia Woolf, "Modern Fiction," in *The Common Reader* (1925; rpt. New York, 1953), p. 154.

7. Ford, *Conrad: A Personal Remembrance,* pp. 180–82. (The spaced periods are in the original; unspaced dots indicate my ellipses.)

8. Ian Watt, "Joseph Conrad: Alienation and Commitment," in *The English Mind,* ed. Hugh Sykes Davies and George Watson (Cambridge, 1964), p. 275.

9. Philip Rieff, *Freud: The Mind of the Moralist* (New York, 1959); Lionel Trilling, "Freud and Literature," in *The Liberal Imagination* (1950; rpt. New York, 1957), pp. 32–54; and "Freud: Within and Beyond Culture," in *Beyond Culture,* pp. 89–118.

10. Trans. W.D. Robson-Scott (1953; rpt. New York, 1957), p. 88.

11. Walter Allen, ed., *The Novelist as Innovator* (London, 1965), Introduction, p. xii.

12. Stevenson, "A Gossip on Romance," *Memories and Portraits, Works* (New York, 1902), 13:329.

13. Ford, *Return to Yesterday,* p. 217.

14. Lionel Trilling, *A Gathering of Fugitives* (New York, 1957), p. 41.

15. *Return to Yesterday,* p. 212. Ford also tells us that James called Marlow "that preposterous master mariner" (*Conrad: A Personal Remembrance,* p. 161).

16. Jean-Aubry, *Conrad: Life and Letters,* 2:55, 91.

17. *The Shadow-Line,* p. 108. The quoted phrase in the next paragraph is from the "Familiar Preface" to *A Personal Record,* p. xxi.

ALLON WHITE

Obscure Writing and Private Life, 1880–1914

If I were to talk to myself out loud in a language not understood by those present my thoughts would be hidden from them.

—Ludwig Wittgenstein

Seek discourse with the shades.

—Joseph Conrad

In his essay on culture, first published in 1883 and immensely popular in England and America, Ralph Waldo Emerson wrote: 'I must have children, I must have events, I must have a social state and a history, or my thinking and speaking want body or basis.' (1) Emerson had two simple things in mind: that social standing imparts weightiness and value to one's words; and that language is social. Unless one is fully part of society, integrated into the heart of its public and private life, linked to it by family relations, by participant action, by social status and by history, then one's discourse is alienated, it is without fixity or firm social origin and is therefore rendered somehow insubstantial. Emerson's is a classic expression of the idea that communication is the possession of the tribe, and that to speak clearly and effectively, with 'body and basis' one must be indisputably of the tribe, speaking to it in its own language. Although he would not have put it in this way, Emerson is making plain a basic socio-linguistic postulate about origins and effective communication—that community and communication share more than a common etymology, and that distance from the norms and values of a language community increases the difficulty of immediate and clear communication with it:(2)

> Familiarity more than any other one thing, would seem to determine clarity. Clarity's model of models, the prose of John Dryden, seems far from clear to a student whose prose reading has started at Thomas Hardy and soared to Ernest Hemingway. Conversely, a psychological report incomprehensible to me opens like a flower to a psychologist ... Familiarity means reassurance. Clarity's first job is to make us feel at home. We want to see where we are.

For the innovative artist, this pact between the community and communication has to be broken. Formal innovation, the infraction of syntactic and narrative rules, the forging of a new lexicon and style, the breaking of established boundaries of genre and judgment, any of these things is simultaneously a removal of self and art from the normative matrices of the language. This is of course a double process, for social alienation makes it correspondingly difficult to adopt the language of the other. Publication under these circumstances becomes a central problem. The reciprocity of values which is understood to guarantee the exchange process underlying publication is thrown into jeopardy by the author's separation from the realm of his addressee, the 'public'. The author has to confront the question of how to communicate without being compromised by the predictable or insidious structure of expectation and value held in the language. The problem of reception—who exactly is one writing for?—raises itself more acutely the further the writer feels himself from the mainstream of the reading public. It is this relation of artistic idiolects to the dominant bourgeois expectations, responses and judgment which became so complicated towards the end of the nineteenth century. (3)

We still have no standard, detailed history of the publication and reception of fiction after the collapse of the three-decker under pressure from the circulating libraries in the decade 1887–97. (4) The circulating libraries, especially the two giants, Mudie's and W.H. Smith, had kept authors, readers and publishers tied into an extremely stable and predictable structure of expectation about novels and novel-reading from the 1840s to the 1880s, and in that period the form flourished. (5) 'We have become a novel-reading people, from the Prime Minister down to the last-appointed scullery-maid,' declared Anthony Trollope in 1870, '... all our other reading put together hardly amounts to what we read in novels.' And in 1892 Edmund Gosse wrote that the tyranny of the novel has never been 'more irresistible', and he added 'the Victorian has been peculiarly the age of the triumph of fiction.' (6) In the 1860s, writers like Bulwer-Lytton, Thackeray, Trollope and George Eliot were receiving four-figure sums for their novels in a period of immense commercial prosperity for fiction.

We are inclined to think of Meredith, Conrad and James as the natural successors to the mid-century novelists, with perhaps a slightly 'elevated' public, but not substantially different from that of their predecessors: the end of the three-decker was more than compensated by the drastic reduction in book prices from 31s.6d. to 6s., which the move to cheap, one-volume novel publication involved.

But there is evidence to show that, by the late 1880s the fiction-reading public had begun to split into two different groups. Of course the so-called 'reading public' is never entirely homogeneous, and as Louis James, Michael Sadleir and Richard Altick (7) have shown, the Victorian novel market was already polarized to a certain extent around the 'respectable' novel and the yellowback. The former was usually published in parts (Dickens's preferred method of publication, and 'Middlemarch' was also sold initially in eight parts) or as a three-decker; the yellowback was either a reprint of the most popular 'respectable' novels or cheap (and often lurid) romances and mystery fiction.

But with the end of the three-decker the market for the 'respectable' novel seems to have split internally into an 'élite' or reviewers' public and the more traditional Victorian public. Again and again in the reviews of Meredith, Conrad and James we meet the same distinction (which to a great extent was in itself formed around these three novelists) between an élite and popular audience:(8)

> Whosoever knows them knows that Mr Meredith's novels are marked by great and rare qualities; but that he makes so constant, so urgent a demand on the imagination, his thought is so subtle and penetrating, and his modes of expression are sometimes so dark with excess of light that he does not succeed very well with the 'ordinary reader'.
> The appearance of a new work from his [Meredith's] pen is hailed by every journal that occupies itself with literature as the great literary event of the day ... [yet] Popular, in the sense in which Dickens and Walter Scott on the one hand were popular,

or on the other in which Miss Braddon and Mr Rider Haggard are popular, he is not and never will be.

The paradox of the position in which Meredith found himself applied with equal force to Conrad and James: that they were 'too intellectual to be popular', that the higher the quality of their work, the less likely they were to appeal to the mass market. This is of no novelty to us, for whom the divorce between a mass culture and high culture is a familiar lament, but at the end of the nineteenth century, with the examples of George Eliot and Dickens so close in the memory, it was a puzzling and sometimes distressing phenomenon. Some reviewers of the time were quick to discern the effects of such a split in the reading public. H.M. Cecil, in an intelligent essay in the 'Free Review' of August 1894, placed Meredith with Wagner and Ibsen as examples of great artists who will never be 'popular', and he uses the idea to account for Meredith's secretiveness and his inclination 'to retire inward upon himself':(9)

> To blame Mr Meredith for his perversities, indeed, would be sometimes to blame the innocent. The guilt for much of it must lie on the shoulders of the public. Cordial recognition of his work in the beginning would have made him less secretive, less inclined to retire inward upon himself, and would have spared us that conviction that he is writing for the select few, whose contempt for the long and hairy-eared public is as great as his own.

Isolation and a lack of recognition from 'the novel-reading public' whilst at the same time being hailed as genius (as 'Shakespeare in modern English' by George Gissing; as 'the most obviously Shakespearean in a certain sense of modern authors' by Percy Lubbock; as 'out and away the greatest force in English letters' by the admiring R.L. Stevenson) became a most trying and bitter paradox for Meredith—the 'Ordeal of George Meredith' as one of his biographers has put it. (10) By the 1880s the British public was beginning to appreciate his work more widely, but even when his reputation was at its highest at the turn of the century, the public remained divided, the majority quite convinced, as one critic put it, that 'Mr Meredith does not write the vernacular.' In a letter to Morley, Swinburne remarked how he thought that Meredith was deliberately reacting to the values of the Victorian novel in a way which necesarily (but, to Swinburne's mind, wrong-headedly) equated the ideal of lucidity with artistic failure:(11)

By dint of revulsion from Trollope on this hand and Braddon on that, he seems to have persuaded himself that limpidity of style must mean shallowness, lucidity of narrative must imply triviality, and simplicity of direct interest or positive incident must involve 'sensationalism'.

This alienation from the bourgeois public is not in any sense a simple cause of Meredith's obscurity, nor is the problem solved by suggesting that it was a result. The two things interpenetrate throughout his career: Meredith's particular psychological estrangement from the public and dominant values held by it in respect of literature made it very difficult for him to write fiction which was both popular and acceptable to himself. He felt constricted by the demands of the public ('The English public will not let me probe deeply into humanity. You must not paint either woman or man: a surface view of the species flat as a wafer is acceptable'). Thus his desire for success (12) conflicted with the conditions necessary for success: Meredith found himself writing for a 'dual addressee', for two different groups with different expectations and values, and his work bears the marks of the compromise which this condition engendered.

This is particularly visible in the conflict between narrative and analysis in his novels, the felt incompatibility between conventions of plot and depth of psychological penetration. For Meredith, stories and plots could not reveal in their sequence of actions the inner secrets of his characters. I do not think that this was merely an inexplicable 'defect', that 'Meredith lacked the sense of construction which should have warned him that he was going wrong.' (13) It is rather that the contrivance of plot seemed to Meredith, much earlier than to most others, a fetter to fiction and not a vehicle for it. His novels bear witness to the modernist mistrust of 'plot', a modernism which either plays up its fabulation and contrivance or neglects it altogether. Meredith did both of these: he was quite conscious that the pressure upon him to tell a good tale conflicted with his inner conviction that 'tales' and 'fiction' were not at all the same thing. The division between novelist and philosopher in 'Sandra Belloni' testifies as much. The novelist is in antagonistic partnership with 'a fellow who will not see things on the surface, and is blind to the fact that the public detest him.' (14) The one preoccupies himself with the public events, with the 'field of action, of battles and conspiracies, nerve and muscle, where life fights for plain issues,' the other protests that such fluency and motion in external events is itself a falsehood, that 'a story should not always flow, or, at least, not to a given measure.' The former then protests that this halting of the story, its hesitation and interpolation will, in itself, destroy the illusion of the fiction, that the characters will be revealed as puppets, their 'golden robe' of illusion reduced to tatters.

This explicit debate on the status and nature of the fiction (in the middle of the fiction) looks back to Sterne and forward to Beckett, Pynchon and Fowles. It is anything but 'Victorian' and it explicitly rejects the contract of illusion between author and reader, that the events are to be seen through the transparent medium of the text. Author, a kind of estranged double, has entered his fiction to reveal himself as a sly manipulator and inept conjuror, like the Rajah and his minister, whom Meredith introduces in chapter 5 of 'One of Our Conquerors' with a satirical double-act to explain the farce of London commuters. In that passage Meredith explicitly associates the self-conscious and elaborate subversion of the story with the accusation of obscurity it will inevitably bring ('princes and the louder members of the grey public are fraternally instant to spurn at the whip of that which they do not immediately comprehend'). In the first chapter of 'The Egoist', Meredith implicitly ironizes this public preference for action by opening the novel with an abstract and essayistic discussion of comedy, leaving the 'real' opening of the story, the mention of the egoistic English gentleman, until the last page of the chapter: he entitles it 'A chapter of which the last page only is of any importance'. It is a technique employed by Robert Musil in the first volume of 'The Man Without Qualities'; chapter 28 is entitled 'A chapter that can be skipped by anyone who has no very high opinion of thinking as an occupation'. In both cases, the self-deprecation is actually at the reader's expense. (15) Yet direct presentation of the action is a function of unity and stability in the act of communication; it requires and projects a unified sender, receiver, code and contact. Communication in Meredith's novels was disintegrating with respect to all of these elements. The receiver was doubled as was the sender; the generic stability of the fiction was in question, and the 'contact', the social relation of the novel's production, was in the process of change.

Meredith's strong sense of being pitted against the public had far-reaching consequences. It was more than just the fact that he had lost faith in the efficacy of narrative continuity and yet the general novel-reading public had not. In his best novels (which for me are 'The Ordeal of Richard Feverel', 'Evan Harrington', 'Beauchamp's Career', 'The Egoist', 'The Tragic Comedians', 'Diana of the Crossways' and 'One of Our Conquerors') Meredith conceives of his characters as victims damaged by public life, sometimes even destroyed by it. His heroes and heroines are either intensely and nervously combative in public, performing desperate feats of verbal warfare, or they hide their inner feelings behind a 'ritual mask of sociability'. His characters are always on the defensive against the public and its opinions.

This tends to split them internally into private, 'natural' beings and public figures covering up their vulnerabilities. In a marvellous phrase, Meredith says that they tend to take refuge in 'that subterranean recess for Nature against the Institutions of Man'. (16) Particularly for his women, 'the Institutions of Man' present a constant threat. The rules of courtship, marriage, propriety and finance Meredith found both offensive and indefensible, and what is striking is that he felt dishonesty and evasion to be morally justified when used to protect oneself from them. Abstract 'truth' is less important than the protection of men and women from the wounding gossip, horrible marriages and powerful social snobberies to which they are subjected in his novels.

The most moving and intensely realized narrative of this opposition between public and private life is Meredith's late novel 'One of Our Conquerors' (1891). In it Victor Radnor has, as a young man, married a rich widow much older than himself and subsequently fallen in love with her companion, Natalia. Victor leaves his wife and lives with Natalia, and they have a fine and courageous daughter, Nesta Victoria. The novel describes the gradually increasing pressure on all three of them under the threat of public exposure: the daughter's relations with her friends and prospective lover are threatened by the knowledge of her illegitimacy and her friendship with Mrs Marsett, a woman of some notoriety but 'more sinned against than sinning'.

Victor and Natalia adopt the two paths which we see taken repeatedly in Meredith's work: combat and withdrawal. Victor, who has become immensely prosperous, 'fronts out' the danger of public attack by building opulent houses and entertaining on a lavish scale, defying scandal with his wealth. Natalia, a timid and sensitive woman, withdraws further into herself, suffers from a progressive nervous exhaustion under the pressures of public encounter and malicious scandal. Finally, the pressures burst these twin defences, Natalia dies and Victor suffers severe mental breakdown. Only their daughter survives the corrosive power of public insinuation and Grundyism.

The novel is one of Meredith's most obscure, and Lionel Johnson was quite correct in saying 'that with Mr Meredith style and subject change or grow together.... In 'Beauchamp's Career', and 'Diana of the Crossways' and 'One of Our Conquerors', it is not too much to say that "the world", or "society", or "the public", or "the nation", seems to rank among the *dramatis personae*.' (17) And they rank as forces to be excluded, to be kept away from the chief characters in the fiction. Open and honest communication in Meredith's world leads to suffering. The world must be kept out:(18)

> Behold! I looked for peace, and thought it near.
> Our inmost hearts had opened, each to each.
> We drank the pure daylight of honest speech.
> Alas! that was the fatal draught, I fear.

The 'pure daylight of honest speech' is the bringer of death and mental breakdown in Meredith, whilst obscurity of language and self-presentation bring the possibility of inner safety. Obscurity, then, is the linguistic defence of vulnerable offenders against public codes. The contract of sincerity between these offenders and the wider society is the key to their failure, it becomes a source of terrible anxiety. Self-revelation in the process of communication almost inevitably brings condemnation and suffering, from Evan Harrington's revelation of his class origins at Beckley Court to Natalia's writhing shame at Lakelands.

This inner connectedness of pain and communication is a major source of obscurity in Meredith and is discussed fully in chapter 4; but the antagonism between an inner and outer language which results from defensive introversion is of paramount importance in the period. In it are rooted the seeds of that fearsome isolation and solipsism which afflict Conrad's characters and later Thomas Mann's Leverkühn and Kafka's Hungry Artist: the dialectic of withdrawal and rejection force one further into the wasteland or wilderness. (19) This modernist phenomenon of what Bradbury and Fletcher have called 'narrative introversion' (20) and 'an internal crisis of presentation', triggers off in the author a dialectical process of increased distance and obliqueness. Both Meredith and James, like James Joyce (and perhaps like Browning before them) become increasingly difficult and resistant in their work with age. The style and the subject grow together inwardly, less concerned with openness towards a public which is felt to be corrosive of one's integrity and alien to one's private desires and needs. (21)

Some of Meredith's difficulty is in the endeavour to catch this mixture of self, never quite in control, never quite 'together'. (22) 'The Tragic Comedians', as the title suggests, required a deliberate collapse of the traditional opposition of tragedy and comedy to describe its protagonists, and the calculated impurity of mode is invoked to express 'a stature and a complexity calling for the junction of the two Modes to name them'. (23) Alvan (taken from a description of the socialist Lassalle upon whose history the novel is based) is described at his death as 'profusely mixed', 'a house of many chambers':(24)

> That mass of humanity profusely mixed of good and evil, of generous ire and mutinous, of the passion for the future of mankind and vanity of person, magnanimity and sensualism, high judgment, reckless indiscipline, chivalry, savagery, solidity, fragmentariness, was dust.

Underlying this profuse mixture is that recurrent doubleness of which I have already spoken, for Alvan is not one but two men, 'the untamed and the candidate for citizenship, in mutual dissension'. The proximity to certain characters in Conrad is unmistakable (one thinks of that mixture of savagery and civilized accomplishment in Kurtz); but whereas in Conrad the incommensurability of these dissenting voices is figured as radically incomprehensible, as 'enigma', in Meredith the duality produces paradox and bizarre juxtapositions. This modal and generic ambiguity in 'The Tragic Comedians' is a confusion of masks, of principles, and processes of reading. Meredith strenuously endeavours to maintain the ludicrous and the elegiac in Alvan, his contradictory drives towards life and death, his private eroticism and public altruism. Our reading is held between the tragic and comic in a way which challenges purity of response and simplicity of affective reception. The reader is placed exactly in the position of those people in Henry James's 'The Sacred Fount' when they discover the picture of the young man holding a mask. The passage is worth quoting in full, for the similarity to the underlying structure of presentation in 'The Tragic Comedians' is striking:(25)

> '.... It's the picture, of all pictures, that most needs an interpreter. Don't we want,' I asked of Mrs. Server, 'to know what it means?' The figure represented is a young man in black—a quaint, tight black dress, fashioned in years long past; with a pale, lean, livid face and a stare, from eyes without eyebrows, like that of some whitened old-world clown. In his hand he holds an object that strikes the spectator at first simply as some obscure, some ambiguous work of art, but that on a second view becomes a representation of a human face, modelled and coloured, in wax, in enamelled metal, in some substance not human. The object thus appears a complete mask, such as might have been fantastically fitted and worn.

'Yes, what in the world does it mean?' Mrs. Server replied. 'One could call it—though that doesn't get one much further— the Mask of Death.'

'Why so? ... Isn't it much rather the Mask of Life? It's the man's own face that's Death. The other one, blooming and beautiful—'

'Ah, but with an awful grimace!' Mrs. Server broke in. [My italics]

The disagreement between Mrs Server and the narrator continues unresolved, we never learn which is the face and which the mask, which life and which death, and the word 'fantastical' which James uses of the mask/face is chosen by Meredith as the key word for 'The Tragic Comedians', it is used to open the novel in an endeavour to reclaim the word from mere pejorative usage. (26) The idea of a fantastical sad clown used to express character as motley and mysterious, as essentially *bizarre*, is common not only to Meredith and James but to Conrad as well. That strange and unlikely harlequin who suddenly emerges from the forests in 'Heart of Darkness' is surely an extravagant and enigmatic symbol of the same kind:(27)

I looked at him, lost in astonishment. There he was before me, in motley, as though he had absconded from a troupe of mimes, enthusiastic, fabulous. His very existence was improbable, inexplicable, and altogether bewildering. He was an insoluble problem.

All three writers thus adopt the harlequin figure to give an emblematic form to the essential and constitutive obscurity of personality, of the self as divided, enigmatic, presenting itself to the world in the form of a question or riddle ('Yes, what in the world does it mean?' asks Mrs Server; 'He was an insoluble problem,' remarks Marlow; 'Oh! she's a riddle of course. I don't pretend to spell every letter of her,' remarks Alvan of Clotilde, the other 'tragic comedian'). Half magus and half clown, the solitary and romantic figure of the harlequin juggles his illusions for a public from which he is always estranged, he crystallizes a fluid and indistinct sense of self. It is used in precisely this sense in the 'Esthétique', (28) of Jules Laforgue, who invented the neologism 's'arlequiner', to behave like or become like a harlequin, and the emblematic adoption of the figure reveals the three novelists at their closest to the symbolist imagination, turning on that remote and haunting image of 'Pierrot Lunaire'. It brings together in one 'fantastical' but determinate cipher, Meredith's sense of a fragmentary self, at once wry and mystical in its inner evasions; James's expression of the 'obscure, the ambiguous work of art', and Conrad's powerful sense of life as infinitely 'questionable', proposing and never answering its own conundrums. It is also an image expressive of the isolation and idiosyncrasy of the artist, his sense of awkwardness with respect to his public. Towards the end of his life Meredith told an interviewer:(29)

> The press has often treated me as a clown or a harlequin - yes, really! and with such little respect that my fellow citizens can scarcely put up with me. Do not cry out! Certainly at this late hour they accord me a little glory: my name is celebrated, but no-one reads my books.

In his short story The Informer, Conrad uses the same structure of the 'double comedian' as Meredith had used for Lassalle. In a remarkably similar narrative, Conrad uses the idea to describe that 'genius of betrayers', Sevrin, the traitor to an anarchist group who is himself betrayed by his love for a dilettante young woman who is flirting with political activism (the similarity to 'The Princess Casamassima' and 'The Tragic Comedians' is striking). Sevrin, like Lassalle and Hyacinth Robinson, is destroyed by an inner doubleness or 'duplicity' which is not mere surface hypocrisy but an internal, 'mutual dissension' which obscures his vision and robs him of his lucidity at the critical moment. He is betrayed by that 'unconscious comedian' hidden within:(30)

> An actor in desperate earnest himself, he must have believed in the absolute value of conventional signs. As to the grossness of the trap into which he fell, the explanation must be that two sentiments of such absorbing magnitude cannot exist in one heart. The danger of that other and unconscious comedian robbed him of his vision, of his perspicacity, of his judgement.

Sevrin is a tragic clown perplexed by the turmoil of private love and political hate, an 'informer' caught between the dangers of conventional signs outside and unconscious desire within. His sudden loss of self-possession tokens the double threat posed to lucidity by the unconscious and by an intrinsic treachery located in the very nature of linguistic communication.

This double insecurity seems to me fundamental to Conrad's writing and his relation to the separation of public and private experience. In his most successful work conscious control, directed energy and concentrated intention in his characters become narrowed to a fragile shell between external and internal hostilities. Cartesian clarity and that solid self-confidence which supports it has almost melted away in his work. Like Sevrin, his characters often feel like actors trapped in their roles, unable to do anything else except act (Marlow feels as though he is trapped in 'some sordid farce acted in front of a sinister back-cloth' in 'Heart of Darkness'). The vertigo of infinitude and endless repetition afflict the actors (and the reader) with a sense of dizzying emptiness. The sinister insubstantiality of categories, signs and rational decisions means that darkness for Conrad was of particular significance, like that primordial darkness which folds round the narrator of 'The Shadow Line', where 'every form was gone ... spar, sail, fittings, rails; everything blotted out in the dreadful smoothness of that absolute night.' In his book 'The Metaphysics of Darkness' (31) Raymond Roussel has traced the pervasive importance of darkness in Conrad's work and amasses impressive evidence that, 'Although it is itself without weight or dimension, [for Conrad] this darkness lies behind all the distinct forms of creation.' He described it in a letter to Cunninghame Graham as 'une ombre sinistre et fuyante dont il est impossible de fixer l'image.' (32)

It is precisely the difficulty of 'fixing the image' which is so terrifying. The agonies of writing, which he recalls endlessly in his gloomy letters to friends and fellow writers, become a torment which in mid-career charted his mental breakdown, it led to him being trapped in the darkness of his own metaphor:(33)

> I see how ill, mentally, I have been these last four months.... This horror ... has destroyed already the little belief in myself I used to have. I am appalled at the absurdity of my situation ... Most appalled to feel that all the doors behind me are shut and that I must remain where I have come blundering in the dark.

This was in 1898, and, by late May, Conrad's close friends had become most concerned about his sanity. His complaints strongly recall Emerson's diagnosis quoted above, that an absence of social identity produces a language wanting 'body or basis'. Not only did Conrad share with Meredith a fearful intuition of inward divisiveness, he also felt a cultural isolation which manifested itself as a fading of subjectivity, an evaporation of anything distinctive either in himself or his writing:(34)

I feel nothing clearly. And I am frightened when I remember that I have to drag it all out of myself. Other writers have some starting point, something to catch hold of ... they lean on dialect —or on tradition—or on history—or on the prejudice or fad of the hour; they trade upon some tie or conviction of their time— or upon the absence of these things—which they can abuse or praise. But at any rate they know something to begin with—while I don't. I have had some impressions, some sensations—in my time—impressions and sensations of common things. And it's all faded—my very being seems faded and thin like the ghost of a blonde and sentimental woman, haunting romantic ruins pervaded by rats. I am exceedingly miserable.

This tragic sense of timelessness, of being a ghost or wanderer outside of any culture, expresses Conrad's anxious sense of exclusion as a literary refugee. Polish, Russian, French, English, remote from any origin and uncomfortably separated from his audience, there are no terms adequate to 'fix the image' and no one close enough for whom it might be clarified.

The bond of familiarity between author and reader which we find in Thackeray and Dickens had almost completely vanished for Conrad. Serial publication had fostered, in Thackeray's words, a 'communion between the writer and the public ... something continual, confidential, something like a personal affection'. (35) It meant that the writer could be immediately responsive to the desires of his reader, even to the point of changing the plot or characters if he felt the public demanded it (as in Thackeray's decision that Clive Newcome might marry Ethel—'What could a fellow do? So many people wanted 'em married'). The familiarity of the bond is striking. In his prefatory note to the concluding number of 'Dombey and Son' Dickens wrote:

I cannot forego my usual opportunity of saying farewell to my readers in this greeting-place, though I have only to acknowledge the unbounded warmth and earnestness of their sympathy in every stage of the journey we have just concluded.

And in Thackeray's preface to 'Pendennis', this closeness is given as a primary reason for the sincerity of the author, it accounts for his 'frankness of expression':

in his constant communication with the reader the writer is forced into frankness of expression, and to speak his own mind

and feelings as they urge him.... It is a sort of confidential talk
between writer and reader.

For Conrad, this confidential talk was impossible; indeed the very idea
of such public confidentiality is a threat. In 'The Return' the London public
is leaving a West End station:(36)

> Outside the big doorway of the street they scattered in all
> directions, walking away fast from one another with the hurried
> air of men fleeing from something compromising; from
> familiarity or confidences; from something suspected and
> concealed—like truth or pestilence.

The linking of compromise with confidence, truth with pestilence, is
symptomatic: the image which Conrad uses to describe the process of writing
is that of addressing a void. 'The work itself' he complained to Sanderson, 'is
only like throwing words into a bottomless hole.' And again, writing to
Sanderson, 'I've taken to writing for the press,.... More words,—another
hole.' (37) The commonplace of artistic alienation which operates with such
evident force in Conrad reaches to the roots of the 'new cryptographic style'.
The more that the addressee of fiction appears dispersed or remote, the more
solipsistic the act of writing seems to become. In his essay on Daudet, Conrad
speaks of the road for the writer of fiction (38) which

> does not lie through the domain of Art or the domain of Science
> where well-known voices quarrel noisily in a misty emptiness; it
> is a path of toilsome silence upon which travel men simple and
> unknown, with closed lips, or, may be, whispering their pain
> softly—only to themselves.

The degree of withdrawal is closely linked to a failure to penetrate the
broad community of common readers, and the more the writer feels himself
to be whispering only to himself, or at best to a small group, the more
vulnerable he becomes to the act of publication. Narrative exposition
becomes self-exposure. Thackeray's 'confidential talk' between writer and
reader becomes Conrad's 'compromising familiarity'. It is not surprising that
the figure of the anarchist agitator became both an attractive and repulsive
subject for these novelists: The anarchist is cut off from all those linkages of
which Emerson spoke (Conrad writes 'Anarchists, I suppose, have no
families—not, at any rate, as we understand that social relation'), and the

conspiratorial intimacy of the political subversive or the informer is an appropriate parallel to the writer's nervous introversion. The Victorian sense of shared language (perhaps quaintly modified by dialect) withers in the absence of the enriching power of social cohesion. Conrad writes:(39)

> we, living, are out of life—utterly out of it ... we don't even know our own thoughts. Half the words we use have no meaning whatever and of the other half each man understands each word after the fashion of his own folly and conceit. Faith is a myth and beliefs shift like mist on the shore; thoughts vanish; words, once pronounced, die; ... only the string of my platitudes seems to have no end.

As the sense of belonging to a single, enfolding culture becomes relativized and distant, all forms of thought and belief lose their substantiality.

This modification in the status of the subject is simultaneously a modification of his relation to communication as such. The shared referentiality of language available to him seems to decrease as the origins and ends of his verbal activity recede into difficulty. Subjective depth gradually replaces both the instrumental and consummatory functions of language, it becomes more and more difficult to gauge when and where the language should stop, how far one can go in interior exploration. The mechanisms of embarrassment (James), shame (Meredith) and guilt (Conrad) are easily triggered by this increasingly personal reference, the risk of self-exposure in forcing the boundary between public and private discourse. I think it no accident that these three men were so reticent about their private lives, even to the point of deliberately misleading people about incidents in their past. (40) Changes in the social relations of production of the fiction combined with the specific trajectories of their lives made novel-writing a constant risk of self-revelation. For Conrad, the art of writing novels was 'the most liable to be obscured by the scruples of its servants and votaries, the one pre-eminently destined to bring trouble to the mind and the heart of the artist.' (41) He felt a strong need to remain hidden within his fiction, to conceal himself behind a veil. E.M. Forster put this most succinctly in his review of Conrad's coy and reticent autobiographical work:(42)

> The character [of Conrad] will never really be clear, for one of two reasons. The first reason has already been indicated; the

writer's dread of intimacy. He has a rigid conception as to where the rights of the public stop, he has determined we shall not be 'all over' him, and has half contemptuously thrown open this vestibule and invited us to mistake it for the private apartment if we choose. We may not see such a character clearly because he does not wish us to see. But we also may not see clearly because it is essentially unclear. This possibility must be considered. Behind the smoke screen of his reticence there may be another obscurity, connected to the foreground by wisps of vapour, yet proceeding from another source, from the central chasm of his tremendous genius. This isn't an aesthetic criticism nor a moral one. Just a suggestion that our difficulties with Mr. Conrad may proceed in part from difficulties of his own. [My italics]

Indeed the difficulties do proceed from 'another obscurity' anterior to the manifest forms of the elusive fiction, an obscurity of authorial voice talking too loudly and insistently amongst the voices of his characters. Conrad's difficulties relate closely to his fear of self-exposure at a time when the nature of fiction somehow altered the relation between writer and the written so that the latter always referred back with uncomfortable rapidity to the former. In 'A Personal Record', Conrad describes how the writer appears to write about the world but in fact only succeeds in writing out himself as that world:(43)

a novelist lives in his work. He stands there, the only reality in an invented world, among imaginary things, happenings and people. Writing about them, he is only writing about himself. But the disclosure is not complete. He remains, to a certain extent, a figure behind a veil, a suspected rather than seen presence—a movement and a voice behind the draperies of fiction.

Conrad is explicit here about the discernible link between the forms of fiction and a new reticence on the part of the author, an unwillingness or inability to communicate himself which upsets the contract of openness between reader and writer. Yet that is perhaps expressing it too simply: communication still takes place but it has a changed relation to the information it bears, it no longer feels able to keep up the fiction of its realism, that it is 'about' something 'outside' and for which the novelist is just a kind of perspicacious and sensitive observer. For Conrad, the author is always writing about himself even when he writes about invented and imaginary things, and his remark is of the utmost significance, not simply for the anxiety it betrays about the visibility of the author in his work, but for the assumption it makes that a reader will consider the fiction a revelation of the psychic state of the author rather than a subjective description of reality.

This vulnerability is connected to a new kind of reading, a new kind of critical attention in the period, whereby the sophisticated read through the text to the psychological state of the author. This was the growth of 'symptomatic reading', an analysis of literature not so much for the accuracy or truth of its rendering of reality, but for the mental disposition of the writer. 'A writer of imaginative prose stands confessed in his work,' (44) Conrad wrote, in writing fiction he writes himself. Literature could thus seem a jejune kind of displacement whereby an author shuffled off his own preoccupations and fantasies into a make-believe world which appeared, precisely, as 'make-believe'. It became increasingly difficult to maintain that heroism of sincerity which had underpinned the desire of the Victorian novelist to be 'honestly transcriptive, veraciously historical'.

This growth of symptomatic reading is inseparable from the growth of psychological understanding in the period. The increasing belief in the existence of the unconscious (or 'subconscious' as it was usually called in the 1880s and 1890s) was linked to a growing revaluation of irrational experience and abnormal mental states. William James's classic book, 'The Varieties of Religious Experience', was taken as arguing strongly for the value of irrational and paranormal states of mind. When Oliver Elton reviewed it in 1904, he made a casual remark which, in the light of the subsequent development of modern literature should be treasured as a prescient understatement:(45)

> Professor James seems to imply that in such a state there may be true revelation, especially from those latent parts of the mind, for which the word 'subconscious' has been found as a metaphor for their imagined sphere or receptacle.

There was a variety of intellectual works appearing in books and periodicals which tended to problematize the barrier between rational and non-rational states of mind. The boundaries of 'true knowledge' were more and more difficult to define or defend. In the same volume of the 'Fortnightly Review' which was serializing Meredith's novel about mental disintegration 'One of Our Conquerors' [Meredith's novel provoked an interesting correspondence about the precise medical form of Victor Radnor's mental illness, and whether it begins with the fall (both physical and

mental) which he sustains right at the outset of the novel.], E.L. Linton
wrote an article called 'Our Illusions', and it is as remarkable a condensed
statement of the dissolving boundary between true and false, rational and
irrational, that can be found anywhere before 1900, not only because it
captures so succinctly a variety of 'fin de siècle' anxiety prevalent at the time,
but because of the way it challenges all absolute notions of truth—moral,
historical and aesthetic. In it she compares the state of mind of a fervent
Christian believer with that of a man suffering from persecution mania. She
concludes that there is essentially no difference between the two:(46)

> When the very presence of Satan is realised by the trembling
> Christian sinner, is he in any way differently held from the
> malefactor pursued by the Furies? The state of mind is the same
> —but the objective truth of the appearance? Was not that maya,
> illusion, in each case alike? If this be not so, then we have no line
> of boundary between madness and sanity. If we affirm the truth
> of spiritual impressions, however we may name them, we open
> the doors of Bedlam and make its haunted inmates free citizens
> like the rest. [My italics]

There was indeed genuine social alarm in the period that insanity was
increasing. A serious debate in the 'Fortnightly Review' in 1896 voiced fears,
supposedly supported by statistical evidence, that there had been a dramatic
increase in the number of insane people in Britain towards the end of the
century, (47) and this had the strange effect of providing a material image of
madness encroaching upon sanity, a statistical and generalized metaphor of
the changing boundary between rationality and irrationality in favour of the
latter. It was of course not only an imputed quantitive change, but, far more
importantly, a qualitative change in the attitude to the irrational. Bearing in
mind that Meredith, Conrad and James all suffered from periods of mental
illness and wrote fictions in which madness is of central importance, (48) the
publication of enormously influential, contemporary work which connected
the psychic condition of the writer with literary creativity is of special
interest.

Two books which were of paramount importance in this respect and
achieved something of a 'succès de scandale' were Professor Lombroso's
'The Man of Genius' (1891) and Max Nordau's 'Degeneration' (1895) which
some years earlier than William James's book had generated enormous
interest. Although she was overestimating somewhat, Helen Zimmern in a
review of Lombroso said that his book had an influence as 'immediate and

decisive' as 'The Origin of Species'. (49) If she had been talking of the general approach to mental phenomena employed by Lombroso, she would not have exaggerated. Nordau's book even stimulated a riposte from A.E. Hake called, predictably enough, 'Regeneration' (50) and despite the fact that Nordau's belligerence often overshadowed his judgment and that Professor Lombroso was not renowned for the accuracy of his scholarship (he was not allowed to forget his statement that 'Milton studiously avoided marriage' by English reviewers!), (51) the books of these men contributed centrally to the debate on the abnormality of genius, the decline of reason and the uncertain psychical bases of intellect. Nordau dedicated his book to Lombroso, and in his dedication wrote:(52)

> Degenerates are not always criminals, prostitutes, anarchists, and pronounced lunatics; they are often authors and artists. These, however, manifest the same mental characteristics and for the most part the same somatic features, as the members of the above-mentioned anthropological family, who satisfy their unhealthy impulses with the knife of the assassin or the bomb of the dynamiter, instead of with pen and pencil....
>
> Thus this book is an attempt at a really scientific criticism, which does not base its judgement of a book upon the purely accidental, capricious and variable emotions it awakens— emotions depending on the temperament and mood of the individual reader—but upon the psychophysiological elements from which it sprang.

Nordau became notorious for his attacks on Ibsen ('not wholly diseased in mind but only a dweller on the borderland—a "mattoid"'); Nietzsche ('insane drivel'); the Parnassians ('egomania of degenerate minds'); and all forms of symbolist aestheticism from Baudelaire to Wilde. Although it is mainly in connection with his violent and malicious attack on decadence that he is now remembered by literary historians, the above extract is an indication of an entirely serious side to his work, symptomatic of an intellectual shift reaching far beyond his bludgeoning criticism of particular literary movements. Nordau did not read these writers for their representation of reality, but read 'through' their work back to the psychic life of the author; he was not so much interested in the mimetic plausibility of the work of art as in the evidence it provided for 'the psychophysiological elements from which it sprang.' Thus he read works of literature as if they were transcriptions of the fantasy life of psychically disturbed patients, and not descriptions, by earnest and rational persons, of some external order of fact and sentiment.

It is difficult to over-estimate the importance of this shift in attention and its concomitant change in the act of reading. It had of course always been a common notion that genius and madness were 'near allied', but within a few years in the 1880s, under the influence of proto-psychology, literary texts were transformed into primary evidence of the inner private fantasies of the author. The sincerity of the relationship between author and middle-class reader (even when the former strongly attacked the latter as, say, George Eliot did in 'Daniel Deronda'), their mutual interest in the honest transcription of the emotional life, was supplemented by a new kind of relationship which made the old contract extremely difficult to keep. The author was suddenly placed at a disadvantage by the sophistication in reader response, he became vulnerable to a certain kind of knowing smile which found in his words the insufficiently disguised evidence of his most intimate preoccupations. As more and more intellectual readers began to regard fiction as a transformation of fantasy by various quasi-defensive devices, the notion of the 'truth' of the text, and the relations between text, author and reader, swiftly changed.

A series of works was published in the 1890s to the effect that, to quote the phrase of a French intellectual Guernsen, 'Genius is a disease of the nerves.' The works of Nordau and Lombroso were central, but to them may be added others also positing the strongest possible link between artistic ability and mental abnormality. J.F. Nisbet's 'The Insanity of Genius' (London, 1891), A.G. Bianchi's 'La Patologia del Genio e gli Scienziati Italiani' (Milan, 1892), Vernon Lee's Beauty and Sanity (1895), P. Radestock's 'Genie und Wahnsinn' (1884), Clifford Allbut's Nervous Diseases and Modern Life (1895), purported to prove the basis of genius in psycho-physiological disorders and erase the boundary between 'delinquency' and artistic production. The assimilation was not always in one direction. Not only was genius considered a (fortunate) kind of insanity, but the work of many insane people was adduced to show how frequently madness was a form of genius. Lombroso in Part III of 'The Man of Genius' (chapter 1: Insane Genius in Literature) quotes over a dozen examples of work executed by inmates of asylums which show the temporary appearance of 'real genius' among the insane. The emphasis of course varied. Whereas Lombroso wished to teach 'respect for the supreme misfortunes of insanity' as well as caution in confronting 'the brilliancy of men of genius', Nordau vociferously attacked modern literary writers as dangerous degenerates, but in both cases one can find, in more or less exaggerated or programmatic form, the explicit statement of a new kind of attention to literature. Lombroso writes:(53)

> What I have hitherto written may, I hope (while remaining within the limits of psychological observation), afford an experimental starting-point for a criticism of artistic and literary, sometimes also of scientific, creations.
>
> Thus, in the fine arts, exaggerated minuteness of detail, the abuse of symbols, inscriptions, or accessories, a preference for some one particular colour, an unrestrained passion for mere novelty, may approach the morbid symptoms of mattoidism. Just so, in literature and science, a tendency to puns and plays upon words, an excessive fondness of systems, a tendency to speak to one's self, and substitute epigram for logic, an extreme predilection for the rhythm and assonance of verse in prose writing, even an exaggerated degree of originality may be considered as morbid phenomena. So also is the mania of writing in Biblical form, in detached verses, and with special favourite words, which are underlined, or repeated many times, and a certain graphic symbolism.

Lombroso's list is an artful compilation of many of the characteristics—given in a remarkably economic and convincing form—of what is now called modernist literature, and among the writers whom he cites as 'suspect' we find Walt Whitman, Hoffman, De Musset, Nerval, Dostoevsky, Poe, Kleist, Baudelaire, Flaubert, the Goncourts and Darwin! Looking even further back to the period of Lamb and Southey, J.F. Nisbet's book 'The Insanity of Genius' (54) which went through six editions by 1912, claimed of its investigation that:

> The result is to place upon a solid basis of fact the long suspected relationship of genius and insanity. Apparently at the opposite poles of the human intellect, genius and insanity are, in reality, but different phases of a morbid susceptibility of, or want of balance in, the cerebro-spinal system.

Although the first of these studies (55), contending that exceptional intellectual ability was organically much the same thing as madness, was written as early as 1859, it was not until the German (56), French and Italian work on the subject began to flood into the country in the 1880s that English writers began to take the notion seriously. It involved a change of critical regard as to what was understood to be the 'origin' of the literary text. It was less and less a case of looking at these texts as either a reflection of the truth or an illuminating source throwing light upon it, but a case of looking through the semi-transparency of the words to the 'real origin' which was the psycho-physiology of the author. This is not the same as simple biographical criticism, which aspired to clarify or amplify the meaning of certain passages in an author's work by a supplement of personal details; this had traditionally endeavoured to be a charitable activity, based upon a sympathetic understanding for the subject on the part of the biographer. There was a direct threat in this new form of attention which shifted the understanding of literature itself, for, to the degree that the source of literature was increasingly located in neurosis, hysteria, hallucination, mattoidism, perversion and other psychological traits, the less 'reality' and 'transcribed truth' could be maintained as the real source of literary production. Even further, if writers persisted in claiming that pure mimesis was their goal and that honest and sincere copying of observable social and emotional events was the novelist's primary activity, then they were either insincere or did not sufficiently understand themselves—the origin of their work was literally 'unconscious', from sources to which rationality was completely secondary. As early as 1895, Vernon Lee (pseud. of Violet Paget, acquaintance of James) wrote in a remarkable article in the 'Fortnightly Review', (57) based on a review of Lombroso:

> When, for instance, shall we recognize that the bulk of our psychic life is unconscious or semi-unconscious, the life of long-organized and automatic functions; and that, while it is absurd to oppose to these the more new, unaccustomed and fluctuating activity called reason, this same reason, this conscious portion of ourselves, may be usefully employed in understanding those powers of nature (powers of chaos sometimes) within us, and in providing that these should turn the wheel of life in the right direction, even like those other powers of nature outside us, which reason cannot repress or diminish but can understand and put to profit. But instead of this, we are ushered into life thinking ourselves thoroughly conscious throughout, conscious beings of a definite and stereotyped pattern; and we are set to do things we do not understand with mechanisms which we have never even been shown!

In another of the major periodicals the same year, T.C. Allbut wrote on the increase in nervous disorders, suicide and insanity in modern life and succinctly summarized the new critical attitude: 'The young poet, who gets rid of the stings of passion by throwing them into verse, is set down as a "sexual pervert"' (58) For writers who had not infringed the prurient code of Victorian morality, to be indicted in this way was really quite new, and to describe a poet in these terms immediately made the act of writing love poetry without guilt or shame a more difficult task. It meant that literature was being read not for its manifest content, which might be quite conventional, but for the 'symptoms' from which could be read off the particular psychic malady of the poet. What it assumed was a certain inner blindness on the part of the writer, whereby what he wrote about, and what the work was 'really' about, were two separate things, and the critic could discover the latter in a way that was impossible for the writer himself because of the unconscious origins from which it sprang. It assumed, in other words, that the novelist or poet could not, by the very nature of artistic production, 'know' the meaning of his own work. Arthur Machen, the novelist and writer of strange 'doppelgänger' stories at the turn of the century, put the argument thus in this acute passage from his 'Hieroglyphics', written in 1899:(59)

> In truth, the problem is simply a problem of the consciousness and sub-consciousness and of the action and interaction between the two. I will not be too dogmatic. We are in misty, uncertain and unexplored regions ... but I am strangely inclined to think that all the quintessence of art is distilled from the sub-conscious and not from the conscious self: or, in other words, that the artificer seldom or never understands the ends and designs and spirit of the artist.

It is a remarkable statement of its time, and in positing a dual voice behind artistic production, the voice of the (unconscious) artificer or constructor (Conrad's 'unconscious comedian') and the voice of the (conscious) artist or designer, it is one of the very few contemporary statements which began to make sense of an obscure 'blurring of voices' in Meredith, Conrad and James. Machen is proposing a 'disjunctive' relation, a relation of non-knowledge at the heart of literary work, 'misty, uncertain and unexplored regions' in the creative space between the twinned makers of a literary text. For the relation of mystery, deception, repression and deceit par excellence is that boundary between the conscious and the unconscious, the boundary between the artistic intent and the psychic origin described by

Nordau, Lombroso, Nisbet and Lee (compared with these writers, Freud had almost negligible influence in England before the turn of the century). (60)

By the beginning of the twentieth century, writing showed clear signs of these antagonistic voices, the controlling poet with his conscious beliefs and designs struggling against the insistent and disruptive mysteries of the unconscious:(61)

> Get hence, you loathsome mystery! Hideous animal get hence!
> You wake in me each bestial sense, you make what I would not be.
>
> You make my creed a barren sham, you wake foul dreams
>   of sensual life,
> And Atys with his blood stained knife were better than
>   the thing I am.

For Oscar Wilde in these verses from The Sphinx, secrecy and mystery, symbolized in the sphinx-enigma, have become internalized as an overt threat to creed, the menace of sexuality within a destabilized psyche, and it is remarkable confirmation of this identification that Wilde's flight from 'loathsome mystery' should find its climax in the figure of Atys, the self-castrator.

The regions of rational control and of honest, sincere description in literature had thus suddenly shrunk. ('How little of the *sapiens* there is in the bulk of humanity, how dependent the *sapientia* is on muscles, nerves and disposition of internal parts....') (62) When literary genius was characterized as a form of psychical abnormality the ability of the artist to tell the truth was thrown into doubt. The Genius was, as Nordau put it, a kind of 'involuntary charlatan' never quite aware of the roots of his own productions. And for Nisbet literary men were 'an enigma even to themselves'. We may recall the words of the great novelist St George in Henry James's story The Lesson of the Master when he says, 'I am a successful charlatan ... most assuredly is the artist in a false position.' And in 'Under Western Eyes' Conrad remarks:(63)

> The falsehood lies deep in the necessities of existence, in secret fears and half-formed ambitions, in the secret confidence combined with a secret mistrust of ourselves ... It seemed to him bizarre that secrecy should play such a large part in the comfort and safety of lives ... A man's most open actions have a secret side to them.

At the same time as anthropology cast doubt upon the universal authenticity of social reality, these early forms of proto-psychology cast doubt upon any literary quest for Truth. The possibility of finding the truth of a literary work passed from the artist to the critic, and between author and critic a sort of mistrustful game of cat-and-mouse develops, whereby the author seeks to make his work opaque to the probing, subtle suggestion of the critic who attempts to see through the artifice.

Henry James came back to this problem several times and it is most perfectly expressed in two stories which he published in the periodical 'Cosmopolis' which flourished between 1896 and 1898, The Figure in the Carpet (1896) and John Delavoy (1898). Both stories relate the close but competitive relationship between a novelist and a young critic and in both, significantly, the critic is frustrated in his passionate aim to reveal the 'essential truth' about the novelist.

John Delavoy is 'the wonderful writer, the immense novelist: the one who died last year.' The characteristic which James insists upon, after Delavoy's genius, is his extreme reticence, his determination that his private life should not be violated. He was, says the young critic, 'my great artist, on whose consistent aloofness from the crowd I needn't touch, any more than on his patience in going his way and attending to his work, the most unadvertised, unreported, uninterviewed, unphotographed, uncriticised of all originals. Was he not the man of the time about whose private life we delightfully knew least?' The young critic produces a critical analysis of Delavoy's work which he feels to be the perfect expression of the novelist, the most penetrating and accurate account of his secretive, intractable subject, and indeed it is an essay of such distinction that it totally wins the approval of the novelist's sister, a woman of exceptional sensitivity and judgment. But to his mortification, the brilliant article, having been at first accepted by the most important journal of the age, 'The Cynosure', is rejected by the editor as 'indecent' and 'indelicate': 'Did you candidly think that we were going to print this? ... We didn't at any rate want indelicacy.'

Two things are at issue here. First, the critic and the novelist's sister subscribe to a completely different moral and aesthetic order to that of the editor, Bullen, and the readership of 'The Cynosure'. Certain paragraphs of the critical article would lose the journal 'five thousand subscribers.' This division of readership between a small intellectual group, the coterie of initiates with its daring explicitness about sexuality and its sophisticated manner of reading, was incompatible with the majority standards of 'ordinary readers'. It was the proof-reader who, with his blue pencil, had first drawn the attention of the editor to offending passages in the essay, and, in this attempted censorship of the writer of the passage by the proof-reader, we have a perfect expression of the conflict between two different readerships.

Second, however, the relationship between the great novelist and the young critic goes back to the game of cat-and-mouse; even though Delavoy, the titular character, is dead throughout the story, in the struggle to preserve his privacy he wins a posthumous battle. The young critic eventually gains the novelist's sister, but she is clearly a sort of compensation prize for his enforced silence. His article is not published, but in its place a small portrait sketch, 'conventional but *sincere*'. The contrast between the original critical essay with its psycho-sexual reading of the novelist (infringing the boundary of 'delicacy') and the 'sincere' portrait sketch which replaces it, gives us a perfect index of the new criticism and the old belle-lettrist biographical tradition which it was beginning to threaten. James spoke of 'our marked collective mistrust of anything like close or analytical appreciation' and he loathed the prying and poking into his private life which seemed a part of this:(64)

> the artist's life's his work, and this is the place to observe him. What he has to tell us he tells us with this perfection ... The best interviewer is the best reader.... Admire him in silence, cultivate him at a distance and secretly appropriate his message.

In the story *The Death of the Lion* (1894) Paraday, the very talented novelist, is hounded to death by the 'universal menagerie' of admirers, he is 'pulled to pieces on the pretext of being applauded.' John Delavoy escapes this fate, his integrity remains unviolated to the end, and neither the readers of 'The Cynosure' nor, more significantly, the readers of Henry James's story John Delavoy get to discover those indelicate revelations which the critic had produced in his analysis of Delavoy's last great novel.

The Figure in the Carpet of two years earlier provides a very similar situation, but with a more teasing, exasperating relation between the young critic and Vereker, the great novelist. Vereker, hardly concealing his disappointment that the critic has completely missed the essential point of his novels, 'the particular thing I've written my books most *for*', sets his oeuvre before the ardent young man as a fascinating enigma, containing, in all its parts, a most marvellous and tantalizing secret which runs through the whole like a pattern in an intricate carpet:(65)

> 'You fire me as I've never been fired', I returned 'you make me determined to do or die'. Then I asked, 'Is it a kind of esoteric

message?' His countenance fell at this—he put out his hand as if to bid me good-night. 'Ah, my dear fellow, it can't be described in cheap journalese.'

Literary criticism is described in the story as an 'initiation' and Vereker's novels are 'only for the initiated'. The relation the novelist creates between himself and his young critic is one of priest to acolyte, Vereker binds the critic to him through a kind of hermeneutic mystery by initiating a search for the word of the master in the myriad patterns of the text. Indeed, at one point the idea of the novelist's work and the creating of a secret are taken as one and the same thing;(66)

> 'And now you quite like it,' I said.
> 'My work?'
> 'Your secret. It's the same thing.'
> 'Your guessing that', Vereker replied, 'is a proof that you're as clever as I say!'

The inscrutable novelist behaves exactly like a Taoist master to his noviciate, answering his questions with oblique, parabolic phrases, fending off his direct approaches to the object. The writer refuses his reader. He rejects all proposals that the young man makes to share the meaning of the work, and indeed eventually what seems to give the work value is precisely its esoteric inviolability, its unbroken code. And once more it is the novelist, who dies during the course of James's story, who wins the battle (for the relation has become an intellectual battle to possess the meaning of the text). The pattern remains still undetected to the end.

Many things are implied in the story. The metaphor of the earnest search for truth so beloved of the Victorians is invoked only to be dismissed with disparaging irony:(67)

> 'Have I got to tell you, after all these years and labours?'
> There was something in the friendly reproach of this—jocosely exaggerated—that made me, as an ardent young seeker for truth, blush to the roots of my hair.

We are in a world where the 'ardent young seeker for truth' suddenly appears gauche and out of place, like an awkward adolescent amongst sophistications he does not understand, and indeed the way in which Vereker places the critic at such an acute disadvantage is important. By obscuring the structure of his work he has turned tables on the new critics, the 'rising young men' who were reading Wagner as a 'neurotic', Mallarmé as 'a nerve-sufferer', Verlaine as a mattoid, Ibsen as 'ego-manic' and Zola as a 'neurasthenic and hysteric'. (68) James employs a rhetoric of enigma to defend the art of the novelist from the many forms of criticism which arose once the trust between reader and author began to break down, and he replaces this trust with the bonds of Tantalus, 'faint wandering notes of a hidden music. That was just the rarity, that was the charm'.

It is manifestly an aesthetic strategy which is taken from Symbolism and Art for Art's Sake, an ideology of rarity which endeavours to value the art object by placing it beyond the reach of the multitude. Vereker even echoes Pater's famous definition of art—'to burn always with a hard, gem-like flame' in describing the hidden pattern in his novels as 'the very passion of his passion, the very part of the business in which, for him, the flame of art burns most intensely....' By indicating that there is a deeply concealed meaning in the work of art and then denying the reader access to it, the modern novelist solicits a hermeneutic attitude towards his work which, as with Symbolism, fends off a direct, immediate assimilation of its meaning. It makes the work more and more densely opaque to the reader, more difficult to see through, constantly eluding the imposition of one fixed and certain meaning. In a letter to Barrett Clark about 'Victory', Conrad consciously adopted this symbolist aesthetic:(69)

> I ... put before you a general proposition, that a work of art is very seldom limited to one exclusive meaning and not necessarily tending to a definite conclusion. And this for the reason that the nearer it approaches art, the more it acquires a symbolic character ... all the great creations of literature have been symbolic, and in that way have gained in complexity, in power, in depth and beauty.

Arthur Symons, in an essay on Mallarmé published in 1898, brought together these two ideas, the vulnerability of the modern writer and the impossibility of writing in the old manner, when he wrote:(70)

> But who, in our time has wrought so subtle a veil, shining on this side, where the few are, a thick cloud on the other, where are the many? The oracles have always had the wisdom to hide their secrets in the obscurity of many meanings, or of what has seemed meaningless; and might it not, after all, be the finest epitaph for a self-respecting man of letters to be able to say, even after the

writing of many books: I have kept my secret, I have not betrayed myself to the multitude? [My italics]

In a marvellous phrase, Mallarmé expressed precisely the dilemma of Vereker and Delavoy (or James, Conrad and Meredith), the dilemma of risking, by the act of writing, some shameful or embarrassing exposure, when he wrote that all publication is 'almost a speculation, on one's modesty, for one's silence'. Symons adds:(71)

> And I, for one, cannot doubt that he was, for the most part, entirely right in his statement and analysis of the new conditions under which we are now privileged or condemned to write.... is it possible for a writer, at the present day, to be quite simple, with the old, objective simplicity, in either thought or expression? To be naïf, to be archaic, is not to be either natural or simple; I affirm that it is not natural to be what is called 'natural' any longer. We have no longer the mental attitude of those to whom a story was but a story, and all stories good.

This dialectic of revelation and concealment dominates the literature of Meredith, Conrad and Henry James. There is in their work the feeling that inner privacies are being cruelly probed and exposed in a way that was quite new. It is sometimes like the distress and fear which the music of Wagner evoked in Victorian listeners, the fear of public 'nakedness', of 'baring one's soul', and not the soul only, but extreme passions normally kept so heavily covered that their existence had been hardly suspected by the persons themselves. Vernon Lee, listening to 'some modern German songs' (probably Wagner or Richard Strauss), wrote that they were a 'violation of the privacy of the human soul'. She continues:(72)

> It is astonishing, when one realizes it, that the charm of music, the good renown it has gained in its more healthful and more decorous days, can make us sit out what we do sit out under its influence; violations of our innermost secrets, revelations of the hidden possibilities of our own nature and the nature of others; stripping away of all the soul's outward forms, melting away of the soul's active structure, its bone and muscle, till there is revealed only the shapeless primaeval nudity of confused instincts, the soul's vague viscera.

Wagner, it was felt, had made music morbid, shameful, excessive. He had gone beyond boundaries which should not have been exceeded (far beyond them), creating the unhealthy, pudic excitement of forbidden indulgence: 'Wagner est une névrose.' For Wagner was also taken as archetypically modern, 'the *modern artist* par excellence, the Cagliostro of modernism', and in London by 1899 one reviewer could write that 'in our capital city at all events, we are now haunted by a kind of Wagner-madness.' (73) It is no accident that 'One of Our Conquerors' adopts the music of Wagner as a fundamental motif, that it should be through Wagner that Victor Radnor can express the depth of his guilt in the confrontation with his peers and that Meredith can express the violation of innermost secrets which eventually destroy Radnor. (74)

The movement from James to Mallarmé, to Meredith and Wagner is not arbitrary. 'Carry the theories of Mallarmé to a practical conclusion, multiply his powers in a direct ratio, and you have Wagner', wrote Symons, who also remarked (as indeed others had done), 'some of Mr Meredith's poems, and occasional passages of his prose, can alone give in English some faint idea of the later prose of Mallarmé.' (75) The mutual adoption of deflective strategy and enigmatic method by so many writers during this period, the exploratory use of secrecy, lying, obscurity, impression and withdrawal, form an interconnection of cultural concern and activity which became a generative complex of modernism. (76) This frequently involves the decision not to tell the truth and the decision not to strive, or perhaps not to hope, for sincere and easy communication with the reader. 'Do you understand me?' asked R.L. Stevenson. 'God knows, I should think it highly improbable.'

NOTES

1. R.W. Emerson, Culture, in 'The Conduct of Life', 1883 (reprinted London, 1905) p. 126. The popularity of this book is evidenced by the fact that it had been reprinted seven times in England by 1905.

2. R.A. Lanham, 'Style, An Anti-Textbook' (New Haven and London, 1974), p. 32.

3. For an extremely intelligent attempt to analyse the meshing of social, textual and psychic changes in the period, see J. Kristeva, L'État et le Mystère, Section C of 'La Révolution du language poétique' (Paris, 1974), pp. 361–435.

4. The standard works (R.D. Altick, 'The English Common Reader: A Social History of the Mass Reading Public, 1800–1900' (Chicago, 1957), and Q.D. Leavis, 'Fiction and the Reading Public' (London, 1932)), give scant coverage to this period and particularly to the specific problems facing Meredith and James with respect to a 'dual addressee'.

5. See G.L. Griest, 'Mudie's Circulating Library and the Victorian Novel' (Bloomington, 1970), for the best study of the forms of distribution of the three-decker.

6. Ibid., p. 3.

7. Louis James, 'Fiction for the Working Man, 1830–1850' (London, 1963); M. Sadleir, 'XIX Century Fiction: a Bibliographical Record' (London, 1951). See also n. 4 above.

8. Unsigned review, 'St. James Gazette', vi, 25 June 1883; unsigned review in 'Temple Bar', xcvii, April, 1893. Both are reprinted in 'Meredith: The Critical Heritage', ed Ioan Williams (London, 1971), pp. 241; 368.

9. Ibid., p. 428.

10. L. Stevenson, 'The Ordeal of George Meredith' (New York, 1953).

11. S. Sassoon, 'Meredith' (London, 1948), p. 125.

12. Meredith described 'The Adventures of Harry Richmond' to his friend Augustus Jessop in 1864 as 'a spanking bid for popularity'.

13. S. Sassoon, 'Meredith', op. cit., p. 74.

14. G. Meredith, 'Sandra Belloni' (entitled 'Emilia in England' until the 1886 reprint), p. 483.

15. Meredith even went so far as to write chapters of his novels to be read differently by different sections of the audience. In chapter 8 of 'The Amazing Marriage' when Gower Woodseer and Lord Fleetwood (two complementary versions of 'sylvan' man, the seer and the man of action) encounter one another and discuss Carinthia Jane. It is requested that the male reader 'bear in mind what wild creature he was in his youth, while the female should marvel credulously.' And indeed, the passionate and idealized male versions of Carinthia which draw the two men together would, I think, elicit different responses from men and women.

16. G. Meredith, 'One of Our Conquerors', p. 120.

17. L. Johnson, review of 'One of Our Conquerors', the 'Academy', xxxix (13 June 1891), cited in 'Meredith: The Critical Heritage', op. cit., pp. 360–3.

18. G. Meredith, 'Modern Love', stanza XLVIII.

19. Meredith wrote of himself in 'Beauchamp's Career': 'Back I go to my wilderness, where, as you may perceive, I have contracted the habit of listening to my own voice more than is good.'

20. J. Fletcher and M. Bradbury, The Introverted Novel, 'Modernism', ed M. Bradbury and J. McFarlane (Harmondsworth, 1976), p. 365.

21. L. Johnson, in his review of 'One of Our Conquerors', ('Meredith: The Critical Heritage', op. cit., p. 360), asked:

Is there no danger that, in a kind of unconscious defiance and challenge, they [the artists] will have gone too far, and grown enamoured of that in their work which the world did well to blame? If the world cried out upon their obscurity, where there was some obscurity but not much, was it not natural in them to have replied with worse obscurities, out of an impatient contempt and exasperation?

22. In an unsigned review of Meredith's poem 'The Empty Purse' the reviewer spoke of 'this new cryptographic style', indicating the degree to which the age was becoming conscious of the new obscurity. It is a function, in many instances, of increasing heterogeneity in the fiction, a dissociation of private experiences from a realm of shared meanings which do not contain the experiences but encroach upon them.

23. This junction of two modes of subjectivity, this 'in-mixing of subjects', refers to the kinds of plural subjectivity which became an important feature of modernist writing. Perhaps the clearest example is in 'Les Chants de Maldoror' by Lautréamont, in which

'characters' are no longer kept separate as stable and discrete entities, but constantly melt into each other in protean, shifting transformations.

24. G. Meredith, 'The Tragic Comedians', pp. 198–9.

25. H. James, 'The Sacred Fount', ed and introd. Leon Edel (London, 1959), pp. 50–1.

26. G. Meredith, 'The Tragic Comedians', preface, p. i:
The word 'fantastical' is accentuated in our tongue to so scornful an utterance that the constant good service it does would make it seem an appointed instrument for reviewers of books or imaginative matter distasteful to those expository pens. Upon examination, claimants to the epithet will be found outside of books and of poets, in many quarters, Nature being one of the most prominent, if not the foremost. Wherever she can get to drink her fill of sunlight she pushes forth fantastically.

27. J. Conrad, 'Heart of Darkness', p. 126.

28. J. Laforgue, 'Oeuvres' (Paris, 1925–62) ed G. Jean-Aubry, II, p. 26.

29. C. Photiades, 'George Meredith: sa vie - son imagination' (Paris, 1910), cited in I. Williams, 'Meredith: The Critical Heritage', op. cit., p. 18. Meredith seems to have been deeply stung by the image of himself as harlequin and he never forgot the term. In a letter of reply (22 July 1887) to a young American critic who had praised his work, Meredith wrote:
In England I am encouraged but by a few enthusiasts. I read in a critical review of some verses of mine the other day that I was 'a harlequin and a performer of antics'. I am accustomed to that kind of writing, as our hustings orator is to the dead cat and the brickbat flung in his face - at which he smiles politely.

30. J. Conrad, The Informer, p. 93.

31. R. Roussel, 'The Metaphysics of Darkness' (Baltimore, 1971), p. 4.

32. 'Joseph Conrad's Letters to R.B. Cunninghame Graham', ed C.T. Watts, (Cambridge, 1969), p. 117.

33. 'Letters from Joseph Conrad, 1895–1924', ed E. Garnett (London, 1928), p. 142.

34. Ibid., p. 59.

35. This and the following extracts from Dickens and Thackeray discussing their relationship to their readers are cited in K. Tillotson, 'Novels of the Eighteen-Forties' (Oxford, 1954), pp. 33 ff.

36. J. Conrad, The Return, in 'Tales of Unrest', p. 119.

37. 'Joseph Conrad: Life and Letters', 2 vols, ed G. Jean-Aubry (New York, 1927), I, p. 227.

38. J. Conrad, Alphonse Daudet, 'Notes on Life and Letters', p. 22.

39. Joseph Conrad, 'Letters to Cunninghame Graham', op. cit., p. 65.

40. Meredith misled the public about his private life in many ways, even extending to his place of birth. See the opening chapter of David Williams's excellent study, 'George Meredith: His Life and Lost Love' (London, 1977); and D. Johnson, 'Lesser Lives' (London, 1973), p. 97. The calculated reticence of both Conrad and James is discussed below, chapters 5 and 6 respectively.

41. J. Conrad, Books, 'Notes on Life and Letters', p. 6.

42. E.M. Forster, Joseph Conrad: A Note, in 'Abinger Harvest' (1936); reprinted (Harmondsworth, 1974), pp. 151–2.

43. J. Conrad, A Familiar Preface, in 'A Personal Record', p. xv.

44. J. Conrad, 'A Personal Record', p. 95.

45. O. Elton, A Note on Mysticism, 'Fortnightly Review', 76 (1904), pp. 462–77, p. 475.

46. Mrs E.L. Linton, Our Illusions, 'Fortnightly Review', 49 (1891), pp. 584–97, pp. 595–6.

47. The following were among the most significant contributions to the periodical literature on the subject: W. J. Corbet, The Increase of Insanity, 'Fortnightly Review', 59 (1896), pp. 431–4; T. Drapes, Is Insanity Increasing?, 'Fortnightly Review', 60 (1896), pp. 483–93. The growing uncertainty of the barrier between sanity, criminality and madness is expressed by Vernon Lee, Deterioration of the Soul, 'Fortnightly Review', 59 (1896), pp. 928–43: 'I think that it is dangerous to draw a hard and fast line between ourselves and any of our fellow creatures, even when we may be obliged, for sheer self-defence, to shut some of them up and chastise them' (p. 931).

48. 'One of Our Conquerors' (1891) is Meredith's remarkable portrayal of mental breakdown, and the work even led to a periodical discussion of the clinical forms of Victor Radnor's breakdown—see chapter 4 (pp. 106–7). Of Conrad's severed depression of 1897–8, Frederick Karl ('Joseph Conrad: The Three Lives', (London, 1979), pp. 424–5) writes:

On March 29, as he was poised to begin something - anything - he wrote a desperate letter to Garnett, demonstrating possibly a more hopeless state of mind than any since his suicide attempt twenty years earlier ... Conrad began to split into pieces,.... Leon Edel ('Henry James, A Biography', 5 vols, London, 1953–72) has documented Henry James's terrible period of depression and despair under the title of The Black Abyss, 1895, in vol. 4 of his biography, 'The Treacherous Years 1895–1900' (London, 1969), pp. 75–100.

49. H. Zimmern, Professor Lombroso's New Theory of Political Crime, 'Blackwood's Magazine', 149 (1891), pp. 202–11.

50. A.E. Hake, 'Regeneration, a reply to Max Nordau', (London, 1895).

51. For an attack on Lombroso's slipshod scholarship and blundering errors of fact see Musing Without Method, 'Blackwood's Magazine', 186 (1909), pp. 843–9. The date of this article should remind us however that the influence and topicality of Lombroso were spread over twenty years or more.

52. M. Nordau, 'Degeneration' (trans. from the 2nd German edn) (London, 1913), pp. vii–viii. The 1st English edn in 1895 went through seven new reprints in the same year and in September 1898 a 'popular' edn was published.

53. C. Lombroso, 'The Man of Genius' (London, 1891), pp. 359–60.

54. J.F. Nisbet, 'The Insanity of Genius' (London, 1891), Preface, p. xv.

55. G. Moreau, 'La Psychologie morbide' (Paris, 1859).

56. F.W. Hagen, Ueber die Verwandtschaft des Genies mit dem Irresein, 'Allgemeine Zeitschrift für Psychiatrie' (1877); P. Radestock, 'Genie und Wahnsinn' (Breslau, 1884).

57. Vernon Lee, Beauty and Sanity, 'Fortnightly Review', 58 (1895), pp. 252–68, p. 253.

58. T. Clifford Allbut, Nervous Diseases and Modern Life, the 'Contemporary Review', 67 (1895), pp. 210–31, p. 225.

59. A. Machen, 'Hieroglyphics: A Note upon Ecstacy in Literature' (London, 1902), p. 120. Essentially a plea for mystical romanticism, it contains some remarkable passages, particularly on the relation of conscious to unconscious expressed in the literary use of the 'Doppelgänger'.

60. The first work of Freud to be translated into English, A New Histological Method

for the Study of Nerve-Tracts in the Brain and Spinal Cord, was contributed to 'Brain' in 1884. In 1893, Dr F.W.H. Myers, one of the leading members of the Society of Psychical Research where he was known as the Spiritualist Don, gave an account of the Freud-Breuer hysteria experiments at a meeting of the Society, the report of which was published in the 'Proceedings' of the Society in its issue of June 1893. In 1896, Dr M. Clarke, a leading British neurologist, published a long review of Freud's study of hysteria in 'Brain'. This review drew the attention of Havelock Ellis to Freud's work. Ellis published a paper, Hysteria in Relation to the Sexual Emotion, in 'The Alienist and Neurologist' in 1898. Ellis was really the prime English mediator of Freud at this time and vol. 1 of his 'Studies in the Psychology of Sex' (1904) referred to Freud's 'fascinating and really important researches'. By contrast Helen Zimmern stated that, by 1891, Professor Lombroso's books had an influence as 'immediate and decisive' as 'The Origin of Species'.

61. Oscar Wilde, The Sphinx (1891), in 'The Works of Oscar Wilde', introd. V. Holland (London, 1966), p. 842.

62. H. Zimmern, Professor Lombroso's New Theory of Political Crime, 'Blackwood's Magazine', 149 (1891), pp. 202–11, p. 211.

63. J. Conrad, 'Under Western Eyes', p. 52.

64. Cited in G. Markow-Totevy, 'Henry James', trans. J. Cummings (London, 1969), pp. 98–9.

65. H. James, The Figure in the Carpet, 'Cosmopolis', 1 (1896), p. 50.

66. Ibid., p. 49.

67. Ibid., pp. 47–8.

68. These descriptions are taken at random from dozens such in Lombroso and Nordau.

69. J. Conrad, 'Life and Letters', op. cit., II, p. 204.

70. A. Symons, Stephane Mallarmé, 'Fortnightly Review', 64 (1898), pp. 677–85, p. 678.

71. Ibid., p. 685.

72. Vernon Lee, Beauty and Sanity, op. cit., p. 260.

73. H.H. Statham, The Writings of Wagner, 'Edinburgh Review', 189 (1899), pp. 96–118, p. 96.

74. For an excellent discussion of the importance of music in 'One of Our Conquerors' see G. Beer, ' "One of Our Conquerors": Language and Music', in 'Meredith Now', ed I. Fletcher (London, 1971), pp. 265–80.

75. A. Symons, Stephane Mallarmé, op. cit., pp. 677, 682.

76. Modernist fiction adopted contrasting strategies in avoiding the dilemma of symptomatic reading and its crisis of intimacy: on the one hand it played up the 'make-believe', it forced fiction further towards radical playfulness (Borges, Nabokov, Beckett, Barth), it concealed the links between writer and written under the formal, ludic elements of structure; on the other hand it positively embraced the idea of fiction as the display of intensely private fantasies and desires, it pushed the psycho-dramatic and confessional nature of writing to extreme limits (Strindberg, Lawrence, Plath, Burroughs).

JOHN BATCHELOR

Edwardian Literature

The phrase 'Edwardian Literature' is not often heard.[1]

An 'age' is a system of agreed meanings in time.[2]

1. 'EDWARDIAN'

To re-read Richard Ellmann's essay, 'The Two Faces of Edward', is to be reminded of the lasting truth of many of its observations and also to note that things have changed since 1959 when it was first published. While it is no longer true that the phrase 'Edwardian literature' is not often heard, it is true, as P.N. Furbank wrote in 1974,[3] that 'Edwardian' is not an established term quite like 'Romantic' or 'Augustan'. The term is still used with circumspection, although there are two distinguished collections of essays by Samuel Hynes, *The Edwardian Turn of Mind* (1968) and *Some Edwardian Occasions* (1972), and the existence of an Edwardian age to which one can confidently refer is assumed in the content, though not in the title, of Bernard Bergonzi's *The Turn of a Century* (1973).

For Cyril Connolly, writing in the 1930s, the Edwardian period had been characterised by 'the struggle between literature and journalism'.[4] He believes that the only Edwardian reputations which had actually been enhanced in the 1930s were those of Forster and Somerset Maugham, while

---

From *The Edwardian Novelists.* © 1982 by John Batchelor.

'Galsworthy, Bennett, Lawrence, Firbank are dead and also out of fashion' (p. 5) and the stocks of Shaw, Wells and Kipling have remained stationary. Frank Swinnerton wrote in 1935 that 'Edwardian' was used in the 1920s as a term of abuse: 'The object was to suggest that Shaw, Wells, Conrad and Bennett were out of date'.[5]

Certainly the 1920s found it necessary to be rude about the Edwardians. Apart from Virginia Woolf's famous attack on Wells, Bennett and Galsworthy in *Mr Bennett and Mrs Brown* (1924) there are Roy Campbell's aside about the 'prophets of Domestic Comfort, Shaw, Wells and Bennett' who have sold the 'experience of the human race' for 'a few patent bath-taps',[6] and Rebecca West's affectionate attack in *The Strange Necessity:* 'All our youth they hung about the houses of our minds like Uncles, the Big Four: H.G. Wells, George Bernard Shaw, John Galsworthy, and Arnold Bennett. They had the generosity, the charm, the loquacity of visiting uncles.'[7]

The Edwardian period is muzzy at the edges. Does it begin in 1895 with the destruction of Wilde and the emergence of Wholesomeness as a literary desideratum? Or does it begin with the death of Queen Victoria? Equally, where does it end? Virginia Woolf had it that human nature changed in 1910, but not everyone would agree with her. 1914 was certainly the end of everything that the Edwardians had taken for granted, but had the sense of literary ending come earlier than that? One could propose at least three frames for the period: the reign of King Edward is not the least important, since writers were conscious of, and affected by, the fact that what Wells spoke of as the 'great paperweight' of Victoria's presence had been removed and that they were working in the virgin years of a new century. Alternatively, the Boer War and the Great War could provide an intelligible frame. The myth of Empire was dented beyond repair by the first, the credibility of the English upper class—with much else—was drastically eroded by the second.

Equally, the Wilde *debâcle* and the first issue of *Blast* could be taken as the parameters. The fall of Wilde signalled the retreat of aestheticism and Edwardian literature can be seen to be casting about for its models and imperatives. If the favoured models are established earlier successes—Wells, Galsworthy and Forster follow Dickens and Meredith, Shaw adapts opera and melodrama, Granville-Barker closely follows Chekhovian musical form—and the imperatives loosely humanist, the period remains notable for its lack of a dominant artistic direction. *Blast*, in 1914, gave a clear new lead.

Exactly what would have happened to literature without the intervention of the Great War is an unanswerable question, but there can be little doubt that Wyndham Lewis and Pound would have had a decisive effect on the direction that it took.

The simple problem presented by the question of dates is compounded by the competing mythologies that the word 'Edwardian' has attracted to itself. Its associations include bloomers, bicycles, Fabians, suburbs, the Liberal Landslide, the People's Budget; garden parties, *Peter Pan*, the upper ten thousand, Lord Russell's imprisonment for bigamy, the King's affairs with Lady Warwick and Mrs Alice Keppel;[8] or realism, mysticism, symbolism, psychical research, high-minded homosexuality, *Principia Ethica* and 'The Free Man's Worship'.

Frank Kermode has claimed that since 1890 to 1900 is very clearly an ending, the next decade may properly be regarded as a beginning: 'You sometimes hear people say, with a certain pride in their clerical resistance to the myth, that the nineteenth century really ended not in 1900 but in 1914. But there are different ways of measuring an epoch. 1914 has obvious qualifications, but if you wanted to defend the neater, more mythical date, you could do very well. In 1900 Nietzsche died; Freud published *The Interpretation of Dreams*; 1900 was the date of Husserl's *Logic*, and of Russell's *Critical Exposition of the Philosophy of Leibnitz*.'[9]

Richard Ellmann in the article referred to above speaks of the self-reliant 'doughtiness' of the Edwardians (p. 114). Of their moral outlook he remarks that they were 'thoroughly secular' and that having rejected Christianity they 'felt free to use it, for while they did not need religion they did need religious metaphors' (p. 116). Their attitude to 'Life' is sacramental: 'The capitalised word for the Edwardians is not "God" but "Life"' (p. 120). The plots of Edwardian novels and plays (he refers particularly to Conrad and Forster) are characterised by sudden transformations, 'secular miracles', alterations of the personality by which the individual attains selfhood (pp. 121 and 130). And in the absence of clear external moral imperatives the writers subordinated themselves to the primacy of their art: 'The Edwardian writer is an artist not because he proclaims he is, as Wilde did, but because his works proclaim it' (p. 129).[10]

The Edwardians inhabited what may be called a contracting moral universe, in which the received moral imperatives had lost their urgency. The Victorian dismantling of Christianity had taken place slowly: its ascendancy in national and institutional life had sustained a series of blows in the latter part of the century. The impact of evolutionary thinking after the publication of Darwin's *Origin of Species* in 1859 remains the biggest single factor in what has been called 'The Disappearance of God'.[11]

George Eliot is quoted as saying that God was inconceivable,

Immortality unbelievable, and Duty 'peremptory and absolute'.[12] Though it would probably be true to say that God no longer functioned as an effective sanction in the lives of most thinking people in the last quarter of the nineteenth century, there is no doubt that after-images which derived their energy from Christian habits of mind survived. George Eliot's sense of duty is one of these, Pater's equally cogent sense of beauty is another.[13] The dethroning of God created strain and distress: it was necessary to put something in his place. These substitutions may be seen as of progressively diminishing grandeur. Duty in the exalted abstract gives way to practical duty to the nation or the empire, duty to the beloved and the family and finally duty to oneself, 'heroic endurance for its own sake'.[14]

In the arts, Pater's passionate conviction that there is an aesthetic 'ecstasy' which can glorify the flux of time and confer 'success in life'[15] gives way to Arthur Symons's claim for the function of the symbol: the expression of the 'ultimate essence', the 'soul of whatever exists and can be realised by the consciousness'. In Symons the substitution of aesthetic principles for Christianity is quite explicit. In its 'revolt against exteriority' symbolism becomes 'a kind of religion, with all the duties and responsibilities of a sacred ritual'.[16]

The Edwardians were conscious of the need to fill the moral vacuum surrounding them. G.E. Moore approached his moral philosophy with the question 'What is Good?' (*Principia Ethica* (1903), Ch. 2 and *passim*). The answer, in his book, is the notion of 'human relationships' which for Bloomsbury was taken to mean close friends, passionate acquaintances and E.M. Forster's 'Love the Beloved Republic'.[17]

For a student of the Edwardian period Moore's answer is less interesting than his question. The fact that the nature of 'good' needed to be considered in terms so radical and pragmatic is at once revealing and representative. Moore's book is a clear instance of a leading Edwardian anxiety, the anxiety over what was good, what was right, where duty lay, what the direction of man should be. Conrad gives his own retrospective account of this anxiety in his 'Author's Note' to *An Outcast of the Islands* (1896): 'The discovery of new values in life is a very chaotic experience; there is a tremendous amount of jostling and confusion and a momentary feeling of darkness' (p. vii).

Some Edwardian novelists write from a specifically Christian viewpoint: notably Chesterton, especially in *The Man Who Was Thursday* (1908) and *Manalive* (1912). Although Christian, Chesterton's perspective was not yet Catholic: he was not received into the Catholic Church until 1922. An interesting minor Catholic novelist of the period is R.H. Benson, whose *Lord of the World* (1907) is a mixture of an invasion novel and a Wellsian utopian prophecy in which a Messiah of the future meets a (German) anti-Christ in an apocalyptic encounter. The most worthwhile of Benson's other books are perhaps *None Other Gods* (1911), the story of a young aristocrat who becomes a vagrant Christian martyr and in some ways anticipates Evelyn Waugh's Sebastian Flyte, and *The Sentimentalists* (1906), a notably temperate novel about his former friend Frederick Rolfe, Baron Corvo (whose attitude to Benson at this date was one of snarling vindictiveness). In Benson's novel Corvo as 'Christopher Dell' is freed from his lacerating and destructive egotism by a form of Christian psychotherapy.[18]

A symptom of the continuing popular taste for Christianity in literature is the enormous commercial success of Robert Hitchens's Catholic novel *The Garden of Allah* (1904).[19] With these obvious exceptions it would seem to be broadly true to say that the Edwardian imagination was secular.

2. EDWARDIAN ANXIETIES

One difference between the Victorian and the Edwardian mind is indicated by the ease with which at Cambridge the young G.E. Moore captured the audience which had formerly attended to the neo-Hegelian 'idealist', J. McT.E. McTaggart. 'It would be too much to say that Moore dethroned McTaggart, who was essentially undethronable, but he did carry the younger men by storm, and caused Lytton Strachey to exclaim, "The age of reason has come!" ... Moore's steady questioning as to what *is* good? What *is* true? had ... torn some large holes in the McTaggartian heaven'.[20]

The freedom celebrated by Forster here and by Russell in, for example, 'The Free Man's Worship'[21] carries an accompanying intensification of anxiety, which characteristically manifested itself as an acute awareness of what Ian Watt has called the 'epistemological crisis' through which the period was passing: 'A crisis most familiar to literary history under the twin rubrics of the disappearance of God and the disappearance of the omniscient author.'[22]

The epistemological crisis is a product of the contracting moral horizons of the period, a steady erosion of the old certainties leaving Edwardian man confronted with the self and nothing beyond the self, unable to trust in anything other than his immediate sense impressions and his own actions. Bertrand Russell's autobiography registers this transition. As the nineteenth century closed he had a confident sense of intellectual territory securely grasped and mapped out: 'The time was one of intellectual intoxication. My sensations resembled those one has after climbing a mountain in a mist, when, on reaching the summit, the mist suddenly clears, and the country becomes visible for forty miles in every direction.'[23]

With the year 1900 came an abrupt change in his outlook: 'Oddly enough, the end of the century marked the end of this sense of triumph, and from that moment onwards I began to be assailed simultaneously by intellectual and emotional problems which plunged me into the darkest despair that I have ever known.'[24]

The popular tradition which sees Edwardian life in terms of Victoria Sackville-West's *The Edwardians* (1930) is at least partly right. The decade was indeed a period of luxury and expanding wealth flavoured with a marked increase of private licentiousness. This growth was accompanied by a terror of the increasingly dispossessed working-class. Literature reflects this in the ubiquitous image of the 'abyss' to describe the life of the urban poor. In *The Time Machine* (1895) H.G. Wells identifies with the aristocratic Eloi, descendants of the Victorian aristocracy, while the terrifying Morlocks who live on the Eloi's flesh are descendants of the industrial proletariat who now live in caverns deep in the earth. There is no doubt that *The Time Machine* reflects and expresses current middle-class anxiety about the urban poor. As Bernard Bergonzi remarks, 'From his schooldays in Bromley he had disliked and feared the working class in a way wholly appropriate to the son of a small tradesman.'[25]

It seems likely that the metaphor of the 'abyss' originated with another Wells fantasy, 'In the Abyss' (*The Plattner Story: and Others*, 1897), in which a deep-sea diver encounters biped intelligent reptiles on the ocean bed; these creatures have a developed urban civilisation and the diver is adopted by them as a visiting deity and worshipped. In the Edwardian period the currency of the word to describe the plight of the urban poor received impetus from C.F.G. Masterman's anonymous pamphlet about slum life, *From the Abyss* (1902), and his 'secular sermon', 'The Social Abyss' (W.H. Hunt (ed.), *Preachers from the Pew* (n.d.), pp.75–84). Jack London's *The People of the Abyss* (1903) uses the image to express with pungency a view of London which becomes central to *Howards End*, Wells's *Tono-Bungay*, Galsworthy's *Fraternity* and C.F.G. Masterman's *The Condition of England*: 'The London Abyss is a vast shambles. Year by year ... rural England pours in a flood of vigorous strong life, that not only does not renew itself, but perishes by the third generation' (p. 38).

City life is causing the population to decline and is damaging the human stock of the nation: it is 'an unnatural life for a human' and produces degenerate children, 'a weak-kneed, narrow chested, listless breed' (pp. 43–5). Forster's Leonard Bast lives on the edge of the 'abyss' in *Howards End* (1910): 'He was not in the abyss, but he could see it, and at times people whom he knew had dropped in, and counted no more' (p. 43). As he develops his portrait of Leonard Bast as an exemplary victim of urban poverty, Forster could almost be quoting Jack London: 'One guessed him as the third generation, grandson to the shepherd or ploughboy whom civilisation had sucked into the town.' Margaret Schlegel notes 'the spine that might have been straight, and the chest that might have broadened' (p. 113).[26]

The metaphor of the 'abyss' is used often by Arthur Morrison in his sensational novel of slum violence, *A Child of the Jago* (1896) and his more romantic, but still violent low-life adventure story *The Hole in the Wall* (1902).[27]

The fear that the race was degenerating had been expressed in such sensational works as Max Nordau's *Degeneration* (published in English in 1895) and *The Malady of the Century* (1896) and is probably one of the reasons for the Edwardians' obsession with their *health*. Tennis, sea-bathing, hot water after meals and 'mind-cures' are among the panaceas of the period. 'Sandow's Exercises', named after Eugene Sandow, an Englishman who made a career for himself in America in the 1890s as a 'body-builder', were the fashion among Edwardian suburban men. William James is entertaining on these trends in *The Varieties of Religious Experience* where he notes the 'Gospel of Relaxation', the 'Don't Worry Movement', and those who say 'Youth, Health, Vigour' as they dress themselves every morning (p. 95). Arnold Bennett, himself a hypochondriac, was exploiting the market for 'health' with his books *Mental Efficiency* (1911; originally published as *The Reasonable Life*, 1907) and *How to Live on Twenty-Four Hours a Day* (1908).

Another dominant anxiety of the period is fear of invasion. 'England and Germany are bound to fight' is one of the themes of *Howards End*, and H.G. Wells's *The War in the Air* (1902) concerns a future war with Germany. The invasion novel is a distinct sub-genre of the period.[28] Germany is usually the aggressor, as in William Le Queux, *The Great War in England in 1897* (1894) and *The Invasion of 1910* (1906). The latter, with an introductory letter by Lord Roberts, is little more than a piece of rearmament propaganda in fictional form. Saki in *When William Came: A Story of London under the Hohenzollerns* (1914) gives a satirical account of England's unpreparedness for war and the social humiliation (curiously mild) of living in London under the Germans. By far the best of this group of novels is Erskine Childers' *The Riddle of the Sands* (1903) in which the Englishman's superior seamanship in small craft enables him to outwit the Germans in the North Sea.

The aggressor was not always Germany: in an extraordinary romance by M.P. Shiel, *The Yellow Danger* (1898), the enemy are the Chinese, and the English victory involves drowning the whole population of China in a monstrous whirlpool. In G.K. Chesterton's *The Flying Inn* (1914) the aggressor is Turkey, and the story concerns a patriotic hero who resists the Turkish occupation of England by travelling the country with a giant cheese and a liquor supply (the 'Flying Inn' of the title) in defiance of Moslem prohibition of alcohol.

The invasion novel was sufficiently clearly established as a form for P.G. Wodehouse to write an effective parody of it in *The Swoop! Or How Clarence Saved England* (1909). The Germans, the Russians, the Chinese and a number of smaller and less likely nations invade England simultaneously and fight each other. The bombardment of London has excellent results: 'The Albert Hall, struck by a merciful shell, had come down with a run, and was now a heap of picturesque ruins ... The burning of the Royal Academy proved a great comfort to all' (p. 42).

3. A PATRIOTIC MYTH:RURAL ENGLAND

The urban poor were felt as a threat from below, 'odours from the abyss' in Margaret Schlegel's phrase (*Howards End*, p. 115). The ambitions of other nations, mainly Germany but also Russia and China, were felt as threats from outside. But how did the literature of the period perceive the England that was being threatened? The positive aspects of English life were seen in terms of two leading, and related, myths: the country house and the land.

Much of the serious literature of the period re-examines and scrutinises these myths. The growth of the cities, and in particular the spread of middle-class suburbs, were facts to which the myth had to accommodate itself. An important insight in Masterman's *The Condition of England*, and one that he shares with Wells and Forster, is the recognition of suburban man as an irreversible feature of modern England. Forster on the whole deplores the suburbs (though he finds virtue in 'half-suburban' Summer Street in *A Room with a View*), Wells in *Tono-Bungay* (1909) sees them as a form of morbid, diseased growth; endless reproductions in miniature of the country house and its aspirations, necessary extensions of Bladesover, the country house which dominates the first part of the novel: 'It is this idea of escaping parts from the seventeenth-century system of Bladesover, of proliferating and overgrowing elements from the Estates, that to this day seems to me the best explanation, not simply of London, but of all England' (p. 80).

Masterman's view of the suburbs is presumably coloured by Wells's (he was a friend of Wells and read the proofs of *Tono-Bungay* while writing *The*

Condition of England) but is awkwardly uncertain, balanced uncomfortably between acceptance and rejection. Suburban man has 'drifted away from the realities of life' and is 'divorced from the ancient sanities of manual or skilful labour, of exercise in the open air, absorbed for the bulk of his day in crowded offices adding sums or writing letters' (p. 94). It closely resembles Jack London's and Forster's lament for the countryman sucked into the town.[29] But Masterman goes on to say that suburban life is at least better than the life of the inner cities. In the suburbs the grip of the city is 'loosened' so that 'something of the large sanities of rural existence could be mingled with the quickness and agility of the town' and the suburbs at their best contain 'clean and virile life' and the 'healthiest and most hopeful promise for the future of modern England' (p. 95).

What Masterman is really saying is that the suburbs were a reasonable compromise between urban and rural life. It is precisely the 'compromised' aspect of suburban life that Forster passionately rejects. Forster, with Kenneth Grahame, Saki, Edward Thomas, W.H. Hudson and Kipling, subscribes to the myth of England as a golden rural world, a place where right feeling is still to be found. Given Forster's satirical and acutely observing intelligence the hold that this myth had on him could only be damaging. It is responsible for the soggier parts of *Howards End* with its romancing about 'yeomen' and the countryside that would vote liberal 'if left to itself' in Hertfordshire, and is seen at its worst in *Maurice* where Maurice and his lover retreat from English suburban life and take refuge in 'the greenwood' to work as woodcutters in a pastoral idyll.[30]

Pastoral and suburban make a fixed, if false, antithesis in the Edwardian mind. Defeated modern man is descended from a heroic past: Masterman's suburb dwellers, Forster's corrupted yeomen, Edward Thomas's agricultural labourer who finds the 'unrelated multitude' of the contemporary urban world an 'endless riddle' (*The South Country*, 1909, p. 65).

Nostalgia is the most striking feature of Thomas's prose works about rural England. In his *The Heart of England* (1906) London's hills are lost to the eye except at night, when 'we can see them as though the streets did not exist' (p. 8). Forster's Leonard Bast has a similar experience in his night walk through the suburban hills in *Howards End*. And *Howards End*'s resentment of the petrol engine is anticipated in Thomas's book: a tramp tries to find a stretch of road where he can 'make a bit of fire' without being disturbed by the stink and dust of the motor-car, which is resented throughout Thomas's book for its disturbance of rural peace (p. 8).[31]

To love the landscape is the act of a patriot. This became particularly clear from the retrospect of the Great War, when the landscape as a threatened ideal was thrown sharply into focus as a pole of the poetic sensibility.[32]

Some of the most vivid expressions of this nostalgia are to be found in the fantasies of the period. Fantasy, 'Fauns and Dryads and slips of the memory ... Pans and puns, all that is medieval this side of the grave',[33] is an irresponsible form, retrogressive, infantile, seeking appropriate arenas in which to escape from the pressures of the day. It is a significant feature of the period if only because so much of it was published: many of Forster's, Saki's and Kipling's short stories, most of the works of such minor writers as Algernon Blackwood, M.P. Shiel and Richard Marsh. Pan is a figure of major importance in these fantasies. In Forster's 'The Story of a Panic' and 'The Curate's Friend' he is an image of sexual freedom,[34] and in James Stephens's *The Crock of Gold* (1912), he is again a sexually liberating, and here mischievous and satirical, force. These pieces draw on the full tradition of Pan, both in what can fairly be called his phallic character (the aspect exploited in Arthur Machen's sensational tale of the macabre, *The Great God Pan* (1894) and in Forrest Reid's homosexual idyll, *The Garden God* (1905)) and in his more decorous literary role as the great custodian of the natural world.

In the extraordinary seventh chapter of *The Wind in the Willows* (1908) Pan, the 'Friend and Helper', appears in person as though to guarantee for ever the nostalgic values of the river-valley in which Rat and Mole live out their lives of innocuous undergraduate friendship (p. 155).

The Wind in the Willows is a completely successful fantasy, a work in which the inner compulsions of the author become locked, at some level well below the surface, with his material: the result is a self-contained and self-sustaining world.

The Toad plot came first, and the river, the wild wood and the Rat and Mole friendship were added later: the stages of this process mark the retreat of Grahame's imagination into a backward-looking arcadia.[35] Toad still has one foot in the adult world, the word of the 'Olympians', the unsympathetic uncles and aunts from Grahame's short story published in *The Golden Age* (1900).

He is the only one of the animals to live in a house rather than a hole (although Badger's hole incorporates a Roman ruin and Mole's has suburban furnishings) and to have adventures involving the human world: the stolen motor-car, the comic-grotesque magistrate, the gaoler's daughter, the barge-woman, the engine-driver. Yet these human figures are heavily distorted, and deprived of the threatening reality that they would have in a 'real' adult world. Toad dresses up as a washer-woman and takes violent revenge on the barge-woman, but only a perversely Freudian critic would read these as fantasies of transvestism and sadism: they are rather expressions of an *infantile* wish to dress up and exercise power. The only opening for something more specifically sexual is in the relationship with the gaoler's daughter, but here Toad is pushed firmly back into his identity as an 'animal', and a 'poor animal' at that, while the rest of adult humanity—policeman, magistrates, engine-driver—treat him as a small but responsible *man*. The gaoler's daughter is a mother to Toad, never a mistress.

The closer Toad gets to the 'real' world the more heavily distorted it becomes. His imprisonment, the most harsh of his contacts with the human world, is elaborately distanced and Gothicised in a sustained pastiche of Wardour Street historical romance: 'Across the hollow-sounding drawbridge, below the spiky portcullis, under the frowning archway of the grim old castle ... up time-worn winding stairs, past men-at-arms in casquet and corselet of steel, darting threatening looks through their vizards' (pp. 141–2) and so on.

The Wind in the Willows is a concentric work. On its circumference is the modern world, the trains, motor-cars and penal systems of the Toad-plot. Within that margin is the more comprehensible but still dangerous Wild Wood, in which Philistine violence has become extinct (the badgers occupy the buried Roman city) but can still have sporadic rebirths (as stoats and weasels). At the centre is the sunlit river valley of the opening chapters in which Rat and Mole preserve intact their own mythical version of rural England. But the author knows that it exists only in a child's gentled fantasy world. Outside that the train whistles, the motor-car roars, the prisons gape for the violent.

4. A PATRIOTIC WRITER: KIPLING'S ENGLAND

Kipling's image of England is at once unique and representative. His Indian and soldier tales of the 1880s and 1890s culminate in *Stalky and Co.* (1899) and *Kim* (1901): on the whole they are aggressive and forward-looking, they celebrate action, they subscribe, although with much subtle qualification (as recent criticism has recognised) to the myth of empire. In his Edwardian stories about Sussex, *Puck of Pook's Hill* (1906), *Rewards and Fairies* (1910), and 'They' (1904), he explores the resources of English myth and the relationships between landscape and personality.

Stalky and Co. is, of course, the unsurpassed account in English of the education that produces successful Imperial administrators. Study Number 5 opposes all comers and resists by stealth the formal values of the school, yet the Headmaster, the 'Prooshian' Bates (whose insight is un-English and would be well suited to England's great imperial competitor) recognises the subversiveness and individualism of Stalky, Beetle and McTurk as exactly the qualities that the empire needs. The early stories in *Stalky* present an innocent, savage world in which the boys take personal revenge on another house by pushing a dead cat under their floor-boards ('An Unsavoury Interlude') and punish a pair of bullies by subjecting them to their own primitive tortures ('The Moral Reformers').

In the last three stories of *Stalky and Co.* the adult world for which the boys are being prepared breaks into this innocence. In 'The Flag of Their Country', a tactless politican 'who has come to address the United Services College on "Patriotism"' (p. 212), tramples on the boys' feelings. He unfurls the Union Jack in front of the assembled school: 'They had certainly seen the thing before ... But the College never displayed it; it was no part of the scheme of their lives; the Head had never alluded to it; their fathers had not declared it unto them. It was a matter shut up, sacred and apart' (p. 213).

Patriotism is like sexual maturity, something they must grow towards and not be forced into prematurely. Any charge of jingoism brought against Kipling must be examined in the light of this story where, in this passage in particular, cheap patriotism is presented as a form of indecent assault.

Kim illustrates the division between the aggressive 1890s Kipling and the nostalgic Edwardian Kipling with an almost mythic neatness. Kim himself, the young white imperialist who is supremely successful in The Game, shares the narrative with the Lama who seeks his spiritual and physical home, his River and the mountains where the 'years fall from him' as he breathes the 'diamond air'.

Kim is the aggressive pragmatist, the Lama the nostalgic idealist. In the early chapters Kim is all eye and ear, an innocent led into experience by The Game and The Road. His knowledge of his identity is limited to the amulet round his neck and his personal myth of a Red Bull on a Green Field. While the Lama's quest for his river is his central preoccupation, Kim's 'quest' for the Red Bull barely holds his attention 'for twenty minutes at a time' (p. 61). His chance encounter with the Mavericks, his father's Regiment (whose flag is the Red Bull of Kim's quest), his re-entry into the world of the Sahibs and his schooling at St Xavier's at Lucknow creates a problem of identity like that of the Indian Prince, Shere Ali, who is sent to Eton and Oxford and as a result rebels against the British when he returns to India in A.E.W. Mason's *The Broken Road* (1908).

The novel weaves continuously, without strain, between the perspectives of Kim and the Lama, while the reader is obliged intermittently to be aware of a third pattern: the conflict between Britain and her enemies in India. If asked to name a famous Edwardian novel about keeping the Russians out of Afghanistan one would be non-plussed: yet that *is Kim*'s plot. It is part of Kipling's unfailing artistry that the work of The Game against the imperial competitors is never obscured but at the same time never allowed to dominate the novel's interest. Angus Wilson believes that there is no 'evil' in *Kim:* my own view is that evil is invisible to Kim and the Lama but present in the novel. The Russian who strikes the Lama is a bullying thug, the priest whom Kim outwits is a systematic parasite representative of vicious, endemic petty corruption in Indian life. The child of thirteen astride Zam-Zammah who has 'known all evil since he could speak' (p. 4) might well grow into an evil parasite himself were it not for his encounters with the Lama and the English. This leads to the simplest and most effective of the book's paradoxes. Kim's value to the British is his talent for duplicity, his capacity to tell lies, to be a Sahib disguised as many kinds of Indian, an agent posing as (as well as actually *being*) the Lama's loyal *chela*, a master of all dialects and manners. But what enslaves his loyalty to both the Lama and the English is that they tell the *truth*.

In Kipling's Edwardian English stories the land itself is the custodian of truth. In *Puck of Pook's Hill* and *Rewards and Fairies*, the history of England is presented to two children, Dan and Una, by Puck, Shakespeare's figure who has become a subversive nature spirit like the Pans and Fauns employed by Forster, Saki and other contemporaries. A field in Sussex belonging to the childrens' father becomes a microcosm for the whole of England. Puck describes his own survival as a minor deity who has always kept close to the earth (compare the Faun in Forster's 'The Curate's Friend', left behind in Wiltshire when the Romans went home). The other deities have not done so well: the God Weland, in 'Weland's Sword', has become a blacksmith shoeing horses for ungrateful farmers: 'Farmers and Weald clay ... are both uncommon cold and sour' (p. 21). Hugh, a novice monk, frees Weland from his immortality by giving him thanks and good wishes: in gratitutde Weland forges Hugh a magic sword and he becomes a warrior, the friend and companion of Sir Richard Dalyngridge, one of the Norman invaders. Between them these two friends bring good management to the land.

Friendship, good management and the power of the land are themes running through the Puck stories. As in *Stalky and Co.* good management is better than high principles: the story of Parnesius, the young centurion who works in an effective but unorthodox way on Hadrian's wall by cooperating closely with the Picts, is a reminder of Kipling's admiration and affection for the young subalterns and administrators who deal with the day-to-day practicalities of India as against the politicians and generals who 'govern' her.

In terms of dramatic dating most of the stories in *Rewards and Fairies* postdate the stories in *Puck of Pook's Hill*. 'The Knife and the Naked Chalk' is an exception. 'Weland's Sword' from the previous volume and 'The Knife and the Naked Chalk' are in a sense complementary versions of the same story, the one magical and the other prehistoric. Weland's magical sword gives power to Sir Hugh and helps bind together Saxon and Norman; stone-age man's need for iron knives leads mankind to collaborate against the wolf, the common enemy. Obviously the notion of uniting against a common enemy to defend England was relevant to the nervous and xenophobic atmosphere of 1910.

Kipling's 'They' (*Traffics and Discoveries*, 1904, pp. 303–5) links the general nostalgia for rural and historical England in the Puck stories with the theme of the country house as the representative of English upper-class values which is a feature of the period, and the interest in the supernatural and extra-sensory perception which characterises some of the earlier stories (notably 'The Brushwood Boy', *The Day's Work*, 1898). It is also a personal story, an indirect expression of Kipling's grief for the death of his six-year-old daughter Josephine in America in the winter of 1898–9.

'The Other Side of the County', East Sussex, where Kipling lived at Bateman's, Burwash, is the world of the living: the contrast between this world and the 'House Beautiful', the Elizabethan house containing a blind woman and the spirits of dead children, is what the story is really about. Angus Wilson praises the story's evocation of landscape,[36] but perhaps stresses insufficiently this contrast between the Elizabethan house and the 'other side of the county'.

The story opens with a sense that the House Beautiful is difficult of access except to those chosen and invited. The narrator is not willing his journey there but is carried by the unfolding of the landscape and the effortless pleasure of riding in his motor-car: 'One view called me to another; one hill top to its fellow' (p. 303).

The symmetry between the blind lady and the puzzled narrator is exact but unobtrusive: the beauty of her setting is closed to her as though she were in a purgatorial state to expiate some unknown sin, but in compensation she is allowed the companionship of the spirit children (although she is unmarried and childless). As the narrator's motor-car breaks into this both paradisal and purgatorial world the language reacts appropriately: 'It was *sacrilege* [my italics] to wake that dreaming house-front with the clatter of machinery' (p. 307). And when he sets out to return to his home the lady has to send her butler (himself a bereaved parent) to guide him back to the world: 'We are *so out of the world* [my italics], I don't wonder you were lost!' (p. 310).

At the end of the story the mystified narrator encounters his dead daughter and at last understands why he has been brought here: the dead child takes his hand, turns it and kisses it in the palm, 'A fragment of the mute code devised long ago' (p. 332). With this comes enlightenment and also the knowledge that it is 'wrong' for him to commune with the dead. The lady intuitively knows this: 'For you it would be wrong'. And she pities him: 'You who must never come here again!' (pp. 334, 335). Angus Wilson regrets this ending: 'He fudges the excellent story a little because none of the answers satisfies him and he hopes to get away with leaving a mystery.'[37]

Perhaps, though, the lines of the story are clearer than this comment suggests. The House Beautiful in 'They' is designed to free the narrator from his personal obsessions in the way that Friars Pardon cures the American millionaire, George Chapin, of his vaguely defined physical and psychological illnesses in 'An Habitation Enforced' (*Actions and Reactions*, 1909, pp. 3–50).

Like the American Chapins, the narrator of 'They' is socially *placed*, and admonished as well as mystified by the House Beautiful. Bits of discreet snobbishness in the narration work *against* the narrator throughout: 'A butler appeared noiselessly at the miracle of old oak that must be called the front door' (p. 310). Socially, the narrator behaves like a provincial tourist: 'If I am not packed off for a trespasser ... Shakespeare and Queen Elizabeth at least must come out of that half-open garden door and ask me to tea' (p. 305).

He is disapproved of by 'the fat woman who sells sweetmeats' in the village (Mrs Madehurst, whose grandchild later dies and joins the spirit children in the House Beautiful); he asks questions about the house and the blind woman and is made to feel that he is an upstart: 'The fat woman ... gave me to understand that people with motor cars had small right to live—much less "go about talking like carriage folk"' (p. 312).

Like 'young Mr Meyer', the Jewish businessman who doesn't know how to shoot properly in 'The Treasure and the Law' (*Puck of Pook's Hill*) the narrator has valuable but crude energies which need to be civilised by the House Beautiful. But if he became a constant visitor to the house his bereavement would narrow his perceptions and become obsessive like that of Helen for her illegitimate son killed in the Great War, in the much later story 'The Gardener' (*Debits and Credits*, 1926). He must leave the House Beautiful and return to the cycle of life suggested by the movement of the car over the landscape and the turning of the year: his last visit is made in the early autumn when the 'elder and the wild rose had fruited'.

The idea of a stranger being *socially* educated by a landscape is taken up and treated centrally in 'An Habitation Enforced'. The American George Chapin has come to Sussex for a complete rest following an illness. His wife Sophie is descended from the Lashmars whose land Sir Walter Conant now owns; as a result Sophie and her husband find themselves accepted into the community of the village despite their wealth and their ignorance of English manners, whereas a Brazilian millionaire who has also moved into the neighbourhood—Sangres the 'nigger'—never will be. Kipling delights in this, in the sense of social distinctions being established by a combination of accidents of history and acts of will.

The story could easily be insufferably snobbish, but fortunately it is handled with sufficient tact and indirection to make its points gracefully. And as with 'They' and 'The Gardener' the fact that the story is *personal* gives it an added dimension, this time a happy one: it is clearly a tribute to Carrie, Kipling's American wife, who had courageously and successfully settled in England for life. Kingsley Amis writes that in his Sussex stories and especially in the poem 'Sussex' Kipling is 'too emphatic', it is 'the work of a man pushing down his roots by will-power'; and of this story in particular 'the tone and content of the story are Anglophile, something which a real Englishman cannot be.'[38]

This seems fair. As well as a tribute to his wife the story can be read as a placebo for personal unease. Among the gentry Kipling himself is an outsider, born in India of parents who were distinctly middle- rather than upper-class. His purchase of Bateman's, a gloomy, grand, damp house is a typical Victorian gesture: the self-made man making himself into a squire. If one accepts this view of Kipling as successful parvenu then his view of the English social order becomes, interestingly, not unlike Wells's (although Wells obviously had further to rise): the envious, resentful, admiring, simplified perception that an intelligent outsider might be expected to have of the life of the English ascendancy.

5. DANDYISM

In the 1890s writers responded to the anxieties of the day by detaching themselves, by insisting on their isolation. They developed the myth of the heroically isolated and doomed artist, Yeats's 'Tragic Generation', or they adopted what Holbrook Jackson describes as the role of the 'Dandy', 'whose media are himself and his own personal appearance [and who] looks upon his personality as a movement in the pageant of life'[30] If one thinks of Wilde, Beardsley, Richard Le Gallienne, Beerbohm, Henry Harland and Corvo, one can see that these two roles, the solitary and the dandy, were closely related. All these writers created for themselves public identities which were loosely upper-class and—this is the important point—detached from the economic and social laws governing modern urban society. Harland and Corvo invented fake aristocratic titles for themselves, Le Gallienne adopted the 'Le' when he moved to London from Liverpool. Wilde's belief in his own detachment from the laws, in both the general and the restricted sense, which governed the rest of mankind can be seen to have contributed substantially to his downfall. After 1900 when, as Yeats put it, 'Everybody got down off his stilts' (introduction to the *Oxford Book of Modern Verse*, 1936) the cult of the *invented* literary personality and the notion of the artist's self-tormenting isolation tended to fade.

Yet there were interesting and important exceptions to this. Arthur Machen and Corvo, for example, perpetuated the 1890s styles in their works and their lives. Arthur Machen was a writer of considerable talent who rightly believed that his career had been eclipsed by the Wilde scandal, and poured his frustrations with the literary life into an important novel, *The Hill of Dreams* (completed by 1897 but not published until 1907).

In the hero of *The Hill of Dreams*, 'Lucian Taylor', Machen creates a figure like Joyce's Stephen Dedalus, an isolated provincial writer seeking an appropriate image. Joyce's Stephen finds his image of the self in the winged figure, the 'fabulous artificer' ascending above Sandymount Strand in the central epiphany of *A Portrait of the Artist as a Young Man* (1916). Lucian finds no such consoling image: instead he becomes lost in a labyrinthine inner world with its own imaginary civilisation–the Roman city of Avallaunius, which is revealed to him beneath the Welsh hills of his home–and its own religion, the practice of Witchcraft.

The Hill of Dreams could be taken to exemplify the epistemological crisis: none of the supposed facts in the novel are reliable, Lucian's hallucinations and the outer reality are indistinguishable until they are put into perspective by the novel's close. Lucian has suffered loss of memory in London and dies of drug-addiction in a slum-house belonging to a prostitute (the witch-mistress of his imagination) who has robbed him. For most of the novel's length the reader is trapped in the inner drama of Lucian's consciousness and finds himself in a treacherous continuum of experience of which the elements are inseparable.

If Machen's Lucian Taylor is an extreme portrait of the self as solitary hero, Corvo's Arthur Rose in *Hadrian VII* (1904) is a striking continuation of the 1890s hero-as-dandy. Corvo's personal life was one of a dandyism by which he formalised his aggressions and secured for himself a social ascendancy based on nothing. The imaginary Italian title, 'Baron Corvo', the non-existent ordination implied by the 'Fr.' to which he contracted his first name, Frederick, the polite Venetian address from which he sent his appeals for money and his pornographic letters (the Bucintoro Rowing Club: Corvo was, indeed, a member and often slept there in a boat when he was penniless and homeless) all contribute to that precarious magnificence wrung from circumstances of awesome humiliation which characterises Corvo's career.

Hadrian VII is a compelling novel up to and including the moment at which George Arthur Rose is elected Pope:

> 'It was on him, on him, that all eyes were, why did he not kneel?
>
> 'Again the voice of the Cardinal-Archdeacon intoned, "Reverend Lord, the Sacred College has elected thee to be the Successor of St Peter. Wilt thou accept pontificality?"
>
> 'There was no mistake. The awful tremendous question was addressed to him.
>
> 'A murmur from the bishop prompted him, "The response is Volo—or Nolo".
>
> 'The surging in his temples, the booming in his ears, miraculously ceased. He took one long slow breath: crossed right hand over left upon his breast: became like a piece of pageant; and responded "I will"' (pp. 84–5).

'Became like a piece of pageant': the phrase anticipates Holbrook Jackson's definition of a Dandy as one who 'looks upon his personality as a movement in the pageant of life' (see above, p. 17). It also points to the novel's central weakness. The difficulty with the novel from this moment onwards is that the plot runs out of invention and the Pope is more 'a piece of pageant' than a human being. Beyond covering the walls of the Vatican with brown paper, impressing the Cardinals by his capacity to digest cream and displaying a childish arbitrariness over details of ritual, Pope Hadrian *does* very little. The novel is like two insignificant islands linked by a disproportionately ornate bridge. The islands are Rose's penury and his shadowy involvement as Pope in European politics—the plot, in short—and the bridge is the obsessive elaboration of his own image as Pope which is the novel's real subject.

Dandyism in its more frivolous sense is continuously present in the minor and popular literature of 1890–1914, as though the differences between Victorian and Edwardian felt in the upper literary atmosphere were scarcely registered in these lower depths. The undergraduate hero of Benson's *The Babe, B.A.: Being the Uneventful History of a Young Gentleman at the University of Cambridge* (1897) is the ancestor of Saki's graceful and infuriating young men Clovis Sangrail in *The Chronicles of Clovis* and Bassington in *The Unbearable Bassington* (both 1912). P.G. Wodehouse's Psmith, the upper-class anarchist who is expelled from Eton, is of the same mould.

Indeed, in Wodehouse's work the dandy, already an 1890s survival into the Edwardian world, was perpetuated for much of the twentieth century. His schoolboy stories of the Edwardian period are taken by Orwell, rightly I think, as works of a precocious maturity in which Wodehouse remained stuck for the rest of his long life (George Orwell, 'In Defence of P.G. Wodehouse', *The Collected Essays*, vol. 3 (Secker and Warburg, 1968), pp. 341–55).

Psmith's characteristics are faintly reminiscent of Stalky's in *Stalky and Co.*, physical courage, disregard of the rules, tribal solidarity and cunning. But unlike Kipling's schoolboys, who are capable of complex emotions (Stalky's sense of personal affront in 'The Flag of Their Country', for example), Wodehouse's figures are capable only of aggression. The dominant motif of the dialogue is the insult, of which there are many good examples. One of the boys says of his adolescent moustache: 'Heaps of people tell me I ought to have it waxed'. 'What it really needs is a top-dressing with guano', replies Psmith (*Mike: A Public-School Story*, 1909, p. 241). Psmith becomes the central figure of the first Wodehouse novel to have an adult setting, *Psmith in the City* (1910). After the Great War Psmith splits into two: his effortless social superiority becomes an attribute of Bertie Wooster, his guile and know-how become characteristics of the indispensable Jeeves.

In the Edwardian romances of high life by Elinor Glyn and Henry Harland dandyism becomes associated with sexual passivity. Three of Harland's Edwardian novels, *The Cardinal's Snuffbox* (1900), *The Lady Paramount* (1902) and *My Friend Prospero* (1904) have identical plots: strong rich girl meets weak rich boy, complications involving mistaken identities are cleared away, they close with each other. Each novel is characterised by enormous wealth, Italian settings, cardinals, and elegant dialogue filled with literary quotations. They are all readable in a tinselly way, and the last novel, *The Royal End*, completed by Harland's widow and published posthumously, has had stronger claims made for it.[40] This novel has a Jamesian heroine, Ruth Adgate, whose personality is filled out with rather more detail than is to be found in the preceding novels and who marries only the *second* richest man in the cast of characters.

While Harland's novels were commercial entertainments Elinor Glyn's

Three Weeks (1907) was the work of a writer who took herself seriously and saw the writing of her sexually explicit novel as an act of personal liberation.[41] Paul Verdayne, her gentleman hero, is 'polished and lazy and strong', a 'clear, insular, arrogant Englishman', a 'Sleeping Beauty' who needs to be sexually awoken by the dominant foreign lady, the 'Imperatskoye', whom he meets in a hotel (p. 64). *Three Weeks* is an uneven, naive, touching work which should not be consigned immediately to the dustbin. Its snobbishness is breath-taking (Paul 'left Oxford with a record for all that should turn a beautiful Englishman into a beautiful athlete' (p. 6)) but its sexual energy is effective where it manages to avoid being absurd.

6. THE IMPERIAL ADVENTURE

The figure of the dandy is balanced by the imperial adventurer who enjoys an equally unbroken continuity in popular literature from the nineteenth to the twentieth centuries. The assumptions underlying Rider Haggard's romances are present and unchanged in such works as A.E.W Mason's *The Broken Road* (1908) and John Buchan's *Prester John* (1910).[42] *Prester John* is a readable and in some ways subtle work. The central protagonists are Davie Crawfurd, the nineteen-year-old Scottish narrator, and his opponent John Laputa, the black Napoleon of Southern Africa who is planning a nationalist rising against the whites. Laputa is a figure of masculine force presented with what seems unmistakable, though presumably unconscious, homoerotic excitement by the adolescent narrator.

Davie Crawfurd sees Laputa stripped naked for the mysterious ceremony in which he puts on the ruby necklet which had belonged to the legendary black King Chaka and originally, it seems, to the Queen of Sheba. Stirred by this sight he acknowledges Laputa as a natural hero: 'I knew that, to the confusion of all talk about equality, God has ordained some men to be kings and others to serve' (*Prester John*, p. 187).

The use of an adolescent narrator is strategically successful. Davie Crawfurd does not have the settled racial attitudes of a mature white imperialist (though he *is*, of course, loyal to the empire) and he can be temporarily demoralised by Laputa's physical presence: 'I longed for a leader who should master me and make my soul his own' (p. 192) he exclaims, and in the course of his lyrical response to Laputa's physical splendour notes that 'he put a hand on my saddle, and I remember noting how slim and fine it was, more like a high-bred woman's than a man's' (p. 150).

When he recovers from this intoxication he quotes (again, presumably unconsciously) the title of Conrad's famous story of a white imperialist's moral collapse: 'Last night I had looked into the heart of darkness, and the sight had terrified me' (p. 200).

The most conspicuous literary debt is to Rider Haggard: the notion of a tradition of heroism handed down to the modern African from an extinct civilisation, the fabulous hidden treasure (the Chaka's necklet) and the mysterious cavern in which Davie is almost trapped are obvious borrowings from *She* and *King Solomon's Mines*. It is possible that the villainous Portuguese trader, Henriques, known to Davie as the Portugoose, owes something to Conrad's Cornelius. But the novel is interesting precisely for the way in which it refuses to be like Conrad. In young Davie it has a potentially Conradian narrator, flexible, pragmatic, emotionally stirred by the force animating the opposing side. But the fundamental imperial assumption of the novel is so secure that Davie's sympathy for Laputa cannot disturb it. The political frame and the emotional energies of the novel exist apart from each other, so to speak, as though unaware of each other's existence.

One of the confusing features of the period, then, is the way in which popular literature continues to reproduce the received dramatic stereotypes as though nothing had changed. With certain obvious exceptions (Wells and Shaw, Chesterton and Belloc) it is broadly true that among the major Edwardian writers there is a tendency for the artist to subordinate his personality to his art. Joyce's perception of the artist-as-hero formulated (though not published) within the decade, is relevant here. The artist is 'like the God of the creation', a remote figure 'paring his fingernails' whose relationship with his work is one of detachment: he is 'within or behind or beyond or above his handiwork'.[43]

With this sense of a need to subordinate the self to the craft went a willingness to collaborate, to work together. In *The Private Papers of Henry Ryecroft* (1903) Gissing describes with stoic detachment the harm that his self-imposed isolation as a writer had done to his art (pp. 21–2). The Edwardians, by contrast, even those who were temperamentally solitaries like Conrad and Ford, were willing to get together. They pooled ideas, they argued about technique, they joined the Fabian movement, they collaborated on periodicals: Forster, though not on the editorial board, worked closely with Lowes Dickinson on *The Independent Review*, Wells and Shaw were associated with *The New Age* (edited by Alfred Orage and Holbrook Jackson), and Conrad can be regarded as a joint founder, with Ford Madox Ford, of *The English Review*.

Simple proximity, too, helped to break down the isolation of these writers' lives: Kipling, Wells, Henry James, Conrad and Ford all lived for a time within easy reach of each other in Kent and Sussex, and attracted a steady flow of literary visitors. And the emergence of the literary agent as an intermediary between author and publisher gave a new kind of cohesiveness and professionalism to the literary life. There is a needed book waiting to be written about J.B. Pinker, the tough Scot who was literary agent to Bennett, Wells, Ford, Conrad, Galsworthy and Henry James. It was easy for a writer to make a living (though Conrad did not find it so): indeed the printed word, as a medium, was enjoying its last few years of undisputed primacy, and it was possible for best-selling writers like Wells and Bennett to enjoy the kind of life-styles that were to be associated with film stars in the 'twenties and 'thirties.

Working in a period of anxiety and acute moral uncertainty, socially integrated but morally bereft, the major Edwardians can be seen to be living a paradox. Their gregariousness is a form of defence from the epistemological crisis. Reliably sensitive to the pressures of his time, C.F.G. Masterman expressed the situation in these terms: 'Belief in religion, as a conception of life dependent upon supernatural sanctions or as a revelation of a purpose and meaning beyond the actual business of the day, is slowly but steadily fading from the modern city race. Tolerance, kindliness, sympathy, civilisation continually improve. Affirmation of any responsibility, beyond that to self and to humanity, continually declines' (*The Condition of England*, 1909, p. 266).

At a personal level tolerance, kindliness and sympathy work very well: the Bloomsbury cult of personal relations, the loyalty that all Conrad's friends showed him in his financial difficulties, the surprising kindness that Wells showed to Gissing are local examples of these virtues in action. But beyond the personal context the period displays a gap, a lack of connection, between moral conviction and effective action. Some commentaries have suggested that this disfunction, or paralysis, is the over-riding factor which permitted England to drift into the Great War.[44]

Individual energy directed to the public arena seems to have been largely fruitless. The enormous labours of Beatrice and Sidney Webb, the powerhouse of the Fabian movement, had little impact on national policy. In prominent altruistic writers like Galsworthy and Granville-Barker there was a vivid awareness of social evils without much in the way of proposals for their correction. Granville-Barker's *Waste* points to the suicidal hypocrisy of a system which can destroy a gifted, innovative politician because of his sexual behaviour. Galsworthy's *Strife* is specific about the evils of industrial conflict and mismanagement but has no clear recommendations to make. The case of Galsworthy's *Justice* is slightly different: it seems likely that

Galsworthy's 'Minute on Separate Confinement' personally forwarded to the Home Secretary by his friend Masterman combined with the publicity attracted by the play did contribute to the reduction of the mandatory term of solitary confinement to a uniform three months for all prisoners.[45]

Wells, of course, had very specific proposals for reordering the nation, but was too impatient to study carefully (as the Webbs did) the political realities he was dealing with. Central to his doctrine in the Edwardian period was the notion that scientific intelligence—himself and those who thought like him—should form an oligarchy to govern the state.[46] Also Wells was too impatient to be politically effective; when people failed to take up his ideas immediately he lost his temper and sulked. Hence the image of the sighted man who is hounded to his death by the blind in 'The Country of the Blind' (1911) and the new master-race of giants who are persecuted by frightened normal-sized humanity in *The Food of the Gods* (1904).

7. THE ROLE OF THE HERO

Effective moral action in the public arena is the role of a hero, and one of the persistent, shared intuitions of the major Edwardians is that the modern world is inhospitable to heroism. Conrad and Ford write with an acute consciousness of the problem of a hero in a world which has no role for him to play. Conrad's Heyst and Ford's Tietjens are the most fully articulated embodiments of this theme, but it is present throughout their work. The whole of *Nostromo* can be seen as an ironic study of traditional male heroic qualities neutered by the conditions of the modern world; and to compound the irony Conrad has set his study of the male will to power and its final ineffectiveness, the self-destructiveness of the pressures within Gould, Nostromo and Decoud, in a South American setting where the word *macho* was coined, a culture which sets supreme value on male force.[47]

In his Victorian novel *Cashel Byron's Profession* (1886, revised 1901) Shaw displays a robust faith in effective male force, aggression, *virtu*. Cashel, the gentleman turned boxer, is personally irresistible, a glamorous violent animal among the inhibited urban males of London: 'His light alert step, and certain gamesome assurance of manner, marked him off from a genteelly promenading middle-aged gentleman, a trudging workman, and a vigorously striding youth' (pp. 152–3).

At the turn of the century and in the Edwardian period, by contrast, Shaw's plays reflect the irrelevance and inefficacy of male force in the modern world. In many of his plays power is vested in the female: Vivie Warren defeating Sir George Crofts in *Mrs Warren's Profession*, Lady Cicely

Waynflete outfacing both Captain Brasshound's romantic vindictiveness and Sir Howard Hallam's impersonal murderousness in *Captain Brassbound's Conversion*, Anne Whitefield subordinating Jack Tanner to the 'eternal purpose'—the perpetuation of the species—in *Man and Superman*, Eliza demonstrating to Henry Higgins that she can do without him in *Pygmalion*.

If the man does win he does so by guile rather than force. Undershaft, in *Major Barbara* (performed 1905, published 1907), is an armaments manufacturer whose career is a triumph of the will, of the doctrine 'thou shalt starve ere I starve' (p. 172). He defeats the play's strong women, his wife Britomart who is an embodiment of aristocratic obstinacy, and his daughter Barbara, the Salvation Army 'Major' of the title whose faith he destroys by demonstrating that the Salvation Army depends on money produced by amoral industrialists like himself. By the end of the play he has won over the whole of his initially outraged family (and his adopted son, the 'foundling' Adolphus Cusins) to his view that 'money and gunpowder' are the 'two things necessary for salvation' (p. 116), and that the seven deadly sins are 'food, clothing, firing, rent, taxes, respectability and children' (p. 172).

Heartbreak House (written 1916–17) gives a retrospect of the theme of heroism in Shaw's Edwardian plays. Undershaft, the Mephistopheles of *Major Barbara*, has become senile Captain Shotover, the octogenarian armaments inventor who is kept going by gin. Captain Brassbound's successor is Hector Hushabye, international adventurer, liar and braggart (both portraits owe something to Cunninghame Graham's reputation). The dominant women of the previous plays are succeeded by Ellie Dunn, the mesmerist who is able to hypnotise and control 'Boss' Mangan, a violent capitalist, and Captain Shotover himself.

These figures, with their different kinds of strength, are powerless in the context of the war. England is a ship navigated by an upper class which has fatally abdicated from its responsibilities:

Captain Shotover: 'The captain is in his bunk, drinking bottled ditch-water; and the crew is gambling in the forecastle. She will strike and sink and split. Do you think the laws of God will be suspended in favour of England because you were born in it?' (p. 177) The image is perhaps a conscious recall of Captain Brassbound's exclamation of despair when he has been deprived of his purpose in life—avenging his mother's death—by Lady Cicely's intervention: 'I was steering a course and had work in hand. Give a man health and a course to steer; and he'll never stop to trouble about whether he's happy or not' (*Captain Brassbound's Conversion* (performed 1900, published 1901, p. 411)).

An endangered ship as an image of humanity's loss of moral direction is a constant feature of Conrad's writing—in *The Nigger of the Narcissus*, 'Typhoon', 'Falk', *Lord Jim*, *Chance*—and is also used with considerable power by Masterman and Bertrand Russell. In Masterman's *The Condition of England* the image is associated with the topical fears of invasion, class war, and the degeneracy of the race:

> 'With the vertical division between nation and nation armed to the teeth, and the horizontal division between rich and poor which has become a cosmopolitan fissure, the future of progress is still doubtful and precarious. Humanity—at best—appears but as a shipwrecked crew which has taken refuge on a narrow ledge of rock, beaten by wind and wave; which cannot tell how many, if any at all, will survive when the long night gives place to morning. The wise man will still go softly all his days; working always for greater economic equality on the one hand, for understanding between estranged peoples on the other; apprehending always how slight an effort of stupidity or violence could strike a death-blow to twentieth-century civilisation, and elevate the forces of destruction triumphant over the ruins of a world' (p. 303).

In his extraordinarily emotional essay, 'The Free Man's Worship', Russell uses a version of the same image to express man's solitariness in a godless universe:

> 'We see, surrounding the narrow raft illumined by the flickering light of human comradeship, the dark ocean on whose rolling waves we toss for a brief hour; from the great night without, a child blast breaks in upon our refuge; all the loneliness of humanity amid hostile forces is concentrated upon the individual soul, which must struggle alone, with what of courage it can command' (pp. 421–2).

Edwardian England, then, is a relatively stable and yet uneasy culture in which 'odours from the abyss' reminded the upper classes of a level of poverty and 'degeneracy' which they preferred not to acknowledge, and in which the threat of a European war was increasingly felt: a culture in which the great Victorian imperatives, Christianity, Monarchy, Empire had largely been replaced by secular consolations which for some writers were still current–rural England, adventure in action, the sense of social ascendancy which expressed itself in dandyism—but for others were themselves devalued and under attack.

NOTES

1. Richard Ellmann, 'The Two Faces of Edward' (1959), in *Golden Codgers* (1973), p.113.

2. J.P. Stern, *On Realism* (1973), p.158.

3. P.N. Furbank, 'Chesterton the Edwardian' *G.K. Chesterton: A Centenary Celebration* (1974), p.16.

4. Cyril Connolly, *Enemies of Promise* (1938), p.23.

5. Frank Swinnerton, *The Georgian Literary Scene, 1910-1935* (1935), p.2.

6. Roy Campbell, 'Contemporary poetry', in Edgell Rickword (ed.), *Scrutinies* (1928), p.169.

7. Rebecca West, *The Strange Necessity: Essays and Reviews* (1928), p.199.

8. For a representative 'high life' treatment of the Edwardian period see R.J. Minney, *The Edwardian Age* (1964).

9. Frank Kermode, *The Sense of an Ending* (1967), p.97.

10. See my discussion of 'Dandyism' below, pp.17–20.

11. See J. Hillis Miller, *The Disappearance of God* (1963). For the impact of Darwin's work on literature and literary criticism see also Leo J. Henkin, *Darwinism in the English Novel, 1860-1910* (1963) and Tom Gibbons, *Rooms in the Darwin Hotel: Studies in English Literary Criticism and Ideas, 1890–1920* (1973).

12. Quoted from F.H.W. Myers by David Daiches, *Some Late Victorian Attitudes* (1967), p.10.

13. See Graham Hough's discussion of aestheticism as an expression of a dethroned religious impulse in *The Last Romantics* (1948).

14. Daiches, p.11.

15. Walter Pater, *The Renaissance* (1873), p.236.

16. Arthur Symons, *The Symbolist Movement in Literature* (1899), p.10. Here the process described by Ellmann in which Christianity, having died, is revived in the form of metaphor, can be seen taking place.

17. For the influence of Moore's book on the Bloomsbury Group, see J.K. Johnstone, *The Bloomsbury Group* (1954).

18. R.H. Benson was a Catholic priest, a convert, the son of an Archbishop of Canterbury, and the brother of two other writers. The Benson brothers occupy a representative minor place in literary scene. E.F. Benson's *The Babe, B.A.* (1897) is a readable comic novel about undergraduate life and his *As we Were* (1930) is a modish memoir of the 1890s and the Edwardian period. A.C. Benson, Master of Magdalene College, Cambridge, and author of the stiflingly complacent don's reminiscences *From a College Window* (1906) also wrote the words for Elgar's 'Land of Hope and Glory'.

19. See the discussion of this novel in Claud Cockburn, *Best-Sellers: The Books that Everyone Read, 1900–1939* (1972).

20. E.M. Forster, *Goldsworthy Lowes Dickinson* (1934), p.92.

21. First published in *The Independent Review*, 1, 3 (December 1903), pp.415–24. This was one of a series of articles by atheist philosophers on religious experience in a Godless world. Goldsworthy Lowes Dickinson, who was on the *Independent's* editorial board,

contributed several such articles between 1903 and 1907. Compare also William James's *The Varieties of Religious Experience: A Study in Human Nature* (1902).

22. Ian Watt, 'Impressionism and symbolism in "Heart of Darkness"', in Norman Sherry (ed.), *Joseph Conrad: A Commemoration* (1974), p.40.

23. Bertrand Russell, *Autobiography* (1970), p.145.

24. Ibid., p.145.

25. Bernard Bergonzi, *The Early H.G. Wells* (1961), p.56.

26. For further examples of the 'abyss' and of the descent into working-class life seen as anthropological exploration, see Peter Keating (ed.), *Into Unknown England 1866-1913* (1976).

27. Somerset Maugham's *Liza of Lambeth* (1897) and Robert Tressell's *The Ragged Trousered Philanthropists* (1914) are similarly based on the degenerative effects of urban poverty, although in these images the specific image of the 'abyss' does not occur in the same way. It is an odd coincidence, incidentally, that the heroine of *Liza of Lambeth* (a story of prostitution and urban violence) and the heroes of *The Hole in the Wall* (a story of smuggling and murder) and of Conrad's and Ford's *Romance* (a story of piracy and adventure) all have the surname 'Kemp'.

28. For an extensive list of invasion novels and a brief discussion of the genre, see Bernard Bergonzi, *The Early H.G. Wells*, pp.12–14.

29. See above, p.7.

30. See my discussion of *Maurice* below, pp.208–13.

31. This was a much discussed topic in enlightened circles. There are several articles deploring the motor-car's encroachment on rural peace in G.M. Trevelyan's *Independent Review* (1903-7), some of them by Forster's friend Goldsworthy Lowes Dickinson. Kipling, on the other hand, loved motoring and writes lyrically about its pleasure in the opening pages of 'They'.

32. See Paul Fussell, *The Great War and Modern Memory* (1975).

33. E.M. Forster, *Aspects of the Novel* (1927) p.115.

34. E.M. Forster, *The Celestial Omnibus: And Other Stories* (1911), pp.1–42, 129–42.

35. See Peter Green, *Kenneth Grahame* (1959).

36. Angus Wilson, *The Strange Ride of Rudyard Kipling* (1977), p.268.

37. Wilson, p.266.

38. Kingsley Amis, *Rudyard Kipling and His World* (1975), pp.97, 98.

39. Holbrook Jackson, *Romance and Reality* (1911), pp.198–9. See also Ellen Moers, *The Dandy* (1960).

40. See Karl Beckson, *Henry Harland: His Life and Work* (1978).

41. Galsworthy's *Joceylyn* is a comparable case; see the discussion of Galsworthy, below pp. 183-8.

42. See the discussion of these novels in Brian V. Street, *The Savage in Literature: Representations of 'Primitive' Society in English Fiction, 1858–1920* (1975).

43. James Joyce, *A Portrait of the Artist as a Young Man* (1916), p.160.

44. See especially George Dangerfield, *The Strange Death of Liberal England* (1935).

45. Catherine Dupré, *John Galsworthy: A Biography* (1976), p.151.

46. See the conception of the 'Samurai', the oligarchy in Wells's *A Modern Utopia* (1905) and the discussion of this idea in the first number of *The New Age* 1, no.1 (2 May 1907), pp.9–11.

47. I am indebted to John Patterson, of Linacre College, Oxford, for this point.

JOHN McCLURE

Problematic Presence:
The Colonial Other in Kipling and Conrad

Serious fiction, as M.M. Bakhtin tells us, dramatises the play of discourses, the competition between different ideologically loaded 'languages' each attempting to set its mark on the world, establish its definitions as authoritative. At the end of the nineteenth century, when Kipling and Conrad were writing some of the most impressive colonial fiction in English, the ethics of imperial expansion was being seriously debated. One issue in the debate was the status of the colonised peoples, the Indians about whom Kipling wrote, the Malays and Africans of Conrad's fiction. Social scientists, liberal humanitarians, missionaries, colonial administrators and planters— each group defined the subject peoples of empire in its own way. But a strong consensus in the west held all peoples of other races to be morally, intellectually and socially inferior to white Europeans, and saw their ostensible inferiority as a justification for domination.

Artists tend to write both within the conventional discourses of their times, and against them. So it is with Kipling and Conrad. Their portraits of other peoples are, to borrow a term from *Heart of Darkness*, inconclusive: drawn now in the conventional terminology of racist discourses, now in terms that challenge these discourses and the image of the other they prescribe. Conrad's especially, is what Kenneth Burke calls 'a disintegrating art': it 'converts each simplicity into a complexity', 'ruins the possibility of ready hierarchies,' and by so doing 'works corrosively upon ... expansionist

From *The Black Presence in English Literature*, edited by David Dabydeen. © 1985 by Manchester University Press.

certainties'.[1] Conrad persistently questions the two basic propositions of European racism: the notion that, as Brian Street puts it, 'a particular "character" could be attributed to a whole people ... a "race" might be gullible, faithful, brave, childlike, savage, bloodthirsty';[2] and the notion that the races are arranged hierarchically, with the white race, or perhaps the Anglo-Saxon race, at the top. In novel after novel Conrad breaks down the crude dichotomies (white/black, civilised/savage, benevolent/blood-thirsty, mature/childish, hardworking/lazy) of racist discourses, ruins the ready racial hierarchies they underwrite, and so undermines the expansionistic certainties of imperialism. In his stories, written in the 1880s and '90s, Kipling uses many of these same crude dichotomies to defend imperialism, but in *Kim* (1901) he breaks with convention, offering instead a powerful criticism of racist modes of representation. In both Kipling's *Kim* and Conrad's Malay novels, we find powerfully persuasive representations of the colonised peoples, representations that identify them neither as innocents nor as demons, but as human beings, complex and difficult, to be approached with sympathy, respect, and caution.

In the much neglected 'Author's Note' to his first novel, *Almayer's Folly* (1895), Joseph Conrad describes a project of representation that informs much of his colonial fiction. Europeans, he insists in the 'Note', have the wrong picture of 'strange peoples' and 'far-off countries.' They 'think that in those distant lands all joy is a yell and a war dance, all pathos is a howl and a ghastly grin of filed teeth, and that the solution of all problems is found in the barrel of a revolver or in the point of an assegai.' But 'it is not so': the 'picture of life' in these far-off lands is essentially 'the same picture' as one sees in Europe, equally elaborate and many-sided. And the 'common mortals' who dwell there deserve respect and sympathy. In short, the fashionable European 'verdict of contemptuous dislike' for these peoples 'has nothing to do with justice.'[3]

The far-off land that Conrad portrays in *Almayer's Folly* is the Malay Archipelago, the strange peoples Malays and Arabs. In spite of its ringing preface, *Almayer's Folly* is full of conventionally dismissive descriptions of these peoples: the omniscient narrator makes much of their 'savage nature' (p. 69) and 'half-formed, savage minds' (p. 116), and uses 'civilised' as if the word referred to a radically different and manifestly superior mode of existence. But the story related by the narrator tends to cast doubt on such dismissive characteristations. The novel's protagonist, a Dutch colonialist named Almayer, prides himself on being, as a white, infinitely superior to the

Malays among whom he dwells. But the story is about Almayer's folly, and events show him to be intellectually and psychologically weaker than the Malays who oppose him.

Almayer's daughter Nina, whose mother is a Malay, occupies a pivotal position between the two opposed communities. She has been given 'a good glimpse of civilised life' (p. 42) in Singapore and an equally intense exposure to Malay culture in the up-river settlement where Almayer works as a trader. Conrad, having established her divided allegiance and unique authority, uses her to challenge Almayer's claims of superiority. Comparing the two communities, Nina at first fails to sees any difference: 'It seemed to Nina', the narrator reports, that 'whether they traded in brick godowns or on the muddy river bank; whether they reached after much or little; whether they made love under the shadows of the great trees or in the shadow of the cathedral on the Singapore promenade' there was no difference, only 'the same manifestations of love and hate and of sordid greed' (p. 43). If Nina has, as the narrator claims, 'lost the power to discriminate' (p. 43), she has gained the power to recognise essential similarities that Europeans such as the narrator are anxious to overlook. This passage is the first of many in Conrad's fiction that insist on the existence of such similarities and dismiss European claims to all but absolute difference and superiority.

Although Nina can find at first no essential difference between 'civilised' and 'savage' ways of life, she ultimately comes to prefer the latter, and her choice has the force of a judgement against European pretences. Nina's mother, who influences her decision, makes her own articulate case against these pretences. Her bitter accusations, dismissed by the narrator as 'savage ravings' (p. 151), reveal the prejudices of the oppressed as well as those of their oppressors. Whites, she tells Nina, '"speak lies. And they think lies because they despise us that are better than they are, but not so strong"' (p. 151). Racism, Conrad suggests, is not an exclusively white phenomenon; but the distinction between speaking lies and thinking them marks Nina's mother's speech as something more than savage raving, and the narrator, by dismissing it as such, only lends weight in the woman's charges.

Almayer's Folly is something of a literary curiosity: I can think of no other novel in which an omniscient narrator's commentaries are consistently undermined by the actions and observations of characters he disparages. Whether Conrad intended to produce this effect or not, he never produces it again. In the novels that follow *Almayer's Folly* the narrators distance themselves from the discourses of racism, adopting them, when they adopt them at all, only provisionally.

An Outcast of the Islands (1896) is set like its predecessor in the remote

Malayan settlement of Sambir. Once again the action centres on a successful Malay counter—offensive against western domination, and once again Conrad depicts the Malays who lead the campaign as patient, resourceful and determined men. Babalatchi, who plans and directs the campaign against Captain Tom Lingard, the English adventurer who monopolises commercial and political power in Sambir, is richly and respectfully drawn. He has been a pirate, his methods are unscrupulous, but they are also brilliantly effective. When Conrad calls him a 'statesman', then, there may be a slightly ironic inflection to his voice, but the irony is pointed at the western reader, not at Babalatchi. Syed Abdulla, Babalatchi's Arab ally, is even more impressive. Conrad speaks of 'the unswerving piety of his heart and ... the religious solemnity of his demeanour', of 'his ability, his will—strong to obstinacy— his wisdom beyond his years', and of his 'great family', which with its various successful trading enterprises lies 'like a network over the islands'.[4] Thus when white characters refer to Asians as 'miserable savages' (p. 126) and boast of their own 'pure and superior descent' (p. 271), the vicious stupidity of racist discourse becomes evident.

Once again in this novel Malay characters offer eloquent and devastating assessments of the white men who rule them. Aissa, a Malay woman courted, compromised and then scorned by Willems, the European 'outcast' of the novel's title, refers repeatedly to Europe as a 'land of lies and evil from which nothing but misfortune ever comes to us—who are not white' (p. 144). Babalatchi's rejoinders to Captain Lingard are even more corrosive of European certainties. Lingard, defending his domination of Sambir, asserts that if he ever spoke to its nominal Malay ruler 'like an elder brother, it was for your good—for the good of all'. 'This is a white man's talk', responds Babalatchi, 'with bitter exultation',

> I know you. That is how you all talk while you load your guns and sharpen your swords; and when you are ready, then to those who are weak, you say: 'Obey me and be happy, or die!' You are strange, you white men. You think it is only your wisdom and your virtue and your happiness that are true. (p. 226)

Babalatchi's searing indictment of European hypocrisy and ethnocentricism is corroborated in a number of ways. The narrator makes it clear, for instance, that Europeans do feel racial antipathy and that the sources of this feeling are irrational. Thus when Willems dreams of escaping from Sambir, his desire is attributed to 'the flood of hate, disgust, and contempt of a white man for that blood which is not his blood, for that race that is not his race'

(p. 152). This flood of feeling, which overmasters Willems' 'reason', resembles the 'feeling of condemnation' that overcomes Lingard when he imagines Willems' illicit relation with Aissa. And this reaction, too, is described as 'illogical'. It is an 'accursed feeling made up of disdain, of anger, and of the sense of superior virtue that leaves us deaf, blind, contemptuous and stupid before anything which is not like ourselves' (p. 254).

If Conrad challenges the European representation of Malays as uniformly savage and inferior, he does not do so in order to replace that representation with an idyllic one. Babalatchi and his comrades, Lakamba and Omar, are Malay adventurers, blood-thirsty, lawless men who consider 'throat cutting, kidnapping, slave-dealing' to be 'manly pursuits' (p. 52). The peace Lingard enforces seems in many ways preferable to the anarchy they admire. But Lingard's peace is also a kind of tyranny, and Adulla's ascension to power seems to restore some degree of freedom without destroying that peace. In the end, then, Conrad suggests that any generalised ennoblement of one race or another is as inappropriate as generalised dismissal: there are certainly differences of custom and belief between cultures, but the most important differences cut across racial lines and render racial affiliation meaningless as an indicator of intelligence, character, or virtue.

This same line of argument is developed in *Lord Jim* (1900),[5] which explores, among other things, the relation between a Malay community and its genuinely popular English ruler. When Jim, another European outcast, arrives in Patusan, another upriver settlement in the Malay Archipelago, three local factions are struggling for dominance: Rajah Allang's local Malays, Doramin's party of Malay settlers from Celebes, and Sherif Ali's forces, drawn from the tribes of the interior. Ambitious and utterly reckless, Jim quickly earns a reputation for valour, allies himself with Doramin's faction, and engineers a military victory over Sherif Ali so dramatic that no second campaign is necessary. By this means he becomes the actual ruler of Patusan, and a widely admired ruler. As a white, a member of the race which has conquered the Archipelago, he is automatically feared and, however grudgingly, respected by the Malays. As a fearless warrior, a successful military leader, a peacemaker, and an even-handed governor, he is widely venerated. Conrad describes Jim's triumph, then, in a manner that makes the Malays' acquiescence and approval seem reasonable, a sign not of innate inferiority but of a reasonable reaction to a complex situation. If a 'Jim-myth' (p. 171) arises, it does so because Jim has saved the community from the bloody deadlock of factional strife, in which 'utter insecurity for life and property was the normal condition' (p. 139).

But Conrad, having exposed the logic of colonial acquiescence, goes on to elucidate the logic of rebellion. Like Lingard in *An Outcast of the Islands*, Jim proclaims his unqualified dedication to the Malay community he rules: 'He declared ... that their welfare was his welfare, their losses his losses, their mourning his mourning' (p. 238). And once again, Conrad tests and refutes this claim to absolute identification. Jim, for reasons that include a misguided sense of racial allegiance, refuses to lead a necessary campaign against piratical white intruders, and these intruders, set free, slaughter a company of Malay warriors, including Doramin's noble son. Conrad's point here, as in *An Outcast of the Islands*, is clear: even the most well-intentioned white ruler will experience a conflict of cultural interests, will be torn between allegiance to his native European community and allegiance to the community he rules. And the resolution of that conflict will be at the expense of his subjects, will justify, ultimately, their resistance to his continued domination.

Conrad makes this point once again in *Heart of Darkness* (1902), but in a most unfortunate way. For here it is the European novelist, Conrad himself, who succumbs to the interests of his own community and betrays his colonial subjects, the Africans he 'represents'. Speaking through Marlow, Conrad identifies the Africans, not consistently but emphatically, as demons and fiends, insists that 'the picture of life' in the Congo forests is appallingly different from the picture in Europe.

In the early stages of Marlow's narrative, the familiar invitations to sympathetic identification with the colonised are still in play. The Congolese are described as victims of a particularly brutal imperialism, compared favourably to their European masters, depicted in ways that stress their kinship with other men. Noting that the villages along the trail to the Central Station are deserted, Marlow remarks, 'Well, if a lot of mysterious niggers armed with all kinds of fearful weapons suddenly took to travelling on the road between Deal and Gravesend, catching the yokels right and left to carry heavy loads for them, I fancy every farm and cottage thereabouts would get empty very soon'.[6] And he suggests that African drumming, 'a sound weird, appealing, suggestive, and wild', may have for Africans 'as profound a meaning as the sound of bells in a Christian country' (p. 20). This is identification with a vengeance.

But as Marlow recounts his voyage up the river to Kurtz at the Inner Station, these familiarising comparisons cease and the emphasis falls more and more emphatically on the savage otherness of the Congolese. Their speech is described as a 'fiendish row' (p. 37) and they are no longer represented as individuals, but rather as 'a whirl of black limbs, a mass of hands clapping, of feet stamping, of bodies swaying, of eyes rolling' (p. 36).

When the idea of kinship is suggested, it is with horror: 'No, they were not inhuman. Well, you know, that was the worst of it—this suspicion of their not being inhuman' (p. 36).

The last images of the Congolese are the most thoroughly distancing: 'Deep within the forest, red gleams partially illuminate many men chanting each to himself some weird incantation' (p. 65) and 'a black figure', a 'sorcerer' with 'horns—antelope horns, I think—on its head' (p. 66). This nightmare vision of 'horned shapes' and the equation of the Congolese with a 'conquering darkness' (p. 75) haunt Marlow long after his return to Europe, and they seem intended to haunt the reader as well.

One could attribute the difference between Conrad's representation of the colonised peoples in the Malay novels and his treatment of them in *Heart of Darkness* to social and biographical factors. The Congo basin, ravaged by centuries of slaving, was undoubtedly horrific, and Conrad seems to have had little opportunity, while he was there, to familiarise himself with the Congolese. Certainly Marlow does not: he insists on more than one occasion that he could not get a clear picture of the Africans, the kind of picture, in other words, that might have enabled him to do justice to them as fellow mortals.

But if Conrad cooperates in the familiar misrepresentation of Africans as demonic others, he does so too, I think, because his commitment to accurate representation comes into conflict with another commitment. The nature of that commitment, which has only recently been recognised by Conrad critics,[7] is best brought out in two passages, one from the manuscript of *Heart of Darkness*, the other from the novel itself. The first has to do with events on board the yacht 'Nellie', where Marlow tells his tale. Just before Marlow begins, the frame narrator recalls,

> A big steamer came down all a long blaze of lights like a town viewed from the sea bound to the uttermost ends of the earth and timed to the day, to the very hour with nothing unknown in her path, no mystery on her way, nothing but a few coaling stations. She went fullspeed, noisily, an angry commotion of the waters followed her ... And the earth suddenly seemed shrunk to the size of a pea spinning in the heart of an immense darkness (p. 7 n.)

The steamer makes a perfect figure of the forces of rationalisation: of science, industrial technology, planning and regimentation. And its voyage offers a poweful image of the consequences of these forces. The ship produces, by its precisely calculated passage to the very ends of the earth, the effect that Max Weber called 'disenchantment': it erases from the world, or from the narrator's imagination of the world, all sense of 'mystery' and wonder, leaves it barren and diminished. Marlow's story, which follows immediately, seems designed as an antidote to this diminution, his steamboat voyage as a counterthrust which reconstitutes, or reenchants, the world shrunk by the steamer. The conclusion of the novel signals the success of this project: looking down the Thames, the frame narrator now remarks that the river 'seemed to lead into the heart of an immense darkness' (p. 79).

By deleting the description of the steamer from the published version of *Heart of Darkness*, Conrad partially obscures this aspect of his fictional design. But some sense of what he is up to is conveyed by a fascinating passage early in the novel. Reminiscing about his childhood passion for maps, Marlow remembers that 'at that time there were many blank spaces on the earth'. Africa was one, 'a blank space of delightful mystery—a white patch for a boy to dream gloriously over' (p. 8). By the time he had grown up, Marlow continues, most such spaces had been filled in, but a sense of the unknown still hung over the upper Congo; it was still not quite charted: still a place of enchantment.

Marlow goes up the river, then, in part because he is dedicated to enchantment, drawn to a world radically different from the world of everyday, predictable familiarity. But this attraction, this need for mystery (which grew ever stronger in Europe as the domain of technological rationalisation expanded) impells Marlow to make something of the Africans that is quite inconsistent with Conrad's project of familiarisation. To preserve a domain of enchantment for himself and his European readers, Conrad has Marlow write 'zone of the demonic' across the 'blank space' of Africa, thus consigning the Africans to a familiar role as demonic others. He sacrifices their needs for adequate representation to his own need for mystery. That Marlow also writes 'zone of the human' across Africa is indisputable, but he does so in fainter script, and by the end of *Heart of Darkness* this script is all but illegible.

Heart of Darkness, then, offers a cruel corroboration of Conrad's warning that no European can be trusted to represent the colonised. Torn between his dedication to accurate and sympathetic representation and his need to affirm the existence of radical moral and epistemological darkness, Conrad makes his African characters bear the burden of that darkness and thus perpetuates identifications that justify European contempt and domination. It is a shame that his most widely read novel should contain his most pejorative representations of the colonised, but a consolation that it offers as well perhaps the most powerful indictment of imperial exploitation in English.

In their time, Kipling and Conrad were frequently compared, but from the distance of some eighty years the differences between their works are more apparent than the similarities. Conrad wrote about the raw edges of empire, Kipling about its great heart. Conrad's fiction is aesthetically ambitious, psychologically oriented, politically sceptical; Kipling's is more conventional, less interested in innerness, and basically affirmative in its treatment of imperial rule. It is not, in other words, a 'disintegrating' art: it sets out to celebrate and defend certain established positions, rather than to work corrosively on them. For the most part the certainties defended are those of imperial ideology. When Kipling criticises the crudest European representations of Indians, he does so on the basis of more sophisticated racist beliefs that still sustain white superiority and right to rule. But Kipling, like Conrad, is inconsistent. In *Kim*, his greatest Indian work, he celebrates a set of certainties that have nothing to do with race, certainties which in fact are directly antagonistic to all doctrines of racial superiority. The reversal becomes apparent when one approaches *Kim* by way of the two decades of stories that precede it.

In 'The Head of the District' (1890), a dying English official, ruler of a frontier district, addresses the Afghan tribesmen he has subdued:

> Men, I'm dying ... but you must be good men when I am not here.... Tallantire Sahib will be with you, but I do not know who takes my place. I speak now true talk, for I am as it were already dead, my children–for though ye be strong men, ye are children.

'And thou art our father and our mother',[8] the Afghan chief replies, apparently satisfied with what Conrad's Babalatchi would have quickly dismissed as 'white man's talk'. But this consensus for dependency is threatened when a Bengali is sent to rule the district. The appointment is interpreted as an insult by the Afghans, who have consented to be ruled by the militarily superior English, but despise Bengalis as weaklings (here, as elsewhere in the stories, Kipling makes much of communal rivalries in India, and mocks the claims of western-educated Bengalis to be ready for posts of responsibility in the Indian Civil Service). 'Dogs you are', a fanatical blind Mullah declares to the Afghans, 'because you listened to Orde Sahib and called him father and behaved as his children' (p. 180). But the Mullah's rebellion, unlike that sponsored by Babalatchi in *An Outcast of the Islands*, fails miserably and is morally, as well as pragmatically, discredited. In the end, after the Mullah has been killed and the unmanly Bengali has fled, the same tribal chief is shown listening, and assenting, to the same paternalistic and racist rhetoric: 'Get hence to the hills—go and wait there, starving, till it shall please the Government to call thy people out for punishment—children and fools that ye be!' (p. 203). The ready hierarchy of imperial domination is thus reconfirmed; the challenge, which is Conrad's work would be authentic and would remain unanswered, is only a pretext for its dramatic re-affirmation.

Indian dependency is affirmed in a different manner in 'His chance in life' (1887), the story of Michele D'Cruze, a young telegraph operator 'with seven-eighths native blood'.[9] A riot breaks out in the town where D'Cruze is posted while the English administrator is away. (Kipling pauses at this point in the story for a cautionary admonition to his audience: 'Never forget that unless the outward and visible signs of Our Authority are always before a native he is as incapable as a child of understanding what authority means' (p. 88).) The Indian police inspector, 'afraid, but obeying the old race instinct which recognizes a drop of White blood as far as it can be diluted' (p. 89), defers to D'Cruze, who astonishes everyone, including himself, by taking charge and putting down the rioters. When an English administrator appears, however, D'Cruze feels 'himself slipping back more and more into the native ... It was the White drop in Michele's veins dying out, though he did not know it' (p. 91). Once again, the contrast to Conrad is instructive: while Conrad uses characters of 'mixed blood' to challenge European claims to superiority, Kipling finds in one such character a pretext for parading racist notions of the distribution of the faculty of rule: responsibility.

A third story, 'The enlightenment of Pagett, M.P.' (1890), shows Kipling working again to make a case for English domination of India. The MP of the story's title is a liberal who has come out to study (and embrace) the National Congress movement, newly founded in 1885. Congress, the organisation that eventually brought independence to India, represented the newly emerging Indian community of western-educated and oriented professionals, men who believed, often correctly, that they were being denied positions in government because of their race. It was only one of a number of nationalist and reform-minded organisations that sprang up in India in the last quarter of the nineteenth century.

But in 'Pagett', Kipling writes as if Congress were an isolated and idiotic institution. Pagett, visiting an old school friend now in the Indian civil service, is 'enlightened' by a series of Indian, British and American witnesses who appear on business and testify enthusiastically against Congress. Some of their criticisms seem plausible, but by no means all of them. And the onesideness of the testimony ultimately betrays the partiality of the whole proceeding: Kipling's unwillingness to let the Congress position be heard at all. Significantly, the only witness to defend Congress, an organisation which numbered among its members numerous well-educated Indians and Englishmen, is a callow school boy, enthusiastic but ill-informed who impresses even the sympathetic Pagett unfavourably.

The other witnesses testify not only against Congress but to the innumerable failings of the Indian people: their religious and racial hatreds, caste exclusiveness, political indifference, corruption, sexism and 'utter indifference to all human suffering'.[10] These disabilities, Kipling suggests, make any talk of equality or of elections mere madness. And they are ineradicable, a kind of racial fatality, 'eternal and inextinguishable' (p. 354).

The racist rhetoric of these three stories, with their stereotypic characterisations, their talk of 'blood', their designation of Indians as 'children', their rejection of all claims to equality, and their refusal to enter into serious dialogue, is typical of Kipling's short fiction in general, the scores of short stories he turned out in the eighties and early nineties. There are impressive Indian characters in a few of these stories, and occasional criticisms of the most brutally dismissive forms of racism. But the good Indians are all also good servants of the raj, and Kipling's own attitude substitutes paternal condescension for contempt. He represents the subject peoples from within the discourse of dependency, the paternalistic rhetoric of racist societies from the American South to the Gangetic Plain.[11]

Something of this tone of condescension lingers in *Kim*. Once again, the positively portrayed Indian characters are all loyal servants of the raj; Congress and the forces it represented seem to have disappeared altogether from the Indian scene. But in *Kim* there is none of the insistence on racial difference and English superiority that we find in so many of the stories. Indeed, in this single work Kipling presses as hard against racist modes of perception and representation as Conrad ever does.

Thus the Church of England chaplain who views the authentically holy lama 'with the triple ringed uninterest of the creed that lumps nine-tenths of the world under the title of "heathen"[12] is depicted as a fool. And so, too, is the young English soldier who calls 'all natives "niggers"' (p. 108) and doesn't know a word of any Indian language. Kipling, who in his stories routinely casts Bengalis as cowardly weaklings, now presents a Bengali secret agent whose feats of courage and endurance 'would astonish folk who mock at his race' (p. 268).

The novel not only repudiates racist modes of characterisation, it dramatises this repudiation. Character after character—the Sahiba, Huree Babu Mokerjee, the Woman of Shamlegh—overcomes his or her racial prejudices. Even Mahbub Ali, the roguish Pathan horse trader and spy, grows more tolerant: he develops, as Mark Kinkead-Weekes has pointed out, 'away from the Pathan ... whose opening words were always "God's curse on all unbelievers" ... towards the Lama's tolerance, [learns] to stop himself with an effort from using his instinctive curse on the "other".'[13] If Kim, 'The Little Friend of All the World' (p. 23), is in one sense the catalyst of all this coming together, he also participates in it, shedding his own prejudices and sense of racial superiority. Throughout the novel, then, Kipling repudiates the hierarchical constructs of racist thinking. What is taken for granted in the earlier fiction is taken down in *Kim*.

Kipling is dreaming, of course, to imagine that the kind of interracial co-operation and comradeship he portrays in *Kim* could take root and grow under British imperial rule: this is E.M. Forster's point in *A Passage to India*. But by blinding himself in this one respect, Kipling is able to see beyond the horizon of his times and portray a world of yet to be realised interracial harmony. For this reason, *Kim* may well be a more effective antidote to racial antipathies than any of Conrad's works, which by their great gloominess tend to corrode at once any belief in racist modes of vision and any hope that they may be abolished.

NOTES

1. Kenneth Burke: *Counter-Statement* (1931, reprinted Berkeley, California, 1968), p. 105.

2. B.V. Street: *The Savage in Literature* (London, 1975), p. 7.

3. Joseph Conrad: *Almayer's Folly* (1895; reprinted New York, 1923), pp. ix–x. Subsequent references to this edition will appear in the text.

4. Joseph Conrad: *An Outcast of the Islands* (1896; reprinted New York, 1926), pp. 109–10. Subsequent references to this edition will appear in the text.

5. Joseph Conrad: *Lord Jim* (1900: reprinted New York, 1968). Subsequent references to this edition will appear in the text.

6. Joseph Conrad: *Heart of Darkness* (1902; reprinted New York, 1963), p. 20. Subsequent references to this edition will appear in the text.

7. See Allon White: *The Uses of Obscurity* (London, 1981) and Jacques Darras: *Joseph Conrad and the West* (London, 1982).

8. Rudyard Kipling: 'The Head of the District', in *In Black and White* (1895; reprinted New York, 1898), p. 172. Subsequent references to this edition will appear in the text.

9. Rudyard Kipling: 'His chance in life', in *Plain Tales From the Hills* (1888; reprinted New York, 1898), p. 86. Subsequent references to this edition will appear in the text.

10. Rudyard Kipling: 'The enlightenments of Pagett, M.P.', in *In Black and White*, p. 383. Subsequent references to this edition will appear in the text.

11. 'There is no originality in Kipling's rudeness to us', wrote Nirad C. Chaudhuri, 'but only a repetition, in the forthright Kiplingian manner, of what was being said in every

mess and club.' Nirad C. Chaudhiri: 'The finest story about India–in English', in *Encounter*, VII (April 1957), p. 47.

12. Rudyard Kipling: *Kim* (1901; reprinted New York, 1959), p. 90. Subsequent references to this edition will appear in the text.

13. Mark Kinkead-Weekes: 'Vision in Kipling's novels', in *Kipling's Mind and Art*, ed. Andrew Rutherford (Stanford, California, 1964), p. 225. For further discussion of Kipling's change of attitude in *Kim*, see K. Bhaskara Rao: *Rudyard Kipling's India* (Norman, Oklahoma, 1967).

L.R. LEAVIS

The Late Nineteenth Century Novel and the Change Towards the Sexual— Gissing, Hardy and Lawrence

Ever since the real beginnings of the English novel in the eighteenth century, and the evolution of the form as a work of art in the nineteenth, it has been intrinsically involved with the relationships between the sexes in society. This of course has been often enough put forward by critics in the past, with emphases ranging from the balanced and flexible to the purely sociological and the crudely sexual—or more recently, the sexist. Certainly, from the outset where the novelist has been preoccupied with the social, the novel has demonstrated an unrivalled grasp of social reality in dramatic terms. This we can see as early as the interests dramatised in the art of Richardson (with his feminine sensibility), in his study of the female predicament and his keen understanding of (for instance) the destructive intelligence of a purely female gathering in tearing to pieces for their entertainment male stupidity and affectation—for the purposes of this brief survey I leave out of consideration the more superficial and extrovertly masculine Fielding and the picaresque novel of the eighteenth century.

Jane Austen took up Richardson's discoveries for her satire, while achieving in her best art a subtle balance of scrupulosity of evaluative judgement and understanding of the predicaments of both sexes. Jane Austen is justly famous for her destructive portraits of both sexes—be they within an eighteenth century satirical tradition or of an intensity peculiar to her—but with few exceptions the reader always senses her clarity of vision and her objectiveness in

From *English Studies: A Journal of English Language and Literature* 66, no. 1 (February 1985). © 1985 by Swets & Zeitlinger B.V.

exploring her own deeply-felt standards in the body of the works. Not in any way sex-centred, Jane Austen's maturity about sexual relations is manifest, and may well be connected with the healthiness of Regency society.

In the Victorian novel one often finds a lack of this balance and healthiness; Mrs. Oliphant, a not untalented writer, and a highly intelligent and formidable woman, displays an attitude to her characters that while apparently rooted in compassion seems in fact to be allied to contempt and, through the writer's sense of superiority, belittlement. From a male standpoint, one would rather be a Mr. Collins, heartily despised by Jane Austen, than one of Mrs. Oliphant's male weaklings so contemptuously stroked by her pitying irony. An explanation for the cause of this distinction between the two writers depends not only on the fact that the later one was surrounded by weak men, and struggling to earn a living, but also on the changed nature of Victorian society, which is bound up with cultural attitudes in the relationship between men and women.

Charlotte Brontë in her Romantic novels was fighting against this very phenomenon, the Victorian attitude towards the sexes, but one might conclude that the influence on the novel of her most striking innovations was delayed until the end of the century. This is not to say that her *Jane Eyre* didn't importantly affect Dickens in his composition of *David Copperfield*, or influence the minor novelist Mrs. Gaskell. However, if one lays *David Copperfield* next to *Jane Eyre*, one can see that with regard to the Victorian novel's coverage of its society Charlotte Brontë was artistically a 'freak'. Whatever Dickens learned from her novel, his is written distinctly in his own terms and focuses solidly on the world of the practical, while Charlotte Brontë's heroine drifts painfully as an outside observer of social reality. For all their great originality neither *Jane Eyre* nor *Villette* contain an adequate equivalent of Betsey Trotwood, a character who insists that Dickens's protagonist should be entrenched in the practical—though we realise that Charlotte Brontë's heroines are deprived of a man's possibilities in the world, and appreciate their frantic efforts to survive and keep a self-respect, while driven on by a puritan refusal to shirk any hostile odds. A less blunt formulation would be that Jane Eyre's adult experience of the world is circumscribed, the book moving on from one enclosed set of circumstances to another. In *Villette* the temporary protector of Lucy Snowe, Miss Marchmont, is herself a refugee from life, and her history proves to set a pattern for the heroine's. One suspects that despite the attempted detachment of the diary-form of her novels, Charlotte Brontë's heroines are close to their author; and Dickens's employment of the same form is more meaningful and functional, not allowing the same suspicion. That Charlotte

Brontë's heroines are observers on the fringe of life is the source of her main creative perceptions, and in exploring their situations her novels show a strange blend of the puritan and the ultra-Romantic, two conflicting qualities which at times hang together uneasily. Despite her puritan temperament Charlotte Brontë was a pioneer of the explicitly sexual in intense psychological poetry, and she came to decisively influence the novel in this way much later, even as late as the time of D.H. Lawrence.

Dickens and George Eliot, the major and most influential novelists of the Victorian period, naturally stand on their own both in their relationships to their societies and in their psychological investigation. Both achieve a dramatic intensity in portraying character, George Eliot intellectually and through realism, Dickens through poetic exaggeration and 'psychological realism'. George Eliot's inward description of Dorothea Brooke's confused emotions during her honeymoon in Rome (Chap. XX, *Middlemarch*) or Dickens's study of Miss Wade in *Little Dorrit* are two clear examples from a profusion of psychological drama encompassing the sexual, being all the more effective for not having an explicitly sexual emphasis.

The stirrings of the late nineteenth and early twentieth century writers of lesser talent in adapting the novel to a new consciousness of life and of society is intriguing. Kingsley had been early with a radical view of aspects of his society in *Alton Locke* (1850) and *Yeast* (1851), both social tracts, but it is when we come to Gissing in the Nineties that we find the beginning of a wave of novelists portraying society with different emphases from the great Victorian novelists. Gissing was influenced profoundly by Dickens and George Eliot, with the rider that like all distinguished minor artists, this influence in his best work was used with individuality and transformed to his own tastes and interests. Once Gissing had got over his early Naturalistic mode it seemed that he was searching for a means to express his particular sensibility without being overwhelmed by the two major Victorian novelists. *New Grub Street* (1891) contains debates among more than one set of characters about the possibility of the novel adapting to new social conditions. One infers that Gissing was through them exploring his position as novelist. Biffen, a novelist of realism, in conversation with Reardon, a failing writer, puts forward his theory of a new objective treatment of low-class life, an anti-heroic realism about what he terms 'the ignobly decent'. Though Gissing (unlike Biffen) no longer endorses 'realism for realism's sake', treating Biffen with a certain amount of irony, one is sure in the light of Gissing's mature writing and of his study of Dickens, that he has great sympathy with that figure's observations:

As I came along by Regent's Park half an hour ago a man and a girl were walking close in front of me, love-making; I passed them slowly, and heard a good deal of their talk ... Now, such a love-scene as that has absolutely never been written down; it was entirely decent, yet vulgar to the nth power. Dickens would have made it ludicrous—a gross injustice. Other men who deal with low-class life would perhaps have preferred idealising it—an absurdity ...

The same character concludes shortly afterwards:

> I shall never write anything like a dramatic scene. Such things do happen in life, but so very rarely that they are nothing to my purpose. Even when they happen, by-the-by, it is in a shape that would be useless to the ordinary novelist; he would have to cut away this circumstance, and add that. Why? I should like to know. Such conventionalism results from stage necessities. Fiction hasn't yet outgrown the influence of the stage on which it originated. Whatever a man writes *for effect* is wrong and bad.

Gissing continued to be interested in 'dramatic scenes', but of a low-key unrhetorical nature in his best work. Within *New Grub Street* the shabby tragedy of the Alfred Yule family is an admirable instance of Gissing's originality in this field. We see a fastidious and pedantic book-worm humiliating his illiterate lower-class wife, while his only child, the sensitive and intelligent Marian looks on in silence. His daughter's subsequent sufferings stem from the pain of her upbringing and her lack of emotional outlet. Several Gissing-experts would see the Yule parents as direct transposition of Gissing's relationship with at least one of his wives. Gissing lived through certain experiences that take a central place in his best novels, but one cannot at least here accept an undiluted 'autobiography embodied in fiction' approach. If one considers the literary influences on Gissing in such scenes, one must appreciate how intelligently yet spontaneously Gissing has employed them. Plainly he has understood the domestic drama (mostly with a comic emphasis, but sometimes as in *Dombey and Son*, tending to melodrama) of Dickens's novels. At the same time George Eliot's *Middlemarch*, with its insistent authorial definition of tragedy which is too common to be called tragic in the accepted sense (especially applied to Casaubon and Dorothea Brooke) must have helped him find a corrective to what he felt was alien to his sensibility in Dickens. Gissing clearly valued her psychological character-studies; as several critics have remarked (to take one instance), Amy Reardon, the villain of *New Grub Street* bears traces of Rosamond Vincy.

While Gissing could be parasitic in his reliance on George Eliot, reducing her to the level of a pot-boiler in *The Whirlpool* (1897), he was acutely aware of the danger of being too much under her spell. As John Halperin shows in his *Gissing, A Life in Books* (New York, 1982) he expressed in his letters a strong reaction against the rationalistic art of George Eliot by turning violently to Charlotte Brontë. We know that he particularly admired *Villette*, re-reading it in 1887. As Halperin suggests, he could see her position as a social-outsider as comparable with his own, and found her poetic treatment of passion congenial. Charlotte Brontë's work may reveal a curious composition of the puritan and Romantic, but Gissing's character appears even more confused and contradictory. He comes across as a mixture of Radical and diehard conservative, his private frustrations turning him against women, yet his decency and non-conformist scrupulosity combined with an acute sensitivity making him understand feminine suffering in feminine terms. Charlotte Brontë's novels must have helped him in *New Grub Street* with his opening portraits of the Milvain sisters (before he disappoints the reader by making them their brother's puppets) and with Marian Yule's love-affair.

The book's sexual outspokenness may have been inspired by Charlotte Brontë's example, but is idiosyncratically expressed. Gissing delineates in his own way the sufferings of the struggling artist and his restricted possibilities with women, pursuing an anti-Romantic path in stressing that for such a person any sexual relation will lead to disaster. Reardon and Biffen turn to classical learning and landscape to compensate for their sexual starvation. Jasper Milvain and Whelpdale provide a new kind of commentary on the state of feeling, typical of the end of the century:

> 'I object to the word "love" altogether. It has been vulgarised. Let us talk about compatibility. Now, I should say that, no doubt, and speaking scientifically, there *is* one particular woman supremely fitted to each man ... If there were any means of discovering this woman in each case, then I have no doubt it would be worth a man's utmost effort to do so, and any amount of erotic jubilation would be reasonable when the discovery was made. But the thing is impossible, and, what's more, we know what ridiculous fallibility people display when they imagine they have found out the best substitute for that indiscoverable. This is what makes me impatient with sentimental talk about marriage. An educated man

mustn't play so into the hands of an ironic destiny. Let him think he *wants* to marry a woman; but don't let him exaggerate his feelings or idealise their nature.'

'There's a good deal in all that,' admitted Whelpdale, though discontentedly.

'There's more than a good deal; there's the last word on the subject. The days of romantic love are gone by. The scientific spirit has put an end to that kind of self-deception. Romantic love was inextricably blended with all sorts of superstitions–belief in personal immortality, in superior beings, in–all the rest of it. What we think of now is moral, and intellectual and physical compatibility; I mean, we are reasonable people ...'

While the main talker here is a selfish cynic who knows that he himself has no moral integrity, Gissing's irony does not disguise the fact that this post-Darwinian position on sexual relations is in keeping with the novel's fatalism.

Born in Exile (1892) continues Gissing's period when he impressively attempted to turn the unhappiness and frustrations of his life into art which novelistically explores the human condition on a level beyond the narrowly personal, however much he asserted to a friend that the book's hero was a phase of himself.

Godwin Peak through temperament and chance becomes cut off from any possibility of fulfilling his talents and ambition in society, even though his brilliant scholastic career promised so much. Bitterly disillusioned with society and himself, he discovers that he is also out of sympathy with the Radical reaction against his times. The novel takes up a theme thrown out in *New Grub Street* of the individualist and déclassé man of talent who gradually finds any position in his society impossible. Peak's desperate attempt at a solution in trying to get into the Church of England (a Church destroyed by loss of faith from the New Science) makes us think of one of the phases of Hardy's *Jude the Obscure* (1895). However Peak lacks Jude's mediæval idealism, and is not dominated by a Sue Bridehead. His woman is a sweet and well-bred upper-class girl, conventional and unintellectual; Peak finds intellectual Radical females sexually repulsive.

The novel ends with the collapse of Peak's ambitions through the hostility of the conventional towards his social position and his hardly-to-be-disguised unconventionality of intellect. He is driven into exile from his own country and dies from emotional starvation. After reading this, one can feel that Dickens could have devoted a whole novel to Pip's predicament after the termination of all his hopes and ambitions (whichever ending one chooses of

Great Expectations) though of course the emphasis of Dickens's novel does not need to entail such a study. One admires the originality of Gissing's treatment of extreme social isolation—one quite different from Arthur Clennam's position in *Little Dorrit*.

The third novel of this successful period [ignoring the sensational *Denzil Quarrier* (1892)] is the more limited *The Odd Women* (1893). Gissing in his earlier work was interested in the position of late-Victorian women, but now devotes a whole novel to the subject. He continues the frank and open discussion of sexual attitudes seen in the previous two books. In *Born in Exile* we encountered Marcella Moxey, an emancipated Radical who was rigidly 'enlightened' and manifestly 'unfeminine'. Rhoda Nunn is a sympathetic study of an intelligent 'new' feminist with a sense of humour and feminine attractiveness below the surface:

> It was a face that invited, that compelled study.
> Self-confidence, intellectual keenness, a bright humour, frank courage, were traits legible enough: and when the lips parted to show their warmth, their fullness, when the eyelids drooped a little in meditation, one became aware of a suggestiveness directed not solely to the intellect, of something like an unfamiliar sexual type, remote indeed from the voluptuous, but hinting a possibility of subtle feminine forces that might be released by circumstance ...

Certainly Gissing has been affected by Charlotte Brontë's Lucy Snowe, but despite his bent in private life of detesting free-thinking women so often cited by his biographers, we see that in *The Odd Women* he could reconsider his judgements.

One reason for qualifying one's estimate of the novel relates to the simplicity of its plot, where the contrast between the story of a conventional woman marrying a jealous and overbearing older man with the attempts of a 'male-chauvinist' philanderer in subduing Miss Nunn is ultimately too schematic. Another is that Gissing has been too markedly affected both by Charlotte Brontë's full-blown Romantic language and by Dickens's theatrical confrontation-scenes to be himself. The would-be seducer of the novel, Everard Bar-foot, is an interesting variant of a villain in the Steerforth mould, but rhetorical confrontation-scenes and passionate outbursts do not fit in to the generally realistic mode of the book. The novel's merit lies in the more muted psychological treatment of the main women's situations, done with an admirable disinterest and understanding.

Hardy's *Jude the Obscure* (1895) is often taken as an important and original novel expressing the new pessimism of its time. However, unlike Gissing, on Hardy's part there seems to be an uncreative or 'journalistic' use of literary influences, which must indicate the work's real stature. One instance is the obtrusiveness of Hardy's emphasis on general 'cosmic pessimism', which has probably originated from *Middlemarch* and its tragedy of the ordinary human condition. Hardy has taken this source and added his own kind of references to Greek Tragedy, backed up by a blatant reliance on coincidence. Gissing himself rejected (and was too much a novelist to affect the same pose in his best writing) the asserted pessimism that characters in *Jude* are made to voice:

> And then he again uneasily saw, as he had latterly seen with more and more frequency, the scorn of Nature for man's finer emotions, and her lack of interest in his aspirations ...

This position (while obviously derivative from) is a long way from George Eliot's:

> But anyone watching keenly the stealthy convergence of human lots, sees a slow preparation of effects from one life on another, which tells like a calculated irony on the indifference or the frozen state with which we look at our unintroduced neighbour. Destiny stands by sarcastic with our *dramatis personae* folded in her hand ... (*Middlemarch*, Chap. XI)

Similar employment of influences is to be met in Hardy's other 'adaptations'; the figure of the boy 'Father Time' is certainly taken from little Paul of *Dombey and Son*, with the subtle delicacy of Dickens's art changed into an insertion, a topical perspective relying on the ramming home of the theme of a typical modern child too old for his years. Indeed, if one compares Dickens's treatment of childhood in his maturity with the childhood of Jude and Father Time, one may feel that in taking over the nineteenth century novel's discovery of childhood from Romantic poetry, Hardy has sensationalised and parodied a tradition, adding nothing original. Again we must surely exempt Gissing from this charge, as he has creatively transformed material in his best work to suit a refined and original sensibility. If this conclusion about Hardy seems too harsh, or unsupported, I can only invite the reader to compare the scene in *Jude* concerning the bohemian support of Phillotson against 'respectable society' (Section VI, 'At Shaston') with Dickens's circus people in *Hard Times*. That a writer can lift material in such a way from other novelists is the mark of a literary vulgariser.

As a social novel, despite its reputation of sweeper-away of conventions, *Jude* is similarly unsatisfactory. Unlike Gissing's best works, the terms which should establish a concrete sense of reality only exist through the bitter observations Jude and Sue make on the social system. When a social reality is offered outside these characters' sense of persecution, the few scenes we get such as of the interior of a Christminster tavern ('real Christminster life') hardly provide a substantial picture. One is left with Hardy's cynicism about marriage, and the attitudes of the main characters, which surely are often mere attitudes, such as Sue's horror of legal wedlock (note that Rhoda Nunn had similar reactions towards marriage), an 'outrageous' challenging of conformity and the Ten Commandments, a questioning of a literal reading of the Bible, and other equally disconnected fragments.

On religious belief in late Victorian England *Born in Exile* has much more to say than *Jude*, and Margaret Maison in her *Search Your Soul, Eustace* (London, 1961) is surely not overstating the case when she remarks:

> Jude's orthodoxy is almost entirely non-combatant—it is a mere Aunt Sally to be knocked down, not by the scientists or the biblical critics, but by the forces of social setbacks and unrestrained fleshly lusts ...

Nevertheless a fascinating and most important aspect of Hardy's novel remains to be mentioned, one which D.H. Lawrence expounded in his *Study of Thomas Hardy*; the relationship between Sue and Jude. Margaret Maison (among others) has pointed out that in the minor Victorian novel there were many 'stories of young women whose scepticism was part of their emancipation, and who proved totally unable to control passion by principle', and cites Olive Schreiner's *The Story of an African farm* (1883) and Mrs. W. D. Humphrey's *Sheba* (1889) as two such popular novels which were near-contemporaries of *Jude*. To these one could add Gissing's *The Odd Women*, especially as it may help to explain certain discrepancies within the character of Sue herself. Lawrence's most interesting study of Hardy's abstract conceptions of women in society has perhaps made of *Jude* a more coherent novel than the one Hardy actually wrote. It is difficult to reconcile the extremes in Hardy's picture of a female militant, who is sexless, even a man-killer as heartless as Amy Reardon in *New Grub Street*, yet is highly impulsive and feminine (a distinctly Hardian emphasis), who has children of her own, who is a relentless Radical crusader, yet ends up in a masochistic conservatism of an insanely puritan nature. *The Odd Women* in contrast intelligently used current interest in the 'new woman' to produce a coherent study. Gissing for this employs two varieties of woman, two friends, one of which is a radical and the other a conventional woman who is in danger of becoming an 'old maid'. While the execution of the novel is too limited, making one wish for more flesh in the book, the ideas behind it are convincing enough. The older man whom the conventional woman (Monica Madden) marries is called Widdowson, a name suspiciously close to Phillotson in *Jude*. The wife comes to rebel against her husband's irrational jealousy, which in the end forces her into the arms of a lover. Monica Madden finds her husband physically repulsive, as Sue does Phillotson. It is this relationship between the Maddens that ends in tragedy.

One suspects that Hardy in drawing on the novelistic convention of the sceptical woman has been affected by Gissing's treatment of sexual relations. Sue Bridehead reads like a curious amalgam of the uncompromising feminist Rhoda Nunn, and her unemancipated man-needing friend Monica Madden, an amalgam that involves too many conflicting elements to be contained in one character. Sue starts off as a Rhoda Nunn and by the end of the novel is thoroughly 'Maddened'. In the process of this transformation Phillotson is rather implausibly made to abandon his movingly described understanding of his young wife's plight and to practise an unnaturally ruthless cruelty upon her, this being 'explained' by his having learned from experience. Widdowson in comparison seems while less sympathetic at least 'all of a piece'. One's sense of Hardy's indebtedness to Gissing is supported by the fact that the two men knew each other and sent each other their novels, Gissing sending Hardy copies of two of his novels as early as 1886. Gissing in fact visited Hardy when he was working on his final version of *Jude*, but little comes out of Gissing's record of that meeting (or indeed of Gissing's note in his diary on first reading *Jude*).

Hardy's importance as a source for D.H. Lawrence's creative innovations has already been well-established in criticism; the unassimilated influence on Lawrence's early work is well-known, and the relationship between his *Study of Thomas Hardy* and the marriage of Will and Anna in *The Rainbow* is a striking example of a great novelist's creative use of material. Perhaps too Hardy's example is distantly behind *Women in Love*. Another sort of novel than *The Rainbow*, *Women in Love* is restricted in its number of characters and relies for its sense of reality on vivid and dramatic conversations. The characters are carefully grouped to make a controlled pattern through the plan of the chapters, while the social implications of

Lawrence's investigation are wide-ranging and ambitious. The apparent result is the range of the social study of a major novel with the poetry of the 'moral fable'. In fact life in England as a background to the main groups of characters is limited to a few brief concrete examples (outside the representative nature of the conversations); the 'A Chair' chapter with its picture of city life seems a sudden switch on Lawrence's part to illustrate a thesis on the state of modern English society. Impossible as it is to come up with a nineteenth century work of a similar nature, one could suggest *Jude* as a possible inspiration—hardly a model—for it (at least) offers to give a study of a whole society through specified encounters and conversations.

In the consideration of literary influences on Lawrence's mature art severe problems arise. On the one hand Lawrence is an original genius who revolutionised the novel, so that in the *execution* of his art he is beyond all simple questions of influence. On the other hand he can be seen as an inheritor of the developments in the novel of the late nineteenth and early twentieth centuries. One can even go as far back as Charlotte Brontë and conclude that her psychological and intensely poetic studies of sexual relations were waiting for a modern and less openly Romantic treatment to enforce the truth of their insights. The strikingly original study of St. John Rivers in *Jane Eyre* is a case in point, and a more specific instance could be seen in a comparison between 'The Cleopatra', a chapter of *Villette* dealing with English and Continental sexual attitudes through the symbolic use of a painting, and Lawrence's treatment of the same area in *The Captain's Doll*. Such a comparison is instructive, despite Lawrence's hostility to Charlotte Brontë when writing on her.

On a lesser level H.G. Well's overtly sexual interest in *Tono Bungay* (1909) and *The New Machiavelli* (1911), while inimical in feeling, must have helped Lawrence in his interest in exploring sexual relationships in the novel—indeed in his comments on Wells in various places he clearly valued him. Wells is directly linked with Gissing, not only because he was an unreliable friend and a reviewer of Gissing's novels, but also because he took the cue from him in dealing with 'the new woman' and in presenting a partially un-Romantic view of sexual relations. Lawrence (a voracious reader) clearly knew his Gissing, and in his letters expressed respect for him while qualifying his admiration with:

Gissing hasn't enough energy, enough sanguinity, to capture me. But I esteem him a good deal ... (to Edward Garnett, 21 Jan. 1912) and 'I've no sympathy with starvers ...' (to same, 12 Jan. 1913). He seems to have read *The Odd Women* in 1909, praising the book in a letter of July 24 1910 to Louie Burrows. *Sons and Lovers* (1913) bears the influence of the nineteenth century, most obviously Thomas Hardy's, but perhaps the schematic presence of Clara Dawes owes not only to Hardy's thesis of woman's conventionality in the face of a rigid social code, but also comes from reading Rhoda Nunn's physical and intellectual challenge to Barfoot, who like Paul wishes to assert his masculinity by conquering the emancipated woman.

It would be fascinating to know if Lawrence had read *Born in Exile*, which stands in interesting contrast to *Women in Love*. Gissing's novel is indeed a pessimistic story of a 'starver', who can find no place in his home-country, and drifts to a death lost abroad in exile. *Women in Love* is permeated by a rejection of English society and its way of life. Parallelling Lawrence's own rejection of England, Birkin and Ursula throw up their jobs to leave England, perhaps for ever. Social conditions are quite different in Gissing's novel, of course. Godwin Peak's classlessness is a drawback in his society, Birkin having a financial independence and being in a society that does not socially stigmatise him and hinder him from finding a suitable mate. Lawrence's novel, while containing a tragic sub-plot, works towards a cautious but defiant optimism in which the individual seems able to exist transplanted from his society. The emphasis is quite unlike the hopeless pessimism of the end of *Born in Exile*.[1]

We come now to consider the revolutionary effect on our time of Lawrence's novels. His art works here in uneasy harness with the Bloomsbury drive against the inhibitions of the Victorian ethos. Lawrence was violently anti-Bloomsbury, but curiously, though not surprisingly, it seems that in our time there is little awareness of a distinction between the two forces; the *Lady Chatterley* trial has helped to establish Lawrence as a debunker of prudish inhibitions. The dangers of being a pioneer of the treatment of relationships with an explicitly sexual emphasis were apparent even in Lawrence's own lifetime, and his reception by admirers of his books as 'the high-priest of sex' seems to have affected Lawrence himself. Unfair and beside the point as it is to blame Lawrence for the present over-awareness and cynically mechanical nature of sex in the contemporary novel, one can't help appreciating the dangers of his historical position. Lawrence is *the* great 'sexual pioneer' of the novel, and the sanest; Gissing (a minor artist) in his sexual emphasis manifestly suffered from his own perverse views arising from his role as a déclassé; Wells's sexual studies only give us the erotic egotism of Wells himself. Lawrence's life is not tainted in *such* a way, nor is his best art (*pace* the cries of 'sexual fascism' levelled at Lawrence). However, when uprooted from England his treatment of relationships went wrong—if all novels after *Women in Love* are not affected in this way, at least *The Plumed Serpent* and *Lady Chatterley's Lover* (written when he was seriously ill) are examples. *Women in Love* is a turning-point in his art and life. It can be read intelligently with widely varying responses. The novel is a puzzling one, exploring in an open and honest way, expressing some of Lawrence's extreme feelings through Birkin, and criticising for its author the limitations and excesses of their nature (Gissing was doing much the same for his position and outlook in minor art in *Born in Exile*). The pattern the novel takes, of the individual voluntarily isolating himself from his society—as Birkin eventually does despite his apparent involvement—has disturbed many readers, not all of them Marxists. Defenders may state that *Women in Love* was analysing the effects of modern society on the individual, taking the analysis further than *The Rainbow*, and providing a prophecy of the state of modern society and the individual. That this is true, does not alleviate one's unease with the novel that alienation from society is too easily achieved and taken too far, especially with the traditional English novel in mind. Lawrence is certainly honest when he shows us Birkin's interview with Will, Ursula's father, in 'Moony', and exhibits the superior arrogance with which Birkin treats the older man. However this honesty does not affect Lawrence's treatment of Birkin's position, nor provide an understanding of Ursula's 'outmoded' family-life. In fact in 'Flitting' Ursula's rupture with her parents is cursorily treated, and she leaves her old home for ever without effort, even with disgust. Lawrence's flight from England with Frieda is colouring the issue here.

To return to the truth inherent in the suggested defence of *Women in Love;* one tends to distrust a 'general truth', here that 'the modern individual is cut off from a strong sense of social unity', particularly as in contemporary fiction it has been repeated so often that it has become a truism. The very function of the novel (if the form is to have any meaning) is never to rest upon one point, but to move on to other positions by challenging generally accepted assumptions. Lawrence can hardly be blamed for modern errors, but with regard to *Women in Love* the duty and stature of a great novelist (which Lawrence is in that novel) demand that he triumph through his art over the conditions of his environment, and his personal history. This last definition is derived from observing the art of Dickens and George Eliot, and relies on the artist achieving an objective realism through personal experience which rejects both utopianism and defeatism. Lawrence was the one who correctly called Gissing 'a starver', perceiving that his art sadly reflected the misery of his life. But one might feel that ultimately *Women in Love* places such an emphasis on the individual that the dazzlingly original exploration of feeling becomes cut off from social responsibility.

One last point in connection with Lawrence is concerned with the issues involved with a fundamental concentration on the sexual. In *The Rainbow* the interrelated changes in society and sexual relationships are unfolded before our eyes, as we follow the development from the marriage of Tom and Lydia to the relationship of Ursula and Skrebensky. Objection has been made that Skrebensky is an unsatisfactory vehicle for the onus placed upon him, even in the novel's terms, where he is an intentionally unsatisfactory figure. He is unsatisfactory as a character and in general conversation, and he often only 'exists' in the highly-charged language describing love-making, scenes which refer back to previous scenes with other characters. 'Lawrence in *Women in Love* succeeds where he fails in *The Rainbow* with the Skrebensky-Ursula relationship' is a shrewd judgement; however in *The Rainbow* the intensity of the love-making scenes stands out disturbingly in their use of Ursula and Skrebensky, in that Lawrence creates an assertive poetry out of a non-living, puppet-figure. This is an indication that the sexual interest carried on from the bulk of the novel has become divorced from its perspective in the human and the real. Later Lawrence was to make a more unbalanced concentration on the sexual divorced from the social and even at times the human, illustrating the difficulties facing a major artist in working on such a level of emphasis. Even in the core of *The Rainbow* lie the seeds of a subsequent abuse of Lawrence's emphases. One is aware of how the later love-making of Will and Anna relates back to their early relationship, and a comparison of their whole marriage with that of Lydia and Tom involves a moral judgement of which the sexual is only one important element. Making the sexual the *only* index to moral and social values is quite another thing, but in an age where sex is no longer regarded with reverence, estimations of characters have become defined solely in terms of the sexual. Even minor writers of integrity, it could be suggested, must be entangled in vulgarities and dishonesties when employing a mode of writing geared to an expression of feeling through highly-charged poetry of physical relationships. All modes of writing are open to exploitation and abuse, some more than others.

History seems to have shifted strangely with regard to the sexual in literature. From the early ponderings of Kingsley over the sexually-repressed adolescence of the sensitive, we have seen a sexual emphasis which would have appalled Lawrence become paramount, self-consciously obsessed by sensation for its own sake, as the thrill of going further in shocking has burnt itself out to end in the mechanical. The act of excreting bodily liquids and solids is not a creative one, but in the modern novel the sexual act has become debased to such a process; and it would be a most dubious and sophistical interpretation to insist on a criticising intention with this emphasis. Meanwhile writers who are less obviously bent on cynical exploitation offer us embarrassing and wooden parodies of Lawrence's revolution in the novel. It is hard to believe that the following passage is not indeed at least half-facetious in its gestures towards Lawrence, but so ponderous is the novel from which it comes (Malamud's *Dubin's Lives* [1979]) that one concludes that the writer hopes to get away with being serious, as do so many prominent writers on both sides of the Atlantic:

> Dubin set the glass down and began to unbraid Fanny's warm hair. She took it out, heavy full. Her shoulders, breasts, youthful legs, were splendid. He loved her glowing flesh. Fanny removed her heart-shaped locket and his bracelet, placing them on the bookcase near the dripping red candle. She kept the ruby ring on. Forcefully she pulled his undershirt over his head; he drew down her black underpants. Fanny kissed his live cock. What they were doing they did as though the experience were new. It was a new experience. He was, in her arms, a youthful figure. On his knees he embraced her legs, kissed her between them.
>
> So geh herein zu mir
> Du mir erwälte Braut! [A Bach cantata is playing on the hifi.]
>
> She led him to bed, flipped aside the blanket. He drew it over
>   their hips ...
> They wrestled in the narrow bed, she with her youth; he with his
>   wiles. At her climax Fanny's mouth slackened; she shut her
>   eyes as though in disbelief and came in silence.
>
> Mit harfen und mit zimbeln schön.
>
> Dubin slept with his arms around her; she with her hand cupping
>   his balls ...

NOTES

1. Many original creative writers have to struggle against a hostile reality and must resist the pressures to succumb to the hopelessness of a 'starver'

(see Wordsworth's *Resolution and Independence*) often for most of their lives. Lawrence was a particularly heroic resister in this respect, though it did lead him into dreams of a model community and to New Mexico.

PETER KEATING

A Woven Tapestry of Interests

'Is that you?' she said, 'from the other side of the county?'
—Rudyard Kipling, 'They', *Traffics and Discoveries* (1904)

'And Rogers came back with a bump and a start to what is called real life.'
—Algernon Blackwood, *A Prisoner in Fairyland* (1913)

One particularly complex aspect of the various attempts by early twentieth-century novelists to contain within their work contrasting phases of contemporary life can be seen in the growth of a new kind of self-conscious regionalism in fiction. The recurrent pattern of social exploration and rejection in novelists like Lawrence, Wells, Mackenzie, Joyce and Bennett was enacted in their lives as well as their novels. The sense of exile that they and their protagonists endorse was not, however, as total as many accounts of 'modernism' tend to assume. There can hardly ever have been a novelist with a more developed commitment to one topographical place than Joyce: in spite of his, and Stephen Dedalus's, dismissal of Dublin as a possible home base, it nonetheless provided Joyce with an inspirational focal point for the whole of his creative life. And in a similar, if less exclusive manner, Lawrence turned repeatedly to Nottinghamshire, Bennett to the Five Towns, Wells to the Home Counties and Mackenzie to Scotland. It was far from uncommon for earlier novelists to become associated in this way with specific areas of the

From *The Haunted Study: A Social History of the English Novel 1875–1914.* © 1989 by Peter Keating.

country, as the major examples of Scott, Austen, Eliot and the Brontës demonstrate. Even important novelists such as these experienced something of the age-old condescension of metropolitan critics towards outsiders, but the opposing view–that the value of their work depended little on whether it was set in Midlothian, Hampshire, Warwickshire or Yorkshire–served as an emphatic corrective. For slightly later novelists this line of defence became irrelevant, not least because they themselves were often contributing to the distinctly pejorative connotations that were now habitually attached to the words 'regional', 'provincial', and 'local'.[1] The rhetoric of exile, of flight from home environments which were denounced as narrow, restricted, repressive, and destructive of the modern artistic spirit, triumphantly established an image of the rootless artist even when his work was still centrally, and often humanely, focused on the home environment which he claimed to be leaving behind him. It is not difficult to identify factors which helped bring about this change of attitude. Matthew Arnold's constant denigration of 'provincial' values made a powerful contribution to it. So did the ever-increasing business and commercial appeal of London as publishing houses and newspaper offices became more centralised.[2] For the young aspiring writer, London offered not only the promise of ultimate fame, but in the meantime many opportunties to earn money from writing. 'There grows in the North Country,' states the opening sentence of Bennett's *A Man from the North*, 'a certain kind of youth of whom it may be said that he is born to be a Londoner,' and the assumption recurs in dozens of novels. In this respect, even French fiction, through its scathing portraits of the meanness of provincial life, was a socially limiting as well as an artistically liberating force. It was all part of the vivisective nature of modernism. If the family, nation and church were on the way out, there was little chance that the regions would be allowed to survive. But, as is usual in such battles, it was the winning side which dictated the terms for the future and created the most persuasive myths. Regional fiction was not only *not* dead, it was actually flourishing.[3] The buoyant fiction market in books and periodicals offered unprecedented opportunities for 'local' authors; and as the publishing industry became centred on London, it was easy to forget that there were active publishers in other English cities, and in Scotland, Wales and Ireland. Regional fiction was often very popular both within the area of the country it portrayed and nationally as well. In 1898 *Literature* devoted a leading article to what it saw as the 'current passion for local colour' among novelists: 'A tendency has already been displayed to divide the map of the United Kingdom amongst them–to every man a parish or two–and to threaten trespassers with all the terrors of the Society of Authors.'[4] *Literature* regarded this trend as epitomising the spread of realism, and it certainly is the case that while many of the leading novelists of the day were turning away from realism, at least one of its several strands found a welcome home in the regions where it survives contentedly to the present day, and is still usually ignored by academic and metropolitan critics.

Not all regional fiction, however, was realistic: nor was the realism of regional fiction all of the same kind. *Literature* had in mind a British version of French naturalism. There was also a far gentler evocation of local manners and customs that looked back to *Our Village* and *Cranford* and, largely because it was not a British version of French naturalism, was greatly enjoyed by large numbers of readers and often dismissed by critics as whimsical or quaint rather than realistic. Falling into either (or neither) of these categories there was, in addition, a considerable body of dialect fiction that attracted a devoted local following while rarely receiving any attention nationally.[5] And although it was becoming common to regard 'regional' as virtually a synonym for 'rural', it was not necessarily the case that regional fiction should deal with country life: in their day, *Dubliners* and *Sons and Lovers* were both regarded as 'regional'. A further problem of classification arises with the late Victorian assumption that realism was concerned preeminently with contemporary life. This had not necessarily been the case for the mid-Victorians whose work was often set in the recent past: nor did it apply to a great deal of late Victorian regional fiction where the 'local colour' came from historical research rather than direct observation. While Scott remained the model of an historical-regional novelist, the immediate late Victorian inspiration was provided by R D. Blackmore's *Lorna Doone* (1869), a rambling, episodic adventure story set in the seventeenth century. *Lorna Doone* was subtitled 'A romance of Exmoor', and Blackmore used the same kind of topographical signposting for his subsequent novels: *Kit and Kitty* (1890), was a 'story of West Middlesex'; *Darvil* (1897) 'A romance of Surrey'. The technique was not exactly new, but Blackmore brought it back into fashion. The huge success of *Lorna Doone* also played a significant part in inspiring a whole school of West Country novelists which included Eden Phillpotts, Sabine Baring-Gould, John Trevena, 'Zack', Quiller-Couch, and, most prominently, Hardy who swiftly took over from Blackmore as the major influence on regional fiction.

Hardy's ambiguous position in this context is an indication of how restrictive the regional label has become. However just the assumption that the work of a writer of major status transcends its local interest, one result of that assumption is to turn the regions into a string of rest-homes for minor literary talents. Addressing this kind of problem, Raymond Williams notes that while 'the Hardy country is of course Wessex', the 'real Hardy country, we soon come to see, is that border country so many of us have been living in: between customs and education, between work and ideas, between love of place and an experience of change'.[6] That is in one sense clearly correct: it defines the transitional experience between rural and urban ways of life that Hardy shares with George Eliot and the Brontës on the one hand, and Lawrence on the other. But the assumption that this is a more 'real' side of Hardy than regional Wessex is somewhat misleading. By birth and background Hardy might well have been expected to live out the career-pattern of flight and exile from the provinces that was characteristic of so many other novelists of the time. In fact his career was a conscious rejection of that possibility. He did not move out to London or Paris, but back into Wessex. Far from restricting his work, this served to heighten the border experience that Williams identifies. It also entailed a commitment to a specific region and culture that found expression in a wide variety of different ways: most strikingly of all, it served to unite a view of life that was disquietingly sensitive to 'the new' and an ancient trust in the communicative power of a strong story. It was a combination that drew patronising comments from a self-conscious modernist like James, though not, significantly, from Woolf, who shared with Hardy the psychological need to belong to a particular place.[7] In one sense, of course, Hardy did not simply write about or from within the area in which he lived: he invented the area because, as he himself explained, the novels he intended to write 'being mainly of the kind called local' they seemed 'to require a territorial definition of some sort to lend unity to their scene'.[8] Wessex was introduced to the reading public in *Far from the Madding Crowd* (1874), and Hardy was soon aware of the opportunity it provided to explore the clash between old and new—or 'the anachronism of imagining a Wessex population living under Queen Victoria' as he described it—and of the way his invented region seemed to take upon itself a heightened air of reality:

> The appellation which I had thought to reserve to the horizons and landscapes of a partly real, partly dream-country, has become more and more popular as a physical provincial definition; and the dream-country has, by degrees, solidified into a utilitarian region which people can go to, take a house in, and write to the papers from.[9]

Outside the novels Hardy contributed actively to the creation of this 'physical provincial definition', not only by public pronouncements on

'Wessex' life and language, but also by his willing support of popularising and commercialising schemes advanced by admirers of the novels. Wessex was featured in exhibitions and books of etchings, paintings and photographs: it also provided the subject for a series of picture-postcards. Hardy was consulted, and often gave very detailed advice, on all of these projects. To the photographer Herman Lea he suggested that it would be worth sending his Wessex photographs to some of the more popular illustrated magazines, adding that if the magazines were American then they might like a title like 'A Fair in Old England': Lea used the title for an article in *Country Life*.[10] By the end of the nineteenth century Hardy was already well on the way to joining novelists like Scott, Dickens and the Brontës who had made specific areas of Britain distinctively their own, and like them his national fame was enhanced by the romanticisation of his 'regionalism', a type of image-making that attracted not only the illustrated periodicals but the growing late Victorian tourist industry as well.

Richard Jefferies stands in marked contrast to Hardy's regional success story, though there are similarities between the two writers. Like Hardy, Jefferies was at first tempted to try his hand at the melodramatic novel of fashionable life before turning to the countryside that he knew so well. He was, in much of his work, a chronicler of the late Victorian agricultural depression, writing about it from the kind of radical viewpoint that is also often present in Hardy. He shared the need to lay literary claim to a region. As he explained in a letter: 'I have worked in many of the traditions of Wiltshire, endeavouring, in fact, in a humble manner to do for that county what Whyte Melville has done for Northampton and Miss Braddon for Yorkshire.'[11] The 'humble' comparisons drawn there are to the point, for while Jefferies continues to be remembered as a writer *of* Wiltshire, he was never able to take possession of it in the way that Hardy possessed Wessex, or Scott the Borders. The best of his novels, *Greene Ferne Farm* (1880), *Bevis* (1882), *After London* (1885) and *Amaryllis at the Fair* (1887) all possess skilfully evoked rural scenes but little development. They are barely novels at all, and their episodic nature emphasises not simply Jefferies's weaknesses, but also his strengths. In Chapter Five there were quoted two admiring contemporary references to Jefferies, neither of them to his fiction. Stephen Reynolds saw him as a leading exponent of autobiografiction, and he was one of the writers who inspired Leonard Bast to spend his uninspiring night under the stars. Through his many collections of journalistic essays and personal reminiscences–of which *The Gamekeeper at Home* (1878), *Wild Life in a Southern County* (1879), *Hodge and his Masters* (1880), *Wood Magic* (1882) and *The Story of my Heart* (1883) are representative–Jefferies contributed two distinctive, and in some senses contradictory, qualities to late Victorian regionalism. On the one hand, there was his loving, detailed exploration of human and animal life in Wiltshire which ranged in tone from the radical to the sentimental; and, on the other hand, a mystical communion with nature that invoked a post-Darwinian despair at mankind's ephemerality in order to heighten the individual's spiritual union with the whole of natural life. The first of these qualities was regional in that it concerned itself with the recreation of the very special conditions of a particular time and place: the second is better described as an expression of ruralism because it exalted the experience of country life above anything that modern science, technology, or the city, could offer.

Jefferies' presence is felt in a good deal of late nineteenth- and early twentieth-century literature. Elements of his lyrical ruralism are observable in writers as diverse as Lawrence, Forster, Edward Carpenter and Kenneth Grahame: the documentary aspect of his studies of village life was further developed by George Bourne in *The Bettesworth Book* (1901), *Memoirs of a Surrey Labourer* (1917) and *Change in the Village* (1912); while W. H. Hudson, in such works as *Nature in Downland* (1900), *Hampshire Days* (1903) and *A Shepherd's Life* (1910), seems often to be following directly in Jefferies' footsteps. Hudson's one outstanding novel, *Green Mansions* (1904), is set in a South American tropical forest, and the story it tells of the explorer Abel's love for the bird-girl Rima may seem to have little in common with British regionalism. Yet in certain important respects *Green Mansions* captures the cult of ruralism more effectively than any other novel of the time. Just as Abel inhabits a personal 'world of nature and of the spirit', so Rima has both the 'beautiful physical brightness' of a wild animal and the 'spiritualising light of mind' that pronounces her human.[12] The 'vast green world' of the novel is both a realistically evoked forest and a symbolic Eden, in which man's fallen state is brought about not by disobedience to God, but by the Darwinian revelation of nature's indifference to man. It is a mythic, romantic variation on the literature of life under the stars or on the open road that Leonard Bast, along with many other Edwardians, longed to experience for himself. Underlying much of this ruralism there is the assumption that modern man needs contact with nature, or with 'the country', or, failing either, with a garden, if he is to live his life to the full, because only in nature will he be able to rediscover the animism that urbanisation and the decline of organised religion have taken away from him.[13] Leonard Bast, yearning for the open road, epitomises in a subdued way the stirring of Pan that is found everywhere in Forster's—and Lawrence's—early fiction. At this level, ruralism and regionalism both actively employ the imagery of exploration that is more readily associated with city literature. Hudson was literally an explorer who reversed the imperial pattern by journeying from South America to discover the neglected wonders of the southern counties of England, and Kipling shared that image. In 1902, just after his move to Bateman's in Sussex, Kipling wrote to Charles Eliot Norton: 'Then we discovered England which we had never done before ... England is a wonderful land. It is the most marvellous of all foreign countries that I have ever been in.'[14] It was characteristic of Kipling's multi-faceted genius that his literary exploration of this newly discovered country of England (or more specifically, Sussex) should have taken many different forms. In stories like 'My Son's Wife' and 'An Habitation Enforced', he examined the theme of outsiders trying to become assimilated into the complex class structure of rural society; in 'Friendly Brook', the lives and superstitions of agricultural labourers; in 'They', county lines are employed supernaturally to denote the uncertain boundaries between life and death; while *Puck of Pook's Hill* (1906) and *Rewards and Fairies* (1910) examine the ways in which a region continues to express the spirit of all the long generations of people—the 'mere uncounted folk' as much as the 'great' and 'wellbespoke'—who have contributed to its specialness.[15]

While the South West of England dominated the late Victorian regional novel, and the southern counties of England were most often the setting for ruralism, it was Scotland that came for a few years at the close of the century to typify regionalism in fiction. What Margaret Oliphant described as the 'field of amusing and picturesque observation first opened by Sir Walter', had been popular throughout the Victorian period.[16] In addition to Oliphant herself, and Stevenson, some notable late Victorian practitioners were William Black, George MacDonald, Jane and Mary Findlater, and Annie S. Swan. Most of these novelists moved easily between Scottish and English subjects, or between local-colour regional fiction and historical or supernatural tales. Not all of their work is adequately covered by the classification 'amusing and picturesque', but at least one strand of it pointed towards the whimsical, sentimental, image of Scotland that was purveyed with spectacular commercial success by 'Kailyard' fiction. The phenomenon was sharply noted by a *Punch* cartoon in 1895. A publisher, on being offered a volume of short stories, asks 'if they are written in any unintelligible Scotch dialect'. 'Certainly not,' responds the indignant author. 'Then,' says the publisher, 'I'm afraid they're not of the slightest use to me.'[17] The label 'Kailyard'—or cabbage-patch—had been coined in the same year as the *Punch* cartoon.[18] It covered such works as J.M. Barrie's *Auld Licht Idylls* (1888), *A Window in Thrums* (1889) and *The Little Minister* (1891); S.R. Crockett's *The*

Stickit Minister (1893) and *The Lilac Sunbonnet* (1894); and Ian Maclaren's *Beside the Bonnie Briar Bush* (1894) and *The Days of Auld Langsyne* (1895). The apotheosis of the kailyard came in 1896 with the publication of *Margaret Ogilvy*, Barrie's biographical study of his mother: it was, the *British Weekly* announced, 'a book which it is almost too sacrilegious to criticise'.[19] In that same book, Barrie told how when nine years earlier he had tried to collect his journalistic 'Auld Licht' sketches into a volume, no publisher 'Scotch or English' would accept it 'as a gift'.[20] By 1896 he must have been enjoying *Punch's* joke that publishers now seemed interested in handling little else. The Kailyard novels were immensely popular not only in Scotland and England, but in America as well where they appeared regularly on best-seller lists. Their success was due in part to skilful publicity engineered by William Robertson Nicoll who was editor of both the *British Weekly*, where much of the Kailyard fiction was first published, and the *Bookman*, the most widely read literary periodical in Britain. The extent of Kailyard popularity cannot, however, be explained solely in terms of the booming activities of one editor, even someone as influential as Nicoll. The real reason lay once again in the public reaction to realism. Barrie's stories, backed by Nicoll's advocacy, began to attract attention shortly after the Vizetelly trial, and the works of Crockett and Maclaren that followed were exactly contemporary with the bowdlerisation of Zola's novels, the hysterical press attacks on Ibsen, Moore and Hardy, and Wilde's trial. Many of the regional novels centred on the South-West of England were also associated with the less acceptable side of realism. There were a few faint hints in *Auld Licht Idylls* that Barrie might be drawn in the same direction, but once that fear was shown to be false, all was well. The Kailyarders were not only harmless, they were notoriously safe.

In true regional style, each of the Kailyard novelists laid claim to a particular part of Scotland—Barrie to Kirriemuir, Maclaren to Perthshire, Crockett to Galloway—but what emerged from their work was not so much regional difference as a collective Scottish image. The Kailyard world was largely rural, backward-looking, sentimental, nostalgic, and essentially domestic, though with a strong bitter-sweet element that was conveyed through the recurrent theme of exile from the beloved home. The Kailyard label was particularly appropriate for the way it designated a type of fiction that relied for its effect entirely on local domestic props, something well understood by Crockett: 'To every Scot, his own house, his own gate-end, his own ingle-nook is always the best, the most interesting, the only thing domestic worth singing about and talking about.'[21] It is no accident that Crockett might have been describing a stereotypical music-hall backcloth for a character sketch by Harry Lauder, who was to carry Kailyard sentimentality into as many English-speaking homes as the novelists themselves. What Nicoll treasured in Kailyard fiction was its gentle yet firm attachment to the moral certainties—epitomised by family, church and community—that were subject to increasingly bitter attacks in other types of fiction. The criticism that the Kailyarders presented a misleadingly unrealistic picture of Scottish life meant nothing at all to Nicoll. In his view realism was morbidly unhealthy, and he spent so much energy promoting the Kailyard precisely because it was not realistic: Kailyard fiction was to serve, in Thomas D. Knowles's words, as 'a bastion against the ungodly aspects of literature'.[22] The very large numbers of readers who rushed to buy the Kailyard novels would not perhaps have shared Nicoll's militant denunciation of realism, but they did share his relief that there were still stories available which assured them that however hard the world may seem there is always more good than bad to be found in it, and that tears are enjoyable when mingled with smiles. It was a long-established best-selling formula that was gathering new life in the late Victorian commercial market.

What the Scottish opponents of Kailyard fiction lacked in numbers, they made up for in the ferocity of their attacks. George Douglas Brown's *The House with the Green Shutters* (1901) was written, at least in part, as a rebuttal of what he described as 'the sentimental slop of Barrie, and Crockett, and Maclaren'.[23] His small Scottish community is mean, squalid, full of gossip, envy and barely-suppressed violence, as also is that of J. MacDougall Hay's *Gillespie* (1914). T.W.H. Crosland in a characteristic piece of facetious debunking, *The Unspeakable Scot* (1902), derided the Kailyard communities as 'little bits of heaven dropped on the map of Scotland', and praised *The House with the Green Shutters* for giving the world a true picture of the modern Scot.[24] But the response of J.H. Millar, who had originally coined the Kailyard label, was more perceptive. Writing in 1903, he noted sadly that Scottish writers now seemed incapable of being 'amusing without being jocose' or 'sympathetic without being maudlin', and looked forward to the day when someone would 'write of Scottish life and character with a minimum of the dreary old wit about ministers and whisky'. Before his book was published Millar rushed to add a footnote to this passage saying that his 'not very lofty ideal had to some extent been realised ... in an unpretending, but excellent, brochure' published in Glasgow.[25] He was referring to John Joy Bell's *Wee Macgreegor* (1902) which was soon joined by two books by Neil Munro, published under his journalistic pen-name of Hugh Foulis, *Erchie* (1904) and *The Vital Spark and Her Queer Crew* (1907). All three books were collections of sketches which had appeared originally in Glasgow newspapers. As Millar noted, they are 'unpretending', but manage to convey genuine, rather folksy humour without excessive resort to either the sentimentality of the Kailyard or the squalid meanness of George Douglas Brown. But, in the emphasis they placed on exactly reproduced accents, national or regional characteristics, and personal idiosyncracies, they also functioned at the level of stereotypes. They were the Scottish equivalent of the tough but good-hearted Cockney popularised by writers such as William Pett Ridge, Edwin Pugh, and W.W. Jacobs.

The relentless fragmentation and categorisation of fiction that typifies the last two decades of the nineteenth century resists any simple explanation. 'Our society has ceased to be homogeneous,' Wells announced in 1903, 'and it has become a heterogeneous confusion, without any secure common grounds of action.'[26] Wells, as usual, was uncertain whether to commit his personal support to collectivism or to pluralism, and at what was usually a less conscious level, his dilemma was one of the main dilemmas of the age. If collectivism had won the struggle for control of the new democracy, then absolutes—though not, certainly, the same absolutes—might have been re-established, but it didn't, and they weren't. Pluralism, or 'heterogeneous confusion', was the triumphant victor. Like most other aspects of British life at the turn of the century, fiction began to splinter into a variety of different forms which were often mutually, and culturally, incompatible, at least according to earlier systems of categorisation: it had become what Wells, in his lecture at The Times Book Club, was to describe memorably as 'a woven tapestry of interests'.[27]

The proliferation of magazines, newspapers and periodicals, directed at very clearly defined groups of readers, encouraged novelists either to specialise in one particular kind of fiction, or, if the writer was exceptionally talented (or facile) to move between different kinds, thus profiting from (or taking advantage of) several sectors of the fragmenting market. One of the best-informed of the literary manuals advised young authors to begin by establishing 'a reputation in the magazines for a special kind of story', and added in support of this advice: 'Mr Kipling is identified with Indian life, Mrs Stannard ("John Strange Winter") with cavalry life, Mr G.R. Sims with London life (of a sort), while Mr Anthony Hope, Mr Machen, and others are all *specialists* in fiction.'[28] The short story played a prominent part in this specialisation, as also did the growing popularity of the one-volume novel, at first in competition with the three-decker and then later in the century as its official replacement. Mid-Victorian novelists, grudgingly concocting the second volume of their three-deckers, had constantly predicted that once this artificial form of publication was got rid of, then formal artistry, based on the natural or inevitable length of a story, would flourish. They were right, but only to the extent of the number of authors available who were capable of striving for artistic perfection, and in that particular sense the prescribed length of a story made little difference. Indeed, for many lesser novelists the one-volume novel served to restrict both social range and literary ambition, with a corresponding loss rather than gain of artistry. It was now all too tempting to focus exclusively on the slum or the suburb, on the lovable Cockney or dour Kailyard Scot, on the city clerk or the New Woman: as we have seen, the reaction against this kind of journalistic and sociological labelling was a major factor in the resurgence of wide-ranging, socially-panoramic realistic fiction in the few years immediately before 1914. There was, however, a more positive result of the commercial tendency towards shorter fiction. A good deal of children's, horror, and adventure fiction had long been published in the one-volume format, for the obvious reason that neither the reader's attention nor narrative suspense could expect to be effectively sustained over a long period of time. This lesson was taken to heart by the late Victorians as literary specialisation began to divide popular fiction into distinctive subgenres.

With a little critical ingenuity it is possible to trace the ancestry of all of these sub-genres—science fiction, ghost stories, adventure tales, fantasy, detective novels, and horror—back beyond the existence of the printed word. So much and so popular a part were they of late Victorian fiction that they often seemed to be inventions of the age, though their archetypal nature was just as important in that popularity. They functioned by bringing age-old fears, longings and aspirations firmly into a modern context through the revivification of myth. The short story or short novel was their natural medium: it provided writers with a limited space within which they could sustain suspense, move swiftly to an horrific climax, or work out an ingenious puzzle. As all of these sub-genres began to establish their own traditions and inspirational texts, the narrative skills became more self-consciously adventurous: they were able to exist within a frame of reference created by their own conventions. No longer were they one element in a large-scale fictional examination of society: instead, they demanded that their exploration of social issues should take place entirely in their own terms. Here again there are losses and gains to record as the size of novels quite visibly shrank. The mid-Victorian 'sensation' novel of M.E. Braddon or Mrs Henry Wood, which was written in the three-decker format and employed the sensational to make larger claims of social portrayal and criticism, was transformed into the brief one-volume 'shocker' like Hugh Conway's *Called Back* (1884) and *Dark Days* (1885), or Richard Marsh's *The Beetle* (1897), which functioned purely at a sensational level, or into works which made more substantial moral demands on the reader but were still clearly part of the new tradition, like Stevenson's *Dr Jekyll and Mr Hyde* and Wilde's *The Picture of Dorian Gray*. In similar fashion mid-Victorian novels such as Dickens's *Bleak House* and Collins's *The Woman in White*, which pioneered the fictional detective but cannot be described adequately as 'detective novels', were rendered down into the tightly controlled solution-solving adventures of a Sherlock Holmes or Father Brown: this trend was initiated by the combined force of Poe's much earlier Dupin stories and Collins's *The Moonstone* (1868). Although strongly pronounced, the appeal of shorter fiction, even in the new sub-genres, was not absolute. The greatest horror novel of the age, Bram Stoker's *Dracula* (1897), is almost as long as many of the older Gothic novels that inspired its creation; and while M.E. Braddon switched effortlessly from three-deckers to the one-volume novel and showed herself perfectly capable of writing up-to-date detective stories, Marie Corelli, taking over something of Braddon's earlier reputation, continued to write massive up-to-date sensation novels. As with almost every other aspect of the late Victorian literary market, the response of novelists was varied and eclectic, but the trend towards shorter fiction was an inspiration as well as a snare to the popular writer.

It was a snare partly because it provided a relatively easy way into the fiction market for any writer who was willing to pander to regional or class stereotypes, or who simply set out to imitate popular literary forms, and partly because once entry had been achieved, the market was reluctant to let any writer deviate from the image of him or her that its own publicity machine had created. Once fixed as a 'slum', 'suburban', 'New Woman', or 'Dartmoor' novelist, an exceptional creative effort was required ever to be regarded as anything else. One of the remarkable features of Stevenson's career is the way that he moved over so many different kinds of fiction, proving a commercial success in most of them, functioning as a powerful influence on their subsequent development, and ignoring the advice of friendly admirers that he should sit still and concentrate on being an Artist. Henry James gave similar advice, for much the same reason, to H.G. Wells. Stevenson and Wells were in effect, being invited to join the 'modernists', the most exclusive of all the specialists. Both declined the invitations and have never been forgiven. Their literary eclecticism was a conscious decision, backed by sufficient talent for them to carry the public with them through various changes of image. Other novelists became inextricably trapped by their success in one particular kind of fiction. The self-consciousness with which these popular literary forms was regarded is apparent at every level of late Victorian fiction. Ray Limbert in Henry James's 'The Next Time', weary of writing highly regarded but commercially unsuccessful novels, decides that the 'next time' he will make a bid for popularity. He writes what he thinks is an '"adventure-story" on approved lines. It was the way they all did the adventure-story that he tried most dauntlessly to emulate.' It turns out to be a 'superb little composition, the shortest of his novels but perhaps the loveliest', and of course, uncommercial.[29] In acknowledging that an 'approved' type of fiction can transcend limiting conventions if the right kind of artistic mind sets to work on it, James was perhaps thinking of Stevenson. Viewed from another angle, the moral of 'The Next Time' is also relevant to Conrad. Throughout his early career Conrad was touchily conscious of sharing the subject-matter of much of his work with the writers of popular adventure fiction. He constantly acknowledged the relationship in order to disown it. *Youth*, he insisted proudly was made out of 'the material of a boys' story', while not being a story written for boys; more bitingly, he points out in *Lord Jim* that Jim's unfulfilled dream of personal heroism can be traced to his adolescent love of 'the sea life of light literature'.[30] Unlike James's Ray Limbert, Conrad wanted popularity only on his own terms. He was determined that it would not be achieved by writing 'approved' adventure stories or 'light literature' of the kind devoured by Jim, but that fact should not be allowed to conceal the irony that *Lord Jim* was serialised in *Blackwood's*, a major purveyor of conventional adventure fiction. In spite of their very different responses to the fragmentation of fiction, both James and Conrad were disturbed by the threat it posed to their own positions as Artists. Other novelists viewed the situation quite differently: the contrasting attitudes of Wells and Stevenson have been mentioned, and their example inspired in turn the work of novelists who were totally uninterested in the idealism and achievement of a James or Conrad. For example, Max Pemberton was a frankly commercial writer. University-educated, though with no definite profession in mind, he studied 'the reading tastes of the masses' and turned to Fleet Street to earn his living. Paragraphs and stories for various magazines led to the editorship of *Chums*: the next inevitable step was a novel. The authors of the day he most admired were Stevenson and Haggard, so he followed their example with *The Iron Pirate* (1893), the first of many commercially successful adventure stories.[31] Haggard himself had nothing of Pemberton's literary opportunism, though the way that he achieved commercial success was not entirely dissimilar. In 1884 he was the author of two unsuccessful novels. Hearing the recently-published *Treasure Island* highly praised, he spoke slightingly of it and was challenged by his brother 'to write anything half so good'.[32] He responded with *King Solomon's*

Mines, which shared with *Treasure Island*, a string of exciting adventures and instant mythic appeal. Although Haggard's tone and view of life were totally unlike those of Stevenson, it was on these two authors more than any others that responsibility fell for saving the country's fiction from the threat of realism. The semi-official doctrine of opposition was labelled 'romance'. It was in many respects an unfortunate choice.

Although the term realism was of relatively recent coinage, its essential meaning had long been understood and used as a standard comparison with romance. The term 'romance' itself, however, had an even more complicated lexical history than realism, and complications were to multiply into total confusion as late Victorian critics and novelists set to work on it. Meredith was a major influence through his opposition to realism, which he described scathingly as 'a conscientious transcription of all the visible, and a repetition of all the audible'; and also through his call for an alternative method which would instil 'philosophy' or 'brainstuff' into fiction by means of sophisticated comedy.[33] A related influence was J.H. Shorthouse, the success of whose historical novel *John Inglesant* in 1881 encouraged him to add a preface to the second edition in which, like Meredith, he called for fiction and philosophy to be united so that eternal truths about mankind could be conveyed effectively to a 'prosaic age'. It was not, however, high comedy that Shorthouse wanted, but a new branch of historical fiction: this literary hybrid he called 'Philosophical Romance'.[34] He was not opposed to realism as the novelist's fundamental method as long as it was imbued with a romantic spirit. 'Yes, it is only a Romance,' he announced, in rhetorical anticipation of his critics, and in the heightened language that was to feature so often in subsequent discussions of the subject: 'It is only the ivory gate falling back at the fairy touch. It is only the leaden sky breaking for a moment above the bowed and weary head, revealing the fathomless Infinite through the gloom.'[35] Kenneth Graham fixes 1887 as 'the year of recognition for the new romance' because in that year George Saintsbury, Rider Haggard and Andrew Lang—the writers who, with the addition of Stevenson, were the major propagandists for romance—issued 'manifestos on its behalf'.[36] All of these writers saw romance as serving to deflect attention away from the dangerous unpleasantness of realism, a classification that in this context allowed for no distinction between Zolaesque documentation and Jamesian psychological analysis: both types of realism were seen as equally guilty of fostering introspection, unmanliness and morbidity, and of favouring a literary method that was mechanical and monotonous. Lang professed to believe that 'any clever man or woman may elaborate a realistic novel according to the rules', while 'romance bloweth where she listeth'.[37] The socially undesirable qualities associated with realism, and its narrow conception of art, are well, if cryptically, expressed there. The fresh wind of romance not only blows away morbidity and brings a return to health, it does this by liberating the imagination, thus making great art possible again. Saintsbury was similarly drawn to imagery of health and cleansing to convey his enthusiasm for romance. The current *malaise* in fiction will not be cured, he announced, 'till we have bathed once more long and well in the romance of adventure and of passion'.[38] There was some talk, by Lang especially, of the battle between realism and romance being fought out to 'the bitter end', but Lang's confidence that romance and realism could be kept apart, that they represented respectively the 'golden' and the 'silver' sides of the 'shield of fiction', was soon undermined.[39] W.E. Henley, a close friend of Stevenson's and a leading spokesman for the 'romance' of imperialism, was also, in his own poetry and as editor of the *National Observer* and the *New Review*, a supporter of certain kinds of realism; while Kipling, who hated literary cliques, and whose early work was predominantly realistic, was immediately enlisted (against his will and approval) into the anti-realist camp because he had introduced the 'romance' of India to the British reading public. Claims for the superior healthiness of romance were further weakened when reviewers began to complain about the lurid descriptions of violence in Haggard's novels.[40] Lang's faith in romance survived not only all of this, but the apparent defection of Stevenson as well. Of *The Ebb-Tide* he observed: 'There is little pleasure in voyaging with such a crew ... But it is not long since Mr Stevenson gave us *Catriona*. May he soon listen to the muir-cocks crying "Come back!" across the heather!'[41]

The conjunction of Lang and Stevenson is of some importance to an understanding of how romance came to carry such high hopes towards the close of the century. Like Kailyard fiction, much of the publicity that surrounded it was skilfully engineered, though Lang, the major publicist, was a far more substantial literary figure than Robertson Nicoll. He was a talented scholar, and regarded respectfully for his contributions to folklore, anthropology and the occult: he was also a leading exponent of the flowery, allusive affected style of writing that was becoming the trademark of literary journalism. He published volumes of graceful poetry; several historical novels under his own name, notably *A Monk of Fife* (1896); a collaborative novel *The World's Desire* (1890) with Rider Haggard; and the collections of fairy stories for which he is probably best remembered today. His prolific output, however, was nothing compared with the energy which went into the advocacy of romance: like Nicoll, Gosse and Clement Shorter, Lang was at heart a literary middleman. His public pulpit was a regular column 'At the

Sign of the Ship' in *Longman's Magazine* which he employed to denigrate
French realism and any British fiction influenced by it, and to praise the
increasingly popular novels of adventure. The same preferences were
pursued in his semi-public or anonymous roles as publisher's reader, literary
adviser and book reviewer. A book or manuscript that met with his approval
might be recommended for publication in England or for serialisation in
America, where he was the English editor of *Harper's*, and once published it
would receive additional publicity in 'At the Sign of the Ship', and possibly
several reviews, signed or anonymous but all by Lang, in different periodicals
and newspapers.[42] The influence that a man like Lang could exert was very
considerable indeed, but it would remain only temporary or local unless it
could focus on a writer of genius who would serve to exemplify and justify
the extravagant theory. This was where Stevenson came in.

The attractiveness of Stevenson rested on his possession of two highly-
developed qualities which are rarely found together. He was an Aesthete and
a writer of exciting stories. In an age which was becoming obsessed with the
need to separate Art from Entertainment, Stevenson spoke and acted on
behalf of both. If the experimental range of his work worried his admirers,
there was still at the heart of it *Treasure Island, Kidnapped, The Black Arrow*
and *The Master of Ballantrae*. They were the perfect antidote to naturalism.
They were absorbing for children and adults; committed to action rather
than analysis; at first, they barely acknowledged that sexuality existed; offered
no disturbing analogies with modernity; linked late Victorian fiction with
Scott on the one hand and with the acceptable French tradition of Dumas on
the other; and, most important of all, since these various qualities could have
been found elsewhere, they were brilliantly written. Stevenson's theories on
the art of fiction were just as acceptable as his practice. Like Wells after him,
Stevenson took public issue with Henry James's claim that art 'competes with
life', but unlike Wells he did not call for fiction to involve itself directly in
life, or for it to reflect the chaotic unorganised quality of life. On the
contrary, he displayed a dedicated belief in organicism:

> From all its chapters, from all its pages, from all its sentences, the
> well-written novel echoes and re-echoes its one creative and
> controlling thought; to this must every incident and character
> contribute; the style must have been pitched in unison with this;
> and if there is anywhere a word that looks another way, the book
> would be stronger, clearer, and (I had almost said) fuller without
> it.[43]

Such views may have been reassuring to those critics who wanted to believe that realism was not carrying all before it, but they were unlikely to convince anyone else. Although Stevenson acknowledged in his early critical essays that realism and romance were essentially different 'technical methods', artistic precedence was given repeatedly to romance, usually by denigrating realism. The novel of 'incident' was set unjustly against a type of fiction that concerned itself with 'the clink of teaspoons and the accent of the curate': the 'great creative writer' was described as someone whose 'stories may be nourished with the realities of life', and then qualified by the insistence that the 'true mark' of those stories was 'to satisfy the nameless longings of the reader, and to obey the ideal laws of the day-dream'. Fiction, he claimed, in a definition that appeared to eliminate any serious adult interest, 'is to the grown man what play is to the child ... when it pleases him with every turn, when he loves to recall it and dwells upon its recollection with entire delight, fiction is called romance'.[44] It was statements such as these that were later to provoke the charges that Stevenson's criticism was mere belletristic chat and his fiction nothing but tales about pirates written for schoolboys, but they were accepted gratefully by Lang and his followers. In spite of Stevenson's more considered critical judgments, it was largely under his influence that 'romance' lost whatever specific meaning it might once have had and became, in effect, almost anything that wasn't realism.

It was the historical novel that Lang and Stevenson had primarily in mind, though, as they understood, not all historical novels were romances, and not all romances historical: furthermore, an historical novel might well be realistic in its method or, in Shorthouse's sense, 'philosophical'. The 'adventure story on approved lines' written by James's Ray Limbert was probably historical and romantic, though, in the late Victorian literary market, it could just as well have been near-contemporary and reasonably realistic. Many romances were fantastic, but 'fantasy' was beginning to insist that it was distinct from other kinds of 'romance'; and in much the same way the 'horror' story was often classified as a romance because it was not 'realistic' and not quite 'supernatural', though, obviously enough, it could be historical or contemporary, and its treatment could be romantic or realistic.[45] The tales of scientific experiment and exploration pioneered by Jules Verne and H.G. Wells were known throughout this period as scientific 'romances' (the term 'science fiction' did not come into general use until the 1920s); tales of ghosts and poltergeists and other supernatural phenomena were often described as 'psychical romances' and there were few late Victorian fictional heroes as truly romantic and a part of their age as the private detective, except perhaps when that dual role was undertaken by the imperial explorer or soldier in an 'adventure' story.

Whereas many reviewers, critics and readers welcomed the new forms of romance as an antidote to the pernicious influence of realism, the novelists themselves were more often motivated by a distrust of realism's scientific and documentary pretensions. 'We have in our police reports realism pushed to its extreme limits,' observes Conan Doyle's surrogate author Dr Watson, 'and yet the result is, it must be confessed, neither fascinating nor artistic.' Holmes agrees with him: 'A certain selection and discretion must be used in producing a realistic effect.'[46] Select and discreet the details may be, but both Holmes and Watson do see the need for the narration of their adventures to remain broadly within the scope of realism. In complete contrast, Walter de la Mare's Henry Brocken rejects realism as in any sense capable of conveying the nature and flavour of his adventures, and apologises to the reader for standing against so powerful a tradition:

> Most travellers, that he ever heard of, were the happy possessors
> of audacity and vigour, a zeal for facts a zeal for Science, a vivid
> faith in powder and gold. Who, then, will bear for a moment with
> an ignorant, pacific adventurer, without even a gun?

For the regions he is to explore, Brocken can 'present neither map nor chart ... latitude nor longitude; can affirm only that their frontier stretches just this side of Dream.'[47] The assumption that facts and modern science have obscured rather than revealed the truth about life is fundamental to much of this fiction. The really worthwhile studies undertaken by the protagonist of George MacDonald's *Lilith* (1895) only begin when he comes down from university: 'Ptolemy, Dante, the two Bacons, and Boyle were even more to me than Darwin or Maxwell, as so much nearer the vanished van breaking into the dark of ignorance.'[48] True knowledge is attained not by marching doggedly forward with each scientific discovery, but by moving further and further back to a point where the mind is no longer corrupted by modern scientific reasoning. Having watched Count Dracula leave his castle by crawling lizard-fashion down the wall, Jonathan Harker feels safe enough to enter details of this latest chilling episode in his diary. As a safeguard he writes in shorthand: 'It is nineteenth century up-to-date with a vengeance. And yet, unless my senses deceive me, the old centuries had, and have, powers of their own which mere "modernity" cannot kill.'[49]

The imagery of exploration was clearly as important to the romance as to the realistic novel and social documentary, and here also it functioned on both a literal and a metaphorical level, though its emphasis was totally different. The realist, the journalist and the sociologist employed exploration imagery to dramatise present social conditions, to draw the reader's attention to neglected areas of contemporary life. In contrast, the writer of romance employed the same imagery in order to escape from the present, or, if he had a point to make of direct contemporary relevance, to set up a process of extrapolation that the reader was expected to follow through. Of the four major kinds of late Victorian romance examined here—historical, scientific, supernatural, detective—only the writer of detective fiction shared the social explorers' preoccupation with present time and conditions. The other three were interested in the present only in so far as it could be placed within the huge vistas of space and time of which it was, if truly understood, merely an insignificant speck. In the process, they divided among themselves not merely types of fiction, but time as well. The historical novelist took as his special province the whole of time past; the writer of science fiction took the whole of time future; while the writer of the supernatural and occult embraced or ignored both time future and time past in his exploration of states of consciousness which were beyond any concept of time available to human understanding.

It was here that the obsession of twentieth-century fiction with the need to find a replacement for linear time can be said to begin. The structural connections between changing concepts of time and the form of fiction did not go unremarked by the writers of the new sub-genres. In many instances time future and time past were used as fairly mechanical means of getting a story under way, but in the hands of such writers as Stevenson, Kipling, MacDonald, Machen and Stoker, formal experiments with multiple narration, radically shifting points of view, and unreliable or misleading narrators, were also being pursued. The modernists were to be too absorbed with the artistic potential of the work itself and too scornful of the literary market-place to give more than an oblique recognition of the popular resurgence and redirection of romance, though James, as we have seen, was fully aware of Stevenson's achievement: he was also fascinated by the artistic possibilities of the supernatural tale. Conrad too was probably more influenced by Stevenson than he cared to admit, though he openly acknowledged the affinities his work had with that of Kipling.[50] The main case to be made out is not, however, one of direct influence, but rather of the complex pattern of interrelationships and separations out of which literary modernism was born. What is to the point, is that while these sub-genres continued to strengthen their independent identities and flourished apart from, and often scorned by modernism, many post-modernist writers, inspired and frustrated by their great modernist predecessors, have turned increasingly, and with experimental admiration, to the alternative forms of popular fiction pioneered by the late Victorians.

It was the historical novel that initiated the late Victorian debate on the spiritually and socially cleansing power of romance, and it was to be the historical novel that proved, ultimately, the greatest literary disappointment. One problem was that among the various forms of late Victorian romance, only historical fiction had to compete with long-established and vital literary traditions. At this time, Scott still provided the virtually automatic standard of comparison for any new historical novel; not far behind was the much-admired Dumas; Dickens, Thackeray and Eliot had all temporarily turned aside from the general mid-Victorian preference for the recent past as the setting for fiction to write historical novels; and, daunting as comparison with these past masters was, the translation into English of Tolstoy's *War and Peace* in 1886 established a contemporary model that no British novelist could begin to challenge. Even so, in the wake of *Lorna Doone*, *John Inglesant*, *Treasure Island* and *Kidnapped*, historical fiction achieved a phenomenal new popularity in Britain. So many historical novels were published that they provoked the compilation of descriptive guides, bibliographies and library handbooks, making the historical novel probably the first type of popular fiction to be treated extensively in this classifying manner.[51] That it was possible to make a comfortable living by writing mainly historical fiction was demonstrated in the 1870s by the successful partnership of Walter Besant and James Rice, and subsequently by a very large number of individual novelists, including Edna Lyall, Stanley Weyman, H.S. Merriman, Quiller-Couch, S.R. Crockett, Neil Munro, Baroness Orczy, Marjorie Bowen and Rafael Sabatini. James, Wells and Bennett held aloof from the trend, but Hardy, Gissing, Morrison, Moore, Ford, and even Conrad eventually, wrote historical novels, while writers like Ouida, Corelli, Caine, Haggard, Doyle and Hewlett alternated between historical and contemporary subjects. The sheer quantity of historical fiction, its variety, and its eclectic use of elements from many different literary genres, make any very precise classification virtually impossible, but in the light of the generalisations already made, certain distinctinve groupings of historical novels can be indicated.

The kind of 'philosophical romance' defined by J.H. Shorthouse made up one strand. Apart from Shorthouse's own *John Inglesant*, the most distinguished contributions were Walter Pater's *Marius the Epicurean* (1885) and *Imaginary Portraits* (1887), and William Morris's late romances or Socialist fables: *A Dream of John Ball* (1988), *The House of the Wolfings* (1889),

News from Nowhere (1891), *The Wood Beyond the World* (1895) and *The Well at the World's End* (1896). Meredith's example was too idiosyncratic to provide a safe model for other writers, though his stylistic influence can be seen in Stevenson's *Prince Otto* (1885), and, mingling with the pastiche Malory that tempted too many historical novelists of the time, in Maurice Hewlett's *The Forest Lovers* (1898) and *Richard Yea-and-Nay* (1900). It was common, if not always correct, to set against these kinds of historical 'romances' the 'realistic' historical novel: this could mean analytical or true-to-life, though it often only meant carefully-researched. The type of the late Victorian researcher-novelist was Conan Doyle, with *Micah Clarke* (1889), *The White Company* (1890), *The Exploits of Brigadier Gerard* (1895) and *Sir Nigel* (1906). Doyle's own reason for thinking *The White Company* and *Sir Nigel*, both of which are set in the fifteenth century, to be the very best of his fiction was that they 'made an accurate picture of that great age'.[52] Among the more successful examples of the 'analytical' historical novel were Maurice Hewlett's *The Queen's Quair* (1904), and Ford Madox Ford's trilogy *The Fifth Queen* (1906), *Privy Seal* (1907) and *The Fifth Queen Crowned* (1908).

The dominant type of historical 'romance' was, however, not primarily 'philosophical', 'analytical', 'accurate', or 'realistic': it was, rather, the loosely-structured collection of exciting episodes and incidents that descended from Stevenson, through Doyle—in spite of his large claims of historical portraiture—and Rider Haggard. The gradual debasement of the high hopes for romance held out by Meredith and Shorthouse can also be traced back to Stevenson's unguarded critical assertions that the greatness of romance lay in its appeal to the 'nameless longings' and 'day-dreams' of the reader, and that it was the adult's version of a child's 'play'. Stevenson could not, however, be held personally responsible for the increasingly strident political tone of this fiction. His historical novels were essentially non-nationalistic, except in so far as they spoke for a lost Scottishness. Furthermore, much of his later work was anti-imperialistic, and it was imperial expansion that created the receptive atmosphere for historical romance, including Stevenson's. It was also imperial expansion that made it increasingly difficult to distinguish in any clear-cut way between an historical and an adventure novel. In one sense, novels like Haggard's *King Solomon's Mines* (1885), A.E.W. Mason's *The Four Feathers* (1902), John Buchan's *Prester John* (1910) and Edgar Wallace's *Sanders of the River* (1911) were firmly contemporary in that the opening up of Africa by Western powers, a subject with which all of these novels dealt, was a familiar daily issue for British readers. But that issue also involved the ancient rights and customs of Africa peoples as well as the constant restructuring of 'tradition' that was so important a part of the mythos of the British Empire: it was frequently difficult (in fiction and in life) to determine where 'history' ended and 'contemporary' adventure began. Ernest Baker said of Flora Annie Steel's novel about the Indian Mutiny *On the Face of the Waters* (1896) that it epitomised 'fiction never interfering with facts', and then added that it also 'pays much attention to sex problems, Ibsenism, and other modern fashions'.[53] The blend of past and present was an inevitable expression of the Empire as history in the making. Nowhere was this more apparent than in the fiction directed at boys, whether in periodicals like the *Union Fack* and *Boy's Own Paper*, or in the adventurous games which featured in fiction that was not ostensibly imperialistic, or, most blatantly, in the novels of writers like W.H.G. Kingston, Gordon Stables, and G.A. Henty, where the message that all boys should be ready to answer the call of Empire was essentially the same whether those boys were expected, to use the evocative titles of Henty's novels, to sail *Under Drake's Flag* (1883) or march *With Roberts to Pretoria* (1902). Although, largely under the influence of Kipling's Indian tales, novelists were beginning to give more attention in their work to the soldier than the sailor and more to war on land than at sea, the traditional British fiction of life at sea—whether experienced by sailors, pirates or fishermen— also saw a revival with such novels as Henry Newbolt's *Taken by the Enemy* (1892), Kipling's *Captains Courageous* (1892) and most interestingly, John Masefield's *Captain Margaret* (1908). The popular apotheosis of historical romance came with Anthony Hope's *The Prisoner of Zenda* (1894), another novel which though contemporary in setting appeared historical because of the quaintness of the Ruritania it portrayed, and with a batch of swashbuckling cloak-and-dagger novels, the most prominent being: Stanley Weyman, *A Gentleman of France* (1893), *Under the Red Robe* (1894), and *The Red Cockade* (1895); Baroness Orczy, *The Scarlet Pimpernel* (1905) and its many sequels; and Jeffrey Farnol's *The Broad Highway* (1910) and *The Amateur Gentleman* (1913). Day-dream and adult play really had taken over.

The social function of a great deal of this historical fiction was perfectly well understood by its authors.[54] First, it had to sustain the mood of adventurous exploration that was necessary for the expansion and maintenance of the British Empire. Secondly, it took upon itself the task of instilling into the new and unformed democracy an appreciation of the long years of progress that had turned Britain into the greatest imperial power the world had ever known. Any period of history, from the Stone Age to the Boer War, could serve these functions. At an individual level the call was for everyone to nurture the qualities of courage, justice and fair play that had made, and would keep, Britain great, and be willing to die for those ideals.

Doyle's Sir Nigel Loring expresses the approved sentiment as the Middle Ages are shown drawing to a close:

> If the end be now come, I have had great fortune in having lived in times when so much glory was to be won, and in knowing so many valiant gentlemen and knights.[55]

Sir Nigel's gallantry and patriotism are a tribute to both his own class, that has for centuries carried the traditions of Britain, and the new democracy that must now take up those traditions. Precisely the same qualities were required because now, as then, the age was one of adventure, excitement and challenge. The code of manliness was, of course, expressed not only in historical fiction, but was also cultivated in schools (both public and board) and in the various youth organisations that were characteristic products of the age.[56] The novelist most commonly associated with the propagation of these attitudes is Kipling; he, certainly, played a conscious part in the process, but the cult of manliness was central in his work for only a short period of time, and there was often little that was truly 'romantic' in his portrayal of the servants of Empire. The more appropriate fictional comparisons are with such characters as Leo Vincey, Sir Henry Curtis, Rudolf Rassendyll and Sir Percy Blakeney, none of whom have equivalents in Kipling. Nor was Kipling's confidence about the ultimate triumph of British imperialism generally as all-embracing as that of many other writers, among them Conan Doyle, whose Lady Tiphaine foresees a future world that is totally Anglicised:

> On I go, and onwards over seas where man hath never yet sailed, and I see a great land under new stars and a stranger sky, and still the land is England. Where have her children not gone? What have they not done? Her banner is planted on ice. Her banner is scorched in the sun. She lies athwart the lands, and her shadow is over the seas.[57]

England's enemy at the time of that fifteenth-century vision was France, and, as far as most late Victorian historical fiction was concerned, France was still the main threat, even though in certain other types of fiction Germany was beginning to take on a new prominence. It was not so much the fear of direct war with France that attracted the attention of novelists as the example that France's more recent history could be made to yield for British readers. The year 1889 marked the centenary of the fall of the Bastille, and over the next twenty or so years hundreds of novels, exploring every possible aspect of France's revolutionary past, were published. Here was everything that late Victorian Britain and the British Empire should learn to avoid—a poverty-stricken maltreated populace, an arrogant aristocracy, violent revolt, a reign of terror, sexual licence, war, dictatorship, and then, with the lesson not learned, a similar pattern repeated over again. Fictional salvation was provided only by dashing debonair Englishmen and the few remnants of the French aristrocracy who had remained true to the principles of justice and honour that most of their fellow-aristocrats had forgotten.

In placing itself so abjectly at the service of dominant late Victorian domestic and imperial ideologies, historical fiction surrended the literary advantages held out to it by radically changing concepts of space and time: it played safe in an age that demanded experiment and speculation. Few novelists understood these demands better than Hardy. As Henry Knight clings desperately to the cliff-face in *A Pair of Blue Eyes* (1873), time closes up 'like a fan before him. He saw himself at one extremity of the years, face to face with the beginning and all the intermediate centuries simultaneously.'[58] In *Two on a Tower* (1882) Hardy has Swithin St Cleeve gazing not at the fossilised remains of long-dead creatures, but at the unknown 'horror' of the sky: 'You would hardly think, at first, that horrid monsters lie up there waiting to be discovered by any moderately penetrating mind–monsters to which those of the oceans bear no sort of comparison.'[59] Hardy's own fictional explorations of these phenomena remained within the contemporary world. For him, such perceptions expressed the torment of modern man, forced constantly to contrast his own ephemerality with the mocking stolidity of the physical world. The scientific romance acknowledged the contemporary crisis posed by Hardy, but focused its attention on the unlimited possibilities of future change. The revival of interest in Utopian and dystopian fiction established fabular forms which enabled writers to speculate freely on the possible ramifications of present social and political developments, and settled, virtually at a stroke, the apparent inability of the realistic novel to deal convincingly with political issues.[60] It was not surprising that the scientific romance should have accepted politics as a natural part of its concerns: it could, after all, trace the necessary connections back to Plato's *Republic*, something that H.G. Wells was particularly conscious of. Its more immediate literary context was provided by Bulwer Lytton's *The Coming Race* (1871), Samuel Butler's *Erewhon* (1872) and a large number of now largely forgotten novels inspired by evolutionary theory; Jules Verne's scientific tales, which in Britain were often regarded as boys' adventure books, and confirmed as such by the serialisation of many of the later ones in the *Boy's Own Paper*; and, from America, Edward Bellamy's *Looking Backward* (1887). It was Bellamy's vision of a future Boston made functionally beautiful by the technological miracles of science that prompted William Morris to offer a very different vision of the future in *News from Nowhere* (1891), while much of Wells's early work—especially *The Time Machine* (1895) and *When the Sleeper Wakes* (1899)—was motivated in part by his opposition to both Bellamy and Morris. The debate initiated here continues to the present day. It was not concerned primarily with fictional form, though nothing exactly comparable to these books had appeared before, but rather with the questions, how will modern democratic society develop, and will it survive at all? Bellamy stepped confidently into the future and announced that the machine would save mankind; Morris acknowledged the importance of the machine, but packed it out of sight so that it could do all the dirty work of life and leave people free to live as near to the ideal, and as beautifully, as his visionary view of the Middle Ages allowed. Wells placed his Time Traveller on an adapted bicycle—one of the most common symbols of social liberation in the 1890s—and sent him pedalling through time and space to a confrontation with a black, round, tentacled 'thing' which he finds 'hopping fitfully' about on a beach, framed against 'the red water of the sea'.[61]

For Bellamy and Morris the potential future of democracy was Utopian, created on the one hand by technological capitalism and on the other by a Marxist-Ruskinian revolution. Wells, attracted as he was by aspects of both of these ideologies, regarded the fate of democracy as being, like the fate of man himself, clothed in impenetrable darkness. There could, in his view, be no single, completed, attainable Utopia, but only stages of progression (or possibly regression) stretching out further into the future than it was possible for the puny mind of man to comprehend.[62] In Wells's hands, the scientific romance became an imaginative exploration of possible options, with futuristic prophecies usually functioning as extrapolations from observable contemporary trends: the claim for immediate relevance was enhanced by the domestic Home Counties setting or starting-point of the stories. No British realist of the time could match Wells's imaginative portrayal of the conflict between Capital and Labour in *The Time Machine*; or the dangers involved in the modern scientist becoming a new kind of God in *The Island of Dr Moreau*; or the nature of mass control in a totalitarian regime in *When the Sleeper Wakes*, a novel which points directly forward to such works as *We*, *Brave New World*, and *Nineteen Eighty-Four*. In a few years of frenzied activity, as the nineteenth century drew to a close, Wells created, or gave memorable modern form to, many of the images and themes that were to be repeated endlessly throughout the twentieth century, in both fiction and film–time travel; interplanetary war; the vast, glass-domed, self-contained city; mass frenzy; the invisible man; voyage to the moon; the morally corrupt or 'mad' scientist; everyday transportation by aeroplane and helicopter; the bombing of metropolitan populations; and, a few years later, atomic warfare. 'Where is *life* in all this, life as I feel it and know it?' Henry James asked of *Anticipantions* (1902), demonstrating, in the saddest possible way, that the modernist novel was ruthlessly determined to be about nothing but itself.[63]

In contrast, the scientific romance at the turn of the century, although on its way to establishing a separate identity, was still a very flexible term. Wells's short stories and romances drew indiscriminately on elements of horror, supernatural, psychological, fantastic and adventure fiction: in his later novels he turned increasingly to the Dialogue, reducing the role of story in order to give greater attention to speculation and prophecy. Certain kinds of narrative which involved journeys into the past rather than the future— Haggard's *She* (1887), Wells's 'The Country of the Blind' (1904), and Doyle's *The Lost World* (1912)—have clear affinities with science-fiction, as also do some of the novels which explored the *Doppelgänger* theme made popular by *Dr Jekyll and Mr Hyde* (1886). Science provides the means of character transformation in Stevenson's fable, and although it has little direct importance apart from that, the ethical and psychological conjecture it indirectly provokes does have a scientific rather than a miraculous origin; at a less imaginative level the mesmerism of du Maurier's *Trilby* (1894) and the drug addiction of the protagonist of Katherine Thurston's *John Chilcote MP* (1904) serve similar purposes. Much closer to later developments in science fiction were Kipling's experiments with non-realistic literary forms. His fascinated interest in technology could be anthropomorphic, as in '.007' and 'The Ship that Found Herself'; mysterious, in 'Mrs Bathurst'; or supernatural, in 'Wireless'. His two stories about the Aerial Board of Control—'With the Night Mail' and 'As Easy as ABC'—are futuristic in the manner of Wells and similarly speculative about the way the world is going. A related experimentation is observable in Kipling's revival of the animal fable. The two *Jungle Books* can be read as exciting tales, an exercise in Darwinism, or as allegorical representations of the type of hierarchical society that must be retained if the lawlessness of the bandar-log is to be controlled: while fables like 'Below the Mill Dam', 'The Mother Hive' and 'Little Foxes' follow the more obvious science-fiction tales in the use of non-realistic forms to voice explicit social criticism.

Both Kipling and Wells drew on the 'invasion novels' which were published in very large numbers throughout this period, and out of which there emerged one of the twentieth century's most characteristic types of formula fiction. Credit for initiating the 'invasion' trend is usually given to Sir George Chesney's *The Battle of Dorking* (1871). As I.F. Clarke has shown, late Victorian interest in fiction that prophesied the nature of future warfare and showed Britain over-run by, or successfully resisting, invading foreign forces, was a direct product of the changing balance of power in Europe–the Franco-Prussian war in 1870; the gradual displacement of France by Germany as Britain's likeliest military foe; the rapid technological developments that led to a naval arms race between Britain and Germany; and the urgent diplomatic manoeuvres in the early years of the present century that took Britain out of 'splendid isolation' and into new kinds of national alignments.[64] The invasion novels ranged from works with an informed interest in military strategy, like *The Battle of Dorking*; through M.P. Shiel's sensational *The Yellow Wave* (1905), and the anti-German propaganda fiction commissioned and serialised by Alfred Harmsworth; to the young P.G. Wodehouse's boy-scout proof *The Swoop! or How Clarence Saved England* (1909). In *The War of the Worlds* (1898) Wells took an imaginative leap— characteristic of him but beyond most authors of invasion novels—and made the enemy not France, Germany, China or Japan, but Mars. The conviction that a European war involving Britain was inevitable sooner or later meant that diplomacy alone could not be trusted. An Army Intelligence Department was formed as early as 1873; it was followed by a Naval Intelligence Board in 1887, the first Official Secrets Act in 1889, the more rigorous Official Secrets Act of 1911, and, in the same year, the formation of MI5 and MI6. Popular novelists like E. Phillips Oppenheim, and especially William Le Queux (who had written invasion novels for Harmsworth's newspapers), were quick to recognise the fictional potential offered by this latest version of the ancient profession of the undercover agent, and with works like Oppenheim's *Mysterious Mr Sabin* (1898) and Le Queux's *Secrets of the Foreign Office* (1903) and *The Man From Downing Street* (1904), the modern spy novel began to take shape. The foreign agent—treacherous, dishonourable and mercenary, of course—was already a familiar figure in invasion fiction: his British counterpart—who was, just as naturally, patriotic, honourable and selfless—made his appearance a little later. David Stafford fixes Duckworth Drew in Le Queux's *Secrets of the Foreign Office* as 'probably ... the first in a long tradition of gentlemanly secret agents' in British fiction.[65] A close relation, and ultimately of more literary significance, was the patriot who gets caught unwillingly and at first uncomprehendingly in intelligence activities. Erskine Childers led the way with *The Riddle of the*

Sands (1903), and was followed by John Buchan's *The Thirty-Nine Steps* (1915).

The ghosts, phantasms, and spirits of various kinds that feature so prominently in the fiction of the period were far older phenomena than even spies and undercover agents: they, however, also seemed new. As one commentator noted in 1900: 'The old spectre of our childhood with his clanking chains has faded into nothingness in this age of inquiry. If he appears again it is in a new character and he must at least be civil to the Society for Psychical Research.'[66] Henry James, the author of several outstanding tales of the supernatural in addition to the incomparable *The Turn of the Screw* (1898) also recognised, in order to dismiss it, 'the new type ... the mere modern "psychical" case ... equipped with credentials' which he saw as destroying 'the dear old sacred terror'[67] Certainly, the influence was not all in one direction, or all of one kind. F.W.H. Myers was so fascinated by *Dr Fekyll and Mr Hyde* that he sent Stevenson detailed comments on the story, together with suggestions for its possible improvement.[68] The appearances of the devil in Stevenson's 'Thrawn Janet' and Corelli's *The Sorrows of Satan* were clearly not prompted by the Society for Psychical Research. Nor did the Society play any part in the development of several branches of supernatural fiction at this time—the semiplayful horror story, for example, that descends from Stevenson's *New Arabian Nights* (1882), to, most notably, Arthur Machen's *The Great God Pan* (1894) and *The Three Impostors* (1895); or the fantasy, fairy, and 'celtic twilight' tales that attracted such diverse writers as George MacDonald, Lord Dunsany, 'Fiona Macleod', J.M. Barrie, Kipling, G.K. Chesterton, Walter de la Mare, E. Nesbit (with novels like *Five Children and It*, 1902, *The Phoenix and the Carpet*, 1904, and *The Enchanted Castle*, 1907), and the side of Algernon Blackwood's neglected talent that found expression in *Jimbo* (1909), *The Human Chord* (1910), *The Centaur* (1911) and *The Prisoner in Fairyland* (1913). The areas of experience covered by the general term 'supernatural' are many and varied, and their fictional representations almost as unclassifiable as the possible types of historical fiction. Yet the impact made by the Society for Psychical Research was immediate and observable. The young Kipling, in India and fascinated by the ancient spiritual and supernatural beliefs he found all around him, would seem to have had no need to refer to the certified case-studies being compiled in London, though in one of the earliest of his Indian stories he has the narrator comment: 'That was more than enough! I had my ghost—a first-hand authenticated article. I would write to the Society for Psychical Research—I would paralyse the Empire with the news!'[69] The narrator is being ironic, and the ghost in question is not really a ghost at all, but already

Kipling's later, more serious involvement with psychical phenomena can be seen establishing itself. Henry James, like Stevenson, corresponded with Myers, and would have had still closer knowledge of the SPR through his brother William James. *The Turn of the Screw* took the form of a classically unverifiable ghost story in order that it should not fall into the trap of being a 'psychical case': even so, for some of the details of his story James probably drew on material in the published papers of the SPR.[70]

It was pointed out in Chapter Two that some of the investigations of the SPR had much in common with early developments in psychoanalysis, and it can be added that the detailed case-studies published in the Society's *Proceedings*, in books by members of the Society like Frank Podmore's *Phantasms of the Living* (1886) and *Modern Spiritualism* (1902), and Myers's *Human Personality* (1903), and in many related books such as Andrew Lang's *Dreams and Ghosts* (1887) and *Cock Lane and Common Sense* (1894), not only read like ghost stories, but also provided many novelists with their raw material. Here were ghosts and hallucinations, *Doppelgängers*, dreams and nightmares, poltergeists and table-rappings, automatic-writing, precognition, hypnotism, materialisations of every conceivable form, and, as was noted earlier, Freud, Breuer, hysteria, and incipient theories of the sub-conscious. There can be little doubt that the new sophistication of the ghost story owed a considerable debt to the SPR, though the wider growth of interest in supernatural phenomena, at least during the Victorian age, had its origins, as did the SPR itself, in the undermining of religious faith by historical and scientific criticism.[71] The popularity of the ghost story increased as the authority of organised religion declined. The responses of SPR investigators and novelists were not, however, identical, with each other or between themselves. For some, the existence of states of consciousness that were not subject to man's control created a challenge that scientific knowledge would ultimately come to understand, if not actually master: for others, it provided evidence that the much-vaunted concept of Victorian progress was finally breaking down, revealing the emptiness of the material world, and with it the vulnerability of fictional realism. Either way, the supernatural provided a means for many writers to come to terms with areas of experience which the destructively analytical tenor of the age appeared to be closing off: in the common language of supernatural fiction, doors were opened, veils raised, and hitherto unsuspected levels of awareness revealed.

There were mysterious Christian allegories (Mrs Oliphant, *A Beleaguered City*, 1979); 'primitive survivals', of the kind identified by anthropologists, masquerading as 'bogles' in the Scottish Highlands (John Buchan, 'No-Man's-Land', 1898); whimsical spirits (Richard Middleton, *The*

Ghost Ship, 1912); spirits wreaking revenge from distant parts of the Empire
(W.W. Jacobs, 'The Monkey's Paw', 1902); the dead taking over the bodies
of the living (Walter de la Mare, *The Return*, 1908); and some highly
convincing erotic ghosts (Robert Hichens, 'How Love Came to Professor
Guildea', in *Tongues of Conscience* (1900); Oliver Onions, 'The Beckoning Fair
One', *Widdershins*, 1911). Algernon Blackwood's lasting contribution to
supernatural fiction came in 1908 with *John Silence*, a collection of five stories
which reintroduced the idea of the Psychic Doctor and initiated a
distinguished series of stories from Blackwood which he described as studies
'of extended or expanded consciousness'[72] M.R. James had nothing of
Blackwood's fascination with the possible causes of supernatural
manifestations: he was concerned solely with effects. If there is to be left 'a
loophole for a natural explanation', James advised, 'let the loophole be so
narrow as not to be quite practicable'.[73] In some ways, that assumption turns
his *Ghost Stories of an Antiquary* (1904) and *More Ghost Stories* (1911) into
exercises in horror rather than supernatural explorations. But the blend that
James achieved of quiet scholarly atmosphere, old towns and flat landscapes
(often East Anglia), and inexplicable malevolent forces, has become, for
many modern readers, the very type of 'English' ghost story. Kipling too
became associated with a particular kind of Englishness, in this area of his
work as in so many others, but the range of his interests, stretched always by
his linguistic and narrative daring, kept him constantly present as the
epitome of the changing nature of consciousness discussed here. The
animism of rural England in 'A Friendly Brook' has to be set against the
inexplicable horror of 'At the End of the Passage' and 'The Mark of the
Beast'; the spiritualistic pathos of 'They'; the telepathy of 'The Dog Hervey';
the metempsychosis of 'The Finest Story in the World'; the Christian
benediction of 'The Gardener'; the power of transforming love granted by
the wraith in 'The Wish House'; and, ultimately, after two decades of
exploring nervous disorder as the type of modern illness, the explicit
Freudianism of 'In the Same Boat'.

Of all the romantic specialists of the age—whether scientist,
sociologist, psychic doctor, journalist, space traveller, alienist, imperial
explorer, spy, modernist, town-planner or psychoanalyst—none offered so
specialised, and yet so comprehensive, a service as the private detective as
personified by Sherlock Holmes. Holmes was by no means the first detective
in fiction.[74] Nor did he lead the way, in any chronological sense, among late
Victorian fictional detectives: throughout the 1870s and 1880s the detective
had been a familiar character in books, penny-dreadfuls, and periodicals.
Holmes first made his appearance in two short novels, *A Study in Scarlet*

(1887) and *The Sign of Four* (1890), but it was not until the publication of the first of the short stories, 'A Scandal in Bohemia' in the *Strand* in July 1891 that his remarkable popularity began. He became almost immediately the most famous detective in the world—though challenged for much of this century, it has been claimed, by another late Victorian creation Sexton Blake—and he remains so to the present day.[75] When Conan Doyle sent Holmes to his apparent death with Moriarty over the Re ichenbach Falls, there were many other writers eager to produce a replacement, but while there were enough readers of detective fiction around to support the work of, among others, Arthur Morrison, Baroness Orczy, Ernest Bramah and R. Austin Freeman, there could be no satisfactory substitute for Holmes. Of his most serious rivals at this time only G.K. Chesterton with *The Innocence of Father Brown* (1911) and *The Wisdom of Father Brown* (1913) came near to creating a detective with the mythic stature of Holmes. Among his other worthwhile challengers were Inspector Hanaud of A.E.W. Mason's *At the Villa Rosa* (1910), and E.W. Hornung's inverted crime stories which feature the criminal rather than the detective, *Raffles: The Amateur Cracksman* (1899) and *Raffles: The Black Mask* (1901). By 1913 the detective story was sufficiently established for E.C. Bentley to publish an enjoyable spoof of the genre, *Trent's Last Case*. Bentley hit many of his targets effectively enough, but not Holmes, who had placed himself beyond the reach of harmful satire or parody.

That the police force had a special and urgent role to play in modern urban society was a mid-Victorian rather than a late Victorian perception: its fictional expression is to be found in Dickens's *Bleak House* and Collins's *The Moonstone*. These detectives are in some respects already the solitary, wide-roaming, tight-lipped unravellers of riddles familiar to twentieth-century readers and film-goers, except that they are also policemen, and, for Dickens especially, their centre of operations is the police station, a spotlessly clean, well-lighted centre of authority and calm in a chaotic urban world.[76] In contrast, Holmes is a 'consulting detective', who only takes up crimes that the police cannot solve and, at his best, succeeds 'where the police of three countries had failed'.[77] This separation of the police and the detective in fiction can to some extent be explained historically. As Ian Ousby has noted, the formation of the Criminal Investigation Department in 1878 gave detectives an expanded role within the police force, and in the 1880s there was a good deal of public disillusionment with the police, especially over the Fenian bomb outrages and the Jack the Ripper murders.[78] Additional contributory factors to the atmosphere of the Holmes stories were the growing tenseness of European diplomatic relations and the increasing use by nations of undercover agents. Holmes was fully aware of the fraught state of international diplomacy, and Watson liked to hint that certain cases he was involved in were diplomatically too sensitive to be revealed to the readers of the *Strand* for some years to come. Not that Holmes himself could ever be identified with anything as limited as an undercover agent: there are some doubts whether he was even human. 'All emotions ... were abhorrent to his cold, precise, but admirably balanced mind,' Watson comments chillingly; 'He was, I take it, the most perfect reasoning and observing machine that the world has seen.'[79] That is, surely, going quite a bit too far: if Holmes were so totally a machine then he could never have served the double role that Julian Symons has well described as a Nietzschean 'Superman' who is simultaneously 'the Great Outsider'.[80] The vision of an Anglicised world given to Lady Tiphaine in *The White Company* would have counted as prophecy within the fifteenth-century setting of that novel, but to the late Victorian Doyle it had become all but a fact. Sherlock Holmes embodied Doyle's own dream that with a good deal of care the world might just stay that way.

Like so many other protagonists of late Victorian fiction, Holmes is an explorer: the greatest of them all. One of the first things that Watson notices about him is his occasional habit of taking long walks 'into the lowest portions of the city'.[81] From those walks he gains his substantial knowledge of Darkest London and recruits the street urchins who serve him as the Baker Street 'irregulars'. His principle area of exploration is, however, his own mind. Most cases he can solve without leaving his room, just as he can recognise someone who has come from Afghanistan without having been there himself. It is sometimes said of Holmes that he is the allround man in an age of specialists, but that is surely not correct: he is the supreme specialist. He believes that 'a man should possess all knowledge which is likely to be useful to him in his work', and take little notice of anything else. He is exceptionally well-informed on 'sensational literature' but not other kinds of literature: he is also a first-class scientist, actor, boxer, and swordsman.[82] One of the things he is not interested in is politics, but that hardly matters as he is an ardent supporter of established governments and the royal families of Europe. The specialism to which all of his formidable knowledge is directed is, of course, the scientific investigation of crime, the activity which more than any other threatens to upset the established order he represents. If he is attracted only to the more arcane and complex crimes, that does not mean that lesser criminals are getting away with anything. On the contrary, his power spreads omnipotently over the modern city: 'He loved to lie in the very centre of five millions of people, with his filaments stretching out and running through them, responsive to every little rumour or suspicion of unsolved crime.'[83] If anyone should get past the police, he is picked up by Sherlock Holmes. 'I am,' he announces, 'the last court of appeal.'[84] When, eventually, the criminal evil he has to confront is so great that it can be defeated in no other way, he willingly sacrifices his own life. In dying with the 'Napoleon of Crime' he vanquishes not only the 'organiser of half that is evil and of nearly all that is undetected in this great city', but the great representative of Britain's traditional national enemy as well.[85]

Shortly before his final battle with Moriarty, Holmes reveals a side of himself that had hitherto been given little prominence. Travelling with Watson on a train high over South London, Holmes gazes down into the working-class abyss, exactly as Masterman was to do a few years later. Holmes, however, finds the sight of 'big, isolated clumps of buildings' rising out of a 'lead-coloured sea' cheering. Watson thinks them 'sordid', and explains that they are Board Schools. As on so many previous occasions, Holmes forcefully corrects his companion: 'Lighthouses, my boy! Beacons of the future! Capsules, with hundreds of bright little seeds in each, out of which will spring the wiser, better England of the future.'[86] It is difficult to imagine that those little English boys could turn out to be wiser or brighter than Holmes, but if that should happen it would be because Holmes had been there to watch over their formative years.

NOTES

1. See, John Lucas, *The Idea of the Provincial* (Loughborough 1981), and *The Literature of Change: Studies in the Nineteenth-Century Provincial Novel* (Hassocks 1977).

2. See, Asa Briggs, *Victorian Cities*, (1963) Chapter Eight.

3. For the gradual growth of interest in, and the various types of, regional fiction, see Lucien Leclaire, *A General Analytical Bibliography of the British Isles* (Clermant-Ferrand 1954).

4. *Literature* II (23 April 1898), p. 463.

5. See, Martha Vicinus, *The Industrial Muse*, Chapter Five.

6. *The Country and the City* (1973), p. 197.

7. See: James, *Letters*, III, 406–7; Woolf, 'The Novels of Thomas Hardy', *Collected Essays*, I, pp. 256–66.

8. Preface to the 1895 edition of *Far From the Madding Crowd*.

9. *Ibid.*

10. *Collected Letters.*

11. Quoted, Roger Ebbatson, *Lawrence and the Nature Tradition* (Brighton 1980), p. 147.

12. *Green Mansions* (1904), pp. 4, 83.

13. For the various manifestations of ruralism at this time, see: Glen Cavaliero, *The Rural Tradition in the English Novel* (1977); John Alcorn, *The Nature Novel from Hardy to*

Lawrence (1977): and the popular books by 'Elizabeth', beginning with *Elizabeth and her German Garden* (1898).

14. Quoted, Charles Carrington, *Rudyard Kipling: His Life and Work* (Harmondsworth 1970), p. 438.

15. 'A Charm', *Rewards and Fairies*, p. ix.

16. 'Scottish National Character', *Blackwood's Magazine*, LXXXVII (June 1860), p. 722.

17. *Punch*, CIX (7 December 1895), p. 274.

18. J.H. Millar, 'The Literature of the Kailyard', *New Review* XII (1895). More generally for the Kailyard, see George Blake, *Barrie and the Kailyard School* (1951); Eric Anderson, 'The Kailyard School', *Nineteenth-Century Scottish Fiction*, edited by Ian Campbell (Manchester 1979); Thomas D. Knowles, *Ideology, Art and Commerce: Aspects of Literary Sociology in the Late Victorian Scottish Kailyard* (Gothenburg 1983).

19. Quoted, Knowles, *Ideology, Art and Commerce*, p. 24.

20. *Margaret Ogilvy* (1896), pp. 73–4.

21. Quoted, Anderson, 'The Kailyard School', *Nineteenth-Century Scottish Fiction*, p. 145.

22. *Ideology, Art and Commerce*, p. 47.

23. Quoted, Ian Campbell, 'George Douglas Brown', *Nineteenth-Century Scottish Fiction*, p. 149.

24. *The Unspeakable Scot* (1902), pp. 87–94.

25. *A Literary History of Scotland* (1903), p. 680.

26. *Mankind in the Making*, p. 359.

27. *Henry James and H.G. Wells*, p. 136.

28. Wagner, *How to Publish*, p. 43.

29. 'The Next Time', *Complete Tales*, IX, 227.

30. *Letters to William Blackwood*, p. 154; *Lord Jim* (Harmondsworth 1982), p. 11.

31. Max Pemberton, *Sixty Years Ago and After* (1936), pp. 94–121.

32. Cohen, *Rider Haggard*, p. 85.

33. *The Egoist*, p. 2; *Diana of the Crossways*, pp. 17–8. See also Meredith's *On the Idea of Comedy and the Uses of the Comic Spirit* (1877).

34. *John Inglesant: A Romance* ('Macmillan Illustrated Pocket Classics', 1905), p. vii.

35. *Ibid.*, ix.

36. *English Criticism of the Novel 1865–1900* (Oxford 1965), p. 66.

37. 'Realism and Romance', *Contemporary Review*, LII (November 1887), p. 691.

38. 'The Present State of the Novel', *Fortnightly Review* XLII (September 1887) p. 417.

39. 'Realism and Romace', pp. 693–4.

40. See, Cohen, *Rider Haggard*, pp. 117, 125.

41. 'At the Sign of the Ship', *Longman's Magazine*, XXV (November 1894), p. 103.

42. For Lang in a wider context, see Roger Lancelyn Green, *Andrew Lang: A Critical Biography* (1946), and *Andrew Lang* (1962).

43. 'A Humble Remonstrance', p. 136.

44. 'A Humble Remonstrance' and 'A Gossip on Romance', *Memories and Portraits* pp. 124, 123, 129. See also, Stevenson's 'A Note on Realism,' *Essays Literary and Critical*.

45. Among many studies, see: Colin Manlove, *Modern Fantasy: Five Studies* (Cambridge 1975); Stephen Prickett, *Victorian Fantasy* (Hassocks 1979); H.P. Lovecraft, *Supernatural Horror in Literature* (1945); David Punter, *The Literature of Terror* (1980).

46. 'A Case of Identity,' *The Adventures of Sherlock Holmes* (Pan Books, 1976), p. 41.

47. *Henry Brocken.*

48. Lilith (1895), p. 5.

49. *Dracula,* p. 37.

50. *Collected Letters,* I, pp. 369–70.

51. For example, Jonathan Nield, *A Guide to the Best Historical Novels and Tales* (1902); Ernest Baker, History in Fiction (2 vols 1907) and *A Guide to Historical Fiction* (1914).

52. *Memories and Adventures* (1924), p. 80.

53. *History in Fiction,* I, p. 192.

54. See, Valerie Chancellor, *History for their Masters: Opinion in the English History Textbook* (1970).

55. *The White Company* ('Author's Edition' 1903), p. 419.

56. See, John Springhall, *Youth, Empire and Society: British Youth Movements 1883–1940* (1977).

57. *The White Company,* p. 399.

58. *A Pair of Blue Eyes,* p. 242.

59. *Two on a Tower,* p. 34.

60. See, Michael Wilding, *Political Fictions* (1980). Among the many surveys of science fiction, see: J.O. Bailey, Pilgrims Through Space and Time (New York 1947); Mark R. Hillegas, *The Future as Nightmare* (New York 1967); Brian Aldiss, *Billion Year Spree* (1973); Darko Suvin, *Metamorphoses of Science Fiction* (new Haven 1980).

61. *The Time Machine,* p. 78.

62. For the development of the Wellsian concept of Utopia, see Roslynn Haynes, *H.G. Wells: Discoverer of the Future* (1980), pp. 82–111.

63. *Henry James and H. G. Wells,* p. 76.

64. See, I.F. Clarke, *Voices Prophesying War 1763–1984* (1966), and *The Pattern of Expectation 1644–2001* (1979).

65. 'Spies and Gentlemen: The Birth of the British Spy Novel, 1893–1914', *Victorian Studies,* XXIV (Summer 1981), p. 490.

66. *Literature,* VI (13 January 1900), p. 50.

67. *The Art of the Novel,* p. 169.

68. The exchange between Myers and Stevenson is reprinted in *Robert Louis Stevenson: The Critical Heritage,* edited by Paul Maixner (1981), pp. 212–22.

69. 'My Own True Ghost Story', *Wee Willie Winkie and Other Stories,* p. 165.

70. See, E.A. Sheppard, *Henry James and The Turn of the Screw* (Oxford 1974), Chapter Eight.

71. See especially, Julia Briggs, *Night Visitors;* also, Dorothy Scarborough, *The Supernatural in Modern English Fiction* (New York 1917), and Peter Penzoldt, *The Supernatural in Fiction* (1952).

72. In his introduction to *The Tales of Algernon Blackwood* (1938), p. xi.

73. Quoted, Briggs, *Night Visitors,* p. 141.

74. For the history of detective fiction, see: *The Development of the Detective Novel* (1958); Julian Symons, *Bloody Murder: From the Detective Story to the Crime Novel* (1972); Ian Ousby, *Bloodhounds of Heaven: The Detective in English Fiction from Godwin to Doyle* (Cambridge, Mass. 1976).

75. E.S. Turner, *Boys will be Boys* (1948), p. 117.

76. See, *Bleak House,* chapter Fifty-Seven, and Collins, *Dickens and Crime,* Chapter 9.

77. *A Study in Scarlet* (1888), p. 21; 'The Reigate Squires', *The Memoirs of Sherlock Holmes* (Harmondsworth 1972), p. 117.

78. *Bloodhounds of Heaven*, pp. 129–32.

79. 'A Scandal in Bohemia', *Adventures of Sherlock Holmes*, p. 15.

80. *Bloody Murder* (Harmondsworth 1974), p. 74.

81. *A Study in Scarlet*, p. 13.

82. *Ibid.*, pp. 16–17.

83. 'The Resident Patient', *Memoirs*, p. 159.

84. 'The Five Orange Pips', *Adventures*, p. 118.

85. 'The Final Problem', *Memoirs*, p. 239.

86. 'The Naval Treaty', *Ibid.*, p. 215.

ANNETTE FEDERICO

The Other Victim:
Jude the Obscure and *The Whirlpool*

"Of course the book is all contrasts—or was meant to be in its original conception," wrote Hardy of his last novel, significantly identifying the contrasts as being not primarily between Jude and Sue, but within each character: "Jude the saint, Jude the sinner; Sue the pagan, Sue the saint; marriage, no marriage." As successful as the novel is in illustrating this principle of opposition, it is, I think, even more effective as a story of fatal imbalances and extremes. In the same letter to Edmund Gosse quoted above, Hardy described Sue Bridehead's "abnormalism" as consisting of "disproportion."[1] Indeed, disproportion and self-absorption control the lives of the main characters to such an extent that their tragedy lies in their own inability to discover an obscure middle way in a modern world represented by antithetical fronts, each fanatically resisting infiltration by the other.

One representation of the contrasts Hardy was occupied with is revealed in the repeated references to ancient and modern, old world and new world, the former symbolizing stability, the latter chaos. Jude and Sue hang somewhere in between, not firmly anchored. Their nomadic lifestyle signifies a restless questing for some kind of equilibrium or poised stability— both objectively, within their society ("marriage, no marriage"), and subjectively, within themselves, especially in their sexual identities.

Gissing's novel, *The Whirlpool* (1897), published two years after Hardy's, is strikingly like *Jude* in its delineation of contrasts and

From *Masculine Identity in Hardy and Gissing.* © 1991 by Associated University Presses, Inc.

disproportions. The protagonist, Harvey Rolfe, clings to his books, to ancient history, to masculine common sense in resistance to Alma Frothingham's emotional identity crisis, and her Sue Bridehead-like nervousness. The impression of split perceptions, of civilization and barbarism, a morally clear-cut old world and a morally confused modern one, is everywhere in the novel, provoking the only happy man in the book, Basil Morton, to utter sagely, "Medio tutissimus"—a middle course is best. But for Harvey Rolfe and Hugh Carnaby, and for virtually every man who collides with the feminine, the middle way is impossible. What lies between "rut and whirlpool"—Rolfe's wonderfully apt names for the division he perceives as inherent in modern life—is a void. As in *Jude*, suicidal behavior informs Gissing's work with a sense of the destructiveness of this moral chaos and the unreasonable pressures men (as well as women) place upon themselves to be happy, either in Wessex, where "mutual butchery" is Nature's law, or in London, where Rolfe stands alone "amid a world of cruelties" (384).

That both Hardy and Gissing should feel depressed about their society may be connected to the fact that very little of the world of Victorian optimism, confidently patriarchal, was easily discoverable after 1890, and what remained of it was rather uneasily organized. Feminism had come out of the newpapers and platforms—the public, political realm—and into the private, personal sphere of men's homes, libraries, and offices, the sanctioned spaces of masculinity. Indeed, Phillotson's anguished moan to Sue Bridehead, "What do I care about J.S. Mill? I only want to lead a quiet life," could very well represent the cry of the exhausted male in the mid-1890s. For men like Phillotson and Harvey Rolfe, who feel not only invaded but baffled by independent-minded women, surrender is preferable to combat. There is no battle of wills between the sexes, as in *The Odd Women*, and no sexual coercion (at least not on the part of men), as in *Tess*. Rolfe gives in to what he feels are his wife's neurotic suggestions, pacifying her, desires and enduring her emotional swings from self-assertion to submission to self-mortification, with almost stoical patience, craving above all a peaceful household. Jude, too, is heroicially unaggressive and indulgent with Sue; we are almost relieved to hear a rare speech of indignation from him: "I've waited with the patience of Job, and I don't see that I've got anything for my self denial," he tells her on one occasion, but more often it is, "My dear one, your happiness is more to me than anything—although we seem to verge on quarrelling so often!—and your will is law to me" (209, 191). But despite their apparent tractability, these male characters are not exactly giving in to feminine aggression. Jude and Rolfe are hardly hen-pecked husbands cowed into submission by argumentative wives. Their way of dealing with women who are seriously confused and struggling with an intense personal need to carve out some place for themselves in their society is to be broadminded, patient, and understanding—in other words, anything but the old-fashioned Victorian tyrant, the man like Phillotson's friend Gillingham, who recommends that Sue "ought to be smacked, and brought to her senses" (185). These modern-minded male protagonists profess their belief in sexual equality, marital independence, and female professionalism. "Do understand and believe me. I don't want to shape you to any model of my own," Rolfe tells Alma before their marriage. "I want you to be your true self, and live the life you are meant for" (118). And Jude, of course, is willing to do whatever Sue wishes, to marry, not to marry, or to marry, but not each other.

Despite the positive implications—men *are* paying attention to what women are feeling—this male martyrdom verges on withdrawal from, not participation in, the reality of women's struggles. Harvey Rolfe, especially, is a weak middle-class man who expresses his dislike for women in general and his exasperation with his wife in particular by avoiding the opposite sex as much as possible. He never imaginatively, sympathetically enters into Alma's terrifyingly empty world; instead he "meditated on Woman" (359), and we can imagine him shaking his head at the riddle. Similarly, for all of Jude's worshipful affection for Sue, there is a sense of baffled condescension in his attitude toward her. She is always "a riddle to him," "one lovely conundrum"—"essentially large-minded and generous on reflection, despite a previous exercise of those narrow womanly humours on impulse that were necessary to give her sex" (108–9, 134). The female and her problems, so mystifying to the male, must be treated delicately, with reasonableness and patience; her very being is stamped, as Hardy says, "the Weaker" (112). Men must treat her, then, with gentle understanding in order to assure their own sexual survival.

In his discussion of *Jude the Obscure in Phoenix*, D.H. Lawrence addresses this problem of men's detachment from women's inner lives by referring to Sue Bridehead's underrated and highly developed individuality:

> Sue had a being, special and beautiful.... Why must man be so utterly irreverent, that he approaches each being as if it were a no-being? Why must it be assumed that Sue is an "ordinary" woman—as if such a thing existed? Why must she feel ashamed if she is specialized? ... She was Sue Bridehead, something very particular. Why was there no place for her?[2]

Sue herself says, "I am not really Mrs. Richard Phillotson, but a woman tossed about, all alone, with aberrant passions, and unaccountable antipathies" (163). The same words could be uttered by Gissing's heroine as she tries to find a place for herself as a free-thinking young woman abroad, as Mrs. Harvey Rolfe in a small house in North Wales, as a professional violinist in London, and as a self-subdued ex-professional, a wife and mother, in the suburbs. These women's experiences are so intense and so personal that they seem neurotic, inconsistent, even cruel from the male point of view. That their nervousness should permeate masculine consciousness is not surprising, especially since men have their own anxieties about changing sexual relations—hence Jude's and especially Rolfe's preoccupation with control, reasonableness, unemotionalism.

The smooth current of institutionalized masculinity itself seems disturbed by women's problems as they are acted out in the private sphere of personal relationships. "You make a personal matter of everything!" cries Jude to Sue at one point in the novel, surprised that she would introduce "personal feeling into mere argument" (122). Perhaps the most intimidating aspect of late-century feminism for men in *Jude* and *The Whirlpool* is precisely this transference by women of abstract political or rhetorical arguments into men's private lives: What does J.S. Mill have to do with us? Basil Ransom, the hero of James's The Bostonians (1886) makes a similar complaint to Verena Tarrant. "There you are—you women—all over; always meaning yourselves, something personal, and always thinking it is meant by others!" (327). It is baffling to men that women should suddenly have become so serious, so thoughtful, and so personal about social ideas.

For Sue Bridehead, obviously, the personal is political, and she is deadly serious when she applies intellectual arguments to her private world. Alma, too, is vocal about her unconventionality, although, like Sue, she fails to live the revolution. The combination of "sweet reasonableness"—Rolfe's initial impression of Alma—or an intellect that "sparkles like diamonds," as Phillotson describes Sue, and unreasonable eccentricities, "colossal inconsistency," and oversensitivity, makes women appear both strong and vulnerable, sexually attractive and sexually perverse to the men who love them. But the men in *Jude* and *The Whirlpool* learn surprisingly little from women's experiences of the world, even though they are intimate witnesses to a gradual process of self-destruction, which is not at all gender-specific, since not only secondary male characters, but the male protagonists themselves, suffer from morbidity and depression, and even exhibit suicidal tendencies. What is designated as modern confusion or feminine inconsistency—Women's Problems—may be an unconscious appropriation of men's own latent hysteria and social/sexual phobias onto women.

Outwardly it is clear how the essential duality of the world is set up in these two novels. Confusion, a complex civilization, and modernity are identified with women, who, appropriately enough, seem nervous, vain, sexually abnormal, and hysterical; nature, simplicity, rationality, and sanity are masculine attributes. Careful readings of the novels reveal that men, too, are standing on the edge of an emotional void, and need only that feminine push to lose themselves altogether. Jude is no less nervous than Sue, and Rolfe suffers from "neuralsia," though the male response to these modern maladies is not "hysteria," but "common sense." There is a strong sense of emotional repression in Jude and Rolfe, and as I will explain later, Gissing's character succeeds in building a wall around his emotional life that finally imprisons him. In one passage in *Jude*, Hardy appears to regret that men must stifle expressions of emotion: "If [Jude] had been a woman he must have screamed under the nervous tension which he was now undergoing. But that relief being denied to his virility, he clenched his teeth in misery" (102). Men are emotionally disenfranchised because of their "virility," the trap of an essentially male-created, gender-defined personality; and men, besides feeling privately oppressed, are beginning to be openly labelled "the oppressor" by New Women (though as Jude tells Sue, men are also victims of socialized sexual identities). For example, Rolfe constantly blames himself for his lapses from idealized manliness—his lack of discretion, common sense, forcefulness, rationality, and courage. Jude is possibly the most self-doubting, passive man in all of Hardy's novels, whom Arabella calls "a tender-hearted fool" (54). Thus the gender-opposition that is the ostensible thematic base of *Jude the Obscure* and *The Whirlpool*—her irrationality, his common sense, her chaotic modernism, his simplified traditionalism—is really gender-reflection: the female is obviously wilfull, restless, nervous, alienated; she is also vain and sexually manipulative. The male role is an inverted reflection of these feminine traits, an intentional pose of masculine sanity meant to balance feminine panic. This kind of sexual "compensation" is developed at the cost of male sexual identity; the potential self is buried under repression and denials, and periodically exposed in men's bouts of self-questioning and their enervated desire for peace, retreat, "a quiet life."

That the men in *Jude* and *The Whirlpool* should feel so defeated, even victimized, is something of a paradox, for the heroines in these two novels are not aggressive, vampirish feminists (as in some late-nineteenth century novels by men).[3] Ironically, it is Sue's feminine nervousness and sexual weakness that Jude finds intimidating, not her feminist polemics: "Her very helplessness seemed to make her so much stronger than he" (120). It is women's femininity, not their unfeminine aggressiveness, that overcomes male common sense and self-mastery, and the male protagonists in Hardy and Gissing are ambivalent about fighting an enemy who is so charming at the same time she is threatening—indeed, dangerous in her very delightfulness. Sue and Alma are anything but caricatures of draconic New Women. In *Jude* and *The Whirlpool*, woman is not the destroyer of man, but rather *mulier est hominis confusio*—man's confusion, and more than in the biblical sense of woman as man's ruin. She is also the confusion of man's senses, a sweet infection of disorder in the rational masculine world. To confound a man's self-possession and intellectuality, at least in these novels, may also enkindle "a fresh and wild pleasure" (as Jude feels at first for Arabella). The exasperating and devastating Sue Bridehead is above all, to Jude, "sweet Sue." Likewise in *The Whirlpool*, Rolfe is mesmerized by Alma's enticing beauty: "His cheek was not far from hers; the faint perfume floated all about him; he could imagine it the natural fragrance of her hair, of her breath" (121). Rolfe's senses are pleasantly besotted, but such self-forgetting emotion in a man who is "all but despising himself for loving her" (120) feels like intellectual defeat.

This contradictory impression of woman as both the delight and the destroyer of male sexuality is treated in *Jude* and *The Whirlpool* quite unexpressionistically and with very little romance. Alma and Sue are not, say, Oscar Wilde's Salome or Bram Stoker's Lucy Westenra. You do not find in Hardy and Gissing the lyrical ruminations of the patriarch, the kind of puzzling exemplified in these lines from a Frenchman's journal: "Since the apple of Eden ... woman has always remained man's enigma, his temptation, his hell and his paradise, his dream and his nightmare, his honey and his gall, his rage and his felicity."[4]

Yet, though hardly as poetically phrased, this feeling of confusion is implicit in Jude's and Rolfe's attitudes toward the women in their lives, and it is ubiquitous in late-century masculine identity. Peter Gay explains,

> Attributing to women confusing and contradictory traits, men found to their astonishment that she was at once timid and threatening, desirable and frightening. With time-honored roles of woman under severe pressure, nineteenth-century men indulged in this projective activity more freely and more desperately than ever. (1984, 170)

The projection of masculine sexual uneasiness onto the bewildering beloved is implicit in male characterization in *Jude* and *The Whirlpool*, as I will later illustrate, but what needs to be processed in that projection is some sense of male involvement in female experience. A reader sympathetic to feminist issues would find Jude's story far more positive than Rolfe's, but because of their complex and contradictory desires, the pull between an emotional life and an intellectual life, between new world and old, both men are unable to fulfill themselves sexually, or know themselves completely, or are unable to find that elusive middle way.

There is a scene in Meredith's novel *The Amazing Marriage*, published the same year as *Jude*, in which the "right-minded great lady" Arpington appropriately scolds another sublime Meredithian egoist, Lord Fleetwood, for abandoning his wife after their wedding (although he first takes her to a prize-fight). Lord Fleetwood, loathing himself for the impulsive proposal, not for the subsequent desertion, plays the injured husband, entrapped by his own romanticism. The aristocratic *tête-à-tête* is a biting expose of "New Men":

> Fleetwood ... betrayed the irritated tyrant ready to decree fire and sword, for the defense or solace of his tender sensibilities....
> "It's a thing to mend as well as one can," Lady Arpington said. "I am not inquisitive: you had your reasons or chose to act without any ... [H]usband you are, if you married her. We'll leave the husband undiscussed: with this reserve, that it seems to me men are now beginning to play the misunderstood." (283)

Meredith's short lecture from the point of view of the *femme sage* in the novel effectively undermines the much longer meditations of the self-antagonized, rationalizing hero. Hardy and Gissing likewise show the new man "beginning to play the misunderstood," but he is an average middle-class (or de-classed) hero, not a spoiled aristocrat. He usually speaks for himself, in a tone that verges on pleading self-pity. In Gissing's novella *Eve's Ransom*, for example, Narramore bemoans the stereotypic image of the innocent maiden and the rapacious suitor: "The day has gone by for a hulking brother to come asking a man about his 'intentions.' As a rule, it's the girl that has intentions. The man is just looking around, anxious to be amiable without making a fool of himself. We're at a great disadvantage" (105). In Hardy, the image of men as victims of their own machinery—that is, patriarchal society's emphasis on success, chivalry, or honor (much like poor Lord Fleetwood's position as a "prisoner of his word")—is early on argued from the male point of view by Henry Knight in *A Pair of Blue Eyes*, only Hardy's third published novel (1873): "I think you will find ... that in actual life it is merely a matter of instinct with men—this trying to push on.

They awake to a recognition that they have, without premeditation, begun to try a little, and they say to themselves, 'Since I have tried thus much, I will try a little more.' They go on because they have begun" (215). *New Grub Street*, of course, is full of men's complaints about unsupportive wives and a soul-murdering society. When his wife suggests that men who fail are men who never struggled to succeed, Edwin Reardon replies, "Darling, they do struggle. But it's as if an ever increasing weight were around their necks; it drags them lower and lower. The world has no pity on a man who can't do or produce something it thinks worth money.... Society is as blind and brutal as fate" (230). Jude, too, complains poignantly—and pointedly:

> "Still, Sue, it's no worse for the woman than for the man. That's what some women fail to see, and instead of protesting against the conditions they protest against the man, the other victim; just as a woman in a crowd will abuse the man who crushes against her, when he is only the helpless transmitter of the pressures put upon him." (227)

Hardy's idea of a man unconsciously pushing on—or being pushed on—and Gissing's image of the man who is dragged into an abyss by the weight of "success" are evocative of a great social and economic tide that threatens to overwhelm men's dignity—what Gissing calls in *The Whirlpool* "life at high pressure." As the narrator of *New Grub Street* says resignedly, "A man has no business to fail.... Those behind will trample over his body; they can't help it; they themselves are borne onwards by resistless pressure" (290). Men such as Jude and Harvey Rolfe feel this same wave of pressure carrying them into a vortex that is somewhat less economically focused than it is morally and sexually. Their interest in classical subjects, in Latin and Greek history, indicate a need to return to a world that is a bastion of uncorrupted masculinity, a world that is stable, serene, mentally balanced. That Jude is unable to enroll in the university at Christminster is not as important as his finally giving up his scholarly ambitions altogether because he has to support a family. And Rolfe's ultimate breakdown, his final inability to concentrate on his old subjects of study, is blamed on Alma's lack of interest in his intellectual pursuits. He is, paradoxically, distracted by her inattention.

Though the pressures of masculinity as experienced by the protagonists in these two novels are primarily sexual, they are nevertheless related to the pressures experienced by "the misunderstood," and are not by any means isolated from the social problems of the 1890s. In fact, pressures of sex and society are closely identified. Despite the rhetoric of Doom and

Fate in both novels, men largely control their own private interpretations of their world, and their anxieties are self-created, as well as externally imposed. In trying to embody a bridge between masculine reason and feminine emotion, male characters erect barriers against their own retreat, blockading the middle way, which can exist neither entirely of intellect nor of sensuality. By assuring their isolation in their own experience of the world, these men see the world itself as split. Even Jude, for all his love, cannot enter into Sue's deepest impressions of life. "Is a woman a thinking unit at all, or a fraction always wanting its integer?" he asks her confusedly. But his implied idea, by contrast, of masculinity as a "unit" is not quite right either. If women's personalities appear fragmented because they are vulnerable to contradictory emotions, men's identities are tense to the breaking point because of the urgent personal need to remain self-protectively whole.

Jude the Obscure and *The Whirlpool* are not only thematically rich and busy with ideas, but grimly expressive of how mid-century notions of masculinity are beginning to erode under the pressure of economic instability, imperialist controversy, and especially feminism. *The Whirlpool*, in particular, comes across as a chronicle of social ills, and incorporates a homicide, three suicides, and one suicide attempt. If *The Whirlpool* seems a chronicle of unhappy men, *Jude* is more like a bleak tapestry of "unhope" (to apply a Hardy neologism), somewhat larger and more suggestive of the past and its unremembered victims. Still, Hardy's provincial-pastoral is no less turbulent than Gissing's urban gyre. Social confusion—the "whirlpool" life of London, or "the sleep of the spinning top" of Christminster and beyond— infects men's private experiences with women, who often seem the bearers of social chaos. Men, though, baffled themselves by changing ideas of what constitutes masculinity, and by a civilization—that patriarchal creation—that is suddenly seen as chaotically feminine, make a mistake by looking too far opposite to orderly retreat and unemotional tranquility. The male novelist's imposition of contrasts and extremes emphasizes the impossibility of compromise between the sexes. It is sadly meaningful that suicides finally sever the central love relationships of both novels. The "homely thing, a satisfactory scheme for the conjunction of the sexes" that Hardy refers to in the Preface to *Jude*, is defeated by a combination of unpredictable human passions and a callous, inhuman society.

Jude Fawley, Hardy's victim of female perversity, is also the male character most sympathetic to feminine experience—experience that illuminates his own sexual identity by laying a light upon male emotions, not just male sexuality. Jude (and Phillotson, too, for that matter) admits that he knows nothing about women, has hardly given any thought to the feminine

point of view, and is as baffled by his own sexual feelings as he is by Sue herself.
Jude also knows very little of the world at large, and indeed the locus of his
private thoughts and actions is obscurity. He is first a dreamy boy and then a
contemplative man who seems to have common human desires that are at once
simple and formidable. The Christminster dream is something for Jude to aim
at, but his real need is much larger than a knowledge of Latin and Greek: it is
"the yearning of his heart to find something to anchor on, to cling to—for
some place which he could call admirable" (23). The yearning for an anchor is
transferred from the place to a particular person when he sees Sue Bridehead.
It is significant that before he even speaks to her, Jude identifies Sue—or the
idea of Sue—using the same language he had used to describe Christminster,
as "an anchorage for his thoughts" and "a kindly star, an elevating power" (74,
73). He wishes to find a feminine freehold after the alarming affair with
Arabella, a sexual initiation that Hardy describes as "a great hitch" interrupting
the "gliding and noiseless current of his life" (37), where Jude feels "as if
materially, a compelling arm of extraordinary muscular power seized hold of
him" that "seemed to care little for his reason and his will, nothing for his so-
called elevated intentions, and moved him along." (38–39). With Arabella, he
is carried along by sensuality, uprooted from his masculine studies because of
this feminine force. Indeed, after his marriage, Jude is rather more
psychologically unsettled and emotionally unanchored than he was as a lonely
and naive boy. But if Jude is seeking an alternate type of stability in Sue, he is
bound to be disappointed, for she is a woman who is "all nervous motion"—in
effect, the sexual embodiment of asexual, intellectualized Christminster. The
two fantasies of place and person, the world and the woman, are linked almost
unconsciously in Jude's imagination. Even as a boy, talking to the carters on the
road, he has become so "romantically attached to Christminster that, like a
young lover alluding to his mistress, he felt bashful at mentioning its name
again" (21). Hardy's language in describing Christminster, Sue, and Jude's
impressions of both is likewise remarkably similar and symbolically mixed. If
the town is likened to "the stillness of infinite motion—the sleep of the
spinning top" (92), Sue is "mobile," of a "nervous temperament" (77), and
always "in a trembling state" (77), though she is "of the type dubbed elegant"
(73), just as Christminster is apostrophized (and note the feminine pronoun):

> Beautiful city! so venerable, so lovely, so unravaged by the fierce
> intellectual life of our century, so serene! ... Her ineffable charm
> keeps ever calling us to the true goal of all of us, to the ideal, to
> perfection.[5]

Jude is attracted by the call to "the ideal," but its sources are imperfect. Both the city and the woman turn out to be anything but "unravaged" by the modern world, and there is something pathetic in Jude's locating his desires in a place and a person more corrupted by contemporary life than he thinks. Indeed, there is something ominous in the old carter's description of this "heavenly Jerusalem" at the beginning of the novel: "Yes, 'tis a serious-minded place. Not but there's wenches in the streets o' nights" (22). The association between the intellectual life and the sensual life evoked in terms of a learned city and its wenches is suggestive not only of a Christminster-Sue connection, but of Jude's psychological split, projected onto these two ideals, between spirituality and passion, the "life of constant internal warfare between flesh and spirit" (155) that Jude himself recognizes as his personal battle.

The psychological equation of Christminster and Sue Bridehead also suggests an artistic attempt to link the central obsessions of the protagonist by using connective symbols and narrative strategies such as foreshadowing—the photograph of Sue, for example, which early in the novel haunts Jude, ultimately forming "a quickening ingredient in his latest intent" to follow Phillotson (63). The implications of the symbolic association of city (intellectual promise) and Sue (sexual promise) become expanded for Jude into the idea of world, of civilization itself, and woman as the representative of the more subliminal forces driving the social machinery. He identifies Sue, in particular, as a product of civilized, modern life, and her nervousness as a symptom of a general social neurosis.

Peter Gay gives a rich treatment of the history of nineteenth-century nervousness in *The Tender Passion*, concluding that "The discovery and promotion of nervousness in the nineteenth century therefore turns out to be largely another eloquent witness to the anxiety that innovation generates" (1986, 349).[6] That Jude's anxiety, his own restlessness, is exacerbated by Sue's innovative morality (partly brought about by his desire for her sexually and her resistance), is another example of his mental association of women and civilization, sex and artificiality, a sophisticated version of Arabella's dimple-making and tail of false hair. The transference of a *zeitgeist* onto women, and onto one woman in particular, operates two ways for Jude: because Sue is so influenced by the modern world, she is not responsible for her perversity, and yet her perversity is what is dragging him back to the barbaric codes of modern life that he disdains. To have Sue is to have in one woman what Basil Ransom in *The Bostonians* identifies as "a feminine, a nervous, hysterical, chattering, canting age" (327); no matter how far Jude and Sue retreat into obscurity, away from the diseases of the age, she will carry with her its whining, womanly, complicated complaints.[7] Like Milton's Satan, which way she flies is Hell: she is herself modernity.

The narrator of Meredith's *The Amazing Marriage* likewise shrewdly comments on men's association of a complex world—or "Life"—with femininity, but in a tone saturated with irony, and so quite different from Hardy's sympathetic portrait of his young hero. Yet the similarities between the intellectual meanderings of the egotistical Lord Fleetwood and the modest, if confused, Jude Fawley (and Gissing's Harvey Rolfe, as well) point to a curious psychological inclination on the part of some late-century males:

> Having established Life as the coldly malignant element, which induces to what it chastises, a loathing of womanhood, the deputed Mother of Life, ensues, by natural sequence. And if there be one among women who disturb the serenity we choose to think our due, she wears for us the sinister aspect of a confidential messenger between Nemesis and the Parcae. (368–69)

In Meredith's ironic interpretation, woman is "sinister" because she brings confusion, she disturbs the cultural current. For Jude, the association of woman with a muddled world is so acute, so imbedded in his consciousness, that he really does not know how to distribute the blame for the confusion of his life and the dissembling of his ambitions:

> Strange that his first aspiration—towards academical proficiency—had been checked by a woman, and that his second aspiration—towards apostleship—had also been checked by a woman. "Is it," he said, "that women are to blame; or is it the artificial system of things, under which the normal sex-impulses are turned into devilish domestic gins and springes to noose and hold back those who want to progress?" (172–73)

One aspect of *Jude the Obscure* attempts to address this male-centered question, typically general and abstract, by putting it in personal terms. If Sue is, in Jude's eyes, "quite a product of civilisation" and "an urban miss" (111), she is to the narrator also a creature defined by her sex, apart from her socialization:

> every face [in Sue's dormitory] bearing the legend "The Weaker" upon it, as the penalty of the sex wherein they were moulded, which by no possible exertion of their willing hearts and abilities

could be made strong while the inexorable laws of nature remain what they are. (112)

One would infer that "the inexorable laws of nature" are also responsible for the opportunities afforded or denied to the male sex as well. If she is molded to submission, must he by necessity be molded to aggression? Sue's attempt to explain men to Jude indicates that from her perspective, he is acting in accordance with natural, biological urges: "An average woman is in this superior to an average man—that she never instigates, only responds.... Your wickedness was only the natural man's desire to possess the woman" (279). Jude rejects Sue's interpretation of men, because for him the prison of the masculine personality is tied to this very notion of male sexual conquest as detached from feminine sensitivity. He replies to Sue passionately, "You have never loved me as I love you—never—never!" (279). Jude is not crushed psychologically because he wants to possess Sue and cannot, but because he feels her equation of masculine sexual desire and "wickedness" omits the possibility of masculine love, narrowing down complicated sexual and emotional needs to men's "grossness."

Though Jude has always recognized that his interest in Sue was "unmistakably of a sexual kind" (80), he is not a seducer (as he later accuses himself) and not an egoist (like Gissing's Tarrant and Elgar) who is controlled by his sensuality. Even more than sexual satisfaction, Jude wants "something to love." "After all," he says, "it is not altogether an *erotolepsy* that is the matter with me, as at that first time ... [I]t is partly a wish for intellectual sympathy, and a craving for loving-kindness in my solitude" (80). Though he is rationalizing his "weakness," Jude is able to distinguish between "that first time" with Arabella, which was purely sexual, and a very different feeling of comradeship, affection, and interest combined with sexual attraction that he calls love. Sue's greatest slight to Jude's masculinity, from the masculine point of view, is not that she refuses to give herself to him sexually, but that she initially prohibits him from loving her ("You mustn't love me—you are to like me, that's all") because she associates male love with sexual proprietorship and aggression.

Thus Hardy's most functionally passive man acquires tragicheroic tones: he blunders toward a selfhood that, in the halfthwarted process of development, is an attempt to redefine his masculinity, to undo the ideology of male sexual dominance, and yet preserve what is truly manly in his sexuality. The love he is able to give to Sue is in his eyes pure, even sacred, and still vaguely linked to his idea of her as a Christ-ministering angel, so to speak, an intellectual and moral guide. Jude tells her fervently, "All that's best and noblest in me loves you, and your freedom from everything that's gross has elevated me" (210). But Sue's obsession with his "natural" desire for sexual penetration, for possession—the same male instinct she fears in her marriage to the anything but lascivious Phillotson—distorts the complex man who is Jude Fawley by focusing on one aspect of him—his sexuality. Jude's "old complaint" is, significantly, not that Sue withholds herself sexually, but that "intimate as they were, he had never once had from her an honest, candid declaration that she loved or could love him" (205).

Sue's fear of being herself confiscated sexually, with which Hardy invites us to sympathize, makes her seem cruel to Jude, who only wants to love her, and be loved by her, the way his "nature," and to some extent his early training with Arabella, encourages a man to love a woman. His generalizations about women and sex in this regard are confused by his confrontations with two particular examples: Arabella provokes his sexuality, and Sue wounds and insults it. Jude feels he is more than a mere cluster of hormonal drives, and also more than a cog in a social machine—more than the "mould civilization fits us into" (163)—and he is striving to synthesize the "natural" man, the sensual, with the "civilized" man. The unbearable irony for Jude is that though he knows he is more than a relative being, defined only by his sexual relationships, the primary referent for his interpretation of society is his sexuality, identified with incoherent emotions and, equally important, with illogical marriage laws.

Indeed, in Jude's mind he is two people: an innocent boy, before the sexual fall, and a postlapsarian sexual adult man. Jude's view of himself as a divided personality is at the source of his masculine identity:

> He could not realize himself. On the old track he seemed to be a boy still, hardly a day older than when he had stood dreaming at the top of that hill, inwardly fired for the first time with ardours for Christminster and scholarship.
>
> "Yet I am a man," he said. "I have a wife. Moreover, I have arrived at the still riper stage of having disagreed with her, disliked her, had a scuffle with her, and parted from her." (61)

Manhood, for Jude, is closely connected to having a wife, a masculine responsibility that is both public and private. Yet Jude feels he cannot "realize himself" in the role of husband, almost as though his boyhood had been ambushed by his sexual urges. Jude's reflections even as a child indicate a discomfort with the prospect of adulthood: growing up brings oppressive social obligations and confrontations with unharmonious laws of nature. In the same way, Rolfe in *The Whirlpool* wishes his own son could remain in "the golden age" and be spared the distressing onslaught of sexual appetites. For Jude, adulthood, and especially sexual maturity, incorporates the whirlpool into private existence, even obscure existence:

> All around you there seemed to be something glaring, garish, rattling, and the noises and glares hit upon the little cell called your life, and shook it, and warped it. If he could only prevent himself growing up! He did not want to be a man. (17)

Jude blunders his way through adolescence full of insecurity and self-abasement. Like Rolfe, he feels he is an exile and a misfit, socially inept and constantly risking humiliation. Jude wishes he had not gone to Arabella's, wishes he had not visited Phillotson, wishes he had not written to the college deans. "Well—I'm an outsider to the end of my days!" he sighs (259). The truth of the utterance is borne out in the novel on every page, and yet it is partly true because Jude does not "realize himself" enough to know where he could belong, even if he had the courage, the confidence, or the opportunity to pull down the walls that shut him out.

In trying to make sense of his social and psychological position, Jude embraces the patriarchal authority of ancient civilizations, the mentally balanced and male-defined worlds of Greece and Rome. Unlike Sue, who is "an epicure in emotions" (she admits, "My curiosity to hunt up a new sensation always leads me into these scrapes"), Jude believes in common sense, consistency, rationality, and practicability—a key word for all the characters in the novel, but for Jude a doctrine he repeatedly fails to follow. The hysterical, emotion-oriented female is opposed to the rational male ideal, but however preoccupied Jude is (and Phillotson, too) with practicability and order, he is up against a "chaos of principles" (258) when it comes to society, and against Sue's "extraordinarily compounded" logic (173) when it comes to his personal relationship with a woman. Jude's lapses into irrationality embarrass and virtually emasculate him; that his actions contradict his theories seems an unforgiveable weakness in a man who bemoans his "bygone, wasted, classical days" when abstract authority and personal experience were neatly defined and separate (214). "It would be just one of those cases in which my experiences go contrary to my dogmas," Jude says, regarding the question of Sue's nuptial "duties." "Speaking as an order-loving man—which I hope I am, though fear I am not" (167). Later he announces to the Remembrance Day crowd, "I am in a chaos of principles—groping in the dark—acting by instinct and not after example" (258).

Phillotson also feels the authority of example is being eroded by his experience with a particular woman. "O, I am not going to be a philosopher any longer! I only see what's under my eyes," he tells the matter-of-fact Gillingham (184). That men's sexual experiences contradict their time-honored beliefs effectively calls into question the whole notion of what constitutes authority, and is the closest Jude and Phillotson come to entering into feminist argument, which sees subjective experience, not objective—and here patriarchal—example, as genuinely authoritative.

The masculine point of view, Jude learns, is only one of several perspectives. This understanding is a major achievement for any of Hardy's male characters, and almost an impossible one for a Gissing protagonist, who, if he does concede something to female subjectivity, does so with a too self-congratulatory air. It is true that Jude still tends to see Sue as the sexual other he cannot quite make out: "Women are different from men in such matters. Was it that they were, instead of more sensitive, as reputed, more callous, and less romantic; or were they more heroic?" (140). Despite his abstraction here, the admission of woman's possible heroism is an important breakthrough in masculine psychology—it is something, for example, Angel Clare cannot immediately accept in relation to Tess, Troy in relation to Fanny, Tarrant to Nancy Lord, or Barfoot to Rhoda Nunn.[8] The erosion of Jude's classical, patriarchal, authoritative ideals is the crack in his socialized masculinity through which a ray of feminine reality can shine.

If experience can be defined as "an encounter of mind with world, as a struggle between conscious perceptions and unconscious dilemmas,"[9] then Jude's experience with society and sexuality can be represented by a struggle between old prejudices and new passions. He tells the Remembrance Day crowd that he is "a sort of success as a frightful example of what not to do," (258) thereby suggesting an awareness of having lived out some kind of story of development. Of course, one of the greatest ironies of *Jude the Obscure* is that the education of the hero comes at the expense of sacrificing the heroine to a perverse reactionism. The "death" of Sue Bridehead is comparable to Alma's drug overdose at the end of *The Whirlpool*. The world is too much for these intelligent and sensitive women, who are without guides or laws or examples—who, in effect, begin by rejecting patriarchal authorities, and yet find their private experience tragically complex. At the end of *Jude the Obscure*, the bedridden protagonist summarily says to the widow Edlin.

> "[Sue] was once a woman whose intellect was to mine like a star
> to a benzoline lamp: who saw all my superstitions as cobwebs that
> she could brush away with a word. Then bitter affliction came to

us, and her intellect broke, and she veered round to darkness. Strange difference of sex, that time and circumstance, which enlarge the views of most men, narrow the views of women almost invariably." (317)

The last sentence is a fairly accurate epitaph to this particular novel, for the intrusion of a feminine personality, which itself finally collapses, broadens the sympathies and dispels many of the prejudices of the last of Hardy's fictional heroes. But however much he seems to have grown in self-awareness—"mentally approaching the position which Sue had occupied when he first met her" (245)—Jude is frustrated and destroyed by the impossibility of balancing his private passions with the prohibitions set up by both his society and the progressive antisocial woman he loves, who paradoxically, is identified with Christminster, the laws of civilization, and with the uncivilizing contradictions of her age and of her sex. Wedged between the Arnoldian "two worlds," Jude's growth is in effect the stirring of unfulfillable desires that are the root of his social and sexual identity. Though he aborts his own potential by suicide, Jude's story affirms the mysteriousness of masculinity: the vulnerability he finds inherent in his "natural" virility is an intolerable awareness of an aspect of himself that goes deeper than socialized roles or self-assumed postures of what it means to be a man.

The Whirlpool is comparable to *Jude the Obscure* in that it is about men and women trying to remake themselves, to balance the emotional life and the rational, the private and the public, the ideal old world and the changing new world. Gissing's male submits to the sexual revolution instead of kicking against it, but he does so with a nostalgic resignation that is even more subversive than open rebellion. Jude's life would have seemed a nightmare of sexual awareness to the protagonist of *The Whirlpool*. Indeed, after reading Hardy's novel, Gissing remarked, "A sad book! Poor Thomas is utterly on the wrong tack, and I fear he will never get back on the right one."[10] The way to deal with feminist reality for Harvey Rolfe is not to accept or sympathize with female subjectivity, as Jude tries to do, but rather to make a show of submission, and then retreat to sealed-off, sane, masculine subjectivity—in other words, to subdue the conflict between the sexes by ignoring women and couching male sexuality under a code of common sense. "What a simple matter life would be, but for women," thinks poor caged-up Hugh Carnaby, expressing what could well be the grim keynote of *The Whirlpool*—and surely there are moments in *Jude the Obscure* where the same thought may have occurred to the hero of that novel. But Jude does not, ever, want to lose touch with Sue's sense of reality, despite her "cruelty" and her frustrating inconsistency. In contrast, virtually all of Rolfe's actions are motivated by a need to get further from, not closer to, the woman he supposedly loves. The only way for a man to survive, Gissing implies, is to stay clear of females and subdue male sexual instincts, a strategy that has its own alienating and destructive side effects for men.

Though evocative of a tempestuous open space, the whirlpool metaphor in Gissing's novel is also an image of stagnation and enclosure. The genuine growth of the protagonist, Harvey Rolfe, is impossible because, despite his proclaimed antithesis, "rut and whirlpool" are the same thing, and are equally destructive. "Yes, I know it too well, the whirlpool way of life," says Mrs. Abbott. "I know how easily one is drawn into it. It isn't only idle people." Rolfe replies, "Of course not. There's the whirlpool of the furiously busy" (156–7). Inertia and industry are self-reflective extremes in this novel, and there is no place to live peacefully in between them for nervous people like Harvey and Alma Rolfe, who exhibit many of the traits exemplified by Jude and Sue, transplanted to the metropolis. But whereas Hardy's man emerges with at least a sense of feminine experience, Gissing's self-occupied, self-protective gentleman remains shut out from the feverish preoccupations of his wife, never opening himself to her confused desires, though he imagines he is an irreproachable modern husband. Gissing appears to want to vindicate Harvey's masculinity, and the whole novel comes across as a miserable warning against feminism, imperialism, financial speculation, modern education, and modern marriage, all of which threaten masculine peace, dignity, and authority. Indeed, one could apply any of these themes to a focused analysis of *The Whirlpool*, not to mention Gissing's declared intention that the book is about fatherhood.[11]

In *Gissing in Context*, Adrian Poole makes a compelling claim for the novel. "*The Whirlpool* is a parable about the necessary failure of the dream of perfect autonomy," he says, adding, "It is precisely the impossibility of Rolfe's fiction of perfect separateness that Gissing is intent on disclosing" (1975, 199, 201). To some extent, this is a precise analysis, but there is a subtle and essential distinction between autonomy, which I understand to mean independence or self-containment, and purposeful alienation, the possibly unconscious urge for estrangement between the self and the objective world. Alma, like Sue Bridehead, wants autonomy, to be self-governed, and to create herself fully, not merely to be completed by a husband. Jude, too, in his relationship with Sue, craves perfect separateness based upon equality and mutual respect. Rolfe, however, appears to want sexual insulation, not sexual autonomy. He is preoccupied with a dissociation from the feminine (i.e., public and social) world, but in constructing barriers to block out that part of reality, he also necessarily has to erect barriers to keep intrusive aspects of his own sexual identity (his "baser appetites," for example) out of his conscious—almost ultra-self conscious—role playing.

Indeed, Rolfe is only the central player in a collection of masculine poseurs in this novel, that, for all its antifeminine rhetoric (Halperin rightly calls *The Whirlpool*, "That most misogynic [*sic*] of Gissing's novels")[12] seems drained of the attractions of a masculine mystique; it is all machismo, without delivering a convincing impression of masculine strength. The retreat from femininity that informs virtually every chapter is, in effect, men's refusal to look inward and explore their own sexuality. The novel is full of psychologically and emotionally numb male impersonators, among whom Rolfe is the most conspicuously self-deceived; he strolls oblivious and untouchable through a sexual battle zone.

If *The Whirlpool* is about a man's "process of enlightenment" (Poole 1975, 201) as is *Jude* in one sense, Poole is correct to emphasize the inconclusiveness of Rolfe's development, which certainly seems suspended between extremes. But if Rolfe is passively arrested in the eye of the hurricane, it is because that is where he wants to be—he is not only unwilling to enter imaginatively into Alma's struggles, but he persistently denies that such struggles exist, both within his wife and especially within himself. He denies or ignores the conflicts that inform his personal existence, wishing to be tepid and undisturbed when what is happening in his marriage is equivalent to Jude's experience of being hit in the ear with a pig's pizzle.

To be sure, Rolfe is an egoist, but he is a unique example in the Gissing gallery for he is virtually without sexual particularity, merely an assemblage of masculine accoutrements, habits, and tastes, free from what Sue Bridehead would call "grossness." The very quality of virility that defines Tarrant, Elgar, and Barfoot seems unnaturally subdued in Harvey Rolfe. His sensuality is dressed up in the habiliments of the late-Victorian gentleman; he seems empty of passion. Yet this character has Gissing's implicit sympathy for he personifies the almost universal male weariness with the complications and intrigues of sexual awareness.

The narrator introduces Rolfe as a "vigorous example" of a "rational man," whose bent is toward an "indolent conservativism" (20, 2). "I have no opinions," he says, and it is almost his refrain in the novel. "My profound ignorance of everything keeps me in a state of perpetual scepticism. It has its advantages, I dare say" (15). Rolfe's cynicism barely conceals his anxiety, and his "fathomless ignorance" and evasiveness are not policy, but conflict. His curious sexual constraint may be the winding down of virility under feminism. He smugly begins where men like Biffen and Reardon (*New Grub Street*) and Peak (*Born in Exile*) tragically end, with subdued appetites and a personality shut off from the world because of conflicting desires and unfulfilled passions. Unlike these men, Rolfe does not appear to be beaten by anything in particular, and certainly not by any mighty love for a woman. He has "no purpose in life, save that of enjoying himself" (2), and yet he is advertized as the victim of something, at the very least of some harassing self doubts.

Rolfe's cool sexual stoicism is not simple obedience to a bourgeois creed: he is no Giles Winterborne. Instead, Rolfe's sealed-off sexual self is part of a thirty-seven-year-old man's conscientious campaign to sabotage debilitating and uncomfortable emotions—to deny his own sexual "instincts" in the interest of escaping "woman's problems." Ironically, in seeking to live a balanced life, Rolfe removes the counterweight. "There is the humiliating point of our human condition," says the male narrator of *The Amazing Marriage*. "We must have beside us and close beside us the woman we have learned to respect.... 'That required other scale of the human balance,' as Woodseer calls her, now that he has got her.... We get no balance without her" (561–62). Apparently unconvinced by the Meredithian notion of human fulfillment and sexual equilibrium, Gissing in *The Whirlpool* seems to suggest that in 1897 male survival has come to mean tenacious sexual suppression. This early description of Rolfe's state of mind, for example, is a key passage:

> Not seldom of late had Harvey flattered himself on the growth of intellectual gusto which proceeded in him together with a perceptible decline of baser appetites, so long his torment and his hindrance. His age was now seven-and-thirty; at forty, he might hope to have utterly trodden under foot the instincts at war with mental calm. He saw before him long years of congenial fellowship, of bracing travel, of well-directed studiousness. Let problems of sex and society go hang! He had found a better way. (21)

Rolfe's "better way," however, is not the middle way; it is instead a path of extreme self-protection that is to a large extent based on a fear of women projected onto something much larger and abstract: society. Rolfe's discomfort in London society is caused almost entirely by his uneasiness around women, and is a direct contrast to the reassuring masculine club with which Gissing sets the scene in chapter 1: men smoking cigars, reading newspapers, and drinking brandy, speculating on the economy, and complaining about "domestic management" (6). It is a bastion of masculinity, a place Rolfe retreats to later in the novel with a sense of real urgency, as if he needs to resurrect his sense of sexual superiority. Even Alma says, quite shrewdly, that her husband is a different person after he's been to the club, he displays "a kind of gaiety ... quite in a boyish way" (172). As the whirlpool—i.e., feminized society—threatens to engulf him,

> as a natural consequence of the feeling of unsettlement, of instability, he had recourse more often than he wished to the old convivial habits, gathering about him once again, at club or restaurant, the kind of society in which he always felt at ease— good, careless, jovial, and often impecunious fellows. (250)

This description complies with John Fowles's view of the Victorian club as an institution that "pandered ... to the adolescent in man" (*The French Lieutenant's Woman*, 235). It also sounds like the robust equivalent of Alma's recourse—also "more often than [she] wished"—to the "little phial with its draught of oblivion" (307). Indeed, a fascinating aspect of Gissing's conception of this character is that he seems to unconsciously reflect the very neuroses he identifies as feminine: vanity, moral weakness, intellectual inconsistency. Rolfe's instinctive need to preserve his identification with maleness, represented by the club, is a recasting of Alma's strong wish to carve out a place for herself as a professional woman, which seems slightly more understandable, given her position, than her husband's heroic reclusiveness.

"The days are past when a man watched over his wife's coming and going as a matter of course," Rolfe tells Carnaby. "We should only make fools of ourselves if we tried it on. It's the new world, my boy; we live in it, and must make the best of it" (215). Apparently progressive, even optimistic, statements like this—only a sampling of Rolfe's modern-minded rhetoric— conceal a deep feeling of male anxiety and distrustfulness of change; the protagonist has persuaded himself that he is both disinterested, or unbiased, as well as uninterested, indifferent to the new order of sexual relationships. Yet he cannot remain psychologically secure in his self-imposed emotional and intellectual isolation. Even more than poor Jude Fawley, "poor old Rolfe" (Carnaby's tender epithet) is fraught with insecurity; his rational pose is a shield against anything that could threaten his patient stoicism. Indeed, the almost constant refrain of this "rational man" is one of self-reproach for being either too rational, or not rational enough. Clearly, he feels uncertain about his sexual identity and about masculine strength. For example, Rolfe repeatedly chastises his "moral cowardice" (24) yet does not assert himself in even the most trivial situations. He is always embarrassed by his "incorrigible want of tact" (153), a foible that seems only the result of a cultivated insensitivity. Certainly on one occasion, after he hears of Bennett Frothingham's suicide, Rolfe feels slightly abashed at his own coldness:

> It occurred to him that it might be a refreshing and salutary change if for once he found himself involved in the anxieties to which other men were subject; this long exemption and security fostered a too exclusive regard of self, an inaptitude for sympathetic emotion, which he recognized as the defect of his character. (45)

It seems that here we have one of Gissing's egoists on the edge of self-awareness; and yet, Rolfe is always and proudly self-possessed, a quality that "differed little from unconcern," according to the narrator, and that eventually traps him in a manly pose of unruffled practicality that alienates him from the emotional—i.e., "feminine"—side of his personality.

Despite his passivity, Rolfe's essential masculinity is never challenged in the novel. He is clearly "manly" in everyone's eyes, and certainly he cannot be called, as Jude is, "a tender-hearted fool." But if Jude is sensitive to the sufferings of others, craving to give and receive love, he is also passionate and sensual. Rolfe, on the other hand, is neither tender-hearted nor sexually vibrant. He is virtually an ascetic, both emotionally and sexually, and he advertises himself as such ("circumstance" is his god and "common sense" his creed), even though he perceives the falseness in the role he plays. It is as though the mask he purposefully wears to protect himself controls or limits his capacity for self-realization.

Perhaps it is because of his own slender awareness of the duplicity in his nature that Rolfe scorns the vulgar hypocrises and poses of society. "What a grossly sensual life was masked by their airs and graces," he thinks while noting the women's "unnaturally lustrous" eyes as they return from supper. "He had half a mind to start tomorrow for the Syrian deserts" (41–42). Clearly the impulse to run away is associated not so much with society life as with female sexuality. He hates himself for attending these social affairs, yet there must be a reason he is attracted (sensually) to such "gross" company. Even as Rolfe delivers diatribe after diatribe against women (or, more accurately, drops nasty remarks—"I hate a dirty, lying, incapable creature, that's all, whether man or woman. No doubt they're more common in petticoats"), he must force himself to avert his eyes from Alma Frothingham for "She stood a fascination, an allurement, to his masculine sense" (32). He dislikes this arousal—indeed, he is ashamed to have "yielded to Alma's fascination" (104), feels "more awkward, more foolish" than he has ever felt, and senses that his male superiority and control have been overcome by female "witchery." The only way to domesticate this wild captivation, for Rolfe, is to marry it, and so satisfy an annoying desire in order to get on with more important masculine pursuits. This is, in effect, a practical application of his private law of self-preservation, the "saving strain of practical rationality which had brought him thus far in life without sheer overthrow" (115). He gets very little pleasure from being in love, and seems quite unaffected by the deliciously turbulent emotions that torture men like Tarrant, Elgar, and Peak, or even Alec d'Urberville and Boldwood. He does not wish to see himself as susceptible to desire—in fact, he wishes to be above sexuality altogether. If a man is unfortunate enough to have sexual longings, the logic goes, he must marry at once so he is not unreasonably distracted by them.

Rolfe here is functioning within the popular precinct of the practical man, an immensely attractive image of masculinity at the turn of the century. He is to some extent playing the part of the efficiency man, but surely Rolfe is anything but a "brain-worker." He is, rather, an idler who produces nothing, not even an original idea. Gissing's hero has a pretension to H. G. Wells's masculine model, and acts upon Wells's formula for controlling inconvenient sexual impulses by gratifying them: "it is better to marry than to burn, a concession to the flesh necessary to secure efficiency," Wells wrote in 1901.[13] Rolfe applies the efficiency code to a troublesome aspect of himself he hardly wishes to recognize—his sexuality—and then dismisses the tension that precipitates and then succeeds his marriage as not worth any energetic attention: "This was love; but of what quality? He no longer cared, or dared, to analyse it" (113).

Shunning self-analysis, Rolfe refines his power of self-deception. It is interesting to come across the following confession very late in the novel:

> in wooing Alma he had obeyed no dictate of the nobler passion; here, too, as at every other crisis of his life, he had acted on motives which would not bear analysis, so large was the alloy of mere temperament, of weak concession to circumstance. (335)

This seems to be an admission of lust in a man who prides himself on his dispassionate sensibility. It is comparable to Jude's disappointment in being unable to match his actions to his theories. Rolfe at this point is certain that he does not love Alma, and possibly has never loved her; yet as a gentleman, he admits he is partly responsible for their mutual estrangement. This does not, however, from Rolfe's point of view, make his marriage a living hell (though Alma feels her life is "a nightmare"), and it is precisely because "he had no sense of hopeless discord in his wedded life" (335) that he is able to contrive a plan of action that will satisfy his own need to maintain the present situation, and remain as much as possible sealed off from "feminine" activities taking place outside the circle of his private experience. "Love did not enter into the matter; his difficulty called for common sense—for rational methods in behavior towards a wife whom he could still respect" (336). The male character's response to a delicate marital problem—which, in fact, far from being ignored, requires above all a "concession" to love—is typically masculine considering the ideologically dominant equation of manliness and "rational methods" in the 1890s. Rolfe approaches his predicament in "an engineering spirit,"[14] self-centered and male-centered, that almost pathologically shuts out feminine subjective experience. Though we may grant Gissing a sympathetic view of this character, and in fact be willing to recognize the pathos of Rolfe's deeply pessimistic nature, all compassion is eclipsed by the repeated, conscious refusal to acknowledge a version of reality separate from his own, and as tragically legitimate. While his wife is ill with grief over the death of her newborn baby, Rolfe privately philosophizes that it is all for the best, and cannot console Alma because he "feared to seem unfeeling" (393). After her agonized penitent pleas to her husband to believe in her fidelity, and on the very night she kills herself, Rolfe says, "we mustn't talk of it. Sit down and be quiet for a little," and feels "all a man's common-sense in revolt" (447). While she is traumatized by a disastrous sequence of events—not the least of which is a devastating feeling of guilt, plus being witness to a murder—Rolfe "was trying to persuade himself that nothing much of moment had come to pass" (445). Such sensible proceedings expose Rolfe's utter rejection of female subjectivity. He is unable or unwilling to see women's experience as contributing to the same world he inhabits, though at the same time his rationalizations expose a reluctance to admit that his version of man-made reality is not hermetic. Gissing views his character's survival strategy with ambivalence—Rolfe is wrong, for example, to ignore his wife's neurosis, just as he is wrong to suppress his own capacity for emotion. The narrator suggests that Rolfe's temperament, though partly due to personal weakness, is also the product of socialized masculinity, an ideology that teaches men to respect women's tender nature, and under the pose of gentle-manliness encourages men to consider the female's delicate constitution and inferior intellect.

Rolfe erred once more in preferring to keep silence about difficulties rather than face the unpleasantness of frankly discussing them.... Like the majority of good and thoughtful men, he could not weigh his female companion in the balance he found good enough for mortals of his own sex. With a little obtuseness to the "finer" feelings, a little native coarseness in his habits towards women, he would have succeeded vastly better amid the complications of his married life. (365)

In other words, men who cannot apply the same moral standards to both sexes are not wilfully prejudiced, but "good and thoughtful," misguided and perhaps unable to view women as equals because society has taught them that women are "the Weaker." Robert Louis Stevenson was one late-century author who perceived the dangers for men of an ideology that implicitly recommends separate codes of ethics for each sex. He pragmatically advised, "It is better to face the fact, and know, when you marry, that you take into your life a creature of equal, if of unlike, frailties; whose weak human heart beats no more tunefully than yours" (1906, 36). It does not occur to Rolfe that Alma's frailties could be anything more than female problems. A confused mix of institutionalized gentlemanliness and his modern belief in marital independence (the rejection of "the old fashioned authority of husbands") prohibits Rolfe from treating his wife as an autonomous individual and a social equal for a man cannot entirely respect what he feels obliged to protect. The irony is that though he permits his wife to pursue a musical career and to move freely in society, Rolfe is still susceptible to sexual prejudices reinforced by patriarchal culture. He is not above classifying Alma as one of "the brainless number of her sex" (382). His habitual, almost unconscious, wish to escape from women thus goes far deeper than his conscious pose as "the pattern of marital wisdom" (336) and the epitome of modern masculine open-mindedness. The shaft of feminine—and feminist—experience that found a chink in the shell of Jude's masculinity fails to illuminate the impervious masculinity, itself pathetically shallow, of Gissing's modern man. But then, as Henry Knight matter of factly says to Elfride Swancourt in *A Pair of Blue Eyes*, "Shallowness has this advantage, that you can't be drowned there" (363).

Gissing appears to grant Rolfe a successful retreat at the end of *The Whirlpool*: his wife conveniently dead, he enjoys a smoke and a philosophical chat about Kipling's *Barrack-Room Ballads* with the Ryecroftian Basil Morton, and then, "Hand in hand, each thinking his own thoughts," walks peacefully and manfully "homeward through the evening sunshine" with his seven-year-old son (453). It is a patriarchal idyll and smacks of male wish-fulfilling fantasies. It does, I think, point to Henry Ryecroft's romance of perfect isolation, but Rolfe's insulation from the sexual traumas that seem to be whirling around him in the "new world" undermine his situation at the end of the novel. Rolfe's whirlpool may be shallow, but it is evocative of the feeling Meredith attributes to one of his heroes, an uncomfortable impression of "the bubbling shallowness of the life about him, and the thought ... of sinister things below it" (*Beauchamp's Career*, 225). There is no genuine sense of Rolfe's development, self-realization, or "conversion" to a broader understanding of gender-specific experiences, but there is a level of real escape from women. Gissing seems to feel—as *The Private Papers of Henry Ryecroft* (written 1900–1) indicates—that this retreat is in itself cherishable, a positive alternative to the peace Jude achieves at the end of his story, which does free men from "sex and society"—the two myths that have become so inextricable, so intricately entangled and identifiable, in the imaginations of many late-nineteenth-century men.

NOTES

1. Quoted in the Norton Critical Edition of *Jude the Obscure* (1978), 349-50.

2. *Phoenix*, 510. Though Lawrence sounds gentle enough in this passage from *Phoenix*, he is finally alienated from Sue Bridehead's neurotic frigidity. An interesting defense of Sue's sexuality that responds to Lawrence's criticism is Mary Jacobus, "Sue the Obscure," *Essays in Criticism*, 25.3 (1975).

3. Peter Gay meticulously documents the history of the *femme fatale*, the vampire-woman, and the unappealing man-woman in nineteenth-century imagination in *The Education of The Senses*, chap. 2, especially pp. 197–213.

4. Quoted from a journal entry by Henri-Frederic Amiel (1849) by Peter Gay in *The Education of the Senses*, 170. Gay sees the ideas expressed by Amiel as characteristic of his time and class.

5. "The words quoted appear in the preface to Matthew Arnold's *Essays in Criticism: First Series* (1865)." Norton Critical Edition of *Jude*, fn. p. 66.

6. See also Sigmund Freud's essay, "Civilized Sexual Morality and Modern Nervous Illness," published in 1908. Freud cites three psychosociologists, Erb, Benswanger, and Von Krafft-Ebing, who each published essays (in 1893, 1896, and 1895, respectively) on the subject of "neurasthenia," an illness that they found to be almost epidemic, and caused primarily by the conditions of modern life. Freud finds the epidemic to be (not surprisingly) caused by the "harmful suppression of the sexual life of civilized peoples (or classes) through the 'civilized' sexual morality prevalent in them." One can imagine an eager, but perhaps reductive, Freudian analysis of the main players in *Jude* based on this essay alone.

7. In their feminist study of fin-de-siècle and modernist literature, No Man's Land, Gilbert and Gubar suggest that in *The Bostonians* James "depicted the escalation in the

battle of the sexes that marked the progress of the nineteenth century," and that he did so with acute paranoia (26; see especially chap. 3). James's novel offers some contrasts between the feminist movement in Great Britain and America from the male novelist's point of view. James's Olive Chancellor and Verena Tarrant are certainly more committed to "the cause" of female emancipation than are Sue Bridehead and Alma Frothingham, for example. But, oddly enough, Jude and Rolfe seem more enlightened about feminist issues and less confident about their masculine prerogative than the closed-minded hero of *The Bostonians*, who faces whole parlors of vocal emancipationists. Perhaps because Hardy and Gissing did not, in *Jude* and *The Whirlpool*, set out to tackle The Woman Question directly, their male characters seem much less combatant and far more confused—the battle lines are not clearly drawn.

8. Rosemarie Morgan argues that Hardy has always sided with his heroines, and that "[f]or all his sympathies with the underprivileged male characters," Hardy finally "treats them with antipathy" are representatives of the status quo. *Women and Sexuality in the Novels of Thomas Hardy*, 162. Morgan's view is compelling, although I see Hardy's treatment of male characters as ambivalent rather than antipathetic.

9. Gay, *Education of the Senses*, 171.

10. Letter to Henry Hick, 27 Nov. 1895, quoted by Morley Roberts, *Henry Maitland*, chap. V. My source is Pierre Coustillas, "Some Unpublished Letters from Gissing to Hardy," *English Literature in Transition*, 1966, 208.

11. Gissing told Morley Roberts that Harvey Rolfe "would probably never have developed at all after a certain stage but for the curious change wrought in his views and sentiments by the fact of his becoming a father." Gissing also wrote to Bertz that in the novel "much stress is laid upon the question of *children*." See Halperin, *Gissing: A Life in Books*, 235 and 242. Interestingly, Gissing made the same claim for *The Whirlpool* to Hardy: "One theme I have in mind—if ever I can get again to a solid book—which I want to treat very seriously. It is the question of a parent's responsibility. This has been forced upon me by the fact that I myself have a little boy, growing out of his infancy." Coustillas, "Some Unpublished Letters...." (dated 3 Sept. 1895), p. 203. Full treatment of Gissing's commitment to the fatherhood theme is beyond the scope of this discussion, but it is certainly relevant that both Hardy and Gissing expressed concern over the inherent morbidity and weakness of the next generation of men, represented by Little Father Time in *Jude the Obscure* and by little Hughie in *The Whirlpool*, with his pale cheeks, his "nervous tendencies," his "too intelligent face" (383, 451). Both novels also touch on men's personal and social responsibilities as parents. Jude, for example, sees "The beggarly question of parentage" as the "excessive regard of parents for their own children, and their *dislike* of other people's... like class-feeling, patriotism, save-your-own-soul-ism, and other virtues, a mean exclusiveness as bottom" (217).

12. Halperin, *George Gissing: A Life in Books*, 240.

13. In *Anticipations*. Quoted in Jonathan Rose, *The Edwardian Temperament*, 142.

14. The apt phrase is from Rose, *The Edwardian Temperament*, 142. His chapter on "The Efficiency Men," though not particularly a study of socialized masculinity, is a fairly good analysis of the social mood in which Gissing's character frequently operates.

EDWARD W. SAID

The Pleasures of Imperialism

Kim is as unique in Rudyard Kipling's life and career as it is in English literature. It appeared in 1901, twelve years after Kipling had left India, the place of his birth and the country with which his name will always be associated. More interestingly, *Kim* was Kipling's only successfully sustained and mature piece of long fiction; although it can be read with enjoyment by adolescents, it can also be read with respect and interest years after adolescence, by the general reader and the critic alike. Kipling's other fiction consists either of short stories (or collections thereof, such as *The Jungle Books*), or deeply flawed longer works (like *Captains Courageous, The Light That Failed*, and *Stalky and Co.*, whose other interest is often overshadowed by failures of coherence, vision, or judgement). Only Conrad, another master stylist, can be considered along with Kipling, his slightly younger peer, to have rendered the experience of empire as the main subject of his work with such force; and even though the two artists are remarkably different in tone and style, they brought to a basically insular and provincial British audience the color, glamor, and romance of the British overseas enterprise, which was well-known to specialized sectors of the home society. Of the two, it is Kipling—less ironic, technically self-conscious, and equivocal than Conrad—who acquired a large audience early on. But both writers have remained a puzzle for scholars of English literature, who find them eccentric, often troubling, better treated with circumspection or even avoidance than

From *Culture and Imperialism.* © 1993 by Edward W. Said.

absorbed into the canon and domesticated along with peers like Dickens and Hardy.

Conrad's major visions of imperialism concern Africa in *Heart of Darkness* (1899), the South Seas in *Lord Jim* (1900), and South America in *Nostromo* (1904), but Kipling's greatest work concentrates on India, a territory Conrad never wrote about. And by the late nineteenth century India had become the greatest, most durable, and most profitable of all British, perhaps even European, colonial possessions. From the time the first British expedition arrived there in 1608 until the last British Viceroy departed in 1947, India had a massive influence on British life, in commerce and trade, industry and politics, ideology and war, culture and the life of imagination. In English literature and thought the list of great names who dealt with and wrote about India is astonishingly impressive, for it includes William Jones, Edmund Burke, William Makepeace Thackeray, Jeremy Bentham, James and John Stuart Mill, Lord Macaulay, Harriet Martineau, and, of course Rudyard Kipling, whose importance in the definition, the imagination, the formulation of what India was to the British empire in its mature phase, just before the whole edifice began to split and crack, is undeniable.

Kipling not only wrote about India, but was *of* it. His father, Lockwood, a refined scholar, teacher, and artist (the model for the kindly curator of the Lahore Museum in Chapter One of *Kim*), was a teacher in British India. Rudyard was born there in 1865, and during the first years of his life he spoke Hindustani and lived a life very much like Kim's, a Sahib in native clothes. At the age of six he and his sister were sent to England to begin school; appallingly traumatic, the experience of his first years in England (in the care of a Mrs. Holloway at Southsea) furnished Kipling with an enduring subject matter, the interaction between youth and unpleasant authority, which he rendered with great complexity and ambivalence throughout his life. Then Kipling went to one of the lesser public schools designed for children of the colonial service, the United Services College at Westward Ho! (the greatest of the schools was Haileybury, reserved for the upper echelons of the colonial elite); he returned to India in 1882. His family was still there, and so for seven years, as he tells of those events in his posthumously published autobiography *Something of Myself,* he worked as a journalist in the Punjab, first on *The Civil and Military Gazette,* later on *The Pioneer.*

His first stories came out of that experience, and were published locally; at that time he also began writing his poetry (what T.S. Eliot has called "verse"), first collected in *Departmental Ditties* (1886). Kipling left

India in 1889, never again to reside there for any length of time, although for the rest of his life his art fed on the memories of his early Indian years. Subsequently, Kipling stayed for a while in the United States (and married an American woman) and South Africa, but settled in England after 1900: *Kim* was written at Bateman, the house he remained in till his death in 1936. He quickly won great fame and a large readership; in 1907 he was awarded the Nobel Prize. His friends were rich and powerful; they included his cousin Stanley Baldwin, King George V, Thomas Hardy; many prominent writers including Henry James and Conrad spoke respectfully of him. After World War One (in which his son John was killed) his vision darkened considerably. Although he remained a Tory imperialist, his bleak visionary stories of England and the future, together with his eccentric animal and quasi-theological stories, forecast also a change in his reputation. At his death, he was accorded the honor reserved by Britain for its greatest writers: he was buried in Westminster Abbey. He has remained an institution in English letters, albeit one always slightly apart from the great central strand, acknowledged but slighted, appreciated but never fully canonized.

Kipling's admires and acolytes have often spoken of his representations of India as if the India he wrote about was a timeless, unchanging, and "essential" locale, a place almost as much poetic as it is actual in geographical concreteness. This, I think, is a radical misreading of his works. If Kipling's India has essential and unchanging qualities, this was because he deliberately saw India that way. After all, we do not assume that Kipling's late stories about England or his Boer War tales are about an essential England or an essential South Africa; rather, we surmise correctly that Kipling was responding to and in effect imaginatively reformulating his sense of these places at particular moments in their histories. The same is true of Kipling's India, which must be interpreted as a territory dominated by Britain for three hundred years, and only then beginning to experience the unrest that would culminate in decolonization and independence.

Two factors must be kept in mind as we interpret *Kim*. One is that, whether we like it or not, its author is writing not just from the dominating viewpoint of a white man in a colonial possession, but from the perspective of a massive colonial system whose economy, functioning, and history had acquired the status of a virtual fact of nature. Kipling assumes a basically uncontested empire. On one side of the colonial divide was a white Christian Europe whose various countries, principally Britain and France, but also Holland, Belgium, Germany, Italy, Russia, Portugal, and Spain, controlled most of the earth's surface. On the other side of the divide, there were an immense variety of territories and races, all of them considered lesser, inferior, dependent, subject. "White" colonies like Ireland and Australia too were considered made up of inferior humans; a famous Daumier drawing, for instance, explicitly connects Irish whites and Jamaican Blacks. Each of these lesser subjects was classified and placed in a scheme of peoples guaranteed scientifically by scholars and scientists like Georges Cuvier, Charles Darwin, and Robert Knox. The division between white and non-white, in India and elsewhere, was absolute, and is alluded to throughout *Kim* as well as the rest of Kipling's work; a Sahib is a Sahib, and no amount of friendship or camaraderie can change the rudiments of racial difference. Kipling would no more have questioned that difference, and the right of the white European to rule, than he would have argued with the Himalayas.

The second factor is that, no less than India itself, Kipling was a historical being as well as a major artist. *Kim* was written at a specific moment in his career, at a time when the relationship between the British and Indian people was changing. *Kim* is central to the quasi-official age of empire and in a way represents it. And even though Kipling resisted this reality, India was already well on its way toward a dynamic of outright opposition to British rule (the Indian National Congress was established in 1885), while among the dominant caste of British colonial officials, military as well as civilian, important changes in attitude were occurring as a result of the 1857 Rebellion. The British and Indians were both evolving, and together. They had a common interdependent history, in which opposition, animosity, and sympathy either kept them apart or brought them together. A remarkable, complex novel like *Kim* is a very illuminating part of that history, filled with emphases, inflections, deliberate inclusions and exclusions as any great work of art is, and made the more interesting because Kipling was not a neutral figure in the Anglo-Indian situation but a prominent actor in it.

Even though India gained its independence (and was partitioned) in 1947, the question of how to interpret Indian and British history in the period after decolonization is still, like all such dense and highly conflicted encounters, a matter of strenuous, if not always edifying, debate. There is the view, for example, that imperialism permanently scarred and distorted Indian life, so that even after decades of independence, the Indian economy, bled by British needs and practices, continues to suffer. Conversely, there are British intellectuals, political figures, and historians who believe that giving up the empire—whose symbols were Suez, Aden, and India—was bad for Britain and bad for "the natives," who both have declined in all sorts of ways ever since.[1]

When we read it today, Kipling's *Kim* can touch on many of these issues. Does Kipling portray the Indians as inferior, or as somehow equal but different? Obviously, an Indian reader will give an answer that focusses on some factors more than others (for example, Kipling's stereotypical views—some would call them racialist—on the Oriental character), whereas English and American readers will stress his affection for Indian life on the Grand Trunk Road. How then do we read *Kim* as a late-nineteenth-century novel, preceded by the works of Scott, Austen, Dickens, and Eliot? We must not forget that the book is after all a novel in a line of novels, that there is more than one history in it to be remembered, that the imperial experience while often regarded as exclusively political also entered into the cultural and aesthetic life of the metropolitan West as well.

A brief summary of the novel's plot may be rehearsed here. Kimball O'Hara is the orphaned son of a sergeant in the Indian army; his mother is also white. He has grown up as a child of the Lahore bazaars, carrying with him an amulet and some papers attesting to his origins. He meets up with a saintly Tibetan monk who is in search of the River where he supposes he will be cleansed of his sins. Kim becomes his chela, or disciple, and the two wander as adventurous mendicants through India, using some help from the English curator of the Lahore Museum. In the meantime Kim becomes involved in a British Secret Service plan to defeat a Russian-inspired conspiracy whose aim is to stir up insurrection in one of the northern Punjabi provinces. Kim is used as a messenger between Mahbub Ali, an Afghan horse dealer who works for the British, and Colonel Creighton, head of the Service, a scholarly ethnographer. Later Kim meets with the other members of Creighton's team in the Great Game, Lurgan Sahib and Hurree Babu, also an ethnographer. By the time that Kim meets Creighton, it is discovered that the boy is white (albeit Irish) and not a native, as he appears, and he is sent to school at St. Xavier's, where his education as a white boy is to be completed. The guru manages to get the money for Kim's tuition, and during the holidays the old man and his young disciple resume their peregrinations. Kim and the old man meet the Russian spies, from whom the boy somehow steals incriminating papers, but not before the "foreigners" strike the holy man. Although the plot has been found out and ended, both the chela and his mentor are disconsolate and ill. They are healed by Kim's restorative powers and a renewed contact with the earth; the old man understands that through Kim he has found the River. As the novel ends Kim returns to the Great Game, and in effect enters the British colonial service full-time.

Some features of *Kim* will strike every reader, regardless of politics and history. It is an overwhelmingly male novel, with two wonderfully attractive men at its center—a boy who grows into early manhood, and an old ascetic priest. Grouped around them are other men, some of them companions, others colleagues and friends; these make up the novel's major, defining reality. Mahbub Ali, Lurgan Sahib, the great Babu, as well as the old Indian soldier and his dashing horse-riding son, plus Colonel Creighton, Mr. Bennett, and Father Victor, to name only a few of the numerous characters in this teeming book: all of them speak the language that men speak among themselves. The women in the novel are remarkably few by comparison, and all of them are somehow debased or unsuitable for male attention—prostitutes, elderly widows, or importunate and lusty women like the widow of Shamlegh; to be "eternally pestered by women," says Kim, is to be hindered in playing the Great Game, which is best played by men alone. We are in a masculine world dominated by travel, trade, adventure, and intrigue, and it is a celibate world, in which the common romance of fiction and the enduring institution of marriage are circumvented, avoided, all but ignored. At best, women help things along: they buy you a ticket, they cook, they tend the ill, and ... they molest men.

Kim himself, although he ages in the novel from thirteen until he is sixteen or seventeen, remains a boy, with a boy's passion for tricks, pranks, clever wordplay, resourcefulness. Kipling seems to have retained a life-long sympathy with himself as a boy beset by the adult world of domineering schoolmasters and priests (Mr. Bennett in *Kim* is an exceptionally unattractive specimen) whose authority must be always reckoned with—until another figure of authority, like Colonel Creighton, comes along and treats the young person with understanding, but no less authoritarian, compassion. The difference between St. Xavier's School, which Kim attends for a time, and service in the Great Game (British intelligence in India) does not lie in the greater freedom of the latter; quite the contrary, the demands of the Great Game are more exacting. The difference lies in the fact that the former imposes a useless authority, whereas the exigencies of the Secret Service demand from Kim an exciting and precise discipline, which he willingly accepts. From Creighton's point of view the Great Game is a sort of political economy of control, in which, as he once tells Kim, the greatest sin is ignorance, not to know. But for Kim the Great Game cannot be perceived in all its complex patterns, although it can be fully enjoyed as a sort of extended prank. The scenes where Kim banters, bargains, repartees with his elders, friendly and hostile alike, are indications of Kipling's seemingly inexhaustible fund of boyish enjoyment in the sheer momentary pleasure of playing a game, any sort of game.

We should not be mistaken about these boyish pleasures. They do not contradict the overall political purpose of British control over India and

Britain's other overseas dominions: on the contrary, *pleasure*, whose steady presence in many forms of imperial-colonial writing as well as figurative and musical art is often left undiscussed, is an undeniable component of *Kim*. A different example of this mixture of fun and single-minded political seriousness is to be found in Lord Baden-Powell's conception of the Boy Scouts, founded and launched in 1907–8. An almost exact contemporary of Kipling, BP, as he was called, was greatly influenced by Kipling's boys generally and Mowgli in particular; BP's ideas about "boyology" fed those images directly into a grand scheme of imperial authority culminating in the great Boy Scout structure "fortifying the wall of empire," which confirmed this inventive conjunction of fun and service in row after row of bright-eyed, eager, and resourceful little middle-class servants of empire.[2] Kim, after all, is both Irish and of an inferior social caste; in Kipling's eyes this enhances his candidacy for service. BP and Kipling concur on two other important points: that boys ultimately should conceive of life and empire as governed by unbreakable Laws, and that service is more enjoyable when thought of less like a story—linear, continuous, temporal—and more like a playing field— many-dimensional, discontinuous, spatial. A recent book by the historian J.A. Mangan sums it up nicely in its title: *The Games Ethic and Imperialism*.[3]

So large is his perspective and so strangely sensitive is Kipling to the range of human possibilities that he offsets this service ethic in *Kim* by giving full rein to another of his emotional predilections, expressed by the strange Tibetan lama and his relationship to the title character. Even though Kim is to be drafted into intelligence work, the gifted boy has already been charmed into becoming the lama's chela at the very outset of the novel. This almost idyllic relationship between two male companions has an interesting genealogy. Like a number of American novels (*Huckleberry Finn*, *Moby-Dick*, and *The Deerslayer* come quickly to mind), *Kim* celebrates the friendship of two men in a difficult, sometimes hostile environment. The American frontier and colonial India are quite different, but both bestow a higher priority on "male bonding" than on a domestic or amorous connection between the sexes. Some critics have speculated on a hidden homosexual motif in these relationships, but there is also the cultural motif long associated with picaresque tales in which a male adventurer (with wife or mother, if either exists, safely at home) and his male companions are engaged in the pursuit of a special dream—like Jason, Odysseus, or, even more compellingly, Don Quixote with Sancho Panza. In the field or on the open road, two men can travel together more easily, and they can come to each other's rescue more credibly than if a woman were along. So the long tradition of adventure stories, from Odysseus and his crew to the Lone Ranger and Tonto, Holmes and Watson, Batman and Robin, seems to hold.

Kim's saintly guru additionally belongs to the overtly religious mode of the pilgrimage or quest, common in all cultures. Kipling, we know, was an admirer of Chaucer's *Canterbury Tales* and Bunyan's *Pilgrim's Progress. Kim* is a good deal more like Chaucer's than like Bunyan's work. Kipling has the Middle English poet's eye for wayward detail, the odd character, the slice of life, the amused sense of human foibles and joys. Unlike either Chaucer or Bunyan, however, Kipling is less interested in religion for its own sake (although we never doubt the Abbot-Lama's piety) than in local color, scrupulous attention to exotic detail, and the all-enclosing realities of the Great Game. It is the greatness of his achievement that quite without selling the old man short or in any way diminishing the quaint sincerity of his Search, Kipling nevertheless firmly places him within the protective orbit of British rule in India. This is symbolized in Chapter 1, when the elderly British museum curator gives the Abbot his spectacles, thus adding to the man's spiritual prestige and authority, consolidating the justness and legitimacy of Britain's benevolent sway.

This view, in my opinion, has been misunderstood and even denied by many of Kipling's readers. But we must not forget that the lama depends on Kim for support and guidance, and that Kim's achievement is neither to have betrayed the lama's values nor to have let up in his work as junior spy. Throughout the novel Kipling is clear to show us that the lama, while a wise and good man, needs Kim's youth, his guidance, his wits; the lama even explicitly acknowledges his absolute, religious need for Kim when, in Benares, toward the end of Chapter 9, he tells the "Jataka," the parable of the young elephant ("The Lord Himself") freeing the old elephant (Ananda) imprisoned in a leg-iron. Clearly, the Abbot-Lama regards Kim as his savior. Later, after the fateful confrontation with the Russian agents who stir up insurrection against Britain, Kim helps (and is helped by) the lama, who in one of the most moving scenes in all Kipling's fiction says, "Child, I have lived on thy strength as an old tree lives on the lime of an old wall." Yet Kim, reciprocally moved by love for his guru, never abandons his duty in the Great Game, although he confesses to the old man that he needs him "for some other things."

Doubtless those "other things" are faith and unbending purpose. In one of its main narrative strands, *Kim* keeps returning to the quest, the lama's search for redemption from the Wheel of Life, a complex diagram of which he carries around in his pocket, and Kim's search for a secure place in colonial service. Kipling condescends to neither. He follows the lama wherever he goes in his wish to be freed from "the delusions of the Body," and it is surely part of our engagement in the novel's Oriental dimension, which Kipling renders with little false exoticism, that we can believe in the novelist's respect for this pilgrim. Indeed, the lama commands attention and esteem from nearly everyone. He honors his word to get the money for Kim's education; he meets Kim at the appointed times and places; he is listened to with veneration and devotion. In an especially nice touch in Chapter 14, Kipling has him tell "a fantastic piled narrative of bewitchment and miracles" about marvelous events in his native Tibetan mountains, events that the novelist courteously forbears from repeating, as if to say that this old saint has a life of his own that cannot be reproduced in sequential English prose.

The lama's search and Kim's illness at the end of the novel are resolved together. Readers of many of Kipling's other tales will be familiar with what the critic J.M.S. Tompkins has rightly called "the theme of healing."[4] Here too the narrative progresses inexorably toward a great crisis. In an unforgettable scene Kim attacks the lama's foreign and defiling assailants, the old man's talisman-like chart is rent, and the two forlorn pilgrims consequently wander through the hills bereft of calm and health. Kim waits to be relieved of his charge, the packet of papers he has stolen from the foreign spy; the lama is unbearably aware of how much longer he must now wait before he can achieve his spiritual goals. Into this heartrending situation, Kipling introduces one of the novel's two great fallen women (the other being the old widow of Kulu), the woman of Shamlegh, abandoned long ago by her "Kerlistian" Sahib, but strong, vital, and passionate nevertheless. (There is a memory here of one of Kipling's most affecting earlier short stories, "Lispeth," which treats the predicament of the native woman loved, but never married, by a departed white man.) The merest hint of a sexual charge between Kim and the lusty Shamlegh woman appears but is quickly dissipated, as Kim and the lama head off once again.

What is the healing process through which Kim and the old lama must pass before they can rest? This extremely complex and interesting question can only be answered slowly and deliberately, so carefully does Kipling *not* insist on the confining limits of a jingoistic imperial solution. Kipling will not abandon Kim and the old monk with impunity to the specious satisfactions of getting credit for a simple job well done. This caution is of course good novelistic practice, but there are other imperatives—emotional, cultural, aesthetic. Kim must be given a station in life commensurate with his stubbornly fought for identity. He has resisted Lurgan Sahib's illusionistic temptations and asserted the fact that *he is Kim*; he has maintained a Sahib's status even while remaining a graceful child of the bazaars and the rooftops; he has played the game well, fought for Britain at some risk to his life and occasionally with brilliance; he has fended off the woman of Shamlegh. Where should he be placed? And where the lovable old cleric?

Readers of Victor Turner's anthropological theories will recognize in Kim's displacements, disguises, and general (usually salutary) shiftiness the essential characteristics of what Turner calls the liminal. Some societies, Turner says, require a mediating character who can knit them together into community, turn them into something more than a collection of administrative or legal structures.

> Liminal [or threshold] entities, such as neophytes in initiation or puberty rites, may be represented as possessing nothing. They may be disguised as monsters, wear only a strip of clothing, or even go naked, to demonstrate that they have no status, property, insignia.... It is as if they are being reduced or groomed down to a uniform condition to be fashioned anew and endowed with additional powers to enable them to cope with their new station in life.[5]

That Kim himself is both an Irish outcast boy and later an essential player in the British Secret Service Great Game suggests Kipling's uncanny understanding of the workings and managing control of societies. According to Turner, societies can be neither rigidly run by "structures" nor completely overrun by marginal, prophetic, and alienated figures, hippies or millenarians; there has to be alternation, so that the sway of one is enhanced or tempered by the inspiration of the other. The liminal *figure* helps to maintain societies, and it is this procedure that Kipling enacts in the climactic moment of the plot and the transformation of Kim's character.

To work out these matters, Kipling engineers Kim's illness and the lama's desolation. There is also the small practical device of having the irrepressible Babu—Herbert Spencer's improbable devotee, Kim's native and secular mentor in the Great Game—turn up to guarantee the success of Kim's exploits. The packet of incriminating papers that prove the Russo-French machinations and the rascally wiles of an Indian prince is safely taken from Kim. Then Kim begins to feel, in Othello's words, the loss of his occupation:

> All that while he felt, though he could not put it into words, that his soul was out of gear with its surroundings—a cog-wheel

unconnected with any machinery, just like the idle cog-wheel of a cheap Beheea sugar-crusher laid by in a corner. The breezes fanned over him, the parrots shrieked at him, the noises of the populated house behind—squables, orders, and reproofs—hit on dead ears.[6]

In effect Kim has died to this world, has, like the epic hero or the liminal personality, descended to a sort of underworld from which, if he is to emerge, he will arise stronger and more in command than before.

The breach between Kim and "this world" must now be healed. The next page may not be the summit of Kipling's art, but it is close to that. The passage is structured around a gradually dawning answer to Kim's question: "I am Kim. And what is Kim?" Here is what happens:

> He did not want to cry—had never felt less like crying in his life—but of a sudden easy, stupid tears trickled down his nose, and with an almost audible click he felt the wheels of his being lock up anew on the world without. Things that rode meaningless on the eyeball an instant before slid into proper proportion. Roads were meant to be walked upon, houses to be lived in, cattle to be driven, fields to be tilled, and men and women to be talked to. They were all real and true—solidly planted upon the feet— perfectly comprehensible—clay of his clay, neither more nor less....[7]

Slowly Kim begins to feel at one with himself and with the world. Kipling goes on:

> There stood an empty bullock-cart on a little knoll half a mile away, with a young banian tree behind—a lookout, as it were, above some new-ploughed levels; and his eyelids, bathed in soft air, grew heavy as he neared it. The ground was good clean dust—not new herbage that, living, is half-way to death already, but the hopeful dust that holds the seed to all life. He felt it between his toes, patted it with his palms, and joint by joint, sighing luxuriously, laid him down full length along in the shadow of the wooden-pinned cart. And Mother Earth was as faithful as the Sahiba [the Widow of Kulu, who has been tending Kim]. She breathed through him to restore the poise he had lost lying so long on a cot cut off from her good currents. His head

lay powerless upon her breast, and his opened hands surrendered
to her strength. The many-rooted tree above him, and even the
dead man-handled wood beside, knew what he sought, as he
himself did not know. Hour upon hour he lay deeper than sleep.[8]

As Kim sleeps, the lama and Mahbub discuss the boy's fate; both men know
he is healed, and so what remains is the disposition of his life. Mahbub wants
him back in service; with that stupefying innocence of his, the lama suggests
to Mahbub that he should join both chela and guru as pilgrims on the way of
righteousness. The novel concludes with the lama revealing to Kim that all
is now well, for having seen

> "all Hind, from Ceylon in the sea to the hills, and my own
> Painted Rocks at Suchzen; I saw every camp and village, to the
> least, where we have rested. I saw them at one time and in one
> place; for they are within the Soul. By this I knew the Soul has
> passed beyond the illusion of Time and Space and of Things. By
> this I knew I was free."[9]

Some of this is mumbo jumbo, of course, but it should not all be
dismissed. The lama's encyclopedic vision of freedom strikingly resembles
Colonel Creighton's Indian Survey, in which every camp and village is duly
noted. The difference is that the positivistic inventory of places and peoples
within the scope of British dominion becomes, in the lama's generous
inclusiveness, a redemptive and, for Kim's sake, therapeutic vision.
Everything is now held together. At its center resides Kim, the boy whose
errant spirit has regrasped things "with an almost audible click." The
mechanical metaphor of the soul being put back on the rails, so to speak,
somewhat violates the elevated and edifying situation, but for an English
writer situating a young white male coming back to earth in a vast country
like India, the figure is apt. After all, the Indian railways were British-built
and assured some greater hold than before over the place.

Other writers before Kipling have written this type of regrasping-of-
life scene, most notably George Eliot in *Middlemarch* and Henry James in
The Portrait of a Lady, the former influencing the latter. In both cases the
heroine (Dorothea Brooke and Isabel Archer) is surprised, not to say
shocked, by the sudden revelation of a lover's betrayal: Dorothea sees Will
Ladislaw apparently flirting with Rosamond Vincy, and Isabel intuits the
dalliance between her husband and Madame Merle. Both epiphanies are
followed by long nights of anguish, not unlike Kim's illness. Then the

women awake to a new awareness of themselves and the world. The scenes in both novels are remarkably similar, and Dorothea Brooke's experience can serve here to describe both. She looks out onto the world past "the narrow cell of her calamity," sees the

> fields beyond, outside the entrance-gates. On the road there was a man with a bundle on his back and a woman carrying a baby ... she felt the largeness of the world and the manifold wakings of men to labour and endurance. She was a part of that involuntary palpitating life, and could neither look out on it from her luxurious shelter as a mere spectator, nor hide her eyes in selfish complaining.[10]

Eliot and James intend such scenes not only as moral reawakenings, but as moments in which the heroine gets past, indeed forgives, her tormentor by seeing herself in the larger scheme of things. Part of Eliot's strategy is to have Dorothea's earlier plans to help her friends be vindicated; the reawakening scene thus confirms the impulse to be in, engage with, the world. Much the same movement occurs in *Kim*, except that the world is defined as liable to a soul's locking up on it. The passage from *Kim* I quoted earlier has a kind of moral triumphalism carried in its accentuated inflections of purpose, will, voluntarism: things slide into proper proportion, roads are meant to be walked on, things are perfectly comprehensible, solidly planted on the feet, and so on. Above the passage are "the wheels" of Kim's being as they "lock up anew on the world without." And this series of motions is subsequently reinforced and consolidated by Mother Earth's blessing upon Kim as he reclines next to the cart: "she breathed through him to restore what had been lost." Kipling renders a powerful, almost instinctual desire to restore the child to its mother in a pre-conscious, undefiled, asexual relationship.

But whereas Dorothea and Isabel are described as inevitably being part of an "involuntary, palpitating life," Kim is portrayed as retaking voluntary hold of his life. The difference is, I think, capital. Kim's newly sharpened apprehension of mastery, of "locking up," of solidity, of moving from liminality to domination is to a very great extent a function of being a Sahib in colonial India: what Kipling has Kim go through is a ceremony of reappropriation, Britain (through a loyal Irish subject) taking hold once again of India. Nature, the involuntary rhythms of restored health, comes to Kim *after* the first, largely political-historical gesture is signalled by Kipling on his behalf. In contrast, for the European or American heroines in Europe, the world is there to be discovered anew; it requires no one in particular to direct it or exert sovereignty over it. This is not the case in British India, which would pass into chaos or insurrection unless roads were walked upon properly, houses lived in the right way, men and women talked to in the correct tones.

In one of the finest critical accounts of *Kim*, Mark Kinkead-Weekes suggests that *Kim* is unique in Kipling's *oeuvre* because what was clearly meant as a resolution for the novel does not really work. Instead, Kinkead-Weekes says, the artistic triumph transcends even the intentions of Kipling the author:

> [The novel] is the product of a peculiar tension between different ways of seeing: the affectionate fascination with the kaleidoscope of external reality for its own sake; the negative capability getting under the skin of attitudes different from one another and one's own; and finally, a product of this last, but at its most intense and creative, the triumphant achievement of an anti-self so powerful that it became a touchstone for everything else—the creation of the Lama. This involved imagining a point of view and a personality almost at the furthest point of view from Kipling himself; yet it is explored so lovingly that it could not but act as a catalyst towards some deeper synthesis. Out of this particular challenge—preventing self-obsession, probing deeper than a merely objective view of reality outside himself, enabling him now to see, think and feel beyond himself—came the new vision of Kim, more inclusive, complex, humanised, and mature than that of any other work.[11]

However much we may agree with some of the insights in this rather subtle reading, it is, in my opinion, rather too ahistorical. Yes, the lama is a kind of anti-self, and, yes, Kipling can get into the skin of others with some sympathy. But no, Kipling never forgets that Kim is an irrefragable part of British India: the Great Game does go on, with Kim a part of it, no matter how many parables the lama fashions. We are naturally entitled to read *Kim* as a novel belonging to the world's greatest literature, free to some degree from its encumbering historical and political circumstances. Yet by the same token, we must not unilaterally abrogate the connections *in it*, and carefully observed by Kipling, to its contemporary actuality. Certainly Kim, Creighton, Mahbub, the Babu, and even the lama see India as Kipling saw it, as a part of the empire. And certainly Kipling minutely preserves the traces of this vision when he has Kim—a humble Irish boy, lower on the hierarchical scale than full-blooded Englishmen—reassert his British priorities well before the lama comes along to bless them.

Readers of Kipling's best work have regularly tried to save him from himself. Frequently this has had the effect of confirming Edmund Wilson's celebrated judgement about *Kim:*

> Now what the reader tends to expect is that Kim will come eventually to realize that he is delivering into bondage to the British invaders those whom he has always considered his own people and that a struggle between allegiances will result. Kipling has established for the reader—and established with considerable dramatic effect—the contrast between the East, with its mysticism and sensuality, its extremes of saintliness and roguery, and the English, with their superior organization, their confidence in modern method, their instinct to brush away like cobwebs the native myths and beliefs. We have been shown two entirely different worlds existing side by side, with neither really understanding the other, and we have watched the oscillation of Kim, as he passes to and fro between them. But the parallel lines never meet; the alternating attractions felt by Kim never give rise to a genuine struggle.... The fiction of Kipling, then, does not dramatise any fundamental conflict because Kipling would never face one.[12]

There is an alternative to these two views, I believe, that is more accurate about and sensitive to the actualities of late-nineteenth-century British India as Kipling, and others, saw them. The conflict between Kim's colonial service and loyalty to his Indian companions is unresolved not because Kipling could not face it, but because for Kipling *there was no conflict;* one purpose of the novel is in fact to show the absence of conflict once Kim is cured of his doubts, the lama of his longing for the River, and India of a few upstarts and foreign agents. That there *might have been* a conflict had Kipling considered India as unhappily subservient to imperialism, we can have no doubt, but he did not: for him it was India's best destiny to be ruled by England. By an equal and opposite reductiveness, if one reads Kipling not simply as an "imperialist minstrel" (which he was not) but as someone who read Frantz Fanon, met Gandhi, absorbed their lessons, and remained stubbornly unconvinced by them, one seriously distorts his context, which he refines, elaborates, and illuminates. It is crucial to remember that there were no appreciable deterrents to the imperialist world-view Kipling held, any more than there were alternatives to imperialism for Conrad, however much he recognized its evils. Kipling was therefore untroubled by the notion of an independent India, although it is true to say that his fiction represents the empire and its conscious legitimizations, which in fiction (as opposed to discursive prose) incur ironies and problems of the kind encountered in Austen or Verdi and, we shall soon see, in Camus. My point in this contrapuntal reading is to emphasize and highlight the disjunctions, not to overlook or play them down.

Consider two episodes in *Kim*. Shortly after the lama and his chela leave Umballa, they meet the elderly, withered former soldier "who had served the Government in the days of the Mutiny." To a contemporary reader "the Mutiny" meant the single most important, well-known, and violent episode of the nineteenth-century Anglo-Indian relationship: the Great Mutiny of 1857, which began in Meerut on May 10 and led to the capture of Delhi. An enormous number of books (e.g., Christopher Hibbert's *The Great Mutiny*), British and Indian, cover the "Mutiny" (referred to as a "Rebellion" by Indian writers). What caused the "Mutiny"—here I shall use the ideologically British designation—was the suspicion of Hindu and Muslim soldiers in the Indian army that their bullets were greased with cow's fat (unclean to Hindus) and pig's fat (unclean to Muslims). In fact the causes of the Mutiny were constitutive to British imperialism itself, to an army largely staffed by natives and officered by Sahibs, to the anomalies of rule by the East India Company. In addition, there was a great deal of underlying resentment about white Christian rule in a country of many other races and cultures, all of whom most probably regarded their subservience to the British as degrading. It was lost on none of the mutineers that numerically they vastly outnumbered their superior officers.

In both Indian and British history, the Mutiny was a clear demarcation. Without going into the complex structure of actions, motives, events, and moralities debated endlessly during and since, we can say that to the British, who brutally and severely put the Mutiny down, all their actions were retaliatory; the mutineers murdered Europeans, they said, and such actions proved, as if proof were necessary, that Indians deserved subjugation by the higher civilization of European Britain; after 1857 the East India Company was replaced by the much more formal Government of India. For the Indians, the Mutiny was a nationalist uprising against British rule, which uncompromisingly reasserted itself despite abuses, exploitation, and seemingly unheeded native complaint. When in 1925 Edward Thompson published his powerful little tract *The Other Side of the Medal*—an impassioned statement against British rule and for Indian independence—he singled out the Mutiny as the great symbolic event by which the two sides, Indian and British, achieved their full and conscious opposition to each other. He dramatically showed that Indian and British history diverged most emphatically on representations of it. The Mutiny, in short, reinforced the difference between colonizer and colonized.

In such a situation of nationalist and self-justifying inflammation, to be an Indian would have meant to feel natural solidarity with the victims of British reprisal. To be British meant to feel repugnance and injury—to say nothing of righteous vindication—given the terrible displays of cruelty by "natives," who fulfilled the roles of savages cast for them. For an Indian, *not* to have had those feelings would have been to belong to a very small minority. It is therefore highly significant that Kipling's choice of an Indian to speak about the Mutiny is a loyalist soldier who views his countrymen's revolt as an act of madness. Not surprisingly, this man is respected by British "Deputy Commissioners" who, Kipling tells us, "turned aside from the main road to visit him." What Kipling eliminates is the likelihood that his compatriots regard him as (at very least) a traitor to his people. And when, a few pages later, the old veteran tells the lama and Kim about the Mutiny, his version of the events is highly charged with the British rationale for what happened:

> A madness ate into all the Army, and they turned against their officers. That was the first evil, but not past remedy if they had then held their hands. But they chose to kill the Sahib's wives and children. Then came the Sahibs from over the sea and called them to most strict account.[13]

To reduce Indian resentment, Indian resistance (as it might have been called) to British insensitivity to "madness," to represent Indian actions as mainly the congenital choice of killing British women and children—these are not merely innocent reductions of the nationalist Indian case but tendentious ones. And when Kipling has the old soldier describe the British counter-revolt—with its horrendous reprisals by white men bent on "moral" action—as "calling" the Indian mutineers "to strict account," we have left the world of history and entered the world of imperialist polemic, in which the native is naturally a delinquent, the white man a stern but moral parent and judge. Thus Kipling gives us the extreme British view on the Mutiny, and puts it in the mouth of an Indian, whose more likely nationalist and aggrieved counterpart is never seen in the novel. (Similarly Mahbub Ali, Creighton's faithful adjutant, belongs to the Pathan people, historically in a state of unpacified insurrection against the British throughout the nineteenth century, yet here represented as happy with British rule, even a collaborator with it.) So far is Kipling from showing two worlds in conflict that he has studiously given us only one, and eliminated any chance of conflict appearing altogether.

The second example confirms the first. Once again it is a small, significant moment. Kim, the lama, and the Widow of Kulu are en route to Saharunpore in Chapter 4. Kim has just been exuberantly described as being "in the middle of it, more awake and more excited than anyone," the "it" of Kipling's description standing for "the world in real truth; this was life as he would have it—bustling and shouting, the buckling of belts, the beating of bullocks and creaking of wheels, lighting of fires and cooking of food, and new sights at every turn of the approving eye."[14] We have already seen a good deal of this side of India, with its color, excitement, and interest exposed in all their variety for the English reader's benefit. Somehow, though, Kipling needs to show some authority over India, perhaps because only a few pages earlier he senses in the old soldier's minatory account of the Mutiny the need to forestall any further "madness." After all India itself is responsible for both the local vitality enjoyed by Kim and the threat to Britain's empire. A District Superintendent of Police trots by, and his appearance occasions this reflection from the Old Widow:

> "These be the sort to oversee justice. They know the land and the customs of the land. The others, all new from Europe, suckled by white women and learning our tongue from books, are worse than the pestilence. They do harm to Kings."[15]

Doubtless some Indians believed that English police officials knew the country better than the natives, and that such officials—rather than Indian rulers—should hold the reins of power. But note that in *Kim* no one challenges British rule, and no one articulates any of the local Indian challenges that must then have been greatly in evidence—even for someone as obdurate as Kipling. Instead we have one character explicitly saying that a colonial police official ought to rule India and adding that she prefers the older style of official who (like Kipling and his family) had lived among the natives and was therefore better than the newer, academically trained bureaucrats. This is a version of the argument of the so-called Orientalists in India, who believed that Indians should be ruled according to Oriental-Indian modes by India "hands," but in the process Kipling dismisses as academic all the philosophical or ideological approaches contending with

Orientalism. Among those discredited styles of rule were Evangelicalism (the missionaries and reformers, parodied in Mr. Bennett), Utilitarianism and Spencerianism (parodied in the Babu), and of course the unnamed academics lampooned as "worse than the pestilence." It is interesting that, phrased the way it is, the widow's approval is wide enough to include police officers like the Superintendent, as well as a flexible educator like Father Victor, and the quietly authoritative figure of Colonel Creighton.

Having the widow express what is in effect a sort of uncontested normative judgement about India and its rulers is Kipling's way of demonstrating that natives accept colonial rule so long as it is the right kind. Historically this has always been how European imperialism made itself palatable to itself, for what could be better for its self-image than native subjects who express assent to the outsider's knowledge and power, implicitly accepting European judgement on the undeveloped, backward, or degenerate nature of their own society? If one reads *Kim* as a boy's adventure or as a rich and lovingly detailed panorama of Indian life, one is not reading the novel that Kipling in fact wrote, so carefully inscribed is it with these considered views, suppressions, and elisions. As Francis Hutchins puts it in *The Illusion of Permanence: British Imperialism in India*, by the late nineteenth century,

> An India of the imagination was created which contained no elements of either social change or political menace. Orientalization was the result of this effort to conceive of Indian society as devoid of elements hostile to the perpetualization of British rule, for it was on the basis of this presumptive India that Orientalizers sought to build a permanent rule.[16]

Kim is a major contribution to this Orientalized India of the imagination, as it is also to what historians have come to call "the invention of tradition."

There is still more to be noted. Dotting *Kim*'s fabric is a scattering of editorial asides on the immutable nature of the Oriental world as distinguished from the white world, no less immutable. Thus, for example, "Kim would lie like an Oriental"; or, a bit later, "all hours of the twenty-four are alike to Orientals"; or, when Kim pays for train tickets with the lama's money he keeps one anna per rupee for himself, which, Kipling says, is "the immemorial commission of Asia"; later still Kipling refers to "the huckster instinct of the East"; at a train platform, Mahbub's retainers "being natives" have not unloaded the trucks which they should have; Kim's ability to sleep as the trains roar is an instance of "the Oriental's indifference to mere noise";

as the camp breaks up, Kipling says that it is done "swiftly—as Orientals understand speed—with long explanations, with abuse and windy talk, carelessly, amid a hundred checks for little things forgotten"; Sikhs are characterized as having a special "love of money"; Hurree Babu equates being a Bengali with being fearful; when he hides the packet taken from the foreign agents, the Babu "stows the entire trove about his body, as only Orientals can."

None of this is unique to Kipling. The most cursory survey of late-nineteenth-century Western culture reveals an immense reservoir of popular wisdom of this sort, a good deal of which, alas, is still very much alive today. Furthermore, as John M. MacKenzie has shown in his valuable book *Propaganda and Empire*, manipulative devices from cigarette cards, postcards, sheet music, almanacs, and manuals to music-hall entertainments, toy soldiers, brass band concerts, and board games extolled the empire and stressed its necessity to England's strategic, moral, and economic well-being, at the same time characterizing the dark or inferior races as unregenerate, in need of suppression, severe rule, indefinite subjugation. The cult of the military personality was prominent, usually because such personalities had managed to bash a few dark heads. Different rationales for holding overseas territories were given; sometimes it was profit, other times strategy or competition with other imperial powers (as in *Kim*: in *The Strange Ride of Rudyard Kipling* Angus Wilson mentions that as early as age sixteen Kipling proposed at a school debate the motion that "the advance of Russia in Central Asia is hostile to British Power").[17] The one thing that remains constant is the subordination of the non-white.

Kim is a work of great aesthetic merit; it cannot be dismissed simply as the racist imagining of one disturbed and ultra-reactionary imperialist. George Orwell was certainly right to comment on Kipling's unique power to have added phrases and concepts to the language—East is East, and West is West; the White Man's Burden; somewhere East of Suez—and right also to say that Kipling's concerns are both vulgar and permanent, of urgent interest.[18] One reason for Kipling's power is that he was an artist of enormous gifts; what he did in his art was to elaborate ideas that would have had far less permanence, for all their vulgarity, without the art. But he was falso supported by (and therefore could use) the authorized monuments of nineteenth-century European culture, and the inferiority of non-white races, the necessity that they be ruled by a superior race, and their absolute unchanging essence was a more or less unquestioned axiom of modern life.

True, there were debates about how the colonies were to be ruled, or whether some of them should be given up. Yet no one with any power to influence public discussion or policy demurred as to the basic superiority of the white European male, who should always retain the upper hand. Statements like "The Hindu is inherently untruthful and lacks moral courage" were expressions of wisdom from which very few, least of all the governors of Bengal, dissented; similarly, when a historian of India like Sir H.M. Elliot planned his work, central to it was the notion of Indian barbarity. Climate and geography dictated certain character traits in the Indian; Orientals, according to Lord Cromer, one of their most redoubtable rulers, could not learn to walk on sidewalks, could not tell the truth, could not use logic; the Malaysian native was essentially lazy, just as the north European was essentially energetic and resourceful. V.G. Kiernan's book *The Lords of Human Kind*, referred to earlier, gives a remarkable picture of how widespread these views were. As I suggested earlier, disciplines like colonial economics, anthropology, history, and sociology were built out of these dicta, with the result that almost to a man and woman the Europeans who dealt with colonies like India became insulated from the facts of change and nationalism. A whole experience—described in meticulous detail in Michael Edwardes's *The Sahibs and the Lotus*—with its own integral history, cuisine, dialect, values, and tropes more or less detached itself from the teeming, contradictory realities of India and perpetuated itself heedlessly. Even Karl Marx succumbed to thoughts of the changeless Asiatic village, or agriculture, or despotism.

A young Englishman sent to India to be a part of the "covenanted" civil service would belong to a class whose national dominance over each and every Indian, no matter how aristocratic and rich, was absolute. He would have heard the same stories, read the same books, learned the same lessons, joined the same clubs as all the other young colonial officials. Yet, Michael Edwardes says, "few really bothered to learn the language of the people they ruled with any fluency, and they were heavily dependent on their native clerks, who had taken the trouble to learn the language of their conquerors, and were, in many cases, not at all unwilling to use their masters' ignorance to their own advantage."[19] Ronny Heaslop in Forster's *A Passage to India* is an effective portrait of such an official.

All of this is relevant to *Kim*, whose main figure of worldly authority is Colonel Creighton. This ethnographer-scholar-soldier is no mere creature of invention, but almost certainly a figure drawn from Kipling's experiences in the Punjab, and he is most interestingly interpreted both as derived from earlier figures of authority in colonial India and as an original figure perfect for Kipling's new purposes. In the first place, although Creighton is seen infrequently and his character is not so fully drawn as Mahbub Ali's or the

Babu's, he is nevertheless present as a point of reference for the action, a discreet director of events, a man whose power is worthy of respect. Yet he is no crude martinet. He takes over Kim's life by persuasion, not by imposition of his rank. He can be flexible when it seems reasonable—who could have wished for a better boss than Creighton during Kim's footloose holidays?— and stern when events require it.

In the second place, it is especially interesting that he is a colonial official and scholar. This union of power and knowledge is contemporary with Doyle's invention of Sherlock Holmes (whose faithful scribe, Dr. Watson, is a veteran of the Northwest Frontier), also a man whose approach to life includes a healthy respect for, and protection of, the law allied with a superior, specialized intellect inclining to science. In both instances, Kipling and Doyle represent for their readers men whose unorthodox style of operation is rationalized by new fields of experience turned into quasi-academic specialties. Colonial rule and crime detection almost gain the respectability and order of the classics or chemistry. When Mahbub Ali turns Kim in for his education, Creighton, overhearing their conversation, thinks "that the boy mustn't be wasted if he is as advertised." He sees the world from a totally systematic viewpoint. Everything about India interests Creighton, because everything in it is significant for his rule. The interchange between ethnography and colonial work in Creighton is fluent; he can study the talented boy both as a future spy and as an anthropological curiosity. Thus when Father Victor wonders whether it might not be too much for Creighton to attend to a bureaucratic detail concerning Kim's education, the colonel dismisses the scruple. "The transformation of a regimental badge like your Red Bull into a sort of fetish that the boy follows is very interesting."

Creighton as anthropologist is important for other reasons. Of all the modern social sciences, anthropology is the one historically most closely tied to colonialism, since it was often the case that anthropologists and ethnologists advised colonial rulers on the manners and mores of the native people. (Claude Levi-Strauss's allusion to anthropology as "the handmaiden of colonialism" recognizes this; the excellent collection of essays edited by Talal Asad, *Anthropology and the Colonial Encounter*, 1973, develops the connections still further; and in Robert Stone's novel on the United States in Latin American affairs, *A Flag for Sunrise*, 1981, the central character is Holliwell, an anthropologist with ambiguous ties to the CIA.) Kipling was one of the first novelists to portray this logical alliance between Western science and political power at work in the colonies.[20] And Kipling always takes Creighton seriously, which is one of the reasons the Babu is there. The native anthropologist, clearly a bright man whose reiterated ambitions to belong to the Royal Society are not unfounded, is almost always funny, or gauche, or somehow caricatural, not because he is incompetent or inept—on the contrary—but because he is not white; that is, he can never be a Creighton. Kipling is very careful about this. Just as he could not imagine an India in historical flux *out of* British control, he could not imagine Indians who could be effective and serious in what he and others of the time considered exclusively Western pursuits. Lovable and admirable as he may be, there remains in the Babu the grimacing stereotype of the ontologically funny native, hopelessly trying to be like "us."

I said that the figure of Creighton is the culmination of a change taking place over generations in the personification of British power in India. Behind Creighton are late-eighteenth-century adventurers and pioneers like Warren Hastings and Robert Clive, whose innovative rule and personal excesses required England to subdue the unrestricted authority of the Raj by law. What survives of Clive and Hastings in Creighton is their sense of freedom, their willingness to improvise, their preference for informality. After such ruthless pioneers came Thomas Munro and Mountstuart Elphinstone, reformers and synthesizers who were among the first senior scholar-administrators whose dominion reflected something resembling expert knowledge. There are also the great scholar figures for whom service in India was an opportunity to study an alien culture—men like Sir William ("Asiatic") Jones, Charles Wilkins, Nathaniel Halhed, Henry Colebrooke, Jonathan Duncan. These men belonged to principally commercial enterprises, and they seemed not to feel, as Creighton (and Kipling) did, that work in India was as patterned and economical (in the literal sense) as running a total system.

Creighton's norms are those of disinterested government, government based not upon whim or personal preference (as was the case for Clive), but upon laws, principles of order and control. Creighton embodies the notion that you cannot govern India unless you know India, and to know India means to understand the way it operates. The understanding developed during William Bentinck's rule as Governor-General and drew on Orientalist as well as Utilitarian principles for ruling the largest number of Indians with the greatest benefits (to Indians as well as the British),[21] but it was always enclosed by the unchanging fact of British imperial authority, which set the Governor apart from ordinary human beings, for whom questions of right and wrong, of virtue and harm are emotionally involving and important. To the government person representing Britain in India, the main thing is not whether something is good or evil, and therefore must be changed or kept, but whether it works or not, whether it helps or hinders in ruling the alien entity. Thus Creighton satisfies the Kipling who had imagined an ideal India, unchanging and attractive, as an eternally integral part of the empire. *This* was an authority one could give in to.

In a celebrated essay, "Kipling's Place in the History of Ideas," Noel Annan presents the notion that Kipling's vision of society was similar to that of the new sociologists—Durkheim, Weber, and Pareto—who

> saw society as a nexus of groups; and the pattern of behaviour which these groups unwittingly established, rather than men's wills or anything so vague as a class, cultural or national tradition, primarily determined men's actions. They asked how these groups promoted order or instability in society, whereas their predecessors had asked whether certain groups helped society to progress.[22]

Annan goes on to say that Kipling was similar to the founders of modern sociological discourse insofar as he believed efficient government in India depended upon "the forces of social control [religion, law, custom, convention, morality] which imposed upon individuals certain rules which they broke at their peril." It had become almost a commonplace of British imperial theory that the British empire was different from (and better than) the Roman Empire in that it was a rigorous system in which order and law prevailed, whereas the latter was mere robbery and profit. Cromer makes the point in *Ancient and Modern Imperialism*, and so does Marlow in *Heart of Darkness*.[23] Creighton understands this perfectly, which is why he works with Muslims, Bengalis, Afghans, Tibetans without appearing ever to belittle their beliefs or slight their differences. It was a natural insight for Kipling to have imagined Creighton as a scientist whose specialty includes the minute workings of a complex society, rather than as either a colonial bureaucrat or a rapacious profiteer. Creighton's Olympian humor, his affectionate but detached attitude to people, his eccentric bearing, are Kipling's embellishments on an ideal Indian official.

Creighton the organization man not only presides over the Great Game (whose ultimate beneficiary is of course the Kaiser-i-Hind, or Queen Empress, and her British people), but also works hand in hand with the novelist himself. If we can ascribe a consistent point of view to Kipling, we can find it in Creighton, more than anyone else. Like Kipling, Creighton respects the distinctions within Indian society. When Mahbub Ali tells Kim that he must never forget that he is a Sahib, he speaks as Creighton's trusted, experienced employee. Like Kipling, Creighton never tampers with the hierarchies, the priorities and privileges of caste, religion, ethnicity, and race; neither do the men and women who work for him. By the late nineteenth century the so-called Warrant of Precedence—which began, according to Geoffrey Moorhouse, by recognizing "fourteen different levels of status"— had expanded to "sixty-one, some reserved for one person, others shared by a number of people."[24] Moorhouse speculates that the love-hate relationship between British and Indians derived from the complex hierarchical attitudes present in both people. "Each grasped the other's basic social premise and not only understood it but subconsciously respected it as a curious variant of their own."[25] One sees this kind of thinking reproduced nearly everywhere in *Kim*—Kipling's patiently detailed register of India's different races and castes, the acceptance by everyone (even the lama) of the doctrine of racial separation, the lines and customs which cannot easily be traversed by outsiders. Everyone in *Kim* is equally an outsider to other groups and an insider in his.

Creighton's appreciation of Kim's abilities—his quickness, his capacity for disguise and for getting into a situation as if it were native to him—is like the novelist's interest in this complex and chameleon-like character, who darts in and out of adventure, intrigue, episode. The ultimate analogy is between the Great Game and the novel itself. To be able to see all India from the vantage of controlled observation: this is one great satisfaction. Another is to have at one's fingertips a character who can sportingly cross lines and invade territories, a little Friend of all the World—Kim O'Hara himself. It is as if by holding Kim at the center of the novel (just as Creighton the spy master holds the boy in the Great Game) Kipling can *have* and enjoy India in a way that even imperialism never dreamed of.

What does this mean in terms of so codified and organized a structure as the late-nineteenth-century realistic novel? Along with Conrad, Kipling is a writer of fiction whose heroes belong to a startlingly unusual world of foreign adventure and personal charisma. Kim, Lord Jim, and Kurtz, say, are creatures with flamboyant wills who presage later adventurers like T.E. Lawrence in *The Seven Pillars of Wisdom* and Malraux's Perken in *La Voie royale*. Conrad's heroes, afflicted as they may be by an unusual power of reflection and cosmic irony, remain in the memory as strong, often heedlessly daring men of action.

And although their fiction belongs to the genre of adventure-imperialism—along with the work of Rider Haggard, Doyle, Charles Reade, Vernon Fielding, G.A. Henty, and dozens of lesser writers—Kipling and Conrad claim serious aesthetic and critical attention.

But one way of grasping what is unusual about Kipling is to recall briefly who his contemporaries were. We have become so used to seeing him alongside Haggard and Buchan that we have forgotten that as an artist he can justifiably be compared with Hardy, Henry James, Meredith, Gissing, the later George Eliot, George Moore, or Samuel Butler. In France, his peers are Flaubert and Zola, even Proust and the early Gide. Yet the works of these writers are essentially novels of disillusion and disenchantment, whereas *Kim* is not. Almost without exception the protagonist of the late-nineteenth-century novel is someone who has realized that his or her life's project—the wish to be great, rich, or distinguished—is mere fancy, illusion, dream. Frédéric Moreau in Flaubert's *Sentimental Education*, or Isabel Archer in *The Portrait of a Lady*, or Ernest Pontifex in Butler's *The Way of All Flesh*—the figure is a young man or woman bitterly awakened from a fancy dream of accomplishment, action, or glory, forced instead to come to terms with a reduced status, betrayed love, and a hideously bourgeois world, crass and philistine.

This awakening is not to be found in *Kim*. Nothing brings the point home more powerfully than a comparison between Kim and his nearly exact contemporary Jude Fawley, the "hero" of Thomas Hardy's *Jude the Obscure* (1894). Both are eccentric orphans objectively at odds with their environment: Kim is an Irishman in India, Jude a minimally gifted rural English boy who is interested more in Greek than in farming. Both imagine lives of appealing attractiveness for themselves, and both try to achieve these lives through apprenticeship of some sort, Kim as chela to the wandering Abbot-Lama, Jude as a supplicant student at the university. But there the comparisons stop. Jude is ensnared by one circumstance after the other; he marries the ill-suited Arabella, falls in love diastrously with Sue Bridehead, conceives children who commit suicide, ends his days as a neglected man after years of pathetic wandering. Kim, by contrast, graduates from one brilliant success to another.

Yet it is important to insist again on the similarities between *Kim* and *Jude the Obscure*. Both boys, Kim and Jude, are singled out for their unusual pedigree; neither is like "normal" boys, whose parents and family assure a smooth passage through life. Central to their predicaments is the problem of identity—what to be, where to go, what to do. Since they cannot be like the others, who are they? They are restless seekers and wanderers, like the archetypal hero of the novel form itself, Don Quixote, who decisively marks off the world of the novel in its fallen, unhappy state, its "lost transcendence," as Lukacs puts it in *The Theory of the Novel*, from the happy, satisfied world of the epic. Every novelistic hero, Lukacs says, attempts to restore the lost world of his or her imagination, which in the late-nineteenth-century novel of disillusionment is an unrealizable dream. [26] Jude, like Frédéric Moreau, Dorothea Brooke, Isabel Archer, Ernest Pontifex, and all the others, is condemned to such a fate. The paradox of personal identity is that it is implicated in that unsuccessful dream. Jude would not be who he is were it not for his futile wish to become a scholar. Escape from being a social non-entity holds out the promise of relief, but that is impossible. The structural irony is precisely that conjunction: what you wish for is exactly what you cannot have. The poignancy and defeated hope at the end of *Jude the Obscure* have become synonymous with Jude's very identity.

Because he gets beyond this paralyzing, dispiriting impasse, Kim O'Hara is so remarkably optimistic a character. Like those of other heroes of imperial fiction, his actions result in victories not defeats. He restores India to health, as the invading foreign agents are apprehended and expelled. Part of his strength is his deep, almost instinctive knowledge of this difference from the Indians around him; he has a special amulet given him during infancy, and unlike the other boys he plays with—this is established at the novel's opening—he is endowed through natal prophecy with a unique fate of which he wishes to make everyone aware. Later he becomes explicitly aware of being a Sahib, a white man, and whenever he wavers there is someone to remind him that he is indeed a Sahib, with all the rights and privileges of that special rank. Kipling even makes the saintly guru affirm the difference between a white man and a non-white.

But that alone does not impart to the novel its curious sense of enjoyment and confidence. Compared with James or Conrad, Kipling was not an introspective writer, nor—from the evidence that we have—did he think of himself, like Joyce, as an Artist. The force of his best writing comes from ease and fluency, the seeming naturalness of his narration and characterization, while the sheer variousness of his creativity rivals that of Dickens and Shakespeare. Language for him was not, as it was for Conrad, a resistant medium; it was transparent, easily capable of many tones and inflections, all of them directly representative of the world he explored. And this language gives Kim his sprightliness and wit, his energy and attractiveness. In many ways Kim resembles a character who might have been drawn much earlier in the nineteenth century, by a writer like Stendhal, for example, whose vivid portrayals of Fabrice del Dongo and Julien Sorel have the same blend of adventure and wistfulness, which Stendhal called *espagnolisme*. For Kim, as for Stendhal's characters and unlike Hardy's Jude, the world is full of possibilities, much like Caliban's island, "full of noises, sounds, and sweet airs, that give delight and hurt not."

At times, that world is restful, even idyllic. So we get not only the bustle and vitality of the Grand Trunk Road, but also the welcoming, gentle pastoralism of the scene en route with the old soldier (Chapter 3) as the little group of travellers reposes peacefully:

> There was a drowsy buzz of small life in hot sunshine, a cooing of doves, and a sleepy drone of well-wheels across the fields. Slowly and impressively the lama began. At the end of ten minutes the old soldier slid from his pony, to hear better as he said, and sat with the reins round his wrist. The lama's voice faltered—the periods lengthened. Kim was busy watching a gray squirrel. When the little scolding bunch of fur, close pressed to the branch, disappeared, preacher and audience were fast asleep, the old officer's strong-cut head pillowed on his arm, the lama's thrown back against the tree bole, where it showed like yellow ivory. A naked child toddled up, stared, and moved by some quick impulse of reverence made a solemn little obeisance before the lama—only the child was so short and fat that it toppled over sideways, and Kim laughed at the sprawling, chubby legs. The child, scared and indignant, yelled aloud.[27]

On all sides of this Edenic composure is the "wonderful spectacle" of the Grand Trunk Road, where, as the old soldier puts it, " 'all castes and kinds of men move ... Brahmins and chumars, bankers and tinkers, barbers and bunnias, pilgrims and potters—all the world coming and going. It is to me as a river from which I am withdrawn like a log after a flood.' "[28]

One fascinating index of Kim's way with this teeming, strangely hospitable world is his remarkable gift for disguise. We first see him perched on the ancient gun in a square in Lahore—where it still stands today—an Indian boy among other Indian boys. Kipling carefully differentiates the religions and backgrounds of each boy (the Muslim, the Hindu, the Irish) but is just as careful to show us that none of these identities, though they may hinder the other boys, is a hindrance to Kim. He can pass from one dialect, one set of values and beliefs, to the other. Throughout the book Kim takes on the dialects of numerous Indian communities; he speaks Urdu, English (Kipling does a superbly funny, gentle mockery of his stilted Anglo-Indian, finely distinguished from the Babu's orotund verbosity), Eurasian, Hindi, and Bengali; when Mahbub speaks Pashtu, Kim gets that too; when the lama speaks Chinese Tibetan, Kim understands that. As orchestrator of this Babel of tongues, this veritable Noah's Ark of Sansis, Kashmiris, Akalis, Sikhs, and many others, Kipling also manages Kim's chameleon-like progress dancing in and out of it all, like a great actor passing through many situations and at home in each.

How very different this all is from the lusterless world of the European bourgeoisie, whose ambiance as every novelist of importance renders it reconfirms the debasement of contemporary life, the extinction of all dreams of passion, success, and exotic adventure. Kipling's fiction offers an antithesis: his world, because it is set in an India dominated by Britain, holds nothing back from the expatriate European. *Kim* shows how a white Sahib can enjoy life in this lush complexity; and, I would argue, the absence of resistance to European intervention in it—symbolized by Kim's abilities to move relatively unscarred through India—is due to its imperialist vision. For what one cannot accomplish in one's own Western environment—where trying to live out the grand dream of a successful quest means coming up against one's own mediocrity and the world's corruption and degradation—one can do abroad. Isn't it possible in India to do everything? be anything? go anywhere with impunity?

Consider the pattern of Kim's wanderings as they affect the structure of the novel. Most of his voyages move within the Punjab, around the axis formed by Lahore and Umballa, a British garrison town on the frontier of the United Provinces. The Grand Trunk Road, built by the great Muslim ruler Sher Shan in the late sixteenth century, runs from Peshawar to Calcutta, although the lama never goes farther south and east than Benares. Kim makes excursions to Simla, to Lucknow, and later to the Kulu valley; with Mahbub he goes as far south as Bombay and as far west as Karachi. But the overall impression created by these voyages is of carefree meandering. Occasionally Kim's trips are punctuated by the requirements of the school year at St. Xavier's, but the only serious agendas, the only equivalents of temporal pressure on the characters, are (a) the Abbot-Lama's Search, which is fairly elastic, and (b) the pursuit and final expulsion of the foreign agents trying to stir up trouble on the Northwest Frontier. There are no scheming money-lenders here, no village prigs, no vicious gossips or unattractive and heartless *parvenus*, as there are in the novels of Kipling's major European contemporaries.

Now contrast *Kim's* rather loose structure, based as it is on a luxurious geographical and spatial expansiveness, with the tight, relentlessly unforgiving temporal structure of the European novels contemporary with it. Time, says Lukacs in *The Theory of the Novel*, is the great ironist, almost a character in these novels, as it drives the protagonist further into illusion and derangement, and also reveals his or her illusions to be groundless, empty, bitterly futile.[29] In *Kim*, you have the impression that time is on your side, because the geography is yours to move about in more or less freely. Certainly Kim feels that, and so does Colonel Creighton, in his patience, and in the sporadic, even vague way he appears and disappears. The opulence of India's space, the commanding British presence there, the sense of freedom communicated by the interaction between these two factors add up to a wonderfully positive atmosphere irradiating the pages of *Kim*. This is not a driven world of hastening disaster, as in Flaubert or Zola.

The novel's ease of atmosphere also comes, I think, from Kipling's own recollected sense of being at home in India. In *Kim* representatives of the Raj seem to have no problem with being "abroad"; India for them requires no self-conscious apologetic, no embarrassment or unease. The French-speaking Russian agents admit that in India, "we have nowhere left our mark yet,"[30] but the British know they have, so much so that Hurree, that self-confessed "Oriental," is agitated by the Russians' conspiracy on behalf of the Raj, not his own people. When the Russians attack the lama and rip apart his map, the defilement is metaphorically of India itself, and Kim corrects this defilement later. Kipling's mind plays over reconciliation, healing, and wholeness in the conclusion, and his means are geographical: the British repossessing India, in order once again to enjoy its spaciousness, to be at home in it again, and again.

There is a striking coincidence between Kipling's reassertion over the geography of India and Camus's in some of his Algerian stories written almost a half century later. Their gestures are symptomatic not of confidence, but of a lurking, often unacknowledged malaise, I believe. For if you belong in a place, you do not have to keep saying and showing it: you just are, like the silent Arabs in *L'Etranger* or the fuzzy-haired Blacks in *Heart of Darkness* or the various Indians in *Kim*. But colonial, i.e., geographical, appropriation requires such assertive inflections, and these emphases are the hallmark of the imperial culture reconfirming itself to and for itself.

Kipling's geographical and spatial governance of *Kim* rather than the temporal one of metropolitan European fiction, gains special eminence by political and historical factors; it expresses an irreducible political judgement on Kipling's part. It is as if he were saying, India is ours and therefore we can see it in this mostly uncontested, meandering, and fulfilling way. India is "other" and, importantly, for all its wonderful size and variety, it is safely held by Britain.

Kipling arranges another aesthetically satisfying coincidence, and it, too, must be taken into account. This is the confluence between Creighton's

Great Game and Kim's inexhaustibly renewed capacity for disguises and adventure; Kipling keeps the two tightly connected. The first is a device of political surveillance and control; the second, at a deeper and interesting level, is a wish-fantasy of someone who would like to think that everything is possible, that one can go anywhere and be anything. TE. Lawrence in *The Seven Pillars of Wisdom* expresses this fantasy over and over, as he reminds us how he—a blond, blue-eyed Englishman—moved among the desert Arabs as if he were one of them.

I call this a fantasy because, as both Kipling and Lawrence endlessly remind us, no one—least of all actual whites and non-whites in the colonies—ever forgets that "going native" or playing the Great Game depends on the rock-like foundations of European power. Was there ever a native fooled by the blue- or green-eyed Kims and T.E. Lawrences who passed among them as agent adventurers? I doubt it, just as I doubt that any white man or woman lived within the orbit of European imperialism who ever forgot that the discrepancy in power between the white rulers and the native subjects was absolute, intended to be unchanging, rooted in cultural, political, and economic reality.

Kim, the positive boy hero who travels in disguise all over India, across boundaries and rooftops, into tents and villages, is everlastingly responsible to British power, represented by Creighton's Great Game. The reason we can see that so clearly is that since *Kim* was written India *has* become independent, just as since the publication of Gide's *The Immoralist* and Camus's *The Stranger* Algeria has become independent of France. To read these major works of the imperial period retrospectively and heterophonically with other histories and traditions counterpointed against them, to read them in the light of decolonization, is neither to slight their great aesthetic force, nor to treat them reductively as imperialist propaganda. Still, it is a much graver mistake to read them stripped of their affiliations with the facts of power which informed and enabled them.

The device invented by Kipling by which British control over India (the Great Game) coincides in detail with Kim's disguise fantasy to be at one with India, and later to heal its defilements, obviously could not have occurred without British imperialism. We must read the novel as the realization of a great cumulative process, which in the closing years of the nineteenth century is reaching its last major moment before Indian independence: on the one hand, surveillance and control over India; on the other, love for and fascinated attention to its every detail. The overlap between the political hold of the one and the aesthetic and psychological pleasure of the other is made possible by British imperialism itself; Kipling understood this, yet many of his later readers refuse to accept this troubling, even embarrassing truth. And it was not just Kipling's recognition of British imperialism in general, but imperialism at that specific moment in its history, when it had almost lost sight of the unfolding dynamics of a human and secular truth: the truth that India had existed before the Europeans arrived, that control was seized by a European power, and that Indian resistance to that power would inevitably struggle out from under British subjugation.

In reading *Kim* today we can watch a great artist in a sense blinded by his own insights about India, confusing the realities that he saw with such color and ingenuity, with the notion that they were permanent and essential. Kipling takes from the novel form qualities that he tries to bend to this basically obfuscatory end. But it is surely a great artistic irony that he does not truly succeed in this obfuscation, and his attempt to use the novel for this purpose reaffirms his aesthetic integrity. *Kim* most assuredly is *not* a political tract. Kipling's choice of the novel form and of his character Kim O'Hara to engage profoundly with an India that he loved but could not properly have— this is what we should keep resolutely as the book's central meaning. Then we can read *Kim* as a great document of its historical moment and, too, an aesthetic milestone along the way to midnight August 14–15, 1947, a moment whose children have done so much to revise our sense of the past's richness and its enduring problems.

NOTES

1. As a sample of this sort of thinking, see J.B. Kelly, *Arabia, the Gulf and the West* (London: Weidenfeld & Nicolson, 1980).

2. Rosenthal, *Character Factory*, p. 52 and *passim*.

3. J.A. Mangan, *The Games Ethic and Imperialism: Aspects of the Diffusion of an Ideal* (Harmondsworth: Viking, 1986).

4. J.M.S. Tompkins, "Kipling's Later Tales: The Theme of Healing," *Modern Language Review* 45 (1950), 18–32.

5. Victor Turner, *Dramas, Fields, and Metaphors: Symbolic Action in Human Society* (Ithaca: Cornell University Press, 1974), pp. 258–59. For a subtle meditation on the problems of color and caste, see S. P. Mohanty, "Kipling's Children and the Colour Line," *Race and Class*, 31, No. 1 (1989), 21–40, also his "Us and Them: On the Philosophical Bases of Political Criticism," *Yale Journal of Criticism* 2, No. 2 (1989), 1–31.

6. Rudyard Kipling, *Kim* (1901; rprt. Garden City: Doubleday, Doran, 1941), p. 516.

7. *Ibid.*, pp. 516–17.

8. *Ibid.*, p. 517.

9. *Ibid.*, p. 523.

10. George Eliot, *Middlemarch*, ed. Bert G. Hornback (New York: Norton, 1977), p. 544.

11. Mark Kinkead-Weekes, "Vision in Kipling's Novels," in *Kipling's Mind and Art*, ed. Andrew Rutherford (London: Oliver & Boyd, 1964).

12. Edmund Wilson, "The Kipling that Nobody Read," *The Wound and the Bow* (New York: Oxford University Press, 1947), pp. 100–1, 103.

13. Kipling, *Kim*, p. 242.

14. *Ibid.*, p. 268.

15. *Ibid.*, p. 271.

16. Francis Hutchins, *The Illusion of Permanence: British Imperialism in India* (Princeton: Princeton University Press, 1967), p. 157. See also George Bearce, *British Attitudes Towards India, 1784–1858* (Oxford: Oxford University Press, 1961), and for the unravelling of the system, see B.R. Tomlinson, *The Political Economy of the Raj, 1914–1947: The Economics of Decolonization in India* (London: Macmillan, 1979).

17. Angus Wilson, *The Strange Ride of Rudyard Kipling* (London: Penguin, 1977), p. 43.

18. George Orwell, "Rudyard Kipling," in *A Collection of Essays* (New York: Doubleday, Anchor, 1954), pp. 133–35.

19. Michael Edwardes, *The Sahibs and the Lotus: The British in India* (London: Constable, 1988), p. 59.

20. See Edward W. Said, "Representing the Colonized: Anthropology's Interlocutors," *Critical Inquiry* 15, No. 2 (Winter 1989), 205–25. See also Lewis D. Wurgaft, *The Imperial Imagination: Magic and Myth in Kipling's India* (Middletown: Wesleyan University Press, 1983), pp. 54–78, and of course the work of Bernard S. Cohn, *Anthropologist Among the Historians*.

21. See Eric Stokes, *The English Utilitarians and India* (Oxford: Clarendon Press, 1959), and Bearce, *British Attitudes Towards India*, pp. 153–74. On Bentinck's educational reform, see Viswanathan, *Masks of Conquest*, pp. 44–47.

22. Noel Annan, "Kipling's Place in the History of Ideas," *Victorian Studies* 3, No. 4 (June 1960), 323.

23. See notes 11 and 12.

24. Geoffrey Moorhouse, *India Britannica* (London: Paladin, 1984), p. 103.

25. *Ibid.*, p. 102.

26. Georg Lukacs, *The Theory of the Novel*, trans. Anna Bostock (Cambridge, Mass: MIT Press, 1971), pp. 35 ff.

27. Kipling, *Kim*, p. 246.

28. *Ibid.*, p. 248.

29. Lukacs, *Theory of the Novel*, pp. 125–26.

30. Kipling, *Kim*, p. 466.

MALCOLM BRADBURY

The Opening World, 1900–1915

Virginia Woolf's sound of "breaking and falling, crashing and destruction," was therefore real enough. By the four years between the beginning of Georgianism and the outbreak of the Great War, the "modern spirit," the sense of *avant-garde* adventure, of new forms opening new windows on a changed world, had once again begun to take hold. New and powerful influences, Dostoevsky and Chekhov, Ibsen and Nietzsche, Bergson and Sorel and Freud, began affecting British writing. For the moment London was recognizably a major centre of artistic cosmopolitanism, and writers and forms flooded in, in what is now remembered as a period of high cultural hospitality and internationalism rare in the modern British arts. Everyone slipped off to Paris. Hueffer came to see himself as German, or French, indeed anything but English. Then there were the expatriates and exiles: Conrad and Gaudier-Brzeska from Poland, S.S. Koteliansky from Russia, Yeats, Shaw and George Moore from Ireland (Joyce took his exile further afield, to the old Habsburg port of Trieste); James, Pound, "H.D.", and later the quiet T.S. Eliot from the USA; Katherine Mansfield from New Zealand, and Wyndham Lewis from God alone knew where (he was appropriately born on a ship at sea). Lawrence made Nottinghamshire sound like a place of exile, followed German literature with passion, and began, like Joyce, on the path of wandering. Now more and more little magazines, generally with strange typographies and abstract covers, began their insecure publication;

From *The Modern British Novel.* © 1993 by Malcolm Bradbury.

more and more movements and manifestos appeared (Imagism, Vorticism), calling in their different ways for energy, explosion, destruction and recommencement, aiming to blast down the past in the hope of blessing the future. The arts were in a mood of rebellious warfare, and their flamboyant putsches, campaigns and counter-putsches won public attention.[1]

Woolf's term for this, "Georgian," was perhaps less than satisfactory. She was speaking of a double revolt, against "Victorianism" and "Edwardianism," but in fact the new movements and tendencies split in many directions, in which Georgianism—everything now was an "ism"—was just one voice. In 1912 came Edward Marsh's *Georgian Poetry*, printing a variety of poets and generations, and claiming that the Georgian period might "take rank in due time with the several great poetic ages of the past." To D.H. Lawrence, who was both in it and reviewed it, the new "Georgian" spirit was one of Nietzschean hope: "The nihilists, the intellectual, hopeless people—Ibsen, Flaubert, Thomas Hardy—represent the dream we are waking from. It was a dream of demolition ... But we are awake again, our lungs are full of new air, our eyes of morning." Others were less sure. Georgianism in verse was soon challenged by Imagism, which was then challenged by Vorticism, each of them with a different view of the distilling form—"image," "vortex," or whatever—of the new. Dreams of the great demolition, the crashing and falling, continued. When Wyndham Lewis started a Vorticist manifesto-magazine in 1914 he called it *Blast:* and in a volley of brief, violent curses and benedictions he blasted the Victorians, rejected Romanticism for Classicism, Georgianism for something harder, tougher, more to do with machines than nature, and blessed the age of the abstract vortex and the cleansing modern explosion. The new excitements intensified year by year, and some of those who had called themselves simply moderns now knew they were Modernists, claiming that a most momentous transformation was fully under way. Small groups gathered, experimental enclaves flourished, hard experimental art-works multiplied, and new small presses and little magazines appeared to exhibit the *avant garde*, printing works by writers whose work seemed to have been shamefully denied, from the new feminists to the exiled James Joyce. Hueffer, who once called himself an "Impressionist," in the manner of Conrad, now called himself a "Vorticist," and used Vorticist methods for his novel *The Good Soldier*, a section of which in turn appeared in *Blast*. *The Egoist*, once a feminist magazine, now had acquired Pound as literary editor; it promoted the movement of "Imagism," and then in 1914, over 24 episodes, ran Joyce's *A Portrait of the Artist as a Young Man*. It was a rare and remarkable period in British writing, in prose and poetry, and in painting and sculpture and dance, all of which linked together in common cause. A prewar Modernist wonderland did exist, and it was indeed like an opening world.

Even so, it is quite possible that all this could have been a brief and seasonal adventure, were it not for one terrible fact. The pre-war writers did not know they *were* pre-war writers, though sometimes it seems they half-intuited what was to come. The *avant garde*, for all its modern prophecies, was not aware of what it was really *avant*. 1914, the year of Joyce's *Dubliners* and the serialization of *A Portrait* ..., saw the excitement reach its peak. Then in August, between the first and second issues of *Blast*, the real blasts sounded. The collapse of the imperial Europe, following the assassination of the Habsburg Archduke in Sarajevo, started; the Great War began. Soon the vortex of new energy ran free, and the young were all transforming themselves into Good Soldiers. Many, including T.E. Hulme, voice of the hard new classicism, and Gaudier-Brzeska, who had declared in *Blast* "The War is a great remedy," died at the front. The abstract metallic explosions, the bursting mechanical violence, the new kinetic energy, became realities; the bombing of the old art cities, the flooding of the museums, that the Futurists had called for turned into fact. Over several literary generations writers had been prophesying the coming of the New Age, the violent end of an epoch, the rule of the destructive element, a war of the worlds. Now an era that thought it was beginning also found that it was ending, that even the springtime new hopes were dashed. An era in culture, the arts and civilization was now in crisis, as Henry James, now at the close of his life, saw. He wrote his story "A Dream of Armageddon," and reflected in a letter of August 1914 to his friend Howard Sturgis "the plunge of civilization into his abyss of blood and darkness ... is a thing that so gives away the whole long age in which we have supposed the world to be, with whatever abatement, gradually bettering, that to have to take it all now for what the treacherous years were all the while really making for and *meaning* is too tragic for any words." Indeed, he noted, "the war has used up words." It was a notion that would resurface grimly after the Holocaust of the Second World War. The words, of course, would come in time. But the realization that they would have to be new words, that the war had drained most of the old ones of signification, that a different language, pared of most of the old romantic and cultural associations, would have to be found, grew as the terrible Great War went on. So it was that the War itself completed what pre-war Modernists had begun to imagine: the sweeping away of Victorianism, and Edwardianism. Georgianism, its eyes full of morning, went too. The war smashed romanticism and sentimentalism, naive notions of patriotism and imperial adventure; they did not outlast the conflict. But, paradoxically, some of the complex aesthetic ideas that had stirred in the years between 1910 and 1914—"hardness," "abstraction," "collage," "fragmentation," "dehumanization"—and the key themes of chaotic history, Dionysian energy, the "destructive element," did help to provide the discourse and forms of the world to come.

1915—the year the war settled into the futility of trench warfare, and Zeppelin airships arrived to bomb London—was the culminating year, both in the war and in the transition of the arts. Some of the key books of the years of experiment appeared, marking a deep change in fictional climate. Conrad's emphatically titled *Victory* came out; so did John Buchan's classic spy story, *The 39 Steps*. Hueffers' farewell to the *belle époque*, the book that he had intended to call *The Saddest Story* (in accordance with its famous opening line, "This is the saddest story I have ever heard"), appeared under the new wartime title of *The Good Soldier*. Virginia Woolf's long-delayed first novel appeared at last as *The Voyage Out*, and Dorothy Richardson opened her long experimental sequence "Pilgrimage" with the volume *Pointed Roofs*. D.H. Lawrence, who had proved himself a writer always interested in apocalyptic moments and signs, the leap from the ruins, the personal resurrection, found the growing darkness of his vision confirmed. Before the War, he had started his most ambitious project so far, *The Sisters*, aided by his reading of Thomas Hardy. Now he divided it into two, to take account of what was happening. "I knew I was writing a destructive work ...," he explained later, "And I knew, as I revised the book, that it was a kind of working up to the dark sensual or Dionysic or Aphrodisic ecstasy, which actually does burst the world, burst the world-consciousness in every individual. What I did through individuals, the world has done through the war. But alas, in the world of Europe I see no Rainbow." In 1915 the first segment of the book, which was called *The Rainbow*, the rainbow being an apocalyptic sign, appeared. It was a work both of crisis and Dionysic sensual ecstasy, developing both in optimism and pessimism on from Hardy. The critics were shocked, perhaps in part by its apparent indifference to the War itself. One thousand and eleven copies were seized and destroyed by the police, and it was banned under the Obscene Publications Act. "The world is gone, extinguished," Lawrence bitterly noted, already planning the path of post-war exile; "It was in 1915 that the old world ended." Many of the fruits of the pre-war experiment had come to birth. So had a new world, bitter and empty, made out of cultural disorder and European ruins. It might be a modern, but it was no longer an opening, world.

It is hardly surprising that the immediately pre-war years became folkloric, for the participants and then for the later critics; so much that is important to the idea of modern literature stirred into existence then. In retrospect, said Wyndham Lewis, looking back from 1937, when he had himself become the "Enemy," at odds with most of what happened thereafter to the Modern movement, it would all appear "an island of incomparable bliss, dwelt by strange shapes labelled 'Pound,' 'Joyce,' 'Weaver,' 'Hulme' ... As people look back at them, out of a very humdrum, cautious, disillusioned society ... the critics of the future will rub their eyes. They will look, to them, so hopelessly avant garde!, so almost madly up and coming! What energy!–what impossibly spartan standards, men will exclaim! ... *We are the first men of a future that has not materialized!*" Whether this is self-serving or not, it is certainly true that we cannot write the history of modern fiction without looking with some care at many of his strange shapes. And there is no doubt that one of the strangest, and most representative, was the one then labelled "Hueffer," though later known as "Ford." Hueffer/Ford always had a gift for metamorphosis, and this brought him into close contact with nearly everything that was interesting and significant about the Modern movement. Lewis, whom he discovered, called him "a flabby lemon and pink giant, who hung his mouth open as though he were an animal at the Zoo inviting buns–especially when ladies were present" (they often were); H.G. Wells, first his friend, then his enemy, described him as "a great system of assumed persona and dramatized selves." Indeed it was true his manner often appeared a disguise, and there somehow seemed to be two or more of him. He was the British writer incarnate, but he was also German, or French. Sometimes he was the foreign bohemian adrift among British philistines; sometimes he was the last British Tory, condemned to travel the great wilderness know as "abroad." At various times he was the Last Pre-Raphaelite, the first Impressionist, a Post-Impressionist, a Vorticist, and a soldier of the Parisian "Revolution of the Word." He wrote extensively about the "critical attitude," but was not a theorist (his companion of the 1920s, Stella Bowen, described him as "a writer—a complete writer—and nothing but a writer"). He collaborated with Conrad, wrote well on James, and had literary friendships (though they often turned, as such things do, into enmities) with most of the major figures of the era—Conrad, James, Hardy, Wells, Pound, Lawrence, Violet Hunt, Rebecca West, May Sinclair, Joyce, Stein, Jean Rhys and Robert Lowell, helping many of them to publication. He was close to every major movement, from Pre-Raphaelitism to Dada, over the fifty years of his writing life. He wrote over eighty books in innumerable genres, children's stories to advanced poetry, from the early 1890s to 1939, the year of his death; thus his writing life more or less matched the main span of Modernism.

He both enacted Modernism's story, and told it–not always accurately, but he was an "Impressionist"—in many books of criticism and reminiscence. He was born in 1873, in a Pre-Raphaelite bohemian household; his father was a German music critic just arrived in Britain, his mother was daughter to the painter Ford Madox Brown. At eighteen, as the Nineties started, he published his first book *The Brown Owl*, a fairy story that owed something to Stevenson, and by 1898, after several more books, met the still little-known Conrad. They collaborated on three commercial novels, *The Inheritors* (1901), *Romance* (1903) and *The Nature of a Crime* (1924), and Hueffer also had a hand in *Heart of Darkness* and *Nostromo*, two of Conrad's finest works. Drawing on the theories of Flaubert, Maupassant and James, they agreed together on the method of "Impressionism": "We accepted the name of impressionists because we saw that life did not narrate but made Impressions on our brains," he later explained. "We in turn, if we wished to produce an effect of life, must not narrate but render impressions."[2] He was also writing novels of his own, and making important literary friendships, with Henry James, H.G. Wells, John Galsworthy and Stephen Crane, the American author of *The Red Badge of Courage*, now living in Britain. Most of these were gathered together, as if for experimental literary security, in the same general area of Kent and Sussex; they visited each other frequently—James on his bicycle, Crane with his six-gun—and formed an important seedbed for the cultivation of the modern, a meeting-place for many of its main ideas and, indeed, its future quarrels.

Between the century's turn and the coming of war, Hueffer—a writer's writer who wrote every day—produced almost forty books, from memoirs and children's books to historical and social novels. Several were in the typical Edwardian form of the "Condition of Engand" novel, explorations of the contemporary social order and its conflicts. But he explored them with "impressionist" techniques, as he did, more surprisingly, the historical romance—above all his fine *Fifth Queen* trilogy, about Katherine Howard, which he completed in 1908, just as he was founding *The English Review*. That magazine brought him into close contact with an entire new generation of writers, including Pound, Lewis, and D.H. Lawrence, all of whom he "discovered": "Ford Madox Hueffer discovered I was a genius," Lawrence wrote, "—don't be alarmed, Hueffer would discover *anything* if he wanted to." He championed the new because it *was* new, original, innovative; the process helped make his own work new. He began to see that an experimental bridge could be built between the older writers of the 1890s and the younger innovators, even those at odds with his own literary philosophy. A declared Impressionist, he gladly published those like Pound

who cried "Death to Impressionism." Though he had total contempt for the
Novel With a Purpose ("A novel should render, not draw morals"), he
published Wells, who after 1900 wrote little else—and before he was done
Hueffer wrote Novels With a Purpose too (his post-war "Parade's End"
sequence had, he said, for its purpose "the obviating of all future wars"). He
believed in Flaubertian French perfection, but he advanced expressionistic
neo-Nietzscheans like D.H. Lawrence. He saw and wrote of an age of
looming sexual chaos, but assisted New Feminist writers like Violet Hunt
(translator of Casanova, and author of the interesting novel of the life of
working women, *The Workaday Woman*, 1906), Rebecca West, Stella Bowen,
and later Jean Rhys. Sometimes his assistance went a very long way, and led
to various unconventional *ménages;* generally he received either too little or
too much in the way of gratitude. It didn't matter; what counted was
"perfection," the "critical attitude," the "serious artist," the "spirit of modern
life." In 1912, he finally and grandly announced his farewell to literature, to
leave the field to newer writers "whose claim or whose need for recognition
and what recognitions bring was greater than my own."

Fortunately, and typically, he soon changed his mind, and so in 1913,
on his fortieth birthday, he resolved to give himself one last chance. "I had
always been mad about writing—about the way writing should be done and
partly alone, partly with the companionship of Conrad, I had even at that
date made exhaustive studies into how words should be handled and books
constructed," he explained, but "I had never really put into any novel of mine
all that I knew about writing." That aim went into his new book, which
proved his finest, his great contribution to the New Novel. He followed the
method of Conrad and later James by dictating some of his story, which
doubtless added to its hesitancies and indirections, its air of fracture and
tension. Excited by Vorticism, he borrowed its "hard" technique, and made
the book polished, "like a steel helmet." Responding to the mood of the time,
he made his theme the dying of the European *belle-époque* world, which he
presented with bitter irony. He gave the book an ambiguous, American
narrator, Dowell, a deceived husband, who declares "Six months age I had
never been to England, and, certainly, I had never sounded the depths of an
English heart." The novel's theme is sounding the false beat of the pre-war
English heart, and the book contains its own ominous warning. Hueffer
ensured that the chief events occur on 4 August of various years—the date of
the outbreak of the Great War, which came as he worked on the novel.

The book, *The Good Soldier,* therefore appeared in 1915, along with
other key books of the pre-war modern movement. The peak of his
experiment, it was also the end of an era. Despite its title, it is a novel not of

war but pre-war. Set mostly in the German spa town of Nauheim (in enemy territory by the time the book appeared), the story is about a man of honour corrupted by sexuality and the social deceits and hypocrisies which surround and disguise it. Two central couples, the British Ashburnhams, the American Dowells, have *mariages blancs*, unconsummated marriages; for different reasons the wives want to protect their sexual sanctity. They pretend to "heart disease" so that, at the spa, various polygamous arrangements can be made. Ashburnham, who seems especially honourable, is the British "good soldier." But married love is conducted through surrogates and intricate systems of deception. Only Dowell, the cuckold narrator, seems unaware of them; the story he tells as it were deceives him. His method of indirect narration also deceives us ("I have, I am aware, told this story in a very rambling way so that it may be difficult for anyone to find their path through what may be a sort of maze. I cannot help it ... when one discusses an affair— a long, sad affair–one goes back, one goes forward ..."). If, as he says, the book's social world is "secret," "subtle," "subterranean," the workings of the sexual world are more obscure still; one critic of the book has remarked that its sexual activity seems always the echo of an echo—now you see it, now you don't. The innocent Dowell is left to unravel the impressions and deceits confronting him. The word "impression" is crucial to the story—there are "all-round impressions," "first impressions," "false impressions." The baffled decoding of impressions—learnt from James and Conrad—gives the difficult fragmented technique. *The Good Soldier* has been called the best French novel in the English language; it is easy to see why. It is what the French critic Roland Barthes calls *scriptible;* we are always aware of the self-conscious method of the writing, the writerly nature of the text. In Jamesian terms (which Hueffer adopted), the story is an "affair," the telling is a "treatment," the method displays James' "baffled relationship between the subject-matter and its emergence." James here was referring to Conrad, but Hueffer takes matters one step further, making his narrator the victim of the story he tells. But in a world of false social surfaces, where everything is deliberately unspoken, it takes an art of great indirection to get to, well, the heart of the matter.

The Good Soldier, one of the culminating books of the pre-war modern movement, was Hueffer's last novel as Hueffer. When he came back from the front he changed his name to Ford; domestic troubles were part of the reason, but, as he rightly said, all identities had changed in the War. He still had twenty more years of writing life, some thirty more books to bring to print, including the excellent "Parade's End" sequence (1924–28), of which more later on. But part of its importance is that it explores the difficult passage, through the battlefields of the Somme, from pre-war to post-war Britain, and suggests why the Condition of England was no longer an easily available subject, why modern forms continued to fragment. By now he was an exile in France; for the "opening world" had plainly closed by now, the London experiment had virtually died, and Britain had banned, silenced or alienated many of its finest and most demanding writers. He would never live permanently in Britain again, and his main work hereafter was done in France, amid the experimental excitements of the 1920s. And by now the modern novel had ceased to be an "affair"; it had become the expression of an historical crisis. The future had indeed materialized, but not in the way its prophets had expected. Hueffer/Ford died in France in 1939, when the Modern experiment was as good as over. Hueffer had seen one half of it; Ford had seen the other. Each had written a major modern work: Hueffer the pre-war *The Good Soldier*; and Ford the post-war "Parade's End." His own reputation had declined by now, but he had done what he meant to do— bring a French perfection to the English novel, and support the changing experiment of British writing. He had crossed with nearly everything that was significant, and midwived many of the main achievements, from start to finish, from Conrad's *Nostromo* and Lawrence's *The White Peacock* to Stein's *The Making of Americans* and Joyce's *Finnegans Wake*. He had written good books and bad ones, and, as he confessed, not done all he intended. But in Modernism's discontinuous continuity he still remains a central figure.

If the young Ford Madox Hueffer who met and collaborated with Joseph Conrad in 1898 was not always to remain Hueffer, the forty-year Polish émigré his path had crossed with had certainly not always been Joseph Conrad. The disorders of imperial middle Europe had brought about his change of name and cultural identity, and they left their mark on all his work. He was born Josef Teodor Konrad Nalecz Korzeniowski, the child of Polish gentry in 1857 in the Russian-occupied Polish Ukraine, a "country that was not a country." His father Apollo was a romantic nationalist who fought against the Tsarist domination, and when he was sent into Russian penal exile he took the young child with him. From this time onward "Conrad" would always remain to some degree exiled and stateless; so would the fiction he came to write. As he grew up he wandered in Europe—he moved to France, went to sea, fought a duel, engaged in gun-running, spent a fortune, attempted suicide. To avoid conscription in the Russian army, he joined the British merchant navy, and sailed the seaways of the imperial and mercantile world, from the Pacific to South America, the British coastal ports to the Congo. That gave him British citizenship, but never quite perfect English;

the fiction he started now would always have, in language as well as vision, a touch of the foreign and the exiled about it. Nonetheless, in a time that was turning to the imperial romance, he evidently possessed perfect exotic material, and a chance meeting with John Galsworthy on an Eastern voyage led him to think of writing a novel. He began a tale about outcast Europeans in the Malayan archipelago, based on personal experience, which he carried about the world; it appeared in 1895 as *Almayer's Folly*. In 1896 he followed it with another similar story of the Pacific, also about Europeans split between two worlds, *An Outcast of the Islands*. Both were romances, but both have a haunting sense of life on its frontier, of existence as isolation and extremity. And a distinctive Conradian note is already struck in a passage in the second novel where he speaks of "the tremendous fact of our isolation, of the loneliness impenetrable and transparent, elusive and everlasting; of the indestructible loneliness that surrounds, envelops, clothes every soul from the cradle to the grave, and perhaps, beyond."

Then in 1898, just round the time Hueffer met him, he produced a quite different kind of book. Today it is uncomfortably dated by its title, *The Nigger of the "Narcissues"*, but it remains a work of unmistakable modernity, the beginning of his major fiction. The story of a homeward voyage from Bombay to London, it tells of nihilistic forces set loose on the ship during the passage, and of the final, necessary restoration of order. Like many of Conrad's later books, it is also a myth—possibly influenced by Herman Melville's remarkable sea-fable "Benito Cereno" (1856)—about an unreliable and doubled world. It was the first of many tales he would set on merchant vessels, seen as microcosms of the social, moral, indeed metaphysical world, where the need for order and discipline conflict with wilderness and threat, not only from the "terrible sea" and the anarchy of life, but from the inner ambiguity of human nature itself. Shipboard society becomes a space where the "essential" values—honour, duty, courage, fidelity ("Those who read me know my conviction that the world, the temporal world, rests on a few simple ideas; so simple they must be as old as the hills," Conrad observed: "It rests notably, among others, on the idea of Fidelity")—are tested to extremity. Pervading the stories is a fearful scepticism, the awareness that civilization soon finds its limits, light turns into darkness, virtue and courage are always at risk, behind every face there is a secret sharer, behind every man there is a darker double. When David Daiches hailed Conrad as "the first important modern novelist in English," was because of the distinctive timbre of his metaphysical vision which means that "the world of significance he creates is at the furthest remove from the world of public significance created by the great Victorian and eighteenth-century novelists." Like the Russian fiction of

Dostoevsky, whose work Conrad claimed to detest ("I don't know what Dostoevsky stands for or reveals, but I do know he is too Russian for me," he said, in a remark that peculiarly resembled the complaints of some critics about his own novels), his novels implanted into social or romantic themes an existential crisis. And with that modern spirit went a modern method, part-born from this alien, metaphysical tone of his writing—a method always indirect, deferring, bred of his dark conviction that he wrote of a gloomy unstable universe in which, as he said, "no explanation is final."

So quite as famous as *The Nigger of the "Narcissus"* is its preface, now taken as one of the most important manifestos of the modern way in fiction. Perhaps stung by H.G. Wells' charge of "obscurity," probably influenced by Stevenson's defence of the "web ... or the pattern" at the heart of fiction ("a web at once sensuous and logical, an elegant and pregnant texture: that is style, that is the foundation of the art of literature"), Conrad made the case for a novel that unified form and content by searching inwardly, self-consciously for its own logic and coherence. A famous phrase declares the symbolist credo: "A work that aspires, however humbly, to the condition of art should carry its justification in every line." A novel should have the magical suggestiveness of music and the plastic arts, should be "an impression conveyed through the senses." And the task of the novelist was to "render." "My task which I am trying to achieve is, by the power of the written word to make you feel—it is, before all, to make you *see*. That—and no more, and it is everything. If I succeed, you shall find there according to your deserts: encouragement, consolation, fear, charm—all you demand— and, perhaps, also that glimpse of truth for which you have forgotten to ask." The aim of art, just like that of life, "is inspiring, difficult—obscured by mists. It is not in the clear logic of a triumphant conclusion; it is not in the unveiling of one of those heartless secrets which are called the Laws of Nature." Art grew not from statement or narrative completeness; it grew from rendering, figuration, "impressions," the pursuit of the symbol. If some unhappy readers thought this simply produced novels that were themselves obscured by mists, others felt this was indeed what James called the new self-consciousness of fiction.

What Conrad had in mind perhaps grew a little clearer when he set off directly for the heart of his darkness. *Heart of Darkness*, the powerful long novella of imperialism he published in magazine form in 1899, and collected in the volume *Youth* in 1902, starts in the gloomy light of London, the imperial city; it returns safely back at last to the drawing-rooms of social fiction. Between comes a cunning allegory of light falling into darkness, a descent through the heart of Africa into human horror and the black places of the soul. In 1890 Conrad had taken part in the new scramble for Africa, sailing to the imperial Belgian outpost in the Congo; he returned ill, shaken, morally outraged by the cruelties and corruption he had seen. "Before the Congo I was only a simple animal," he said. The story follows his experience almost exactly, taking its narrator, Marlow, on a "night journey" from London, via a sinister Brussels, to the grim Congo and the "Inner Station"— a journey that moves from civilization through futility and carelessness to evil, darkness, exploitation, and "the earliest beginnings of the world." In the Congo Marlow finds his tragic double, Mr Kurtz, an idealist who had dreamt of bringing civilization to Africa, been drawn into its savagery–"The wilderness had patted him on the head"—and comes to the ultimate abyss, declared in his dying cry of "The horror! The horror!" Kurtz bequeaths Marlow a moral dilemma; when he returns to London he has to report his death to Kurtz's *fiancée*, "the Intended," who asks what his last words were. Marlow chooses a saving lie over a revelation of the moral anarchy he has seen: "The last word he spoke was—your name," he says. But the story contains a second story, of its own telling. Marlow recounts it all, on a ship in a London port, to a chosen audience, an Imperial trio: a Lawyer, an Accountant and a Director of Companies, to whom he reveals that London too has been, is, one of the earth's dark places. Marlow—the angled, ironic narrator who first appeared in the earlier story "Youth"—is the key to the tale. He is, Conrad explained, a man "with whom my relations have grown very intimate in the course of years ... He haunts my hours of solitude when, in silence, we lay our heads together in great comfort and harmony; but as we part at the end of a tale I am never sure that it may not be for the last time." He is, effectively, the storyteller as method, not just the experiencer of the tale, but its constructor, interpreter, investigator, decoder, an intruded presence between tale and reader. He has his own view of story: "The meaning of an episode is not inside like a kernel but outside, enveloping the tale which brought it out only as a glow brings out a haze, in the likeness of one of those misty halos that sometimes are made visible by the spectral illumination of moonshine." This may sound like a defence of Romanticism, but the point, of course, is that "episodes" do not have one simple meaning, but are refracted. This was what readers otherwise admiring of Conrad often challenged. "Is there not also a central obscurity, something noble, heroic, beautiful, inspiring half-a-dozen great books, but obscure, obscure?" asked E.M. Forster. To others this became the essence of modern fiction itself, what James, also writing of Conrad, called the baffled relation between the story and its emergence, which made the novel not an action but an "affair."

A novel should be not a "superficial how" but a "fundamental why," suggests Marlow, when he returns, one of several narrators, to tell the story of *Lord Jim* (1900). Jim, the hero who fails to be a hero, abandons his vessel, the *Patna*, loaded with pilgrims en route for Mecca, when he thinks it is sinking, and so violates a fundamental law of duty and responsibility. The ship is rescued, and his cowardice and shame exposed, at an official enquiry. But this fails to satisfy Marlow, who sees Jim as "one of us" and looks for what this tells us about human nature: "Why I longed to go grubbing after the deplorable details of an occurrence which, after all, concerned me no more than as a member of an obscure body of men [sailors] held together by a community of inglorious toil and by fidelity to a certain standard of conduct, I can't explain," he tells us: " ... Perhaps, unconsciously, I hoped I would find that something, some profound and redeeming cause, some merciful explanation, some convincing shadow of an excuse." The book changes from seafaring adventure into a psychological and metaphysical investigation, and develops not to a final resolution but to a deep uncertainty about human complexity. Marlow teases the story backward and forward, seeking the essence among the multiplied meanings of Jim—coward and hero, outcast and *tuan*, the man who tries to redeem his moral crime by confronting the "destructive element," and finally meets the positive and negative faces of his own self in an apparently senseless act of sacrifice. The book's time-scale, and its viewpoint, move back and forth, through indirections and curious retellings. These indirect methods are of the essence, functioning in the story just as Marlow does: to fill out an expanding world of values and ambiguities against which Jim is tested, and has tested himself, and which leaves him and the story "inscrutable at heart," real and yet disembodied.

Later in life Conrad would describe his art as lying "almost wholly in my unconventional grouping and perspective," explain that he was concerned for "effects" rather than "mere directness of narrative." Complexity was becoming the essence of his novels; like his own Captain Giles in *The Shadow Line* (1917), Conrad had chosen to be an expert in "intricate navigation." If readers found them difficult, as they did, this was not only because of oblique tactics—his breaking of conventional time-codes, his refusal of safe endings, his multiplication of viewpoints—nor because of his sense that life and human action were enigmatic, "inscrutable at heart." There was also something that could aptly be called "foreign" about his writing, a double vision, displayed in the spirit of irony—a spirit seemingly at odds with the best hopes and public themes of the Edwardian age, when in fact he produced his finest work. *Nostromo* (1904) is often though his best novel, an ultimate fable of New World imperialism. It is set in the imaginary South American republic of Costaguana—otherwise "the dung coast," dominated by its silver mine, the ever-ambiguous symbol of New World adventuring—and written in the mode of what we now call "magical realism." Conrad gives his imaginary land a complex Borgesian history, drawn, he says, from Don José Avellanos' *History of Fifty Years of Misrule*, a lost work whose pages float away across the harbour in the course of the novel. "I am in fact the only person in the world possessed of its contents," Conrad says in the preface, " ... I hope my accuracy can be trusted." It has to be, since, as he also says, "There was not a single brick, stone, or grain of sand in its soil I had not placed into position with my own hands." Like the New World itself, Costaguana is an invented space of history and myth: it is pastoral, virgin land, the placid gulf, an American dream, a half-blank page on which history is still to be written, "a twilight country ... with its high shadowy Sierra and its misty campo for mute witness of events flowing from the passions of men short-sighted in good and evil."

It also has a very modern politics, and if its history is still being written, many try to write it: the old colonists and the new European adventurers, who bring the usual mixtures of idealism and materialism, buccaneering exploitation and liberal dreams, social reform and violent revolution, hope and depravity, "violent efforts for an idea and sullen acquiescence in every form of corruption." "Liberals! The words one knows so well have a nightmarish meaning in this country," we learn; all the causes prove to have "a flavour of folly and murder," and no one survives very long. Western civilization intrudes with its apparent principles of order and reason, bringing the steamship company, the railroad, the exploitation of the San Tomé silver mine, otherwise known as "material interests." "Silver" is the novel's key word, intricately coded into the book. It is a moral ideal, and a source of European and North American wealth; a dream of redemption and the corrupting instrument of an age of capitalism and individualism. The source of identity, it destroys everyone—Charles Gould, Decoud, above all Nostromo, "our man," the Man of the People, the figure of "unbroken fidelity, rectitude and courage" whose fidelity and bravery are corrupted and rendered an artifice: "Nostromo had lost his peace; the genuineness of all his qualities was destroyed." Nature and civilization becalm each other, producing a collapse of ideals and dreams, love and will, creating indifference and nihilism. *Nostromo* is a dark book—in its vision of human nature and desire, its view of modern history, its doubt of all political systems. At the end the United States still waits in the wings ("We shall run the world's business whether the world likes it or not"), and the name of the corrupted Nostromo still rings ambiguously over the dark gulf. This is the work of a man who sees that history does not work by progressive liberal evolution nor by revolution, that idealistic virtues and political dreams rarely survive pure but betray or are betrayed from within or without: an ironist indeed.

His next book, *The Secret Agent* (1907), brought that irony far closer to home. He turned to a British subject, given him by Hueffer, with a Russian flavour, explaining his conception like this: "The vision of an enormous town presented itself, of a monstrous town more populous than some continents and in its man-made might as if indifferent to heaven's frowns and smiles: a cruel devourer of the world's light. There was room enough here to place any story, depth enough for any passion, variety enough there for any setting, darkness enough to bury five millions of lives." The "monstrous town" is London, the darkness holds grim political secrets as well as obscure and furtive lives. The theme is anarchism, the central situation based on a bizarre and futile attempt made in 1894 on Greenwich Observatory—the sailor's sanctuary, the place where the temporal mean is set—when the terrorist had been blown up by his own bomb. This was the stuff of the sensational novel and the detective story; Conrad described his task as one of "applying an ironic method to a subject of this kind." The irony he applied is universal: there is irony of character (all the figures in the book are somehow examples of paradox, contradiction and futility), irony of plot (nothing ever works out as intended), irony of narrative perspective (the outcome of the story is an emotional nihilism), irony of existence (life, as Mrs Verloc discovers, is not worth looking into). Anarchism unwraps into the empty void of its own nihilism, and is in any case the product of safe bourgeois values; the book distances all the human agents, even the gentle simpleton Stevie, and spares neither civilization nor the revolutionary aspirations that threaten it. Frank Kermode describes the book as "a story with an enormous hole in the plot"; other critics have seen it as a novel without a hero, and a work without a perspective. But as Thomas Mann saw, when he wrote the preface for the German translation, the perspective is that of irony itself. It was a work neither of political liberalism nor revolutionary utopianism, both tempting attitudes of the day; it uses what Mann calls the method of "the tragic grotesque," the viewpoint of dismayed distance, the modern tone. There was one further irony; Conrad had subtitled the book "a simple tale," and hoped his melodrama would lift his disappointing sales; it did not. Chesterton was affronted enough to counter the book with his *The Man Who Was Thursday*; it may well have stimulated Wells, to whom it is dedicated, to write his more buoyant version of the monstrous town in *Tono-Bungay*. Conrad explained the book to Galsworthy as "an honourable failure ... I suppose there is something in me that is unsympathetic to the general public ... Foreignness, I suppose."

And "foreignness," the fact that not all the world is to be seen under Western eyes, was the theme of his next novel, *Under Western Eyes* (1911). This surely is Conrad's real masterpiece, even though it has its obvious imperfections, enough to drive its author to a nervous breakdown after writing it. It is an exile's book, in which he returns to the source of his own exile, Russia, that land of heroic romance and empty futility, tyranny and anarchy, "spectral dreams and disembodied aspirations," a work that links his fiction back to Dostoevsky and forward to Nabokov. Conrad added a preface to the book after the Bolshevik Revolution of 1917, explaining its underlying prophecy: an autocratic state founded on total moral anarchism had now been upturned by its "imbecile opposite," a proletarian and utopian revolution that went for destruction as the first means to hand. The book unlocks the hidden implication behind many of his other novels—that, if you happen to see the world with not quite Western eyes, not with the conventional assumptions of British liberalism or good-hearted reform, political order is generally a thin film on the top of chaos, and political sentiment quickly leads to a world of guilt and treachery. For all that he dismissed the works of Dostoevsky (just being translated in Britain as his book appeared), his fiction, and the tradition of the Russian novel, is imprinted on this novel: in the divided ideology, split between conservatism and revolution, in the romantic turmoil of soul, and the search for a metaphysic between contradictory, violent extremes. Razumov, the book's central character, directly recalls the Raskolnikov of *Crime and Punishment*, with his introspective and tormented consciousness, and his need to confess and purge the crime he has committed; both writers deal with the theme of the psychological purging of the self in a world that itself lacks all moral substance—a modern existential theme that has been central to the modern novel.

But there is one essential and fundamental difference, which makes the book into a dual text (as Nabokov's *Ada*, imprinting the landscape of Russia on America, the Russian novel on the American novel, is a dual text). The vivid tale of Razumov's student life, his encounter with revolution, and his betrayal in Saint Petersburg, and then his confession and expiation among the revolutionary exiles of the city of exiles, Geneva, is a Russian story. But the story is told to be interpreted and read under Western eyes. The book's narrator, a British teacher of languages in Geneva, is a latter-day Marlow, trying to tell and read the tale that has come his way. "To the teacher of languages there comes a time when the world is but a place of many words and man appears to be a mere talking animal not much more wonderful than a parrot," he tells us at the start; words are, he confesses, "the great foes of reality." It is his distance from the inner secrets of so many words that make him a less than reliable narrator, for though he is a student of many grammars there is much he cannot see with his "Western eyes." Thus the book layers two stories, from two narrative traditions, two different political and moral cultures. There is the language teacher's story, and that of Razumov, which he draws from his written confessions or his partial witnessing of events. Thus the story is filled with hidden secrets, which he doubly attempts to decode: making what sense he can of Razumov's tale, and making the experience understandable to readers who have only Western eyes. He uses Razumov's diary to extend his eyewitness material, but also develops and comments on it. The difficulty, not always narratively successful, becomes part of the virtuosity of the telling. It was not entirely surprising that British readers had some trouble with Conrad's "obscurity." When his own narrator has such problems in reading and interpreting a tale so dense with confusions and secrets, when that story concerns a different and alien world with a different sense of history, then it takes care and time to read with Western eyes a story that questions the gaze of Western eyes.

Conrad's obscurity, in short, was more than a technical obscurity; it had also to do with a challenge to Western culture his readers took some time to accept. Nonetheless they did accept it; with his next novel, *Chance* (1913), Conrad had at last his first popular success. Thereafter his audience magically widened. His last group of books—*Victory* (1915), *The Shadow Line* (1917), *The Arrow of Gold* (1919), *The Rescue* (1920), *The Rover* (1920)–satisfied the audience at last; where earlier books had runs of less than three thousand five hundred copies, *The Rescue* had a first run of twenty-five thousand. By now he had returned, largely, to sea stories, and his famous obscurity seemed to have turned into a dense and satisfying Romantic haze. His technique had muted, turning into what one great admirer, Virginia Woolf, called "old nobilities and sonorities ... a little wearily reiterated, as if times had changed." In his final years he became one of Britain's most famous writers, revered abroad, offered a knighthood (mysteriously refused) in 1924; he died later that year. His greatest importance as a writer had lain in two things. One was the vision of a world of disorder, which challenged our sense of humanity and politics, and demanded an obscure new faith. The other was his obscurity itself, or rather what he made of it as a meaning for the writing of fiction. His best books remain those that, as the painter Max Ernst recommended, make the audience "a spectator at the birth of the work." Or, as Mark Schorer put it: "The virtue of the modern novelist—from James and Conrad down—is not only that he pays so much attention to his medium, but that, when he pays most, he discovers through it a new subject-matter, and a greater one ... the final lesson of the modern novel is that technique is not the secondary thing it seemed to Wells, some external machination, a mechanical affair, but a deep and primary operation; not only that technique *contains* intellectual and moral implications, but that it *discovers* them."[3] And if by the close of the Edwardian period the novel was beginning to be acknowledged not simply as a mimetic but an autotelic form, that is, an internally coherent struggle to construct, from its own discovering means, its own discovering expression, Conrad indeed remains of profound importance.

Edwardian readers who had difficulty with the obscurity and pessimism of Joseph Conrad plainly had none with the bright brash new world of H.G. Wells. By the early years of the century he had no more belief in the value of the obscure novel. "I have never taken any great pains about writing," he explained. "Long ago, living in close conversational proximity to Henry James, Joseph Conrad, and Mr Ford Madox Hueffer, I escaped from under their immense artistic preoccupations by calling myself a journalist." In 1900, the year of *Lord Jim* and Freud's *Interpretation of Dreams*, he stepped away from his scientific romance to publish *Love and Mr Lewisham*, the story of a very ordinary schoolmaster caught between Great Ideas and the Instinct of Sex. This was the first of a row of novels Wells produced rapidly over the Edwardian period, all with somewhat similar themes, all about the excitement of life in a time of change and promise. Wells was above all readable; he was the novelist of ordinariness and familiarity, which he made excitingly unordinary and unfamiliar. His stories were mostly based on autobiographical materials, born out of the lower-middle-class London suburban world from which he came, tales of aspiring, opportunity-seeking young men and women who were taking on the adventure of social, educational, commercial, and sexual self-transformation. The basic plot is plain: a young person from modest beginnings is helped by political awareness, scientific knowledge and sexual openness to face the widening prospects of life, challenging convention and the stuffy inheritance of the British past in the process. There is usually a Big Idea on hand—Science, Evolution, Socialism, Feminism, Free Love, Modernity, or just a great new commercial invention. Some of the stories, like *Kipps* (1905) or *The History of Mr Polly* (1910), are larky and Dickensian, and Wells brought a welcome note of comic relief to the general solemnity of fiction. Others, like *Ann Veronica (1909)*, a portrait of a free new woman who takes what she wants, or *Tono-Bungay* (also 1909), a remarkable analysis of contemporary British culture, are more deeply serious. The Wellsian message is also unmistakable. If we are timid or unlucky, we return to the prison of convention or dull domesticity, but the real promise is the rule of positive evolution, stated in *The History of Mr Polly*: "... when a man has once broken through the paper walls of everyday circumstance, those unsubstantial walls that hold so many of us securely prisoned from the cradle to the grave, he has made a discovery," Wells tells us: "If the world does not please you, *you can change it.*"

Wells, we know, along with Arnold Bennett, John Galsworthy, and some others, wrote the Edwardian novel. But what then was the Edwardian novel? Plainly it was not the new self-conscious fiction James, Conrad and Hueffer were commonly expounding. But this did not mean its authors were ignorant of the claim that the novel was, as James said, an "affair." Wells had kept good company with "the immense artistic preoccupations" of these writers, and had given some considerable support to them; for example, he hailed Stephen Crane's highly Impressionist *The Red Badge of Courage* (1895) as a new kind of writing, "the expression in art of certain enormous repudiations." He sustained his friendship with Conrad, who dedicated *The Secret Agent* to Wells as "the historian of ages to come" (he likewise dedicated *Nostromo* to John Galsworthy, who had indeed encouraged him to begin writing). Wells believed he was constructing a radical experiment in fiction, as did Galsworthy and above all Bennett, who had signalled himself as "the latest disciple of the Goncourts," had devoted himself during the 1890s to what he called "conscious pleasure in technique," and always asserted there was no conflict between experimental artist and commercial literary adventurer. The experiment was above all a revolt against Victorianism, the nineteenth-century notion of the novelist. The question was the direction in which that revolt led the new writer. While the authors of "immense artistic preoccupations" followed the course of Impressionism, the Edwardians felt they had inherited the sweeping, reforming spirit of Naturalism. For a period in the 1890s the two seemed to be reconciled. By the early twentieth century the choice seemed to be between the one or the other: on the one hand "the beautiful difficulties of art," which dissolved materiality in fiction, and on the other the reforming passion born of Nietzscheanism, which moved on beyond Darwinian pessimism to a new evolutionary optimism. If the Symbolists claimed "art," the Edwardians claimed life: as Wells put it, imperially, "Before we have done, we will have all life within the scope of the novel."

"Life," from the Naturalists on, obviously meant more than just life, ongoing existence. It meant evolutionary energies, people seen in their environment and history, as representatives of the workings of the world; it was love and death and sex and marriage, plainly and frankly, objectively and critically seen. It was material mass, houses and goods and class relations, detail on detail amassed and considered and ordered. It was material in another sense, the telling facts of social activity and human behaviour the writer had noted, by being there and finding out. It was the world with all its facts challenged and its statements investigated, everything checked and taken down in evidence. It was literature supported by the investigative skills of journalism, the scepticism of science; it was not sentimental, or if it was sentimental it was in the interest of radical expectations. Readers then and since agreed that life was, indeed, just like this.[4] One thing was clear; it was not seeking a Flaubertian perfection of art. "Literature is not jewelry, it has quite other aims than perfection, and the more one thinks of 'how it is done' the less one gets it done," said Wells: "These critical indulgences lie along a fatal path ..." "What I'am trying to render is nothing more or less than Life," explains George Ponderevo, the very self-conscious narrator of *Tono-Bungay*. Arnold Bennett entitled an entire section of *The Old Wives' Tale* (1908) "What Life Is"—the answer was in fact a long, slow, melancholy decline into age and death—and insisted his first concern was with life's feel and texture, "the interestingness of existence." Amongst other things it was clear that what life required of the writer was not aesthetic wholeness or even Conradian incompleteness but a plain openness. "I fail to see how I can be other than a lax, undisciplined storyteller," asserts George Ponderevo. "I must sprawl and flounder, comment and theorize, if I am to get the thing out I have in mind." Where James said that art made life, these writers purposefully insisted that life, observed, made art. And when Virginia Woolf said that the novel is not like that because life is not like that, she was arguing against writers who had already made their own confident declaration of what life actually is.

But equally this was not a return to the middle ground of Victorian realism, even though these novels do often inspire reference back to Dickens or Hardy. For Wells, the open "sprawling" method was a way of dealing with the shapelessness and lack of social coherence that was Edwardian England, when "all that is modern and different has come in as a thing intruded or as a gloss upon [the] predominant formula." As he put it himself, the traditional English novel has been formed within a fixed social frame; now, with "the new instability," that frame had splintered and itself become part of the picture. As Raymond Williams explains it, the Victorian novel was created out of community, a social and moral compact that linked individual and social life; in the Edwardian period the communicable society had dissolved, and individual and society lived in a fluid and atomized world. If the Edwardian novel carried realism forward, it carried it into new social conditions. God the benevolently omniscient narrator was still there, but now He was God the Scientist, God the Sociologist, God the Journalist. He was interested in progress, evolution and social change, and was always a meticulous external observer of the world as it worked. In Edwardian fiction—and it goes on being written still—the observer is everywhere, a presence between writer and reader. "The opening chapter does not concern itself with Love—indeed that antagonist does not appear until the third— and Mr Lewisham is seen at his studies," begins *Love and Mr Lewisham*, telling us about Mr Lewisham at his studies. "Those privileged to be present at a family festival of the Forsytes have seen that charming and instructive sight—an upper middle class family in full plumage," announces Galsworthy the novelist at the start of *The Man of Property* (1906), going on to tell us that these observers would see a spectacle "not only delightful in itself, but illustrative of an obscure human problem"; in fact they would have "a vision of the dim road of social progress." "On an autumn afternoon of 1919 a hatless man with a slight limp might have been observed ascending the gentle, broad declivity of Riceyman steps," commences Arnold Bennett's *Riceyman Steps* (1923), and this positioned observer is kept busily moving and, of course, observing, for the rest of this objectified novel.

In Edwardian fiction, chapters concern themselves with topics, obscure human problems are illustrated, visions of the dim road of social progress are regularly offered. Characters are seen from the exterior, their dominant characteristics signalled ("a hatless man with a slight limp"), as if they exist more for their social representativeness than any felt life within. They live unconsciously as symptoms of a larger case, become what D.H. Lawrence, writing on Galsworthy, called "a subjective-objective reality, a divided being hinged together, but not strictly individual." "A character has to be conventionalized," Bennett explained: "You can't put the whole of a character in a book, unless the book were of inordinate length and the reader of infinite patience. You must select traits ..." "I have come to see myself from outside, my country from outside—without illusions," says Ponderevo. The result of this is a distinctive way of writing fiction, no less fictional, of course, than any other. It is, as Virginia Woolf fairly says, material realism—dense with social life, rich in illustrative detail, filled with exteriorized observations which are also generalizations, dealing with social types in a transforming political order. It also mirrors a sense of change as an involuntary and formless growth. In many of the novels of the Nineties, and in the fiction of James and Conrad, individuals, living in a world of "things" or "material interests," are often drawn back into an existential subjectivity. In Edwardian fiction, the individual, though often solitary and exposed, is generally caught up completely in the padded mahogany furniture, the busy streets and commerce, of an age of materiality. It could be said that "Edwardian fiction" not only revived realism, but ensured its survival as a means of twentieth-century writing. Like the work of Dreiser in the United States, it created a dialectic with a more abstract modernity that has remained powerful in the evolution of modern fiction.

That said, it becomes apparent when we look more closely at the best Edwardian fiction—and it seems fair to take Galsworthy's *The Man of Property* (1906), Bennett's *The Old Wives' Tale* (1908) and Wells' *Tono-Bungay* (1909) as eminent examples—that "Edwardian fiction" was never a single thing, as those who challenged it later sometimes suggested. John Galsworthy's *The Man of Property*—which by a very appropriate process of dynastic evolution turned first into the three and then the nine volumes of "The Forsyte Saga" (1906–34)—is a still readable family saga that details the disintegration of the property-owning middle classes from the mid-1880s to the 1930s, and it chronicles a significant social change. "*The Forsyte Saga* has great importance as the mirror of the British high bourgeoisie," observes Herr Birenbaum, a character in Angus Wilson's novel *No Laughing Matter* (1967), which both pastiches and parodies the form. If, as has so often been said, the English novel is first and foremost the burgher epic, then this is that form in a kind of self-conscious disintegration. The Forsytes start as the representatives of the rising class of their age: "the middlemen, the commercials, the pillars of society, the corner-stones of convention," the people whose wealth and security makes everything possible, "makes your art possible, makes literature, science, even religion, possible. Without the Forsytes, who believe in none of these things, where should we be?" Galsworthy catches them at the peak of their power, which is corrupted from within by the possessive code of property, and threatened from outside by what usually threatens such things—adulterous love and divorce. Like Thomas Mann in his remarkable *Buddenbrooks* (1900), Galsworthy at first seemed to write the story of the collapse of the bourgeois age, as historical forces undermine it, and his observation at first is detached and highly ironic. And perhaps, if there had been a major social revolution in Britain, Galsworthy would have been its great chronicler. But Britain remained and remains a bourgeois society, and as the sequence evolved the tone grew less critical, as the characters became more attractive to the readers and clearly to their author. The critique of a class turns into a family saga, following the family over three generations, through peace to war and uncomfortable peace again. Because the fundamental world remains whole, there is no crisis of form (as there is in Mann's fiction), and Galsworthy stayed an Edwardian novelist into post-Edwardian times. He became the great chronicler of middle Britain, and as such won the Nobel Prize for literature in 1932.

Bennett's social history has quite different cultural roots. He was above all the self-made author, the solicitor's son from the Five Towns who watched the dissolution of the weighty, moral, confining Victorian age through the eyes of someone who has been carried upward by social change and his own effective career. The story of an age in motion from limited provincial lower-middle-class life to the promises and disappointments of the "newfangled days" is the heart of his theme as a serious writer, the most memorable part of his large human comedy. He belonged to the age of regional realism, that opening out of the wider world to honest literary treatment that was one urgent justification for Naturalism; he brought the spirit of the Goncourt brothers to the British literary provinces, and British provincial fiction has depended on this ever since. But he divested the task of much of its theory, in accordance, no doubt, with his own claim that "The novelist should cherish and burnish this faculty of seeing crudely, simply, artlessly, ignorantly." At best this made him a novelist of deep social honesty, at worst an aspiring vulgarian. In 1902 he produced two utterly contrasting works. One was *Anna of the Five Towns*, the story of a miser's daughter in the Potteries of his childhood, intimately charting a process of social change from the 1880s to the present; the other was *The Grand Babylon Hotel*, a high-life fantasy obviously written to display sophistication and frankly written for money. His work went up and down in quality, but onward and upward in commercial success; he admitted he had set out to become "an engine for the production of literature," and he made his literary fortune. In that same year he moved to Paris, which provided him with the essential contrast of one of his finest books, *The Old Wives' Tale*. It began, his preface tells us, in Paris in 1903, in the Naturalist way; observing a ridiculous old woman in a Paris restaurant, he realized she had once been slim and beautiful. To explore her story, he gave her a sister, also fat; one of the sisters would live "ordinarily," fulfilling a life of provincial virtue, the other would become a Parisian and a whore. "Neither has any imagination," he noted. "The two lives would intertwine." Constance and Sophia Baines, daughters of a Bursley draper, with their two very different, ageing lives, were born from these thoughts. The story of dutiful Constance, who stays at home, and rebellious Sophia, lured by a travelling salesman to Paris, becomes a long, loving chronicle over the forty years from the 1860s to the 1900s; at first a shared heredity and environment appear to produce two quite different destinies, but they unwind, over the slow and erosive passage of time, and through the later stages of the industrial revolution and through the French empire, to one common human fate. The novel skilfully bridges not just British provincial and French experience, but French techniques and a British subject-matter, the commonplace Staffordshire world becoming ever more brighly lit in the gaze from Paris. As Henry James admiringly said, this was all done clearly and effortlessly and became the method of "saturation," achieved with a power of demonstration "so familiar and quiet that truth and poetry ... melt utterly together." It also showed the limitations of the method of "hugging the shores of the real." But it is not when he hugs the shores of the real—as he so successfully did here, and again in *Clayhanger* (1910) and *Riceyman Steps* (1923)—but when he sets sail on the sea of the fanciful that Bennett is disappointing; and "hugging the shores of the real," disclosing the novel as a felt moral and social history, is, as John Updike has said, one of the essences of fiction.

Bennett, of course, did not see his art as artless; and no more did Wells when he wrote *Tono-Bungay*, the book in which he put the largest part of his vision, and which lies at the heart of his claim on fiction. It owed, he said, something to Balzac, certainly a good deal to Dickens, and, in its comedy of impertinence, something also to Mark Twain, who also wrote of the age of the entrepreneur and advertising—above all in the mocking comedy of *A Connecticut Yankee in King Arthur's Court* (1889), where the era of the machine and the bomb violently intrudes into the timeless chivalric wonderland of Camelot, so reassuring to Victorian imaginations. In Wells the land of timeless Englishness is the "Bladesover System"—"great house, the church, the village, and the labourers and the servants in their stations and degrees ..."—in which nonetheless change moves unseen, even though "all that is modern and different has come in as a thing intruded or as a gloss on this predominant formula, either impertinently or apologetically." This is really the principle of the novel, which takes the "predominant formula," equally found in fiction, and subjects it to impertinence and rewriting. For, as the narrator George Ponderevo tells us, this is a story of "this immense process of social disintegration in which we live"; the "ordered scheme" is going. Bladesover has been "outgrown and overgrown," and a "modern mercantile investing civilization" has rapidly taken its place. The book that Ponderevo now writes is thus "something in the nature of a novel," its apparent formlessness resembling the condition of England itself. Formlessness is in fact not just the method of the book, but its central metaphor. "I suppose what I'm really trying to render is nothing more or less than Life—as one man has found it." George tells us in the now familiar way, adding, "I want to tell—*myself*, and my impressions of the thing as a whole, to say things I have come to feel intensely of the laws, traditions, usages, and ideas we call society, and how we poor individuals get driven and lured among these windy, perplexing shoals and channels." So his book is "just an agglomeration," "not a constructed tale." It is the lively, funny story of George's Uncle Edward Ponderevo, a Mr Toad-like entrepreneur and adventurer, "the Napoleon of domestic conveniences," who pursues wealth, fame, power and social position by peddling a worthless, maybe even harmful, patent medicine that offers to cure the new ailments of the changing age. As Uncle Teddy deceives a society that has already begun to deceive itself, George himself turns into a scientific inventor, a figure out of Wells' earlier future fiction who is involved in the invention of a flying machine, a radioactive compound called "quap," and at last a "destroyer" on which everyone can sail away after the collapse of the artificial Tono-Bungay empire. Like the earlier scientific romances, the book contains an important social allegory about the splits, divisions and conflicting, potentially destructive forces of an age dissolving into the future.

Tono-Bungay is, of course, a "Condition of England" novel, and one of the finest, a panoramic satire of its age. Its random energy is portrayed best in its portrait of London itself, in a version that contrasts interestingly with Conrad's in *The Secret Agent*. Here is "the richest town in the world, the biggest port, the greatest manufacturing town, the Imperial city—the centre of civilization, the heart of the world!" The "whole illimitable place" teems with "suggestions of indefinite and sometimes outrageous possibility, of hidden but magnificent meanings," but it is also a tentacular chaos, spreading, teeming, "unstructured" and "cancerous." "Factory chimneys smoke right against Westminster with an air of carelessly not having permission, and the whole effect of industrial London and of all London east of Temple Bar and of the huge dingy immensity of London port, is to me of something disproportionately large, something morbidly expanded, without plan or intention," George reports, creating an analogy between the city and the activities of the two Ponderevos themselves. "All these aspects have suggested to my mind ... the unorganized, abundant substance of some tumourous growth-process ... To this day I ask myself will those masses ever become structural, will they indeed shape into anything new whatever ..." London too is formless, but filled with chaotic energies, which Wells presents with a delighted wonder, opening the story up to include science and shopping, the building of fortunes and the building of houses, loveless marriages and so "freer" sexual relations, social contrast and the implicit danger of war. But, for all that it needs reform, modern life remains a great and "impertinent" adventure. And it is on further formlessness that the book ends: "I fell into a thought that was nearly formless," George declares, as he departs the shores of Britain on his "destroyer," looking for something else new. The solution, of course, lies where Wells himself would put it, in science, machinery and invention. "I decided that in power and knowledge lay the salvation of my life; the secret that would fill my need; that to these things I would give myself," he concludes.

This could, in its way, be taken as Wells' own farewell to the real experiment of the novel, even though he wrote a good many more. *Ann Veronica*, also published in 1909, created a public scandal with its story of a free woman seeking free love; he retrieved his comic reputation with *The History of Mr Polly* in 1910, another story about the little man breaking loose. However Wells was increasingly giving himself elsewhere, to science, political prophecy, world visions, and the bounds of the novel were proving too small. *The New Machiavelli* in 1911 is an endeavour to write a political novel about the making of the state: "The state-making dream is a very old dream indeed in the world's history," says its narrator: "It plays too small a part in novels." The book deals with the struggle between a Great Idea and a Great Love, with feminism and the transformation of the modern family, with military policy and apocalyptic warnings—all to come true—about war with Germany and the break-up of Empire; it has a chaotic force, but none of the aesthetic care that was shaping other novels of the modern. That year Wells declared his position in a lecture on "The Contemporary Novel," in which he attacked the cult of "artistic perfection," separated himself from the self-conscious artists, and urged that the task of fiction was to deal with "political questions and religious questions and social questions." Here was the basis for the famous quarrel of 1915 with Henry James; for Wells was, in effect, now taking on the whole idea of the "literary imagination" itself, and the way in which it stood apart from "the world." The "world," as Wells saw it, meant science and technology, politics and history, the formation of new societies and the shaping of the new world order. The novels he wrote, and continued to write, if with diminishing force, toward the year of his death in 1946, were, as he said, frankly instrumental, means in a larger argument. It became an argument between literature and science ("the two cultures"), between pessimism and optimism, between the moral crisis of progress and progress itself. It was part of a split in the fortunes of the modern novel which was also a split in British culture itself, one to which writers would continually return. To understand the novels of Wells, and Bennett and Galsworthy, you had merely to read them and perceive their view of life, society and politics. But to understand the work of James, Conrad, Woolf and Joyce, you needed to grasp an entire conception of art itself, and its distinctive modern task.

If the British novel and the British culture of 1910 seemed split and in need of reconciliation, then it was offered one kind of answer in the work of E.M. Forster, whose *Howards End*–with its epigraph of "Only connect ..." ("Only connect the prose and the passion")—appeared that year. Forster, who said he belonged to "the fag-end of Victorian liberalism," the late-Victorian dissenting intelligentsia whose members included "philanthropists, bishops, clergy, members of parliament, Miss Hannah Moore," possessed an Arnoldian desire to see life steadily and see it whole. He had been (like many of the Bloomsbury Group, with whom he was half-associated) at Cambridge, and come under the influence of the philosopher G.E. Moore, who emphasized "aesthetic states" and "personal relations" as the standards of life; he had read and been shaped by the works of Samuel Butler, with his "undogmatic outlook," and George Meredith, who urged that "the cause of comedy and the cause of truth are the same." By 1910 he had already published three social comedies—*Where Angels Fear to Tread* (1905), *The Longest Journey* (1907), and *A Room With a View* (1908)—which challenged social dullness and philistinism, sexual convention and the undeveloped English heart, and emerged as an important comic voice of a new humanism. His moral comedy was illuminated by a sharp liberal intelligence and a symbolist inclination, and these three were novels of new feeling. But it was plain that with *Howards End* a new ambitiousness had entered his fiction, and that here was a work that confronted Masterman's "Condition of England," and not with the larky splendour of Wells' *Tono-Bungay* but with an urgent desire to relate and unify a formless culture split in many directions: between class and class, culture and commerce, materialism and idealism, head and heart, muddle and mystery, society and consciousness, or culture seen as cancerous and formless and culture as meaning and wholeness.

The question at the heart of *Howards End* was "Who shall inherit England?"—a question to which it gave complex answers. "Does she belong to those who have moulded her and made her feared by other lands, or to those who have added nothing to her power, but have somehow seen her, seen the whole island at once, lying as a jewel in a silver sea, sailing as a ship of souls, with all the brave world's fleet accompanying her towards eternity?" the book asks. Like Wells, it acknowledges that something new is happening to England: in the "Age of Property," a new "civilization of luggage" is advancing, and modern discontinuity is accelerating, driven by commercial enterprise, new industrialism and technology, and the potential clash of world imperialism. Here too there is a tentacular growth, as the "red rust" of London's suburbia spreads over the land and sprawls toward Howards End, the ancient farmhouse that is the central symbol of the novel. Forster embodies this split world in a story of two families. There are the Wilcoxes, energetic people, male-dominated, rushing by car round the nation to do the work of Empire; and there are the Schlegels, represented by two sisters–the intelligent Margaret, the impulsive Helen—who are emancipated, humane, of foreign stock, and devoted to ideas. They take from their German father a sense of idealism and a faith that materialism can be dissolved by "the mild intellectual light," and "In their own fashion they cared deeply about politics, but not as the politicians would have us think; they desired that public life should mirror whatever is good in the life within." The book's theme is the relation of these two, and of both to a third. For at Howards End lives Mrs Wilcox, different from them all. She has faint mystical properties, is linked not with the busy present but with the yeoman past, and attached to some of the book's main "symbols"—the house Howards End, with its Druidic spirit, the wych-elm tree, and the hay in the meadow—though these symbols are carefully contained within the human: "House and tree ... kept within the limits of the human. Their message was not of eternity, but of hope on this side of the grave."

The novel is the story of these two families, who are drawn toward each other through various personal relationships, but become divided. When Mrs Wilcox dies she wills Howards End to Margaret, hoping for a reconciliation. Margaret eventually marries the widower Mr Wilcox, and an ambiguous unity is achieved. Meanwhile her sister Helen has had an affair with a lowly Wellsian clerk, Leonard Bast, and had an illegitimate child. At first Mr Wilcox refuses to give any help. But the story ends with Mr Wilcox ill, Margaret triumphant, and Helen's child likely to inherit Howards End. Barely told, the story sounds schematic, but the book is a complex and ironic comedy, and in Forster's world nothing is simple. For this is a world split in many ways, between the whole and the part, the eternal and the "flux," "infinity" and "panic and emptiness," the note of spiritual anarchy that sounds out of Beethoven's Fifth Symphony. And Forster gives the novel a large panoramic sweep. It is deeply set in the Edwardian period (it *is* an Edwardian novel) and amid the forces active in it: the economic race with Germany, the process of imperial expansion and commercial growth, the technological destructions of the motor car, the intellectual pressures shifting people from liberalism to socialism. In the three main settings of the book–the metropolitan intellectual world of the Schlegels, the commuter world of the Wilcoxes, the clerkly suburbia of Leonard Bast—change is moving fast. A key theme of the novel is moving house and rebuilding; Wickham Place, where the Schlegels live, is to be pulled down for flats ("Can what we call civilization be right if people mayn't die where they were born?"

asks Mrs Wilcox), and "the civilization of luggage" is nearing Howards End, as the nearby railway station shows ("The station ... struck an indeterminate note. Into which country will it lead, England or Suburbia? It was new, it had island platforms and a subway, and the superficial comfort exacted by business men ..."). Margaret looks for "infinity" in King's Cross station, and hopes to "live in fragments no longer"; but she too lives the life of "gibbering monkeys," and zig-zags "with her friends over Thought and Art." Motion and muddle threaten any idea of culture or the infinite, and Margaret sees that the places of solid life are "survivals, and the melting-pot was being prepared for them. Logically, they had no right to be alive. One's hope was in the weakness of logic." Forster's endeavour is to reconcile two worlds not naturally akin, the worlds of "life by time" and "life by value," and recognizes—it is an essential part of his comic vision–that they rarely converge.

As the American critic Lionel Trilling was later to see, Forster is one of the great novelists of modern liberalism, a writer of checks and balances, who extends his liberal scepticism even to the most cherished of liberal principles, like the Wellsian faith in progress or science. In *Howards End* nothing is eternally reconciled; history upsets eternity, muddle upsets mystery, and panic and emptiness question the symbols of wholeness that float through the book. The will to vision, the liberal wish for right reason, the claim of the holiness of the heart's affections—all are consistently confronted with ambiguity. The same scepticism applies to his style, which is always dialectical. Forster had not dispensed with realism and familiarity, but opened it out to wider things. So poetry resides with comedy, symbolism with realism, and, says Trilling, where "the plot speaks of clear certainties, the manner resolutely insists that nothing can be so simple."[5] *Howards End* lies, "liberally," midway between Wells' assertively progressive novel, the carrier of history, and the symbolist novel of late James or Woolf, the carrier of form, between social and moral comedy and something more symbolist or metaphysical. The book works in a double form—an attempt to connect not only the prose to the passion of life, but realism to the "musicalization" of fiction. And so one way the book can be read is as Forster's attempt to reconcile, through his distinctive comic humanism, the two directions in which the novel was now pulling: toward social and political realism, and pure wholeness of form. "Yes—oh dear, yes—the novel tells a story," Forster was to say in his admirable study *Aspects of the Novel* (1927), and that means it must satisfy realism, familiar recognition, and story's narrative "and then ... and then ..." But the novel can also be a form of "pattern" and "rhythm," and reach for "expansion": "That is the idea the novelist must cling to. Not completion. Not rounding off but opening out." By the time Forster returned to the public with his novel of Empire *A Passage to India* in 1924, the world of his Edwardian novel had already dissolved. British empiricism and German idealism had not met, or not in the way he imagined; the civilization of luggage, and "panic and emptiness," were here to stay. Symbolism has become more ambiguous, confronting a greater nullity; the machine of civilization persistently breaks down and turns into stone, and not just the political world but the earth itself resists wholeness. Keeping his saving comic irony, his belief in the moral world of personal relations, Forster had passed from being a liberal novelist to a Modernist. Thereafter, from 1924 till his death in 1970, he wrote no more novels, saying that the world his fiction comprehended had gone. But he also had a striking influence on his successors; writer after writer, from Christopher Isherwood to Angus Wilson and Doris Lessing, has since returned to the mode of the liberal novel. And this still left *Howards End* a classic of pre-war liberal fiction, *A Passage to India* a classic of Modernist fiction: two of the more important British novels of the century.

NOTES

1. A good recent record of this era is Julian Symons, *Makers of the New: the Revolution of Literature, 1912–1939* (London, 1987). Also see Frank Swinnerton's bluff but interesting *The Georgian Literary Scene* (London, 1938).

2. Ford Madox Ford, *Joseph Conrad: A Personal Reminiscence* (London, 1924).

3. Mark Schorer, "Technique as Discovery," in *The World We Imagine: Selected Essays* (London, 1969).

4. "I can feel with this [Wells' creative energy] strongly, as I felt strongly with Lewisham many years ago making schedules for exams: the first character in fiction I ever fully identified with." Raymond Williams, *The English Novel from Dickens to Lawrence*, cited above.

5. See Lionel Trilling, *E.M. Forster* (Norfolk, Conn., 1943; London, 1944). And also see the essays of his collection *The Liberal Imagination: Essays on Literature and Society* (New York, 1950).

DAVID TROTTER

The Avoidance of Naturalism:
Gissing, Moore, Grand, Bennett, and Others

By the end of 1895, Emily Morse Symonds had published, as George Paston, three mildly advanced novels which, if not outstandingly successful, had at least been reviewed favorably by Arnold Bennett, then literary editor of *Woman*. They met in January 1896 and immediately recognized each other as fellow professionals, exchanging "tips" and talking "shop" for hours on end. On December 23, 1896, he took her out to dinner and the theater. "Her book is going rather well, & she is half through her next (a tale of literary life) which she says will be her best."

The tale of literary life, *A Writer of Books* (1898) is indeed her best. Like the novel Bennett himself had completed in May 1896, *A Man from the North*, it is about a writer from the provinces arriving in London to make a name. Cosima Chudleigh, left to fend for herself when her father dies, wants to "get away from her present surroundings, begin a new existence, and lay the foundations of a career." The career, not marriage, will provide the new existence. Writing, in her view, involves research. She decides that she must witness an operation, as the "French realists" had done, in case any of her characters ends up on the operating table. She takes it for granted that the novelist should be a "scientific observer."

These assumptions reveal the continuing influence, in England in the 1890s, of French naturalism; that is, of the view that writers should not flinch from unpoetic subject matter and that they should treat whatever they write

From *The Columbia History of the British Novel*, edited by John Richetti. © 1994 Columbia University Press.

about with "scientific" exactitude and objectivity. The assumptions, however, are Cosima Chudleigh's, not Symonds's. Cosima is eventually persuaded, by the man she loves, a critic of force and integrity, to abandon them and to develop instead the "personal flavour" that has always characterized English fiction.

French naturalism, resolutely unpoetic, exhaustively researched, was something English writers of any ambition measured themselves against. They could not ignore it. But unlike their American counterparts (Stephen Crane, Frank Norris, Theodore Dreiser) they did not, in the end, assimilate it. The story of that resistance, that avoidance, is, to some extent, the story of English fiction in the final decades of the nineteenth century.

In 1896, George Gissing reported that there was "no public for translated novels—except those of Zola." In England, Zola *was* naturalism. He had articulated the creed of objectivity in *Le roman expérimental* (1880). "We must operate with characters, passions, human and social data as the chemist and physicist work on inert bodies, as the physiologist works on living bodies." No subject matter was beyond him. He had "done" peasant life in *La terre*, the stock exchange in *L'Argent*, Bohemia in *L'Oeuvre*, heavy industry in *Germinal*, and so on. But it wasn't, finally, the methodology or the choice of subject matter that made Zola such a force. English writers have always found method, when proclaimed as such, fairly resistible. It was, rather, the view of existence written into, and encoded by, his narratives.

For the naturalist fiction that began to appear in France in the 1870s added a new pattern to the small stock of curves describing the shape lives take (or adapted an old one from Classical and Racinian tragedy): the plot of decline, of physical and moral exhaustion. Most nineteenth-century novels divided existence into a long rise stretching to the age of sixty, measured in social and moral terms, and a short (physical) decline. Naturalist fiction envisaged instead a rapid physical rise to the moment of reproduction in the twenties, then a long redundancy, a morbidity accelerated by the emergence of some innate physical and moral "flaw." Its narratives are shaped not by a process of moral and social adjustment but by the reiteration of genetic inheritance.

Zola's Rougon-Macquart novels (1871–1893) described the effects of heredity and environment on the members of a single family, tracing the passage of a genetic "flaw" down the legitimate line of the Rougons and the illegitimate line of the Macquarts. Henry James pointed out that the development of each section of the long chronicle was "*physiologically* determined by previous combinations." In each generation, the inherited flaw topples an individual life into a downward spiral of disease, alcoholism, poverty, or madness. This downward spiral is the way in which naturalist novels, in Europe and America, spoke about individual and social development.

Physiological narratives fed an anxiety about social decline whose formal expression was the theory of "degeneration" that began to emerge, in the natural and medical sciences, during the second half of the nineteenth century. The age of "evolution," "progress," and "reform" developed an urgent interest in regression, atavism, and decline. Indeed, it was Darwin's theory of evolution by natural selection that, in Britain at any rate, provided a context. At first, the theory had seemed to suggest that evolution was inevitably progressive, slowly but surely transforming the simple into the complex, the primitive into the civilized. Increasingly, however, Darwin and his followers came to realize that evolution was not synonymous with progress. Environment operated in various ways to different effects, and the most adaptive inherited characteristics were not necessarily the "highest" or most "civilized" ones. Gradually, attention shifted to examples of regression. In *Degeneration: A Chapter in Darwinism* (1880), Darwin's disciple Edwin Ray Lankester pointed out that parasites, which necessarily postdate their host organisms, are nonetheless "*simpler* and *lower* in structure" than those organisms.

The implications for social theory seemed distressingly clear. Lankester himself talked of the decline of the "white races" into parasitism. Paradigms of regression created by the natural and medical sciences began to play an important part in the analysis of social change. Degeneration was seen as a self-reproducing pathological process: not the effect, but the cause of crime, poverty, disease (and experimental literature). Max Nordau's *Degeneration*, a lurid and influential treatise published in translation in 1895, proclaimed the end of civilization in biblical cadence. But his conviction that the European races were degenerating derived from medical science rather than from the Bible. Physicians, he said, had recognized in the behavior of the European elites a "confluence" of "degeneracy" and "hysteria." All the new tendencies in the arts could safely be regarded as "manifestations" of this confluence.

In 1910, Henry Adams pointed out that Europeans had become obsessed with "supposed social decrepitude," particularly in the cities. "A great newspaper opens the discussion of a social reform by the axiom that 'there are unmistakeable signs of deterioration in the race.' The County Council of London publishes a yearly volume of elaborate statistics, only to prove, according to the London *Times*, that 'the great city of today,' of which

Berlin is the most significant type, 'exhibits a constantly diminishing vitality.'" Evidence of diminishing vitality included not only the poor standard of health among army recruits, but also the falling birth rate, the decline of the rural population and the prevalence of alcoholism and nervous exhaustion. More or less any social "problem" could be attributed to it.

Naturalism's decline plot was the perfect match to the social narrative articulated by degeneration theory; too perfect a match, in fact, since it was itself regarded, by Nordau and others, as a symptom of degeneracy. British writers, then, were not simply competing with a new literary technique, a method and a choice of subject matter. Rather, they had to decide whether to exploit or moderate or deny an anxiety about social decline that was already a habit of mind among their readers.

Henry James, in Paris in 1884, told W.D. Howells that he respected Zola, despite his pessimism and his "handling of unclean things." It was the handling of unclean things that at first dictated the British response to Zola. Henry Vizetelly began to issue translations in the same year; he was tried for publishing obscene books in 1889, convicted, and sent to prison for three months. By that time, however, the other feature noted by James—the pessimism inscribed in naturalism's decline plots—had made its mark on the English novel.

Like Zola, George Gissing researched his subjects assiduously. His diary shows him going over "a die-sinker's place" in Clerkenwell, in preparation for *The Nether World* (1889), and getting some "useful ideas." Gissing was proud that Charles Booth had used his novels as a source of information about working-class life, and he returned the compliment by studying *Life and Labour of the People in London* (1892–1903) in the British Museum; he was both flattered and irritated to discover that the Reverend Arthur Osborne Jay's *Social Problem* (1893) had incorporated, without acknowledgment, a long passage from *The Nether World*. Like Zola, he tended to "do" a subject per novel: the literary marketplace in *New Grub Street* (1891), suburban life in *In the Year of Jubilee* (1894), and so on.

The subject he returned to most frequently during the 1880s, in *Workers in the Dawn* (1880), *The Unclassed* (1884), *Demos* (1886), *Thyrza* (1887), and *The Nether World*, was urban deprivation. Gissing said that he wanted to capture "the very spirit of London working-class life," and he came closer to doing so than any other Victorian novelist except Margaret Harkness. Gissing's slums exist for us in their carefully differentiated sounds and smells, in the desires and anxieties that only an implacably earnest investigator would have troubled to disentangle from the received view of universal brutality and ignorance. He could always, and always meant to, tell the difference.

And yet the story told by these novels does not, in the end, differ all that much from the stories told by Zola and by degeneration theory. In *Workers in the Dawn* Arthur Golding, a would-be friend of the people, marries and attempts to reform a young prostitute, Carrie Mitchell. But his grammar lessons have no effect on a woman who is genetically programmed for a life of whoring and brandy drinking. When she leaves him for another man, he sadly pictures to himself the downward spiral of her future career: "how her passions, now set free from every restraint, would scourge her on from degradation to degradation, till she met her end in some abyss of unspeakable horror." Gissing's slums contain a residue of degenerates who so far exceed the norms of social classification that they can only be regarded as members of a different species. Clem Peckover, in *The Nether World*, is compared to a "savage," and to a "rank, evilly-fostered growth." "Civilisation could bring no charge against this young woman; it and she had no common criterion."

Gissing's methodical approach, and his degeneration plots, align him with Zola. But he never eradicated the personal flavor that was thought to distinguish English from French fiction. Carrie Mitchell was based on Nell Harrison, a young prostitute he himself had married and tried unsuccessfully to reform. Osmond Waymark, the hero of *The Unclassed*, recapitulates Gissing's own development from political radicalism through disillusionment to an increasingly bitter denunciation of universal vulgarity. Social commentary, in these novels, ebbs and flows according to the state of the author's investment in elite culture. Furthermore, "French" methods had always to contend with "English" moralism, with an inherited faith in the power of imaginative sympathy. The conclusion of *The Nether World*—a man and woman resolving to bring what comfort they can to those less resourceful than themselves—echoes the conclusions of Dickens's *Little Dorrit* (1857), Eliot's *Middlemarch* (1872), and, more distantly, Milton's *Paradise Lost*. Characteristically, however, Gissing does not allow his man and woman the comfort of each other; they go their own solitary ways.

In the early 1880s George Moore, the eldest son of a wealthy Liberal M.P. and stable owner, having failed to establish himself as an artist in Paris, took up naturalism. His first novel, *A Modern Lover* (1883), the story of a young artist, was, according to the *Spectator*, a frank homage to "Zola and his odious school." The initial situation of *A Mummer's Wife* (1885) reproduces, with equal frankness, the initial situation of Zola's *Thérèse Raquin* (1867), which Moore had thought of translating: sickly husband, neurotic wife, interfering mother-in-law, assertive lover, all penned in desolate rooms above a shop. Kate Ede elopes with an actor, Dick Lennox, and achieves some success on the stage. Now divorced and pregnant, she marries Lennox. But she has taken to drink, and her baby dies. Moore places her exactly on the curve of the degeneration plot. "She had met Dick in her seven-and-twentieth year, when the sap of her slowly-developing nature was rising to its highest point." After the climax of elopement, the taste of freedom, it's downhill all the way. The dissolute life of the traveling players wears her out. Abandoned by Lennox, she declines into alcoholism and prostitution, eventually dying a loathsome death. *A Mummer's Wife* is the nearest thing to French naturalism in English literature. It was duly banned by the circulating libraries.

In March 1887, Beatrice Potter shared a railway carriage with the historian and Liberal M.P. Sir George Trevelyan. "I begged him to go into a smoking carriage ... for had I not in the pocket of my sealskin not only a volume of Zola, but my case of cigarettes! neither of which could I enjoy in his distinguished presence." The novel was *Au bonheur des dames*, in which Zola "did" department stores. Sir George eventually settled down with *The Princess Casamassima* (1887), James's stab at an unpoetic subject matter. Potter, who became, in partnership with Sidney Webb, the leading sociologist of her day, remained enthusiastic about Zola—as, indeed, did several writers with more consistently polemical intentions than Gissing or Moore.

Potter's cousin, Margaret Harkness (as John Law) published Zolaesque novels—*A City Girl* (1887), *Out of Work* (1888), *In Darkest London* (1889), *A Manchester Shirtmaker* (1890)—that earned the respect of Friedrich Engels. The influence of *Germinal* on mining novels like W.E. Tirebuck's *Miss Grace of All Souls'* (1895) or Joseph Keating's *Son of Judith* (1900) is evident enough. But working-class, or socialist, fiction never achieved the same prominence as two other genres shaped by polemical intent: slum fiction and New Woman fiction.

Slum fiction, pioneered in the 1880s by Gissing and Walter Besant, and developed in the 1890s by Rudyard Kipling, Arthur Morrison, Somerset Maugham and others, incorporated the decline plot wholesale but shifted the emphasis from heredity to environment. A number of stories—Gissing's *Demos*, Kipling's "The Record of Badalia Herodsfoot" (1890), Morrison's "Lizerunt" (1894), Maugham's *Liza of Lambeth* (1897)—concern women whose lives follow a similar pattern: courtship, and a glimpse of freedom, then marriage, marital violence, abandonment, and finally prostitution or death. These heroines are not degenerate. They are spirited women who have the vitality beaten out of them by an inhospitable environment and a series of brutal men. The contrast between female virtue and institutionalized violence allows for "English" pathos as well as "French" realism.

However, the remorseless downward spiral of the plot still carries the message that there is no escape, no possibility of transformation. In Morrison's *Child of the Jago* (1896), heredity combines with environment to corrupt the young hero. Morrison wanted to distinguish between a degenerate working class and one that is organically sound but damaged by its environment. The novel's reforming priest, Father Sturt, is based on the same Reverend Jay who had lifted a passage from *The Nether World*; Morrison later endorsed Jay's plan to establish penal settlements in isolated parts of the country where working-class degenerates could be confined for life and prevented from reproducing their "type."

Heredity was also a crucial concern in the New Woman novels that began to appear toward the end of the 1880s. Julia Frankau (writing as Frank Danby) out-Zolaed Zola in *A Babe in Bohemia* (1889). Lucilla Lewesham, a young girl brought up by her decadent father and his shrieking mistress, escapes moral contamination but not hereditary epilepsy. The book was savagely denounced in the press, and banned by the circulating libraries. Degeneration theory served Frankau's sensationalism admirably. Meeting her in 1911, Arnold Bennett found her "very chic"—and thoroughly ashamed of her novels. But even those New Woman novelists who had no reason to feel ashamed of their novels—George Egerton (i.e., Mary Chavelita Dunne), Emma Frances Brooke, Mona Caird, Ménie Muriel Dowie—had much to say about (male) degeneracy.

"Doctors-spiritual must face the horrors of the dissecting-room," Sarah Grand declared in the preface to *Ideala* (1888). Her heroine decides that the future of the race is a question of morality and health. "Perhaps I should ... say a question of health and morality, since the latter is so dependent on the former." Both heroine and author deploy the biomedical categories of late nineteenth-century social psychology. Ideala believes that the British Empire, like the Roman, has decayed internally, and that the solution is not reform, but a program of physical and moral regeneration.

Grand's third novel, *The Heavenly Twins* (1894), was hugely successful and established her as one of the leading writers of the day. It has been claimed as a precursor of modernism, and does experiment with tone and point of view. But the experiments are largely confined to one of its three loosely connected case studies, the story of the "heavenly twins" Angelica and Diavolo. The other case studies can best be understood as versions of the naturalist degeneration plot. Edith Beale marries Sir Mosley Menteith, a syphilitic degenerate, gives birth to a child famously likened to a "speckled toad," and dies. The deformed child was a popular motif in naturalist fiction, incarnating degeneracy. Evadne Frayling marries one of Menteith's fellow officers. More worldly-wise than Edith, she recognizes his unsuitability at once, and declines to consummate the marriage. She remains unfulfilled, and cannot find a way to redeem her husband, whose habits are "the outcome of his nature."

Book 6 of *The Heavenly Twins* is narrated by Doctor Galbraith, a specialist in nervous disorders who examines and befriends Evadne. If Edith's story is a case study in degeneracy, Evadne's is a case study in that other modern disease, "hysteria." After her husband's death, Galbraith marries Evadne. But the outcome of his efforts to restore her to health remains uncertain. Paying a call in the neighborhood, Evadne encounters the "speckled toad" once again, and suffers a relapse. Degeneracy and hysteria may yet have the last word.

As, indeed, they threaten to do in the conservative polemic of contemporary popular fiction. Stevenson's Mr. Hyde gives "an impression of deformity without any namable malformation." In his concluding statment of the case, Dr. Jekyll speaks of the "bestial avidity" with which his monstrous double would relish the infliction of torture. Professor Moriarty, in Conan Doyle's Sherlock Holmes stories, has "hereditary tendencies of the most diabolical kind," a criminal "strain" in the blood. According to Van Helsing, in Bram Stoker's *Dracula* (1897), the Count himself is a degenerate. "Lombroso and Nordau would so classify him." Dracula's invasion of England dramatizes anxieties that were the stock in trade of theorists like Nordau and Cesare Lombroso. He aims to pollute the entire English race, beginning with his natural allies, the parasites, outcasts, and madmen. Mary Shelley's Frankenstein had produced a monster by perverting Science and violating Nature; these fin-de-siècle monsters are the product of Nature, and can only be mastered by a combination of Science, faith, and bourgeois shrewdness.

Vizatelly's imprisonment seems to have taken the sting out of the moral objections to Zola. Thereafter, open hostility receded. In 1893, Zola was invited to London by the Institute of Journalists, and, much to Gissing's amusement, received by the Lord Mayor. Gissing noted that no prominent author had played any part in the welcome and that a testimonial dinner arranged by the Authors' Club was "in the hands of a lot of new and young men."

The young writer most likely to further the cause of naturalism in England was Hubert Crackanthorpe, who the year before had conducted a long and respectful interview with Zola, which he published in his experimental magazine, the *Albermarle*. He certainly made full use of the decline plot. In "A Conflict of Egoisms," in *Wreckage* (1893), degeneracy destroys a New Woman, the neglected wife of a novelist suffering from "brain exhaustion." Professionally mature but emotionally immature, she cannot cope with her husband's indifference, and retaliates by destroying the manuscript of his latest novel. He decides on suicide, but exhaustion gets him first; he drops dead as he is about to leap off a bridge. Crackanthorpe seems to have taken his own narratives a little too seriously. He drowned himself in the Seine in 1896.

Crackanthorpe, however, was an isolated enthusiast. Naturalism's more seasoned champions had long since ceased to champion. During the 1890s, Gissing concentrated on stories of intellectual life and middle-class rebellion. In 1891, Moore accused Zola of selling out. He now sailed under the flag not of Zola, but of Zola's erstwhile disciple, Huysmans—whose *A rebours* (1884) was a dandyish pastiche of naturalism—and of Wagner. From *Confessions of a Young Man* (1888) through to *Evelyn Innes* (1898) and *Sister Teresa* (1901), Moore's major concern was the pathology of faith and creativity.

And yet there is *Esther Waters* (1894), a peculiar hybrid of the "French" and "English" traditions. Esther is, in the French manner, the victim of forces beyond her control; but she has been equipped, in the English manner, with moral resilience. Moore's mixed feelings led him to anatomize working-class life by means of a decline plot, and yet at the same time to draw back from the apocalyptic determinism usually inscribed in such plots. William Latch's seduction and abandonment of Esther would not have been out of place in a novel by Mrs. Gaskell or George Eliot. When she subsequently returns, pregnant and impoverished, to her equally impoverished family and immediately quarrels with her drunken, brutal stepfather, it seems as though she has entered a different kind of novel altogether. Mr. Saunders, however, is, by a cunning displacement, merely her *step*father: the bloodlines through which contamination invariably flows in naturalist fiction have been cut.

In this novel, identities are made rather than inherited. Esther creates an identity by managing a business and bringing up her child. For every degenerate like Mr. Saunders, there is someone who has identified, and been identified by, a talent or an occupation. Lanky, narrow-chested Arthur Barfield, the son of Esther's first employer, comes into his own whenever he mounts a horse. In naturalist novels, people don't "come into" a new identity. In English novels, they do, but not, on the whole, by mounting a horse. Moore avoided both "French" determinism and the "English" conviction that the only paths to self-discovery are introspection and marriage.

In chapter 44, Esther, now a widow and once again destitute, returns to Woodview, the home of the Barfield family, which has itself been destroyed by gambling. The opening paragraph repeats word for word the opening paragraph of the first chapter, which describes Esther's arrival at the local station. In chapter 1, the first sentence of the second paragraph—"An oblong box painted reddish brown and tied with a rough rope lay on the seat beside her"—is full of anticipation; the person it refers to has not yet been identified, and we read on eagerly, seeking clues. In chapter 44, the sentence has been expanded. "An oblong box painted reddish brown lay on the seat beside a woman of seven or eight and thirty, stout and strongly built, short arms and hard-worked hands, dressed in dingy black skirt and a threadbare jacket too thin for the dampness of a November day." Now there is nothing left to anticipate: the older Esther is the sum of the experiences that have shaped her appearance. The narrative loop confirms the decline plot, returning her, roughened and diminished, to her starting point. But she is not defeated. Her decline cannot be attributed to the emergence of some moral or physical flaw. We are closer to the formal recapitulations of Henry James and James Joyce than to Zola's apocalypse.

Another writer who modified an earlier adherence to naturalism was Sarah Grand. *The Beth Book* (1897) reworks the Evadne story from *The Heavenly Twins*. Like Evadne, Beth Caldwell, cramped by lack of education and experience, marries a man, Dr. Dan Maclure, who turns out to be disreputable and corrupt. He has an affair with one of his patients, whom Beth regards as a "parasite." Both her husband and her most ardent admirer, a neurotic writer, are well embarked on decline: "The one was earning atrophy for himself, the other fatty degeneration."

But Beth, like Esther Waters, refuses to decline along with her menfolk. Nurtured by a community of intellectual women that includes the heroines of Grand's earlier novels, she discovers a talent for writing and public speaking. Grand cleverly alters the proportions of the decline plot by devoting more than half the novel to Beth's childhood and youth. The talents and pleasures Beth develops are grounded in those early experiences. The book's conclusion, however, a mystical reunion with a man she has fallen in love with, somewhat qualifies the carefully accumulated emphasis on independence, female community, and ordinariness.

Gissing, Moore, and Grand all seem half-persuaded by Zola's determinism, by the plausibility of genetic explanations. But in the end they refuse apocalypse; partly, I think, because apocalypse seemed like a foreign invention. Galbraith reappears to counsel Beth, and to offer some gruff literary advice. Her husband is predictably fond of French novels. Galbraith, like Quentin Mallory, thinks that French novels have destroyed the French nation. Grand supports him, in a footnote, with an account of the cowardly behavior of Frenchmen during a recent emergency. The revaluation of Englishness that was in progress at the time undoubtedly reinforced the determination of British writers to steer clear of naturalism. Gissing relied heavily on it in his most popular novel, the semiautobiographical *Private Papers of Henry Ryecroft* (1903). As for Moore, well, he learned to despise the English during the Boer War, and took up Irishness instead.

Gissing, Moore, and Grand fell back on English moralism. Other writers tried to sidestep the downward spiral of the decline plot without committing themselves to the counterbalance of moral absolutes. Oscar Wilde's *Picture of Dorian Gray* (1891), for example, makes dazzling play with the idea of degeneracy. Constantly collapsing the metaphoric into the literal, the metaphysical into the organic, it nonetheless refuses to come clean, to own up, to disavow appearances. For Wilde himself, however, the metaphor became distressingly literal. Max Nordau had classified him as a decadent and an egomaniac, claiming that his "personal eccentricities" were the "pathological aberration of a racial instinct." Wilde, at the end of his tether, complied with the metaphor. Submitting a plea for release from prison, he confessed to sexual madness and endorsed Nordau's classification of him as a degenerate.

Thomas Hardy came closer than Wilde, in his fiction if not in his life, to acknowledging that sin is a disease. In *Tess of the D'Urbervilles* (1891), Angel Clare characterizes Tess as the product of a degenerate family. He invokes against her the degeneration plot that the novel harbors all along, but which it has so far resisted through its emphasis on her singularity. Hardy can scarcely be said to endorse Angel's point of view. But one might argue that Angel's degeneration plot takes the novel over, carrying Tess through "relapse" to murder and beyond.

One review of *Jude the Obscure* (1896), headed "Hardy the Degenerate," claimed that the author had depicted a humanity "largely compounded of hoggishness and hysteria." Jude does seem cloudily aware of degeneration theory. Depressed by interminable quarrels with Arabella, he decides that the best way to express his "degraded position" is to get drunk. "Drinking was the regular, stereotyped resource of the despairing worthless." Jude will do what he thinks the hero of a naturalist novel would do. Appropriately enough, it is he who conveys the medical verdict on Father Time's massacre. Jude merely *quotes* degeneration theory. But he quotes it so convincingly that one cannot altogether avoid the suspicion that Hardy might have seen some truth in it. It would have suited his temperament. And *Jude the Obscure* does sometimes seem like a novel written by Angel Clare.

H.G. Wells took a more explicit interest in social and biological theory than Hardy or Wilde. *The Time Machine* (1895) explores the implications of the second law of thermodynamics, formulated in the 1850s, which envisages the gradual heat death of the universe. But its most gripping passages concern social rather than physical deterioration. When the time traveler reaches the year 802,701, he emerges into the middle of a crisis in the long-drawn-out feud between two degenerate species, the Eloi and the Morlocks (hysteria and hoggishness, again). Wells told Huxley that he had tried to represent "degeneration following security." *The Time Machine* is a vision of social apocalypse framed within a vision of global entropy, and the rhetoric of apocalypse overshadows the rhetoric of entropy.

Later writers distanced themselves less equivocally. In *The Secret Agent* (1907), it is the loutish anarchist Ossipon who characterizes Stevie and Winnie as degenerates. On the latter occasion, Conrad speaks contemptuously of Ossipon invoking Lombroso "as an Italian peasant recommends himself to his favourite saint." In Joyce's *Ulysses* (1922), it is Mr. Deasy, the bullying Anglo-Irish headmaster, who bends Stephen Dedalus's ear with a diatribe against the degeneracy of the Jews: "They are the signs of a nation's decay. Wherever they gather they eat up the nation's vital strength ... Old England is dying." By that time, degeneration theory no doubt seemed less compelling, if only through overuse.

Another response that requires some discussion, because it had profound consequences for the twentieth-century novel, was present in the philosophy of the New Woman writers in the early 1890s but not developed into a new narrative form until somewhat later. Grant Allen, whose *Woman Who Did* (1895) was probably the most notorious of all the New Woman novels, preached a New Hedonism, a revision of sexual relationships that would eliminate "race degradation" and promote "race preservation." Women had either to separate themselves from men or to mate with those men who were still, despite everything, racially sound. Thus the heroine of Sarah Grand's "Eugenia" (1894), who is herself racially sound, rejects Lord Brinkhampton, a "neuropath" and degenerate, and proposes to the aptly named Saxon Wake. Wake is a "yeoman," but makes up racially for what he lacks socially. This will be the race-preserving, the eugenic—the Eugeniac—marriage. Such racially sound marriages should preferably be complemented, as Allen's language suggests and as the conclusion to *The Beth Book* makes clear, by a mystical union.

Mystical-eugenic unions were all very well, but they did presuppose an abundant supply of healthy, strong-willed young men and women. Narratives promoting race preservation had to balance the dream of a New

Hedonism against the reality, as it was perceived, of social decrepitude. Whereas the New Woman novelists tended to pair different types of degeneracy—the hoggish and the hysterical, Morlock and Eloi—their successors tended to pair a couple seeking regeneration with a couple or couples doomed to degeneracy. This new pairing emerges tentatively in Gissing's *Odd Women* (1893) and *In the Year of Jubilee* (1894), then more strongly in Forster and Lawrence.

Forster's *Longest Journey* (1907) incorporates two separate plots, which just happen to coincide at a place called suburbia. In the first, sensitive Rickie Elliot's marriage to suburban Agnes Pembroke merely confirms the fatality of his physical disablement (hereditary lameness). Together, like a couple in a New Woman novel, they produce a horribly crippled daughter who soon dies. Thereafter Rickie "deteriorates." Rickie's race will die out, but his half brother, Stephen Wonham, the product of a more eugenic union with a staunch yeoman farmer, may yet flourish. Distanced genetically from Rickie, as Esther Waters is from her stepfather, Stephen belongs to a different bloodline, a different plot. The genetic distance is also a moral and emotional distance. Agnes Pembroke, who has already drained the life out of Rickie, regards Stephen as a monster. "He was illicit, abnormal, worse than a man diseased." Forster defends Stephen's abnormality against suburban convention, because he believes that it alone will preserve the race.

In Lawrence's *Women in Love* (1920), the degeneration plot and the regeneration plot seem about to fuse, as Ursula is paired momentarily with Gudrn, Birkin with Crich. But in the end they diverge as emphatically as the bloodlines, the histories, of Rickie Elliot and Stephen Wonham. Degeneration theory circumscribes the "barren tragedy" of Gerald's life. It surfaces in chapter 2, when the wedding party adjourns to Shortlands, and the talk turns to questions of race and nationality. Birkin has agreed with Gerald that "race is the essential element in nationality," and is caught "thinking about race or national death" when called upon to make a speech. Nobody else has mentioned race or national *death*. The thought disappears as Birkin rises to make his speech, but reappears in chapter 5. Birkin finds Gerald reading the *Daily Telegraph* at Nottingham Station. Gerald draws his attention to an essay arguing that "there must arise a man who will give new values to things, give us new truths, a new attitude to life, or else we shall be a crumbling nothingness in a few years, a country in ruin." Asked whether he thinks it's true, Birkin shrugs. His own analysis of national death, and his new gospel, are a good deal more radical than anything envisaged by the leader-writer of the *Daily Telegraph*, or indeed any other newspaper. But he cannot very well dispute the contention that the country is in ruin, and that a new attitude to life is required, since this is what he himself believes. Birkin's shrug is also the text's.

Gerald Crich will act out this analysis of race and national death. He is no degenerate. He does not suffer from some inherited flaw. But he is constantly placed, both as an individual and as the member of a class, by quotations from the discourse of race and national death. His great achievement has been to make the mines profitable, breaking with his father's mid-Victorian philosophy of paternalism and muddling-through, and promoting a new creed of organization and efficiency. One of the issues that separates father from son is the proper attitude toward the "whining, parasitic" poor. Thomas Crich feeds the supplicants; his wife and his son both want to turn them away. But the issue is framed in the son's terms rather than the father's, in the language of Lankester's Social Darwinism.

Gerald himself can be associated with early twentieth-century campaigns for "national efficiency": physical health; scientific and technological training; military and naval preparedness; industrial modernization; a government of national unity. Gudrun imagines that she might inspire him to become the Napoleon or the Bismarck of modern Britain. "She would marry him, he would go into Parliament in the Conservative interest, he would clear up the great muddle of labour and industry." The application of business ethics and methods to public policy was one of the causes promoted by the national efficiency movement. That would be Gerald's "new gospel," if he could only bring himself to mean it.

That he cannot is due to his failure to form relationships. Gerald is not a degenerate destroyed by some inherited genetic flaw. He is a conditional degenerate—he often behaves *as if* he were drunk—who is corrupted by the degenerate environments he encounters. Degeneracy exists in the two bohemias—Halliday's and Loerke's—he inhabits briefly at the beginning and at the end of the novel. Halliday's circle is the kind that might easily have got itself denounced in Nordau's *Degeneration*. Lawrence makes sure we get the point about Halliday: "His face was uplifted, degenerate, perhaps slightly disintegrate, and yet with a moving beauty of its own." While Birkin observes bohemia coolly, then passes on, Gerald lingers, intrigued, appalled, fascinated, drawn inexorably into moral, sexual, and physical conflict. He loses Minette to Halliday just as he will later lose Gudrun to Loerke.

Loerke, the "mud-child," the "very stuff of the underworld of life," is Lawrence's best shot at a degenerate. Extravagantly Jewish and homosexual, he fulfils to an almost parodic degree the requirements of stereotype. He is an evolutionary test case, a parasite, a creature developed at once beyond and below humanity, into pure destructiveness. Gudrun succumbs to Loerke;

Gerald fights him and loses. Never himself a degenerate, Gerald, unlike Birkin, cannot create an alternative to degeneracy. His failure propels him, like Jude, into the final spiral of the degeneration plot. His desire for "finality" drives him on to a conclusion, but his "decay of strength" ensures that the conclusion will be death.

Gerald's story exemplifies the degeneration theory that glosses it so consistently. Rupert and Ursula's story, on the other hand, looks back to those tentative imaginings of mystical-eugenic union in Gissing and Grand, in George Egerton's "The Regeneration of Two" (1894), in Forster. Lawrence's parallel narratives are sometimes seen as part of a literary revolution, as distinctively modernist. But they might also be regarded as the solution, at once formal and ideological, to a problem first articulated thirty years before.

A passage in Arnold Bennett's journal for June 15, 1896, describes the aged male inmates of the Fulham Road workhouse. "Strange that the faces of most of them afford no vindication of the manner of their downfall to pauperdom! I looked in vain for general traces either of physical excess or of moral weakness." Well-read in French fiction, an admirer of novels like *A Mummer's Wife*, Bennett naturally looks for evidence of degeneracy in the undeserving poor. But he cannot find any. To his eyes, the faces reveal wear and tear, not monstrosity. Like his friend Emily Symonds, Bennett may have wondered whether he ought not to behave more like a naturalist. But temperament, and the relative eclipse of naturalism, dictated that his novels, beginning with *A Man from the North* (1898), should confine themselves to mundane wear and tear. Unlike Zola, or Gissing, or Moore, he did not attempt any "vindication" of biomedical theory.

By the end of the 1890s, the brief phase of the slum novel was effectively over. The East End of London was still a point of automatic reference in many novels, but the portrayal of working-class life became increasingly lighthearted. Symptomatic of the new mood was the instant success of William de Morgan's genial, old-fashioned romances. Dickens, not Zola, was the model. Addressing the Boz Club, William Pett Ridge claimed that Dickens had revealed the "romance" and the "cheerfulness" in the lives of "hard-up people." Some writers, he went on, described the poor as though they were "gibbering apes." But such "naturalism" was outmoded. "The reading public knows better; it knows that the Dickens view is the right view." Ridge, like Edwin Pugh and W.W. Jacobs, was proud to be considered a disciple of Dickens. His best-known working-class novel, *Mord Em'ly* (1898), is a sentimental, facetious tale about a slum girl whose vitality is nourished rather than impaired by London life.

At the same time, a new territory and a new class had become visible, as suburbia spread out from London and the major industrial centers and coastal resorts, boosted by railway expansion and the advent of the motorcar. Suburbia was as tribal as the slums, as tempting to the cultural anthropologist; more so, perhaps, since the new tribe was composed of avid novel-readers. The result was a flourishing genre of fiction which, taking its tone from Jerome's *Three Men in a Boat* (1889) and the Grossmith's *Diary of a Nobody* (1892), celebrated or gently mocked suburban life-styles and values.

Critics of suburban life seized on its monotony. Ruskin put the objection pithily when he alluded to "those gloomy rows of formalised minuteness, alike without difference and without fellowship, as solitary as similar." Suburbia permitted neither difference nor community. It denied the vision fostered by Romanticism and embedded in nineteenth-century social theory, the vision of a society united by common human bonds but differentiated according to individual capacities and desires.

Suburban uniformity could be regarded as benevolent, according to the Dickens view, or petty and destructive, according to the Ruskin view. The real challenge was to see in the suburbs something other than uniformity. Bennett rose to the challenge—perhaps not in *A Man from the North*, which is written according to the Ruskin view, but certainly in *Clayhanger* (1910), *Hilda Lessways* (1911), and *The Card* (1911). There is nothing very startling about Bennett's point that suburbia exists in the eye of the beholder. But it is symptomatic of a new emphasis in English fiction that he should choose to write about suburbs rather than slums, and that he should discover in his chosen territory no more than the faintest trace of monstrosity.

Most unusually for a novelist, Bennett was interested in the way people remain in ignorance of themselves, and in the way such ignorance creates an identity. This interest required a new kind of plot. Many, if not most, plots—and certainly those favored by the great nineteenth-century English novelists—turn on moments of revelation, when the illusions nurtured by timidity, prejudice, or habit fall away, and a naked self confronts a naked world. These are the moments when identity is begun, renewed, or completed. French naturalism had added a different plot, in which the revelation is gradual, and of something already known but temporarily concealed: a moral or physical flaw, an organic "lesion." Both kinds of plot favor awareness. Illusions are there to be stripped away. There can be no self-discovery, no personal development, whether into enlightenment or into degeneracy, until they have been stripped away.

A curious episode in *The Old Wives' Tale* (1908) suggests that Bennett was never really very happy with either kind of plot. Grouchy, fallible, cautiously opportunistic, waveringly tyrannical Samuel Povey is summoned from his bed one night by his more expansive cousin, Daniel, and transferred, in effect, to another novel. Daniel begins by confessing that his wife is an alcoholic, and so tears to pieces in a moment "the veil of thirty years' weaving." Hinting at even darker horrors, he leads Samuel through his shop and into the house behind, where his son, one leg broken by a fall, and his wife, whom he has murdered in a fit of rage, lie sprawled. The "vile" Mrs. Povey isn't merely drunken, and dead—she is an emblem of degeneracy.

The experience transforms Samuel. He regards Daniel as a martyr, a man goaded beyond endurance. "Samuel, in his greying middle age, had inherited the eternal youth of the apostle." His new conviction makes him, for the first time in his life, a public figure. He launches a campaign to vindicate Daniel and secure his release. During the campaign, which fails, he contracts pneumonia and dies. His death provokes the narrator into a startling display of mawkishness.

Bennett finds himself caught between two traditions, French naturalism (Mrs. Povey's degeneracy) and English moralism (Samuel's transformation), neither of which suits him at all. The whole episode seems like a lengthy quotation from a second-rate novel by someone else. One moment only sounds like Bennett. On the night of the murder, halfway through an anguished debate with Samuel, Daniel meticulously empties the surplus of the corn he had used to throw at Samuel's bedroom window out of his jacket pocket into its receptacle. Bennett characterizes him, at this moment of crisis, through the part of his mind that doesn't yet realize what has happened. Crises are supposed to reveal, to set naked self against naked world. Bennett is more interested in the illusions that remain.

A new kind of plot was needed to demonstrate how such illusions—such nescience—might form a personality. Bennett's protagonists advance their hollowness into a world which, as they age, becomes ever more crowded, ever more impenetrable. They feel the changes in pressure within them, but the shell of their nescience never cracks, as it would in a "French" novel; nor is it ever filled up, with hard-earned wisdom, with love, as it would be in an "English" novel. The heroine of *Leonora* (1903), watching her husband die, realizes that she has been created not by love but by the "constant uninterrupted familiarity" of married life. It is an acknowledgment produced not by abrupt revelation but by illusions mutually adjusted over a long period of time.

The term Bennett found for lives not shaped by development or degeneration was "declension." A chapter in *Hilda Lessways* is entitled "Miss Gailey in Declension" and describes the deterioration of Hilda's dancing instructor. Declension involves a gradual loss of energy, will, presence, significance. But there is a gain to be had from the erosion of these qualities, which constantly demand that one live up to an ideal or self-image, or fashion oneself according to social convention. It is a gain of definiteness, of irreducible difference. I don't know whether Bennett had the grammatical sense of declension in mind. That sense is appropriate, because the declensions he portrays are not merely disablements, but variations in the form a person's life can take.

In the end, in Bennett's novels, loss and gain are hard to distinguish, as they are in many people's lives. Miss Gailey is a spinster, and his spinsters (Janet Orgreave, for example, in the Clayhanger series) remind us that an identity created by not willing, by not signifying, is at once, and inextricably, formation and deformation. Few people in Bennett's fiction escape declension. At the end of *Whom God Hath Joined* (1906), Laurence Ridware, who has just survived a punishing divorce, wonders whether he should propose to a much younger woman, Annunciata Fearns. But he simply doesn't have the energy. Edwin Clayhanger is motivated during his youth by a fierce hatred of Methodism. But by the time he is asked, in *These Twain* (1916), to serve as District Treasurer of the Additional Chapels Fund, he doesn't even have enough animosity left for a contemptuous refusal. His ambition goes the same way: "His life seemed to be a life of half-measures, a continual falling-short." Yet he is in his way fulfilled, even assertive.

Bennett regarded marriage as the test, and the fulfillment, of the identity that declension creates. Toward the end of *These Twain*, Hilda wants to move to the country, and she persists in her arguments even though she knows perfectly well that Edwin wants to stay in town. Edwin has to come to terms with the fact that his wife, in denying his clearly stated preference, is denying him.

If Hilda had not been unjust in the assertion of her own individuality, there could be no merit in yielding to her. To yield to a just claim was not meritorious, though to withstand it would be wicked. He was objecting to injustice as a child objects to rain on a holiday. Injustice was a tremendous actuality! It had to be faced and accepted. (He himself was unjust. At any rate he intellectually conceived that he must be unjust, though honestly he could remember no instance of injustice on his part.) To reconcile oneself to injustice was the master achievement.

To reconcile oneself to injustice is to acknowledge the irreducible difference of other people, an acknowledgment enforced not by revelation but by long familiarity. The passage brilliantly renders Edwin's habits of mind: the faint pomposity, the honesty that compels him *not* to confess to injustice and so claim the authenticity of sudden illumination. These habits are his difference from Hilda, and what she loves in him.

One final example will demonstrate the extent to which Bennett deviated from a degeneration plot, which was nonetheless very much in his mind. *The Old Wives' Tale* follows the destinies of the two Baines sisters: cautious, commonsensical Constance, who inherits her father's haberdashery store and marries the chief apprentice, Samuel Povey; and passionate, unsettled Sophia, who elopes to Paris with a commercial traveler, Gerald Scales. Bennett's treatment of sexual desire, which, traditionally, either reveals us to ourselves as we really are or destroys us, tested his faith in declension to the limit. Frank Harris expressed disappointment that there wasn't more of the "superb wild animal" about Sophia; Bennett thought him dismally sentimental.

Bennett undid the wild animal in Sophia by, so to speak, writing his declension plot *over* the degeneration plot of Zola's *Nana*, the story of the spectacular rise and fall of a courtesan. Sophia's Paris is Nana's Paris, Paris during the last celebrations before the calamity of 1870. The mob yelling "To Berlin! To Berlin!" while Nana dies horribly of smallpox is the mob Sophia encounters at the Place de la Concorde. Zola said that his novel described a pack of hounds after a bitch who is not even in heat. Sophia, the object of "inconvenient desires," walks unscathed amid the "frothing hounds" as though protected by a spell. Sophia, unlike Nana, does not sell herself to the men who pursue her. It is the courtesan Madame Foucault, resplendent when first encountered, but increasingly abject, and reduced finally to an "obscene wreck," who plays Nana's part. Heredity dooms Nana, the degenerate daughter of degenerate parents, but the Baines stock is sound.

Even so, desire has left its mark on that inheritance. One day Sophia, now the prosperous owner of the Pension Frensham, wakes up semiparalyzed. Struggling to the foot of the bed, she examines herself in the wardrobe mirror and sees that the lower part of her face has been twisted out of shape. The doctor offers a swift diagnosis. "*Paralysie glossolabiolaryngée* was the phrase he used." By the early 1890s, facial, and specifically glossolabial, paralysis had been recognized as one of the major symptoms of hysteria. Sophia realizes that the attack has been triggered by an encounter with a young man from Bursley, which destroys the barrier painstakingly erected between her two lives.

The second half of the nineteenth century has been described as the belle époque of hysteria, and Paris and Vienna, the classic fin-de-siècle capitals, as its native environment. In Paris, the master of ceremonies was Jean-Martin Charcot, who began to treat hysterics at the Saltpetrière in

1870. By observation, examination, and the use of hypnosis, he proved that their symptoms were genuine and genuinely disabling. Freud, who studied at the Saltpetrière from October 1885 to February 1886, credited Charcot with establishing the legitimacy of hysteria as a disorder. Charcot demonstrated that it afflicted men as well as women and was not simply related, as tradition had it, to the vagaries of the female reproductive system (the wandering womb). Even so, hysteria remained symbolically, if not medically, a female malady, and one associated with sexual disorders.

In an obituary written shortly after Charcot's death in 1893, Freud summed up his mentor's understanding of the etiology of hysteria: "Heredity was to be regarded as the sole cause." French psychiatrists, like their English counterparts, were wholehearted advocates of degeneration theory. Charcot's narratives of hysteria, with their genealogical trees full of interconnecting cases of alcoholism, epilepsy, criminality, and suicide, resemble the story line of Zola's Rougon-Macquart novels.

Freud argued, in a series of papers published in the 1890s and in *Studies on Hysteria* (1895), that Charcot and his followers had been "dazzled" by the apparently all-encompassing concept of heredity. In this, he added, they were responding to a pervasive belief in the degeneracy of Western societies. To reject heredity as a cause of mental illness, as Freud did, was to reject determinism; that is, a life story shaped by events not merely beyond the individual's control but beyond his or her experience.

Freud began to study cases of "acquired" rather than inherited hysteria, and to uncover a rather different story line. He decided that hysteria did not begin in the life of an ancestor, with an organic "lesion," but in the life of the patient, with a traumatic experience. During that experience, the patient was confronted with a feeling which she could not bring herself to acknowledge, and which she repressed, thus dividing her consciousness. This feeling, which could neither be acknowledged nor ignored, was then converted, after a period of latency, into hysterical symptoms.

Hysteria, then, began and ended within individual experience. Where women were concerned, Freud said, the "incompatible ideas" that produced trauma were likely to "arise chiefly on the soil of sexual experience or sensation." He gave two examples: a girl who blamed herself because, while nursing her sick father, she had thought about a young man; and a governess who had fallen in love with her employer. These two cases, written up in *Studies on Hysteria*, reveal the new story line: the origin in trauma, the latency period, the physical symptoms.

We might compare the first to the case of Sophia. Left alone in the house to watch her paralyzed father, Sophia spots Gerald and rushes down to speak to him. The encounter confirms her desire, her sexual awakening. When she goes back upstairs, she finds her father dead. Her body expresses the intensity of a guilt she can neither acknowledge nor ignore. "As she stood on the mat outside the bedroom door she tried to draw her mother and Constance and Mr. Povey by magnetic force out of the wakes into the house, and her muscles were contracted in this strange effort." Split between desire and remorse, she represses the latter and elopes with Gerald. But it is surely the remorse that returns, converted into facial paralysis. Sophia's hysteria begins in trauma and ends in physical symptoms. If Zola's narratives resemble Charcot's, then Bennett's resemble Freud's; and that is a measure of the lengths to which English fiction had gone, by the turn of the century, in its avoidance of naturalism.

SELECTED BIBLIOGRAPHY

Baguley, David. *Naturalist Fiction.* Cambridge: Cambridge University Press, 1990.

Bjorhovde, Gerd. *Rebellious Structures: Women Writers and the Crisis of the Novel 1880–1900.* Oxford: Norwegian University Press, 1987.

Cave, Richard. *A Study of the Novels of George Moore.* Gerrards Cross: Colin Smythe, 1978.

Keating, Peter. *The Haunted Study: A Social History of the English Novel 1875–1914.* London: Secker and Warburg, 1989.

Klaus, H. Gustav, ed. *The Rise of Socialist Fiction 1880–1914.* Brighton: Harvester, 1987.

Pick, Daniel. *Faces of Degeneration.* Cambridge: Cambridge University Press, 1989.

Poole, Adrian. *Gissing in Context.* London: Macmillan, 1975.

Sutherland, John. *The Longman Companion to Victorian Fiction.* London: Longman, 1988.

Trotter, David. *The English Novel in History 1895–1920.* London: Routledge, 1993.

NICHOLAS DALY

Incorporated Bodies:
Dracula and the
Rise of Professionalism

The dinner was very long, and the conversation was about the aristocracy—and Blood. Mrs Waterbrook repeatedly told us that if she had a weakness, it was Blood.

—David Copperfield

In the popular adventure fiction of the *fin de siècle*, dubbed the "revival of romance" by contemporary critics, we have tended to see a literature of anxiety. Our accounts of such fiction generally trust to the period's self-presentation as a period of crisis. The monstrous anachronisms of *She*, *Dracula*, and *Dr Jekyll and Mr Hyde* consequently seem to mirror a whole set of anxieties: the collapse of empire, the degeneration of the race in the light of evolutionary theory, and the rise of the New Woman, to name but a few. These are indeed anxious texts, but I want to argue that they produce and manage anxiety rather than express it. In this essay I will give an account of the way one of these romances, Bram Stoker's *Dracula*, uses anxiety to produce as both necessary and natural a particular form of professional, male, homosocial combination—the team of experts.[1] I will also be advocating a reconsideration of the *fin de siècle* as a period of crisis. Despite the rhetoric of crisis, Britain was far from collapse. On the contrary, the British empire grew dramatically during this period; at home, state power was also undergoing a phase of expansion. This latter phenomenon depended on the existence of a

From *Texas Studies in Literature and Language* 39, no. 2 (Summer 1997). © 1997 by the University of Texas Press.

new class of experts, and it is in the formation of this professional class that
the adventure romances played their cultural part. At the center of the
romance is not, as criticism has often assumed, the monster, but the
monster's nemesis, the closely knit team of men whose principal weapons are
knowledge and "power of combination," as Van Helsing phrases it in
Dracula. The adventure romance is thus one component of what Harold
Perkin has called the "rise of professional society," a historical shift that links
such apparently disparate phenomena as the dramatic increase in the number
of professional associations, the expansion of the state sector, and the birth
of high modernism. If as literary artifacts, then, the romances of Stoker,
Haggard, and their rivals look back to the Gothic romances of Horace
Walpole and Ann Radcliffe, ideologically they belong to the specifically
modernist culture that we associate with the work of Joyce, Woolf, and
Eliot.[2]

Attempts to historicize the "revival of romance" too often take the *fin
de siècle* at its own estimate. Patrick Brantlinger's assessment of the "revival"
in *Rule of Darkness* typifies this approach. Arguing for the use of the term
"imperial Gothic" to describe the romances of Stoker, Haggard, and others,
Brantlinger suggests that after the mid-Victorian era the British found their
own myths of progress to be increasingly unconvincing. Instead they began
to worry about "the degeneration of their institutions, their culture, their
'racial stock.'"[3] He continues, "Apocalyptic themes and images are
characteristic of imperial Gothic, in which, despite the consciously pro-
Empire values of many authors, the feeling emerges that 'we are those upon
whom the ends of the earth are come.'" Images of cultural and physical
degeneration certainly did circulate widely in the late nineteenth century,
abetted by theories which built on Darwin's speculations on the possibility of
species "reversion" in *The Descent of Man*. Max Nordau, prophet of cultural
decline, found a wide audience for his *Degeneration* (1893). Bram Dijkstra's
study of the female body in *fin-de-siècle* art is just one account that
demonstrates how pervasive such theories were in late Victorian culture.[4]
This rhetoric of decline became familiar enough for Oscar Wilde to recast it
in an ironic light in the following well-known exchange from *The Picture of
Dorian Gray*. Lady Narborough, like many late-nineteenth-century
commentators, sees changes in sexual mores as the harbingers of decline:

> "Nowadays all the married men live like bachelors, and all
> the bachelors like married men."
> "*Fin de siècle*," murmured Lord Henry.
> "*Fin du globe*," answered his hostess.

"I wish it were the *fin du globe*," said Dorian with a sigh. "Life is a great disappointment."[5]

Wilde appears to be keenly aware of something that Brantlinger and other present-day critics overlook—that reiterations of crisis and imminent apocalypse may conceal real continuities. I would go further and suggest that the specter of decline may be put to work during periods of development. The heyday of Brantlinger's "imperial Gothic" coincided with a period of actual imperial expansion. Anxious or not, Britain added to its empire some 750,000 square miles in Asia and the South Pacific, and another 4,400,000 square miles in Africa between 1870 and 1900.[6] Within Britain's own borders, these same years witnessed an extension of state government into regions previously treated either as part of the private sphere or as part of the free market. The decline of liberalism as an ideology was accompanied by a marked increase in the willingness of the state to concern itself with the family and with the relations of employers and employees. A wave of social legislation was one symptom of this shift; the appearance of an army of experts familiar with the new theoretical tools of psychology and eugenics— that is to say, a group capable of overseeing the new relations of the state and the private sphere—was another.[7] Widespread warnings that things fall apart coincided with signs that the center was not only holding but also entering a phase of expansion.

This paradox may be resolved by taking a taking a close look at one historical example. Seen through the lens of crisis, the Boer War strikes one as a traumatic national event; fears for the degeneration of the race and the security of the nation were apparently borne out when considerable numbers of British recruits were rejected as unfit for service.[8] Nevertheless, the end result of the war was not only management of the trauma but also an expansion and consolidation of certain power structures. Evidently, anxiety provided the occasion for state intervention on a grand scale. While the Committee on Physical Deterioration set up after the war found no evidence of actual physical or mental degeneration, it did see environmental factors as affecting the health of the poor. The outcome was new legislation whose influence Harold Perkin describes in these terms:

> The Report on Physical Deterioration was one of the most influential social documents of the age, and many of its recommendations, including school meals for poor children, medical inspection, physical education for both sexes, cookery and domestic science for girls in schools, tighter control of the

milk supply and food adulteration, social education of mothers by midwives and health visitors, juvenile courts, and a ban on the sale of alcohol and tobacco to children, all passed into law before the [1914] war.[9]

Fears there may well have been of the decline of Englishness within England, as well as assaults from without, but these fears had the effect of buttressing—not enfeebling—the power of the state. Of equal importance, these fears established a mission for a new group of professionals in human management, whose area of expertise would extend into that which liberal ideology had once designated as the private sphere.

While we cannot ignore the existence of a *fin-de-siècle* discourse of crisis and anxiety, then, neither can we take it at face value. Additional problems attach to the labeling of late-nineteenth-century adventure fiction as Gothic, Victorian Gothic, or imperial Gothic. This move situates the *fin-de-siècle* romance within a "Gothic tradition" perceived as deriving from the classic Gothic fiction of the late eighteenth century. Accounts of Gothic have tended to view it as a literature of crisis, in which the anxieties of a culture find their most explicit expression. The Marquis de Sade may have been the first to impose this construction on the Gothic fiction of "Monk" Lewis and others, describing it as "the fruit of the revolution of which all Europe felt the shock."[10] More recent criticism endorses the general tenor of the Marquis's comments, while offering different views as to what revolutionary crisis is at stake. Thus David Punter, for example, suggests that Gothic reflects the social trauma of the industrial revolution.[11] Psychoanalytic criticism treats Gothic fiction in the same way, while effectively privatizing the revolution; Gothic becomes the textual arena in which the sexual anxieties of an age are rehearsed. Whether in its Marxist or psychoanalytic/feminist versions, the basic theory of the functioning of fiction remains the same: anxiety exists "out there" somewhere beyond the text, generated by some impending crisis in the culture; the dominant representations of a culture obscure this, but in Gothic this anxiety returns as the "repressed" of the culture. Criticism's role, then, by an etymological coincidence,[12] is to identify the particular crisis that bubbles below the surface of any given culture and to show how the anxiety generated by this crisis is expressed in a particular text.

A glance at critical accounts of *Dracula* from the last twenty or so years confirms that this theory of Gothic fiction, which we might call anxiety theory, has dominated the interpretation of the novel. For a novel that enjoys a rather ambivalent relation to the canon, *Dracula* seems to solicit interpretation, and critics have been generous in obliging. Psychoanalysis, Marxism, feminism, gender studies, and other varieties of critical thought have each taken at least one turn at reading the text. In this respect the critical fate of *Dracula* resembles that of *Frankenstein*, a text in which the monster who dominates the action has been seen to embody threats ranging from the emerging working class to language itself.[13] In the pandemonium of interpretive activity around Stoker's novel, Count Dracula has appeared as the embodiment of fears about degeneration, the influx of eastern European Jews into late Victorian England, a subversive female sexuality, reverse colonization, nascent media culture, male penetration, and monopoly capital, among other things. However, the apparent diversity of critical conclusions masks a broad consensus that Stoker's text reflects certain anxieties, be they late Victorian or universal. The reading practice that accompanies this theory of Gothic fiction is allegorical: the text mirrors extratextual anxieties; the vampire is the figure in the text for those anxieties; criticism decodes the figure to reveal its real referent. For example, Richard Wasson writing in 1966 argues that "Count Dracula ... represents those forces in Eastern Europe which seek to overthrow, through violence and subversion, the more progressive democratic civilization of the West."[14] It may be easy to smile at this, to say the least, overdetermined reading of the text, which tells us more about Cold War America than about the novel, but the basic trope recurs again and again in the criticism. Writing eleven years later, Phyllis Roth sees the novel as reflecting pre-Oedipal anxieties, while Judith Weissman sees it as representing a fear "that women's sexual appetites are greater than men's."[15] More recently still, Christopher Craft confidently traces the novel's origins to "Victorian culture's anxiety about desire's potential indifference to the prescriptions of gender."[16] The tenor in these readings of the monster becomes more complicated, but the basic tenor/vehicle relation returns in a way that is itself more numbing than uncanny.

The tendency to see *Dracula* in relation to specific late-nineteenth-century historical contexts marks the most recent accounts of the text. Stephen Arata describes his essay on the novel as moving from the psychoanalytic to the historical in order to identify the text with a late Victorian "anxiety of reverse colonization."[17] *Dracula*, he argues, is one of the stories that culture tells itself in order to "assuage the anxiety attendant upon cultural decay."[18] Jennifer Wicke takes the refreshing tack of seeing the novel as looking forward to the twentieth century rather than back to the nineteenth. Yet she too is drawn into allegory, this time rewriting the text as a liminal modernist artifact:

the social force most analogous to Count Dracula's as depicted in the novel is none other than mass culture, the developing technologies of the media in its many forms, as mass transport, tourism, photography and lithography in image production, and mass-produced narrative.[19]

It may be doing a certain violence to Wicke's careful prose to rewrite her characterization of the novel as "refract[ing] hysterical images of modernity" (469) as yet another version of the anxiety story, but that is what it seems to be, nonetheless.

In what follows, I will try to leave the anxiety story behind, reading the text as more performative than reflective, as providing a cultural narrative that reshapes society rather than mirroring social anxieties. Questioning the separation of text and history, I will be taking for granted that, as Ann Cvetkovich puts it, "the work of ... novels is itself a part of Victorian history."[20] In the end it may appear that I am simply producing another allegory of the text, one with the "little band of men" at its center in place of the monster. The difference between a reading that places the text outside of the historical processes it supposedly reflects and a reading that makes it part of those processes is in practice a difficult one to maintain—*Dracula* as myth of origins may look very much like *Dracula* as historical allegory. But if the text still appears as an allegory in my account, it is an allegory of the future, or rather an allegory that helped to construct the future that its own narrative could then be seen to reflect.

In suggesting that this is the way to read *Dracula*, I am also proposing that we treat late-nineteenth-century romances as part of their moment—the moment of modernism. If we pay less attention to the formal links to Gothic fiction and stress instead the way in which such a narrative engages its moment, we can discover what *Dracula* shares with novels included in the canon of modernist fiction. The moment of modernism is primarily defined by a new concentration of metropolitan power, a new imperialism, the spread of consumerism, and the expansion of a culture of experts. While all of these are at some level related, it is this last aspect of modernist culture that I want to concentrate on here.[21] As Thomas Strychacz has shown, the culture of the expert, when translated into the field of literary practice, possesses its most obvious equivalent in the specialized languages of experimental modernism. As Strychacz puts it, "If a body of formal knowledge underpins a professional's power within a mass society, then the idiom of modernist writing—arcane allusion, juxtaposition, opaque writing, indeterminacy, and so on—performs precisely this function within mass culture."[22] The rise of a culture of experts, then, coincides with the appearance of texts that seem to demand of the reader an ability to master their private languages. Joyce's *Finnegans Wake* is perhaps the ultimate product of this trend, but the pattern is established much earlier, in the work of James and Conrad for example. In this essay, however, I will be arguing that *Dracula*, a text more often seen as the polar opposite of the modernist novel, is equally concerned with the culture of the expert. Specifically, *Dracula* provides a myth of origins for such a culture.

THE POWER OF COMBINATION

Where does one begin a reading of *Dracula?* Well, why not at the end? If the text has accomplished something, let us catch it tallying up its gains. The last word lies with Jonathan Harker, in a note appended to Mina's typewritten account of the adventure and the other vestiges of events seven years earlier. Harker begins his note thus:

> Seven years ago we all went through the flames; and the happiness of some of us since then is, we think, well worth the pain we endured. It is an added joy to Mina and to me that our boy's birthday is the same day as that on which Quincey Morris died. His mother holds, I know, the secret belief that some of our brave friend's spirit has passed into him. His bundle of names links all our little band of men together; but we call him Quincey ... We could hardly ask anyone, even did we wish to, to accept these as proofs of so wild a story. Van Helsing summed it all up as he said, with our boy on his knee:—"We want no proofs; we ask none to believe us! This boy will some day know what a brave and gallant woman his mother is. Already he knows her sweetness and loving care; later on he will understand how some men so loved her, that they did dare much for her sake."[23]

The novel ends with Quincey, son of Jonathan and Mina; he is at once sign of the promise of the future and a souvenir, through his "bundle of names," of the past.[24] But we know that other blood flows in his veins. The giving and taking of blood throughout the novel means that more than the original Quincey Morris's spirit "has passed into him." Mina has drunk Dracula's blood, Dracula has drunk Lucy's, Lucy has had transfusion of blood from all the novel's main characters except Jonathan.[25] In other words Quincey stands as a record of the adventure in more than his "bundle of names." But this also means that the vampire's blood flows is little Quincey's veins, which suggests, not to put too fine a point on it, that Quincey is part vampire. What then has been accomplished? Society has been saved from the vampire; Quincey, emblem of the society of the future *is*—at least partly—a vampire.

This would scarcely seem to represent a triumph over the nosferat$$ But what if we consider that the real accomplishment of the novel is bringing that "little band of men" together? What if the threat of the vampire has largely been an instrument for the formation of an association between these men? As the ending of the novel shows, the team of men does not simply wither away once the vampire has been destroyed. The little band is also brought together by their common love of Mina ("some men so loved her, that they did dare much for her sake"). To avert a threat poses by a monster, to save a "gallant woman" from that monster: this is the charter for this league of men. I want to argue that the vulnerable woman is, like the vampire, needed by the narrative.[26] At the same time, thought as we shall see, the celebration of the mother of the future generation dissimulates the text's investment in producing an exclusively male (and disembodied) model of social reproduction. The female body becomes in fact the exemplary object for the expertise of the team of men. Not surprisingly, then, the home, the feminine sphere for most of the nineteenth century, becomes the privileged site for their activities.

Let us consider the sorts of men who are united by their loathing of the vampire and their love of Mina, and consider also the way their positions change in the course of the narrative. Jonathan Harker introduce himself to us first as a young solicitor and becomes in the course of the narrative the successor to his employer, Hawkins. Upon the death of Mr. Hawkins, the Harkers become wealthy beyond their modest dream with a suddenness that shocks Mina:

> It seems only yesterday that the last entry was made, and yet how much between them, in Whitby and all the world before me, Jonathan away and no news of him; and now, married to Jonathan, Jonathan a solicitor, a partner, rich, master of his business, Mr Hawkins dead and buried ... The service [for Hawkins] was very simple and very solemn. There were only ourselves and the servants there, one or two old friends ... and a gentleman representing Sir John Paxton, the President of the Incorporated Law Society. (206)

One generation passes away, and another succeeds it. But succession is not based on biological ties between father and son: one professional is replaced by another, the transition sanctioned by the relevant professional body, in this case the Incorporated Law Society. The biological body is replaced by the legal body as the agent of reproduction.

This is not the only case of succession in the novel, nor is the older "biological" model completely defunct, at least in the case of non-middle-class characters. Throughout there is the sense that one social formation, as represented by one generation, is being replaced by another. Mr. Hawkins's death occurs at the same time as two others: that of Lord Godalming and that of Mrs. Westenra, Lucy's mother. Arthur in turn becomes Lord Godalming, the new generation of aristocrat. Lord Godalming is the team's equivalent for "Sir John Paxton, the President of the Incorporated Law Society": his presence confers a suitable air of dignity and respect-ability on the business in which he is engaged, in this case the hunting of Dracula.[27] Lucy does not replace Mrs. Westenra in the same way, of course; as Lucy herself dies at the same time (due to the depredations of Dracula), Arthur, Lord Godalming, comes to inherit that estate too under Mrs. Westenra's will. Male succession seems to be a far less problematical matter than female succession, for reasons that I hope will become apparent.

Consider the novel's other "leading men": Dr. Seward, Professor Van Helsing, and Quincey Morris. Two of the three, Seward and Van Helsing, are, like Jonathan, professional men. Seward is the new medical professional: an alienist and physician, at an early age (it would seem) he has reached the top of his profession, having charge of his own asylum for the insane. He is also, in a sense, the professional offspring of Van Helsing, as he has learnt his craft at the latter's feet. He is Van Helsing's "disciple" even according to the rules of vampiric influence, as he has on an earlier occasion sucked Van Helsing's blood to save him from infection after a surgical accident. For Seward the latter is "my old friend and master, Professor Van Helsing" (137). Van Helsing also thinks fondly of those good old days, while acknowledging Seward's full professional status in the present: "You were always a careful student, and your case-book was ever more full than the rest. You were only student then; now you are master ..." (146). Van Helsing is the professional *ne plus ultra*. He is "the great specialist" (144). In addition to his qualifications as a doctor and scientist, we also learn that he is a qualified lawyer: "You forget that I am a lawyer as well as a doctor" (197). Thus it is that this super-professional is the natural leader of this new social group composed largely of professional men.

Quincey P. Morris, the Texan adventurer, is the only real outsider in this group. Significantly, he is also the only expendable member of the team.

Not before he proves his usefulness, though. Quincey, after all, is the one who finally "stakes" Dracula, as Mina tells us: "on the instant, came the sweep and flash of Jonathan's great knife. I shrieked as I saw it shear through the throat; whilst at the same moment Mr Morris' bowie knife plunged in the heart" (447). This staking is a necessary task for the closure of the narrative, but one that it skirts around gingerly. In Mina's account the weapons themselves seem to be doing the work without the effort of the men who wield them. While Jonathan's decapitating of the monster is part of the protocol, it is clear enough from the earlier "saving" of Lucy that it is the actual staking that is symbolically central. But whereas elsewhere in the novel this symbolic penetration is performed on females by males, here the act is male-male. This seems to threaten the homosocial arrangement of the text, and it should not be surprising that Quincey, who is "only too happy to have been of any service" (448) does not survive to take a part in the new order.

I have not yet explained Mina's role in this professional order. Mina evidently, is not part of the "little band of men"; rather she is meant to be the ideal center around which it revolves. She is, however, related to the society of professionals who are ostensibly protecting her. In fact if Seward, Van Helsing, and Harker resemble the new ruling class, an elite group of "experts" whose power lies in education and affiliation to various incorporeal bodies, Mina may be seen as a soldier in the army of cheay (here, free) female labor that sustains that group. Mina begins the narrative as a teacher, more accurately as an "assistant schoolmistress" (70), on part of the cheap female labor force, but in the course of the novel she becomes stenographer, typist and nurse to the band of men.[28] This is not, of course, viewed as in any way exploitative in the text: Mina's interests are seen to be literally married to Jonathan's.

> I have been working very hard lately, because I want to keep up with Jonathan's studies, and I have been practising shorthand very assiduously. When we are married I shall be able to be useful to Jonathan and if I can stenograph well enough I can take down what he wants to say in this way and write it out for him on the typewriter, at which am also practising very hard. (71)

Later, too, she happily embraces her secretarial work for the team; after all, as Van Helsing himself tells us at the end, the men are daring all for her sake.

While the nonprofessional Texan is ultimately killed off, and while Mina's gender disqualifies her from team-membership, their selflessness is nevertheless entirely in keeping with the logic of the new order. Part of the novel's ideological program is the abnegation of simple self-interest. Van Helsing's final eulogy on the men's "salvation" of Mina ("some men so loved her, that they did dare much for her sake" [449]) places their self-sacrificing mission on a par with the divine ("And God so loved the world ..."). Earlier, one of the greatest compliments that Van Helsing finds to bestow on Mina is that she is not selfish:

> She is one of God's women fashioned by his own hand to show us men and other women that there is a heaven where we can enter, and that its light can be here on earth. So true, so sweet, so noble, so little an egoist—and that let me tell you is much in this age, so sceptical and selfish. (227)

This occurs in a conversation between Van Helsing and Mina's husband, Jonathan. Dizzying heights of homosocial rhetoric are reached, and once again Mina's role, even—or perhaps especially—in her absence, is to bond men emotionally. Jonathan is nearly overcome: "We shook hands, and he was so earnest and so kind that it made me quite choky" (227).

Selfishness is in fact a vice of the generation/social formation that is displaced by the new professionals. The self-centeredness of the dying Mrs. Westenra is partly responsible for her negligence in caring for Lucy after the latter has become the Count's victim. Seward is inclined to take a benign view of this sort of egoism:

> Here, in a case where any shock may prove fatal, matters are so ordered that, from some cause or other, the things not personal— even the terrible changes in her daughter to whom she is so vitally attached—do not seem to reach her. It is something like the way Dame Nature gathers round a foreign body an envelope of some insensitive tissue which can protect from evil that which it would otherwise harm by contact. If this be an ordered selfishness, then we should pause before we condemn any one for the vice of egoism.... (147)

Subsequent events prove the dangers of this magnanimous view of things: through her ignorance of Lucy's condition, Mrs. Westenra is on more than one occasion responsible for the vampire's access to Lucy. Not once, but twice does she remove the garlic flowers from Lucy's neck, the first time opening the window as well to inadvertently admit Dracula. The defensive selfishness that Seward sees at work in her behavior turns out to be fatal to others.

It would appear that Mrs. Westenra is an emblem of decadence as it comes to be defined in the work of Paul Bourget, circulated in English in the writings of Havelock Ellis. The pseudo-scientific language used also comes to be the master discourse of *Dracula*. Here is Ellis's version of Bourget on decadence:

> A society should be like an organism. Like an organism, in fact, it may be resolved into a federation of smaller organisms, which may themselves be resolved into a federation of cells. The individual is the social cell. In order that the organism should perform its functions with energy, but with a subordinated energy, and in order that these lesser organisms should themselves perform their functions with energy, it is necessary that the cells comprising them should perform their functions with energy, but with a subordinated energy. If the energy of the cells becomes independent, the lesser organisms will likewise cease to subordinate their energy to the total energy and the anarchy which is established constitutes the *decadence* of the whole The social organism does not escape this law and enters into *decadence* as soon as the individual life becomes exaggerated beneath the influence of acquired well-being and of heredity.[29]

The sort of thinking that *Dracula* produces, then, is coming to be familiar to an English readership in this period from other discourses. Mrs. Westenra's egoism, however excusable it may seem initially to Seward, produces damage to the social organism. Her behavior links her to the text's ultimate egoist, Dracula himself. As Van Helsing describes it, the fight against the vampire is the struggle of "combination" against selfish individualism:

> we too are not without strength. We have on our side *power of combination*—a power denied the vampire kind; we have resources of science; we are free to act and think; and the hours of the day and the night are ours equally ... We have self-devotion in a cause, and an end to achieve that is not a selfish one. These things are much. (285; emphasis added)

Van Helsing, and the professional middle class which he comes from, are not above learning a lesson from the working class, it seems. Combination, which as E.P. Thompson shows once evoked middle-class and aristocratic fears of Jacobin conspiracy as well as of unionization, is here reborn as the cornerstone of professional middle-class power.[30] If the aristocratic prestige of a Lord Godalming can be remodeled as a useful tool for this enterprise, some of the attributes of the working class can be similarly refashioned.

THE RISE OF PROFESSIONALISM

Franco Moretti has argued that Dracula represents the threat of monopoly capitalism itself, against which the more "traditional" forces represented by Van Helsing's team set themselves.[31] From what we have seen of the text, it seems more likely that Dracula is the individualist monster who is seen as archaic or traditional. The little band of men formed in the text are an emergent formation; they are part of the emergence of monopoly capital, in the specific form that takes in the professional monopolies.

Professionalism is a rather difficult concept to pin down.[32] Histories of professionalism run the risk of assuming a false continuity between its pre-industrial and its nineteenth-century varieties, or between its relatively independent nineteenth-century practitioners and the modern corporate professional. The sociology of the professions has to strive to distinguish between the objective attributes of professionalism and the profession's own self-image. Magali Larson provides a useful definition of professionalism as "the attempt to translate one order of scarce resource—special knowledge and skills—into another—social and economic rewards."[33] This translation cannot work without certain conditions, notably state endorsement of the particular monopoly of resources being established. Even for the most "traditional" of the market-oriented professions (which excludes the military and the clergy), these conditions are not established until well into the nineteenth century. Of more concern to us here, though, is the remarkable rise of occupations that designated themselves professions in the late Victorian period. There are two different processes at work in the rise of professional ideologies in the late nineteenth century. On the one hand, there is a considerable increase in the number of what we might call dependent professionals. (This is an awkward usage, since it is the way in which these groups begin to define themselves as professionals that is of interest—potential professionals might be a better term.) As Harold Perkin describes,

> [These] were growing with the expansion of service occupations during the Victorian age. By 1911, if we add the lesser

professionals and technicians to the higher ones, the professions were 4.1 per cent of the occupied population, not much short of the 4.6 per cent who were "employers" in the census of industrial status, and if we add "managers and administrators" the figure rises to 7.5 per cent, larger than the category of "employers and proprietors" (6.7 per cent).[34]

What is more significant for our purposes, however, is that more and more individuals who depended for their livelihood on the marketing of particular specialized knowledges began to amalgamate along the lines of the existing "liberal professions," such as medicine and law. At work here is the professional ideology of the self-regulating organization of experts, but also the more general collectivist ethos of the late nineteenth century. The last quarter of the nineteenth century is generally recognized as the moment of combination in industry and business, of the formation of cartels, syndicates, and trusts. Even Britain, which was losing ground as the pace of industrial and economic development increased elsewhere, participated in this international trend toward concentration of capital. As Eric Hobsbawm puts it: "From 1880 on the pattern of distribution was revolutionized. 'Grocer' and 'butcher' now meant not simply a small shopkeeper but increasingly a nationwide or international firm with hundreds of branches."[35] There was a similar tendency toward combination among those who possessed educational "capital." Professional associations of all sorts proliferated. To name only those involved in the sphere of literary production, the late nineteenth century saw the appearance of the Associated Booksellers of Great Britain and Ireland (1895), the Publisher's Association (1895), and the Society of Authors (1883). Perkin charts the dimensions of this transformation:

> To the seven qualifying associations of 1800—four Inns of Court for barristers, two Royal Colleges and the society of Apothecaries for medical doctors—the first eighty years of the nineteenth century had added only twenty more, for solicitors, architects, builders (not successful as a profession), pharmacists, veterinary surgeons, actuaries surveyors, chemists, librarians, bankers (another unsuccessful attempt) accountants, and eight types of engineer. From 1880 down to the First World War there appeared no less than thirty-nine, from chartered accountants, auctioneers and estate agents, company secretaries and hospital administrators to marine, mining, water, sanitary, heating and

ventilating, and locomotive design engineers, insurance brokers, sales managers, and town planners. To these we should add the non-qualifying associations ... which often combined professional aspirations with something of the character of trade unions or employers' associations.[36]

A large section of the middle class who were not owners of capital in the traditional sense, and who clearly did not see themselves as clerks, begar to define themselves in the terms of expertise that had only relatively recently been fully appropriated by the "real" professions.[37] As Perkin suggests, the dream of professionalism is of resources (knowledge and skill) which in theory at least are susceptible to almost infinite extension: everyone can be a capitalist where human capital is in question. Medicine (and to a lesser extent law) was the profession that offered the dominant model for the new groups of experts to aspire to: high social status, the ideal of public service, self-regulation, and the idea of expertise based on a developing scientific field were all highly attractive to these groups.[38]

This synecdochic tendency of medicine is important for an attempt to understand the particular contribution which *Dracula* makes to the social imaginary. While, as I have noted, its protagonists are for the most part professionals of the (somewhat) more established sort, this narrative of the deployment of expertise and the power of combination spoke to all those other groups for whom medical expertise provided the ideological image of their own specialized knowledge. The men's collectivity of Stoker's text, then, speaks to a more general movement in middle-class England, providing them with an origin myth and with a fantasy of control through expertise. Rather than representing the last gasp of liberal English culture against monopoly capital, as Franco Moretti would have it, those led by Van Helsing *are* the new men, an increasingly fraternal, and in specific ways patriarchal, group. The threat that ostensibly unites them is, so to speak, a back-formation; and the woman in whose service they claim to be provides the secretarial and other support services that sustain them. It is in this sense that we can speak of the text's using fear toward a particular end, rather than expressing it.

THE VAMPIRE AS FIGURE

While I am arguing that we can to some extent decode the significance of the "little band of men," I also want to insist that the figure of the vampire is better understood as just that—a figure. In other words, I want to shift the emphasis from what the vampire and vampirism might represent to the mode of representation, to the particular form that the vampire gives to danger.[39] In the vampire we confront a monster whose primary usefulness depends on his capacity to *embody* threats, not so much in his own body, which remains elusively protean, but in the bodies of his victims. Once a threat has been properly embodied, it can be dealt with. We can approach this aspect of *Dracula* by reconsidering some of the literary materials Stoker draws on to produce his monster, in this case his own earlier adventure romance, *The Snake's Pass* (1890). In this, his first novel, he blends adventure romance after the fashion of H. Rider Haggard with an interethnic marriage plot. His English hero, Arthur Severn, becomes embroiled in a land dispute and a search for treasure while visiting the west of Ireland. Seven eventually finds the treasure and marries Norah Joyce, the daughter of an Irish peasant.[40] One of the most striking aspects of the text, though, is the amount of space devoted to describing the peculiar shifting bog which dominates the landscape. An old schoolfriend of Severn's, Dick Sutherland, is engaged in research into the bogs of Ireland, and through their conversations we are given a wealth of bog-lore. While the novel has a conventional villain, the moneylender Black Murdock, the only force in the text analogous to the threat of Dracula is in fact the shifting bog. The bog is, in its own way, a killer, as the following dialogue between Severn and his old schoolfriend shows:

> "Is it a dangerous bog?" I queried.
>
> "Rather! It is just as bad a bit of soft bog as ever I saw. I wouldn't like to see anyone or anything that I cared for try to cross it ... [b]ecause at any moment they might sink through it; and then, goodbye—no human strength or skill could ever save them."
>
> "Is it a quagmire, then? or like a quicksand?"
>
> "... Nay! it is more treacherous than either. You may call it, if you are poetically inclined, a 'carpet of death!' ... It will bear up a certain weight, for there is a degree of cohesion in it; but it is not all of equal cohesive power, and if one were to step in the wrong spot—" He was silent. "... A body suddenly immersed would, when the air of the lungs had escaped and the rigor mortis had set in, probably sink a considerable distance; then it would rise after nine days, when decomposition began to generate gases.... Not succeeding in this, it would ultimately waste away, and the bones would become *incorporated* with the existing

vegetation somewhere about the roots, or would lie among the slime at the bottom."

"Well," said I, "for real cold-blooded horror, commend me to your men of science."[41]

In this passage it is clear that the threat posed by the bog is of the dissolution of identity through a negative version of "incorporation." The bog, like the vampire, has the capacity to assimilate foreign bodies, to incorporate matter into its own substance. To be drained by the vampire is to have your blood circulate with his, to have your essence preserved, yet to be personally destroyed. In the case of the victim of the shifting bog "the bones ... become incorporated with the existing vegetation somewhere about the roots." The threat of the bog functions in specific ways in *The Snake's Pass* that do not concern us here, but the earlier novel does allow us to see how the figure of the vampire is a more successful reworking of the earlier figure.

The bog is in many ways a greater threat than the vampire, or more accurately, the text has yet to evolve strategies for its successful control: the professional ideal is not as effective there as in the case of *Dracula*. It is not that the ideal is unavailable, as the following passage indicates. Dick Sutherland is explaining how to reclaim bogland:

> "In fine we cure bog by both a surgical and a medical process. We drain it so that its mechanical action as a sponge may be stopped, and we put in lime to kill the vital principle of its growth. Without the other, neither process is sufficient; but together, scientific and executive man asserts his dominance."
>
> "Hear! Hear!" said Andy. "Musha but Docther Wilde himself, Rest his sowl! couldn't have put it aisier to grip. It's a *purfessionaler* the young gintleman is intirely." (56; emphasis added)

The draining operations undertaken, though, are on a less treacherous bog than the one described above. Eventually lime does become available in abundant quantities to further the work of reclamation, but only when the shifting bog has slid off into the sea: "scientific and executive man" can only do their work when the real "monster" of the text has been conveniently removed. The monstrous, shifting bog represents a threat that has not been adequately embodied, one that in fact threatens to erase the boundaries of any corporeal self. While the collectivities of *Dracula* seem to provide a version of incorporation that is untroubling for the subjects of the novel, the incorporating bog, like the Count himself, threatens identity.

Unlike the more properly abject bog, though, the threat of the vampire can be localized and overcome in the bodies of his female victims. We can discern both a continuity with the professional techniques of the engineer, Sutherland, and an advance over them in the shift from the language of the engineer to that of the doctor: cutting and draining are the equivalent to decapitation and staking in the control of the vampire; adding lime the equivalent of filling the mouth with garlic. One process stops the "mechanical action," the other the "vital principle." Significantly, we only have one example in the text of all of these protocols being followed: the staking of the only English vampire, Lucy, in the tomb. As I have suggested, this localization of the danger in the body of women demonstrates the extent to which the threat of the vampire is custom-built for a certain emergent form of power: the collectivity is formed to deal with the threat of the outsider/foreign body, but its most important activities are directed at extending its power "at home." Van Helsing, the vampire expert, but also professionally interested in Lucy as her physician, is the one who explains the means of her "reclamation" in the following passage.[42] As in the case of Dick Sutherland's account of the treatment of the bog, the master language is provided by science. Professional knowledge distinguishes Seward and Van Helsing from Quincey and Lord Godalming, especially when the medical instruments used take on a strikingly domestic character:

> Van Helsing, in his methodical manner, began taking the various contents from his bag and placing them ready for use. First he took out a soldering iron and some plumbing solder, and then a small oil lamp ... then his operating knives ... and last a round stake some two and a half or three inches thick and about three feet long ... With this stake came a heavy hammer, such as in households is used in the coal-cellar for breaking the lumps. To me, a doctor's preparations for work of any kind are stimulating and bracing, but the effect of these things on both Arthur and Quincey was to cause them a sort of consternation. (256–7)

The techniques of surgery (the operating knives) meet those of the handy man (solder, coal-hammer, stake), the latter magically transformed by the alchemy of professionalism. There are further rituals: the actual staking performed by Arthur under Van Helsing's direction, is accompanied by "prayer for the dead" (surely inappropriate if Lucy is not yet really dead and the final touches are added by the doctors: "the Professor and I sawed the top off the stake, leaving the point of it in the body. Then we cut off the head and filled the mouth with garlic" (260). This is a far more elaborate process than that which is required to treat the other vampires, including the Count himself. The staking of Dracula is by comparison a very rushed affair, and even the destruction of the three vampire women who still inhabit Dracula's castle in Transylvania is handled without a number of the steps followed in Lucy's case. The English woman is the only proper object of these techniques. As we discovered through the fate of Quincey Morris the staker of Dracula, the use of these same professional procedures against males, even against the monstrous Count, is fraught with danger and run counter to the logic of the narrative's project. In a very real sense, *Dracula* turns out to be not about Dracula at all: his staking is the least important in the text.

Vampirism is a back-formation justifying a certain type of intervention, a new type of discipline, a new place for the qualified professional who straddles the public and private realms. Since vampirism is already within the home, the professional must follow it there. Since women are the vampire's natural prey, they must become the special objects of the professional's watchfulness. Besides Dracula's castle, we are offered only two models of domesticity in the novel. The first is the Westenras's home where the Count's attacks on Lucy necessitate (and this making necessary is very much the text's project) turning the home into a hospital: alternatively watched over by Dr. Seward and Professor Van Helsing at first, and later guarded by the full male team excluding Harker, Lucy can scarcely by regarded as living in a private house any longer. Later in the novel, the novel's principal institution, Seward's asylum for the insane, becomes home: Mina and the band of men all come to live in the institution. The domestic merges with the institutional and the institutional merges with the domestic, which of course is only appropriate in a novel where the single marriage, that of Mina and Jonathan, takes place in a hospital.[43] Both of these carefully administered spaces, the institutional house and the domestic institution, have as their ostensible goal the protection of the vulnerable female body from the vampire, yet in both cases the Count manages to enter relatively effortlessly. But in this failure lies the strength of Van Helsing's group: it is only when the vampire-threat comes to be located within the female body that it can be properly treated. Similarly, it is only when the female body has been infected by vampirism that it can be a proper object of expert treatment: where there is no crisis, there can be no intervention.

The late Victorian romance constructs a certain male, professional, homosocial order: *Dracula* provides an exemplary instance of how this is accomplished, though *King Solomon's Mines, She, The Lost World, Treasure Island,* and arguably *The Adventures of Sherlock Holmes* all take part in this process. The expedition, the treasure hunt, the investigation—all posit a suitable threat in response to which the team of men can be summoned. Whether it is the immortal Ayesha or the degenerate criminal that provides the alibi, the constitution of the male group follows the same pattern. In *Dracula* the figure of the vampire is remodeled by Stoker to bring the putative resistance to modernity closer to home: his team of men are as comfortable policing the houses of London as they are tracking the vampire across Europe. But this aspect of *Dracula* allows us to see that imperial novels like *King Solomon's Mines* or *The Lost World* also have a domestic address: the professional at home can see his own exotic reflection in the resourceful imperial team member.

Of course the seamless way in which the male order establishes itself in *Dracula* glosses over the far more conflicted process of the consolidation of professional power. The rise of professional culture lacked the strong narrative drive of Stoker's novel: there were subplots and *longueurs*, not to mention problems of closure. Even in the profession of medicine, which the novel makes its master-profession, women disputed male control almost as soon as it was first secured by the Medical (Registration) Act of 1868.[44] Nevertheless, the strategies of exclusion and the specific disposition of power/knowledge that *Dracula* presents in nascent form have proved to be extremely resilient. Moreover, while the shape of the crisis keeps changing, crisis narratives continue to provide terms in which professional intervention can be explained. And while the Count enjoys an impressive afterlife in popular culture, the real survivors of the novel are the "little band of men": in countless films, books, and television shows, the model of the team of men, each member possessing some particular skill, is reproduced.[45] Revamped in war stories, westerns, and police procedurals, the narrative of professional combination shows no signs of dying out.

NOTES

1. By male homosocial I mean those ties between men which, while promoting close and even intense bonds between them, proscribe homoerotic contact. See Eve Kosofsky Sedgwick, *Between Men: English Literature and Male Homosocial Desire* (New York: Columbia University Press, 1985), chapter 1 passim.

2. I would agree with Jon Thompson's contention that there exists in the late nineteenth and twentieth century "a larger culture of modernism that includes popular culture and is not limited to institutionalized high art." See *Fiction, Crime and Empire: Clues to Modernity and Postmodernism* (Urbana and Chicago: University of Illinois Press, 1993), 28.

3. Patrick Brantlinger, *Rule of Darkness: British Literature and Imperialism, 1830–1914* (Ithaca: Cornell University Press, 1988), 230.

4. Bram Dijkstra, *Idols of Perversity: Fantasies of Feminine Evil in Fin-de-Siècle Culture* (Oxford: Oxford University Press, 1986), chapter 7. See also Daniel Pick, *Faces of Degeneration: A European Disorder, c.1848–c.1918* (Cambridge: Cambridge University Press, 1989).

5. *The Picture of Dorian Gray* (1891; New York: Airmont, 1964), 178.

6. These figures are taken from Walter A. Arnstein's *Britain Yesterday and Today: 1830 to the Present* (1966; Lexington: D.C. Heath, 1988), 164.

7. See for example the essays in Mary Langan and Bill Schwartz, eds., *Crises in the British State 1880–1930* (London: Hutchinson, 1985).

8. See Harold Perkin, *The Rise of Professional Society: England Since 1880* (Routledge: London and New York, 1989), 56.

9. Ibid., 59.

10. Quoted in Devendra P. Varma, *The Gothic Flame* (London: Arthur Baker, 1957), 217.

11. David Punter, *The Literature of Terror* (London: Longman, 1980).

12. Both criticism and crisis have their origins in the Greek verb *krino*, to decide.

13. The resonances between these two nineteenth-century fictional monsters have been remarked on before now. Franco Moretti treats the two together in his fine essay "The Dialectic of Fear" in *Signs Taken for Wonders*. William Veeder notes in his foreword to an anthology solely devoted to *Dracula* criticism, *Dracula: The Vampire and the Critics*, ed. Margaret Carter (Ann Arbor: UMI Research Press, 1988), that *Frankenstein* had earlier achieved this same mark of critical attention with Levine and Knoepflmacher's *The Endurance of Frankenstein*.

14. Richard Wasson, "The Politics of Dracula," in Carter, *Dracula: The Vampire and the Critics*, 19–23.

15. Phyllis A. Roth, "Suddenly Sexual Women in Bram Stoker's *Dracula*," in Carter, *Dracula: The Vampire and the Critics*, 57–67, Judith Weissman, "Women and Vampires: *Dracula* as a Victorian Novel," in Carter, *Dracula: The Vampire and the Critics*, 69–77.

16. Christopher Craft, "'Kiss me with those Red Lips': Gender and Inversion in Bram Stoker's *Dracula*," in Carter, *Dracula: The Vampire and the Critics*, 167–90 [190].

17. Stephen D. Arata, "The Occidental Tourist: *Dracula* and the Anxiety of Reverse Colonization," *Victorian Studies* (1990): 621–45.

18. Ibid., 623.

19. Jennifer Wicke, "Vampiric Typewriting: *Dracula* and its Media," *ELH* 59 (1992): 467–93.

20. See Ann Cvetkovich, *Mixed Feelings: Feminism, Mass Culture, and Victorian Sensationalism* (New Brunswick, N.J.: Rutgers University Press, 1992). For an exemplary account of the way in which the novel anticipates and participates in historical change rather than reflecting it, see Nancy Armstrong's *Desire and Domestic Fiction: A Political History of the Novel* (Oxford: Oxford University Press, 1987).

21. On the connections between modernism and the new prominence of the imperial metropolis, see Raymond Williams, *The Politics of Modernism: Against the New Conformists* (London: Verso, 1989), 37–48. On the complexity of the relations of professionalism, literary criticism, and modernism, see Bruce Robbins, *Secular Vocations: Intellectuals, Professionalism, Culture* (London: Verso, 1993), chapter 2.

22. Thomas Strychacz, *Modernism, Mass Culture and Professionalism* (Cambridge: Cambridge University Press, 1993), 27. Strychacz is mostly concerned with American

modernism, but his argument for the connection between modernist style and professional private languages applies equally well to British modernism.

23. Bram Stoker, *Dracula* (1897; Harmondsworth: Penguin, 1985), 449. Subsequent references in the text.

24. We are never given little Quincey's full name, but we can assume it is something like Quincey Jonathan Arthur John Abraham (or Van Helsing) Harker. The name Abraham, of course, also links him to another professional family: that of Bram (Abraham) Stoker himself, a lawyer, and brother of two doctors.

25. Wicke and Craft also comment on the question of little Quincey's origins: for Wicke his multiple parentage suggests the simulacra that are (almost) all that remain of the adventure's record; Craft sees Quincey as the displaced product of the symbolic gang-rape of Lucy in the tomb.

26. As Ann Cvetkovich has described, this narrative in which a particular construction of the woman enables certain strategies of professionalized male intervention is produced earlier in the century in the sensation novel. See *Mixed Feelings*, chapter 3. However, the scientific/medical discourse that appears toward the end of *Lady Audley's Secret* to justify Lady Audley's incarceration operates as the master-discourse of *Dracula* almost from the beginning.

27. The English aristocracy was certainly lending its prestige to the world of business in the 1890s. In 1896 167 English noblemen, one quarter of the active peerage, were company directors. See Perkin, *Rise of Professional Society*, 366.

28. Though before she assumes her new role the doctors themselves play the parts of nurse. While tending Lucy, Van Helsing assures Seward: "We are the best nurses, you and I" (151). This is before Jonathan and Mina join forces with them.

29. Quoted in R.K.R. Thornton, *The Decadent Dilemma* (London: Edward Arnold, 1983), 39, from an Ellis essay of 1889. As Thornton remarks, the italics and the explanatory nature of the passage in which it occurs suggest that this may be the first use of the word in this sense in English. Ellis, of course, is largely interested in using decadence as a stylistic term.

30. See *The Making of the English Working Class* (New York: Random House, 1966). On the subsequent history of the figure of combination see Nancy Armstrong, *Desire and Domestic Fiction: A Political History of the Novel* (New York: Oxford University Press, 1987), chapter 4.

31. Franco Moretti, *Signs Taken for Wonders: Essays in the Sociology of Literary Forms* (London: Verso, 1988), 83–108.

32. For the discussion which follows I have relied mostly on Magali Sarfatti Larson's *The Rise of Professionalism: A Sociological Analysis* (Berkeley: University of California Press, 1977), and Harold Perkin's *The Rise of Professional Society: England Since 1880*; references in the text. Larson offers an analytical account of the ideology of professionalism as well as useful historical material on nineteenth-century English professionalism. Perkin's account is more historically dense, but he is less clear about the specific characteristics of professionalism, tending to treat most of the non-owning section of the middle class as professional. Annie Witz's *Professions of Patriarchy* (London: Routledge, 1992) treats the connections between professionalism and gender, something largely ignored by Larson and Perkin.

33. Larson, *Rise of Professionalism*, xvii.

34. Perkin, *Rise of Professional Society*, 85.

35. Eric Hobsbawm, *The Age of Empire 1875–1914* (New York: Random House, 1989), 44.

36. Perkin, *Rise of Professional Society*, 85–6.

37. Medicine is a case in point. The government-backed educational monopoly that alone could grant any title to expert status for doctors was not formalized until the passing of the 1858 Medical Act.

38. Larson argues that because of the universal need it serves medicine became "one of the principal diffusors of the stereotyped image of profession among the public" (39). The tendency to see medicine as the exemplary profession has continued to operate in sociological approaches to professions.

39. To some extent form in this sense is important for the little band too, insofar as the form of their collectivity is extremely important in itself, outside of any reading of the particular professions that constitute it.

40. David Glover's "'Dark enough fur any man': Bram Stoker's Sexual Ethnology and the Question of Irish Nationalism," in *Late Imperial Culture*, ed. Roman de la Campa, E. Ann Kaplan, and Michael Sprinker (London: Verso, 1995), provides an excellent account of the politics of *The Snake's Pass*. I am grateful to David Glover for allowing me to read an early draft of this essay.

41. Bram Stoker, *The Snake's Pass* (1890; Dingle, Ireland: Brandon Press, 1990), 59; further references in the text.

42. Cf. Van Helsing's convincing Lord Godalming of the necessity of Lucy's staking by describing his own attachment to her: "I gave what you gave: the blood of my veins; I gave it, I, who was not, like you, her lover, but only her physician and her friend. I gave her my nights and days—before death, after death; and if my death can do her good even now, when she is the dead Un-Dead, she shall have it freely" (248).

43. Seward's asylum seems to lie halfway between the two models of the asylum which Elaine Showalter describes as dominating Victorian England. In the period between 1830 and the rise of Darwinist thought, the prevalent model was that of the asylum as home, with a regime of paternal therapy. After Darwinist thought began to enter medical discourse, the paternal model was replaced by what Showalter, after Foucault, calls psychiatric policing. See Showalter, *The Female Malady: Women, Madness and English Culture* (New York: Pantheon, 1985), especially chapters 3, 4, and 5. The policing model, with its possibilities for intervention within and outside the asylum, seems to be in the ascendant in *Dracula*.

44. See Witz, *Professions of Patriarchy*, chapter 3.

45. See for example Bruce Robbins's reading of the 1966 Western, *The Professionals* in *Secular Vocations*, 29–56.

WORKS CITED

Arata, Stephen D. "The Occidental Tourist: *Dracula* and the Anxiety of Reverse Colonization." *Victorian Studies* (1990): 621–45.

Armstrong, Nancy. *Desire and Domestic Fiction: A Political History of the Novel*. New York: Oxford University Press, 1987.

Arnstein, Walter A. *Britain Yesterday and Today: 1830 to the Present*. 1966; Lexington: D.C. Heath, 1988.

Brantlinger, Patrick. *Rule of Darkness: British Literature and Imperialism, 1830–1914*. Ithaca: Cornell University Press, 1988.

Carter, Margaret. *Dracula: The Vampire and the Critics*. Ann Arbor: UMI Research Press, 1988.

Conan Doyle, Sir Arthur. *The Lost World*. London: Hodder and Stoughton, n.d.

Craft, Christopher. "'Kiss Me With Those Red Lips': Gender and Inversion in Bram Stoker's *Dracula*." In *Dracula: The Vampire and the Critics*, edited by Margaret Carter, 167–94. Ann Arbor: UMI Research Press, 1988.

Dijkstra, Bram. *Idols of Perversity: Fantasies of Feminine Evil in Fin-de-Siècle Culture*. New York: Oxford University Press, 1986.

Fraser, W. Hamish. *The Coming of the Mass Market, 1850–1914*. Hamden: Archon, 1981.

Hobsbawm, Eric. *The Age of Empire 1875–1914*. New York: Vintage Books, 1989.

Langan, Mary, and Bill Schwartz, eds. *Crises in the British State 1880–1930*. London: Hutchinson, 1985.

Larson, Magali Sarfatti. *The Rise of Professionalism: A Sociological Analysis*. Berkeley: University of California Press, 1977.

Moretti, Franco. *Signs Taken for Wonders: Essays in the Sociology of Literary Forms*. London: Verso, 1988.

Perkin, Harold. *The Rise of Professional Society: England Since 1880*. London: Routledge, 1989.

Punter, David. *The Literature of Terror*. London: Longman, 1980.

Robbins, Bruce. *Secular Vocations: Intellectuals, Professionalism, and Culture*. London: Verso, 1993.

Roth, Phyllis A. "Suddenly Sexual Women in Bram Stoker's *Dracula*." In *Dracula: The Vampire and the Critics*, edited by Margaret Carter, 57–67. Ann Arbor: UMI Research Press, 1988.

Sedgwick, Eve Kosofsky. *Between Men: English Literature and Male Homosocial Desire*. New York: Columbia University Press, 1985.

Showalter, Elaine. *The Female Malady: Women, Madness and English Culture*. New York: Pantheon, 1985.

Stevenson, Robert Louis. *Treasure Island*. London: Cassell, 1883.

Stoker, Bram. *The Snake's Pass*. 1890; Dingle: Brandon, 1990.

———. *Dracula*. 1897; Harmondsworth: Penguin, 1985.

Thompson, E.P. *The Making of the English Working Class*. New York: Vintage Books, 1966.

Thompson, Jon. *Fiction, Crime and Empire: Clues to Modernity and Postmodernism*. Urbana: University of Illinois Press, 1993.

Thornton, R.K.R. *The Decadent Dilemma*. London: Edward Arnold, 1983.

Wasson, Richard, "The Politics of *Dracula*." In *Dracula: The Vampire and the Critics*, edited by Margaret Carter, 19–23. Ann Arbor: UMI Research Press, 1988.

Weissman, Judith. "Women and Vampires: *Dracula* as a Victorian Novel." In *Dracula: The Vampire and the Critics*, edited by Margaret Carter, 69–77. Ann Arbor: UMI Research Press, 1988.

Wicke, Jennifer. "Vampiric Typewriting: Dracula and its Media." *ELH* 59 (1992): 467–93.

Wilde, Oscar. *The Picture of Dorian Gray* (1891). New York: Airmont, 1964.

Witz, Anne. *Professions and Patriarchy*. London: Routledge, 1992.

JOHN PAUL RIQUELME

Oscar Wilde's Aesthetic Gothic: Walter Pater, Dark Enlightenment, and *The Picture of Dorian Gray*

"J'ai soif de ta beauté."

—Oscar Wilde, *Salomé*[1]

It was from within, apparently, that the foulness and horror had come.

—Oscar Wilde, *The Picture of Dorian Gray*

GOTHIC CHIAROSCURO AND REALISM

The Picture of Dorian Gray proceeds against the background of Walter Pater's aesthetic writings, but also against Pater in a stronger sense.[2] It provides in narrative form a dark, revealing double for Pater's aestheticism that emerges from a potential for dark doubling and reversal within aestheticism itself. The duplication produces not a repetition of Pater but a new version of his views that says what he cannot or will not articulate, including a recognition of the dark dynamics of doubling and reversal that inhabit those views. That recognition includes the possibility that the process of doubling and reversal will continue. In the novel, Wilde responds to Pater by projecting the dark implications of Pater's attitudes and formulations in a mythic Gothic narrative of destruction and self-destruction. Wilde simultaneously aestheticizes the Gothic and gothicizes the aesthetic. The merger is possible, and inevitable, because of the tendency of Gothic writing to present a

From *Modern Fiction Studies* 46, no. 3 (Fall 2000). © 2000 by the Purdue Research Foundation.

fantastic world of indulgence and boundary-crossing and the tendency of the aesthetic, in Pater, to press beyond conventional boundaries and to recognize terror within beauty. As an avatar of Narcissus, Dorian Gray embodies both tendencies in a poisonous, self-negating confluence signifying madness. But the madness is not his alone. He shares it with others in the narrative and with the fantastic quality of his story. No one is immune from the madness and its effects. In this allegory about art, Wilde's book and its producer are themselves implicated. They cannot stand apart in a realm of clarity that is somehow insulated from the darkness they portray and embody. Despite the mannered elegance of the book's characters and its style, it sheds only partial light on its subject, which includes itself.

The novel's narrative concerns a dark and darkening recognition that transforms Dorian's life by actualizing a potential that was already there in his family, a potential that is one truth about British society.[3] This dark enlightenment is rendered in a narrative that provides the equivalent of chiaroscuro, understood with reference to painting as a combination of light and clarity with enigmatic darkness and obscurity in a space that undermines the coherence and implied sanity of a representational geometry. By combining clarity and obscurity, often in a shallowly rendered space, chiaroscuro provides an alternative and a challenge to visual representations that rely on general illumination, the appearance of a coherent Cartesian geometry, and a vanishing point. The impression can be enigmatic or frightening for the person whose vision is impeded, because terror tends to arise when insufficient or uneven light creates a sense of disorientation and confusion. Edmund Burke makes this point in his treatise on the sublime and the beautiful.[4] Things that go bump in the night scare us, especially if we cannot see them clearly and understand them by means of familiar categories.

The alternative and the challenge to realism in Wilde's literary chiaroscuro concern realism's reliance on positive knowledge and on believable representations that create for the reader an impression of sanity, intelligibility, and control. The narrative provides in the painting and the book a look at the dark as well as the light, at something disturbing that exceeds, as Gothic writing regularly does, the boundaries of realistic representation and the limits of bourgeois values. As a Gothic revisionary interpretation of Pater's late Romanticism, this particular instance of excess marks a turning point in literary history toward literary modernism. The reliance on doubling as a symptom of a darkness within both culture and the mind follows Robert Louis Stevenson's *The Strange Case of Dr Jekyll and Mr Hyde* (1886) and anticipates Bram Stoker's *Dracula* (1897) and Joseph

Conrad's writings, especially *Heart of Darkness* (1902) and *The Secret Sharer* (1910). The conjoining of light and dark occurs as the narrative of a doubling that becomes visible through acts of aesthetic making and aesthetic response. The collaborative act of creating the painting brings into being something apparently new, original, and masterful that turns out to be not only beautiful but also atavistic and terrifyingly at odds with the public values of the society that applauds its beautiful appearance. That collaborative act parallels and engages with our own act of reading. It comes to an end at the same time as our engagement with the book reaches closure, once Dorian and his painting are finished.

PATER AGAINST WILDE: POE, THE FRENCH CONNECTION, AND DOUBLING

In *Oscar Wilde*, an award-winning biography, Richard Ellmann claims that in his review of *The Picture of Dorian Gray*, Pater objects only to the portrayal of "Lord Henry Wotton, who speaks so many of Pater's sentences." "But otherwise he was delighted with the book" (323). This is one of Ellmann's least convincing readings, since it is deaf to the irony of Pater's response, which is defensive, prejudicial, and patronizing. Like many other critics, Ellmann reads Pater's review as positive.[5] In fact, Wilde and Pater had exchanged compliments about some of their earlier writings. Pater wrote admiringly to Wilde about *The Happy Prince* in June 1888 (Wilde, *Letters* 219). And Wilde's anonymous review of Pater's *Imaginary Portraits* a year earlier refers to the prose as "wonderful," though he comments that it is ascetic and in danger of becoming "somewhat laborious" (qtd. in Ellmann 289). But in his later review of Pater's *Appreciations* in March 1890, Wilde's criticisms are blunter and more frequent. He says that "Style," though the "most interesting" of the essays, is also "the least successful, because the subject is too abstract" (*Artist* 230); that Charles Lamb "perhaps [...] himself would have had some difficulty in recognising the portrait given of him"; that the essay on Samuel Taylor Coleridge "is in style and substance a very blameless work" (232); and that the essay on William Wordsworth "requires re-reading" (234), though he does not say why. Most damning are his comments on Pater's style: "Occasionally one may be inclined to think that there is, here and there, a sentence which is somewhat long, and possibly, if one may venture to say so, a little heavy and cumbersome in movement" (231). Wilde ends with apparently high praise by saying that Pater's work is "inimitable," but also that "he has escaped disciples" (234), presumably including Wilde himself.

Critics who emphasize the positive character of Walter Pater's review of the novel may do primarily because many of the other reviews were more pointedly negative, even censoriously so.[6] Only by contrast with the hostile reviews can Pater's be called favorable. On the one hand, Pater was generously siding with Wilde against his troglodytic detractors. But considering Wilde's review of *Appreciations* and his echoing of Pater's views in the words of Lord Henry Wotton, Pater had reasons to be displeased and to pay Wilde back. Ellmann does trace Wilde's shift from an enthusiastic, admiring response to Pater's writings and to aestheticism at Oxford toward his later, more critical stance, but he does not suggest that Pater would have sensed the rift and responded in kind.[7] The details of the review indicate that he did.

In his review, Pater writes as though he were immune from the book's implications, or as though he wishes he were. Taking into account Lord Henry's repetition of Pater's language, which Ellmann mentions without detailing, it becomes clear that Pater could not have missed the novel's challenge to his own attitudes. Unlike Lamb, he recognized his own portrait. Pater attempts to turn aside the book's force in various ways. Like Lord Henry Wotton and Basil Hallward in their responses to Dorian and his portrait, Pater does not want to admit the bearing that Wilde's Gothic rendering has on his own ideals. He takes exception to Wilde's portrayal of an aesthetic hedonism but not by strategies that effectively answer the challenge, for Wilde's resistance approaches the absolute in its ironic probing of Paterian views and the British society into which they fit all too comfortably. Wilde anticipates Pater's response to seeing his own portrait in *Picture*. In chapter 13, Dorian murders the artist who has painted him, in effect murdering the man who, like a father or mentor, has contributed in a significant way to making him what he is. Just before he dies, Basil Hallward sees the painting late at night by the light of a "half-burned candle" (314) in the former schoolroom of Dorian's house, in a scene that would require for visual rendering a candlelit chiaroscuro like that of paintings by Georges de La Tour (1593–1652). By the "dim light," Hallward sees "a hideous face on the canvas grinning at him" that combines "horror" with "marvellous beauty" in a portrayal of its subject that includes "his own brush-work" and a frame of "his own design" (314–15). When he holds the lighted candle to the picture, he finds "his own name" as signature. Hallward's response anticipates Pater's review of the book, for the painter sees at first only "some foul parody" that he feels cannot be his work: "He had never done that. Still, it was his own picture" (315). As subjective and objective genitive, the phrase "his own picture" suggests both that the painting is one he has produced and that it portrays him.

Like Hallward in the schoolroom, Pater finds in Wilde's *Picture* "a satiric sketch," especially with regard to Lord Henry, in which the presentation of "Epicurean theory" "fails" because it abandons "the moral sense." While Pater finds Dorian "a beautiful creation," he calls him "a quite unsuccessful experiment in Epicureanism, in life as a fine art" ("Novel" 265). In his closing statement, having already mentioned the "Doppelgänger," or "double life," as central to Wilde's narrative, Pater is right to associate Wilde's work "with that of Edgar Poe, and with some good French work of the same kind, done, probably, in more or less conscious imitation of it" (266). His assertion implies that *Picture* is also an act of imitation, but of American and French sources, not a British original. Wilde, in fact, does not *imitate* a British writer; he *echoes* his writing. He does so for the same reason that the mythological figure Echo repeats already existing language: in order to say something quite different. Pater would rather not admit that his own writings are at least as important as Poe's in the texture of Wilde's novel and that they are the object of the satire. He also faces only indirectly how thoroughly Wilde's transformation of aesthetic theory is fused with anti-British attitudes. Pater makes the non-British character of the book and its author clear at the start and the end of the review. Besides closing by drawing attention to foreign models rather than one that is much closer to home, Pater begins with comments that situate Wilde prejudicially as an Irish writer. The book putatively produced on non-British patterns by an Irish writer is, not surprisingly, filled with anti-British sentiments. Wilde has turned the critical direction of the Gothic inward, toward England and toward art as an English writer presents it.

At the start of the review, by means of irony and implication, Pater comes close to responding directly in kind to the book's national antagonism, closer than he ever comes to articulating openly his individual antagonism about the transforming of his own work. He may well have sensed that Wilde's skepticism about the British and about Pater's aestheticism were not separable. Misrepresenting or misunderstanding Wilde's emphatic differences from Matthew Arnold, which are as strong as his differences from Pater's aestheticism, Pater suggests that Wilde "carries on, more perhaps than any other writer, the brilliant critical work of Matthew Arnold" ("Novel" 263). Because Pater's own critical directions include significant disagreements with Arnold, by aligning Wilde with Arnold, he distances the younger writer from himself. He would have been intent on doing that in order to separate his own version of aestheticism from the dark version Wilde attributes to him by implication in the novel. Pater describes the ostensible carrying forward of Arnold as "startling" Wilde's '"countrymen."'

By putting "countrymen" in quotation marks, Pater implies ambiguously that, by following in the footsteps of an English critic who had written about the inevitable, necessary "fusion of all the inhabitants of these islands into one homogeneous, English-speaking whole" (Arnold, "On" 296), Wilde surprises his adoptive countrymen, the British, whose countryman he is not, and that he surprises his real countrymen, the Irish, from whom he must have estranged himself by his switching of allegiance.[8] Pater's antagonism toward his younger contemporary is clear in the review's first two sentences. He suggests that Wilde is "an excellent talker," presumably like all the other voluble Irish, whose work relies on the paradox that written dialogue presents itself as spoken. That paradox participates, according to Pater, in a "crudity" that is acceptable only because of what he terms, drawing on another cliché about the Irish, Wilde's "genial, laughter-loving sense of life and its enjoyable intercourse" ("Novel" 263). Under attack, Pater reacts prejudicially to a work by an Irish author who echoes negatively Pater's own writing as part of its presentation of British society's hypocrisy. Although Pater might be willing to admit some of the ills of British society, he cannot do so in a way that implicates himself. Hallward recognizes when he holds "the light up again to the canvas" that "[i]t was from within, apparently, that the foulness and horror had come" (*Picture* 316). Although Wilde's character locates the source of the horror inside, the major British proponent of aestheticism turns away from the implication. Pater also writes about something within emerging to the surface when he describes the Mona Lisa in a passage that Wilde takes as his antithetical model: "It is a beauty wrought out from within upon the flesh [...]" (*Renaissance* 80).

When Pater comments on the Doppelgänger in the novel as the experience "not of two *persons*, in this case, but of the man and his portrait" ("Novel" 266) he points toward but does not describe the novel's complex antirealistic structure of doublings.[9] Rather than presenting the book's alternative to realism in its combination of antirealistic and realistic detail, Pater praises and blames the realistic elements as an "intrusion of real life" that, because it is "managed, of course, cleverly enough," "should make his books popular" (264). Pater damns by faint praise when he suggests that Wilde's writing is cleverly crude enough to attract a crowd. In fact, the combination of realistic and antirealistic elements is a pervasive stylistic sign of the novel's dual quality. The doubling structure of the narrative and the narration implicates the reader of *Picture*, including the reviewer of the book, as the counterpart of the picture's viewer. Instead of bringing out the book's complexity, relying on the hierarchical presuppositions of evolutionary thinking about culture, Pater criticizes Wilde for moving away from a "true

Epicureanism" toward something "less complex," and presumably less valuable (264). The narrative's intricate doublings, which derive not only from Poe but from Pater's comments on the Mona Lisa, include a multitude of parallels that anticipate a related complexity in *Dracula*. Because the parallels are so numerous and sometimes involve apparent reversals of position, as is often the case in the modern Gothic, the clear distinction between victim and perpetrator, innocent and guilty, blurs, especially when they change roles. As with the doublings of *Dracula*, the reader is invited to feel implicated.

Central to the novel's structure is the doubling not only of person and painting that Pater mentions but also of picture and book, both the book within the narrative that Lord Henry gives Dorian, and the book we read that is also a *Picture*. The doublings include Basil Hallward and Lord Henry Wotton as fraternal collaborators in the production of the painting and as doubles of different kinds for Dorian himself. Hallward and Wotton split up the dual role that Leonardo da Vinci fills as the quintessential artist-scientist. As a detached experimenter with human lives, Wotton is an avatar of Victor Frankenstein, who produces an ugly, destructive double of himself. There is, as well, the parallel between Dorian Gray and Sybil Vane, as attractive young people to whom unpleasant, destructive revelations are made. Complicating that parallel is the fact that Dorian stands in relation to Sybil as Lord Henry does to him as the revealer of something harsh and damaging. Dorian also stands eventually in the same relation to Basil, whom he destroys, as he has already destroyed Sybil. At the end, he stands in that same destructive relation to himself. Although Dorian prevents Basil from ripping up the painting with a knife near the end of chapter 2, he ultimately stabs the painter, who says he has revealed himself in the painting, and he pursues Hallward's intention from chapter 2 by trying to stab the painting in the book's final chapter and thereby stabbing its subject. This is ekphrasis with a vengeance and the revenge of the ekphrastic object, which strikes out at the artist and viewer, who wish also to strike it.[10] The roles in revolution become indistinguishable.

So many doublings and shifts of position undermine the possibility of reading the book as realistic, that is, as containing primarily intelligible patterns and answers rather than enigmas that cannot be readily resolved. There is no ultimately controlling perspective based on a geometry of narrative relations that allows us to find a stable, resolving point of vantage. In this narrative garden of forking paths, there appears to be a virus that replicates itself in double, antithetical forms within a maze that leads us not to an exit but to an impasse. The narrative oscillations and echoes arising from and as multiple parallels, reversals, and blurrings are modernist in character, but important details identify the writings of Pater as one of their origins. The brushstrokes and the frame are his. As Wilde says in his "Preface," "[I]t is the spectator, and not life, that art really mirrors" (*Picture*, 139). And as he suggests in another epigram, the reader as Caliban who sees his face in the mirror of art is likely to be enraged or, like Dorian, driven mad. These epigrams pertain to Pater as an inevitable early reader of the novel and to us.

WILDE AGAINST PATER: ECHO AGAINST NARCISSUS

As I have already suggested, Wilde neither imitates nor follows Pater in his aesthetic Gothic narrative. Instead, he echoes him as a way to evoke, refuse, and transform what he finds in the earlier writer. This is the work of Echo, whose story is bound up with that of Narcissus. In *Picture*, Wilde provides an early example of what T.S. Eliot called "the mythical method," a defining element of modernism that Eliot locates in James Joyce's *Ulysses* and earlier in some of William Butler Yeats's poems.[11] In fact, the first examples of the mythical method antedate considerably the examples that Eliot gives. As early as Thomas Hardy's *The Mayor of Casterbridge* (1886), we find a long narrative set in recent times that is constructed around extended mythic and literary parallels. Wilde also constructs his narrative around a myth, that of Echo and Narcissus. At first it might seem that Narcissus is the primary mythic figure in *Picture* and that the resulting narrative is not comparable in its mythic dimension to either *A Portrait of the Artist as a Young Man* or *Ulysses*, because the myths surrounding Daedalus and Odysseus are more various and extended than that of Narcissus. But, in fact, Echo and Narcissus, however different from each other, are counterparts, whose stories constitute a single compound myth. Echo as well as Narcissus plays a continuing role in Wilde's novel because of the style's echoic character. By echoing Pater's writings frequently and strategically, Wilde projects the story of a contemporary Narcissus as one truth about Paterian aestheticism. He echoes Pater not in order to agree with the older British writer's views but to present them darkly, in shades of gray, as at base contradictory in destructive and self-destructive ways.

Wilde begins his novel by evoking Pater's aestheticism through a series of statements about beauty and through allusions to the bestknown passages of Pater's writing: the "Conclusion" of *Studies in the History of the Renaissance* (1873)[12] and the description of Mona Lisa from the essay on Leonardo da Vinci in that volume. The first epigram in the "Preface," which asserts that "[t]he artist is the creator of beautiful things" (*Picture* 138), is followed in the remaining epigrams by numerous references to "beauty," "beautiful things," and "beautiful meanings." As the reader soon discovers, the narrative is permeated by the aesthetic, since it concerns throughout the desire to create, experience, possess or destroy beauty. Almost immediately, in the second paragraph of chapter I, we learn that Lord Henry Wotton sees, along with "the fantastic shadows of birds in flight," laburnum blossoms "whose tremulous branches seemed hardly able to bear the burden of a beauty so flame-like as theirs" (140). On the one hand, the branches are personified as undergoing an ecstatic experience in which they can hardly endure the deep impression that the blossoms, which they have yielded, or borne, make on them. But their experience is not unalloyed, for it is also the bearing, or carrying, not of a joy but of a heavy, awkward "burden" that can hardly be sustained. Further, the experience includes the play of light and dark in the "fantastic shadows" of something "in flight," either merely flying or trying to escape.

The passage is of particular note because it contains the first instances of personification (branches that feel; bees "shouldering their way" through grass) in a narrative that includes centrally the terrifying coming-to-life of something inanimate. The crossing of the boundaries between human, animal, and insect in the rhetorical figures of the book's second paragraph anticipates what eventually becomes a matter of animation involving creating and destroying life and a matter of the limits defining the human and civilization. Wilde has merged the aesthetic with issues that regularly arise in Gothic writing, issues that are anthropological, aesthetic, and scientific: the creation of the new and the character of the human. Later in chapter I, when Hallward tells his friend Lord Henry Wotton about his first encounter with Dorian Gray, he indicates his agreement with something Wotton had told him about the difference between "savages" and "being civilized." The distinction is superficial, since everything depends on appearances: "With an evening coat and a white tie, as you told me once, anybody, even a stock-broker, can gain a reputation for being civilized" (145). Harry had gone out for the evening in public to help prove that "poor artists [...] are not savages." They may not be, but in Basil's case, which asks to be taken as representative, the artist contributes to an ostensibly civilized process of creating art that turns out to unleash a destructive, self-destructive savagery antithetical to the principles of civilization itself. In a typically modern transformation of Gothic narrative, the threat in Wilde's novel comes from within culture and within British society, not from foreigners who can be treated as savages. As an Irish writer, Wilde would have been particularly aware of the distinctions the British tended to draw between themselves and ostensibly less civilized racial and national groups who might in some way pose a crude threat, Calibanlike, to British aspirations and identity.

The passage about laburnum is also notable because it initiates three kinds of echoing within the style of the novel. One occurs as language that literally echoes: "blossoms [...] laburnum [...] branches [...] bear [...] burden [...] beauty [...] birds" and "flame-like [...] fantastic [...] flight flitted" (140). The echoic quality of the prose finds one origin in the stories of Poe, the most echoic stylist among earlier prominent figures in the Gothic tradition. In "The Fall of the House of Usher," for example, the opening sentence begins "During the whole of a *dull, dark, and soundless day* [...] (95). And the title of the story, "*Willi*am *Wil*son," about a man with a double, which provides one precursor for *Picture*, includes an echoic doubling. The second form of echo involves repetition of the passage's language or similar language later in the book. Burdens, flames, and shadows occur regularly, often in passages that are significant and significantly related. The phrase "fantastic shadows," with its evocation of the visual impression of chiaroscuro, returns in a way that punctuates at times the stages in Dorian's destructive attempt to hide and to experience who he is. In the opening of chapter 13, when Dorian and Hallward mount the stairs toward the schoolroom in which Dorian will murder the artist, the "lamp cast fantastic shadows" (313). Later, when Dorian visits opium dens in an attempt to forget, he sees mostly dark windows, "but now and then fantastic shadows were silhouetted against some lamp-lit blind": "They moved like monstrous marionettes, and made gestures like live things" (348–49). These shadows are cast neither by birds nor marionettes but by human beings. The implications of personification have been reversed from the book's opening, since now the human is marked by the loss of consciousness that is memory in Dorian's will to forget and by a monstrous loss of agency.

The word "burden" also occurs at important moments, sometimes in combination with the word "shadow," which becomes associated with the painting as Dorian's double. In chapter 2, when Dorian first looks carefully at the completed painting and appears "with cheeks flushed," "as if he had recognized himself for the first time," he is described as "gazing at the shadow of his own loveliness" (167). The portrait is a kind of mirror that contains not his image with inflamed cheeks but a dark version, a shadow. In chapter 7, Lord Henry sees something similar in Sybil when a "faint blush, like the shadow of a rose in a mirror of silver, came to her cheeks" (231). Toward the end of chapter 8, Dorian thinks that the "portrait was to bear the burden of his shame" (258). After having "lost control" "almost entirely"

(282) in chapter 9, Dorian oscillates in a darkly narcissistic way between looking at the portrait with "loathing" and gazing "with secret pleasure, at the misshapen shadow that had to bear the burden that should have been his own" (298).

"Burden" also reappears at very nearly the novel's end, when Dorian castigates Lord Henry for being willing to "sacrifice anybody [...] for the sake of an epigram" (370). When Lord Henry responds that "[t]he world goes to the altar of its own accord," his language suggests most obviously a sacrificial altar, but considering Dorian's immediate confession that he has forgotten how to love and wishes he could recover his passion, the word "altar" resonates with the notion of marriage in addition to and together with that of the pain of a sacrifice. In his brief confession, Dorian says that his "own personality has become a burden" and admits his own narcissism: "I am too much concentrated on myself" (370). Lord Henry's similar preoccupation with himself results, as we learn in the next chapter, in his "divorce-case" (377), because his wife has left him for another man. When Dorian meets Victoria, Lord Henry's wife, early in the novel, Lord Henry makes cynical fun of marriage and women as he commands Dorian: "Never marry at all." Dorian readily agrees because he is "putting into practice" "one of your aphorisms," "as I do everything that you say" (191). That latter statement means both that he puts all of Lord Henry's aphorisms into practice and that he obeys Lord Henry's commands, like a slave. The phrasing echoes the marriage ceremony's vow, "I do," but not to signify the union of partners in a marriage. Shortly before this exchange, Victoria Wotton has commented that Dorian has just repeated "'one of Harry's views'" and that she always hears "'Harry's views from his friends'" (190). The details of these various scenes involving marriage and self-concern bear on the relation of Wilde's narrative to the story of Echo and Narcissus and to the Gothic tradition.

Gothic narratives regularly include attitudes and situations that challenge the institution of marriage. In this regard, they provide a dark reflection of the concern with domesticity in the history of the realistic novel. Wilde's Gothic narrative is no exception in its presentation of attitudes that make meaningful marriage impossible. Among Wilde's modern innovations is the fusing of a Gothic emphasis on impediments to marriage with the myth of Narcissus, which includes centrally the refusal of Echo's advances. Narcissus would rather not be distracted from gazing at himself. Wilde merges aesthetic narcissism with the Gothic tradition's representation of marriage's difficulty or even impossibility. Further, Victoria Wotton's comment about Dorian's parroting of Lord Henry's views reveals Dorian to be an empty echo, one without a mind of its own. Instead of repeating in order to transform or even counter meaningfully someone else's words, Dorian is the slave of another's attitudes. Echo as a mythological figure represents the possibility of choice under difficult circumstances. Dorian's behavior and his thinking are, by contrast, chosen for him, just as he chooses and manipulates the actions and thoughts of others.

The third type of echo initiated by the laburnum passage is the repeating of words from Pater's aesthetic writings. Throughout his career, Wilde had a reputation for using other writers' language in ways that drew comments amounting to the charge of plagiarism.[13] In that respect, his writing anticipates Eliot's later sometimes unacknowledged borrowings, which challenge Romantic views of the artist's originality. In the case of both writers, their modernist, anti-Romantic borrowings are intentional, motivated, and, because of the new implications of the repeated language, creative. In the laburnum passage, the compound "flamelike" in association with la*burn*um and with birds who are escaping or departing creates a clear echoic link to the "Conclusion" of *The Renaissance*. There Pater closes his first paragraph with the oddly phrased, memorable statement that "[t]his at least of flame-like our life has, that it is but the concurrence, renewed from moment to moment of forces parting sooner or later on their ways" (150). Fire, so prominent in Pater's "Conclusion" in both "flame-like" and "to burn always with this hard, gem-like flame" (152), appears in Dorian's retrospective insight about his boyhood: "Life suddenly became fiery-coloured to him. It seemed to him that he had been walking in fire. Why had he not known it?" (*Picture* 160). Later, Lord Henry thinks in an apparently positive way about "his friend's young fiery-coloured life" (206). But Dorian's flame-like experiences as a child and later are painful or even infernal, not ecstatic in the way that Pater's "Conclusion" suggests. Wilde's references to flame evoke Pater, but the implications have been reversed. In *Picture*, it is not the flame of art and passion that we choose as our future. Instead, flames of an unpleasant kind have already made us what we are. The flame and its passionate intensity are destructive in Wilde, rather than being the salvation from destruction or a consolation for it.

Dorian's fiery experience also connects him to Narcissus. Lord Henry has already identified Dorian with Narcissus in chapter I, when he contrasts Basil with Dorian and intellect with beauty: "'Why my dear Basil, he is a Narcissus, and you—well, of course you have an intellectual expression, and all that. But beauty, real beauty, ends where an intellectual expression begins. Intellect is in itself a mode of exaggeration, and destroys the harmony of any face" (142). Like separating creativity from criticism, which Wilde addresses in "The Critic as Artist" (*Artist* 340–408), severing the tie between beauty and thinking is a mistake that Wilde does not let stand. In Ovid, Narcissus is *inflamed* by his own beauty, which leads him to self-destruction.[14] In Wilde, as later in part III of Eliot's *The Waste Land*, the modern Narcissus is grotesque: a young man with a physically and morally ugly double in Wilde; a young man with an inflamed, carbuncular face who inhabits an infernal contemporary city in Eliot. When Wilde's Narcissus looks into the mirror of his painting, coproduced by his older friends, Basil and Henry, he becomes fascinated first with his own beauty but then with a growing ugliness that he recognizes as also himself.

Mona Lisa as Dark Narcissus/Narcissus as Medusa

The details of Wilde's narration imply that the intense experience central to Paterian aestheticism evoked in the "Conclusion" of *The Renaissance* is narcissistic in character. Wilde established the connection to Pater primarily, as Ellmann points out, by having Lord Henry speak "many of Pater's sentences," or, at least, many sentences that echo Pater. But Lord Henry speaks many of Wilde's sentences as well, and some of those Wildean sentences mimic Pater in their phrasing. Since at Oxford Wilde "adopted 'flamelike' as one of his favorite adjectives" (Ellmann 48), the sentence about the laburnum echoes ambiguously both Pater and Wilde. Although we may be inclined to judge Lord Henry more harshly than the novelist because of his evident misogyny and his general moral blindness, Lord Henry's wit is often in the mode of Oscar Wilde. There is a critical portrait of the artist in progress, as well as a critical portrayal of someone else. In one of his letters, Wilde himself points to his suffused identification with all the major characters in the novel: "I am so glad you like that strange coloured book of mine: it contains much of me in it. Basil Hallward is what I think I am: Lord Henry what the world thinks me: Dorian what I would like to be—in other ages, perhaps" (*Letters* 352). Though Wilde holds Pater's views up for inspection, even mockingly, he does not do so in a self-congratulatory, distanced, or morally superior way. By blurring the distinction between the observer and the subject being observed, Wilde participates in the book's logic of doubling and reversal. If he did not, he would risk adopting a morally superior stance that occupies a position outside the process he presents. The dynamics of his literary chiaroscuro prevent his becoming merely a spectator of the sort that Lord Henry seems to think he is. The critical observer's uncertainty extends to the observer's perspective. Otherwise, that perspective can be narcissistic and blind to its own tendencies, in the way that Lord Henry's self-delusion is, even late in the novel. In the penultimate chapter, despite abundant evidence of Dorian's crimes, Lord Henry refuses to see his dark side, calling him "the young Apollo" (383).

Wilde constructs his narrative around an experience that resembles not only the one Narcissus undergoes but the one that Pater mentions in the final paragraph of the "Conclusion" (153) when he turns to the "awakening" in Jean Jacques Rousseau of "the literary sense" that is described in Rousseau's *Confessions*. Pater devotes part of the paragraph to relating how fear of death inspired Rousseau to "make as much as possible of the interval that remained." He concludes that "our one chance lies in expanding the interval, in getting as many pulsations as possible into the given time." Wilde models Dorian Gray's recognition, as he is sitting for his portrait, and the direction that his life takes on Pater's rendition of Rousseau's life story, but Wilde's version is unremittingly dark by comparison with Pater's. Even the name "Dorian Gray" captures the darkening of what should be a bright beauty, since "Dorian" obviously suggests a Greek form, while "Gray" as a color stands in contrast to Apollonian brightness. In writing about the Renaissance, which involves centrally a revival of classical art and thinking, Pater aligns himself with a cultural heritage that includes the "Dorian," but not with tones of gray, understood as either neutral or dark. As Linda Dowling argues, because of the work of Karl Otfried Müller as transmitted by Benjamin Jowett at Oxford, in the latter part of the nineteenth century, the surname "Dorian" also carried suggestions of pederasty deriving from Greek culture.[15] "Dorian Gray" is oxymoronic in a Paterian context. "Gray" blunts the force and implications of "Dorian," and it does so without suggesting vividly a fruitful merger of opposites of the sort that we find in Joyce's revisionary evocation and extension of Pater at the conclusion of part four of *A Portrait of the Artist as a Young Man*. In that climactic portion of Joyce's narrative, whose title echoes the title and the tale of Wilde's book as "a portrait of the artist" (*Picture* 144), Stephen Dedalus, who like Dorian has a Greek name, sees a rim of the moon on the horizon as if stuck into the earth in a union of heaven and earth that is compared to a "silver hoop embedded in grey sand" (Joyce 173). The grayness of Dorian's story yields no such positive, generative mergers. Joyce's modernist mergings in *A Portrait* combine elements of a Paterian prose style with a myth about a creator and with realistic writing. Wilde's antecedent mergings in *The Picture* combine similar elements, though the myth concerns self-absorption, with the Gothic in a darkly modernist move away from aestheticism and late Romanticism, a move that echoes Pater but also exorcises him.

The echoing as exorcism proceeds through the combining of the light and the dark from Pater in a narrative of recognition and delusion structured around the myth of Narcissus. Rousseau's awakening through literature brings into the narrative an optimistic element from Pater's "Conclusion" that for Dorian is dark. The book that Harry gives him is poisonous. But the narrative is more the story of a painting than a book, though the book is important, as it is in both of Pater's long narratives, *Marius the Epicurean* (1885) and *Gaston de Latour* (1896).[16] When Lord Henry calls the portrait "the finest portrait of modern times" (166), the comparison to the Mona Lisa is inevitable. The work is a new Mona Lisa. The story of the picture's creation, however, fuses details from Pater's description of the Mona Lisa with Rousseau's moment of recognition that has become the experience of Narcissus recognizing his own beauty. Pater suggests that Mona Lisa's sitting for her portrait was possible only through an accompaniment: "by artificial means, the presence of mimes and flute-players, that subtle expression was protracted on the face" (*Renaissance* 79). As Lord Henry talks to Dorian, Hallward realizes that "a look had come into the lad's face that he had never seen there before" (159). Dorian compares the effect to that of music but realizes that it was created by words (160), as if a literary text were being performed. The recognition that this male version of Mona Lisa experiences is clearly that of Narcissus: "A look of joy came into his eyes, as if he had recognized himself for the first time. [...] The sense of his own beauty came on him like a revelation" (167). But the recognition is equally of something dark: "There was a look of fear in his eyes, such as people have when they are suddenly awakened" (162). Although that fear comes from Dorian's recognition of his mortality, for which Rousseau found compensation in words, it comes as well from recognizing something monstrously threatening. When Pater looks at the Mona Lisa, he sees not unalloyed beauty but "the unfathomable smile, always with a touch of something sinister in it, which plays over all Leonardo's work" (*Renaissance* 79). This is a beauty that the Greeks would "be troubled by," a "beauty into which the soul with all its maladies has passed." Finally, this is a beauty inseparable from monstrosity: "like the vampire, she has been dead many times, and learned the secrets of the grave" (80).

Late in the novel, Wilde reiterates the connection to the Mona Lisa as Pater presents the painting. Just after calling Dorian "Apollo," Lord Henry says to him that "it has all been to you no more than the sound of music"; he goes on that "[l]ife is a question of nerves, and fibres and slowly built-up cells" (383). As Pater says of Mona Lisa, her vampiric experience "has been to her but as the sound of lyres and flutes." In the same passage, he claims that "it is a beauty wrought out from within upon the flesh, the deposit, little cell by cell, of strange thoughts and fantastic reveries and exquisite passions"

(*Renaissance* 80). The darkness is already there, within the painting, waiting for the sitter, Narcissus-like, to behold, to fear, and to desire. Like Patrick Bateman, who videotapes some of his crimes in *American Psycho*, Dorian imagines that "there would be real pleasure in watching it" (259). Later, we hear more about Dorian's desires in passages that echo Pater on the Mona Lisa but with reversed valences. The vocabulary of "cell" and "thought" is still there, but ugliness has displaced beauty. We learn that a single "thought" "crept" from "cell to cell of his brain": "Ugliness that had once been hateful to him because it made things real, became dear to him now for that very reason. Ugliness was the one reality" (349). But Dorian is wrong. There are always two realities, and they are perpetually turning into each other.

The novel is replete with evocations of Narcissus, from Lord Henry's early statement to Basil (142) to Dorian's gazing in the final chapter into the "curiously carved mirror" (387), given to him by Lord Henry, just before he breaks it. In that last chapter, however, the mythic references undergo a metamorphosis when Dorian thinks of the mirror as a "polished shield" immediately prior to discarding it. He has earlier thought of the picture itself as a mirror or has compared himself in a mirror to his deformed image in the undead portrait. At the end of chapter 8, it is "the most magical of mirrors" (259) for observing secrets. Two chapters later, the double image of his laughing face in the mirror and "the evil and aging face" of the portrait pleases him: "The very sharpness of the contrast used to quicken his sense of pleasure" (282). In the ultimate chapter, Dorian is not pleased with the mirror or the painting. The myth of Echo and Narcissus has now merged with that of Medusa and Perseus, whose protection includes a polished shield. Dorian as Narcissus-become-Perseus is about to look at himself-as-Medusa without benefit of his shield and with a knife rather than a sword in hand. The introduction of Medusa here again takes up a prominent detail from Pater's writing and puts it to new use. In the Leonardo essay, Pater devotes an entire vivid paragraph to Leonardo's painting of *Medusa* rendered "as the head of a corpse" (*Renaissance* 68). The paragraph culminates the part of the essay in which Pater evokes the "interfusion of the extremes of beauty and terror" in "grotesques" (67). He says of the painting that "the fascination of corruption penetrates in every touch its exquisitely finished beauty" (68). In *Marius the Epicurean*, Pater uses the image again prominently three times. In the last, most memorable instance, in the closing of chapter 21, he merges Medusa implicitly with Narcissus: "Might this new vision, like the malignant beauty of pagan Medusa, be exclusive of any admiring gaze upon anything but itself?" (*Marius* 202).

Dorian is about to experience the effect of Medusa, which is himself, but, in fact, he has already had this experience. The morning after he murders Basil, while he waits impatiently for Alan Campbell to arrive, Dorian turns his eyes inward, where his "imagination, made grotesque by terror" has become merely a "puppet," the inanimate but dancing image of a person. Time dies and drags "a hideous future from its grave," which it shows to him: "He stared at it. Its very horror made him stone" (327). Like Pater's vampiric Mona Lisa, he has "learned the secrets of the grave" (*Renaissance* 80). Like Medusa, the terrifyingly attractive recognition of his mortality turns him to stone; it dehumanizes him by robbing him of his ordinary human passion. Long before the book's final chapter, Dorian has become undead, still living but not alive as a human being. When Dorian looks at the painting a final time after breaking the mirror, he understands that the Medusa-like truth about the painting is the truth about him. The enraged self-destruction that follows is the demise of Medusa were she able to look at her own poisonous self or, Perseus-like, to use a sharp weapon against herself. On the one hand, the ending restores order and sanity to the narrative by apparently re-establishing the difference between art and life, between the inanimate and the living, between the beautiful and the ugly. But within the seemingly restored realism, a myth darker than the story of Narcissus that involves a mirror has fused with the tale of Narcissus and taken up residence within the ostensible realism, from which it cannot be separated.

If the vampire can live within Mona Lisa, the death of Dorian Gray can be the death of Medusa. In addition to this odd ultimate brushstroke in the novel's mythic surface, which resists explanation, other details of the ending remain enigmatic. We still do not know where we stand in relation to the darkness and the light. There is no vanishing point and no orienting perspective. The beautiful creature became a destroyer who eventually destroyed himself. But how are we to understand and name the avenger's act of revenge against himself, a dark Narcissus's divorce from himself, a suicidal Medusa's look at herself that is also a suicidal Perseus's gazing at Medusa without a shield: as a fit of madness? as a mistake? as an action consciously intended? All we know is that art and life, the beautiful and the ugly, the light and the dark, those counterparts whose relations have been unstable throughout the narrative, have changed places once again. For readers, there is no more consolation, resolution, or explanation in the ending than Basil Hallward experiences when he gazes at "his own picture" and realizes that "It was from within, apparently, that the foulness and the horror had come" (316).

NOTES

I wish to thank Dora Goss of the Boston University Department of English for her detailed response to a late version of this essay.

1. "I am thirsty for thy beauty" (80; my translation). Salomé speaks these words to the severed head of John the Baptist near the end of the play just before Herod orders her to be killed. I cite from the French version of the play, originally published in Paris in 1893, as the only published version indisputably of Wilde's sole authorship. In *The Writings of Oscar Wilde*, Isobel Murray describes briefly the publication history of the play in her statement concerning the text that accompanies her reprinting of the English translation published in Wilde's lifetime (614).

2. Many critics who write about Wilde or Pater touch on the relation their works bear to each other. Critics who deal at some length with Wilde and Pater include Julia Prewitt Brown, Denis Donoghue, Richard Ellmann, and Christopher S. Nassaar. Nassaar maintains that Pater's "*The Renaissance* casts a long, sinister shadow across *Picture*, and the entire novel seems to be structured with Pater's book as its focal point" (39). The conclusion that Nassaar draws, however, that Wilde saw art's exploration of evil as somehow separable from life needs more defense than he provides. Brown and Donoghue focus on Wilde's significant swerves from Pater concerning art (Brown) or on the less-than-amicable turn in their relations (Donoghue). Brown cites *Oscar Wilde's Oxford Notebooks* (14–17) as providing "a succinct summary of the major differences between Wilde and Pater" (115n4). In the preface to her study of Wilde, Brown gives the following overview: "Walter Pater's place in the particular intellectual history already alluded to here is relatively minor, and [...] far less is said in the following pages about Pater's influence on Wilde than about Wilde's divergence from Pater. With attention to the philosophical significance of Wilde's career, this loosening of the long-established tie between Pater and Wilde constitutes the main revisionary thrust of this book" (xvii). See also Brown 3–4, 49, 59–60. In his main discussion of Wilde's relations with Pater in his biography of Pater, Donoghue maintains that "Pater never really liked Wilde" (81) and that "[t]he friendship [...] virtually came to an end in the winter of 1891" (83). I find the argument for significant, defining differences between Wilde and Pater convincing. I pursue some of the differences as they emerge in specific texts in the present essay and in my essay on *Salomé*.

3. Lord Henry investigates Dorian's family background in chapter 3 (175–77), where we learn that it includes passion and violence, as well as class antagonism and a disregard of conventional behavior. Dorian's mother married a subaltern without financial resources, obviously against her father's will. As a consequence, her father, Lord Kelso, arranged to have the subaltern killed in a duel. Dorian's decision to store the portrait in the room set up for him by his grandfather to keep him out of the way after his mother's death suggests that the portrait's meaning emerges in part from the family's history.

4. In section 3 of *A Philosophical Inquiry*, "Obscurity," Burke states: "To make any thing very terrible, obscurity seems in general to be necessary. When we know the full extent of any danger, when we can accustom our eyes to it, a great deal of the apprehension vanishes. Every one will be sensible of this, who considers how greatly night adds to our dread [...]" (54).

5. In the midst of reprinting Wilde's letters to editors responding to the antagonistic reviews of his novel, Rupert Hart-Davis includes a footnote that quotes the opening sentence of Pater's review as an example of "some of the most welcome praise," which "came later" (Wilde, *Letters* 270n1). Donald H. Eriksen refers to "Walter Pater's favorable review in the *Bookman*" (99). By contrast, Donoghue sees the praise in later portions of the review as Pater's being "generous" (85) after he had taken "the occasion to repudiate not only Lord Henry but his creator" (84).

6. Rupert Hart-Davis identifies and describes some of the negative reviews when he publishes Wilde's lengthy letters to the editors of the journals in *Letters* (257-72).

7. Ellmann points out that Wilde sent Pater a presentation copy of *Salomé* when it was published in French (374). But Denis Donoghue mentions that "[t]here is no evidence that Pater acknowledged the gift" (85).

8. Arnold expresses these sentiments in "On the Study of Celtic Literature" (291–386). In his use of the word "countrymen," Pater may well have been echoing Arnold's use of that word ("my own countrymen"; "Introduction" 391) to refer unambiguously to the English in his introduction to his study of Celtic literature (387–95).

9. See Chris Baldick's *In Frankenstein's Shadow* for a sketch of some of the book's significant doublings related to the one I provide but emphasizing monstrosity and the multiform character of identity rather than anti-realism and the implicating of the reader (148–152).

10. For studies of the ekphrastic tradition, see Krieger and Hollander.

11. Eliot uses the term in his review of Joyce's *Ulysses*, "Ulysses, Order, and Myth," originally published in *The Dial* (November, 1923).

12. The title of Pater's *Studies* later became *The Renaissance: Studies in Art and Poetry*. As is well known, Pater withdrew his "Conclusion" after the first edition but restored it in revised form for the third edition (1888) and subsequent editions. Donoghue describes the uproar over the "Conclusion" and the steps Pater took in response (48–67).

13. In the introduction to his study of Wilde, Peter Raby describes Wilde's habitual borrowings and the charge leveled against them (9).

14. In Book III of Ovid's *Metamorphoses*, we find: "uror amore mei: flammas moveoque feroque" ("I am inflamed with love for myself: the flames I both fan and bear"; 463) and "sic attenuatus amore / liquitur et tecto paulatim carpitur igni" ("thus ravaged by his love, he melts away, and gradually he is devoured by that buried fire"; 489–90). I am grateful to Melanie Benson of the Boston University Department of English for drawing my attention to the flame imagery in Ovid's presentation of Narcissus and for her translation of the relevant phrases.

15. See especially Dowling 124–125, but also 74 and 79, where she comments on the influence of Müller's *Die Dorier: Geschicten hellnischer Stämme und Städte*.

16. Isobel Murray points out the importance of books to Pater's protagonists in her introduction to Wilde's novel (ix).

WORKS CITED

Arnold, Matthew. *Lectures and Essays in Criticism. The Complete Prose Works of Matthew Arnold*. Vol. III. Ed. R.H. Super. Ann Arbor: U of Michigan P, 1962.

Baldick, Chris. *In Frankenstein's Shadow: Myth, Monstrosity, and Nineteeth-century Writing*. Oxford: Clarendon, 1987.

Brown, Julia Prewitt. *Cosmopolitan Criticism: Oscar Wilde's Philosophy of Art*. Charlottesville: UP of Virginia, 1997.

Burke, Edmund. *A Philosophical Inquiry into the Origin of Our Ideas of the Sublime and Beautiful*. 1759. Ed. Adam Phillips. Oxford: Oxford UP, 1990.

Conrad, Joseph. *Heart of Darkness*. 1902. New York: Norton, 1978.

———. *The Secret Sharer*. 1910. Ed. Daniel R. Schwarz. Boston: Bedford, 1997.

Donoghue, Denis. *Walter Pater: Lover of Strange Souls*. New York: Knopf, 1995.

Dowling, Linda. *Hellenism and Homosexuality in Victorian Oxford*. Ithaca: Cornell UP, 1994.

Eliot, T.S. "Ulysses, Order, and Myth." *James Joyce: Two Decades of Criticism*. Ed. Seon Givens. New York: Vanguard, 1963. 198–202.

Ellis, Bret Easton. *American Psycho: A Novel*. New York: Vintage, 1991.

Ellmann, Richard. *Oscar Wilde*. New York: Knopf, 1988.

Ericksen, Donald H. *Oscar Wilde*. Boston: Twayne, 1977.

Hardy, Thomas. *The Mayor of Casterbridge*. 1886. Ed. Dale Kramer. New York: Oxford UP, 1987.

Hollander, John. *The Gozer's Spirit: Poems Speaking to Silent Works of Art*. Chicago: U of Chicago P, 1995.

Joyce, James. *"A Portrait of the Artist as a Young Man"; Text, Criticism, and Notes*. Ed. Chester G. Anderson. New York: Viking, 1968.

Krieger, Murray. *Ekphrasis: The Illusion of the Natural Sign*. Baltimore: Johns Hopkins UP, 1992.

Murray, Isobel. "Introduction." *The Picture of Dorian Gray*. Ed. Isobel Murray. Oxford: Oxford UP, 1981. vii–xvi.

Nassaar, Christopher S. *Into the Demon Universe:A Literary Exploration of Oscar Wilde*. New Haven: Yale UP, 1974.

Ovid. *Metamorphoses. Liber 1–5. Ovid's Metamorphoses. Books 1–5*. Ed. William S. Anderson. Norman: U of Oklahoma P, 1997.

Pater,Walter. *Gaston de Latour: an unfinished romance*. Ed. Charles L. Shadwell. London: Macmillan, 1896.

———. *Marius the Epicurean, His Sensations and Ideas*. 1885. Ed. Ian Small. Oxford: Oxford UP, 1986.

———. "A Novel by Mr. Oscar Wilde." *Selected Writings of Walter Pater*. Ed. Harold Bloom. New York: Columbia UP, 1974.

———. *The Renaissance: Studies in Art and Poetry*. 1893. 4th ed. Ed. Adam Phillips. Oxford: Oxford UP, 1986.

Poe, Edgar Allan. *Selected Writings of Edgar Allan Poe*. Ed. Edward H. Davidson. Boston: Houghton Mifflin, 1956.

Raby, Peter. *Oscar Wilde*. Cambridge: Cambridge UP, 1988.

Riquelme, John Paul. "Shalom/Solomon/Salomé: Modernism and Wilde's Aesthetic Politics." *The Centennial Review* 39 (1995): 575–610.

Stevenson, Robert Louis. *The Strange Case of Dr Jekyll and Mr Hyde*. 1886. New York: Dell, 1966.

Stoker, Bram. *Dracula*. London: Archibald Constable, 1897.

Wilde, Oscar. *The Artist as Critic: Critical Writings of Oscar Wilde*. 1969. Ed. Richard Ellmann. Chicago: U of Chicago P, 1982.

———. *The Letters of Oscar Wilde*. Ed. Rupert Hart-Davis. New York: Harcourt, 1962.

———. *Oscar Wilde's Oxford Notebooks: A Portrait of a Mind in the Making*. Ed. Philip E. Smith and Michael S. Helfand. New York: Oxford UP, 1989.

———. *The Picture of Dorian Gray. The Portable Oscar Wilde*. 1946. Ed. Richard Aldington. New York: Viking, 1965.

———. *Salomé. A Florentine Tragedy. Vera. The First Collected Edition of the Works of Oscar Wilde*. 1908. Vol. I. Ed. Robert Ross. London: Dawsons of Pall Mall, 1969.

———. *The Writings of Oscar Wilde*. Ed. Isobel Murray. Oxford: Oxford UP, 1989.

JIL LARSON

Emotion, Gender, and Ethics in Fiction by Thomas Hardy and the New Woman Writers

> Flirtation, if it can be sustained, is a way of cultivating wishes, of playing for time. Deferral can make room.
>
> —Adam Phillips[1]

In the fiction published in the 1880s and 90s that focuses on the "New Woman" or late Victorian feminist, the break from traditional assumptions about women and ethics is sharp but not definitive. Likewise the rejection of conventional aesthetic choices often leads these writers not to narrative methods that are wholly innovative and successful but to strange experiments. In this transitional literature, written during a period of cultural upheaval, the exaggerated and the extravagant invade realism, as if to startle readers out of their complacency.[2] Formal innovations enable the exploration of a new sexual ethics. In keeping with Victorian novelistic tradition, the New Woman writers tell stories about love and marriage. But marriage is no longer the goal toward which everything inevitably tends; it is, instead, an object of the text's ethical scrutiny. As Teresa Mangum notes in her study of Sarah Grand and the New Woman novel, "Promoting the interests of women, these novels work to remake marriage, a framework shaping so many women's lives, into a fictional structure and an institution that would give women power, control, authority, security, respect, and, most significantly, agency."[3] As in other latecentury fiction, New Women writing

From *Ethics and Narrative in the English Novel, 1880–1914.* © 2001 by Jil Larson.

betrays an insecurity about choice and agency, provoked in this case by the political and social consequences of gender inequity.

The characters in New Woman novels are self-conscious about the awkwardness of rejecting old beliefs and values when the new ones are so inchoate. These are the conditions that make agency problematic. In the words of Waldo's Stranger in Olive Schreiner's *The Story of an African Farm* (1883), "To all who have been born in the old faith there comes a time of danger, when the old slips from us, and we have not yet planted our feet on the new" (135). Evadne, in Sarah Grand's *The Heavenly Twins* (1893), notes something similar when she observes to her husband that he is not to blame for ruining her life: "It is not our fault that we form the junction of the old abuses and the new modes of thought. Some two people must have met as we have for the benefit of others" (340). In her analysis of late Victorian feminism in the context of this mid-air, transitional historical moment, Sally Ledger points out that "the recurrent theme of the cultural politics of the *fin de siècle* was instability, and gender was arguably the most destabilizing category. It is no coincidence that the New Woman materialized alongside the decadent and the dandy. Whilst the New Woman was perceived as a direct threat to classic Victorian definitions of femininity, the decadent and the dandy undermined the Victorians' valorization of a robust, muscular brand of British masculinity deemed to be crucial to the maintenance of the British Empire."[4] Not only were gender categories destabilized at the end of the century, though; these new threats to stability were themselves elusive and complex, difficult to categorize. Both in fiction and in the periodical press, representations of the New Woman were multiple and contradictory. She was sometimes stereotyped as intellectual, masculine, and asexual, other times as sexually voracious and unable to control her emotions. She was aligned both with the free love movement and with the campaign for the reform of marriage laws, which was characterized by insistence upon monogamy within marriage for both men and women. Patricia Ingham offers one theory about why the varied representations of New Women in fiction reflect an inevitable reality: "All escapes or attempts to escape into unmapped territory are necessarily erratic; where there is no established route, self-assertion will be idiosyncratic."[5] The confusion within this effort to redefine gender and sexual morality reflects confusion and ideological fragmentation within cultural politics as a whole during this period; the periodical press lumped together the New Women, the decadents, and the socialists in the 1890s, but the challenges they posed were, as Ledger argues, "ultimately too fragmented to form a coherent ideological programme to that posed by the monolithic grand narrative of Victorianism" ("New

Woman and the Crisis of Victorianism" 41). Still, narrative efforts to tell new stories, to experiment, to slip from the hold of dominant cultural assumptions—even if only temporarily and imperfectly—enabled these *fin-de-siècle* writers the chance to cultivate wishes and play for time, to flirt with possibilities. And while that is very different from establishing a sound, ideologically coherent plan for change that would dovetail with other radical movements, it was what was possible at this point in history. Drawing on Foucault's idea of a reverse discourse, Ledger argues that the Victorian periodical press unwittingly opened a discursive space, through its attacks and ridicule, for voices in support of the New Woman and her claims.[6] If nothing else, this space for dialogue between dominant and suppressed discourses created room to maneuver and awareness, in the words of Grand's heroine, of one's position at the junction of old and new.

The painful struggle of Evadne and other characters in New Woman fiction reflects the challenge these authors faced when striving to write honestly about women's experience and to benefit those who would continue this endeavor in the future; such an endeavor, as Patricia Stubbs points out, entailed "a political as well as an aesthetic struggle ... The inoffensive heroine who could shock no one was a highly political creature, and only the most determined of writers were prepared to modify, let alone transform her."[7] If the transitional groping of the New Woman writing mars it aesthetically and dooms its heroines to frustration, thus weakening its political impact, the fiction nevertheless merits our attention for what it reveals about the ethical concerns of late Victorian feminism.

EMOTION, REASON, AND GENDER

New woman writing is an emotional literature that afforded its audience a fresh way of thinking about emotion. As Lyn Pykett emphasizes in her study of the sensation novel and New Woman fiction, "to some of its earliest readers and critics the New Woman writing simply was feeling; it was an hysterical literature, written (and read) on the nerves."[8] In addition to being emotionally charged, however, this fiction often takes emotion as its subject, investigating the interplay of feeling and reason in women's choices. As Pykett argues, many of these writers "simultaneously celebrate the feminine and/as feeling, and problematise the conventional association of woman with feeling" (174). In that sense, these writers not only represent a particular historical moment in the making of the modern identity (to adopt Charles Taylor's phrase), they also anticipate the concerns of twentieth-century feminists by exploring the relevance of gender to ideas about subjectivity and agency.

One influential tradition in philosophical thought views emotions as irrational, animal, and feminine. Designated unruly and disruptive of ethical deliberation, emotions must be controlled and educated by reason. Current work in philosophy and cognitive psychology, however, influenced by an Aristotelian philosophical tradition, suggests that far from being merely a hindrance to responsible thought and action, emotion plays an instrumental role in ethical decision-making.[9] The popularity of Daniel Goleman's recent book, *Emotional Intelligence*, results from the promise for social and ethical change inherent in a better understanding of the role emotions play in our lives. Goleman identifies "a pressing moral imperative" as his impetus for writing a book concerned to preserve "the goodness of our communal lives" from the selfishness and violence currently threatening it.[10] Emotional intelligence, as Goleman defines it, involves not only learning to manage feelings and control impulses, but also becoming aware of one's own emotions–especially as they relate to beliefs, judgments, and actions–and better attuned to the feelings of others. This new respect for the ethical value of emotion stems from greater understanding of the complex cognitive dimension of emotion than is possible if one adheres to the dualistic view that separates reason and feeling, associating the former with masculinity and power and the later with femininity and nurturance.

The Victorian ideology of separate spheres was, of course, predicated on this assumed difference between men and women. By calling attention to the ethical implications of this ideology, New Woman writing began to redefine the role of emotion in the lives of women while dramatizing in their fiction how gender socialization continued to thwart and isolate even the most rebellious and progressive of the new heroines. In a sense Carol Gilligan's work on women's moral development takes up the very questions that interested the New Woman writers: How differently do men and women define moral problems? Is there a new way to speak about ethics "in a different voice," one that accords as much importance to emotions, context, and relatedness as to individualistic rights? In an interdisciplinary forum on Gilligan's work published in *Signs* in 1986, many of the critics of *In a Different Voice* misunderstand the goal of the study, which is not to prove statistically that men and women are different, or to argue for the value of separate spheres. Rather, her work seeks to redefine morality so that women's experiences, which have shaped women's psychological development, are not ignored or devalued, as they were in studies by Lawrence Kohlberg, Erik Erikson, and others. The "voice" referred to in her title is "identified not by gender but by theme."[11] What she is furthering is a different model of ethical deliberation for men and women both, one that includes emotions, particularly those of empathy and compassion, instead of rejecting them as irrational.

Reading Thomas Hardy's late novels, especially *Tess of the d'Urbervilles* (1891) and *Jude the Obscure* (1895), in the context of the fiction of the New Woman has been an ongoing project of Victorianists at least since Penny Boumelha's 1982 study of sexual ideology in Hardy's novels. One of the most intriguing of the recent efforts to contextualize Hardy's fiction in this fashion occurs in John Kucich's 1994 book on Victorian ethics, *The Power of Lies*. Unlike Kucich and other literary critics who attribute the ethical contradictions of Hardy's novels to his gender and describe him as significantly less feminist than his female contemporaries, I argue that preconceptions about women, emotions, and ethics have kept too many critics from recognizing what Hardy has in common with such late-century women writers as Olive Schreiner and Sarah Grand.[12]

Kucich considers Hardy to be a detached aesthete who scapegoats women and who distances himself from emotion, sexual desire, and subjectivity, thereby safeguarding his own moral position. This reading betrays an assumption not shared by the narrators and implied authors of Hardy's novels–the belief that emotion and desire interfere with responsible ethical choice. As I interpret Hardy's fiction, one of its central ideas is that reason and emotion are not truly "separate spheres." Hardy rejects the totalizing, absolute nature of the Victorian doctrine of separate spheres, constructing instead a contextual ethics of particularity. Like Grand and Schreiner, he seeks to forge new definitions of what can constitute gender identity and sexual morality. In contrast to earlier Victorian novelists, these writers critique a sexual ideology that punishes women for acting on their emotions and desires. Admittedly, however, several features of New Woman writing tend to obscure this critique or even to render it self-doubting. For that reason it will be helpful to sort out the various strands of my argument about this complex body of *fin-de-siècle* literature.

First, this fiction often resists the separate spheres of belief that women are naturally associated with feeling and men are naturally associated with reason. These writers question such a stereotype. But they also seek to redeem the ethical and cognitive potential of emotion. They associate emotion with women but no longer diminish women's power by doing so. Second, because a woman's emotions can make her vulnerable, this fiction often contrasts women whose intellect and education arm them with direct methods of self-defense to women who rely more exclusively on emotions and desires that lead them to indirect forms of influence and manipulation. What this contrast obscures, however, is the role played by emotion in the intellectual development of these New Women, the degree to which feeling and reason are interrelated. Third, the fiction dramatizes a new kind of flirtation: unlike the traditional coquette, the late Victorian feminist flirts not only to attract attention and indulge her desires but also to experiment and learn. This is, admittedly, a controversial claim, and I realize that by making it I am aligning myself with contemporary critics of the New Woman who, through sexist misreading, diminished her by categorizing her as a mere flirt. What interests me, however, is the novelists' appropriation of flirtation for their new sexual ethics; by reinscribing this familiar, often frivolous activity as a trope for something more radical and significant, they seem to give readers what they expect only to disconcert them. Finally, the heroines rarely escape punishment or emotionally crushing defeat of some sort, though this could be said to be a mark of the honesty of the fiction, a clear-eyed acknowledgment of all that thwarted even the most progressive of late-century women.

I argue, then, that in its treatment of emotions and sexual relationships, Hardy's *Jude the Obscure* shares both the feminist concerns of the New Woman writing and its ethically complex treatment of emotion, reason, and gender. To test the validity of this argument, I offer a reading of Hardy's novel in the context of Olive Schreiner's "The Buddhist Priest's Wife" and *The Story of an African Farm* and Sarah Grand's *The Heavenly Twins*.

EMOTION AND ETHICAL CHOICE

"The Buddhist Priest's Wife" tells the story of a New Woman leaving for India who must say goodbye to the man she loves without letting him know that she loves him. Like *Jude the Obscure*, this story critiques the ideology of separate spheres and the double standard, even as it demonstrates that in their relationships with men women may appear powerful when they are actually at the mercy of inflexible patriarchal rules and ingrained assumptions about gender. The intellect seems more educable than the emotions and drives; hence, according to Schreiner's heroine, men and women are most alike intellectually. In keeping with separate-spheres imagery, the story's New Woman imagines circular disks representing the sexes. When it comes to their power to reason, men and women are equal, and that half of each disk is identical, a bright red. But the red shades into different colors, blue in one and green in the other, when it is a matter of the personal and sexual, areas in which men and women, according to the heroine, are most starkly different in their emotions and behavior. True to the values of most New Woman writing, influenced as it was by social Darwinism, the story attributes this difference to "nature":[13] "it's not the man's fault," says the heroine, "it's nature's."[14] But if the story accepts this as a reality, it also makes it seem cruel and unfair, for this difference empowers the man and strips the woman of agency. The fiction suggests that in sexual relationships a measure of power and influence is granted to the woman who ethically compromises herself through passive manipulation. Schreiner's heroine refuses to play this game:

> If a man loves a woman, he has a right to try to make her love him because he can do it openly, directly, without bending. There need be no subtlety, no indirectness. With a woman it's not so; she can take no love that is not laid openly, simply, at her feet. Nature ordains that she should never show what she feels; the woman who had told a man she loved him would have put between them a barrier once and for ever that could not be crossed; and if she subtly drew him towards her, using the woman's means—silence, finesse, the dropped handkerchief, the surprise visit, the gentle assertion she had not thought to see him when she had come a long way to meet him, then she would be damned; she would hold the love, but she would have desecrated it by subtlety; it would have no value. (92)

Schreiner reveals here how the New Woman differs from the traditional woman: she is ethically more scrupulous, but her capacity for love is at once her strength and her tragedy, for the depth of her thwarted emotional longing combined with her intelligence means that "in one way she was alone all her life" (84). Like other New Women, this heroine finds that she is unable to address both her intellectual and her emotional needs. Complexly interrelated as these needs are, Victorian culture nevertheless structures them as antithetical and mutually exclusive. As Laura Chrisman points out, the man in Schreiner's story is oblivious of the woman's love for him and "all of their intellectual discoursing on the nature of love develops this irony, together with the irony of the gap between intellectual and emotional expression."[15] In one sense, the story is about the paradox of this gap, which is unnecessary and hurtful to women and yet helpful as well, for the division of the intellectual from the affective provides Victorian women with a defensive strategy, a way to gain control over their emotions and the men who have the potential to agitate these emotions.[16]

Schreiner's heroine is too intelligent to blunder into the trap of simply acting like a man, directly expressing what she feels and wants and thereby alienating herself from the more conventional man she loves, but she is also too emotional, and too deeply in love, to rest content with being this man's friend. The story is dominated by its heroine's efforts to intellectualize and rationalize her pain, to control it through an ability to understand it. Clearly, her emotions and her attachment to a particular person have led her to her ideas about gender, sexuality, and ethics, though as she sees it, the intellectual life is apart from emotions; it allows a woman to "drop her shackles a little" (93). In that, it is like death. The story begins and ends with reference to the heroine's beauty in death. "Death means so much more to a woman than a man," she says; "when you knew you were dying, to look round on the world and feel the bond of sex that has broken and crushed you all your life gone, nothing but the human left, no woman any more ..." (93). Escaping the shackles of sex, whether through cogitation or through death, is but one aspiration of this New Woman.[17] An equally strong aspiration arises from her desire to be loved by the man who hurts her when he denies her sexuality, when he says, "You're the only woman with whom I never realise that she is a woman" (93). Given the norms of late Victorian society, once gender difference is overcome and a man recognizes the humanity of a woman, she no long represents romantic or sexual possibilities for him. The protagonist of "The Buddhist Priest's Wife" is thus caught in a double-bind: wanting this man's love but refusing the assumptions about gender differences that seem to make it possible.[18] The solution is to emigrate to India, to remove oneself from the culture responsible for this double-bind. As Chrisman remarks, there is a eugenicist twist implicit in the story's ending: "India serves Schreiner, arguably, as a repository for evolutionarily overdeveloped women, who are marked out as being unsuitable wifely and maternal material. Sexual and familial activity is to be denied them as a wastage of their resources; they can make the greatest social contribution through their intellect" ("Empire, 'Race', and Feminism" 58). But the ethical import of the story is conveyed through the woman's emotional pain, masked as it is by her intellectual defenses. The story encourages us to question why intellectual women could not also be loving wives and mothers; thus the story erects gendered antinomies only to deconstruct them.[19] Joyce Avrech Berkman has compared Schreiner to current poststructuralists in this regard, noting that "unlike present-day thinkers, who can marshal a plethora of twentieth-century scientific, historical, and philosophical evidence for their views on the cultural construction of gender, class, and race, Schreiner attacked widely held assumptions about human difference without such scholarly support."[20]

Like Schreiner's story, *Jude the Obscure* takes as its subject "the inseparability of emotional and intellectual aspiration,"[21] and again the characters muse on the possibility of friendship across gender lines: "If he could only get over the sense of her sex," Jude Fawley thinks about Sue Bridehead, "... what a comrade she would make."[22] But like the woman in Schreiner's story, he finds that his desire makes this impossible. In contrast to his uncomplicated physical attraction to Arabella, his feelings for Sue include both intellectual and emotional affinity. In part the connection he feels with Sue arises from their shared sensitivity, their emotional response to life, of which Hardy thoroughly approves despite the pain that accompanies their capacity for love, fellow-feeling, and empathy. Kucich claims that in Hardy's fiction desire and emotionalism, especially as they are associated with women, interfere with honesty (*Power of Lies* 228). The trouble with this argument is that it obscures Hardy's critique of the assumption that rationality, with its often inflexible regard for principle, is superior to emotion and awareness of multiple perspectives, including those shaped by the feelings that arise from particular attachments.[23]

The chapter of *Jude the Obscure* that is key to an understanding of this dimension of the novel's ethics is the one that focuses on Richard Phillotson's deliberations about Sue's request for a separation from him. Hardy's belief in the importance of emotion in ethical decision-making is particularly clear at this pivotal moment in the narrative. In conversation with Gillingham, Phillotson explains his decision to release his wife from her marriage vows so she can live with her lover. His friend attempts to reason with him, to talk him out of this unconventional decision, but Phillotson responds, "I am only a feeler, not a reasoner" (243). As the chapter makes clear, however, Phillotson is indeed reasoning, but his thinking is guided by emotion: by his love for Sue, by his empathetic responsiveness to her pain (which he metaphorically alludes to as her "cries for help" [241]), and by his intuitive recognition that she and Jude share an "extraordinary sympathy or similarity" (241).[24] "I simply am going to act by instinct, and let principles take care of themselves," Phillotson declares. The implied author leaves us in no doubt that this is a responsible, compassionate decision.

Kucich argues that "Hardy's women are regularly aligned with emotionalism, as opposed to the customary rationality of his men" (*Power of Lies* 228), but he begs the question by assuming that emotion is emotionalism and therefore suspect, and also by opposing feeling and reason, which, as in this chapter of the novel, are only apparent opposites. Moreover, Hardy's novel subverts the separate spheres of ideology by creating men, such as Jude and Phillotson, who are as tender-hearted and emotional as the female characters, and women who are intellectuals. Kucich is right that Sue loses her capacity for moral reasoning by the end of the novel, as Tess does by the end of *Tess of the d'Urbervilles*, while the male characters gain philosophical wisdom (230), but it is too often overlooked that Sue, the novel's New Woman, educates both Jude and Phillotson through her intellectual superiority. Jude describes her as "a woman whose intellect was to mine like a star to a benzoline lamp" (422). Phillotson admits that "her intellect sparkles like diamonds, while [his] smoulders like brown paper" (241). And when he comes up with the radical idea that a woman and her children could very well be a family without a man, he realizes that he has "out-Sued Sue" in his thinking (243). As John Goode comments about Sue, comparing her to Jude, "she does not seek the City of Light—she has it already" (*Thomas Hardy* 158). Unfortunately, her intellectual superiority, like that of the heroines of Grand and Schreiner, creates emotionally traumatizing problems for her, even as it illuminates the minds of those who come to know her.

A traditional role for women is to influence men, and in that sense Sue is not unlike other Victorian heroines. Where she differs from them, however, is that her moral influence is not only as intellectual as it is emotional: it is thoroughly unconventional. Her collapse at the end of the novel into guilt-ridden hysteria is a symptom of her emotional susceptibility. Ironically, though, it is this very susceptibility that has made her such a sensitive teacher of radical ideas. After this breakdown, she unsuccessfully attempts to reverse the ethical education she has provided for Phillotson and Jude. Only as a force of conventional influence is Sue ineffectual. Through his heroine, Hardy subverts the paradigm of traditional feminine influence, but influence remains important to the ethics of the novel. When Sue tries to persuade Phillotson to release her from the marriage bond, for example, she seeks to influence him, as she has been influenced, by John Stuart Mill's ideas about liberty. Mill himself was saved by influence, as he describes in his *Autobiography*: following a nervous breakdown, he found medicine in Wordsworth's poems because they expressed "thought coloured by feeling" (104) and helped him restore balance to his overly analytic mind, a product of his Utilitarian education. Sue's breakdown represents a different kind of imbalance: thought distorted by feeling. Prior to this crisis, though, Sue is not at all the cold and unsympathetic character that some readers perceive her to be. Her ideas are imbued with emotion and therefore potently influential. Ingham emphasizes the "fruitful ambiguity" in Hardy's language and characterization in this novel, which she considers his most feminist; what she refers to as the "kaleidoscope of critical Sue (mis)construing" (*Thomas Hardy* 78) is symptomatic of readers still caught in categorical thinking about gender, not open to the ambiguity of this kind of emotional–intellectual influence.

If Sue is "a harp which the least wind of emotion from another's heart could make to vibrate as readily as a radical stir in her own" (*Jude the Obscure* 293), if, in other words, she is as susceptible to the emotions of others as they are to her ideas, then she is inconstant, as Kucich points out. But Hardy's novel stresses that constancy is an unrealistic ideal for sexual relationships, and sexuality is a strong component in the complex of forces that doom the relationship of Jude and Sue. The empathy that moves Sue to shed tears at the sight of Father Time's tears is what makes her a sympathetic character (lovingkindness, in Hardy, often counter-balances the misery associated with erotic attraction), despite the cruelty that results from her vacillations in her relationships with men. Similarly, her reasons for withholding in sexual relationships are contradictory and often difficult to understand, but as Ingham points out, Sue's strength and integrity are evident in her ability to claim "her right to say no whatever the reason" (*Thomas Hardy* 76). Although it is difficult to generalize about New Women, the heroines I focus on in the fiction of Schreiner, Grand, and Hardy all attempt to overcome their lack of agency, often at great risk to themselves and those they love. These attempts result only in imperfect success and ultimate failure, largely because gendered paradigms, even by the end of the nineteenth century, were extremely difficult to resist, but also because Victorian culture did nothing to encourage the blending and balancing of emotion and intellect so essential to a responsible ethical life for women and men, especially in romantic relationships and marriage.

FLIRTATION

Emotion in the fiction of Schreiner and Hardy is indeed associated with women, but it is a vital component of their intellectual and ethical lives. *Jude the Obscure* develops another theme prominent in the fiction of late-century women writers: the idea that the New Woman's intellect becomes a weapon she turns against men as a means of defending herself against patriarchal injustice and freeing herself from constraints. In her relationships this exercise of power leads the New Woman to become what Hardy calls "an epicure in emotions" (180), usually with cruel consequences for the man or men in love with her.

Sarah Grand's *The Heavenly Twins*, like "The Buddhist Priest's Wife" and *Jude*, poses the question of what it would be like for a woman to be in a relationship with a man without the complications of gender and sexuality. Grand's Angelica Hamilton-Wells employs her cleverness as a child to secure rights equal to those of her twin brother. She grows up well-educated but restless, without intellectual challenges. Like Sue's feeling that Jude is her counterpart and Lyndall's bond with Waldo in *The Story of an African Farm*, Angelica's twinship with a boy is key to her understanding of gendered identity.[25] As Teresa Mangum notes in her discussion of the novel, "Angelica ... possesses potential for resistance because she has experienced the formation of gender and the systematic devaluing of women it enforces firsthand as an opposite sex twin" (*Married, Middlebrow, and Militant* 134). When the newly arrived choir tenor falls in love with her at first sight, she disguises herself as her brother and develops a close friendship with him. Later she is unable to account for her behavior, though she admits to her desire for excitement and her rebellion against those who would domesticate her. Cross-dressing allows her a luxurious physical freedom; it also enables a rare sort of intellectual liberty.[26] She says to the tenor, "I have enjoyed the benefit of free intercourse with your masculine mind undiluted by your masculine prejudices and proclivities with regard to my sex."[27] The consequences for her are therefore positive, despite the guilt she suffers after her exposure. For the tenor, however, the prank has psychologically painful repercussions, and his experience with Angelica eventually leads to his death.

Lyndall, the New Woman in *The Story of an African Farm*, shares Angelica's yearning for more possibilities than life offers a woman. Lyndall's mind and imagination help her satisfy this emotional hunger. Instead of literal role-playing, she mentally multiplies herself by participating in forms of life completely unlike her own—transcending time, gender, and race, imagining herself a medieval monk, a Kaffir witch-doctor, and a variety of other selves. "I like to see it all; I feel it run through me—that life belongs to me; it makes my little life larger; it breaks down the narrow walls that shut me in" (182). As both Lyn Pykett and Ann Ardis have noted, this disruption of stable feminine identity occurs in much of the New Woman writing and is often reinforced by its unconventional narrative strategies.[28] Although selflessness was expected of the traditional Victorian woman, the late-century New Woman paradoxically seeks to escape self through intellectual and emotional experiments in self-actualization, even when these experiments are hurtful to others.

Lyndall's restlessness is evident as well in her relationship with the man she loves. She explains her feelings for him by stressing his strength and power, even as she exerts her own power by refusing to marry him, though she is pregnant with his child, and by confessing that she became involved with him because "I like to experience, I like to try" (206). This adventurousness, which is at once calculating and emotionally self-indulgent, is what leads her to describe herself as having no conscience (176), certainly an unfair self-assessment, though it is true that she hurts those close to her through her unconventional choices. She has enough of a conscience to wish she were a better person, to prefer being good to being loved (201). Schreiner encourages us to recognize Lyndall's burden of guilt but also to question where the New Woman's responsibility begins and ends in a patriarchal society that so circumscribes women's freedom.

In her relationship with Jude, Sue is very much like Angelica and Lyndall because she too feels emotional restlessness followed by compunction. Like these other New Women, Sue is "venture-some with men" (182). She enjoys tormenting Jude by having him walk down the aisle with her as practice for her marriage to Phillotson. She explains that she likes to do interesting things that "have probably never been done before" (180). But her pleasure evaporates when she realizes that her "curiosity to hunt up a new sensation" causes Jude pain (180). Living with an openness to possibility, Sue also strives to be responsible and compassionate. The novel shows us how difficult it is for her to balance concern for her own needs with her desire to avoid hurting others. The ethical problems in her life exercise her emotional intelligence, particularly within late Victorian culture with its confusing mixture of old and new expectations for women.

All three of the women in these novels evade commitment and seek to gain emotional satisfaction from their relationships with men in daring, unpredictable, intellectually self-conscious ways. Their behavior is understandable but also sadistically flirtatious.[29] The novels waver between evoking admiration for these New Women, and the new ethics of possibility that they bring to their relationships, and judging them for turning their backs on a traditionally feminine ethics of care. In her study of Sarah Grand, Teresa Mangum deplores "the critic's power of erasure" when quoting Hugh Stutfield, a literary critic for *Blackwood's Magazine*, who patronizes Grand's characters in particular and the New Woman in general. But there is nothing inaccurate in Stutfield's observations of the complex, flirtatious character of this new brand of literary heroine:

> The glory of the women of to-day as portrayed in the sex-problem literature is her "complicatedness." To be subtle, inscrutable, complex–irrational possibly, but at any rate incomprehensible—to puzzle the adoring male, to make him scratch his head in vexation and wonderment as to what on earth she will be up to next,—this is the ambition of the latter-day heroine, (quoted in Mangum, *Married, Middlebrow, and Militant* 32)

Although I agree with Mangum about the sexist tone of this commentary, I am not convinced that Stutfield's reading of "the political struggles of the New Woman as a new and fairly trans-parent form of flirtation" is "a distinctly sexist misreading" (32). The flirtation in these novels is fascinating because it serves the political aims of these late-century women, even if only in a compromised way. Far from being the agents of purposeful change that Mangum's interpretation makes them, Grand's heroines, like Schreiner's and Hardy's, are indeed the "victims of restless dis-satisfaction" of Stutfield's description, though they are not merely that. Their restlessness and experiments with new forms of flirtation prompt their agency, which is exploratory and performative rather than purposeful. They alternate between being victims and agents.[30] This instability is a mark both of their complexity and of their *fin-de-siècle* predicament.

This fiction encourages us to view flirtation, traditionally thought of as ethically suspect (perhaps especially by feminists), in a new light. In the New Woman novels I consider here, flirtation coincides with the heroines' moments of advantage, power, and self-fashioning, while the foreclosure of possibility that puts an end to their intellectual and emotional playfulness and unpredictability coincides with cultural containment and loss of even limited agency. Writing about flirtation, Adam Phillips asks, "what does commitment leave out of the picture that we might want? If our descriptions of sexuality are tyrannized by various stories of committed purpose—sex as reproduction, sex as heterosexual intercourse, sex as intimacy—flirtation puts in disarray our sense of an ending. In flirtation you never know whether the beginning of a story—the story of the relationship—will be the end; flirtation, that is to say, exploits the idea of surprise" (*On Flirtation* xviii–xix). Surprise is sprung on the man by the woman in each of these novels: Angelica surprises the tenor when he realizes that she is a woman, not an enchanting boy. By refusing to marry or to make a commitment, Lyndall surprises the father of her baby, who, she realizes, will continue to love her as long as she resists his mastery. And Sue surprises the men in her life at every turn: by marrying Phillotson as a way of getting back at Jude for concealing his own marriage, by refusing to sleep with Jude even after leaving her husband for him, by returning to Phillotson as a penance after the death of her children. In each novel, the story of the relationship is shaped not by the man's choice, but by the woman's restless discontent and unwillingness to be the traditional heroine in such a story.

Although the men are hurt by this new kind of flirtation that takes away their power, the novels also encourage us to recognize the positive ethical consequences of a "flirtation that puts in disarray our sense of an ending."

Temporarily, all three heroines win for themselves a better kind of love and relationship by avoiding commitment and imagining and enacting their own agency. The sexual equality, friendship, and freedom that they achieve in their relationships with the men they love is short-lived and contingent on material conditions and circumstances beyond their control. But this new kind of romantic relationship energizes potential, even if it is potential that never fully blooms. Thus in New Woman fiction, flirtation, a stage of courtship that the respectable, modest Victorian woman was advised to disdain, ironically enough plays a critical role in the development of a more feminist sexual ethics.

OUR SENSE OF AN ENDING

If these experimentally flirtatious women characters "put in disarray our sense of an ending," their stories and the norms of late Victorian culture eventually manage to contain them. The emotion that has informed the thinking of these women does indeed become debilitating in the end, though it is important to see that, depressing as it is, the punishing plot reveals not the authors' beliefs about what the New Woman's fate should be, but his or her recognition of what it most often was.

Both *The Story of an African Farm* and *Jude the Obscure* counter-point the New Woman character with a traditional woman, Em and Arabella respectively, and in both novels the conventional, respect-able woman thrives while Lyndall and Sue suffer, one literally dying and the other metaphorically dying through self-sacrifice. *The Heavenly Twins* also focuses primarily on two women, though as Kucich points out, the counternarratives of Angelica and Evadne are self-canceling (*The Power of Lies* 252). They reveal Grand to be more conservative than Schreiner or Hardy because not only are both of her heroines punished and subdued by social strictures, both are redeemed by the superior wisdom of men. The resolutions of their stories underscore the novel's emphasis on the interdependence of women's and men's ethics. As Evadne points out in her criticism of gendered moral education, "So long as men believe that women will forgive anything they will do anything" (92). Once women's morality changes, men's will too.[31] This point is not canceled when it is reversed: with their greater power and education, men can do much to help women socially, intellectually, and ethically. But what is disturbing about Grand's conclusion is that both Angelica and Evadne cling pathetically to their male rescuers—in contrast to Sue and Lyndall who make choices that defy the men they love.

The Heavenly Twins begins with a portrait of Evadne as a reader and thinker but also a loving, warm-hearted person, who fears that her unusualness as an intellectual woman will have painful emotional consequences: "I don't want to despise my fellow-creatures. I would rather share their ignorance and conceit and be sociable than find myself isolated even by a very real superiority" (37). Mangum points up the irony: "For the intellectual woman success can only be failure" (*Married, Middlebrow, and Militant* 107). Like the heroine of "The Buddhist Priest's Wife," Evadne finds that for much of her life her fate is to be alone, stranded because of her difference and her principled stands, including her refusal to consummate her marriage to her syphilitic husband, with whom she nevertheless lives because of her father's skill at exploiting her emotionally.[32] Once she promises her husband not to involve herself publicly in intellectual or political work, Evadne is left with no outlet for the tremendous energies apparent from the novel's opening study of her mind and character. By the end of *The Heavenly Twins*, the early focus on Evadne's reading has given way to Dr. Galbraith's narration—his reading of her life as a broken spirit, a woman who has collapsed into hysteria.[33] Her state is very much like that of Sue Bridehead's at the end of *Jude the Obscure*. Sue becomes "creed drunk," as Jude describes her, clinging not to a man but to the religious and moral orthodoxies she had rejected all her life. Schreiner's heroine similarly turns against herself. After having lost her baby as Sue loses hers, Lyndall struggles with a wasting illness and judges herself "weak" and "selfish" (247); the "old clear intellect" (252) resurfaces moments before her death, but her final psychological state, like that of the other New Women in this fiction, is marked by desperate yearning.[34] Countering the stereotype of the New Woman as merely an "intellectualized, emancipated bundle of nerves" (Hardy's Preface to the First Edition of *Jude*, xxxviii), Grand, Hardy, and Schreiner all depict the late Victorian feminist as someone who feels as deeply as she thinks and, in fact, suffers not from mere high-strung nervousness but from unresolvable moral dilemmas created by gendered cultural politics and an uneasy transition between old and new definitions of friendship, love, and marriage.[35]

The cultural containment of these women that occurs at the end of each novel reestablishes separate spheres ideology by associating women with emotion that overwhelms reason. As we have seen, however, the novels attempt to counter this stereotype while also acknowledging its destructive power. Schreiner, Grand, and Hardy delineate a subtle, complex, and ethically promising relationship between emotion and reason in the lives of these early feminists only to expose all that militates against this new sense of self: social ostracism with its attendant guilt and isolation, the fear of causing pain to loved ones, and perhaps above all the internalized social norm of the woman as emotional and therefore not capable of reason–or if intellectual then not truly feminine.

Hardy deplored what he described as the cosmic joke that emotions were allowed to develop in a such a defective world, and yet he recognized the ethical force of emotion. Too often critics who stress Hardy's difference from the New Women writers slip into a twentieth-century version of separate spheres thinking, characterizing Hardy as on the side of reason, wary of the feminine and the emotional, even though there is little in his novels to support such an interpretation. Like Olive Schreiner and Sarah Grand, Hardy encouraged his readers to rethink conventional ideas about women and feeling, as difficult as that was during an age just beginning to understand women's aspirations without fathoming how they could be realized.

NOTES

1. Adam Phillips, *On Flirtation* (Cambridge, MA: Harvard University Press, 1994), xix.

2. As John Goode notes in his reading of Hardy's New Woman novel, *Jude the Obscure*, in *Thomas Hardy: The Offensive Truth* (Oxford: Blackwell, 1988), "again and again the novel breaks out of its frame" (139), deploying strategies of illusion-breaking to create something new that will shake up readers lulled by realism and an attendant acceptance of the status quo. Lloyd Fernando, in his *"New Women" in the Late Victorian Novel* (University Park, PA: Pennsylvania State University Press, 1977), remarks that "rarely in the history of the English novel had opinions and attitudes rendered such service in lieu of art on behalf of a contemporary movement" (133), dismissing the ethical content of New Woman novels as "opinions and attitudes" detrimental to the aesthetic quality of the majority of this late-century fiction, though important for its influence on George Gissing and Hardy. Fernando, like many of the contemporary critics of these novels, seems to miss the point of the New Woman writers' need to refuse old forms, true as it may be that this need did not always result in a pleasing aesthetic experience for readers. For an excellent discussion of the complex question of the political effectiveness of antinarrative strategies in Olive Schreiner's work and, more generally, that of women and minority cultures, see Janet Galligani Casey's "Power, Agency, Desire: Olive Schreiner and the Pre-Modern Narrative Moment," *Narrative* 4.2 (May 1996): 124–41.

3. Teresa Mangum, *Married, Middlebrow, and Militant: Sarah Grand and the New Woman Novel* (Ann Arbor, MI: University of Michigan Press, 1998), 16.

4. Sally Ledger, "The New Woman and the Crisis of Victorianism," in Ledger and McCracken, eds., *Cultural Politics*, 22.

5. Patricia Ingham, *Thomas Hardy* (Atlantic Highlands, NJ: Humanities Press International, 1990), 90.

6. Sally Ledger, *The New Woman: Fiction and Feminism at the Fin de Siècle* (Manchester: Manchester University Press, 1997), 9. Ledger points out, however, that for

New Woman writers the language of the marginal and the discourse of dominant ideology were equally compromised and problematic ("The New Woman" 34). Janet Galligani Casey also stresses the problems for late Victorian feminists of "attempting to articulate one's liminal status through genres that will at once remain faithful to that liminality and yet project it within the dominant culture" ("Power, Agency, Desire" 131).

7. Patricia Stubbs, *Women and Fiction: Feminism and the Novel, 1880–1920* (Sussex: Harvester, 1979), 25.

8. Lyn Pykett, *The 'Improper' Feminine: The Women's Sensation Novel and the New Woman Writing* (London and New York: Routledge, 1992), 169.

9. For an instructive description of these traditions and their arguments see chapter 3, "Rational Emotions," of Martha C. Nussbaum, *Poetic Justice: The Literary Imagination and Public Life* (Boston: Beacon, 1995), 53–78.

10. Daniel Goleman, *Emotional Intelligence* (New York: Bantam, 1995), xii.

11. "Forum on *In a Different Voice,*" *Signs* 11.2 (1986), 327.

12. Gail Cunningham's discussion of Hardy in the context of New Woman writing is representative of the many critics who describe Hardy's approach as something other than feminist: "The areas of interest which led his novels to converge on the New Woman fiction were sexual morality in general, and a pervading cynicism about marriage. Neither of these need necessarily imply a specifically feminist approach: indeed in many of his novels Hardy's view of women, and his ideas about sex and marriage, seem to pull him uncomfortably in different directions" (Cunningham, *The New Woman and the Victorian Novel* [New York: Harper and Row, 1978], 81). I wonder, though, if Hardy himself is "uncomfortably" ambivalent, or if some readers are made uncomfortable by the challenge his heroines—especially Sue Bridehead—present to their assumptions about women and feminism.

13. Like other New Women writers, Schreiner was influenced by the evolutionary theories of Herbert Spencer and Charles Darwin, and after an early crisis of religious faith embraced science, sometimes with ethically troubling implications, as Sally Ledger demonstrates in her analysis of Schreiner's "deployment of eugenic theory in the name of feminism" (*New Woman: Fiction and Feminism* 73). Charles Taylor offers a trenchant discussion of scientism as a constituent of modern culture, emphasizing that it signals not a loss of faith or a sharp break with mid-Victorian Christianity—for scientism "itself requires a leap of faith"—so much as "a new militant moral outlook growing out of the old and taking its place beside it as a fighting alternative" (*Source of the Self* 404).

14. Olive Schreiner, "The Buddhist Priest's Wife," in *Daughters of Decadence: Women Writers of the Fin de Siècle*, ed. Elaine Showalter (New Brunswick, NJ: Rutgers University Press, 1993), 92.

15. Laura Chrisman, "Empire, 'Race,' and Feminism at the Fin-de-Siècle: The Work of George Egerton and Olive Schreiner," in Ledger and McCracken, eds., *Cultural Politics*, 57.

16. Janet Galligani Casey focuses on similar strategies in Schreiner's unfinished novel, *From Man to Man*. For Rebekah, the heroine of this novel, intellectual pursuits (and writing in particular) afford an eroticized, highly private refuge. Writing diary entries and letters, full of polemics and philosophical ruminations as well as highly emotional expressions of love for her husband, who is unfaithful to her, is for the heroine "an act that comes to embody all of the emotional and sexual energy that is thwarted in her daily existence" ("Power, Agency, Desire" 136). Casey's point is that this private writing distracts

Rebekah from public writing, which is true, but it is also interesting to note how the personal, traditionally feminine and emotional genres of letter and diary are intellectualized and made strange, fascinating, even erotically compelling, in late Victorian feminist writing.

17. Victorian women poets similarly sought comfort and a sense of agency and control in intellectual detachment and in imagining their own deaths. In several of her lyric poems, Christina Rossetti's speaker, for instance, assures her beloved from beyond the grave that it is now a matter of indifference to her if he remembers or forgets her. Similarly, Charlotte Mew seeks what she call the "inhuman thing" (quoted in Angela Leighton, *Victorian Women Poets: Writing Against the Heart* [Charlottesville and London: University Press of Virginia, 1992], 287), the white space of "vision and desolation ... which turns experience into art" (Leighton, *Victorian Women* 287), not only as a retreat from relationships and the pain of emotional entanglement and rejection in a patriarchal society, but also as a position of power and invulnerability. In the words of Angela Leighton, who beautifully draws out this dimension of both poets' work, "to miss life itself is to gain, in its place, the free time of the dream" (163). Even though the New Woman writers turned more openly and defiantly against Victorian patriarchy, these strategies of "free time," imagination, play, flirtation, and indirection are clearly evident in the lives of all of the late-century heroines I consider.

18. I agree with Laura Chrisman's assessment of the depressing dead end of this story and of the "essentially monologic and isolationist perspective" of Schreiner's stories in general, despite their experimental combining of realism and symbolism and their dialogues between men and women. As Chrisman notes, "the speech patterns expose the impossibility of social communication and an integrated feminist identity and collectivity" ("Empire, 'Race,' and Feminism" 47).

19. In her discussion of Schreiner's *Woman and Labour,* Ledger points out that Schreiner attempted to bring her eugenicist thinking in line with her feminism: "The evolutionary arrest of woman, the denial of intellectual activity and traditionally 'masculine' pursuits, would sound a death knell for human evolution. As mothers of the human race, the evolutionary development–bodily and intellectual–of women was, for Schreiner, crucial" (*New Woman: Fiction and Feminism* 24).

20 Joyce Avrech Berkman, *The Healing Imagination of Olive Schreiner: Beyond South African Colonialism* (Amherst, MA: University of Massachusetts Press, 1989), 231.

21. Laura Green, "'Strange [In]difference of Sex': Thomas Hardy, the Victorian Man of Letters, and the Temptations of Androgyny," *Victorian Studies* 38.4 (Summer 1995), 544.

22. Thomas Hardy, *Jude the Obscure* (New York: Oxford University Press, 1987), 159.

23. Sheila Berger stresses Hardy's "antagonism toward consistency and rationality" in her reading of the novelist's reflections on his aesthetic values. For example, Hardy "appreciates drama in literature because it 'appeal[s] to the emotional reason rather than to the logical reason; for by their emotions men are acted upon, and act upon others'" (Berger, *Thomas Hardy and Visual Structures: Framing, Disruption, Process* [New York and London: New York University Press, 1990], 4).

24. In her *Thomas Hardy and Women: Sexual Ideology and Narrative Form* (Sussex: Harvester, 1982), Penny Boumelha observes that the similarity of Jude and Sue marks a change in Hardy's fiction: "There is no sense that Jude and Sue inhabit different

ideological structures as there is in the cases of Clym and Eustacia, or even Angel and Tess"
(141). Green also identifies this similarity between its male and female protagonists as one
of the features of *Jude* that make it the most radical of Hardy's novels ("Strange
[In]difference" 527).

25. A fascinating dimension of all of the New Woman novels I consider is the
characterization of the New Man. Angelica's twin Diavolo (like everything else about
them, their names are, ironically, more fitting if reversed) supports his sister's feminism
and cross-dresses himself even as he takes his own privileges for granted. Jude and Waldo
are tender-hearted men who hate injustice of any sort and are thus sympathetic to the
cause of the women they love. But Jude occasionally utters essentialist, limiting ideas about
women (which critics wrongly confound with Hardy's own ideas), and Waldo is dreamy
and often merely bewildered by Lyndall's political ideas. Most importantly, the men in the
novels demonstrate the tragic reality that cross-gender friendships were not viable in late
Victorian culture. Ledger writes of Waldo and Lyndall, "theirs is a powerful brother/sister
type of relationship, an emotional and intellectual bond which, like Sue Bridehead and
Jude Fawley's, is shown not to be possible in the world represented by the novel's
discourses" (*New Woman: Fiction and Feminism* 83). And I think Mangum is right to
question whether Angelica's desire for friendship between men and women "on terms
unimaginable to the Victorians" would be perceived as any more realizable now than it was
then (*Married, Middlebrow, and Militant* 136).

26. Sue similarly experiments with cross-dressing when she is compelled to wear
Jude's clothes after a act of rebellion results in a drenching of her own. As Goode points
out in his comparison of Sue and Angelica, "Sue gets caught between image and utterance.
It is the requirement of clothes and image that she leaps out of" (*Thomas Hardy* 158).
Goode's excellent chapter on *Jude* in his book on Hardy intricately traces Sue's more
complex efforts to leap into a voice; like other critics describing the tension between old
and new in the New Woman fiction, Goode notes that "the heterodox voice is the voice
of the future tied dependently into the discourse of the present" (170).

27. Sarah Grand, *The Heavenly Twins* (Ann Arbor, MI: University of Michigan
Press, 1992), 458.

28. Pykett makes this point in her discussion of George Egerton's fiction (*The
'Improper' Feminine* 173). Ardis observes, more generally, that in New Woman writing
heterogeneity has replaced "the humanistic model of integrated selfhood or 'character.' A
monolithic model of New Womanliness [is] not … substituted for the old model of the
'pure woman'" (*New Women* 113–14).

29. Green makes the intriguing point that "linguistic pedantry occurs with
remarkable frequency in moments of flirtation or jockeying for position between male and
female characters" ("Strange [In]difference" 536). In Schreiner's novel, too, flirtation is as
intellectual as it is emotional—and distinctively different from the flirtation of the mid-
Victorian coquette. Lyndall's lover says to her, "I like you when you grow metaphysical and
analytical," and she thinks, "he was trying to turn her own weapons against her" (204).

30. See Scott McCracken, "Stages of Sand and Blood: The Performance of
Gendered Subjectivity in Olive Schreiner's Colonial Allegories," in Alice Jenkins and Juliet
John, eds., *Rereading Victorian Fiction* (London: Macmillan, 2000), 145–56, for an
intriguing argument about New Woman identities as performances self-consciously
played out within a context (or on a stage) of material conditions that limited agency.

31. George Bernard Shaw praised Grand for demanding that "the man shall come

to the woman exactly as moral as he insists that she shall come to him" (Mangum, *Married, Middlebrow, and Militant* 89).

32. A.R. Cunningham identifies two main types of New Women heroines: the "bachelor girl," a designation appropriate for Sue, Lyndall, and Angelica, since this type was thoroughly unconventional in her thinking; and the New Woman of the "purity school," a designation that fits Evadne since she is unusually intelligent but not willing to abandon traditional Victorian moral values and ideals. See A.R. Cunningham, "The 'New Woman Fiction' of the 1890s," *Victorian Studies* 17 (1973): 176–86.

33. Even as a reader, Evadne, like Jude, is an autodidact for whom "the reading experience is structured as an alternative to education rather than a means to education" (Mangum, *Married, Middlebrow, and Militant* 103). Goode's point that *Jude* raises the question of education as a leading out and an admission of the obscure to "the garden of bourgeois order" (*Thomas Hardy* 103) is equally relevant to Evadne, whose difficulty acquiring books and isolation in reading them reveal the constraints on her agency, even as her bold, feminist notes on her reading—like Jude's enthusiasm and freshness of perspective as a young scholar—underscore the advantage of exclusion from the bourgeois order. Unfortunately, the trajectory of both characters as readers is far from hopeful. Evadne, for instance, goes from an active, curious critical thinker, to a woman who reads to escape, to a nonreader whose life is a casebook read by Dr. Galbraith.

34. See Mangum, *Married, Middlebrow, and Militant* 30–35, for an account of how contemporary psychological theories were deployed to silence New Woman characters and their creators.

35. It would be instructive to compare the dramatic psychological breakdowns of these New Women to the emotional collapse suffered by heroines of earlier Victorian novels, such as Gwendolen Harleth in George Eliot's *Daniel Deronda* (New York: Penguin, 1995). Unlike Evadne, Gwendolen glories in the superiority that isolates her from others until that isolation breaks her spirit. Then, like Evadne, she is overcome by hysteria. Reaching out to Deronda for moral guidance and advice about how to establish loving connections with others, Gwendolen, unlike Sue and Lyndall, moves hopefully into the future. Eliot's heroine suffers for her difference, but she is not so different that she cannot reintegrate herself into society. These New Women are unable to do so because their efforts to conform lack conviction and authenticity. They reject gender expectations more rebelliously than even the most rebellious of earlier Victorian heroines. For a discussion of Eliot's "emotional intellect" and her sexual ethics in relation to the Woman Question, see Fernando, *"New Women" in the Late Victorian Novel*, chapter 2.

RUTH ROBBINS

Conclusions? *Rainbow's* End:
The Janus Period

The title of this chapter has several points of reference. In the first instance, it relates to the titles of novels by E.M. Forster and D.H. Lawrence, *Howards End* and *The Rainbow* respectively. But the rainbow's end is also a mythological place—it does not exist, but if it did, and you were ever to find it, there would be a pot of gold there. As I have argued, the usual history of the late Victorians, the Edwardians and the Georgians is one which presents the late Victorians as belated, more minor figures than their immediate forebears, and as much less significant than their inheritors. Modernism, the story goes, is the pot of gold at the end of the Victorian rainbow. Modernism, however, did not come from nowhere. Many of the conditions of modernity were Victorian in origin and the Victorians were the first to confront them. Although there may be a kind of Oedipal resistance to the acknowledgement of the influence wielded by the forefathers and foremothers of the Modernist novel and Modernist poetry, the story of Modernism's development is certainly one of transitions and continuities, not of sudden breaks with the past. Making it new depends absolutely on knowledge of the past. And the 1890s had already made it new, proliferating uses of the word 'new' as Holbrook Jackson demonstrated in 1913 (Jackson 1987, 23).

Forster and Lawrence do not at first sight seem like particularly comparable novelists. They came from very different backgrounds—both social and educational; and the aesthetics of the novels that they wrote are

From *Pater to Forster, 1873–1924.* © 2003 by Ruth Robbins.

also worlds apart. Lawrence's *Sons and Lovers* (1913) and *The Rainbow* (1915) are set in the provincial English East Midlands, in a landscape of industry as much as of agriculture. His characters are often working class, distanced by material circumstances, geography and temperament from the attitudes of the capital. The Brangwens of *The Rainbow* are further up the social ladder than Paul Morel, the coalminer's son in *Sons and Lovers;* but the Brangwens are not the social equals of the Schlegels in Forster's *Howards End,* nor of the Anglo-Indian community in *A Passage to India.* They have capital, but they could not live on it; they own land, but they have to work the land; they receive an education both from the state in the wake of the 1870 Education Act, and in a grammar school, for which their families must pay. That education, however, does not quite buy them the 'cultural capital' the Schlegels enjoy, with their rich European heritage derived from their intellectual German father, their artistic home, and their access to music and books. The Schlegels, as Forster is honest enough to admit, derive their outlook from very different conditions than these. As Margaret says to her women's group in London: 'so few of us think clearly about our own private incomes, and admit that independent thoughts are in nine cases out of ten the result of independent means' (Forster 1989a, 134). Lawrence, perhaps, was an example of the tenth case. His independence of thought leads to a distinctive iconoclasm in his fiction, where Forster, with more at stake in the social status quo, attempts to maintain some of the traditions of the past. Neither man, however, in their best fictions at any rate, makes the fictional world entirely anew.

One symptom of the relationship they each had with their immediate predecessors as well as with their contemporaries is the continuity of the thematic concerns of their fictions with those that preceded them. Lawrence's *Rainbow* describes the effects of the Victorian expansions of industry and urban centres on the families at Marsh farm. *Howards End* is partially concerned with the creeping spread of suburban London which threatens to engulf the rural community that surrounds the edenic house from which the novel takes its title. As Lyn Pykett argues, in a phrase which belongs to a much earlier period of literary history, both novels are 'condition of England novels', a comment that surely also connects Lawrence and Forster to Bennett and Wells as well as the English novelists of the so-called 'Hungry' 1840s such as Gaskell, Disraeli and Kingsley. They describe a society in crisis, and they both—though very differently—return to explanatory models from earlier kinds of fiction to make their critique of contemporary England. Degeneration theory might not be quite named in either book; but arguments about heredity, race and blood, underlie both of their accounts of modernity. The Schlegel sisters are half-German, and that half is their 'cultured half', the part of them that allows them to appreciate art, music and books. Ursula Brangwen might be bred and brought up on the Nottinghamshire–Derbyshire border, but as well as being the Anglo-Saxon daughter of that Brangwen soil, she gets part of her racial inheritance from her Polish grandmother and mother, which is an unspoken—but nonetheless potent—explanatory myth for her modernist sense of alienation from and restlessness within the landscape she lives in.[1]

Both novelists are partially also concerned with the figure of the New Woman. The Schlegel sisters attend a women's debating club for the improvement of their minds. Adela Quested who takes the passage to India is named as one of their friends who meets them in such activities and who is similarly hysterical. Similarly, Ursula Brangwen, as both Dorothea Brooke in *Middlemarch* and Sophia Baines in Bennett's *Old Wives' Tale* had done before her, wishes to 'do' something with her life, rather than settle into the old conventional mould of marriage and family imaged in her mother who 'was so complacent, so utterly fulfilled in her breeding'.

And Imperialism, that most 'Victorian' of discourses, is also present in both works, though slightly offstage in both *The Rainbow* and *Howards End*. In *Howards End*, the guests at Evie Wilcox's wedding include some rather appalling colonial types of the sort who would be more ruthlessly and thoroughly dissected in *A Passage to India* (1924). Paul Wilcox cannot marry Helen—even if he wanted to—because he must go and do the work of Empire in Nigeria. *The Rainbow* describes the alienating effects of Anton Skrebensky's tour of duty in Africa during that imperialist war, the Boer conflict (1899–1902), and he discovers that Africa is indeed a Heart of Darkness (Lawrence 1995, 413). He ends up in India, presumably enjoying the social life of the Anglo-Indian that Forster satirized in his later novel, and that is also part of the dissolute backdrop of Ford's *The Good Soldier*.

In addition, both novels are basically realist in technique. In *Howards End* and *The Rainbow*, the stories are told with an eye to their message; a point is being made through narrative which can be largely recuperated through paraphrase: we are not seeing steadily or whole, and the manner of the narrative does not always tell in a clear way. But the 'decent' values of a cultured liberal humanism are nonetheless preached by Forster; the more revolutionary concepts of emotional and sexual refashionings are part of Lawrence's message. In the works of both novelists, characters remain the sum of environment, heredity and experience as well as of any intrinsic personality; explanations for their motivations and behaviour are offered with varying degrees of straightforwardness. These are transitional texts which face, as it were, both ways, Janus-like, drawing on both fictional pasts and futures.

TIME AND CHARACTER IN *THE RAINBOW*

In a very famous and much-quoted letter to Edward Garnett in June 1914, Lawrence defended his conception of character in the novel that was to become *The Rainbow*. He wrote:

> You mustn't look in my novel for the old stable *ego*—of the character. There is another *ego*, according to whose action the individual is unrecognisable, and passes through, as it were, allotropic states which it needs a deeper sense than any we've been used to exercise to discover are states of the same single radically unchanged element. (Like as diamond and coal are the same single element of carbon. The ordinary novel would trace the history of the diamond—but I say, 'Diamond, what! This is carbon.' And my diamond might be coal or soot, and my theme is carbon.) (Lawrence 1962, 282)

One cannot say of Lawrence's characters, to paraphrase Woolf, that they are simply 'this or that'. The influence of Freudian psychoanalysis, even though explicitly disavowed by Lawrence as a reductive reading in discussions of *Sons and Lovers* in his letters, permeates his fictional people, arguing for a complexity in the making of personality that cannot be reduced to social factors.[2] The life of instinct—of the body, of sexual appetite—is formative in *The Rainbow*, not in opposition to the realist explanations of character, but in relation to them. The conception of character in *The Rainbow* looks both backwards and forwards. Lawrence in part makes use of realist conception, constructing his novel on the ideas of social causes and their social consequences, in much the same way as earlier fiction writers had done. But for Lawrence, both causes and consequences depend on a radically different way of seeing character. Something of the old bourgeois individual survives in this conception, but it is destabilized—hence Lawrence's description of character in terms of the chemical properties of the allotrope, an element (and therefore unchangeable) that can exist in two or more different forms.

The reasons for a different mode of characterization are embedded in a different conception of the effects of time in the novel. For traditional realist fiction, events unfold chronologically and therefore logically until an endpoint is reached from which explanations can be safely furnished, but in

Lawrence's novel, time itself is multiple, and furnishes no simple superstructure. In *Howards End*, Margaret comes to realize 'the chaotic nature of our daily life, and its difference from the orderly sequence that has been fabricated by historians' (Forster 1989a, 115). Lawrence's novel works on a much bigger scale than Forster's, and dramatizes the complications of the relationships between time and telling. At its simplest, Lawrence's work evades simplistic chronology. *The Rainbow* has a broadly chronological organization in that each generation is dealt with in its turn; but it also organizes itself thematically, narrating events out of their proper order, circling backwards and forwards in a structure which dramatizes the presence of the past.

Thus, although in many ways *The Rainbow* is constructed on the realist foundations of telling causes and effects, it locates causes rather differently. In the traditional realist novel, the most common construction is of a story focussed on an individual character placed within a specific social, geographical, economic and cultural milieu. For the Lawrence of *Sons and Lovers*, as for Bennett and Wells before him, the fictional universe he wished to portray was not known in the traditional realist way, at least partly on the simple basis of the fact that he, like them, describes a different social milieu from that most common in Victorian and Edwardian fiction. *Sons and Lovers*, as Sagar notes, opens 'with a socio-economic history of Eastwood, followed by a meticulous placing of the Morel household within the industrial landscape'. He does this because 'he cannot assume that typical novel-reader would know anything about "small homes"; still less about miners' (Sagar 1985, 77).

The Rainbow opens in a similar way, though the language is more lyrical and less grounded in either the declarative structures of realism or the mechanical precision of its construction of causal sequences. It offers slightly but importantly different explanatory mechanisms. It opens with a description of the traditional way of life of a particular farming family living in the English East Midlands. In that opening—'The Brangwens had lived for generations on the Marsh Farm' (Lawrence 1995, 9)—the timescale is non-specific. It is impossible to say with certainty *when* the story opens because Lawrence suggests in his opening that the Brangwens' way of life had been the same since before time could be measured. Official time, the measured time of clocks, calendars and history, changes people and brings them painfully to individuality and self-consciousness. Tom Brangwen, representing the first generation of Brangwen men to live with the effects of industrialization, urbanization and the mechanistic regulation of clock time, is also the first Brangwen to be represented as an individual with a personal history in this family saga. The notion of significant events in time having their effects on particular human beings is a direct inheritance from the realist tradition.

Time, however it is measured, is a central preoccupation of modern consciousness, and became therefore a central preoccupation of modernist aesthetics. It is no accident that clock time is the regular beat that pitilessly organizes Woolf's *Mrs Dalloway* (1925)—a novel that was originally to be called *The Hours*; nor that clocks striking nine and five regulate the flow of the crowds over the London bridges in T.S. Eliot's *The Waste Land* (1922). For Lawrence, too, time is far more complex than a clock or calendar, or even an historical epoch, can measure. *The Rainbow* conflates various measures of time as part of the attempt to explain the crisis of modernity. The Brangwens are farmers and are therefore 'naturally' and explicitly associated with the natural cycles of the seasons:

> They felt the rush of the sap in spring, they knew the wave which cannot halt, but every year throws forward the seed to begetting, and, falling back, leaves the young-born on the earth. They knew the intercourse between heaven and earth, sunshine drawn into the breast and bowels, the rain sucked up in the day time, nakedness that comes under the wind in autumn, showing the birds' nest no longer worth hiding. Their life and inter-relations were such ... (Lawrence 1995, 9–10)

Seasonal time is repetitive time, or continuous time. Every spring, there is the rush of sap, every autumn the dying away of life. The cycle is always the same. In his description of this kind of time, with its insistently sensual and sexual metaphors, Lawrence associates natural or cyclical time with fecundity and fulfilment, though it is a narrow fulfilment, dependent on narrowed horizons. All the same, no one can be immune to the forces of history as they approach the farm in the railway, the canal and the expanding town.

Alongside historical (or progressive, linear) time and natural (cyclical, seasonal) time, *The Rainbow* also places its events into other time frames. One is the frame of evolutionary time. In the course of the novel, the focus shifts from Marsh Farm to the new generations of Brangwens living first in the village of Cossethay, and finally in a redbrick house in Ilkeston—an evolutionary movement from primeval slime to 'civilization', if a red-brick house in Ilkeston counts as civilization. Evolution—just like historical movements—does not necessarily imply progress: degeneration is a powerful if scarcely articulated fear in the text.

The other important time frame is mythical time, expressed through the continuing references to the Book of Genesis. Lawrence had a 'mythic method', in which he too 'manipulated a continuous parallel between contemporaneity and antiquity' before Joyce did, and before T.S. Eliot described Joyce's method in his essay '*Ulysses*, Order and Myth' in 1923 (Eliot 1975, 177). Myths are shared stories expressing the continuity of communal values and providing explanatory contexts for the observed world and for lived experience. In this context, the Bible has a particular resonance for the Bible stories are also regulatory myths, describing a way of life and an ethical system that not only does continue, but one that *should* continue, timelessly as it were, because its final reference point is the eternal time of God. In a novel called *The Rainbow*, the symbol of God's promise never again to destroy his creation in flood, the Genesis story is a backdrop of continuity to the historical changes the fiction recounts. In this frame, far from being Primeval slime, Marsh Farm is an Eden in which man and nature are in perfect harmony, and where woman—like Eve—is vaguely dissatisfied, presented in her ambition for knowledge and a wider horizon than the farm can provide.

The three generations with which the novel deals—Lydia and Tom, Will and Anna, and Ursula and Skrebensky—represent continuity in the sense that the same battles are played out between husbands and wives, and between parents and children through the different generations. Husbands and wives fight for individual needs until they learn to complement each other; children rail against parental authority. But where Anna escapes Tom's parenting through her marriage to Will, her daughter escapes Anna's parenting through work, education, and a secret sexual life without the benefit of clergy: the times, they were a-changing. Anna's escape is one sanctioned by her community. Ursula's escape is based on individualism, on breaking free—eventually in *Women in Love*, from 'the "nets" which enfold characters in *The Rainbow*: the nets of custom, family and loyalty between a single man and a single woman' (Torgovnick 2001, 41). In other words, there is repetition with difference. The cyclical and repetitious nature of human relations are modified by their contact with history rather more than they are modified by the individual temperaments of the different individuals in each generation.

One of the changes wrought by large historical forces on local individual circumstances is the failure of the Polish rebellion which makes Lydia Lensky and her daughter into refugees, and which brings them into the orbit of Marsh Farm. This historical event is presented in terms of its local effects. Their arrival in Cossethay is the decisive new element which alters the Brangwens. The Lenskys are culturally and politically sophisticated

aristocrats; Lydia is half-German and half-Polish–a distinctive new bloodline
in the Brangwen gene pool the narrative implies. Poland, which had
disappeared off the map as an independent state in the eighteenth century is
a kind of 'non' place, often used in English fiction as a shorthand for very
different, often temperamental, romantic and unstable, unEnglish people.
Lydia and Tom fight as well as love each other, their battle based on the
traditional, organic stable values of English life (which may also be stultifying)
represented by Tom and the sophisticated European values and insights of the
uprooted Lydia. The couple reaches an accommodation with each other by
valuing and accepting the differences between them, mostly based on Lydia's
compromise. She has suffered much from the instability of Polish values, is
tired of travelling and rootlessness epitomized by her husband, and recognizes
the good in stability at Marsh Farm on that basis. Lydia's intense grief when
Tom is drowned is symptomatic of the balance they have found in their
relationship, a balance between masculine and feminine, stability and flux,
also expressed in Tom's drunken speech at Anna's wedding, where he
describes—comically but sincerely—the complementarity of husband and
wife in the composite figure of the angel (129).

    It is in the next generation that the battle between the sexes becomes
particularly bitter, in Anna and Will's marriage. Neither member of this
couple has a secure anchor in tradition and continuity. Will's family might be
Brangwens, but they are 'Nottingham Brangwens' who have left the land and
gone to live in the town. Anna is by birth, if not by upbringing, a foreigner,
deracinated from the traditions of her own family by death and emigration.
She finds in Tom a wonderful surrogate who can comfort her by reference to
his own natural element—the natural world. But in leaving the family home,
she also leaves behind her tenuous rootedness. Her marriage to Will—whose
name is certainly not accidental; he is wilfulness personified—is based on
conflict. Each of them battles for dominance over the other, whereas the
parents' generation had battled towards equilibrium, not for victory. They
are diametrically opposed in terms of temperament, signalled by reference to
their opposing attitudes towards organized religion and the art that
symbolizes it. Will's relationship with God is spiritual, not intellectual–he
never listens to the sermons, Anna says (149), but he glories in church
architecture. Anna in contrast has a practical attitude, resenting Will's
transports of aesthetic pleasure in part because they exclude her, and in part
because, not feeling them herself, she believes they are a sham.

    The contested narratives of Lawrence's evolving present clearly have
specific pasts. One kind of past we all share, though we obviously share it
very differently, is our personal past of childhood. In his depiction of Ursula,

which makes up the bulk of *The Rainbow*, Lawrence presents an acutely realized description of what it is like to be a child. Childhood is a period of multiple repetitions in a context of change. The developing child experiences routines of family life as both comfort to nestle in and as a controlling structure to evade. In multiple vignettes of family life, Ursula's developing consciousness is described. Her relationship with her father—special and meaningful—is evoked as both passion and failure, for example in her failed attempts to help him plant potatoes in the garden. She tries hard, but 'the grown-up power to work deliberately was a mystery to her' (207). She is incompetent in this small task, and her disappointment at her failure, out of all proportion with its cause, is nonetheless precisely what a small child would feel.

Just like Stephen Dedalus in *A Portrait of the Artist as a Young Man*, Ursula has flights of fancy in which she escapes from mundane existence into romantic fantasy (*The Idylls of the King* in her case) but from which she must always return with a bump. The discovery that dreams cannot be lived in is made repeatedly, though never quite realized by Ursula. The grammar school is a place of dreams until she discovers that her fellow pupils are not romantic maidens but catty adolescent girls. The university feeds a similar kind of romantic Medieval fantasy in which the professors 'were black-gowned priests of knowledge, serving forever in a remote hushed temple' (400), until she is forced to recognize its mercantile basis as 'a little apprentice-shop where one was further equipped for making money ... a little slovenly laboratory for the factory' which is not redeemed by its 'spurious Gothic arches, spurious peace, spurious Latinity ... spurious naïveté of Chaucer' (403). For a while, Skrebensky makes a pretty good substitute for Sir Lancelot, until she realizes that being with him means acquiescing in the social world she despises, which turns her love into contempt. Ideals provide a framework which is repeatedly dismantled by experience, though experience does not stop Ursula from dreaming.

The process of growing up in Ursula's case is a process of both discovering relationships between causes and effects—seeds die if you tread on them when you are a child; much later, you fail your exams if you spend all your time with your lover—and deciding that such things do not matter much. And this is the real difference between Lawrence's conception of time and character and that found in other earlier novelists. Growing up for most people, and for the people in most realist fiction, is the process of accepting causal relationships and learning to live with them; for Ursula, maturity comes when she refuses the connection, a position the novel itself validates. Against the backdrop of her miserable teaching career (also very impressively realized), her university education, her love affairs with Winifred Inger and Anton Skrebensky, her rejection of both of them, and her discovery that she is pregnant, Ursula is shown breaking away from the conventions or 'nets' of her own society. She tests out the various roles that tradition has bequeathed her: good daughter, apt pupil, teacher, possible wife and mother, and finds them all wanting. In those conventional terms, at the end of *The Rainbow*, her life is a failure. She has tested out new social roles—become a New Woman, indeed—and found them wanting; she has fought her parents and her lover; she has failed her university course, and she is pregnant with her lover's child. She is adrift. Her experiences have not led to the usual conclusions about how to live life and 'new' conclusions are not quite forthcoming in this novel—they will be played out in *Women in Love*. Whatever lessons she has learned, she has not learned for all time. It is perfectly possible that she will continue to relive those problems in slightly different forms (and the battles with Birkin in the later novel are not very dissimilar from those with Skrebensky), suggesting a conception of character which is cyclical in its development rather than straightforwardly linear or progressive. Just as Will and Anna's accommodation of each other is cyclical—periods of calm and contentment followed by periods of brutal conflict—Ursula's life threatens to be a repetitive failure: repetitive in the sense that it might just replicate the old patterns inherited from the previous generations, and in the sense that she might just keep making the same mistakes.

But in a daring act of falsification as irresponsible—though not as cheerful—as anything to be found in Wells's unearned conclusions to his novels, Lawrence fabricates a happy ending, projected onto the future as a happy beginning, for Ursula. For no reason that is explained to the reader unless it is that she has been frightened by horses, she discovers that she is not, after all, pregnant. Pregnancy would certainly be one of the nets that might keep Ursula earthbound. Instead, Lawrence gives her the vision of the rainbow, a contemporary Ark of the Covenant promising a better future. As Ursula recovers from her miscarriage she sits expectantly to watch a new creation, having discovered through her experiences that she need not relive the old models of the past, particularly the models of coupledom her parents and grandparents represented. Watching colliers and their wives as they cross the countryside, in a passage which clearly owes a great deal to the ending of Zola's naturalist novel *Germinal* (1885), she sees a new life, not realized, but in potential: 'In the still, silenced forms of the colliers she saw a sort of suspense, a waiting in pain for the new liberation: she saw the same in the false hard confidence of the women. The confidence of the women was brittle. It would break quickly to reveal the strength and patient effort of the new germination' (458). And then she sees the rainbow, and like Lily Briscoe in Woolf's *To the Lighthouse*, has her vision. Sadly, just as with Lily, the vision is frankly vague, despite the sonorous biblical cadences in which it is expressed. It is a vision of the sweeping away of modernity—the houses and collieries disappearing in an apocalypse that will leave people free. Quite how this is to come about is not described or imagined: enough that the vision has been vouchsafed. But in the next narrated episodes of Ursula's life in the opening chapters of *Women in Love*, the cycle of repetition recurs, and she comes back to earth with a bump. The collieries and the colliers have not been swept away, not here, not yet, probably not ever. Realizing this, Ursula and her sister leave their roots, conditioned by them, reacting against them, but not accepting their limitations.

FORSTER'S CONNECTIONS

> The reality that lends itself to narrative representation is the conflict between desire and the law. (White 1987, 12)

Forster's fiction is much less iconoclastic than Lawrence's and it shares neither the mystical attempt to break free from the past and the present in its thematic concerns, nor the sense of straining form in which Lawrence partially articulates his vision. *Howards End* and *A Room With a View* (1908) are far closer to Galsworthy than to Woolf not least because Forster's fictions accept, as Lawrence's do not, at least a minimal ethical requirement for the individual to take into consideration the individuality of others. In other words, there is a conventional acquiescence to the condition of maturity as the acceptance of limitations on freedom of personal action. In the terms of the Hayden White quotation, the conflict between desire and duty, or desire and the law, is best resolved in Forster's fiction by deferring to others. For Forster though, 'the law' is a dangerous abstraction; the others to whom one must defer are personal others—friends and lovers, not nation state, not impersonal propriety, not unexamined conventions—a position stated in *Two Cheers for Democracy* (1951) as the belief that given the choice between betraying one's country (an abstraction) and betraying one's friend (a person), the proper choice is to betray one's country. For Helen Schlegel, as for the Emersons in *A Room with a View*, 'personal relations are the important thing for ever and ever, and not this outer life of telegrams and anger' (Forster 1989a, 176). At the same time, though, Margaret responds to contradict her sister. The Wilcoxes might well be part of the outer world, but—and this the point of 'connection':

If Wilcoxes hadn't worked and died in England for thousands of
years, you and I couldn't sit here without having our throats cut.
There would be no trains, no ships to carry us literary people
about, no fields even. Just savagery ... More and more do I refuse
to draw my income and sneer at those who guarantee it. (Forster
1989a, 177–8)

Making that connection between material circumstances and the labour
which produces them eventually makes Margaret a heroine. She rescues her
sister from her impetuousness, and Mr Wilcox from his inhuman obtuseness
about human relations. It is a small, local and individual victory over the kind
of futility and anarchy that Eliot refers to (Eliot 1975, 177). Its smallness is a
function of the domesticated nature of this particular fiction, and it shows the
limitations of Forster's vision. All the same, I do not see any reason to think
that Forster's vision is less significant than Woolf's or Lawrence's, the former
equally limited in social reach, and the latter unrealizable.

But Forster also knew that his vision was limited, and in *A Passage to
India*, the last novel he published in his lifetime, he set out to test its
limitations against a broader canvas. India cannot be the kind of knowable
community represented by the village at Howards End. And what becomes
of personal relationships if the conditions under which they operate are not
conditions of fairly basic equality and freedom? Or, to put it another way,
Aziz and his friends enter the novel in 'a very sad talk ... they were discussing
as to whether or no it is possible to be friends with an Englishman' (Forster
1989c, 33). The answer at the end of the novel is 'not yet ... not there' (316);
personal relationships do not survive, but that is an argument that the
conditions, in this case the conditions of imperialism in India, must be
changed, not that the basic principle of personal relationships is wrong.

The Indian setting provides a powerful backdrop for the examination
of alternative identities and positions, radically destabilizing the known and
knowable conditions of England. India is presented as a space of
epistemological crisis, where everything is a mystery or a muddle, but
Forster's is not a nihilistic view, because he holds open the possibility that
sense can be made of all of this even as he registers the absence of coherence
from his own narrative project. *A Passage to India* has the most modernist
credentials in Forster's fiction. In his adaptation of the title of a poem by
Walt Whitman as his title for the book—from 'Passage to India' to *A Passage
to India*—Forster's addition of the indefinite article signals that what is to be
presented is one version of events amongst many possible versions. The
novel's central event, the assault on Miss Quested in the Marabar Caves, may

or may not have happened at all. As Fielding puts it to Adela, there are four possibilities, each of which has internal evidence for its own validity as an account of what actually happened: 'Either Aziz is guilty, which is what your friends think; or you invented the charge out of malice, which is what my friends think; or you had an hallucination' (240). The fourth possibility is that it was 'somebody else' (242). No definitive answer is ever given, and none of the principles can give a coherent account of the event, if indeed it was an event. One of the central questions we are accustomed to ask about novels—the sign of the declarative purpose in the realist tradition—is 'what is it about?' We are accustomed to be able to answer that question in terms of simple paraphrase. Typically in modernist writing, however, that question becomes more difficult to respond to, and Forster's novel is 'modernist' at least to the extent that it evades the clear telling of a story.

The setting is similarly unstable. The limited geographical reach and small social groupings of the knowable community do not apply to India. Over and over again characters on both sides of the racial divide describe the vastness and diversity of the subcontinent, seeing it very unsteadily and not at all whole, inassimilable by any individual mind. There is no one order of reality which is *the* truth about India, no single entity which represents the 'real' India that Adela Quested wishes to discover. This point is emphasized from the novel's first page. Chandrapore, the city in which the action (such as it is) is set, cannot be defined or adequately described. Its geography defies the classifications which a realist novelist takes for granted in creating solidity of specification. The town is radically non-specific, described largely through negatives: it 'presents nothing extraordinary', except for the Marabar Caves, but no one can explain why they are special. The Ganges, holy river of India, 'happens not to be holy there.' 'The streets are mean, the temples ineffective.' It is only when the perspective of distance is introduced that the city has anything remarkable about it, and even perspective does not give certainty of judgement.

If events and setting are unstable, then character is also problematized, dependent on context, on racial and social grouping, and on the responses of others to the individual, at least as much as on any intrinsic or essential qualities. In that first conversation between Aziz and his friends when they ask the all-important question about friendship with an Englishman, Mahmoud Ali, who has never left India, says it is not possible. His experience of Englishmen tells him that they are dictatorial and unpleasant. Hamidullah, educated in England, says it is possible—but only in England.

Forster's presentation deliberately presents the world of feeling and instinct as preferable to that of rules and empirical evidence. Sympathetic characters, notably Mrs Moore and Fielding, are defined as 'oriental', because they act on feelings not on rules. The struggle of the Anglo-Indians is to impose their own version of reality on the multiple groupings of subject peoples. As part of the matrix which maintains power, it is not permissible for them ever to admit they are wrong. They present themselves as figures of enlightenment and empirical evidence, bringing law and education to the benighted savages. As such, they are rule-bound, conventional, utterly dependent on a concept of observable 'facts' for their interpretation of India, in contrast to the Indians who are presented as instinctive and feeling beings.[3] Throughout the novel, then, and specifically with regard to the 'evidence' concerning Aziz's alleged guilt, Forster mounts a devastating critique of realism's presumption that facts speak for themselves, and that there is only ever one possible version of events. For all their insistence on the facts, the English have responded emotionally to an idea (that a 'young girl, fresh from England' has been assaulted), rather than dispassionately to highly circumstantial evidence.

The readers outside the text, however, know that each of the pieces of evidence against Aziz is open to more than one interpretation. The trip to the caves was conceived not out of lust for the white woman, whom Aziz anyway thinks is ugly, but out of shame that he cannot invite anyone to his house which is unswept and dirty. We know too, that Aziz did not plan that his other guests would miss the train and was distressed by Godbole and Fielding missing the train, spoiling his hospitable purpose. We also know that although Aziz gave orders for the English ladies' servant to be left behind, it was at their request, not with any malicious purpose. Mrs Moore did not accompany them to the fateful final cave because she felt unwell, not because Aziz plotted to leave her behind. The vaunted logic of Europe is submerged in herd instinct: 'All over Chandrapore [the day of the alleged assault], the Europeans were putting aside their normal personalities and sinking themselves in their community. Pity, wrath, heroism, filled them, but the power of putting two and two together was annihilated' (175). Ironically it is Aziz's Indian friend Hamidullah who thinks in Western terms: '[He] loved Aziz and knew he was calumniated; but faith did not rule his heart, and he prated of "policy" and "evidence" in a way that saddened [Fielding]' (181).

Fielding is the only character who can actively see 'both sides'. The English as a group, though far less sympathetically portrayed, are not so very dissimilar to the Indians, presented as 'better' in part because they are subjected not rulers of their own destiny. If the Anglo-Indians see all Indians as the 'same', the Indians perform similar acts of stereotyping on their colonial rulers: 'Turtons and Burtons are all the same' (266) says Aziz in the aftermath of the trial. The surnames are similar, virtually indistinguishable. This is the Indian version of the white racist comment 'they all look the same to me'. Fielding refuses any such simplistic seeing and is active in putting forward a philosophy that the two sides must meet. He comes to India, we are told, with a public role as a teacher, and, unlike Ronny, as an experienced man. When he is introduced, we are told:

> This Mr Fielding had been caught by India late. He was over forty when he entered that oddest portal, the Victoria terminus at Bombay, and–having bribed a European ticket-inspector–took his luggage into the compartment of his first tropical train. The journey remained in mind as significant. Of his two carriage companions, one was a youth, fresh to the East like himself, the other a seasoned Anglo-Indian of his own age. A gulf divided him from either: he had seen too many cities and men to be the first or to become the second. (Forster 1989c, 79)

Fielding is in all senses of the phrase a man of the world: he has travelled widely, and he has had wide experience (including sexual experience, we are told). He is unmarried, and so has no personal baggage to encumber him on his journey east, no girl fresh from England to protect with manly but unthinking vigour. As he tells Aziz, he travels light. But he also trusts his emotions, finding friendship and ties based on mutual affection more important than allegiance to abstract ideals such as country or social set. To use a metaphor from reading, Fielding does not see the world in black and white: 'The remark that did him most harm at the club,' comments the narrator, 'was a silly aside to the effect that the so-called white races are really pinko-grey' (80). The shades of grey are important for they are what connect disparate and oppositional world views. Also, unlike any other character in the novel, with the possible exception of Miss Quested, he has no faith in God. Consequently, he has no faith to lose–and it is loss of faith in her 'poor little talkative Christianity' which disables Mrs Moore as a power for active good in the text (161). But lack of religious allegiance also means inclusiveness. There may be many mansions in the Christian heaven, but Christianity 'must exclude someone from [its] gathering' (58), as Islam also does. Hinduism comes close to embracing the universe, but also excludes certain elements and even Professor Godbole cannot include inanimate matter in his scheme of heaven. Fielding does not much care about inanimate matter, but he can include all people in his view of a world based on trust and affection. Circumstances defeat him. His only regret over supporting Aziz is that it will now be possible for people to label him a 'pro-Indian' or as anti-British, and on the basis of that label, they will exclude him from their gatherings.

In the end, the single individual cannot alter the force of history. Fielding wants to be Aziz's friend, but is disabled by historical circumstance. The novel ends with a kind of rainbow-like promise for a better future. If Aziz cannot be friends with Fielding here and now, perhaps his children can be friends with Fielding's children then and there, when the world has changed again, and when India has achieved its independence. The poem from which the novel takes its title, Whitman's 'Passage to India', is a celebration of modernity:

> Singing my days
> Singing the great achievement of the present,
> Singing the strong light works of engineers,
> Our modern wonders, (the antique ponderous Seven outvied,)
> In the Old World the East the Suez canal,
> The New by its mighty railroad spann'd,
> The seas inlaid with eloquent gentle wires
> (Whitman 1975, 429)

These achievements make connection across racial and national divides possible–English men and Indian men can only be friends if they can meet. As yet, though, this modernity is an ambivalent gift. The remarkable technological feats of the Suez Canal, of the building of the railroad across the United States, and of the spanning of the Atlantic with the telegraph cable, all speak of a world defined by a communication revolution, at least to the West. Native Americans, Indians and Egyptians, amongst others though, certainly had reason to feel much more uncertain that technological advance represented progress. What the West saw as advancement, it also saw as evidence of its superiority, and without equality there cannot be friendship.

To return, then, to the rainbow's end of Modernism. The aesthetics of Modernism, the attempt to make it new, to tear down the old conventions and find alternative modes of being in the world, and to find new ways of describing the world, represent a very attractive proposition. No one wants to be an old stick-in-the-mud in the primeval slime at Marsh Farm. Taking flight from those old certainties, which were never that certain anyway, though, leaves fictional characters–and in a modified way, their readers–at sea. What is being assented to when Molly Bloom ends her soliloquy in the final pages of *Ulysses* (1922) with an apparently triumphant 'yes'? What does

Lily Briscoe's 'vision' amount to in *To the Lighthouse* (1927)? Is Ursula Brangwen really on the threshold of a better life in either of her two fictional endings? When T.S. Eliot glosses 'Shantih, Shantih, Shantih' as the peace that defies understanding in his notes to *The Waste Land* (1922), is it supposed to be comforting?

At the end of Fielding's tea party in *A Passage to India*, Professor Godbole sings a strange and haunting song: 'At times there seemed rhythm, at times there was the illusion of Western melody. But the ear, baffled repeatedly, soon lost any clue, and wandered in maze of noises, none harsh or unpleasant, none intelligible' (95). The Professor offers to explain 'in detail':

> It was a religious song. I placed myself in the position of a milkmaiden. I say to Shri Krishna: 'Come! Come to me only.' The God refuses to come. I grow humble and say: 'Do not come to me only. Multiply yourself into a hundred Krishnas, and let one go to each of my hundred companions, but one, O Lord of the Universe, come to me.' He refuses to come. This is repeated several times ... I say to him, Come, come, come, come, come, come, come. He neglects to come. (Forster 1989c, 96)

His explanation is as baffling as the song itself. In its evasion of telos—in the absence of that structured ending that Western narratives usually provided—it appears to be a narrative without a point, expressive of the muddle or mystery of India rather than explanatory or elucidatory. A request is made and is not answered. The kinds of answer that come from neatly tied up endings in those realist narratives against which Modernists railed are obviously falsifications, not least because real lives do not begin and end so neatly. But I'm not always convinced that those other endings described in Modernist writing aren't just as false and misleading. The world did not change after all on the basis of the individual epiphanies that fictional characters experienced. The old illusions and the new illusions still really saw the same old world even if they saw it differently.

NOTES

1. By the same token, degeneration explanations are at the heart of *Sons and Lovers*. It is surely not accidental that the family's name is Morel—a name they share with one of the foremost thinkers of degeneration theory, Bénédicte Augustin Morel (1809–73). The reasons for William Morel's death—the split in him between the cultured life his mother aspires to and the life of the body epitomized by his father—are part of a Lamarckian

scheme. Lamarck (1744–1829) had suggested that the acquired characteristics of parents could be passed down to their children in a kind cultural hereditarian schema. William inherits two incompatible tendencies and cannot support the contradiction.

2. Complexes, he wrote, are 'vicious half-statements ... When you've said Mutter complex [mother complex], you've said nothing ... A complex is not simply a sex relation: far from it–My poor book: it was, as art, a fairly complete truth: so they carve a half lie out of it and say "Voilà". Swine!' (qtd in Sagar 1985, 93–4).

3. This, of course, is one of the problems of the book. The schema Forster establishes is dangerously close to inscribing an essentialist concept of race based on what Edward Said calls 'orientalism'. This idea refers to the habit of the western academy–scholars, artists, anthropologists, novelists and poets–to find in the 'East' (a mythical place that is not Europe or the US), the ideas and feeling that they expected to find there. Orientalism leads to essentializing stereotyping in the representation of non-white, non-Western peoples. See Said 1991 and 1994 for these arguments. Sara Sulieri's *The Rhetoric of English India* takes up Said's theme and develops it further.

Chronology

1880	Liberal administration formed by Gladstone.
1881	Pablo Picasso born. P.G. Wodehouse born.
1882	Charles Darwin dies. Virginia Woolf and James Joyce born. Married Woman's Property Act passed.
1883	Karl Marx dies. Robert Louis Stevenson publishes *Treasure Island*.
1884	*Oxford English Dictionary* first published. Berlin Conference on the division of African territories.
1885	D.H. Lawrence born. Walter Pater publishes *Marius the Epicurean*. First internal combustion engine for gasoline.
1886	Stevenson publishes *The Strange Case of Dr. Jekyll and Mr. Hyde* and *Kidnapped*. Thomas Hardy publishes *The Mayor of Casterbridge*. Marx's *Capital* published in English. Defeat of the Irish Home Rule Bill; Gladstone loses election.
1887	Bloody Sunday in Trafalgar Square.
1888	Katherine Mansfield born. Wilde publishes *The Happy Prince and Other Tales*. Jack the Ripper murders in London
1891	George Gissing publishes *New Grub Street*. Hardy publishes *Tess of the D'Urbervilles*. Oscar Wilde publishes *The Picture of Dorian Gray*.
1892	Arthur Conan Doyle publishes *The Adventures of Sherlock Holmes*.

1893	Gissing publishes *The Odd Women*. Henry Ford manufactures first automobile. Independent Labour Party formed.
1894	Deaths of Stevenson and Pater. Kipling publishes *The Jungle Book*.
1895	Oscar Wilde publishes *The Importance of Being Earnest*. Hardy publishes *Jude the Obscure*; H.G. Wells publishes *The Time Machine*. Wilde tried for sexual offenses and imprisoned.
1897	Bram Stoker publishes *Dracula*. Wells publishes *The Invisible Man*. Gissing publishes *The Whirlpool*.
1898	Wells publishes *The War of the Worlds*.
1899	Boer War begins.
1900	Deaths of Wilde and Nietzsche. Conrad publishes *Lord Jim*. Freud publishes *The Interpretation of Dreams*. British Labour Party founded.
1901	Queen Victoria dies and Edward VII accedes to the throne. Kipling publishes *Kim*.
1902	Boer War ends. Conrad publishes *Typhoon* and "Heart of Darkness"; Arnold Bennett publishes *Anna of the Five Towns*. *Times Literary Supplement* founded. Secondary schools established by Education Act for England and Wales.
1903	Gissing dies. Samuel Butler's *The Way of All Flesh* published. Orville and Wilbur Wright make first flight. The Women's Social and Political Union founded.
1904	Conrad publishes *Nostromo*.
1905	Liberal administration wins election on platform of radical reform. Doyle publishes *The Return of Sherlock Holmes*.
1906	Samuel Beckett born. Henrik Ibsen dies. Self-government granted to Transvaal and Orange colonies in South Africa. Galsworthy publishes *The Man of Property*, the first volume of the trilogy *The Forsyte Saga*.
1907	Kipling awarded the Nobel Prize for literature. Conrad publishes *The Secret Agent*. First Cubist art exhibition in Paris.
1908	Forster publishes *A Room with a View*. Chesterton publishes *The Man Who Was Thursday*. Bennett publishes *The Old Wives' Tale*.
1910	Edward VII dies; George V becomes king. Leo Tolstoy dies. Forster publishes *Howards End*. Bennett publishes *Clayhanger*.

1911	Conrad publishes *Under Western Eyes*. Katherine Mansfield publishes *In a German Pension*. House of Lords partially reformed by liberal government. Suffragette riots in London.
1912	Stoker dies. C.G. Jung publishes *The Theory of Psychoanalysis*. House of Commons rejects Women's Franchise Bill.
1913	Panama Canal opens. Suffragette demonstrations in London.
1914	World War I begins.

Contributors

HAROLD BLOOM is Sterling Professor of the Humanities at Yale University. He is the author of over 20 books, including *Shelley's Mythmaking* (1959), *The Visionary Company* (1961), *Blake's Apocalypse* (1963), *Yeats* (1970), *A Map of Misreading* (1975), *Kabbalah and Criticism* (1975), *Agon: Toward a Theory of Revisionism* (1982), *The American Religion* (1992), *The Western Canon* (1994), and *Omens of Millennium: The Gnosis of Angels, Dreams, and Resurrection* (1996). *The Anxiety of Influence* (1973) sets forth Professor Bloom's provocative theory of the literary relationships between the great writers and their predecessors. His most recent books include *Shakespeare: The Invention of the Human* (1998), a 1998 National Book Award finalist, *How to Read and Why* (2000), *Genius: A Mosaic of One Hundred Exemplary Creative Minds* (2002), and *Hamlet: Poem Unlimited* (2003). In 1999, Professor Bloom received the prestigious American Academy of Arts and Letters Gold Medal for Criticism, and in 2002 he received the Catalonia International Prize.

HENRY JAMES was the noted author of numerous novels, short stories, plays, and works of literary criticism, including *The Portrait of a Lady*, *Daisy Miller*, and "The Turn of the Screw."

RAYMOND WILLIAMS was a fellow of Jesus College, Cambridge, and the author of more than thirty titles and more than five hundred articles and reviews. His books include *The Long Revolution*, *Modern Tragedy*, and *Drama from Ibsen to Brecht*.

DAVID THORBURN teaches at the Massachusetts Institute of Technology. He is a joint editor of a title on Romanticism and the co-author of a collection of essays on John Updike.

ALLON WHITE was an influential literary and cultural critic. He is the author of *Carnival, Hysteria, and Writing* and wrote on Dickens, Pynchon, and others.

JOHN BATCHELOR has been a fellow at New College, Oxford. He has written on Conrad and John Ruskin and served as editor for an edition of Conrad's work.

JOHN McCLURE teaches at Rutgers University and is the author of *Late Imperial Romance* and works on Conrad and Kipling.

L.R. LEAVIS teaches at the University of Nijmegen in the Netherlands. His research centers on nineteenth- and twentieth-century English literature, and focuses on literature, culture, and the media.

PETER KEATING is the author or editor of numerous titles and has written a book on George Gissing and *The Working Classes in Victorian Fiction*. He has edited anthologies and editions of works by authors such as Kipling, Arnold, and Gaskell. He is also a translator.

ANNETTE FEDERICO teaches English at James Madison University. She is the author of *Masculine Identity in Hardy and Gissing* and *Idol of Suburbia: Marie Corelli and Late-Victorian Literary Culture*.

EDWARD W. SAID served as Old Dominion Professor of Humanities at Columbia University. He wrote *Joseph Conrad and the Fiction of Autobiography* and *The World, the Text, and the Critic*. He also edited editions of the works of Kipling, Henry James, and others.

MALCOLM BRADBURY has been a critic, part-time Professor of American Studies at the University of East Anglia, and a novelist. His critical works include *The Modern British Novel* and *No, Not Bloomsbury*; he also has edited *The Penguin Book of Modern British Short Stories* and co-edited a book on modernism.

DAVID TROTTER has been Quain Professor of English Language and Literature at University College, London. He has published several titles, including *The English Novel in History, 1895–1920*, and *English and Irish Poetry*.

NICHOLAS DALY has taught at Trinity College, Dublin. He is the author of *Literature, Technology, and Modernity, 1860–2000*, and *Modernism, Romance and the "Fin de Siècle."*

JOHN PAUL RIQUELME is Professor of English at Boston University. He has written studies of *Tess of the D'Urbervilles* and *Dracula* as well as a book on T.S. Eliot and Romanticism.

JIL LARSON teaches English at Western Michigan University. She was the managing editor of *Victorian Studies* and has written on Hardy and Conrad.

RUTH ROBBINS teaches English at University College Northampton. She is the author of *Victorian Gothic: Literary and Cultural Manifestations in the Nineteenth Century* and *Literary Feminisms*.

Bibliography

Anderson, Linda R. *Bennett, Wells and Conrad: Narrative in Transition*. NY: St. Martin's, 1988.

Brooker, Peter and Peter Widdowson. "A Literature for England." In *Englishness: Politics and Culture 1880–1920*, edited by Robert Colls and Philip Dodd, 116–63. London: Croom Helm, 1986.

Carracciolo, Peter. "Buddhist Teaching Stories and Their Influence on Conrad, Wells, and Kipling: The Reception of the Jataka and Allied Genres in Victorian Culture." *The Conradian* 11, no. 1 (May 1986): 24–34.

Colón, Susan. "Professionalism and Domesticity in George Gissing's *The Odd Women*." *English Literature in Transition (1880–1920)* 44, no. 4 (2001): 441–58.

Costa, Richard Haver. "Edwardian Intimations of the Shape of Fiction to Come: Mr. Britling/Job Huss as Wellsian Central Intelligences." *English Literature in Transition (1880–1920)* 18 (1975): 229–42.

DeMille, Barbara. "Cruel Illusions: Nietzsche, Conrad, Hardy, and the 'Shadowy Ideal.'" *Studies in English Literature 1500–1900* 30, no. 4 (Autumn 1990): 697–714.

Ellman, Richard, and Charles Feidelson, eds. The Modern Tradition: Backgrounds of Modern Literature 1965.

Gannon, Charles E. "American Dreams and Edwardian Aspirations: Technological Innovation and Temporal Uncertainty in Narratives of Expectation." In *Histories of the Future: Studies in Fact, Fantasy and*

Science Fiction, edited by Alan Sandison, 91–111. Basingstoke, England: Palgrave, 2000.

Gindin, James. *Harvest of a Quiet Eye: the Novel of Compassion*. Bloomington: Indiana University Press, 1971.

Gorra, Michael. "Rudyard Kipling to Salman Rushdie: Imperialism to Postcolonialism." In *The Columbia History of the British Novel*, edited by John Richetti, 631–57. NY: Columbia University Press, 1994.

Hartveit, Lars. *The Art of Persuasion: A Study of Six Novels*. Oslo: Universitets Forlaget, 1977.

Howe, Irving. *Politics and the Novel*. New York: Horizon Press, 1960.

Hunter, Jefferson. *Edwardian Fiction*. Cambridge, Mass.: Harvard University Press, 1982.

James, Henry. *The Art of Fiction: And Other Essays*. New York: Oxford University Press, 1948.

Kaplan, Carola, and Anne B. Simpson, eds. *Seeing Double: Revisioning Edwardian and Modernist Literature*. NY: St. Martin's, 1996.

Karl, Frederick R. "Conrad, Wells, and the Two Voices." *Publications of the Modern Language Association of America* 88, no. 5 (October 1973): 1049–65.

Kaye, Richard A. *The Flirt's Tragedy: Desire without End in Victorian and Edwardian Fiction*. Charlottesville, VA: University Press of Virginia, 2002.

Kestner, Joseph A. *Sherlock's Sisters: The British Female Detective, 1864–1913*. Aldershot, England: Ashgate, 2003.

Kramer, Dale, ed. *The Cambridge Companion to Thomas Hardy*. Cambridge, England: Cambridge University Press, 1999.

Leavis, F.R. "Marriage, Murder, and Morality: *The Secret Agent* and *Tess*." *Neophilologus* 80, no. 1 (January 1996): 161–69.

Levenson, Michael. *A Genealogy of Modernism: A Study of English Literary Doctrine 1908–1922*. Cambridge: Cambridge University Press, 1984.

Levine, George. *The Realistic Imagination: English Fiction from Frankenstein to Lady Chatterley*. Chicago: University of Chicago Press, 1981.

Lothe, Jakob. "Repetition and Narrative Method: Hardy, Conrad, Faulkner." In *Narrative: From Malory to Motion Pictures*, edited by Jeremy Hawthorn, 116–31. London: Arnold, 1985.

McClure, John A. "Late Imperial Romance." *Raritan* 10, no. 4 (Spring 1991): 111–30.

Miller, D.A. *Narrative and Its Discontents: Problems of Closure in the Traditional Novel.* Princeton: Princeton University Press, 1981.

Miller, J. Hillis. *Fiction and Repetition: Seven English Novels.* Cambridge: Harvard University Press, 1982.

Myers, Mitzi. "'Servants as They Are Now Educated': Women Writers and Georgian Pedagogy." *Essays in Literature* 16, no. 1 (Spring 1989): 51–69.

O'Grady, Walter. "On Plot in Modern Fiction: Hardy, James, and Conrad." *Modern Fiction Studies* 11 (1965): 107–115.

O'Malley, Patrick R. "Oxford's Ghosts: *Jude the Obscure* and the End of the Gothic." *Modern Fiction Studies* 46, no. 3 (Fall 2000): 646–71.

Orel, Harold. "Joseph Conrad and H.G. Wells: Two Different Concepts of the Short-Story Genre." *Literary Half-Yearly* 27, no. 2 (July 1986): 2–25.

Parrinder, Patrick. "Edwardian Awakenings: H.G. Wells's Apocalyptic Romances (1898–1915)." In *Imagining Apocalypse: Studies in Cultural Crisis*, edited by David Seed, 62–74. Basingstoke, England: Macmillan; NY: St. Martin's, 2000.

Perry, Carolyn J. "A Voice of the Past: Ruskin's Pervasive Presence in Gissing's *The Odd Women.*" *Publications of the Missouri Philological Association* 13 (1998): 63–70.

Polhemus, Robert M. *Comic Faith: The Great Tradition from Austen to Joyce.* Chicago: University of Chicago Press, 1980.

Raskin, Jonah. *The Mythology of Imperialism: Rudyard Kipling, Joseph Conrad, E.M. Forster, D.H. Lawrence and Joyce Cary.* NY: Random House, 1971.

Reynolds, Kimberley. "Fatal Fantasies: The Death of Children in Victorian and Edwardian Fantasy Writing." In *Representations of Childhood Death*, edited by Gillian Avery and Kimberley Reynolds, 169–88. Basingstoke, England: Macmillan; NY: St. Martin's, 2000.

Robbins, Ruth. *Literary Feminisms.* NY: St. Martin's, 2000.

Rose, Jonathan. *The Edwardian Temperament 1895–1919.* Athens: Ohio University Press, 1986.

Said, Edward W. "The Text, the World, the Critic." *The Bulletin of the Midwest Modern Language Association* 8, no. 2 (1975): 1–23.

———. "The Text, the World, the Critic." In *The Horizon of Literature*, edited by Paul Hernadi, 125–55. Lincoln: University of Nebraska Press, 1982.

Schieck, William J. "Schopenhauerian Compassion, Fictional Structure, and the Reader: The Example of Hardy and Conrad." In *Twilight of Dawn: Studies in English Literature in Transition*, edited by O.M. Brack Jr., 45–67. Tucson: University of Arizona Press, 1987.

Seed, David. "Disorientation and Commitment in the Fiction of Empire: Kipling and Orwell." *Dutch Quarterly Review of Anglo-American Letters* 14, no. 4 (1984): 269–80.

Smith, Warren S. *The London Heretics 1870–1914*. London: Constable, 1967.

Smith, Warren S., ed. *British Novelists, 1890–1929: Traditionalists*. Detroit: Gale, 1985.

Solomon, Eric. "Notes toward a Definition of the Colonial Novel." *North Dakota Quarterly* 57, no. 3 (Summer 1989): 16–23.

Wilt, Judith. "The Imperial Mouth: Imperialism, the Gothic, and Science Fiction." *Journal of Popular Culture* 14, no. 4 (1981): 618–28.

Yeazell, Ruth Bernard, ed. *Sex, Politics, and Science in the Nineteenth-Century Novel*. Baltimore: Johns Hopkins University Press, 1985.

Acknowledgments

"The New Novel" by Henry James. From *Notes on Novelists*: 317–351. © 1914 by Charles Scribner's Sons. Reprinted by permission.

"A Parting of the Ways" by Raymond Williams. From *The English Novel: From Dickens to Lawrence*: 119–39. © 1970 by Raymond Williams. Reprinted by permission of Oxford University Press.

"Conrad and Modern English Fiction" by David Thorburn. From *Conrad's Romanticism*: 153–65. © 1974 by Yale University. Reprinted by permission.

"Obscure Writing and Private Life, 1880–1914" by Allon White. From *The Uses of Obscurity: The Fiction of Early Modernism*: 30–54. © 1981 by Allon White. Reprinted by permission.

"Edwardian Literature" by John Batchelor. From *The Edwardian Novelists*: 1–26. © 1982 by John Batchelor. Reprinted by permission.

"Problematic Presence: the Colonial Other in Kipling and Conrad" by John McClure. From *The Black Presence in English Literature*, edited by David Dabydeen: 154–67. © 1985 by Manchester University Press. Reprinted by permission.

"The Late Nineteenth Century Novel and the Change Towards the Sexual— Gissing, Hardy and Lawrence" by L.R. Leavis. From *English Studies* 66, no.

1 (February 1985): 36–47. © 1985 by Swets & Zeitlinger B.V. Reprinted by permission.

"A Woven Tapestry of Interests" by Peter Keating. From *The Haunted Study: A Social History of the English Novel 1875–1914*: 330–366. © 1989 by Peter Keating. Reprinted by permission.

"The Other Victim: *Jude the Obscure* and *The Whirlpool*" by Annette Federico. From *Masculine Identity in Hardy and Gissing*: 102–129. © 1991 by Associated University Presses, Inc. Reprinted by permission.

"The Pleasures of Imperialism" by Edward W. Said. From *Culture and Imperialism*: 132–62. © 1993 by Edward W. Said. Reprinted by permission.

"The Opening World, 1900–1915" by Malcolm Bradbury. From *The Modern British Novel*: 81–119. © 1993 by Malcolm Bradbury. Reprinted by permission. of Curtis Brown Group Ltd, London on behalf of Malcolm Bradbury.

"The Avoidance of Naturalism: Gissing, Moore, Grand, Bennett, and Others," by David Trotter. From *The Columbia History of the British Novel*, edited by John Richetti: 608–630. © 1994 by Columbia University Press. Reprinted by permission.

"Incorporated Bodies: *Dracula* and the Rise of Professionalism," by Nicholas Daly. From *Texas Studies in Literature and Language* 39, no. 2 (Summer 1997): 181–203. © 1997 by the University of Texas Press. All rights reserved. Reprinted by permission.

"Oscar Wilde's Aesthetic Gothic: Walter Pater, Dark Enlightenment, and *The Picture of Dorian Gray*" by John Paul Riquelme. From *Modern Fiction Studies* 46, no. 3 (Fall 2000): 609–631. © 2000 by the Purdue Research Foundation. Reprinted by permission.

"Emotion, Gender, and Ethics in Fiction by Thomas Hardy and the New Woman Writers" by Jil Larson. From *Ethics and Narrative in the English Novel, 1880–1914*: 44–63. © 2001 by Jil Larson. Reprinted by permission.

"Conclusions? *Rainbow*'s End: The Janus Period" by Ruth Robbins. From *Pater to Forster, 1873–1924*: 192–209. © 2003 by Ruth Robbins. Reprinted by permission.

Index

429